John Patrick, Edward Knott, John Patrick

The Religion Of Protestants

A Safe Way To Salvation

John Patrick, Edward Knott, John Patrick

The Religion Of Protestants
A Safe Way To Salvation

ISBN/EAN: 9783742814272

Manufactured in Europe, USA, Canada, Australia, Japa

Cover: Foto ©Lupo / pixelio.de

Manufactured and distributed by brebook publishing software (www.brebook.com)

John Patrick, Edward Knott, John Patrick

The Religion Of Protestants

CALLED THE
Religion of Protestants
A SAFE WAY TO
SALVATION,

Made more generally useful by omitting Perfonal Contefts, but inferting whatfoever concerns the common Caufe of *Proteftants*, or defends the Church of *England*.

WITH
An ADDITION of fome genuine Pieces of Mr. *Chillingworth*'s never before Printed.

Ifaac. Cafaub. in Ep. ad Card. *Perron.* Reg. *Jac.* nomine fcripta.

Rex arbitratur rerum abfolutè neceffariarum ad falutem non magnum effe numerum. Quare exiftimat ejus Majeftas, nullam ad ineundem concordiam breviorem viam fore, quàm fi diligentèr feparentur neceffaria à non neceffariis, & ut de neceffariis conveniat, omnis opera infumatur: in non neceffariis libertati Chriftianæ locus detur, Simpliciter neceffaria Rex appellat, quæ vel expreffe verbum Dei præcipit credenda faciendave, vel ex verbo Dei neceffariâ confequentiâ vetus Ecclefia elicuit. — Si ad decidendas hodiernas Controverfias hæc diftinctio adhiberetur, & jus divinum à pofitivo feu Ecclefiaftico candidè fepararetur; non videtur de iis quæ funt abfolutè neceffaria, inter pios & moderatos viros, longa aut acris contentio futura. Nam & pauca illa funt, ut modò dicebamus, & fere ex æquo omnibus probantur, qui fe Chriftianos dici poftulant. Atque iftam diftinctionem Sereniff. Rex tanti putat effe momenti ad minuendas Controverfias, quæ hodie Ecclefiam Dei tantopere exercent, ut omnium pacis ftudioforum judicet officium effe, diligentiffimè hanc explicare, docere, urgere.

London, Printed for R. *Chifwell*, at the Rofe and Crown in S.*Pauls* Church-yard, C. *Harper*, at the Flower de-Luce in *Fleetftreet*, *W.Crook*, at the Green-Dragon without *Temple-Bar*, and *J. Adamfon* at the Angel in S.*Paul's* Church-yard. 1687.

An Advertisement concerning this Edition.

I Hope I shall incur no blame from those who deservedly value this Excellent BOOK of Mr. Chillingworth, for having made it of a lesser bulk and an easier purchase than before, after I have told them my way of proceeding herein: I have not Epitomized it in the usual way, by contracting any where his sense, and giving it more briefly in words of my own; which would have been indeed an injury to him, who knew so well how to express his own sense fully and perspicuously beyond most men, without any redundancy of style; but by paring off and leaving out some parts of it, which I thought might be well spared, and make the Reading of his Book more pleasant, as well as more generally useful, when his defence of the Protestant Doctrins and the cause of the Reformation lay more closely together not being interrupted with so many pages spent to justifie Dr. Potter in the personal contests betwixt him and his adversary; or in detecting the sophistry, frauds and falsities of the Jesuit, where the matter was not of common concern. But where I thought it was, I have been scrupulously careful to omit nothing: so far from it, that I am apt upon a review to think, that the pleasure of reading his admirable Confutation, has bribed me to insert more than was needful, in pursuance of my first design.

The reason why the Jesuits Book which Mr. Chillingworth answers is not here reprinted, was partly because it is too tedious and wordy, abounding in impertinent cavils, and affecting to fetch a great compass to amuse and lose the

Advertisement.

Reader before he comes to the point in Question, which he scarce ever attempts closely to prove; and chiefly because Mr. Chillingworth *has commonly all along set down in a different Character, as much of his words, as was needful to let the Reader see, what it is he makes a Reply to, and where I found any omission of this kind, I have transcribed out of the Jesuits Book such passages and citations, as might give further light to it: besides, that every one who has a mind, or any doubt remaining about this matter, may easily consult the Folio Edition & satisfie himself.*

I have added a large **Table of Contents** *at the end which was wanting before, whereby the Reader may find any Argument or head of Discourse therein contained, with little or no trouble; which* Table *will serve any Edition of the Book, because the numbers after the Chapter refer to the divisions of the Chapters at the side, not to the Pages at the top.*

As for the Additional pieces that follow the Book, and were never before printed, he that reads them will find by the clearness of expression, the close way of arguing and strength of reasoning, sufficient to convince him that they are not spurious, but the genuine productions of this great Man; but yet for his further satisfaction he may know, that the Manuscript out of which most of them were faithfully transcribed, is an Original of Mr. Chillingworths *own hand-writing, and now in the custody of the Reverend Dr.* Tennison, *to whom he is beholden for their present Publication.* Farewel.

TO

TO THE
Most High and Mighty Prince,
CHARLES
BY THE GRACE OF GOD,

KING of Great *Brittain*, *France* and *Ireland*, Defender of the Faith, &c.

May it please Your most Excellent Majesty,

I Present, with all humility to Your most sacred Hands, a Defence of that Cause which is and ought to be infinitely dearer to you, than all the world: Not doubting but upon this Dedication I shall be censured for a double boldness; both for undertaking so great a Work, so far beyond my weak abilities, and again, for presenting it to such a Patron, whose judgment I ought to fear more than any Adversary. But for the first, it is a satisfaction to my self, and may be to others, that I was not drawn to it out of any vain opinion of my self, (whose personal defects are the only thing which I presume to know,) but undertook it in obedience to Him, who said, *Tu Conversus confirma fratres*, not to *S. Peter* only but to all men: being encouraged also to it by the goodness of the Cause, which is able to make a weak man strong. To the belief hereof I was not led partially or by chance, as many are, by the prejudice and prepossession of their Country, Education and such like inducements, which if they lead to truth in one place, perhaps lead to error in a hundred; but having with the greatest equality and indifferency, made enquiry and search into the grounds on both sides, I was willing to impart to

others

The Epistle Dedicatory.

others that satisfaction which was given to my self. For my inscribing to it your Majesties sacred Name, I should labour much in my excuse of it from high presumption, had it not some appearance of Title to your Majesties Patronage and protection as being a Defence of that Book, which by special Order from Your Majesty was written some years since chiefly for the general good, but peradventure not without some aim at the recovery of One of your meanest Subjects from a dangerous deviation, and so due unto your Majesty, as the fruit of your own High humility and most Royal Charity. Besides, it is in a manner nothing else, but a pursuance of, and a superstruction upon that blessed Doctrin, wherewith I have adorn'd and arm'd the Frontispiece of my Book, which was so earnestly recommended by your Royal Father of happy memory, to all the lovers of Truth and Peace, that is to all that were like himself, as the only hopeful means of healing the breaches of Christendom, whereof the Enemy of souls makes such pestilent advantage. The lustre of this blessed Doctrin I have here endeavoured to uncloud and unveil, and to free it from those mists and fumes which have been rais'd to obscure it, by that Order, which envenoms even poison it self, and makes the *Roman* Religion much more malignant and turbulent than otherwise it would be; whose very Rule and Doctrin, obliges them to make all men, as much as lies in them, subjects unto Kings, and servants unto Christ, no farther than it shall please the Pope. So that whether Your Majesty be considered, either as a pious Son towards your Royal Father K. *James,* or as a tender hearted and compassionate Son towards your distressed Mother, the Catholick Church, or as a King of your Subjects, or as a Servant unto Christ, this work, (to which I can give no other commendation, but that it was intended to do you service in all these capacities,) may pretend not unreasonably to your Gracious acceptance.

The Epistle Dedicatory.

ceptance. Lastly being a Defence of that whole Church and Religion you profess, it could not be so proper to any Patron as to the great Defender of it; which stile Your Majesty hath ever so exactly made good, both in securing it from all dangers, and in vindicating it (by the well ordering and rectifying this Church) from all the foul aspersions both of Domestick and Forrein enemies, of which they can have no ground, but their own malice and want of Charity. But it's an argument of a despairing and lost cause to support it self with these impetuous outcries and clamors, the faint refuges of those that want better arguments; like that Stoick in *Lucian* that cried Ω̃ κατάρατε, *O damn'd villain*, when he could say nothing else. Neither is it credible the wiser sort of them should believe this their own horrid assertion, That a God of goodness should damn to eternal torments, those that love him and love truth, for errors which they fall into through humane frailty! But this they must say, otherwise their only great argument from their damning us, and our not being so peremptory in damning them, because we hope unaffected Ignorance may excuse them, would be lost: and therefore they are engaged to act on this Tragical part, only to fright the simple and ignorant, as we do little children by telling them that bites, which we would not have them meddle with. And truly that herein they do but act a part, and know themselves to do so, and deal with us here as they do with the King of *Spain* at *Rome*, whom they accurse and Excommunicate for fashion sake on *Maundy-Thursday*, for detaining part of *S.Peters* Patrimony, and absolve him without satisfaction on *Good-Friday*, methinks their faltring and inconstancy herein, makes it very apparent. For though for the most part, they speak nothing but thunder and lightning to us, and damn us all without mercy or exception, yet sometimes to serve other purposes, they can be content to speak to us in a milder

strain,

The Epistle Dedicatory.

strain, and tell us, as my adversary does, more than once, *That they allow Protestants as much Charity as Protestants allow them.* Neither is this the only contradiction which I have discovered in this uncharitable Work; but have shewed that by forgetting himself, and retracting most of the principal grounds he builds upon, he hath saved me the labour of a confutation; which yet I have not in any place found any such labour or difficulty, but that it was undertakeable by a man of very mean, that is, of my abilities. And the reason is, because it is Truth I plead for; which is so strong an argument for it self, that it needs only light to discover it: whereas it concerns Falshood and Error to use disguises and shadowings and all the fetches of Art and Sophistry, and therefore it stands in need of abler men, to give that a colour at least, which hath no real body to subsist by. If my endeavors in this kind may contribute any thing to this discovery, and the making plain that Truth (which my Charity perswades me the most part of them disaffect only, because it has not been well represented to them,) I have the fruit of my labour, and my wish; who desire to live to no other end, than to do service to Gods Church and Your most Sacred Majesty, in the quality of

Your Majesties most faithful Subject,

and most humble and devoted Servant

WILLIAM CHILLINGWORTH.

THE

THE PREFACE TO THE AUTHOR OF
Charity Maintained.

With an Anſwer to his Direction to *N. N.*

SIR,

UPON the firſt news of the publication of your Book, I uſed all diligence with ſpeed to procure it; and came with ſuch a mind to the reading of it, as *S. Auſtin* before he was a ſetled Catholick, brought to his conference with *Fauſtus* the Manichee. For as he thought, that if any thing more then ordinary might be ſaid in defence of the Manichean Doctrine, *Fauſtus* was the man from whom it was to be expected: So my perſuaſion concerning you was,

Si Pergama dextrâ defendi poſſunt, certè hac defenſa videbo.
   If *Troy* by any Power could ſtand,
   'Twould be defended by your hand.

1. For I conceived that among the Champions of the Roman Church, the *Engliſh* in Reaſon muſt be the beſt, or equal to the beſt, as being by moſt expert Maſters trained up purpoſely for this war, and perpetually practiſed in it. Among the *Engliſh*, I ſaw the Jeſuits would yield the firſt place to none; and Men ſo wiſe in their generation as the Jeſuits were, if they had any *Achilles* among them, I preſumed, would make choice of him for this ſervice. And beſides, I had good aſſurance that in the framing of this building, though you were the only Architect, yet you
wanted

wanted not the assistance of many diligent hands to bring you in choice materials towards it; nor of many careful and watchful eyes to correct the errors of your work, if any should chance to escape you. Great reason therefore had I to expect great matters from you, and that your Book should have in it the Spirit and Elixir of all that can be said in defence of your Church and Doctrin; and to assure my self, that if my resolution not to believe it, were not built upon the rock of evident grounds and reasons, but only upon some sandy and deceitful appearances, now the Wind and Storm and Floods were coming, which would undoubtedly overthrow it.

2. Neither truly were you more willing to effect such an alteration in me than I was to have it effected. For my desire is to go the right way to *Eternal Happiness*. But whether this way lie on the right-hand or the left, or strait forwards; whether it be by following a living Guide, or by seeking my directions in a Book, or by hearkening to the secret whisper of some private Spirit, to me it is indifferent. And he that is otherwise affected, and has not a Travellers indifference, which *Epictetus* requires in all that would find the truth, but much desires in respect of his ease, or pleasure, or profit, or advancement, or satisfaction of friends, or any human consideration, that one way should be true rather than another; it is odds but he will take his desire that it should be so, for an assurance that it is so. But I for my part, unless I deceive my self, was and still am so affected as I have made profession: not willing I confess to take any thing upon trust, and to believe it without asking my self why; no, nor able to command my self (were I never so willing) to follow, like a sheep, every shepheard that should take upon him to guide me; or every Flock that should chance to go before me: but most apt and most willing to be led by reason to any way, or from it; and always submitting all other Reasons to this one, God hath said so, therefore it is true. Nor yet was I so unreasonable as to expect Mathematical demonstrations from you in matters plainly incapable of them, such as are to be *believed*, and if we speak properly, cannot
be

be *known* ; such therefore I expected not. For as he is an unreasonable Master, who requires a stronger assent to his conclusions than his arguments deserve; so I conceive him a froward and undisciplin'd Scholar, who desires stronger arguments for a conclusion than the matter will bear. But had you represented to my understanding such reasons of your Doctrine, as being weighed in an even ballance, held by an even hand, with those on the other side, would have turned the Scale, and have made your Religion more credible than the contrary; certainly I should have despised the shame of one more alteration, and with both mine armes and all my heart most readily have embraced it. Such was my expectation from you, and such my preparation, which I brought with me to the reading of your Book.

3. Would you know now what the event was, what effect was wrought in me by the perusal and consideration of it? To deal truly and ingenuously with you, I fell somwhat in my good opinion both of your sufficiency and sincerity: but was exceedingly confirmed in the ill opinion of the Cause maintained by you. I found every where Snares that might ▓▓▓▓ and Colours that might deceive the Simple; ▓▓▓▓ing that might persuade, and very little that m▓▓▓▓e an understanding Man, and one that can di▓ern between Discourse and Sophistry. In short, I was verily perswaded that I plainly saw and could make it appear, to all dispassionate and unprejudicate Judges, that a vein of Sophistry and Calumny did run clean through it from the beginning to the end. And this I undertook with a full resolution to be an adversary to your Errors, but a Friend and Servant to your Person: and so much the more a Friend to your Person, by how much the severer and more rigid Adversary I was to your Errors.

4. In this work, my Conscience bears me witness, that I have according to your advice *proceeded always with this consideration, that I am to give a most strict account of every line, and word that passeth under my Pen*; and therefore have been precisely careful for *the matter* of my Book to defend

truth

truth only, and only by Truth. And then scrupulously fearful of Scandalizing you or any Man with the *manner* of handling it.

6. In your Pamphlet of Directions to *N. N.* you have loaded not only my person in particular, but all the Learned and Moderate Divines of the Church of *England*, and all Protestants in general, nay all wise Men of all Religions but your own, with unworthy Contumelies, and a Mass of portentous and execrable Calumnies.

7. To begin with the last, you stick not in the beginning of your first Chapter, to fasten the imputation *of Atheism and Irreligion upon all wise and gallant Men, that are not of your own Religion.* In which uncharitable and unchristian Judgment, void of all colour or shadow of probability, I know yet by experience that very many of the *Bigots* of your Faction are partakers with you. God forbid I should think the like of you! Yet if I should say, that in your Religion there want not some temptations unto, and some Principles of Irreligion and Atheism, I am sure I could make my Assertion much more probable than you have done, or can make this horrible imputation.

8. For to pass by *first*, that which experience justifies, that where and when your Religion hath most absolutely commanded, there and then Atheism hath most abounded; To say nothing *Secondly*, of your notorious and confessed forging of so many false Miracles, and so many lying Legends, which is not unlikely to make suspitious men to question the truth of all: Nor to object to you *Thirdly*, the abundance of your weak and silly Ceremonies and ridiculous Observances in your Religion, which in all probability cannot but beget secret contempt and scorn of it in wise and considering men, and consequently Atheism and Impiety, if they have this persuasion setled in them (which is too rife among you, and which you account a piece of *Wisdom and Gallantry*) that if they be not of your Religion, they were as good be of none at all: Nor to trouble you *Fourthly* with this, that a great part of your Doctrine, especially in the Points contested,

tested, makes apparently for the temporal ends of the teachers of it; which yet I fear is a great scandal to many *Beaux Esprits* among you: Only I should desire you to consider attentively when you conclude so often from the differences of Protestants, that they have no certainty of any part of their Religion, no not of those Points wherein they agree, whether you do not that which so magisterially you direct me not to do, that is, proceed *a destructive way, and object arguments against your adversaries, which tend to the overthrow of all Religion?* And whether as you argue thus, *Protestants differ in many things, therefore they have no certainty of any thing:* So an Atheist or a Sceptick may not conclude as well, Christians, and the Professors of all Religions differ in many things, therefore they have no certainty of any thing? Again, I should desire you to tell me ingenuously, whether it be not too probable that your portentous Doctrine of Transubstantiation, joyn'd with your foremention'd perswasion of, *No Papists no Christians,* hath brought a great many others as well as himself, to *Averroes*'s resolution, *Quandoquidem Christiani adorant quod comedunt, sit anima mea cum Philosophis? Forasmuch as the Christians worship that which they eat, let my Soul be with the Philosophers.* Whether your requiring men upon only probable and *Prudential motives,* to yield a *most certain assent* unto things in humane reason impossible, and telling them, as you do too often, that they were as good not believe at all, as believe with any lower degree of Faith, be not a likely way to make considering men scorn your Religion, (and consequently all, if they know no other) as requiring things contradictory, and impossible to be performed? Lastly, Whether your pretence that there is no good ground to believe Scripture, but your Churches infallibility, joyn'd with your pretending no ground for this but some Texts of Scripture, be not a fair way to make them that understand themselves, believe neither Church nor Scripture?

9. Your Calumnies against Protestants in general are set down in these words, Chap. 2. §. 2. *The very doctrine*

The Preface to the Author of Charity maintain'd

of Proteſtants, if it be followed cloſely, and with coherence to it ſelf, muſt of neceſſity induce Socinianiſm. *This I ſay confidently, and evidently prove, by inſtancing in one Error, which may well be termed the Capital and Mother-hereſie, from which all other muſt follow at eaſe; I mean, their Hereſie in affirming that the perpetual viſible Church of Chriſt, deſcended by a never interrupted Succeſſion from our Saviour to this day, is not infallible in all that it propoſeth to be believed as revealed truths.*

For if the Infallibility *of ſuch a publick* Authority *be once impeached; what remains, but that every man is given over to his own* wit *and* diſcourſe? *and talk not here of holy Scripture, for if the true Church may err, in defining what Scriptures be Canonical; or in delivering the ſenſe and meaning thereof, we are ſtill devolved, either upon the* private Spirit *(a foolery now exploded out of* England, *which finally leaving every man to his own conceits, ends in* Socinianiſm) *or elſe epon* natural wit *and* judgment, *for examining and determining what Scriptures contain true or falſe Doctrine, and in that reſpect ought to be received or rejected. And indeed, take away the authority of Gods Church, no man can be aſſured, that any one Book or parcel of Scripture was written by Divine Inſpiration; or that all the Contents are infallibly true, which are the direct Errors of* Socinians. *If it were but for this reaſon alone, no man, who regards the eternal ſalvation of his Soul, would live or die in* Proteſtancy, *from which, ſo vaſt abſurdities as theſe of the* Socinians *muſt inevitably follow. And it ought to be an unſpeakable comfort to all us Catholicks, while we conſider, that none can deny the infallible authority of our Church, but jointly he muſt be left to his own wit and ways, and muſt abandon all* infuſed Faith *and true Religion, if he do but underſtand himſelf aright.* In all which Diſcourſe, the only true word you ſpeak, is, *This I ſay confidently:* As for *proving evidently,* that I believe you reſerved for ſome other opportunity : for the preſent I am ſure you have been very ſparing of it.

10. You ſay indeed confidently enough, that *the denyal of the Churches infallibility is the Mother-hereſie, from which all other muſt follow at eaſe;* which is ſo far from being

being a necessary truth, as you make it, that it is indeed a manifest falshood. Neither is it possible for the wit of man by any good, or so much as probable consequence, from the denial of the Churches Infallibility to deduce any one of the ancient Heresies, or any one Error of the *Socinians*, which are the Heresies here entreated of: For who would not laugh at him that should argue thus, Neither the Church of *Rome*, nor any other Church is infallible, *Ergo*, The Doctrine of *Arrius, Pelagius, Eutyches, Nestorius, Photinus, Manichæus*, was true Doctrine? On the other side, it may be truly said, and justified by very good and effectual reason, that he that affirms with you the Popes Infallibility, puts himself into his hands and power to be led by him at his ease and pleasure into all Heresie, and even to Hell it self, and cannot with reason say, (so long as he is constant to his grounds) *Domine cur ita facis?* Sir, *Why do you thus?* but must believe *white to be black, and black to be white ; vertue to be vice, and vice to be vertue*; nay (which is a horrible, but a most certain truth) Christ to be Antichrist, and Antichrist to be Christ, if it be possible for the Pope to say so: Which I say and will maintain, howsoever you daub and disguise it, is indeed to make men apostate from Christ to his pretended Vicar, but real Enemy: For that name, and no better, (if we may speak truth without offence) I presume he deserves, who under pretence of interpreting the Law of Christ, (which Authority, without any word of express warrant, he hath taken upon himself) doth in many parts evacuate and dissolve it : So dethroning Christ from his dominion over mens consciences, and instead of Christ setting up himself. In as much as he that requires that his Interpretations of any Law should be obeyed as true and genuine, seem they to mens understandings never so dissonant and discordant from it, (as the Bishop of *Rome* does) requires indeed that *his Interpretations* should be the *Laws* ; and he that is firmly prepared in mind to believe and receive all such Interpretations without judging of them, and though to his private judgment they seem unreasonable, is indeed congruously disposed

posed to hold Adultery a venial sin, and Fornication no sin, whensoever the Pope and his adherents shall so declare. And whatsoever he may plead, yet either wittingly or ignorantly he makes the Law and the Law-maker both stales, and obeys only the Interpreter. As if I should submit to the Laws of the King of *England*, but should indeed resolve to obey them in that sence which the King of *France* should put upon them whatsoever it were; I presume every understanding man would say that I did indeed obey the King of *France* and not the King of *England*. If I should pretend to believe the Bible, but that I would understand it accordingly to the sense which the chief Mufty should put upon it, who would not say that I were a Christian in pretence only, but indeed a Mahumetan?

11. Nor will it be to purpose for you to pretend that the precepts of Christ are so plain that it cannot be feared, that any Pope should ever go about to dissolve them and pretend to be a Christian: For, not to say that you now pretend the contrary, (to wit), *that the Law of Christ is obscure, even in things necessary to be believed and done*; and by saying so, have made a fair way for any foul interpretation of any part of it: certainly that which the Church of *Rome* hath already done in this kind, is an evident argument, (that if she once had this Power unquestioned and made expedite and ready for use, by being contracted to the Pope) she may do what she pleaseth with it. Who that had lived in the Primative Church, would not have thought it as utterly improbable, that ever they should have brought in the Worship of Images and Picturing of God, as now it is that they should legitimate Fornication? Why may we not think they may in time take away the whole Communion from the Laity, as well as they have taken away half of it? Why may we not think that any Text and any sense may not be accorded, as well as the whole 14. *Ch.* of the *Ep.* of S. *Paul* to the *Corinth.* is reconciled to the Latine service? How is it possible any thing should be plainer forbidden, than the *Worship of Angels*, in the *Ep.* to the *Colossians*? than *the teaching for Doctrines*

Ērines Mens commands in the Gospel of *S. Mark?* And therefore seeing we see these things done which hardly any man would have believed, that had not seen them, why should we not fear that this unlimited Power may not be used hereafter with as little moderation? Seeing devices have been invented how Men may worship Images without Idolatry, and Kill Innocent Men under pretence of Heresie without Murther, who knows not that some tricks may not be hereafter devised, by which lying with other Mens Wives shall be no Adultery, taking away other Mens Goods no Theft? I conclude therefore, that if *Solomon* himself were here, and were to determine the difference, which is more likely to be Mother of all Heresie, the *denial* of the *Churches*, or the *affirming* of the *Popes Infallibility*, that he would certainly say, *this is the Mother, give her the Child*.

12. You say again confidently, that *if this Infallibility be once impeached, every Man is given over to his own Wit and Discourse*: which, if you mean, *Discourse*, not guiding it selfe by Scripture, but only by principles of Nature, or perhaps by prejudices and popular errors, and drawing consequences not by rule but chance, is by no means true; if you mean by Discourse, right reason, grounded on Divine revelation and common notions, written by God in the hearts of all Men, and deducing, according to the never failing rules of Logick, consequent deductions from them, if this be it, which you mean by *Discourse*, it is very meet and reasonable and necessary that Men, as in all their actions, so especially in that of greatest importance, the choice of their way to happiness, should be left unto it: and he that follows this in all his opinions and actions, and does not only seem to do so, follows alwaies God; whereas he that followeth a Company of Men, may oftimes follow a Company of Beasts. And in saying this, I say no more than *S. John* to all Christians in these words, *Dearly beloved, Believe not every spirit, but try the spirits, whether they be of God, or no*: and the rule he gives them to make this tryal by, is to consider whether they confess *Jesus to be the Christ*; that is, the Guide of their Faith, and

C   Lord

Lord of their actions; not whether they acknowledg the *Pope* to be his Vicar: I say no more than S. *Paul* in exhorting all Christians, *to try all things and to hold fast that which is good*; than S. *Peter* in commanding all Christians, *to be ready to give a reason of the hope that is in them*: than *our Saviour* himself in forewarning all his followers, that *if they blindly followed blind Guides, both leaders and followers should fall into the Ditch*; and again in saying even to the People, *Yea and why of your selves Judge ye not what is right?* And though by passion, or precipitation, or prejudice; by want of Reason, or not using that they have, Men may be and are oftentimes led into Error and mischief; yet that they cannot be misguided by discourse truly so called, such as I have described, you your self have given them security. For what is discourse, but drawing conclusions out of premises by good consequence? Now the principles which we have setled, to wit, the *Scriptures*, are on all sides agreed to be infallibly true. And you have told us in the fourth chap. of this Pamphlet, that *from truth no man can by good consequence infer falshood*; Therefore by discourse no Man can possibly be led to Error: but if he Err in his conclusions, he must of necessity either Err in his principles, (which here cannot have place,) or commit some Error in his discourse; that is indeed, not discourse but seem to do so.

13. You say thirdly, with sufficient confidence, that *if the true Churh may Err in defining what Scriptures be Canonical, or in delivering the sense thereof, then we must follow either the private Spirit, or else natural wit and Judgment, and by them examine what Scriptures contain true or false Doctrine, and in that respect ought to be received or rejected:* All which is apparently untrue, neither can any proof of it be pretended. For though the present Church may possibly Err in her judgment touching this matter, yet have we other Directions in it, besides the private spirit, and the examination of the Contents, (which latter way may conclude the negative very strongly, to wit, that such or such a Book cannot come from God, because it contains irreconcilable contradictions, but the affirmative

it

it cannot conclude, becaufe the Contents of a Book may be all true, and yet the Book not written by Divine infpiration:) other Direction therefore I fay we have, befides either of thefe three, and that is, the Teftimony of the Primitive Chriftians.

14. You fay Fourthly, with convenient boldnefs, That *this infallible Authority of your Church being denied, no man can be affured, that any parcel of Scripture was written by Divine infpiration* : Which is an untruth, for which no proof is pretended, and befides, void of modefty and full of impiety. The firft, becaufe the experience of innumerable Chriftians is againft it, who are fufficiently affured, that the Scripture is Divinely infpired, and yet deny the infallible Authority of your Church or any other. The fecond, becaufe if I cannot have ground to be affured of the Divine Authority of Scripture, unlefs I firft believe your Church infallible, then I can have no ground at all to believe it: becaufe there is no ground, nor can any be pretended, why I fhould believe your Church *Infallible,* unlefs I firft believe the Scripture Divine.

16. Had I a mind to recriminate now, and to charge Papifts (as you do Proteftants) that they lead Men to Socinianifm, I could certainly make a much fairer fhew of evidence than you have done. For I would not tell you, you deny the Infallibility of the Church of *England, Ergo,* you lead to Socinianifm, which yet is altogether as good an Argument as this; Proteftants deny the Infallibility of the *Roman* Church, *Ergo,* they induce Socinianifm: Nor would I refume my former Argument, and urge you, that by holding the *Popes* Infallibility, you fubmit your felf to that Capital and Mother Herefie, by advantage whereof, he may lead you at eafe to believe *vertue vice,* and *vice vertue,* to believe Antichriftianity Chriftianifm, and Chriftianity Antichriftian; he may lead you to Socinianifm, to Turcifm, nay, to the Divel himfelf if he have a mind to it: But I would fhew you that divers ways the Doctors of your Church do the principal and proper work of the Socinians for them, undermining the Doctrine of the Trinity, by denying it to be fuppor-

ted by those Pillars of the Faith, which alone are fit and able to support it, I mean Scripture, and the Consent of the Ancient Doctors.

17. For *Scripture*, your Men deny very plainly and frequently, that this Doctrine can be proved by it. See if you please, this plainly taught, and urged very earnestly by Cardinal *Hosius*, *De Author. Sac. Scrip. l.* 3. *p.* 53. By *Gordonius Huntlæus*, *Contr. Tom.* 1. *Controv.* 1. *De verbo Dei C.* 19. by *Gretserus* and *Tanerus*, *in Colloquio Ratesbon*: And also by *Vega*, *Possevin*, *Wiekus*, and *Others*.

18. And then for *the Consent of the Ancients*, that that also delivers it not, by whom are we taught but by Papists only? Who is it that makes known to all the World, that *Eusebius* that great searcher and devourer of the Christian Libraries *was an Arrian*? Is it not your great *Achilles*, *Cardinal Perron*, in his 3. Book 2. Chap. of his Reply to K. *James*? Who is it that informs us that *Origen* (who never was questioned for any Error in this matter, in or near his time) *denyed the Divinity of the Son and the Holy Ghost*? Is it not the same great Cardinal, in his Book *of the Eucharist* against *M. du Plessis. l.* 2. *c.* 7 ? Who is it that pretends that *Irenæus hath said those things, which he that should now hold, would be esteemed an Arrian?* Is it not the same *Perron* in his Reply to K. *James*, in the Fifth Chap. of his Fourth Observation? And does he not in the same place peach *Tertullian* also, and in a manner give him away to the *Arrians*? And pronounce generally of the *Fathers before the Council of Nice*, That *the* Arrians *would gladly be tryed by them*? And are not your fellow Jesuits also, even the Prime Men of your Order, prevaricators in this point as well as others? Doth not your Friend M. *Fisher*, or M. *Flued* in his Book of the Nine Questions proposed to him by K. *James* speak dangerously to the same purpose, in his Discourse *of the Resolution of Faith*, towards the end? Giving us to understand, *That the new Reformed* Arrians *bring very many Testimonies of the Ancient Fathers, to prove that in this Point they did contradict themselves, and were contrary one to another: which places whosoever shall read will clearly see, that to*

common

with an answer to his Direction to N. N.

common People they are unanswerable, yea, that common People are not capable of the Answers that Learned Men yield unto such obscure passages. And hath not your great Antiquary *Petavius,* in his Notes upon *Epiphanius in Hær.* 69. been very liberal to the Adversaries of the Doctrine of the Trinity, and in a manner given them for Patrons and Advocates, first *Justin Martyr,* and then almost all the Fathers before the Council of *Nice,* whose Speeches he says, touching this point, *cum Orthodoxæ fidei regula minime consentiunt*: *Are no way agreeable to the rule of Orthodox Faith.* Hereunto I might add, that the Dominicans and Jesuits between them in another matter of great importance, viz. *Gods Prescience of future contingents,* give the *Socinians* the premises, out of which their conclusion doth unavoidably follow. For the *Dominicans* maintain on the one Side, that *God can foresee nothing but what he Decrees*: The Jesuits on the other Side, that *he doth not Decree all things*: And from hence the *Socinians* conclude (as it is obvious for them to do) that *he doth not foresee all things.* Lastly, I might adjoyn this, that you agree with one consent, and settle for a rule unquestionable, that no part of Religion can be repugnant to Reason, whereunto you in particular subscribe unawares in saying, *From truth no Man can by good consequence infer falshood,* which is to say in effect, that Reason can never lead any Man to Error: And after you have done so, you proclaim to all the World (as you in this Pamphlet do very frequently,) that *if Men follow their Reason and Discourse,* they will (if they understand themselves) be led to *Socinianism.* And thus you see with what probable matter I might furnish out and justifie my accusation, if I should charge you with leading Men to *Socinianism*! Yet I do not conceive that I have ground enough for this odious imputation. And much less should you have charged *Protestants* with it, whom you confess to abhor and detest it: and who fight against it, not with the broken Reeds, and out of the Paper Fortresses of an imaginary Infallibility, which were only to make sport for their Adversaries; but with the *Sword of the Spirit, the Word of God:* of which we may
say

The Preface to the Author of Charity maintain'd,
say most truly, what *David* said of *Goliah's* Sword, offered him by *Abilech, non est sicut iste,* There is none comparable to it.

19. Thus *Protestants* in general, I hope, are sufficiently vindicated from your Calumny: I proceed now to do the same service for the Divines of *England*; whom you question first in point of Learning and Sufficiency, and then in point of Conscience and Honesty, as prevaricating in the Religion which they profess, and inclining to *Popery.* Their Learning (you say) consists only in *some superficial Talent of Preaching, Languages, and Elocution, and not in any deep knowledg of Philosophy, especially of Metaphysicks, and much less of that most solid, profitable, subtile,* & (O rem ridiculam *Cato* & jocosam!) *succinct method of School Divinity.* Wherein you have discovered in your self the true Genius and Spirit of detraction. For taking advantage from that wherein envy it self cannot deny but they are very eminent, and which requires great sufficiency of substantial Learning, you disparage them as insufficient in all things else. As if Forsooth, because they dispute not eternally. *Utrum Chimæra bombinans in vacuo, possit comedere secundas Intentiones? Whether a Million of Angels may not sit upon a Needles point?* Because they fill not their Brains with notions that signifie nothing, to the utter extermination of all reason and common sence, and spend not an Age in weaving and un-weaving subtile Cobwebs, fitter to catch Flies than Souls; therefore they have no deep knowledge in the Acroamatical part of Learning! But I have too much honoured the poorness of this detraction to take notice of it.

20. The other Part of your accusation strikes deeper, and is more considerable: And that tells us that, *Protestantism waxeth weary of it self; that the Professors of it, they especially of greatest Worth, Learning, and Authority, love temper and moderation: and are at this time more unresolved where to fasten, than at the Infancy of their Church: That their Churches begin to look with a New Face: Their Walls to Speak a New Language: Their Doctrine to be altered in many things, for which their Progenitors forsook the then Visible*

Visible Church of Christ: For example, the Pope *not Antichrist*: Prayer for the Dead : Limbus Patrum : Pictures : That the Church hath Authority in determining Controversies of Faith, and to interpret Scripture ; about Freewil, Predestination, Universal Grace : That all our Works are not Sins : Merit of good Works : Inherent *Justice* : Faith alone doth not justifie : Charity to be preferred before knowledg : Traditions : Commandments possible to be kept : That their thirty nine Articles are patient, nay ambitious of some sence wherein they may seem Catholick : That to Alledge the necessity of Wife and Children in these days, is but a weak Plea for a Married Minister to compass a Benefice : That *Calvinism is* at length accounted Heresie, and little less than .Treason : That *Men in Talk and Writing use* willingly the once fearful Names of Priests and Altars : That they are now put in mind, that for exposition of Scripture, they are by Canon bound to follow the Fathers : which if they do with sincerity, it is easie to tell what Doom will pass against Protestants ; seeing by the confession of Protestants, the Fathers are on the Papists side, which the Answerer to some so clearly demonstrated, that they remained convinced : In fine, as the Samaritans *saw in the* Disciples countenances, that they meant to go to Hierusalem, so you pretend it *is even legible in the* Fore-heads of these Men, that they are even going, nay making hast to Rome. Which scurrilous Libel void of all Truth, Discretion and Honesty, what effect it may have wrought, what credit it may have gained with credulous *Papists,* (who dream what they desire, and believe their own dreams,) or with ill-affected, jealous, and weak *Protestants,* I cannot tell : But one thing I dare boldly say, that you your self did never believe it.

21. The truth is, they that run to extreams in opposition against you, they that pull down your Infallibility and set up their own, they that declaim against your Tyranny, and exercise it themselves over others, are the Adversaries that give you the greatest advantage, and such as you love to deal with : whereas upon Men of temper and moderation, such as will oppose nothing because you maintain it, but will draw as near to you, that they

may

may draw you to them, as the Truth will suffer them: such as require of Christians to believe only in Christ, and will Damn no Man nor Doctrine without express and certain warrant from Gods Word: upon such as these you know not how to fasten; but if you chance to have conference with any such, (which yet as much as possibly you can you avoid and decline,) you are very speedily put to silence, and see the indefensible weakness of your cause laid open to all Men. And this I verily believe is the true Reason that you thus rave and rage against them, as foreseeing your time of prevailing, or even of subsisting, would be short, if other adversaries gave you no more advantage than they do.

22. In which perswasion also I am much confirmed by consideration of the Silliness and Poorness of those suggestions, and partly of the apparent vanity and Falshood of them, which you offer in justification of this wicked Calumny. For what if out of Devotion towards God; out of a desire that He should be Worshiped as *in Spirit and Truth* in the first place, so also *in the Beauty of Holiness*? what if out of fear, that too much Simplicity and Nakedness in the publick Service of God may beget in the ordinary sort of Men a dull and stupid irreverence, and out of hope that the outward State and Glory of it, being well disposed and wisely moderated, may ingender, quicken, encrease and nourish the inward reverence, respect and devotion which is due unto Gods Sovereign Majesty and Power? What if out of a persuasion and desire that *Papists* may be won over to us the sooner, by the removing of this Scandal out of their way; and out of an Holy Jealousie, that the weaker sort of *Protestants* might be the easier seduced to them by the Magnificence and Pomp of their Church-service in case it were not removed? I say, what if out of these considerations, the Governors of our Church, more of late than formerly, have set themselves to adorn and beautifie the places *where Gods Honour dwells*, and to make them as Heavenly as they can with Earthly Ornaments? Is this a sign that they are warping towards *Popery*? Is this Devotion

in the Church of *England*, an argument that She is coming over to the Church of *Rome*? Sir *Edwin Sands*, I presume every Man will grant, had no inclination that way; yet He Forty Years since highly commended this part of Devotion in *Papists*, and makes no scruple of proposing it to the imitation of *Protestants*: little thinking that they who would follow his Counsel, and endeavour to take away this disparagement of *Protestants*, and this Glorying of *Papists*, should have been censured for it, as making way and inclining to *Popery*. His Words to this purpose are excellent Words, and because they shew plainly, that what is now practised was approved by Zealous *Protestants* so long ago, I will here set them down.

Survey of Religion.

23. *This one thing I cannot but highly commend in that sort and Order: They spare nothing which either cost can perform in enriching, or skill in adorning the Temple of God, or to set out his Service with the greatest Pomp and magnificence that can be devised. And although, for the most part, much Baseness and Childishness is predominant in the Masters and contrivers of their Ceremonies, yet this outward State and Glory being well disposed, doth ingender, quicken, increase, and nourish the inward reverence, respect and Devotion, which is due unto Sovereign Majesty and Power. And although I am not ignorant that many Men well reputed have embraced the thrifty Opinion of that Disciple, who thought all to be wasted that was bestowed upon Christ in that sort, and that it were much better bestowed upon him on the Poor, (yet with an eye perhaps that themselves would be his quarter Almoners,) notwithstanding I must confess, it will never sink into my Heart, that in proportion of Reason, the allowance for furnishing out of the Service of God should be measured by the scant and strict rule of meer necessity, (a proportion so low that Nature to other most bountiful in matter of necessity, hath not failed no not the most ignoble Creatures of the World,) and that for our selves no measure of heaping but the most we can get, no rule of expence but to the utmost Pomp we list: Or that God himself had so inriched the lower parts of the World with such wonderfull varieties of Beauty and Glory, that they might serve only to the Pampering of Mortal Man in his Pride; and that*

that in the Service of the High Creator Lord and giver, (*the outward Glory of whose higher Pallace may appear by the very Lamps that we see so far off Burning gloriously in it*) *only the Simpler, Baser, Cheaper, Less Noble, Less Beautiful, Less Glorious things should be imployed. Especially seeing as in Princes Courts, so in the Service of God also, this outward State and Glory, being well disposed, doth* (*as I have said*) *ingender, quicken, increase and nourish the inward reverence, respect and Devotion, which is due to so Sovereign Majesty and Power. Which those whom the use thereof cannot persuade unto, would easily by the want of it be brought to confess; for which cause I crave leave to be excused by them herein, if in Zeal to the common Lord of all, I choose rather to commend the vertue of an Enemy than to flatter the vice and imbecility of a Friend.* And so much for this matter.

24. Again, what if the Names of the *Priests* and *Altars* so frequent in the Ancient Fathers, though not in the now *Popish* sense, be now resumed and more commonly used in *England* than of late times they were: that so the colourable argument of their conformity, which is but nominal, with the Ancient Church, and our inconformity, which the Governors of the Church would not have so much as nominal, may be taken away from them; and the Church of *England* may be put in a State, in this regard more justifiable against the *Roman* than formerly it was, being hereby enabled to say to *Papists* (whensoever these Names are objected,) we also use the Names of *Priests* and *Altars*, and yet believe neither the Corporal Presence, nor any Proper and propitiatory Sacrifice?

25. What if *Protestants* be now put in mind, that for exposition of Scripture, they are bound by a *Canon to follow the Ancient Fathers*: which whosoever doth with sincerity, it is utterly impossible he should be a *Papist*? And it is most falsly said by you, that you know that to some *Protestants* I clearly demonstrated, or ever so much as undertook, or went about to demonstrate the contrary. What if the Centurists be censured somewhat roundly by a *Protestant* Divine for affirming, that *the keeping of the Lords day was a thing indifferent for two Hundren Years*? Is there in
all

all this or any part of it any kind of proof of this scandalous Calumny?

26. As for the points of Doctrine wherein you pretend that these Divines begin of late to falter, and to comply with the Church of *Rome*, upon a due examination of particulars it will presently appear, *First*, that part of them always have been, and now are held constantly one way by them; as the Authority of the Church in determining Controversies of Faith, though not the Infallibility of it: That there is Inherent Justice, though so imperfect that it cannot justifie: That there are Traditions, though none necessary: That Charity is to be preferred before knowledg: That good Works are not properly meritorious: And lastly, that Faith alone justifies, though that Faith justifies not which is alone. And *Secondly*, for the remainder that they, every one of them, have been Anciently without breach of Charity disputed among *Protestants*, such for example were the Questions about the *Popes* being the Antichrist, the Lawfulness of some kind of Prayers for the Dead, the Estate of the Fathers Souls, before Christs Ascension; Freewil, Predestination, Universal Grace: the Possibility of keeping Gods Commandments. The use of Pictures in the Church: Wherein that there hath been anciently diversity of opinion amongst *Protestants*, it is justified to my hand by a witness, with you, beyond exception, even your great Friend M. *Brerely*, *whose care, exactness and fidelity* (you say in your Preface) *is so extraordinary great*. Consult him therefore: Tract. 3. Sect. 7. of his *Apology*: And in the 9, 10, 11. 14. 24. 26. 27. 37. Subdivisions of that *Section*, you shall see as in a mirror, your self proved an egregious calumniator, for charging *Protestants* with innovation and inclining to *Popery*, under pretence forsooth, that their Doctrine begins of late to be altered in these points. Whereas, M *Brerely* will inform you, they have been anciently, and even from the begininng of the Reformation, controverted amongst them, though perhaps the Stream and Current of their Doctors run one way, and only some Brook or Rivulet of them the other.

27. It remains now in the laſt place, that I bring my ſelf fairly off from your foul Aſperſions, that ſo my Perſon may not be any diſparagement to the Cauſe, nor any ſcandal to weak Chriſtians.

28. Firſt upon Hearſay, you charge me with a great number of falſe and impious Doctrines, which I will not name in particular, becauſe I will not aſſiſt you ſo far in the ſpreading of my own undeſerved defamation: but whoſoever teaches or holds them *let him be Anathema!* The Summ of them all is this, *Nothing ought or can be certainly believed, farther than it may be proved by evidence of Natural Reaſon:* (where I conceive Natural reaſon it oppoſed to ſupernatural Revelation) and whoſoever holds ſo *let him be Anathema!* And moreover to clear my ſelf once for all, from all imputations of this nature, which charge me injuriouſly with denial of Supernatural Verities, I profeſs ſincerely, that I believe all thoſe Books of Scripture, which the Church of *England* accounts Canonical, to be the Infallible Word of God: I believe all things evidently contained in them; all things evidently, or even probably deducible from them: I acknowledge all that to be Hereſie, which by the Act of Parliament *primo of Q. Eliz.* is declared to be ſo, and only to be ſo: And though in ſuch points which may be held diverſly of divers men *ſalvâ Fidei compage,* I would not take any Mans Liberty from him, and humbly beſeech all men, that they would not take mine from me! Yet thus much I can ſay (which I hope will ſatisfie any man of reaſon,) that whatſoever hath been held neceſſary to Salvation, either by the Catholick Church of all ages, or by the conſent of Fathers, meaſured by *Vincentius Lyrinenſis* his rule, or is held neceſſary either by the Catholick Church of this age, or by the conſent of *Proteſtants,* or even by the Church of *England,* that, againſt the *Socinians,* and all others whatſoever, I do verily believe and embrace.

29. But what are all Perſonal matters to the buſineſs in hand? If it could be proved that Cardinal *Bellarmine* was indeed a *Jew,* or that Cardinal *Perron* was an *Atheiſt,* yet I preſume you would not accept of this for an Anſwer

to all their writings in defence of your Religion. Let then my actions and intentions and opinions be what they will, yet I hope truth is nevertheless Truth, nor reason ever the less Reason because I speak it. And therefore the Christian Reader, knowing that his Salvation or Damnation depends upon his impartial and sincere judgment of these things, will guard himself I hope from these Impostures, and regard not the Person but the cause and the reasons of it; not who speaks but what is spoken: Which is all the favour I desire of him, as knowing that I am desirous not to persuade him, unless it be truth whereunto I persuade him.

30. The last Accusation is, That *I answer out of Principles which* Protestants *themselves will profess to detest* : which indeed were to the purpose if it could be justified. But, besides that it is confuted by my whole Book, and made ridiculous by the Approbations premised unto it, it is very easie for me out of your own Mouth and Words to prove it a most injurious calumny. For what one Conclusion is there in the whole Fabrick of my Discourse, that is not naturally deducible out of this one Principle, That *all things necessary to Salvation are evidently contained in Scripture?* Or what one Conclusion almost of importance is there in your Book, which is not by this one clearly confutable? Grant this, and it will presently follow in opposition to your first Conclusion, and the argument of your first Ch : that amongst men of different opinions, touching the obscure and controverted Questions of Religion, such as may with probability be disputed on both Sides (and such as are the disputes of *Protestants;*) Good men and lovers of truth of all Sides may be saved; because all necessary things being supposed evident, concerning them, with men so qualified, there will be no difference : There being no more certain sign that a Point is not evident, than that honest and understanding and indifferent men, and such as give themselves liberty, of judgment, after a mature consideration of the matter differ about it.

31. Grant

The Preface to the Author of Charity maintain'd,

31. Grant this, and it will appear, *Secondly*, that the means whereby the revealed Truths of God are conveyed to our understanding, and which are to determine all Controversies in Faith, necessary to be determined, may be, for any thing you have said to the contrary, not a Church but the Scripture; which contradicts the Doctrine of your *Second Chapter*.

32. Grant this, and the distinction of points Fundamental and not Fundamental, will appear very good and pertinent. For those truths will be Fundamental, which are evidently delivered in Scripture, and commanded to be Preached to all men; Those not Fundamental which are obscure. And nothing will hinder, but that the Catholick Church may Err in the latter kind of the said points: because Truths not necessary to the Salvation, cannot be necessary to the being of a Church; and because it is not absolutely necessary that God should assist his Church any farther than to bring Her to Salvation; neither will there be any necessity at all of any Infallible Guide, either to consign unwritten Traditions, or to declare the obscurities of the Faith. Not for the former end, because this Principle being granted true, nothing unwritten can be necessary to be consigned. Nor for the latter, because nothing that is obscure can be necessary to be understood, or not mistaken. And so the discourse of your whole *Third Chap:* will presently vanish.

33. *Fourthly*, for the Creed's containing the Fundamentals of simple belief, though I see not how it may be deduced from this principle, yet the granting of this plainly renders the whole dispute touching the Creed necessary. For if all necessary things of all sorts, whether of simple belief or practice be confessed to be clearly contained in Scripture, what imports it whether those of one sort be contained in the Creed?

34. *Fifthly*, let this be granted, and the immediate Corollary in opposition to your Fifth Chap. will be and must be, That, not Protestants for rejecting, but the Church of *Rome* for imposing upon the Faith of Christians, Doctrines unwritten and unnecessary, and for disturbing

with an answer to his Directions to N. N.

sturbing the Churches Peace, and dividing Unity for such matters, is in a high degree presumptuous and Schismatical.

35. Grant this, *sixthly*, and it will follow unavoidably that *Protestants* cannot possibly be Hereticks, seeing they believe all things evidently contained in Scripture, which are supposed to be all that is necessary to be believed: and so your *Sixth Chapter* is clearly confuted.

36. Grant this Lastly, and it will be undoubtedly consequent, in contradiction of your *Seventh Chapter*, that no Man can shew more Charity to himself than by continuing a *Protestant*, seeing *Protestants* are supposed to believe, and therefore may accordingly practice, at least by their Religion are not hindered from practising and performing all things necessary to Salvation.

37. So that the position of this one Principle, is the direct overthrow of your whole Book, and therefore I needed not, nor indeed have I made use of any other. Now this principle, which is not only the Corner-stone or chief Pillar, but even the base, and adequate Foundation of my Answer; and which while it stands firm and unmovable, cannot but be the supporter of my Book, and the certain ruin of yours, is so far from being, according to your pretence, detested by all *Protestants*, that all *Protestants* whatsoever, as you may see in their Harmony of Confessions, unanimously profess and maintain it. And you your self, C. 6. § 30. plainly confess as much, in saying, *The whole Edifice of the Faith of* Protestants *is setled on these two Principles: These particular Books are Canonical Scripture: And the sense and meaning of them is plain and evident at least in all points necessary to Salvation.*

38. And thus your Venom against me is in a manner spent, saving only that there remain two little impertinences, whereby you would disable me from being a fit advocate for the cause of *Protestants*. The first, because I refuse to subscribe the Artic. of the Ch. of *England*: The second, because I have set down in writing, motives which sometime induced me to forsake Protestantism, and hitherto have not answered them.

39. By

39. By the former of which objections it should seem, that either you conceive the 39 Articles the common Doctrine of all Protestants, and if they be, why have you so often upbraided them with their many and great differences? Or else that it is the peculiar defence of the Church of *England*, and not the common cause of all *Protestants*, which is here undertaken by me: which are certainly very gross mistakes. And yet, why he who makes scruple of subscribing the truth of one or two Propositions, may not yet be fit enough to maintain, that those who do subscribe them, are in a saveable condition, I do not understand. Now though I hold not the Doctrine of all *Protestants* absolutely true, (which with reason cannot be required of me while they hold contradictions,) yet I hold it free from all impiety, and from all Error destructive of Salvation, or in it self damnable: And this I think in reason may sufficiently qualifie me, for a maintainer of this assertion, that *Protestancy destroys not Salvation*. For the Church of *England*, I am persuaded that the constant Doctrine of it is so pure and Orthodox, that whosoever believes it and lives according to it, undoubtedly he shall be saved; and that there is no Error in it which may necessitate or warrant any Man to disturb the peace or renounce the Communion of it. This in my opinion is all intended by Subscription, and thus much if you conceive me not ready to subscribe, your *Charity* I assure you is much *mistaken*.

40. Your other Objection is yet more impertinent and frivolous than the former: Unless perhaps it be a just exception against a Physitian, that himself was sometimes in, and recovered himself from that Disease which he undertakes to cure; or against a Guide in a way, that at first before he had experience, himself mistook it, and afterwards found his error and amended it. That noble writer *Michael de Montai'gne*, was surely of a far different mind; for he will hardly allow any Physitian competent, but only for such Diseases as himself had passed through: And a far greater than *Montai'gne*, even he that said, *Tu conversus confirma fratres, when thou art converted, strengthen thy*

by *Brethren,* gives us sufficiently to understand, that they which have themselves been in such a state as to need Conversion, are not thereby made incapable of, but rather engaged, and obliged unto, and qualified for this Charitable Function.

41. The Motives then, hitherto not answered, were these.

42. *I. Because perpetual visible profession, which could never be wanting to the Religion of Christ, nor any part of it, is apparently wanting to* Protestant *Religion, so far as concerns the points in contestation.*

II. Because Luther *and his followers, separating from the Church of* Rome, *separated also from all Churches, pure or impure, true or false then being in the world; upon which ground I conclude, that either Gods promises did fail of performance, if there were then no Church in the World, which held all things necessary, and nothing repugnant to Salvation; or else that* Luther *and his Sectaries, separating from all Churches then in the World, and so from the true, if there were any true, were* damnable Schismaticks.

III. Because, if any credit may be given to as credible records, as any are extant, the Doctrine of Catholicks hath been frequently confirmed; and the opposite Doctrine of Protestants, *confounded with supernatural and Divine Miracles.*

IV. Because many points of Protestant *Doctrine, are the damned Opinions of Hereticks, condemned by the Primitive Church.*

V. Because the Prophecies of the Old Testament, *touching the Conversion of Kings and Nations to the true Religion of Christ, have been accomplished in and by the Catholick* Roman *Religion, and the Professors of it; and not by* Protestant *Religion, and the Professors of it.*

VI. Because the Doctrine of the Church of Rome *is conformable, and the Doctrine of* Protestants *contrary, to the Doctrine of the* Fathers *of the Primitive* Church, *even by the Confession of* Protestants *themselves; I mean, those Fathers, who lived within the compass of the first* 600. *years; to whom* Protestants *themselves do very frequently, and very confidently appeal.*

VII. Because the first pretended Reformers had neither extraordinary Commission *from God, nor ordinary* Mission *from the Church, to Preach* Protestant Doctrine.

VIII. Because Luther, *to Preach against the Maß* (*which contains the most material points now in controversie*) *was perswaded by reasons suggested to him by the Devil himself, disputing with him.* So *himself professeth in his Book* de Missa Privata. *That all men might take heed of following him, who professeth himself to follow the Devil.*

IX. Because the Protestant *cause is now, and hath been from the beginning, maintained with grosse falsifications, and Calumnies ; whereof their prime Controversie writers, are notoriously, and in high degree guilty.*

X. Because by denying all humane Authority, either of Pope, *or Councils, or Church, to determine Controversies of Faith, they have abolished all possible means of suppressing Heresie, or restoring Unity to the Church.*

These are the Motives ; now my Answers to them follow briefly and in order.

43. To the first : God hath neither decreed nor foretold, that his true Doctrine should *de facto* be alwaies visibly professed, without any mixture of falshood.

To the second : God hath neither decreed nor foretold, that there shall be alwaies a visible Company of Men free from all Error in it self Damnable. Neither is it alwaies of necessity Schismatical to separate from the external Communion of a Church, though wanting nothing necessary : For if this Church supposed to want nothing necessary, require me to profess against my Conscience, that I believe some Error, tho never so small and innocent, which I do not believe, and will not allow me Her Communion, but upon this condition : In this case, the Church for requiring this condition is Schismatical, and not I for separating from the Church.

To the third : If any credit may be given to Records far more creditable than these, the Doctrine of *Protestants*, that is, the Bible hath been confirmed, and the Doctrine of *Papists*, which is in many points plainly opposite to it, confounded with Supernatural and Divine Miracles, which for number and Glory, out-shine *Popish* pretended Miracles, as much as the Sun doth an *Ignis fatuus*, those I mean which were wrought by our Saviour Christ and his Apostles,

ſtles: Now this Book, by the Confeſſion of all ſides confirmed by innumerous Miracles, foretels me plainly, that in after Ages, great Signs and Wonders ſhall be wrought in confirmation of falſe Doctrine, and that I am not to believe any Doctrine which ſeems to my underſtanding repugnant to the firſt, though an Angel from Heaven ſhould teach it; which were certainly as great a Miracle as any that was ever wrought in atteſtation of any part of the Doctrine of the Church of *Rome*: But that true Doctrine ſhould in all Ages have the teſtimony of Miracles, that I am no where taught; So that I have more reaſon to ſuſpect and be afraid of pretended Miracles, as ſigns of falſe Doctrine, then much to regard them as certain arguments of the truth. Beſides, ſetting aſide the Bible, and the Tradition of it, there is as good ſtory for Miracles wrought by thoſe who lived and died in oppoſition to the Doctrine of the *Roman* Church, (as by S. *Cyprian*, *Colmannus*, *Columbanus*, *Aidanus* and others,) as there is for thoſe that are pretended to be wrought by the Members of that Church. Laſtly, it ſeems to me no ſtrange thing, that God in his Juſtice ſhould permit ſome true Miracles to be wrought to delude them, who have forged ſo many, as apparently the Profeſſors of the *Roman* Doctrine have to abuſe the World.

To the Fourth: All thoſe were not *Hereticks which by *Philaſtrius*, *Epiphanius*, or S. *Auſtine* were put in the Catalogue of Hereticks.

*See this acknowledged by Bellar: *de Scrip: Eccleſ. in Philaſtrio: by Petavius Animad. in Epiph. de inſcrip. operis: By S. Auſtin. Lib. de Hæref. Hær. 80.

To the Fifth: Kings and Nations have been, and may be Converted by Men of contrary Religions.

To the Sixth: The Doctrine of *Papiſts*, is confeſſed by *Papiſts* contrary to the Fathers in many points.

To the Seventh: The Paſtors of a Church cannot but have Authority from it, to Preach againſt the abuſes of it, whether in Doctrine or Practice, if there be any in it: Neither can any Chriſtian want an ordinary commiſſion from God to do a neceſſary work of Charity after a peacable manner, when there is no body elſe that can or will do it. In extraordinary caſes, extraordinary courſes are not to be diſallowed. If ſome Chriſtian Lay-man should come into a Country of Infidels, and had ability to perfuade them to Chriftianity, who would fay he might not ufe it for want of Commiffion!

To the Eighth: *Luthers* conference with the Devil might be, for ought I know, nothing but a Melancholy Dream: If it were real, the Devil might perfuade *Luther* from the Mafs, hoping by doing fo to keep him conftant to it : Or that others would make his diffuafion from it an argument for it, (as we fee *Papifts* do) and be afraid of following *Luther*, as confeffing himfelf to have been perfuaded by the Devil.

To the Ninth: *Iliacos intra muros peccatur & extra*. *Papifts* are more guilty of this fault than *Proteftants*. Even this very Author in this very Pamphlet, hath not fo many leaves as falfifications and Calumnies.

To the Tenth : Let all Men believe the Scripture and that only, and endeavour to believe it in the true fenfe, and require no more of others, and they fhall find this not only a better, but the only means to fupprefs Herefie, and reftore Unity. For he that believes the Scripture fincerely, and endeavours to believe it in the true fenfe, cannot poffibly be an Heretick : And if no more than this were required of any Man, to make him capable of the Churches Communion, then all Men fo qualified, though they were different in opinion, yet notwithftanding any fuch difference, muft be of neceffity one in Communion.

THE ANSWER TO THE PREFACE.

TO *the First, and Second.* §. If beginnings be ominous (as they say they are,) D. *Potter* hath cause to look for great store of uningenuous dealing from you; the very first words you speak of him, *viz. That he hath not so much as once truly and really fallen upon the point in question,* being a most unjust and immodest imputation.

2. For the point in question was not that which you pretend, *Whether both* Papists *and* Protestants *can be saved in their several Professions* ? But, *whether you may without uncharitableneß affirm that Protestancy unrepented destroys Salvation?* For there is no incongruity but that it may be true, *That you and we cannot both be Saved:* and yet as Ttrue, *That without uncharitableness you cannot pronounce us Damned.* And therefore though the Author of *Charity Mistaken* had proved as strongly as he hath done weakly, *that one Heaven could not receive* Protestants *and* Papists *both*, yet certainly, it was very hastily and unwarrantably, and therefore uncharitably concluded, that *Protestants* were the part that was to be excluded. As, though Jews and Christians cannot both be saved, yet a Jew cannot justly, and therefore not charitably pronounce a Christian Damned.

3. Neither may you or *C. M.* conclude him from hence (as covertly you do,) *an Enemy to Souls by deceiving them with ungrounded false hopes of Salvation*; seeing the hope of Salvation cannot be ungrounded, which requires and supposes belief and practise of all things absolutely necessary

to

to Salvation, and repentance of those Sins and Errors which we fall into by humane frailty: Nor a *friend to indifferency in Religions*, seeing he gives them only hope of pardon of Errors who are desirous, and according to the proportion of their opportunities and abilities industrious to find the truth, or at least truly repentant, that they have not been so. Which Doctrine is very fit to excite men to a constant and impartial search of truth, and very far from teaching them, that it is indifferent what Religion they are of, and without all controversie very honourable to the goodness of God, with which how it can consist, not to be satisfied with his Servants true endeavours to know his will and do it, without full and exact performance, I leave it to you and all good men to judge.

5. You say *he was loth to affirm plainly, that generally both* Catholicks *and* Protestants *may be saved:* which yet is manifest he doth affirm plainly, of *Protestants* throughout his Book; and of Erring *Papists*, that have *sincerely sought the truth and failed of it, and Die with a general repentance :* p. 77. 78. And yet you deceive your self, if you conveive he had any other necessity to do so, but only that he thought it true. For we may and do pretend that before Luther *there were many true Churches, besides the* Roman, which agreed not with her: in particular, *The Greek Church.* So that what you say is evidently true, is indeed evidently false. Besides if he had had any necessity to make use of you in this matter, he needed not for this end to say that now in your Church, Salvation may be had; but onely that before *Luthers* time it might be: Then when your means of knowing the truth were not so great, and when your ignorance might be more invincible, and therefore more excusable. So that you may see if you please, it is not for ends, but for the love of truth, that we are thus charitable to you.

6. Neither is it material what you alledge, that they are not *Fundamental Errors*, and then, *what imports it whether we hold them or no, forasmuch as concerns our possibility to be Saved.* As if we were not bound by the Love of God and the love of truth, to be zealous in the defence of all Truths,

The Answer to the Preface.

Truths, that are any way profitable, though not simply necessary to Salvation. Or as if any good man could satisfie his Conscience with being so affected and resolved. Our Saviour himself having assured us, * That *he that shall break one of his least Commandments* (some whereof you pretend are concerning venial sins, and consequently the keeping of them not necessary to Salvation) *and shall so teach men, shall be called the least in the Kingdom of Heaven.*

7. But then it imports very much, though not for the *possibility that you may be saved*, yet for the *probability that you will be so:* because the holding of these Errors, though it did not *merit*, migh yet *occasion* Damnation. As the Doctrine of Indulgences may take away the fear of Purgatory, and the Doctrine of Purgatory the fear of Hell; as you well know it does too frequently. So that though a godly man might be saved *with these* Errors, yet by *means of them,* many are made vicious and so damned. *By them* I say, though *not for them.* No godly Lay-man who is verily persuaded that there is neither impiety nor superstition in the use of your Latin Service, shall be Damned, I hope, for being present at it; yet the want of that Devotion which the frequent hearing the Offices understood, might happily beget in them, the want of that instruction and edification which it might afford them, may very probably hinder the Salvation of many which otherwise might have been saved. Besides, though the matter of an Error may be only something profitable, not necessary, yet the neglect of it may be a damnable Sin. As not to regard Venial Sins is in the Doctrine of your Schools, mortal. Lastly, as Venial Sins, you say, dispose men to mortal; so the erring from some profitable, though lesser truth, may dispose a man to Error in greater matters. As for example: The Belief of the *Popes* Infallibility is, I hope, not unpardonably damnable to every one that holds it; yet if it be a falshood (as most certainly it is) it puts a man into a very congruous disposition to believe *Antichrist,* if he should chance to get into that See.

8. To

The Answer to the Preface.

8. *To the third §*] *In his distinction of points Fundamental and not Fundamental, he may seem, you say, to have touched the point, but does not so indeed. Because though he saies there are some points so Fundamental, as that all are obliged to believe them explicitely, yet he tells you not, whether a man may disbelieve any other points of Faith, which are sufficiently presented to his understanding, as Truths revealed by Almighty God.* Touching this matter of *Sufficient Proposal*, if you mean by *sufficiently presented to his understanding as revealed by God*, that which, all things considered, is so proposed to him, that he might and should and would believe it to be true and revealed by God, were it not for some voluntary and avoidable fault of his that interposeth it self between his understanding and the truth presented to it : if you speak of truths thus proposed and rejected, let it be as damnable as you please to deny or disbelieve them. But it amazes me to hear you say, that Dr. *Potter* declines this Question, seeing the Light it self is not more clear, then Dr. *Potters* Declaration of himself (p. 245, 246. *&c.* of his Book) beginning his discourse thus. " *It seems Fundamental to the Faith, and for the Salvation of*
" *every member of the Church, that he acknowledge and believe*
" *all such points of Faith, as whereof he may be convinced that*
" *they belong to the Doctrine of Jesus Christ.*

" To this conviction he requires three things. *Clear*
" *Revelation* ; *Sufficient Proposition, and Capacity and under-*
" *standing in the hearer. For want of clear Revelation, he*
" *frees the Church before Christ and the Disciples of Christ*
" *from any damnable Error, though they believed not those*
" *things which he that should now deny were no Christian. To*
" *sufficient Proposition, he requires two things.* 1. *That the*
" *points be perspicuously laid open in themselves.* 2. *So forci-*
" *bly, as may serve to remove reasonable doubts to the contra-*
" *ry, and to satisfie a teachable mind concerning it, against the*
" *Principles in which he hath been bred to the contrary. This*
" *Proposition he says is not limited to the* Pope *or* Church, *but*
" *extended to all means whatsoever, by which a man may be*
" *convinced in Conscience, that the matter proposed is Divine*
" *Revelation* ; *which he professes to be done sufficiently, not*
" *only*

"only when his Conscience doth expresly bear witness to the
"truth; but when it would do so, if it were not choaked, and
"blinded by some unruly and unmortified lust in the will. The
"difference being not great between him that is wilfully blind,
"and him that knowingly gainsaieth the Truth. The 3 thing
"he requires is Capacity and Ability to apprehend the Proposal,
"and the Reasons of it: the want whereof excuseth Fools and
"Madmen, &c. But where there is no such impediment, and
"the will of God is sufficiently propounded, there (saith he) he
"that opposeth is convinced of Error; and he who is thus
"convinced is an Heretick: and Heresie is a work of the
"Flesh, which excludeth from Salvation, (he means without
"Repentance,) And hence it followeth, that it is Funda-
"mental to a Christians Faith, and necessary for his Salvati-
"on, that he believe all revealed truths of God, whereof he
"may be convinced that they are from God.

Again, it is almost as strange to me, why you should say, this was the only thing in question, *Whether a Man may deny or disbelieve any point of Faith, sufficiently presented to his understanding as a truth revealed by God.* For to say, that any thing is a thing in question, methinks at the first hearing of the words, imports, that it is by some affirmed, and denied by others. Now you affirm I grant, but what *Protestant* ever denied, that it was a sin to give God the lie? Which is the first and most obvious sense of these Words. Or which of them ever doubted, that to disbelieve is then a fault, when the matter is so proposed to a Man, that he might and should, and were it not for his own fault, would believe it? Certainly he that questions either of these, justly deserves to have his wits called in question. Produce any one *Protestant* that ever did so, and I will give you leave to say it is the only thing in question. But then I must tell you, that your ensuing Argument, viz: *To deny a truth witnessed by God is damnable, But of two that disagree, one must of necessity deny some such truth, Therefore one only can be saved;* is built upon a ground clean different from this postulate. For though it be always a fault to deny what either I do know, or should know, to be testified by God; yet that which by a

F   cleanly

The Answer to the Preface.

cleanly conveyance you put in the place hereof, *To deny a Truth witnessed by God* simply, without the circumstance of *being known or sufficienly proposed,* is so far from being certainly Damnable, that it may be many times done without any the least fault at all. As if God should testifie something to a man in the *Indies,* I that had no assurance of this testification should not be obliged to believe it. For in such cases the Rule of the Law has place, *Idem est non esse & non apparere:* not to be at all and not to appear to me, is to me all one. *If I had not come and spoken unto you* (saith our Saviour) *you had had no sin.*

10. As little necessity is there for that which follows: *That of two disagreeing in a matter of Faith one must deny some such truth.* Whether by [such] you understand, *Testified at all by God*; or *testified and sufficiently propounded.* For it is very possible the matter in controversie may be such a thing wherein God hath not at all declared himself, or not so fully and clearly as to oblige all Men to hold one way; and yet be so overvalued by the parties in variance, as to be esteemed a matter *of Faith,* and one of those things of which our Saviour says, *He that believeth not shall be Damned.* Who sees not that it is possible two Churches may excommunicate and Damn each other for keeping *Christmas* Ten days sooner or later; as well as *Victor* excommunicated the Churches of *Asia,* for differing from him about *Easter-Day* ? And yet I believe you will confess, that God had not then declared himself about *Easter*; nor hath now about *Christmas.* Anciently some good Catholick Bishops excommunicated and Damned others for *holding there were Antipodes :* and in this questiom I would fain know on which side was the sufficient proposal. *The contra-Remonstrants* differ from the *Remonstrants* about the points of Predetermination as a matter of Faith: I would know in this thing also, which way God hath declared himself; whether for Predetermination or against it. *Stephen Bishop of* Rome held it as a matter of Faith and Apostolick tradition, *That Hereticks gave true Baptism*: Others there were, and they as good Catholicks as he, that held that this was neither matter of *Faith* nor matter of *Truth*. *Justin Martyr and*

The Answer to the Preface.

and *Irenæus* held the Doctrine of the *Millenaries* as a matter of *Faith*: and though *Justin Martyr* deny it, yet you, I hope, will affirm, that some good Christians held the contrary. S. *Augustine*, I am sure, held *the communicating of Infants*, as much Apostolick tradition, as the Baptising of them: whether the Bishop and the Church of *Rome* of his time, held so too, or held otherwise, I desire you to determine. But, sure I am, the Church of *Rome* at this present holds the contrary. The same S. *Austin* held it no matter of Faith, that the *Bishops of* Rome *were Judges of Appeals* from all parts of the Church Catholick, no not in *Major Causes and Major Persons*: whether the Bishop or Church of *Rome* did then hold the contrary do you resolve me; but now I am resolved they do so. In all these differences, the point in question is esteemed and proposed by one side at least as a matter of *Faith*, and by the other rejected as not so: and either this is to disagree in matters of Faith, or you will have no means to shew that we do disagree. Now then to shew you how weak and sandy the Foundation is, on which the whole Fabrick both of your Book and Church depends, answer me briefly to this *Dilemma*. Either in these oppositions one of the opposite Parts erred damnably, and denied Gods truth sufficiently propounded or they did not. If they did, than they which do deny Gods truth sufficiently propounded, may go to heaven; and then you are rash and uncharitable in excluding us, though we were guilty of this fault. If not, then there is no such necessity, that of two disagreeing about a matter of Faith, one should deny Gods truth sufficiently propounded. And so the Major and Minor of your Argument, are proved false. Yet, though they were as true as Gospel, and as evident as Mathematical Principles, the conclusion (so impertinent is it to the Premises) might still be false. For that which naturally issues from these propositions is not, *Therefore one only can be saved*: But, *Therefore one of them does something that is damnable*. But with what Logick or what Charity you can infer either as the immediate production of the former premises, or as a Corollary from this conclusion, Therefore *one only can be saved,*

ved, I do not understand; unless you will pretend that this consequence is good, such a one doth something damnable, therefore he shall certainly be damned: which whether it be not to overthrow the Article of our Faith, which promises remission of sins upon repentance, and consequently to ruin the Gospel of Christ, I leave it to the *Pope* and the *Cardinals* to determine. For if against this it be alledged, that no man can repent of the sin wherein he Dies: This muce I have already stopped, by shewing that if it be a sin of Ignorance, this is no way incongruous.

13. Ad 6. §.] In your sixth *Parag.* I let all pass saving only this, *That a perswasion that men of different Religions* (you must mean Christians of different Opinions or Communions) *may be saved, is a most pernicious Heresie, and even a ground of Atheism.* What strange extractions Chymistry can make I know not; but sure I am, he that by reason would infer this Conclusion, *That there is no God*; from this ground,*That God will save men in different Religions*, must have a higher strain of Logick, than you for I have hitherto made shew of. In my apprehension, the other part of the contradiction, *That there is a God*, should much rather follow from it; and I say and will maintain, that to say, *That Christians of different Opinions and Communions (such I mean, who hold all those things that are simply necessary to Salvation) may not obtain Pardon for the Errors wherein they Die ignorantly, by a general Repentance*; is so far from being a ground of Atheism, that to say the contrary, is to cross in Diameter a main *Article of our Creed*, and to overthrow the *Gospel of Christ*.

14. Ad 7. §.] To what you say, of some *Protestants* that *hold it necessary to be able to prove a perpetual Visible Church distinct from Yours.* I answer, Some perhaps undertake to do so, as a matter of courtesie; but I believe you will be much to seek for any one that holds it necessary. For though you say that Christ hath promised there shall be a Perpetual Visible Church; yet you your selves do not pretend that he hath promised there shall be Histories and Records always extant of the Professors of it in

all

all Ages: nor that he hath any where enjoyned us to read those Histories that we may be able to shew them.

17. To your ensuing demands, though some of them be very captious and ensnaring; yet I will give you as clear and plain and Ingenuous Answers as possibly I can.

18. Ad 11. §.] To the First then, about *the Perpetuity of the visible Church*, my Answer is: That I believe our Saviour, ever since his Ascension, hath had in some place or other a Visible true Church on Earth: I mean a Company of Men, that professed at least so much truth as was absolutely necessary for their Salvation. And I believe that there will be somewhere or other such a Church to the Worlds end. But the contrary Doctrine I do at no hand believe to be a damnable Heresie.

19. Ad 12. §.] To the Second, what *Visible Church there was before* Luther *disagreeing from the* Roman? I answer, that before *Luther* there were many Visible Churches in many things disagreeing from the *Roman*: But not that the whole Catholick Church disagreed from Her, because She her self was a Part of the Whole, though much corrupted. And to undertake to name a Catholick Church disagreeing from Her, is to make her no Part of it, which we do not, nor need not pretend. And *for men agreeing with* Protestants *in all points*, we will then produce them, when you shall either prove it necessary to be done, which you know we absolutely deny; or when you shall produce a perpetual succession of Professors, which in all points have agreed with you, and disagreed from you in nothing. But this my promise, to deal plainly with you, I conceive, and so intended it to be very like his, who undertook to drink up the Sea, upon condition, that he, to whom the promise was made, should first stop the Rivers from runing in. For this unreasonable request which you make to us is to your selves so impossible, that in the very next Age after the Apostles, you will never be able to name a Man, whom you can prove to have agreed with you in all things, nay (if you speak of such, whose Works are extant and unquestioned) whom we cannot prove to have disagreed from you.

vou in many things. Which I am so certain of, that I will venture my Credit, and my Life upon it.

20. Ad 13. §.] To the Third, *Whether, seeing there cannot be assigned any Visible true Church distinct from the Roman, it follows not that She Erred not Fundamentally.* I say, in our sense of the word *Fundamental,* it does follow. For if it be true, that there was then no Church distinct from the *Roman,* then it must be, either because there was no Church at all, which we deny: Or because the *Roman* Church was the whole Church, which we also deny: Or because She was a Part of the Whole, which we grant. And if She were a true Part of the Church than She retained those truths which were simply necessary to Salvation, and held no Errors which were inevitably and unpardonably destructive of it. For this is precisely necessary to constitute any man or any Church a member of the Church Catholick. In our sense therefore of the Word *Fundamental,* I hope She erred not Fundamentally: but in your sense of the word, I fear she did. That is, She held something to be Divine Revelation, which was not; something not to be which was.

21. Ad 14. §.] To the Fourth. *How it could be damnable to maintain her Errors, if they were not Fundamental?* I answer. 1. Though it were not damnable, yet if it were a fault, it was not to be done. For a Venial sin, with you is not damnable; yet you say, it is not to be committed for the procuring any good. *Non est faciendum malum vel minimum, ut eveniat bonum vel maximum.* 2. It is damnable to maintain an error against Conscience, though the error in it self, and to him that believes it, be not damnable. Nay, the profession not only of an error, but even of a truth, if not believed, when you think on it again, I believe you will confess to be a mortal sin; unless you will say, Hypocrisie and Simulation in Religion is not so. 3. Though we say, the Errors of the *Roman* Church were not destructive of Salvation, but pardonable even to them that Dyed in them, upon a general repentance: yet we deny not but in *themselves they were damnable.* Nay, the very saying they were pardonable,
implie

implies they needed pardon, and therefore in themselves were damnable: damnable *meritoriously*, though not *effectually*. As a poyson may be deadly in it self, and yet not kill him, that together with the Poyson takes an Antidote: or as Fellony may deserve Death, and yet not bring it on him that obtains the Kings Pardon.

22. Ad 15. §] To the Fifth. *How they can be excused from Schism, who forsook her Communion upon pretence of Errors which were not damnable!* I answer. All that we forsake in you, is only the Belief, and Practice, and profession of your Errors. Hereupon, you cast us out of your Communion. And then with a strange, and contradictious and ridiculous Hypocrisie, complain that we forsake it. As if a man should thrust his friend out of doors, and then be offended at his departure. But for us not to forsake the belief of your Errors, having discovered them to be Errors, was impossible; and therefore to do so could not be damnable, believing them to be Errors. Not to forsake the practice and profession of them, had been damnable Heresie; supposing that (which you vainly run away with, and take for granted) those Errors in themselves were not damnable. Now to do so, and as matters now stand, not to forsake your Communion, is apparently contradictious: seeing the condition of your Communion is, that we must profess to believe all your Doctrines, not only not to be damnable Errors (which will not content you,) but also to be certain and necessary and revealed truths. So that to demand why we forsake your Communion upon pretence of Errors which were not damnable, is in effect to demand why we forsook it upon our forsaking it! For to pretend that there are Errors in your Church though not damnable, is *ipso facto* to forsake your Communion, and to do that which both in your account, and as you think in Gods account, puts him as does so, out of your Communion. So that either you must free your Church from requiring the belief of any Error whatsoever, damnable and not damnable, or whether you will or no, you must free us from Schism. For Schism there cannot be in

leaving

leaving your Communion, unless we were obliged to continue in it. Man cannot be obliged by Man, but to what either formally or virtually he is obliged by God, for all just power is from God. God the Eternal truth neither can nor will oblige us to believe any the least and the most innocent falshood to be a Divine truth, that is, to Err; nor, to profess a known Error, which is to lie. So that if you require the belief of any Error among the conditions of your Communion, our obligation to communicate with you ceaseth, and so the imputation of Schism to us, vanisheth into nothing: but lies heavy upon you for making our separation from you just and necessary, by requiring unnecessary and unlawful conditions of your Communion. Hereafter therefore, I intreat you, let not your demand be, how could we forsake your Communion without Schism, seeing you Erred not damnably? But how we could do so without Schism, seeing you Erred not at all? which if either you do prove, or we cannot disprove it, we will (I at least will for my part) return to your Communion, or subscribe my self Schismatick. In the mean time, μένωμεν ὥσπερ ἐσμέν, we continue where we are.

23. Yet notwithstanding all your Errors we do not renounce your Communion *totally* and absolutely, but only leave Communicating with you in the practice and profession of your Errors. The tryal whereof will be to propose some form of worshiping God, taken wholly out of Scripture; and herein if we refuse to joyn with you, then, and not till then, may we justly say we have utterly and absolutely abandoned your Communion.

25. Ad 17. §.] To the Seventh, *Whether Error against any one truth sufficiently propounded as testified by God, destroy not the Nature and Unity of Faith, or at least, is not a grievous offence excluding Salvation* ! I answer, if you suppose, as you seem to do the proposition so sufficient, that the party to whom it is made is convinced that it is from God, so that the denyal of it involves also with it the denial of Gods veracity; any such Error destroys both Faith and Salvation. But if the Proposal be only so
sufficient,

The Answer to the Preface.

sufficient, not, that the party to whom it is made is convinced, but only that he should, and but for his own fault would have been convinced of the Divine verity of the Doctrine proposed: The crime then is not so great, for the belief of Gods veracity may well consist with such an Error. Yet a fault I confess it is and (without Repentance) damnable, if all circumstances considered the proposal be sufficient. But then I must tell you that the proposal of the present *Roman* Church is only pretended to be sufficient for this purpose, but is not so: especially all the Rayes of the Divinity, which they pretend to shine so conspicuously in her proposals, being so darkned and even extinguished with a cloud of contradiction, from Scripture, Reason, and the Ancient Church.

26. Ad 18. §.] To the Eighth. *How of disagreeing* Protestants, *both parts may hope for Salvation, seeing some of them must needs Err against some Truth testified by God?* I answer, 1. The most disagreeing *Protestants* that are, yet thus far agree, that these Books of Scripture which were never doubted of in the Church, are the undoubted Word of God, and a perfect rule of Faith. 2. That the sense of them, which God intended, whatsoever it is, is certainly true. So that they believe implicitely even those very truths against which they Err; and why an implicit Faith in Christ and his Word, should not suffice as well as an implicit Faith in your Church, I have desired to be resolved by many of your Side, but never could.

3. That they are to use their best endeavours to believe the Scripture in the true sense and to live according to it. This if they perform (as I hope many on all Sides do) truly and sincerely, it is impossible but that they should believe aright in all things necessary to Salvation: that is, in all those things which appertain to the Covenant between God and man in Christ, for so much, is not only plainly but frequently contained in Scripture. And believing aright touching the Covenant, if they for their parts perform the condition required of them, which is sincere obedience, why should they not expect that God will perform his promise and give them Salvation?

For, as for other things which lie without the Covenant, and are therefore less necessary, if by reason of the seeming conflict which is oftentimes between Scripture and Reason, and Authority on the one side, and Scripture, Reason, and Authority on the other; if by reason of the variety of tempers, Abilities, Educations, and unavoidable prejudices, whereby mens understandings are variously formed and fashioned, they do embrace several Opinions, whereof some must be erroneous; to say that God will Damn them for such Errors, who are lovers of him, and lovers of truth, is to rob man of his comfort, and God of his goodness; it is to make Man desperate and God a Tyrant. *But they deny Truths testified by God, and therefore shall be Damned.* Yes, if they knew them to be thus testified by him, and yet would deny them, that were to give God the lie, and questionless damnable. But if you should deny a truth which God had testified but only to a Man in the *Indies,* (as I said before) and this testification you had never heard of, or at least had no sufficient reason to believe that God had so testified, would not you think it a hard case to be Damned for such a denial? Yet consider I pray a little more attentively the difference between them, and you will presently acknowledge, the question between them is not at any time, or in any thing, Whether God says true or no? or whether he says this or no? But supposing he says this, and says true, whether he means this or no? As for example, between *Lutherans, Calvinists,* and *Zwinglians,* it is agreed that Christ spake these Words, *This is my Body* ; and that whatsoever he meant in saying so is true : But what he meant and how he is to be understood, that's the question. So that though some of them deny a truth by God intended, yet you can with no reason or justice accuse them of denying the truth of Gods Testimony, unless you can plainly shew that God hath declared, and that plainly and clearly, what was his meaning in these Words. I say *plainly and clearly.* For he that speaks obscurely and ambiguously, and no where declares himself plainly, sure he hath no reason to be much offended if he be mistaken. When therefore you can shew, that

in

The Answer to the Preface.

in this and all other their Controversies, God hath interposed his Testimony on one side or other; so that either they do see it, and will not; or were it not for their own voluntary and avoidable fault, might and should see it and do not; let all such Errors be as damnable as you please to make them. In the mean while, if they suffer themselves neither to be betraid into their Errors, nor kept in them by any sin of their will; if they do their best endeavour to free themselves from all Errors, and yet fail of it through humane frailty; so well am I persuaded of the goodness of God, that if in me alone, should meet a confluence of all such Errors of all the *Protestants* in the World, that were thus qualified, I should not be so much afraid of them all, as I should be to ask pardon for them. For, whereas that which you affright us with of calling Gods Veracity in Question, is but a Panick fear, a fault that no man thus qualified, is, or can be guilty of; to ask pardon of simple and purely involuntary errors is tacitely to imply that God is angry with us for them, and that to impute to him the strange Tyranny of *requiring Brick, when he gives no Straw; of expecting to gather, where he strewed not; to reap where he sowed not*: of being offended with us for not doing what he knows we cannot do. This I say upon a supposition, that they do their best endeavours to know Gods will and do it; which he that denys to be possible, knows not what he says; for he says in effect, that Men cannot do, what they can do; for to do what a Man can do, is to do his best endeavour. But because this supposition, though certainly possible, is very rare, and admirable, I say secondly, that I am verily persuaded, that God will not impute Errors to them, as sins, who use such a measure of industry, in finding truth, as humane *prudence* and ordinary *discretion* (their abilities and opportunities, their distractions and hindrances, and all other things considered) shall advise them unto, in a matter of such consequence. But if herein also we fail, then our Errors begin to be malignant, and justly imputable, as offences against God, and that love of his truth which he requires

The Answer to the Preface.

in us. You will say then, that for those Erring *Protestants*, which are in this case, which evidently are far the greater part, they sin damnably in Erring, and therefore there is little hope of their Salvation. To which I answer, that the consequence of this Reason, is somewhat strong against a *Protestant*; but much weakned by coming out of the Mouth of a *Papist*. For all Sins with you are not damnable. But yet out of courtesie to you, we will remove this rubb out of your way; and for the present suppose them *mortal Sins*; and is there then no hope of Salvation, for him that commits them? Not, you will say, if he Die in them without repentance; and such *Protestants* you speak of, *who without Repentance Die in their Errors*. Yea but what if they Die in their Errors with Repentance? than I hope you will have Charity enough to think they may be saved. *Charity Mist.* takes it indeed for granted, that this supposition is distructive of it self; and that it is impossible, and incongruous, that a Man should repent of those Errors wherein he Dies; or Die in those whereof he repents. But it was wisely done of Him to take it for granted; for most certainly He could not have spoken one word of sense for the confirmation of it. For seeing *Protestants* believe, as well as you, Gods infinite and most admirable perfections in himself, more than most worthy of all possible love: seeing they believe, as well as you, his infinite goodness to them, in Creating them of nothing; in Creating them according to his own Image; in Creating all things for their use and benefit; in streaming down his Favours on them every moment of their Lives; in designing them, if they serve him, to infinite and Eternal Happiness; in Redeeming them, not with corruptible things, but the Pretious Blood of his beloved Son: seeing they believe, as well as you, His infinite goodness, and Patience towards them, in expecting their Conversion; in Wooing, Alluring, Leading, and by all means, which his Wisdom can Suggest unto him, and Mans nature is capable of, drawing them to Repentance and Salvation: Seeing they believe these things as well as you, and for ought you know,

In the place above quoted.

know, consider them as much as you, (and if they do not, it is not their Religion, but they that are to blame,) what can hinder, but that the consideration of Gods most infinite goodness to them, and their own almost infinite wickedness against him, Gods Spirit cooperating with them, may raise them to a true and sincere and a cordial love of God? And seeing sorrow for having injured or offended the Person beloved, or when we fear we may have offended him, is the most natural effect of true love; what can hinder, but that love which hath oftimes constrained them, to lay down their lives for God (which our Saviour assures us is the noblest Sacrifice we can offer,) may produce in them an universal sorrow for all their sins, both which they know they have committed, and which they fear they may have? In which number, their being negligent, or not dispassionate, or not unprejudicate enough in seeking the truth, and the effect thereof, their Errors, if they be sins, cannot but be compriz'd. In a word, what should hinder, but that, that Prayer---- *Delicta sua quis intelligit? who can understand his faults? Lord cleanse thou me from my secret sins*, may be heard and accepted by God, as well from a *Protestant* that Dies in some Errors, as from a *Papist* that Dies in some other sins of Ignorance, which perhaps he might more easily have discovered to be sins, than a *Protestant* could his Errors to be Errors? As well from a *Protestant*, that held some Error, which (as he conceived) Gods Word and his Reason, (which is also in some sort Gods Word) led him unto; as from a *Dominican*, who perhaps took up his opinion upon trust, not because he had reason to believe it true, but because it was the opinion of his *Order*; for the same man if he had light upon another Order, would in all probability, have been of the other Opinion. For what else is the cause, that generally *all the Dominicans are of one Opinion, and all the Jesuits of the other?* I say, from a *Dominican* who took up his Opinion upon trust; and that such an Opinion (if we believe the writers of your Order) as if it be granted true, it were not a point matter, what Opinions any man held, or what actions any man did, for the best would be as bad as the worst, and the worst as good as the best. And yet such is the partiality of your Hypocrisie, that of disagreeing *Papists*, neither shall deny the truth testified by God, but both may hope for Salvation: but of disagreeing *Protestants* (though they differ in the same thing,) one side must deny Gods Testimony and be incapable of Salvation. That a *Dominican* through culpable negligence, living and dying in his Error, may repent of it, though he knows it not; or be saved though he do not: But if a *Protestant* do the very same thing, in the very same point, and Die in his Error, his case is desperate. The Sum of all that hath been said to this Demand is this. 1. That no Erring *Protestant* denys any truth testified by God, under this formality, *as testified by him*; nor which they know or believe to be testified by him. And therefore it is a horrible Calumny in you to say, *They call Gods Veracity in question*. For Gods undoubted and unquestioned Veracity, is to them the ground, why they hold all they do hold: neither do they hold any Opinion so stifly, but they will forgoe it rather than this one, *That all which God says is true*. 2. God hath not so clearly and plainly declared himself in most of these things which are in controversie between *Protestants*, but that an honest man, whose heart is right to God, and one that is a true lover of God, and of his truth, may by reason of the conflict of contrary Reasons on both sides, very easily, and therefore excusably mistake, and embrace Error for Truth, and reject Truth for Error. 3. If any *Protestant* or *Papist* be betrayed into, or kept in any Error, by any sin of his will (as it is to be feared many Millions are) such Error is, as the cause of it, sinful and damnable: yet not exclusive of all hope of Salvation, but pardonable if discovered, upon a particular explicite repentance; if not discovered, upon a general and implicite repentance for all Sins known and unknown: in which number all sinful Errors must of necessity be contained.

27. Ad 19. §.] To the Ninth. Wherein you are so urgent for a *particular Catalogue of Fundamentals*: I answer

The Answer to the Preface. 47

(we almost in your own words, that we also constantly urge and require to have a particular Catalogue of your Fundamentals, whether they be written Verities, or unwritten Traditions, or Church Definitions? all which, you say integrate the material Object of your Faith: In a word of all such Points as are defined and sufficiently proposed; so that whosoever denys, or doubts of any of them, is certainly in the state of damnation. A Catalogue I say in particular of the Proposals: and not only some general definition, or description, under which you lurk deceitfully, of what, and what only is sufficiently proposed: wherein yet you do not very well agree. For many of you hold the *Popes* Proposal *Ex Cathedra*, to be sufficient and obliging: Some a Council without a *Pope*: Some, of neither of them severally, but only both together: Some not this neither in matter of manners, which *Bellarmine* acknowledges, and tells us it is all one in effect, as if they denyed it sufficient in matter of Faith: Some not in matter of Faith, neither think this Proposal Infallible, without the acceptation of the Church Universal: Some deny the Infallibility of the Present Church, and only make the Tradition of all Ages the *Infallible Propounder*. Yet if you were agreed *what and what only is the Infallible Propounder*, this would not satisfie us; nor yet to say, *that All is Fundamental which is propounded sufficiently by him*. For though agreeing in this, yet you might still disagree *whether such or such a Doctrine were propounded or not: or if propounded, whether sufficiently, or only insufficiently.* And it is so known a thing, that in many points you do so, that I assure my self you will not deny it. Therefore we constantly urge and require a particular and perfect Inventory of all these Divine Revelations, which you say *are sufficiently propounded, and that such a one to which all of your Church will subscribe as neither redundant, nor deficient;* which when you give in with one hand, you shall receive a particular Catalogue of such Points as I call *Fundamental* with the other. Neither may you think me unreasonable in this demand, seeing upon such a particular Catalogue of your sufficient Proposals

This great diversity of Opinions among you, touching this matter, if any man doubt of it, let him read *Franciscus Picus Mirandula in l. Theorem. in Expofit. Theor. quarti.* and *Tho. Waldensis. Tom. 3. De Sacramentalibus. doct. 3. fol. 5.* and he shall be fully satisfied that I have done you no injury.

as

as much depends, as upon a particular Catalogue of our *Fundamentals.* As for example. Whether or no a man do not Err in some point defined and sufficiently proposed: and whether or no those that differ among you, differ in *Fundamentals*; which if they do *One Heaven* (by your own Rule) *cannot receive them All.* Perhaps you will here complain, that this is not to satisfie your demand, but to avoid it, and to put you off as the *Areopagites* did hard Causes *ad diem longissimum,* and bid you come again a Hundred Years hence: To deal truly, I did so intend it should be. Neither can you say, my dealing with you is injurious, seeing I require nothing of you, but that, what you require of others, you should shew it possible to be done, and just and necessary to be required. For, for my part, I have great reason to suspect, it is neither the one nor the other. For whereas the Verities which are delivered in Scripture, may be very fitly divided into *such as were written because they were necessary to be believed,* Of which rank are those only which constitute and make up the Covenant between God and Man in Christ: and then *such as are necessary to be believed not in themselves but only by accident, because they were written.* Of which rank are many matters of History, of Prophecy, of Mystery, of Policy, of Oeconomy, and such like, which are evidently not *intrinsecal* to the Covenant. Now to sever exactly and punctally these Verities one from the other: what is *necessary in it self* and antecedently to the writing, from what is but only profitable in it self, and *necessary only because written,* is a business of extream great difficulty, and extream little necessity. For first he that will go about to distinguish especially in the story of our Saviour, what was written because it was *profitable,* from what was written because *necessary,* shall find an intricate peice of business of it, and almost impossible that he should be certain he hath done it, when he hath done it. And then it is apparently unnecessary to go about it, seeing he that believes all, certainly believes all that is necessary. And he that doth not believe all (I mean all the undoubted parts of the undoubted Books of Scripture) can hardly

believe

believe any, neither have we reason to believe he doth so. So that, that *Protestants* give you not a Catalogue of *Fundamentals*, it is not from Tergiversation (as you suspect, who for want of Charity to them always suspect the worst,) but from Wisdom and Necessity. For they may very easily Err in doing it; because though all which is necessary be plain in Scripture, yet all which is plain is not therefore written because it was necessary. For what greater necessity was there that I should know S. *Paul left his Cloak at* Troas, than those *Worlds of Miracles*, which our Saviour did, which were never written. And when they had done it, it had been to no purpose; There being as matters now stand, as great necessity, of believing those truths of Scripture, which are not Fundamental, as those that are. You see then what reason we have to decline this hard labour, which you a rigid Task-master have here put upon us. Yet instead of giving you a Catalogue of Fundamentals, with which I dare say you are resolved before it come, never to be satisfied, I will say that to you, which if you please may do you as much service; and this it is. That it is sufficient for any Mans Salvation that he believe the Scripture: That he endeavour to believe it in the true sense of it, as far as concerns his Duty: And that he conform his Life unto it either by Obedience or Repentance. He that does so (and all *Protestants* according to the *Dictamen* of their Religion should do so,) may be secure that he cannot Err Fundamentally. And they that do so cannot differ in Fundamentals. So that notwithstanding their differences, and your presumption, *the same Heaven may receive them All.*

28. Ad 20. §.] Your Tenth and last request is, *to know distinctly what is the Doctrine of the* Protestant *English Church, in these points; and what my private Opinion.* Which shall be satisfied when the Church of *England* hath expressed her self in them; or when you have told us what is the Doctrine of your Church, in the Question of *Predetermination*, or the *Immaculate Conception*.

29. Ad 21. and 22. §.] These answers I hope in the judgment of indifferent men are satisfactory to your Questions though not to you, For I have either answered them, or given you a reason why I have not. Neither, for ought I can see, *have I flitted from things considered in their own nature, to accidental or rare Circumstances,* But told you my Opinion plainly what I thought of your Errors in themselves: and what as they were qualified or malignified with good or bad Circumstances.

CHAP. I.

The ANSWER to the First CHAPTER.

Shewing that the Adversary grants the Old Question and proposeth a New one. And that there is no reason, why among Men of different Opinions and Communions, one Side only can be saved.

1. AD 1. §.] *Protestants* are here accused of uncharitableness while they accuse you of it: and you make good this charge in this manner. Protestants *charge the* Roman *Church with many and great Errors, judge reconciliation of their Doctrine and ours impossible, and that for them who are convicted in Conscience of her Errors, not to forsake her in them, or to be reconciled unto her, is damnable. Therefore if* Roman Catholicks *be convicted in Conscience of the Errors of* Protestants, *they may and must judge a reconciliation with them damnable, and consequently, to judge so is no more uncharitable in them, than it is in* Protestants *to judge as they do.*

CHIL. All this I grant; nor would any *Protestant* accuse you of *want of Charity* if you went no further. If you be perswaded in Conscience that our Religion is erroneous, the profession of it, though in it self most true, to you would be damnable. For it is no uncharitableness to judge *Hypocrisie a damnable Sin.* Let Hypocrite then and Dissemblers on both Sides pass. It is not

towards

towards them, but good Christians; not to *Protestant* Professors but Believers, that we require your Charity. What think you of those that believe so verily the truth of our Religion, that they are resolved to Die in it, and if occasion were to Die for it? What Charity have you for them? What think you of those that in the Days of our Fathers, laid down their Lives for it? are you content that they shall be saved, or do you hope they may be so? Will you grant that notwithstanding their Errors, there is good hope they might Die with Repentance? and if they did so, certainly they are saved. If you will do so, this Controversie is ended. No man will hereafter charge you with *want of Charity*. This is as much as either we give you, or expect of you, while you remain in your Religion. But then you must leave abusing silly People, with telling them (as your fashion is) that *Protestants confess* Papists *may be saved, but* Papists *confess not so much of* Protestants; *therefore yours is the safer way, and in Wisdom and Charity to our own Souls we are bound to follow it.* For granting this, you grant as much hope of Salvation to *Protestants,* as *Protestants* do to you. If you will not, but still affirm, as *C. M.* does, that *Protestants* (not dissemblers but *believers*) *without a particular Repentance of their Religion cannot be saved*: This I say, is a *want of Charity.*

But I pray Sir what dependance is there between these Propositions: We that hold *Protestant* Religion false should be damned if we should profess it, Therefore they also shall be damned, that hold it true? Just as if you should conclude, *Because he that doubts is Damned if he Eat,* Therefore he that does not doubt is damned also if he Eat. And therefore though your Religion to us, or ours to you, if professed against Conscience would be damnable; yet may it well be uncharitable to define it shall be so, to them that profess either this or that according to Conscience.

3. Ad 3. 4. 5. 6. §.] C. M. *Our meaning is not, that we give* Protestants *over to reprobation; that we offer no Prayers in hope of their Salvation; that we hold their Case desperate.* God forbid, &c.

CHIL. I wish with all my Heart that you had expressed your self in this matter more fully and plainly. Yet that which you say, doth plainly enough afford us these Corollaries. 1. That whatsoever *Protestant* wanteth Capacity, or having it, wanteth sufficient means of instruction to convince his Conscience of the falshood of his own, and the truth of the *Roman* Religion, by the confession of his most rigid Adversaries, may be saved, notwithstanding any Error in his Religion. 2. That nothing hinders but that a *Protestant* Dying a *Protestant* may Die with contrition for all his Sins. 3. That if he Die with Contrition, he may and shall be saved.

4. All these acknowledgments we have from you, while you are, as you say, stating, but, as I conceive granting the very point in question. So that according to your Doctrine, the heavy sentence shall remain upon *such only, as either were, or but for their own fault, might have been sufficiently convinced of the truth of your Religion, and the falshood of their own, and yet Die in it without contrition.* Which Doctrine if you would stand to, and not pull down, and pull back with one hand, what you give and build with the other, this controversie were ended; and I should willingly acknowledge, that which follows in your fourth paragraph; *That you allow* Protestants *as much Charity as* D. Potter *allows you.* But then I must intreat you to alter the *argument of this Chapter*, and not to go about to give us reasons, *why amongst Men of different Religions, one side only can be saved absolutely*, which your Reasons drive at: But you must temper the crudeness of your Assertion by saying, *One Side only can be saved, unless want of Conviction, or else Repentance excuse the other.* Besides you must not only abstain from damning any *Protestant* in particular, but from affirming in general, that Protestants *Dying in their Religion cannot be saved*; for you must always remember to add this caution, unless *they were excusably ignorant of the falshood of it, or Died with contrition.* And then considering that you cannot know, whether or no, all things considered, they were convinced sufficiently of the truth of your Religion and the

falshood

falshood of their own, you are obliged by Charity to judge the best, and hope they are not. Considering again, that notwithstanding their Errors, they may Die with contrition, and that it is no way improbable that they do so, and the contrary you cannot be certain of, You are bound in Charity to judge and hope they do so. Considering thirdly and lastly, that if they Die not with *Contrition*, yet it is very probable they may Die with *Attrition*, and that this pretence of yours, that *Contrition will serve without actual Confession, but Attrition will not*, is but a Nicety or Phansie, or rather to give it the true name, a Device of your own, to serve ends and purposes; (God having no where declared himself, but that wheresoever he will accept of that Repentance, which you are pleased to call *Contrition*, he will accept of that which you call *Attrition*; For though he like best the bright Flaming Holocaust of Love, yet he rejects not, he quenches not the smoaking Flax of that Repentance (if it be true and effectual) which proceeds from hope and fear:) These things I say, considered, (unless you will have the Charity of your Doctrine rise up in judgment against your uncharitable Practice) you must not only not be peremptory, in damning *Protestants*, but you must hope well of their Salvation: and out of this hope, you must do for them as well as others, those, as you conceive, Charitable offices, of Praying, giving Alms and offering Sacrifice, which usually you do, for those of whose Salvation you are well and Charitably persuaded; (for I believe you will never conceive so well of Protestants, as to assure your selves they go directly to Heaven.) These things when you do I shall believe you think as Charitably as you speak. But until then, as he said in the Comedy, *Quid verba audiam cum facta videam?* so may I say to you, *Quid verba audiam cum facta non videam?* To what purpose should you give us Charitable Words, which presently you retract again, by denying us your Charitable Actions. And as these things you must do, if you will stand to and make good this pretended Charity, so must I tell you again and again, that one thing you must not doe; I mean you must not affright poor People out of their Religion, with telling them, that *by the Confession of both sides, your way is safe, but in your judgment, ours undoubtedly damnable.* Seeing neither you deny Salvation to *Protestants Dying with repentance*, nor we promise it to you, *if ye Die without it.* For to deal plainly with you, I know no *Protestant* that hath any other hope of your Salvation, but upon these grounds, that *unaffected ignorance* may excuse you, or *true repentance* obtain pardon for you; neither do the heavy censures which *Protestants* (you say) pass upon your Errors, any way hinder but they may hope as well of you, upon repentance, as I do. For the *fierce Doctrine*, which, God knows who, teaches, that *Christ for many Ages before* Luther *had no visible Church upon Earth*; will be mild enough, if you conceive them to mean (as perhaps they do) by *no visible Church, none pure and free from corruptions*, which in your judgment is all one with no Church. But the truth is the *corruption* of the Church, and the *destruction* of it, is not all one. For if a particular man or Church may (as you confess they may) hold some particular Errors, and yet be a member of the Church Universal: why may not the Church hold some Universal Error, and yet be still the Church? especially, seeing you say, it is nothing but *opposing the Doctrine of the Church, that makes an Error damnable*, and it is impossible that the Church should oppose the Church, I mean that the present Church should oppose it self. And then for the *English Protestants*, though they censure your Errors deeply, yet, by your favour, with their deepest censures it may well consist that *invincible ignorance* may excuse you from damnation for them. For you your self confess *that ignorance may excuse Errors, even in Fundamental Articles of Faith: so that a man so erring shall not offend at all in such his ignorance or Error*; they are your own words. p. 19. And again with their heaviest censures it may well consist, that your Errors though in themselves damnable, yet may prove *not damning* to you, if you Die with true repentance, for all your sins known and unknown.

5. Thus

5. Thus much Charity therefore, if you stand to what you have said, is interchangeably granted by each Side to the other, that Neither Religion is so fatally *destructive*, but that by ignorance or repentance Salvation may be had on both Sides: though with a difference that keeps *Papists* still on the more uncharitable Side. For whereas we conceive a lower degree of repentance (that which they call *Attrition*) if it be true, and effectual, and convert the Heart of the Penitent, will serve in them: They pretend (even this *Author* which is most charitable towards us,) that *without Contrition* there is no hope for us: But though *Protestants* may not obtain this purchase at so easie a rate as *Papists*, yet (even *Papists* being Judges) they may obtain it; and though there is no entrance for them but at the only door of *Contrition*, yet they may enter, Heaven is not inaccessible to them. Their Errors are no such impenetrable Isthmus's between them and Salvation, but that *Contrition* may make a way through them. All their Schism and Heresie is no such fatal Poyson, but that if a man joyn with it the Antidote of a general repentance, he may Die in it, and live for ever. Thus much then being acknowledged, I appeal to any indifferent reader, whether C. M. be not by this *Hyperaspist* forsaken in the plain Field, and the point in question granted to D. *Potter*, viz. *That Protestancy even without a particular repentance, is not destructive of Salvation*; so that all the Controversie remaining now, is, not simply whether *Protestancy unrepented destroys Salvation?* as it was at first proposed, but *Whether Protestancy in it self* (that is *abstracting from ignorance and contrition*) *destroys Salvation?* So that as a foolish Fellow who gave a Knight the Lie, desiring withal leave of him to set his Knighthood aside, was answered by him, that he would not suffer any thing to be set aside that belonged unto him: So might we justly take it amiss, that conceiving as you do Ignorance and Repentance such necessary things for us, you are not more willing to consider us with them, than without them. For my part such is my Charity to you, that considering what great necessity *You* have, as much as any

Christian

Christian Society in the *World*, that these Sanctuaries of *Ignorance* and *Repentance* should always stand open, I can very hardly perswade my self so much as in my most secret consideration to devest you of these so needful qualifications: But whensoever your Errors, superstitions and impieties come into my mind, (and besides the general bonds of humanity and Christianity, my own particular Obligations to many of you, such and so great, that you cannot perish without a part of my self,) my only comfort is amidst these Agonies, that the Doctrine and Practice too of Repentance, is yet remaining in your Church: And that though you put on a Face of confidence of your Innocence in point of Doctrine, yet you will be glad to stand in the Eye of Mercy as well as your fellows, and not be so stout, as to refuse either Gods pardon or the Kings.

6. But for the present, Protestancy is called to the Barr, and though not sentenced by you to Death without Mercy, yet arraigned of so much natural malignity (if not corrected by *Ignorance* or *Contrition*) as to be *in it self destructive of Salvation*. Which controversie I am content to dispute with you; only remembring you, that the adding of this limitation [*in it self*] hath made this a new Question, and that this is not the conclusion for which you were charged with *want of Charity*.

7. Ad 7. and 8. §.] C. M. *Now this is our gradation of reasons. Almighty God having ordained mankind to a supernatural end of Eternal Felicity, hath in his providence setled competent Means*, &c.

CHIL. In your gradation I shall rise so far with you as to grant, *that Christ founded a visible Church, stored with all helps necessary to Salvation, particularly with sufficient means to beget and conserve Faith, to maintain Unity, and compose Schisms, to discover and condemn Heresies, and to determine all controversies in Religion*, which were necessary to be determined. For all these purposes, he gave at the beginning (as we may see in the Ep. to the *Ephesians*) *Apostles, Prophets, Evangelists, Pastors, and Doctors*: who by word of mouth taught their contemporaries, and by writings

tings (wrote indeed by some, but approved by all of them) taught their Christian posterity to the Worlds End, how all these ends, and that which is the End of all these ends, Salvation, is to be atchieved. And these means the Providence of God hath still preserved, and so preserved, that they are sufficient for all these intents. I say *sufficient*, though, through the Malice of Men, not always *effectual*, for that the same means may be sufficient for the compassing an end, and not effectual, you must not deny, who hold that *God gives all men sufficient means of Salvation, and yet that all are not saved.* I said also, sufficient to determine all controversies, which *were necessary to be determined.* For if some controversies may for many Ages be undetermined, and yet in the mean while men be saved; why should, or how can the Churches being furnished with effectual means to determine *all* Controversies in Religion be necessary to Salvation, the end it self, to which these means are ordained being as experience shews not necessary? Plain sense will teach every man, that the necessity of the means must always be measured by, and can never exceed the necessity of the end. As if eating be necessary, only that I may live, then certainly if I have no necessity to live, I have no necessity to eat. If I have no need to be at *London*, I have no need of a Horse to carry me thither. If I have no need to Fly, I have no need of Wings. Answer me then I pray directly, and Categorically, Is it necessary that all Controversies in Religion should be determined, or is it not? If it be, why is the question of *Predetermination*, of the *immaculate conception*, of the *Popes indirect power in temporalties*, so long undetermined? if not, what is it but Hypocrisie to pretend such great necessity of such effectual means, for the atchieving that end, which is it self not necessary. Christians therefore have and shall have *means sufficient* (though not always effectual) *to determine* not all *controversies* but *all necessary to be determined.* I proceed on farther with you, and grant that this means to decide controversies in Faith and Religion, must be indued with an Universal Infallibility in whatsoever it propoundeth

I

poundeth for a Divine truth. For if it may be false in any one thing of this nature, in any thing which God requires men to believe, we can yield unto it but a wavering and fearful assent in any thing. These grounds therefore I grant very readily, and give you free leave to make your best advantage of them. And yet, to deal truly, I do not perceive how from the denial of any of them it would follow that Faith is Opinion: or from the granting them, that it is not so. But for my part, whatsoever clamour you have raised against me, I think no otherwise of the Nature of Faith, I mean *Historical Faith*, than generally both *Protestants* and *Papists* do; for I conceive it *an assent to Divine Revelations upon the Authority of the revealer*. Which though in many things it differ from Opinion, (as commonly the Word *Opinion* is understood) yet in some things, I doubt not but you will confess, that it agrees with it. As first, that as Opinion is an Assent, so is Faith also. Secondly, that as Opinion, so Faith is always built upon less evidence than that of Sence or Science. Which assertion you not only grant but mainly contend for in your *sixth Ch*. Thirdly and lastly, that as Opinion, so Faith admits degrees; and that as there may be a strong and weak Opinion, so there may be a strong and weak Faith. These things if you will grant (as sure if you be in your right mind you will not deny any of them) I am well contented that this ill-sounding Word, *Opinion*, should be discarded, and that among the Intellectual habits you should seek out some other *Genus* for Faith. For I will never contend with any man about Words, who grants my meaning.

8. *But though the Essence of Faith exclude not all weakness and imperfection, yet may it be enquired, whether any certainty of Faith, under the highest degree may be sufficient to please God and attain Salvation*. Whereunto I answer, that though men are unreasonable, God requires not any thing but Reason. They will not be pleased without a down weight, but God is contented if the Scale be turned. They pretend, that Heavenly things cannot be seen to any purpose, but by the mid-day-light: But God will be satisfied,

ed, if we receive any degree of light which makes us leave the *Works of Darkness and walk as Children of the Light.* They exact a certainty of Faith above that of Sence or Science, God desires only that we believe the conclusion, as much as the premises deserve, that the strength of our Faith be equal or proportionable to the credibility of the Motives to it. Now though I have and ought to have an absolute certainty of this Thesis, *All which God reveals for truth is true,* being a proposition that may be demonstrated, or rather so evident to any one that understands it, that it needs it not; Yet of this Hypothesis, *That all the Articles of our Faith were revealed by God,* we cannot ordinarily have any rational and acquired certainty, more than moral, founded upon these considerations: First that the goodness of the precepts of Christianity, and the greatness of the promises of it, shews it, of all other Religions, most likely to come from the Fountain of goodness. And then that a constant, famous and very general Tradition, so credible, that no Wise Man doubts of any other, which hath but the Fortieth part of the credibility of this, such and so credible a Tradition, tells us, that God himself hath set his Hand and Seal to the Truth of this Doctrine, by doing great, and glorious, and frequent miracles in confirmation of it. Now our Faith is an assent to this conclusion, that *the Doctrine of Christianity is true,* which being deduced from the former *Thesis,* which is Metapyhsically certain, and from the former *Hypothesis,* whereof we can have but a Moral certainty, we cannot possibly by natural means be more certain of it than of the weaker of the premises; as a River will not rise higher than the Fountain from which it flows. For the conclusion always follows the worser part, if there be any worse: and must be Negative, Particular, Contingent, or but Morally certain, if any of the Propositions, from whence it is derived be so: Neither can we be certain of it in the highest degree, unless we be thus certain of all the principles whereon it is grounded. As a man cannot go or stand strongly, if either of his Legs be weak. Or as a building cannot be stable, if any one of the necessary Pillars thereof be infirm and instable. Or as, If a message be brought me, from a man of absolute credit with me, but by a messenger that is not so, my confidence of the Truth of the Relation, cannot but be rebated and lessened, by my diffidence in the Relator.

9. Yet all this I say not as if I doubted, that the Spirit of God, being implored by devout and humble Prayer and sincere obedience, may, and will by degrees, advance his servants higher, and give them a certainty of adherence, beyond their certainty of evidence. But what God gives as a reward to believers, is one thing: and what he requires of all men, as their duty, is another: and what he will accept of out of grace and favour, is yet another. To those that believe and live according to their Faith, he gives by degrees the *spirit of obsignation and confirmation*, which makes them know (though how they know not) what they did but believe: And to be as fully and resolutely assured of the Gospel of Christ, as those which heard it from Christ himself with their Ears, which saw it with their Eyes, which looked upon it, and whose hands handled the Word of Life. He requires of all, that their Faith should be (as I have said) proportionable to the motives and Reasons enforcing to it; he will accept of the weakest and lowest degree of Faith, if it be living and effectual unto true obedience. For he it is that *will not quench the smoaking Flax, nor break the bruised Reed*. He did not reject the Prayer of that distressed man that cried unto him, *Lord I believe, Lord help my unbelief*. He commands us to *receive them that are weak in Faith*, and thereby declares that he receives them. And as nothing avails with him, but Faith *wich worketh by love*: So any Faith, if it be but as a *grain of Mustard seed*, if it *work by love*, shall certainly avail with him and be accepted of him. Some experience makes me fear, that the Faith of considering and discoursing men, is like to be crackt with too much straining: And that being possessed with this *false* Principle, that it is in vain to believe the Gospel of Christ, with such a kind or degree of assent, as they yield to other matters of Tradition: And finding that their Faith of it,

is to them undifcernable, from the belief they give to the truth of other Stories; are in danger either not to believe at all, thinking not at all as good as to no purpofe, or elfe, though indeed they do believe it, yet to think they do not, and to caft themfelves into wretched agonies and perplexities, as fearing they have not that, without which it is impoffible to pleafe God and obtain Eternal happinefs. Confideration of this advantage, which the Devil probably may make of this Phanfie, made me willing to infift fomewhat largely upon the Refutation of it.

10. I return now thither from whence I have digreffed, and affure you, concerning the grounds afore-laid, which were, that there is a *Rule of Faith, whereby controverfies may be decided, which are neceffary to be decided,* and that *this rule is Univerfally infallible,* That notwithftanding any Opinion I hold, touching Faith, or any thing elfe, I may, and do believe them, as firmly as you pretend to do. And therefore you may build on, in Gods name, for by Gods help, I fhall always embrace, whatfoever ftructure is naturally and rationally laid upon them, whatfoever conclufion may, to my underftanding, be evidently deduced from them. You fay, out of them it undeniably follows, *That of two difagreeing in matter of Faith, the one cannot be faved, but by Repentance or Ignorance.* I anfwer by diftinction of thofe terms, *two diffenting in a matter of Faith.* For it may be either in a thing which is indeed a *matter of Faith,* in the ftricteft fenfe, that is, fomething, the Belief whereof God requires under pain of damnation: And fo the conclufion is true, though the Confequence of it from your former premiffes either is none at all, or fo obfcure, that I can hardly difcern it. Or it may be as it oftens falls out concerning a thing which being indeed *no matter of Faith, is yet overvalued* by the Parties at variance, and efteemed to be fo. And in this fenfe it is neither confequent nor true. The untruth of it I have already declared in my examination of your Preface. The inconfequence of it is of it felf evident; for who ever heard of a wilder Collection than this ——

God

God hath provided means sufficient to decide all Controversies in Religion, necessary to be decided;
This means is Universally infallible,
Therefore of two, that differ in any thing which they esteem a matter of Faith, one cannot be saved.

He that can find any connection between these Propositions, I believe will be able to find good coherence between the Deaf Plantiff's Accusation, in the *Greek* Epigram, and the Deaf Defendants Answer, and the Deaf Judges Sentence: And to contrive them all into a formal Categorical Syllogism.

11. Indeed if the matter in agitation were plainly decided, by this infallible means of deciding Controversies, and the Parties in variance knew it to be so, and yet would stand out in their dissention; this were in one of them, direct opposition to the Testimony of God, and undoubtedly a damnable sin. But if you take the liberty to suppose what you please, you may very easily conclude what you list. For who is so foolish as to grant you these unreasonable Postulates, that every emergent Controversie of Faith, is plainly decided by the means of dicision which God hath appointed, and that of the Parties litigant, one is always such a convicted Recusant as you pretend! Certainly, if you say so, having no better warrant than you have, or can have for it, this is more proper and formal uncharitableness, than ever was charged upon you. Methinks, with much more Reason, and much more Charity, you might suppose, that many of these Controversies which are now disputed among Christians (all which profess themselves lovers of Christ, and truly desirous to know his Will and do it) are either *not decidable* by that means which God hath provided, and so not necessary to be decided : Or if they be, yet *not so plainly and evidently*, as to oblige all men to hold one way : or Lastly, if decidable, and evidently decided, yet you may hope that the erring part, by reason of some Vail before his Eyes, *some excusable ignorance or unavoidable prejudice,* does not see the Question to be decided against him, and so opposes not that which He

doth

doth know to be the word of God, but only that which You know to be so, and which he might know, were he void of prejudice. Which is a fault I confess, but a fault which is incident even to good and honest men very often: and not of such a gigantick disposition as you make it, to fly directly upon God Almighty, and to give him the Lie to his Face.

12. Ad 9, 10, 11, 12, 13, 14, 15, 16. §.] In all this long discourse you only tell us what you will do, but do nothing, but reserve them to the Chapters following, and there they shall be examined. The Sum of all collected by your self, §. 16. is this.

That *the Infallible means of determining Controversies, is the Visible Church.*

That *the distinction of points Fundamental, and not Fundamental, maketh nothing to the present Question.*

That *to say the Creed containeth all Fundamentals, is neither pertinent nor true.*

That *whosoever persist in Division from the Communion and Faith of the* Roman *Church are guilty of Schism and Heresie.*

That *in regard of the Precept of Charity towards one self,* Protestants *are in state of Sin, while they remain divided from the* Roman *Chruch.*

To all these Assertions I will content my self for the present to oppose this one, That *not one of them all is true.* Only I may not omit to tell you, that if the first of them were as true as the *Pope* himself desires it should be, yet the Corollary which you deduce from it, would be utterly inconsequent, That *whosoever denys any point proposed by the Church, is injurious to Gods Divine Majesty, as if he could deceive, or be deceived.* For though your Church were indeed as *Infallible a Propounder of Divine Truths* as it pretends to be, yet if it appeared not to me to be so, I might very well believe God most true, and your Church most false. As though the Gospel of S. *Matthew* be the Word of God, yet if I neither knew it to be so, nor believed it, I might believe in God, and yet think that Gospel a Fable. Hereafter therefore I must entreat you to remember,

remember, that our being guilty of this impiety, depends not only upon your being, but upon our knowing that you are so. Neither must you argue thus, *The Church of Rome is the Infallible Propounder of Divine Verities, therefore he that opposes Her calls Gods Truth in Question:* But thus rather; The *Church of* Rome *is so, and* Protestants *know it to be so, therefore in opposing Her, they impute to God, that either he deceives them, or is deceived himself.* For as I may deny something which you upon your knowledg have affirmed, and yet never disparage your honesty, if I never knew that you affirmed it: So I may be undoubtedly certain of Gods Omniscience, and Veracity, and yet doubt of something which he hath revealed, provided I do not know, nor believe that he hath revealed it. So, that though your Church be the appointed witness of Gods Revelations; yet until you know, that we know she is so, you cannot without foul Calumny impute to us, That *we charge God blasphemously with deceiving, or being deceived.* You will say perhaps, That this is directly consequent from our Doctrine, That the *Church may Err,* which is directed by God in all Her proposals. True, if we knew it to be directed by him, otherwise not; much less if we believe, and know the contrary. But then if it were consequent from our Opinion, have you so little Charity as to say, that men are *justly chargeable with all the consequences of their Opinions.*; Such consequences, I mean, as they do not own but disclaim, and if there were a necessity of doing either, would much rather forsake their Opinion than embrace these Consequences? What Opinion is there that draws after it such a Train of *portentous Blasphemies,* as that of the *Dominicans,* by the judgment of the best Writers of your own *Order?* And will you say now that the *Dominicans* are justly chargeable with all these Blasphemies? If not, seeing our case (take it at the worst) is but the same, why should not your judgment of us be the same? I appeal to all those *Protestants* that have gone over to your Side; whether when they were most averse from it, they did ever deny or doubt of *Gods omniscience or veracity*;

whe-

whether they did ever believe, or were taught, that *God did deceive them, or was deceived himself.* Nay, I provoke to you your self, and desire you to deal truly, and to tell Us whether you do in your Heart believe, that we do indeed not believe the Eternal Veracity of the Eternal Verity? And if you judge so strangely of us, having no better ground for it, than you have or can have, we shall not need any farther proof of your uncharitableness towards us, this being the extremity of true uncharitableness. If not, then I hope having no other ground but this (which sure is none at all) to pronounce us *damnable Hereticks*, you will cease to do so; and hereafter (as, if your ground be true, you may do with more truth and Charity) Collect thus, *They only Err damnably, who oppose what they know God hath testified,* But Protestants *sure do not oppose what they know God hath testified, at least we cannot with Charity say they do, Therefore they either do not Err damnably, or with Charity we cannot say they do so.*

13. Ad 17. §.] *Protestants* (you say) *according to their own grounds must hold that of Persons contrary in whatsoever point of belief one part only can be saved, therefore it is strangely done of them to charge* Papists *with want of Charity for holding the same.* The consequence I acknowledg, but wonder much what it should be that lays upon *Protestants* any necessity to do so! You tell us it is their holding Scripture *the sole Rule of Faith* : for this, you say, obligeth them to pronounce them damned, that oppose any least point *delivered in Scripture*. This I grant, If they oppose it after sufficient declaration, so that either they *know it to be contained in Scripture,* or have no just probable Reason, and which may move an honest man to doubt whether or no it be there contained. For to oppose in the first Case in a man that believes the Scripture to be the Word of God, is to give God the Lie. To oppose in the second, is to be obstinate against Reason, and therefore a sin though not so great as the former. But then this is nothing to the purpose of the necessity of damning all those that are of contrary belief; and that for these Reasons. First, because the contrary belief may be touch-

K   ing

ing a point not at all mentioned in Scripture; and such points, though indeed they be not *matters of Faith*, yet by men in variance are often over-valued and esteemed to be so. So that, though it were damnable to oppose any point contained in Scripture; yet Persons of a contrary belief (as *Victor* and *Polycrates*, S. *Cyprian*, and *Stephen*) might both be saved, because their contrary belief was not touching any point contained in Scripture. Secondly, because the contrary belief may be about the sense of some place of Scripture which is ambiguous, and with probability capable of diverse Senses; and in such Cases it is no marvel, and sure no Sin, if several men go several ways. Thirdly, because the contrary belief may be concerning points wherein Scripture may with so great probability be alledged on both sides, (which is a sure note of a point *not necessary*) that men of honest and upright Hearts, true lovers of God and of truth, such as desire, above all things, to know Gods Will and to do it, may, without any fault at all, some go one way, and some another, and some (and those as good men as either of the former) suspend their judgments, and expect some *Elias to solve doubts*, and reconcile repugnances. Now in all such Questions one side or other (which soever it is) holds that which indeed is opposite to the sense of the Scripture, which God intended; for it is impossible that God should intend Contradictions. But then this intended Sense is not so fully declared, but that they which oppose it may verily believe that they indeed maintain it, and have great shew of reason to induce them to believe so; and therefore are not to be damned, as men opposing that which they either know to be a truth delivered in Scripture, or have no probable Reason to believe the contrary; but rather in Charity to be acquitted and absolved, as men who endeavour to find the Truth, but fail of it through humane frailty.

This ground being laid, the Answer to your ensuing Interrogatories, which you conceive impossible, is very obvious and easie.

14. *To the first, Whether it be not in any man a grievous sin to deny any any one Truth contained in holy Writ?* I answer, Yes, if he knew it to be so, or have no probable Reason to doubt of it: otherwise not.

15. *To the second, Whether there be in such denial any distinction between Fundamental and not Fundamental sufficient to excuse from Heresie?* I answer, Yes, There is such a distinction. But the Reason is, because these points, either in themselves, or by accident, are *Fundamental*, which are *evidently contained in Scripture, to him that knows them to be so*: Those not Fundamental which are there-hence deducible but probably only, not evidently.

16. *To the third, Whether it be not impertinent to alledge the Creed as containing all Fundamental points of Faith, as if believing it alone we were at Liberty to deny all other Points of Scripture?* I answer, It was never alledged to any such purpose; but only as a sufficient, or rather more than a sufficient Summary of those points of Faith, which were of necessity to be believed actually and explicitely; and that only of such which were meerly and purely *Credenda*, and not *Agenda*.

17. *To the fourth*, drawn as a Corollary from the former, *Whether this be not to say, that of Persons contrary in belief, one part only can be saved?* I answer, By no means. For they may differ about points *not contained in Scripture*: They may differ about the *sense of some ambiguous Texts* of Scripture: They may differ about some Doctrines, for and against which Scriptures may be alledged with *so great probability*, as may justly excuse either Part from Heresie, and a self-condemning obstinacy. And therefore, though D. *Potter* do not take it ill, that you believe your selves may be saved in your Religion; yet notwithstanding all that hath yet been pretended to the contrary, he may justly condemn you, and that out of your own principles, of *uncharitable presumption*, for affirming as you do, that *no man can be saved out of it*.

CHAP.

CHAP. II.

The ANSWER to the Second CHAPTER.

Concerning the means, whereby the revealed Truths of God are conveyed to our understanding; and which must determine Controversies in Faith and Religion.

C. M. Of our estimation, respect and reverence to holy Scripture, even Protestants themselves give Testimony, while they possess it from us, and take it upon the integrity of our custody, &c.

CHIL. Ad §. 1.] He that would Usurp an absolute Lordship and Tyranny over any People, need not put himself to the trouble and difficulty of abrogating and disanulling the Laws, made to maintain the Common Liberty; for he may frustrate their intent, and compass his own design as well, if he can get the Power and Authority to interpret them as he pleases, and add to them what he pleases, and to have his interpretations and additions stand for Laws; if he can rule his People by his Laws, and his Laws by his Lawyers. So the *Church of* Rome, to establish Her Tyranny over mens Consciences, needed not either to abolish or corrupt the Holy Scriptures, the Pillars and Supporters of Christian Liberty (which in regard of the numerous multitude of Copies dispersed through all places, Translated into almost all Languages, guarded with all sollicitous care and industry, had been an impossible attempt;) But the more expedite way, and therefore more likely to be successful, was to gain the opinion and esteem of the *publick and authorized interpreter* of them, and the Authority of adding to them what Doctrine she pleased under the Title of *Traditions* or *Definitions.* For by this means, she might both serve her self of all those causes of Scripture, which might be drawn to cast a favourable countenance upon Her ambitious pretences, which in case the Scripture had been abolished, she could not have done; and yet be secure enough of having

having either her Power limitted, or her corruptions and abuses reformed by them; this being once setled in the minds of men, that *unwritten Doctrines, if proposed by her, were to be received with equal reverence to those that were written*: and that *the sense of Scripture was not that which seemed to mens reason and understanding to be so, but that which the Church of Rome should declare to be so, seemed it never so unreasonable, and incongruous*. The matter being once thus ordered, and the holy Scriptures being made in effect not your Directors and Judges (no farther than you please) but your *Servants and Instruments*, always prest and in readiness to advance your designs, and disabled wholly with minds so qualified to prejudice or impeach them; it is safe for you to put a Crown on their head, and a Reed in their Hands, and to bow before them, and cry, *Hail King of the* Jews! to pretend a great deal of *esteem, and respect, and reverence* to them, as here you do. But to little purpose is verbal reverence without entire submission and sincere obedience; and, as our Saviour said of some, so the Scripture, could it speak, I believe would say to you, Why *call ye me Lord, Lord, and do not that which I command you?* Cast away the vain and arrogant pretence of *Infallibility*, which makes your Errors incurable. Leave Picturing God, and Worshiping him by Pictures. *Teach not for Doctrine the Commandments of men.* Debar not the Laity of the Testament of Christ's Blood. Let your publick *Prayers*, and *Psalms* and *Hymes* be in such Language as is for the Edification of the Assistants. Take not from the Clergy that Liberty of Marriage which Christ hath left them. Do not impose upon men that *Humility of Worshiping Angels* which S. *Paul* condemns. Teach no more proper Sacrifices of Christ but one. Acknowledge them *that Die in Christ to be blessed, and to rest from their Labours*. Acknowledge the Sacrament after Consecration, to be Bread and Wine, as well as Christs Body and Blood. Acknowledge the gift of continency without Marriage not to be given to all. Let not the Weapons of your Warfare be Carnal; such as are Massacres, Treasons, Persecutions, and in a word all means

either

either violent or fraudulent: These and other things, which the Scripture commands you, do, and then we shall willingly give you such Testimony as you deserve; but till you do so, to talk of estimation, respect, and reverence to the Scripture, is nothing else but talk.

2. For neither is that true which you pretend, *That we possess the Scripture from you, or take it upon the integrity of your Custody*, but upon *Universal Tradition*, of which you are but a little part. Neither, If it were true that *Protestants* acknowledged, *The integrity of it to have been guarded by your alone Custody*, were this any argument of your reverence towards them. For first, you might preserve them entire, not for want of Will, but of Power to corrupt them, *as it is a hard thing to Poyson the Sea*. And then having prevailed so far with men, as either not to look at all into them, or but only through such spectacles as you should please to make for them, and to see nothing in them, though as clear as the Sun, if it any way made against you, you might keep them entire, without any thought or care to conform your Doctrine to them, or reform it by them (which were indeed to reverence the Scriptures) but out of a persuasion, that you could qualifie them well enough with your glosses and interpretations, and make them sufficiently conformable to your present Doctrine, at least, in their judgment, who were prepossessed with this persuasion, that *your Church was to judge of the sense of Scripture, not to be judged by it*.

3. Whereas you say, *No cause imaginable could avert your will from giving the function of Supream and sole judge to holy Writ, but that the thing is impossible, and that by this means controversies are encreased and not ended*. What indifferent and unprejudiced man may not easily conceive another cause which (I do not say does, but certainly) may prevert your Wills, and avert your understandings from submitting your Religion and Church to a *Tryal by Scripture*. I mean the great and apparent and unavoidable danger which by this means you would fall into, of losing the Opinion which men have of your Infallibility, and consequently your Power and Authority over mens Consciences,

sciences, and all that depends upon it; so that though *Diana of the Ephesians* be cryed up, yet it may be feared that with a great many among you (though I censure or judge no man) the other cause which wrought upon *Demetrius* and the *Craftsmen*, may have with you also the more effectual, though more secret influence: and that is, that *by this craft we have our living*; by this craft, I mean of keeping your Proselytes from an indifferent Tryal of your Religion by Scripture, and making them yield up and captivate their judgment unto yours.

As for the impossibility of Scriptures being the sole Judge of Controversies, that is, *the sole rule for man to judge them by* (for we mean nothing else) you only affirm it without proof, as if the thing were evident of it self. And therefore I, conceiving the contrary to be more evident, might well content my self to deny it without refutation. Yet I cannot but desire you to tell me, If Scripture cannot be the Judge of any Controversie, how shall that touching the *Church and the Notes of it* be determined? And if it be the sole Judge of this one, why may it not of others? Why not of All? Those only excepted wherein the Scripture it self is the subject of the Question, which cannot be determined but by natural reason, the only Principle, beside Scripture, which is common to Christians.

4. Then for the Imputation of *increasing contentions and not ending them*, Scripture is innocent of it; as also this Opinion; *That Controversies are to be decided by Scripture*. For if men did really and sincerely submit their judgments to Scripture, and that only, and would require no more of any man but to do so, it were impossible but that all Controversies, touching things necessary and very profitable should be ended: and if others were continued or increased, it were no matter.

5. In the next Words we have direct *Boyes-play*; a thing given with one hand and taken away with the other; an acknowledgment made in one line, and retracted in the next. *We acknowledge* (say you) *Scripture to be a perfect rule, for as much as a writing can be a Rule,*
only

only we deny that it excludes unwritten Tradition. As if you should have said, we acknowledge it to be as perfect a Rule as a writing can be; only we deny it to be as perfect a Rule as a writing may be. Either therefore you must revoke your acknowledgment, or retract your retractation of it; for both cannot possibly stand together. For if you will stand to what you have granted, That *Scripture is as perfect a Rule of Faith as a Writing can be*: you must then grant it both so *Compleat*, that it needs no addition, and so *evident*, that it needs no interpretation: For both these properties are requisite to a *perfect rule*; and a Writing is capable of both these properties.

6. That both these Properties are requisite to a *perfect rule*, it is apparent: Because that is not perfect in any kind which wants some parts belonging to its integrity: As he is not a perfect man that wants any part appertaining to the Integrity of a Man; and therefore that which wants any accession to make it a perfect rule, of its self is not a perfect Rule. And then, the end of a *rule* is to regulate and direct. Now every instrument is more or less perfect in its kind, as it is more or less fit to attain the end for which it is ordained: But nothing obscure or unevident while it is so, is fit to regulate and direct them to whom it is so: Therefore it is requisite also to a *rule* (so far as it is a Rule) to be evident; otherwise indeed it is no *rule*, because it cannot serve for direction. I conclude therefore, that both these properties are required to a perfect Rule: both to be so compleat as to need no Addition; and to be so evident as to need no Interpretation.

7. Now that a Writing is capable of both these perfections, it is so plain, that I am even ashamed to prove it. For he that denies it must say, That *something may be spoken which cannot be written*. For if such a compleat and evident rule of Faith may be delivered by word of mouth, as you pretend it may, and is; and whatsoever is delivered by word of mouth may also be written; then such a compleat and evident rule of Faith may also be written. If you will have more light added to the Sun, answer me then to these Questions. Whether your Church can set down in writing

ting all these, which she pretends to be Divine unwritten Traditions, and add them to the verities already written? And whether she can let us down such interpretations of all obscurities in the Faith as shall need no farther interpretations? If she cannot, then she hath not that power which you pretend she hath, of being an *Infallible Teacher of all Divine verities*, and an infallible interpreter of obscurities in the Faith: for she cannot teach us all Divine verities, if she cannot write them down; neither is that an interpretation which needs again to be interpreted: If she can; Let her do it, and then we shall have a writing, not only capable of, but, actually endowed with both these perfections, of being both so compleat as to need no Addition, and so evident as to need no Interpretation. Lastly, whatsoever your Church can do or not do, no man can without Blasphemy deny, that *Christ Jesus*, if he had pleased, could have writ us a rule of Faith so plain and perfect, as that it should have wanted neither any part to make up its integrity, nor any clearness to make it sufficiently intelligible: And if Christ could have done this, then the thing might have been done; a writing there might have been indowed with both these properties. Thus therefore I conclude, a writing may be so perfect a Rule, as to need neither Addition nor Interpretation; But the *Scripture you acknowledge a perfect Rule for as much as a writing can be a Rule*, therefore it needs neither Addition nor Interpretation.

8. You will say, *that though a writing be never so perfect a Rule of Faith, yet it must be beholden to Tradition to give it this Testimony, that it is a Rule of Faith, and the Word of God.* I answer: First, there is no absolute necessity of this. For God might, if he thought good, give it the attestation of perpetual Miracles. Secondly, that it is one thing to be a perfect Rule of Faith, another to be proved so unto us. And thus though a writing could not be proved to us to be a perfect rule of Faith, by its own saying so, for nothing is proved true by being said or written in a Book, but only by Tradition which is a thing credible of it self; yet it may be so in it self, and contain

all the material Objects, all the particular Articles of our Faith, without any dependance upon Tradition; even this also not excepted, that *this Writing doth contain the rule of Faith*. Now when *Protestants* affirm against *Papists*, that *Scripture is a perfect rule of Faith*, their meaning is not, that by Scripture all things absolutely may be proved, which are to be believed : For it can never be proved by Scripture to a gainsayer, that there is a God, or that the Book called Scripture is the Word of God; For he that will deny these Assertions when they are spoken, will believe them never a whit the more because you can shew them written : But their meaning is, that the Scripture, to them which presuppose it Divine, and a Rule of Faith, as *Papists* and *Protestants* do, contains all the material Objects of Faith; is a compleat and Total, and not only an imperfect and a partial Rule.

9. *But every Book and Chapter, and Text of Scripture is Infallible and wants no due perfection, and yet excludes not the Addition of other Book, of Scripture; Therefore the perfection of the whole Scripture excludes not the Addition of unwritten Tradition.* I answer; Every Text of Scripture though it have the perfection belonging to a Text of Scripture, yet it hath not the perfection requisite to a *perfect Rule of Faith*; and that only is the perfection which is the subject of our discourse. So that this is to abuse your Reader with the ambiguity of the word *Perfect*. In effect, as if you should say, a Text of Scripture may be a perfect Text, though there be others beside it; therefore the whole Scripture may be a perfect Rule of Faith, though there be other parts of this Rule, besides the Scripture, and though the Scripture be but a part of it.

10. The next Argument to the same purpose is, for Sophistry, Cosin German to the former. *When the first Books of Scripture were written, they did not exclude unwritten Tradition: Therefore now also, that all the Books of Scripture are written, Traditions are not excluded.* The sense of which Argument (if it have any) must be this. When only a part of the Scripture was written, then a part of the Divine Doctrine was unwritten; Therefore now when

when all the Scripture is written, yet some part of the Divine Doctrine is yet unwritten. If you say, your conclusion is not that it is so, but without disparagement to Scripture, may be so: without disparagement to the truth of Scripture, I grant it; but without disparagement to the Scriptures being a *perfect Rule*, I deny it. And now the Question is not of the Truth, but the perfection of it; which are very different things, though you would fain confound them. For Scripture might very well be all true, though it contain not all necessary Divine Truth. But unless it do so, it cannot be a *perfect Rule of Faith*; for that which wants any thing is not perfect. For I hope you do not imagine, that we conceive any Antipathy between Gods Word Written and unwritten, but that both might very well stand together. All that we say is this, that we have reason to believe that God *de Facto*, hath ordered the matter so, that all the Gospel of Christ, the whole Covenant between God and Man, is now Written. Whereas if he had pleased, he might so have disposed it, that part might have been written, and part unwritten: but then he would have taken order, to whom we should have had recourse, for that part of it which was not written; which seeing he hath not done (as the Progress shall demonstrate) it is evident he hath left no part of it unwritten. We know no man therefore that says, It were any injury to the written Word to be joyned with the unwritten, if there were any wherewith it might be joyned; but that we deny. The fidelity of a Keeper may very well consist with the Authority of the thing committed to his Custody. But we know no one Society of Christians that is such a faithful Keeper as you pretend. The Scripture it self was not kept so faithfully by you, but that you suffered infinite variety of Readings to creep into it; all which could not possibly be Divine, and yet, in several parts of your Church, all of them, until the last Age, were so esteemed. The interpretations of obscure places of Scripture, which without Question, the Apostles taught the Primitive Christians are wholly lost; there remains no certainty scarce of any one. Those *Worlds of Miracles*, which our Saviour did, which were not written, for want of writing are vanished out of the memory of men. And many profitable things which the Apostles taught and writ not, as that which S. *Paul* glances at, in his *second Epistle to the* Thesalon. of the *cause of the hindrance of the coming of Antichrist*, are wholly lost and extinguished. So unfaithful or negligent hath been this keeper of Divine verities; whose eyes, like the Keepers of *Israel* (you say) have *never Slumbred nor Slept*. Lastly, we deny not but a Judge and a Law might well stand together, but we deny that there is any such Judge of Gods appointment. Had he intended any such Judge, he would have named him, lest otherwise (as now it is) our *Judge of Controversies* should be our greatest Controversie.

11. Ad 2, 3, 4, 5, 6. §.] In your second Paragraph, you sum up those arguments wherewith you intend to prove, that *Scripture alone cannot be Judge in Controversies*. Wherein I profess unto you before hand, that you will fight without an Adversary. For though *Protestants*, being warranted by some of the Fathers, have called Scripture the *Judge of Controversies*; and you in saying here, That Scripture *alone* cannot be Judge, imply that it may be called in some sense a Judge, though not alone: Yet to speak properly (as men should speak when they write of Controversies in Religion) the Scripture is not a Judge of Controversies, but *a Rule only and the only Rule for Christians to judge them by*. Every man is to Judge for himself with the *Judgment of Discretion*, and to choose either his Religion first, and then his Church, as we say: or as you, his Church first, and then his Religion. But by the consent of both sides, every man is to judge and choose: and the Rule whereby he is to guide his choice, if he be a natural man, is Reason, if he be already a Christian, Scripture, which we say is the Rule to judge Controversies by. Yet not all simply, but all the Controversies of Christians, of those, that are already agreed upon This first Principle that, *the Scripture is the Word of God*. But that there is any man, or any company of men appoint-

ed

ed to be judge for all men, that we deny, and that I believe you will never prove. The very truth is, we say no more in this matter, than evidence of Truth hath made you confess in plain terms in the beginning of this chap. *viz.* That *Scripture is a perfect Rule of Faith, for as much as a writing can be a Rule.* So that all your reasons whereby you labour to dethrone the Scripture from this office of *Judging,* we might let pass as impertinent to the conclusion which we maintain, and you have already granted; yet out of courtesie we will consider them.

12. Your first is this; *a Judge must be a person fit to end Controversies, but the Scripture is not a person, nor fit to end Controversies, no more than the Law would be without the Judges, therefore though it may be a Rule it cannot be a Judge.* Which conclusion I have already granted. Only my request is, that you will permit Scripture to have the properties of a Rule, that is, to be fit to direct every one that will make the best use of it, to that end for which it was ordained. And that is as much as we need desire. For as if I were to go a Journey and had a guide which could not Err, I needed not to know my way: so on the other side, if I know my way or have a plain rule to know it by, I shall need no guide. Grant therefore Scripture to be such a Rule, and it will quickly take away all necessity of having an Infallible guide. But *without a living Judge it will be no fitter* (you say) *to end Controversies, than the Law alone to end Suits.* I answer, if the Law were plain and perfect, and men honest and desirous to understand aright, and obey it, he that says it were not fit to end Controversies, must either want understanding himself, or think the World wants it. Now the Scripture, we pretend, *in things necessary is plain and perfect,* and men, we say, are obliged, under pain of Damnation, to seek the true sense of it, and not to wrest it to their preconceived Phansies. Such a Law therefore to such men cannot but be very fit to end all Controversies, necessary to be ended. For others that are not so, they will end when the World ends, and that is time enough.

13. Your

13. Your next encounter is with them, who acknowledging the Scripture a Rule only and not a Judge, make the Holy Ghost, (speaking in Scripture, the judge of Controversies. Which you disprove by saying, *That the Holy Ghost speaking only in Scripture is no more intelligible to us, than the Scripture in which he speaks.* But by this reason neither the *Pope*, nor a Council can be a Judge neither. For first, denying the Scriptures, the writings of the Holy Ghost, to be Judges, you will not I hope offer to pretend, that their decrees, the writings of men are more capable of this function: the same exceptions at least, if not more, and greater lying against them as do against Scripture. And then what you Object against the Holy Ghost, speaking in Scripture, to exclude him from this office, The same I return upon them and their decrees, to debar them from it; that they speaking unto us only in their decrees, are no more intelligible than the decrees in which they speak. And therefore if the Holy Ghost speaking in Scripture may not be a judge for this reason; neither may they, speaking in their decrees, be Judges for the same Reason. *If the* Popes *decrees (you will say) be obscure, he can explain himself, and so the Scripture cannot.* But the Holy Ghost, that speaks in Scripture, can do so, if he please, and when he is pleased will do so. In the mean time it will be fit for you to wait his leisure, and to be content, that those things of Scripture which are plain should be so, and those which are obscure should remain obscure, until he please to declare them. Besides he can (which you cannot warrant me of the *Pope* or a Coucil) speak at first so plainly, that his Words shall need no farther explanation; and so in things necessary we believe he has done. And if you say, *the Decrees of Councils touching Controversies, though they be not the Judge, yet they are the Judges Sentence:* So, I say, the Scripture, though not the Judge, is the Sentence of the Judge. When therefore you conclude, *That to say a Judge is necessary for deciding Controversies, about the meaning of Scripture, is as much as to say, he is necessary to decide what the Holy Ghost speaks in Scripture:*

ture: This I grant is true, but I may not grant that a Judge (such a one as we dispute of) is necessary either to do the one, or the other. For if the Scripture (as it is in things necessary) be plain, why should it be more necessary to have a judge to interpret them in plain places, than to have a judge to interpret the meaning of a Councils decrees, and others to interpret their Interpretations, and others to interpret theirs, and so on for ever? And where they are not plain, there if we, using diligence to find the truth, do yet miss of it and fall into Error, there is no danger in it. They that Err, and they that do not Err may both be saved. So that those places which contain things necessary, and wherein Error were dangerous, need no Infallible interpreter because they are plain: and those that are obscure need none because they contain not things necessary, neither is Error in them dangerous.

The Law-maker speaking in the Law, I grant it, *is no more easily understood than the Law it self,* for his Speech is nothing else but the Law: I grant it *very necessary, that besides the Law-maker speaking in the Law, there should be other Judges to determine Civil and Criminal Controversies, and to give every man that Justice which the Law allows him.* But your Argument drawn from hence to shew a necessity of a visible Judge in Controversies of Religion, I say is Sophistical: and that for many Reasons.

14. First, Because the variety of Civil cases is infinite, and therefore there cannot be possibly Laws enough provided for the determination of them: and therefore there must be a Judge to supply out of the Principles of Reason the interpretation of the Law, where it is defective. But the Scripture (we say) is a perfect Rule of Faith, and therefore needs no supply of the defects of it.

15. Secondly, To execute the Letter of the Law, according to rigour, would be many times unjust, and therefore there is need of a Judge to moderate it; whereof in Religion there is no use at all.

16. Thirdly, In Civil and Criminal causes the parties have for the most part so much interest, and very often so little honesty, that they will not submit to a Law though

never

never so plain, if it be against them; or will not see it to be against them, though it be so never so plainly: whereas if men were honest, and the Law were plain and extended to all cases, there would be little need of Judges. Now in matters of Religion, when the Question is, whether every man be a fit Judge and chooser for himself, we suppose men honest, and such as understand the difference between a Moment and Eternity. And such men, we conceive, will think it highly concerns them to be of the true Religion, but nothing at all that this or that Religion should be the true. And then we suppose that all the necessary points of Religion are plain and easie, and consequently every man in this cause to be a competent Judge for himself; because it concerns himself to judge right as much as Eternal happiness is worth. And if through his own default he judge amiss he alone shall suffer for it.

17. Fourthly, in Civil Controversies we are obliged only to external passive obedience, and not to an internal and active. We are bound to obey the Sentence of the Judge, or not to resist it, but not always to believe it just. But in matters of Religion, such a Judge is required whom we should be obliged to believe, to have judged right. So that in Civil Controversies every honest understanding man is fit to be a Judge; But in Religion none but he that is infallible.

18. Fifthly, in Civil Causes there is means and power, when the Judge has decreed, to compel men to obey his Sentence: otherwise, I believe, Laws alone, would be to as much purpose, for the ending of differences, as Laws and Judges both. But all the Power in the World is neither fit to convince, nor able to compel a mans Conscience to consent to any thing. Worldly terror may prevail so far as to make men profess a Religion which they believe not, (such men I mean, who know not that there is a Heaven provided for Martyrs, and a Hell for those that dissemble such truths as are necessary to be professed:) But to force, either any man to believe what he believes not, or any honest man to dissemble what he does believe

(if

(if God commands him to profess it,) or to profess what he does not believe, all the Powers in the World are too weak, with all the Powers of Hell, to assist them.

19. Sixthly, in Civil Controversies the case cannot be so put, but there may be a Judge to end it, who is not a party: In Controversies of Religion, it is in a manner impossible to be avoided but the Judge must be a party. For this must be the first, whether he be a Judge or no, and in that he must be a party. Sure I am, the *Pope*, in the Controversies of our time, is a chief party; for it highly concerns him, even as much as his Popedom is worth, not to yield any one point of his Religion to be Erroneous. And he is a man subject to like passions with other men. And therefore we may justly decline his Sentence, for fear temporal respects should either blind his judgment, or make him pronounce against it.

20. Seventhly, in Civil Controversies, it is impossible *Titius* should hold the land in question and *Sempronius* too: and therefore either the Plantiff must injure the Defendant, by disquieting his possession, or the Defendant wrong the Plantiff by keeping his right from him. But in Controversies of Religion the Case is otherwise. I may hold my Opinion and do you no wrong, and you yours and do me none. Nay we may both of us hold our Opinion, and yet do our selves no harm; provided, the difference be not touching any thing necessary to Salvation, and that we love truth so well, as to be diligent to inform our Conscience, and constant in following it.

21. Eightly, For the ending of Civil Controversies, who does not see it is absolutely necessary, that not only Judges should be appointed, but that it should be known and unquestioned who they are? Thus all the Judges of our Land are known men, known to be Judges, and no man can doubt or question, but these are the Men. Otherwise if it were a disputable thing, who were these Judges, and they had no certain warrant for their Authority, but only some Topical congruities, would not any man say such Judges, in all likelihood, would rather multiply Controversies, then end them?

22. Ninthly,

22. Ninthly, and laftly, For the deciding of Civil Controverfies men may appoint themfelves a judge. But in matters of Religion, this office may be given to none but whom God hath defigned for it: who doth not always give us thofe things which we conceive moft expedient for our felves.

23. So likewife if our Saviour, the King of Heaven, had intended that all Controverfies in Religion fhould be by fome Vifible Judge finally determined, who can doubt, but in plain terms he would have expreffed himfelf about this matter? He would have faid plainly. *The Bifhop of Rome I have appointed to decide all emergent Controverfies.* For that our Saviour defigned the *Bifhop of Rome* to this Office, and yet would not fay fo, nor caufe it to be written *ad Rei memoriam*---- by any of the *Evangelifts* or *Apoftles,* fo much as once; but leave it to be drawn out of uncertain Principles, by thirteen or fourteen more uncertain confequences, He that can believe it, let him. All thefe Reafons, I hope, will convince you, that though we have, and have great neceffity of, Judges in Civil and Criminal caufes: yet you may not conclude from thence, that there is any publick authorized Judge to determine Controverfies in Religion, nor any neceffity there fhould be any.

24. *But the Scripture ftands in need of fome watchful and unerring eye to guard it, by means of whofe affured vigilancy we may undoubtedly receive it fincere and pure.* Very true, but this is no other than the watchful Eye of Divine providence: the goodnefs whereof will never fuffer, that the Scriptures fhould be depraved and corrupted, but that in them fhould be always extant a confpicuous and plain way to Eternal happinefs. Neither can any thing be more palpably unconfiftent with his goodnefs, than to fuffer Scripture to be undifcernably corrupted in any matter of moment, and yet to exact of men the belief of thofe verities, which without their fault, or knowledge, or poffibility of prevention, were defaced out of them. So that God requiring of men to believe Scripture in its purity, ingages himfelf to fee it preferved in fufficient purity, and you need not fear but he will fatisfie his ingagement.

You

Scripture the only Rule for Judging Controversies.

You say, *we can have no assurance of this but your Churches Vigilancy*. But if we had no other we were in a hard case; for who could then assure us that your Church has been so vigilant, as to guard Scripture from any the least alteration? There being various Lections in the ancient Copies of your Bibles, what security can your new raised *Office of Assurance* give us, that, that reading is true which you now receive, and that false which you reject? Certainly they that anciently received and made use of these divers Copies, were not all guarded by the Churches vigilancy from having their Scripture altered from the purity of the Original in many places. For of different readings, it is not in nature impossible that all should be false, but more than one cannot possibly be true. Yet the want of such a protection was no hindrance to their Salvation, and why then shall the having of it be necessary for ours? But then this Vigilancy of your Church, what means have we to be ascertain'd of it? First, the thing is not evident of it self; which is evident, because many do not believe it. Neither can any thing be pretended to give evidence to it, but only some places of Scripture; of whose incorruption more than any other what is it that can secure me? If you say the Churches vigilancy, you are in a Circle, proving the Scriptures uncorrupted by the Churches vigilancy, and the Churches vigilancy by the incorruption of some places of Scripture, and again the incorruption of those places by the Churches vigilancy. If you name any other means, than that means which secures me of the Scriptures incorruption in those places, will also serve to assure me of the same in other places. For my part, abstracting from Divine Providence, which will never suffer the way to Heaven to be blocked up or made invisible, I know no other means (I mean no other natural and rational means) to be assured hereof, than I have that any other Book is uncorrupted. For though I have a greater degree of rational and humane Assurance of that than this, in regard of divers considerations which make it more credible, *That the Scripture hath been preserved from any material alteration*; yet my assurance of

M 2   both

both is of the same kind and condition, both Moral assurances, and neither Physical or Mathematical.

25. To the next argument the Reply is obvious; *That though we do not believe the Books of Scripture to be Canonical because they say so*, (For other Books that are not Canonical may say they are, and those that are so may say nothing of it:) yet we believe not this upon the Authority of your Church, but upon the Credibility of *Universal Tradition*, which is a thing *Credible of it self*, and therefore fit to be rested on; whereas the Authority of your Church is not so. And therefore your rest thereon is not rational but meerly voluntary. I might as well rest upon the judgment of the next man I meet, or upon a chance of a Lottery for it. For by this means I only know I might Err, but by relying on you I know I should Err. But yet (to return you one suppose for another) suppose I should for this and all other things submit to her direction, how could she assure me that I should not be mis-led by doing so? She pretends indeed infallibility herein, but how can she assure us that she hath it? What, by Scriptures. That you say cannot assure us of its own Infallibility, and therefore not of yours. What then, by Reason? That you say may deceive in other things, and why not in this? How then will she assure us hereof, By saying so? Of this very affirmation there will remain the same Question still, How it can prove it self to be infallibly true. Neither can there be an end of the like multiplied Demands, till we rest in something evident of it self, which demonstrates to the World that this Church is infallible. And seeing there is no such Rock for the Infallibility of this Church to be setled on, it must of necessity, like the Island of *Delos*, flote up and down for ever. And yet upon this point according to *Papists* all other Controversies in Faith depend.

26. To the 7, 8, 9, 10, 11, 12, 13, 14, 15, 16, §.] The sum and substance of the Ten next Paragraphs is this, *That it appears, by the Confessions of some* Protestants, *and the Contentions of others, that the Questions about the Canon of Scripture, what it is: and about the Various reading and Transla-*

Scripture the only Rule for Judging Controversies. 85

Tranſlations of it, which is true and which not, are not to be determined by Scripture, and therefore that all Controverſies of Religion are not decidable by Scripture.

27. To which I have already anſwered ſaying, That when Scripture is affirmed to be the rule by which all Controverſies of Religion are to be decided, Thoſe are to be excepted out of this generality which are concerning the Scripture it ſelf. For as that general ſaying of Scripture, *He hath put all things under his Feet,* is moſt true, though yet S. *Paul* tells us, *That when it is ſaid, he hath put all things under him, it is manifeſt he is excepted who did put all things under him:* So when we ſay that all Controverſies of Religion are decidable by the Scripture, it is manifeſt to all, but *Cavillers*, that we do and muſt except from this generality, thoſe which are *touching the Scripture it ſelf.* Juſt as a Merchant ſhewing a Ship of his own, may ſay, all my ſubſtance is in this Ship; and yet never intended to deny, that his Ship is part of his ſubſtance, nor yet to ſay that his Ship is in it ſelf. Or as a man may ſay, that a whole Houſe is ſupported by the Foundation, and yet never mean to exclude the Foundation from being a part of the Houſe, or to ſay that it is ſupported by it ſelf. Or as you your ſelves uſe to ſay, that the Biſhop of *Rome* is head of the whole Church, and yet would think us but Captious Sophiſters ſhould we infer from hence, that either you made him no part of the whole, or elſe made him head of himſelf. Your negative concluſion therefore, that theſe *Queſtions touching Scripture, are not decidable by Scripture,* you needed not have cited any Authorities, nor urged any reaſon to prove it; it is evident of it ſelf, and I grant it without more ado. But your Corollary from it, which you would inſinuate to your unwary reader, *that therefore they are to be decided by your, or any Viſible Church,* is a meer inconſequence, and very like his collection, who becauſe *Pamphilus* was not to have *Glycerium* for his Wife, preſently concluded that he muſt have her; as if there had been no more men in the World but *Pamphilus* and himſelf. For ſo you as if there were nothing in the World capable of this Office, but the

Scripture,

Scripture, or the present Church, having concluded against Scripture, you conceive, but too hastily, that you have concluded for the Church. But the truth is, neither the one nor the other have any thing to do with this matter. For first, the Question *whether such or such a Book be Canonical Scripture*, though it may be decided negatively out of Scripture, by shewing apparent and irreconcilable contradictions between it and some other Book confessedly Canonical; yet affirmatively it cannot but only by the Testimonies of the ancient Churches : any Book being to be received as undoubtedly Canonical, or to be doubted of as uncertain, or rejected as Apocryphal, according as it was received, or doubted of, or rejected by them. Then for the Question, *of various readings which is the true*, it is in reason evident and confessed by your own *Pope*, that there is no possible determination of it, but only by comparison with ancient Copies. And lastly for Controversies about different Translations of Scripture, the Learned have the same means to satisfie themselves in it, as in the Questions which happen about the Translation of any other Author, that is, skill in the Language of the Original, and comparing Translations with it. In which way if there be no certainty, I would know what certainty you have, that your *Doway* Old, and *Rhemish* New *Testament* are true Translations? And then for the unlearned those on your Side are subject to as much, nay the very same uncertainty with those on ours. Neither is there any reason imaginable, why an ignorant *English Protestant* may not be as secure of the Translation of our Church, that it is free from Error, if not absolutely, yet in matters of moment, as an ignorant *English Papist* can be of his *Rhemish Testament*, or *Doway Bible*. The best direction I can give them is to compare both together, & where there is no real difference (as in the Translation of controverted places I believe there is very little) there to be confident, that they are right; where they differ, therefore to be prudent in the choice of the guides they follow. Which way of proceeding, if it be subject to some possible Error, is it the best that either we, or you have; and it is not required that we use any better than the best we have.   28. You

28. You will say, *Dependance on your Churches infallibility is a better.* I answer, it would be so, if we could be infallibly certain, that your Church is infallible, that is, if it were either evident of it self, and seen by its own light, or could be reduced unto and setled upon some Principle that is so. But seeing you your selves do not so much as pretend, to enforce us to the belief hereof, by any proofs infallible and convincing, but only to induce us to it, by such as are, by your confession, only probable, and *prudential motives*; certainly it will be to very little purpose, to put off your uncertainty for the first turn, and to fall upon it at the second: to please your selves in building your House upon an imaginary Rock, when you your selves see and confess, that this very Rock stands it self at the best but upon a frame of Timber. I answer secondly, that this cannot be a better way, because we are infallibly certain that your Church is not infallible, and indeed hath not the real prescription of this priviledge, but only pleaseth her self with a false imagination and vain presumption of it: as I shall hereafter demonstrate by may unanswerable arguments.

31. But, *seeing the belief of the Scripture is a necessary thing, and cannot be proved by Scripture, how can the Church of England teach, as she doth, Art.* 6. *That all things necessary are contained in Scripture?*

32. I have answered this already. And here again I say, That all but Cavillers will easily understand the meaning of the Article to be, That all the Divine Verities, which Christ revealed to his Apostles, and the Apostles taught the Churches, are contained in Scripture. That is, all the material Objects of our Faith; whereof the Scripture is none, but only the means of conveying them unto us: which we believe not finally, and for it self, but for the matter contained in it. So that if men did believe the Doctrine contained in Scripture, it should no way hinder their Salvation, not to know whether their were any Scripture or no. Those Barbarous Nations *Irenæus* speaks of were in this case, and yet no doubt but they might be saved. The end that God aims at, is the belief of the Gospel,

the

the Covenant between God and Man; the Scripture he hath provided as a means for this end, and this also we are to believe, but not as the last Object of our Faith, but as the instrument of it. When therefore we subscribe to the 6. *Art.* you must understand that, by *Articles of Faith*, they mean the final and ultimate Objects of it, and not the means and instrumental Objects;

33. But, *Protestants agree not in assigning the Canon of Holy Scripture*. Luther *and* Illyricus *reject the Epistle of* S. James. Kemnitius, *and other Luth. the second of* Peter, *the second and third of* John. *The Epistle to the* Heb. *the Epistle of* James, *of* Jude, *and the Apocalyps. Therefore without the Authority of the Church, no certainty can be had what Scripture is Canonical.*

34. So also the *Ancient Fathers*, and not only Fathers, but *whole Churches* differed about the certainty of the Authority of the very same Books: and by their difference shewed, they knew no necessity of conforming themselves herein to the judgment of your or any Church. For had they done so, they must have agreed all with that Church, and consequently among themselves. Now I pray tell me plainly, Had they sufficient certainty what Scripture was Canonical, or had they not? If they had not, it seems there is no such great harm or danger in not having such a certainty whether some Books be Canonical or no, as you require: If they had, why may not *Protestants*, notwithstanding their differences, have sufficient certainty hereof, as well as the Ancient Fathers and Churches, notwithstanding theirs?

35. You proceed. And whereas the *Protestants* of *England* in the 6. *Art.* have these Words, *In the name of the Holy Scripture we do understand those Books, of whose Authority was never any doubt in the Church*; you demand, *what they mean by them?* Whether that by the Churches consent they are assured what Scriptures be Canonical? I Answer for them. Yes, they are so. And whereas you infer from hence, *This is to make the Church Judge*: I have told you already, That *of this Controversie we make the Church the Judge*; but not the present Church, much less

the

the present *Roman* Church, but the consent and Testimony of the *Ancient and Primitive Church*. Which though it be but a highly probable inducement, and no demonstrative enforcement, yet methinks you should not deny but it may be a sufficient ground of Faith: Whose Faith, even of the Foundation of all your Faith, your Churches Authority, is built lastly and wholly upon *Prudential Motives*.

36. But *by this Rule the whole Book of* Esther *must quit the Canon; because it was excluded by some in the Church:* by *Melito, Athanasius,* and *Gregory Nazianzen*. Then for ought I know he that should think he had reason to exclude it now, might be still in the Church as well as *Melito, Athanasius, Nazianzen* were. And while you thus inveigh against *Luther*, and charge him with Luciferian Heresies, for doing that which you in this very place confess that Saints in Heaven before him have done, *are you not partial and a Judge of evil thoughts?*

37. *Luther's* censures of *Ecclesiastes, Job,* and the *Prophets*, though you make such Tragedies with them, I see none of them but is capable of a tolerable construction, and far from having in them any Fundamental Heresie. He that condemns him for saying, the Book of *Ecclesiastes is not full, That it hath many abrupt things*, condemns him, for ought I can see, for speaking truth. And the rest of the censure is but a bold and blunt expression of the same thing. The Book of *Job* may be a true History, and yet as many true Stories are, and have been an Argument of a Fable to set before us an example of Patience. And though the Books of the Prophets were not written by themselves, but by their Disciples, yet it does not follow that they were written casually: (Though I hope you will not damn all for Hereticks, that say, some Books of Scripture were written casually.) Neither is there any reason they should the sooner be called in question for being written by their Disciples, seeing being so written they had attestation from themselves. Was the Prophesie of *Jeremy* the less Canonical, for being written by *Baruch?* Or because S. *Peter* the Master dictated the Gospel,

Gospel, and S. *Mark* the Scholar writ it, is it the more likely to be called in Question?

38. But leaving *Luther*, you return to our *English* Canon of Scripture; And tell us, that in *the New Testament, by the above mentioned rule, (of whose Authority was never any doubt in the Church) divers Books must be discanonized.* Not so. For I may believe even those questioned Books to have been written by the Apostles and to be Canonical: but I cannot in Reason believe this of them so undoubtedly, as of *those Books which were never questioned.* At least I have no warrant to damn any man that shall doubt of them or deny them now: having the example of Saints in Heaven, either to justifie, or excuse such their doubting or denial.

39. You observe in the next place, that *our sixth Article, specifying by name all the Books of the* Old Testament, *shuffles over these of the* New *with this generality --- All the Books of the* New Testament, *as they are commonly received, we do receive, and account them Canonical:* And in this you fancy to your self *a mystery of iniquity.* But if this be all the shuffling that the Church of *England* is guilty of, I believe the Church, as well as the King, may give for her Motto, *Honi soit qui mal y pense.* For all the Bibles which since the Composing of the Articles have been used and allowed by the *Church of England,* do testifie and even proclaim to the World, that by -- *Commonly received,* they meant, *received by the Church of* Rome, *and other Churches before the Reformation.* I pray take the pains to look in them, and there you shall find the Books which the Church of *England* counts Apocryphal marked out and severed from the rest, with this Title in the beginning, *The Books called Apocrypha*; and with this close or Seal in the End, *The End of the Apocrypha.* And having told you by name, and in particular, what Books only She Esteems *Apocryphal,* I hope you will not put Her to the trouble of telling you that the rest are in Her judgment *Canonical.*

40. But if by *Commonly received,* She meant, *by the Church of* Rome; *Then by the same reason, must She receive divers Books of the* Old Testament *which She rejects.* Cer-

41. Certainly a very good Consequence. The Church of *England* receives the Books of the *New Testament*, which the Church of *Rome* receives; Therefore she must receive the Books of the *Old Testament* which she receives. As if you should say, If you will do as we, in one thing, you must in all things. If you will pray to God with us, you must pray to Saints with us. If you hold with us, when we have reason on our side, you must do so, when we have no reason.

43. But, *with what Coherence can we say in the former part of the Article, That by Scripture we mean those Books that were never doubted of; and in the latter say, We receive all the Books of the* New Testament, *as they are commonly received, whereas of them many were doubted?* I answer. When they say, *of whose Authority there was never any doubt in the Church,*. They mean not, those only of whose Authority there was simply no doubt at all, by any man in the Church; But such as were not at any time doubted of by the whole Church, or by all Churches, but had attestation, though not Universal, yet at least sufficient to make considering men receive them for Canonical. In which number they may well reckon those Epistles which were sometimes doubted of by some, yet whose number and Authority was not so great, as to prevail against the contrary suffrages.

44. But, *if to be commonly received, pass for a good Rule to know the Canon of the* New Testament *by, why not of the Old?* You conclude many times very well, but still when you do so, it is out of principles which no man grants. For who ever told you, that to be *commonly* received is a good Rule to know the Canon of the *New Testament* by? Have you been trained up in Schools of subtilty, and cannot you see a great difference, between these two, We receive the Books of the *New Testament as they are* commonly received, and we receive those that are commonly received, *because they are so?* To say this, were indeed to make, *being commonly received,* a Rule or Reason to know the Canon by. But to say the former, doth no more make it a Rule, than you should make the Church of *England* the rule of your receiving them, if you should say,

say, as you may, The Books of the *New Testament* we receive for Canonical, as they are received by the Church of *England*.

45. You demand, *upon what infallible ground we agree with* Luther *against you, in some, and with you against* Luther *in others?* And I also demand upon what infallible ground you hold your Canon, and agree neither with us, nor *Luther?* For sure your differing from us both, is of it self no more apparently reasonable, than our agreeing with you in part, and in part with *Luther.* If you say, your Churches Infallibility is your ground : I demand again some Infallible ground both for the Churches Infallibility, and for this, that *Yours is the Church;* and shall never cease multiplying demands upon demands, until you settle me upon a Rock; I mean, give such an answer, whose Truth is so evident that it needs no further evidence. If you say, *This is Universal Tradition :* I reply, your Churches Infallibility is not built upon it, and that the Canon of Scripture, as we receive it, is. For we do not profess our selves so absolutely, and undoubtedly certain; neither do we urge others to be so, of those Books, which have been doubted, as of those that never have.

46. The Conclusion of your Tenth. §. is, That *the Divinity of a writing cannot be known from it self alone, but by some extrinsecal Authority* : Which you need not prove, for no Wise Man denies it. But then this authority is that of *Universal Tradition,* not of your Church. For to me it is altogether as αὐτόπιστον, that the Gospel of *Saint Matthew* is the Word of God, as that all which your Church says is true.

47. That Believers of the Scripture, by considering the Divine matter, the excellent precepts, the glorious promises contained in it, may be confirmed in their Faith, of the Scriptures Divine Authority; and that among other inducements and inforcements hereunto, internal arguments have their place and force, certainly no man of understandeng can deny. For my part I profess, if the Doctrine of the Scripture were not as good, and as fit to come from the Fountain of goodness, as
the

the Miracles, by which it was confirmed, were great, I should want one main pillar of my Faith, and for want of it, I fear should be much staggered in it. Now this and nothing else did the *Doctor* mean in saying, *The Believer sees, by that glorious beam of Divine light which shines in Scripture, and by many internal Arguments, that the Scripture is of Divine Authority.* By *this* (faith he) *he sees it*, that is, he is moved to, and strengthened in his belief of it: and by this partly, not wholly; by this, not alone, but with the concurrence of other Arguments. He that will quarrel with him for saying so, must find fault with the *Master of the Sentences*, and all his *Scholars*, for they all say the same.

48. In the next Division, out of your liberality, you will suppose, that Scripture, like to a corporal light, is *by it self alone* able to determine and move our understanding to assent: yet notwithstanding this supposal, *Faith still* (you say) *must go before Scripture, because as the light is visible only to those that have eyes: so the Scripture only to those that have the Eye of Faith.* But to my understanding, if Scripture do move and determine our Understanding to assent, then the Scripture, and its moving must be before this assent, as the cause must be before its own effect; now this very assent is nothing else but Faith, and Faith nothing else than the Understandings assent. And therefore (upon this supposal) Faith doth, and must originally proceed from Scripture, as the effect from its proper cause: and the influence and efficacy of Scripture is to be presupposed before the assent of Faith, unto which it moves and determines, and consequently if this supposition of yours were true, there should need no other means precedent to Scripture to beget Faith, Scripture it self being able (as here you suppose) to determine and move the understanding to assent, that is to believe them, and the Verities contained in them. Neither is this to say, that the Eyes with which we see, are made by the light by which we see. For you are mistaken much, if you conceive that in this comparison, Faith answers to the Eye. But if you will not pervert it, the Analogy

must

must stand thus-; Scripture must answer to light; The Eye of the Soul, that is the Understanding, or the faculty of assenting, to the bodily Eye; And lastly assenting or believing to the Act of seeing. As therefore the light, determining the Eye to see, though it presupposes the Eye which it determines, as every Action doth the Object on which it is imployed, yet it self is presupposed and antecedent to the Act of seeing, as the cause is always to its effect: So, if you will suppose that Scripture, like light, moves the understanding to assent, The Understanding (that's the Eye and Object on which it works) must be before this influence upon it; But the Assent, that is the belief whereof the Scripture moves, and the understanding is moved, which answers to the Act of seeing, must come after. For if it did assent already, to what purpose should the Scripture do that which was done before? Nay indeed how were it possible it should be so, any more than a Father can beget a Son that he hath already? Or an Architect build an House that is built already? Or than this very world can be made again before it be unmade? Transubstantiation indeed is fruitful of such Monsters. But they that have not sworn themselves to the defence of Error, will easily perceive, that *Jam factum facere*, and *Factum infectum facere*, are equally impossible. But I digress.

49. The close of this Paragraph, is a fit cover for such a Dish. There you tell us, That *if there must be some other means precedent to Scripture to beget Faith, this can be no other than the Church.* By the Church, we know you do, and must understand the *Roman Church*: so that in effect you say, no man can have Faith, but he must be moved to it by your Churches Authority. And that is to say, that the King and all other *Protestants*, to whom you write, though they verily think they are Christians and believe the Gospel, because they assent to the truth of it, and would willingly Die for it, yet indeed are Infidels and believe nothing. The Scripture tells us, *The Heart of man knoweth no Man, but the Spirit of Man which is in him.* And who are you, to take upon you to make us

believe

believe, that we do not believe, what we know we do? But if I may think verily that I believe the Scripture, and yet not believe it; how know you that you believe the *Roman Church?* I am as verily, and as strongly perswaded that I believe the Scripture, as you are that you believe the Church. And if I may be deceived, why may not you? Again, what more ridiculous, and against sense and experience, than to affirm, That there are not Millions amongst you and us that believe, upon no other reason than their Education, and the authority of their Parents and Teachers, and the Opinion they have of them? The tenderness of the subject, and aptness to receive impressions, supplying the defect and imperfection of the Agent! And will you proscribe from Heaven all those believers of your own Creed, who do indeed lay the Foundation of their Faith (for I cannot call it by any other name) no deeper than upon the Authority of their Father, or Master, or Parish Priest? Certainly, if these have no true Faith, your Church is very full of Infidels. Suppose *Xaverius* by the Holiness of his Life had converted some *Indians* to Christianity, who could (for so I will suppose) have no knowledge of your Church but from him, and therefore must last of all build their Faith of the Church upon their Opinion of *Xaverius*: Do these remain as very *Pagans* after their Conversion, as they were before? Are they brought to assent in their Souls, and obey in their Lives the Gospel of Christ, only to be Tantalized and not saved, and not benefited but deluded by it, because, forsooth, it is a man and not the Church that begets Faith in them? What if their motive to believe be not in reason sufficient? Do they therefore not believe what they do believe, because they do it upon sufficient motives? They choose the Faith imprudently parhaps, but yet they do choose it. Unless you will have us believe that, that which is done, is not done, because it is not done upon good reason: which is to say, that never any man living ever did a foolish action. But yet I know not why the Authority of one Holy Man, which apparently has no ends upon me, joyned with the goodness

goodness of the Christian Faith, might not be a far greater and more rational motive to me to embrace Christianity, than any I can have to continue in *Paganism*. And therefore for shame, if not for Love of Truth, you must recant this fancy when you write again: and suffer true Faith to be many times, where your Churches Infallibility has no hand in the begetting of it. And be content to tell us hereafter, that we believe not enough, and not go about to persuade us, we believe nothing, for fear with telling us what we know to be manifestly false, you should gain only this, *Not to be believed when you speak truth.* Some pretty Sophisms you may happily bring us to make us believe, we believe nothing: but Wise men know that Reason against Experience is alwaies Sophistical. And therefore as he that could not answer *Zeno's* subtilties against the existence of Motion, could yet confute them by doing that, which he pretended could not be done: So if you should give me a hundred Arguments to persuade me, because I do not believe Transubstantiation, I do not believe in God, and the *Knots* of them I could not unty, yet I should cut them in pieces with doing that, and knowing that I do so, which you pretend I cannot do.

53. It is superfluous for you to prove *out of* S. Athanasius, *and* Austine *that we must receive the sacred Canon upon the credit of Gods Church.* Understanding by Church, as here you explain your self, *The Credit of Tradition.* And that not the Tradition of the Present Church, which we pretend may deviate from the Ancient, but *such a Tradition, which involves an evidence of Fact, and from Hand to Hand, from Age to Age, bringing us up to the times and Persons of the Apostles, and our Saviour Himself, commeth to be confirmed by all these Miracles, and other Arguments, whereby they convinced their Doctrine to be true.* Thus you. Now prove the Canon of Scripture which you receive by such Tradition and we will allow it. Prove your whole Doctrine, or the Infallibility of your Church by such a Tradition, and we will yield to you in all things. Take the alledged places of S. *Athanasius,* and S. *Austin,* in this

sense,

sense, (which is your own,) and they will not press us any thing at all. We will say, with *Athanasius*, *That only four Gospels are to be received, because the Canons of the Holy and Catholick Church* (understand of *all Ages* since the perfection of the Canon) *have so determined*.

54. We will subscribe to S. *Austin*, and say, That *we also would not believe the Gospel, unless the Authority of the Catholick Church did move us*, (meaning by the Church, the Church of all Ages, and that succession of Christians which takes in *Christ himself* and his *Apostles*.) Neither would *Zwinglius* have needed to cry out upon this saying, had he conceived as you now do, that by the Catholick Church, the Church of all Ages, since Christ, was to be understood. As for the Council of *Carthage*, it may speak not of such Books only, as were certainly Canonical, and for the regulating of Faith, but also of those which were only profitable, and lawful to be read in the Church. Which in *England* is a very slender Argument that the Book is Canonical, where every body knows that Apocryphal Books are read as well as Canonical. But howsoever, if you understand by Fathers, not only their immediate Fathers and Predecessors in the Gospel, but the succession of them from the Apostles; they are right in the Thesis, that *whatsoever is received from these Fathers, as Canonical, is to be so esteemed*; Though in the application of it, to this or that particular Book they may happily Err, and think that Book received as Canonical, which was only received as Profitable to be read; and think that Book, received alwaies, and by all, which was rejected by some, and doubted of by many.

55. *But we cannot be certain, in what Language the Scriptures remain uncorrupted.* C H I L. Not so certain, I grant, as of that which we can demonstrate: But certain enough, morally certain, as certain as the nature of the thing will bear. So certain we may be, and God requires no more. We may be as certain as S. *Austin* was, who in his *second Book of Baptism, against the Donatists*, c. 3. plainly implies, *the Scripture might possibly be corrupted*. He means sure in matters of little moment, such as con-

certain not the Covenant between God and Man. But thus he saith. The same S. *Austin* in his 48. *Epist.* clearly intimates, [a] *That in his judgment, the only preservative of the Scriptures integrity, was the Translating it into so many Languages, and the general and perpetual use and reading of it in the Church: for want whereof the works of particular Doctors were more exposed to danger in this kind*; but the Canonical Scripture being by this means guarded with Universal care and dilligence was not obnoxious to such attempts. And this assurance of the Scriptures incorruption, is common to us with him; we therefore are as certain hereof as S. *Austin* was, and that I hope was certain enough. Yet if this does not satisfie you, I say farther, We are as certain hereof as your own *Pope Sixtus Quintus* was. He in his *Preface to his Bible* tells us, [b] *That in the prevestigation of the true and genuine Text, it was perspicuously manifest to all men, that there was no Argument more firm and certain to be relied upon, than the Faith of Ancient Books.* Now this ground we have to build upon as well as He had: and therefore our certainty is as great, and stands upon as certain ground as his did.

[a] *Neque enim sic posuit integritas atque notitia literarum quamlibet illustris Episcopi, e stoliri, quemadmodum scriptura Canonica tot linguarum literis & ordine & successione celebrationis Ecclesiasticæ custoditur; contra quam defuerunt tamen, qui sub nominibus Apostolorum multa confingerent. Frustra quidem; Quia illa sic commendata, sic celebrata, sic nota est. Verum quid possit adversus literas non Canonica authoritate fundatas etiam hinc demonstrabit impiæ conatus audaciæ, quod & adversus eos quæ tanta notitiæ mole firmatæ sunt, sese erigere non prætermisit.* Aug. ep. 48. ad Vincent. contra Donat & Rogat. [b] *In hac Germani textus pervestigatione, satis perspicue inter omnes constat, nullum argumentum esse certius ac firmius, quam antiquorem probatorum codicum latinorum fidem, &c.* sic Sixtus in præfat.

56. This is not all I have to say in this matter. For I will add moreover, that we are as certain in what Language the Scripture is uncorrupted, as any man in your Church was, until *Clement* the 8th set forth your own approved *Edition of your Vulgar* Translation. For you do not, nor cannot, without extreme impudence deny, that until then, there was great variety of Copies currant in divers parts of your Church, and those very frequent in various lections: all which Copies might possibly be false in some things, but more than one sort of them, could not possibly be true in all things. Neither were it less impudence

impudence to pretend, that any man in your Church, could until *Clements*'s time have any certainty what that one true Copy and reading was (if there were any one perfectly true.) Some indeed that had got *Sixtus his Bible*, might after the Edition of that very likely think themselves cock-sure of a perfect true uncorrupted Translation, without being beholden to *Clement*; but how fouly they were abused and deceived that thought so, the Edition of *Clemens*, differing from that of *Sixtus* in a great multitude of places, doth sufficiently demonstrate.

57. This certainty therefore in what Language the Scripture remains uncorrupted, is it necessary to have it, or is it not? If it be not, I hope we may do well enough without it. If it be necessary, what became of your Church for 1500 Years together? All which time you must confess she had no such certainty: no one man being able truly and upon good ground to say, *This or that Copy of the Bible is pure, and perfect, and uncorrupted in all things.* And now at this present, though some of you are grown to a higher degree of Presumption in this point, yet are you as far as ever, from any true and real, and rational assurance of the absolute purity of your Authentick Translation: which I suppose my self to have proved unanswerably in divers places.

58. Ad 16. §.] *C. M.* Objects to *Protestants*, That *their Translations of the Scripture are very different, and by each other mutually condemned.* Luthers *Translation by* Zwinglius, *and others:* That *of the* Zwinglians *by* Luther. *The Translation of* Oecolampadius, *by the Divines of* Basil: *that of* Castalio *by* Beza: *That of* Beza *by* Castalio. *That of* Calvin, *by* Carolus Molinæus. *That of* Geneva *by* M. Parks, *and* King James. *And lastly one of our Translations by the* Puritans.

59. *CHIL.* All which might have been as justly objected against that great variety of Translations extant in the Primitive Church, and made use of by the Fathers and Doctors of it. For which I desire not that my word, but S. *Austins* may be taken. *They which have Translated the Scriptures out of the* Hebrew *into* Greek, *may be numbred,*

bred, but the Latine *Interpreters are innumerable.* For *whensoever any one, in the first times of Christianity, met with a* Greek Bible, *and seemed to himself to have some ability in both Languages, he presently ventured upon an Interpretation.* So *He,* in his *second Book of Christian Doctrine. Cap.* 11. Of all these, that which was called the *Italian Translation* was esteemed best; so we may learn from the same S. *Austin in the* 15. *Chap. of the same Book. Amongst all these Interpretations* (saith he) *let the* Italian *be preferred: for it keeps closer to the Letter, and is perspicuous in the sense.* Yet so far was the Church of that time from presuming upon the absolute purity and perfection, even of this best Translation, that S. *Hierome* thought it necessary to make a new Translation of the *Old Testament,* out of the *Hebrew* Fountain, (which himself testifies in his Book *de Viris Illustribus,*) And to correct the vulgar version of the *New Testament,* according to the truth of the Original Greek; amending many Errors which had crept into it, whether by the mistake of the Author, or the negligence of the Transcribers; which work he undertook and performed at the request of *Damasus,* Bishop of *Rome.* You *constrain me* (saith he) *to make a new Work of an old: that after the Copies of the Scriptures have been dispersed through the whole World, I should sit as it were an Arbitrator amongst them, and because they vary among themselves, should determine what are those things* (in them) *which consent with the* Greek *verity.* And after: *Therefore this present Preface promises the four Gospels only corrected by collation with* Greek *Copies. But that they might not be very dissonant from the Custome of the* Latine *reading, I have so tempered with my stile, the Translation of the Ancients, that, those things amended wich did seem to change the sense, other things I have suffered to remain as they were.* So that in this matter *Protestants* must either stand or fall with the Primitive Church.

62. C. M. *But the Faith of* Protestants *relies upon Scripture alone; Scripture is delivered to most of them by Translations; Translations depend upon the skill and honesty of Men, who certainly may Err because they are Men, and certainly*

Scripture the only Rule for Judging Controversies.

do Err, at least some of them, because their Translations are contrary. It seems then the Faith, and consequently the Salvation of Protestants relies upon fallible and uncertain grounds.

63. CHIL. This Objection, though it may seem to do you great service for the present; yet I fear you will repent the time that ever you urged it against us as a fault, that we make mens salvation *depend upon uncertainties*. For the Objection returns upon you many ways, as first thus; The Salvation of many Millions of *Papists* (as they suppose and teach) depends upon their having the Sacrament of Pennance truly administred unto them. This again upon the Minister's being a true Priest. That such or such a man is Priest, not himself, much less any other can have any possible certainty: for it depends upon a great many contingent and uncertain supposals. He that will pretend to be certain of it, must undertake to know for a certain all these things that follow.

64. First that he was Baptized with due matter. Secondly, with the due form of Words, (which he cannot know, unless he were both present and attentive.) Thirdly, he must know that he was Baptized with due Intention, and that is, that the Minister of his Baptism was not a secret *Jew*, nor a *Moore*, nor an *Atheist*, (of all which kinds, I fear experience gives you just cause to fear, that *Italy* and *Spain* have Priests not a few,) but a Christian in Heart, as well as Profession; (otherwise believing the Sacrament to be nothing, in giving it he could intend to give nothing.) nor a *Samosatenian*, nor an *Arrian*: but one that was capable of having due intention, from which they that believe not the Doctrine of the Trinity are excluded by you. And lastly, that he was neither Drunk nor Distracted at the administration of the Sacrament, nor out of negligence or malice omitted his intention.

65. Fourthly, he must undertake to know, that the Bishop which ordained him Priest, ordained him compleatly with due Matter, Form and Intention: and consequently, that he again was neither *Jew*, nor *Moore*, nor *Atheist*, nor liable to any such exception, as is unconsistent with due Intention in giving the Sacrament of Orders. 66.

66. Fifthly, he must undertake to know, that the Bishop which made him Priest, was a Priest himself, for your rule is, *Nihil dat quod non habet*: And consequently, that there was again none of the former nullities in his Baptism, which might make him incapable of Ordination; nor no invalidity in his Ordination, but a true Priest to ordain him again, the requisite matter and form and due intention all concurring.

67. Lastly, he must pretend to know the same of him that made him Priest, and him that made Him Priest, even until he comes to the very Fountain of Priesthood. For take any one in the whole train and succession of Ordainers, and suppose him, by reason of any defect, only a supposed and not a true Priest, then according to your Doctrine he could not give a true, but only a supposed Priesthood; and they that receive it of him, and again, they that derive it from them, can give no better than they received; receiving nothing but a name and shadow, can give nothing but a name and shadow: and so from Age to Age, from Generation to Generation being equivocal Fathers, beget only equivocal Sons; No Principle in Geometry being more certain than this, That *the unsuppliable defect of any necessary Antecedent, must needs cause a nullity of all those Consequences which depend upon it.* In fine, to know this one thing, you must first know Ten Thousand others, whereof not any one is a thing that can be known; there being no necessity that it should be true, which only can qualifie any thing for an Object of Science, but only, at the best, a high degree of probability that it is so. But then, that of Ten Thousand probables no one should be false; that of Ten Thousand requisites, whereof any one may fail, not one should be wanting, this to me is extremely improbable, and even Cousin-german to Impossible. So that the assurance hereof is like a Machine composed of an innumerable multitude of pieces, of which it is strangely unlikely but some will be out of order; and yet if any one be so, the whole Fabrick of necessity falls to the ground. And he that shall put together, and maturely consider all the possible

ways

Scripture the only Rule for Judging Controversies.

ways of lapsing, and nullifying a Priesthood in the Church of *Rome*, I believe will be very inclinable to think, that it is an hundred to one, that amongst a hundred seeming Priests, there is not one true one. Nay, that it is not a thing very improbable, that amongst those many millions, which make up the *Romish Hierarchy*, there are *not twenty* true. But be the truth in this what it will be, once this is certain, that They which makes mens Salvation (as you do) depend upon Priestly Absolution, and this again (as you do) upon the Truth and reality of the Priesthood that gives it, and this lastly upon a great multitude of apparent uncertainties, are not the fittest men in the World, to object to others as a horrible crime, *That they make mens Salvation depend upon fallible and uncertain Foundations.* And let this be the first retortion of your Argument.

68. But suppose this difficulty assoiled, and that an Angel from Heaven should ascertain you (for other assurances you can have none) that the Person, you make use of, is a true Priest, and a competent Minister of the Sacrament of Pennance; yet still the doubt will remain, whether he will do you that good which he can do, whether he will pronounce the absolving words with intent to absolve you? For perhaps he may bear you some secret malice, and project to himself your damnation, for a compleat *Italian* revenge. Parhaps (as the tale is of a Priest that was lately burnt in *France*) he may upon some conditions have compacted with the Devil to give no Sacraments with Intention. Lastly, he may be (for ought you can possibly know) a secret *Jew*, or *Moor*, or *Anti-Trinitarian*, or perhaps such a one as is so far from intending your forgiveness of sins and Salvation by this Sacrament, that in his heart he laughs at all these things, and thinks Sin nothing, and Salvation a word. All these doubts you must have clearly resolved (which can hardly be done but by another Revelation,) before you can upon good grounds assure your self, that your true Priest gives you true and effectual absolution. So that when you have done as much as God requires for your Salvation, yet can you by no means be secure, but that you may have the

ill luck to be Damned: which is to make Salvation a matter of chance, and not of choice, and which a man may fail of, not only by an ill life, but by ill Fortune. Verily a most comfortable Doctrine for a considering man lying upon Death bed, who either feels or fears that his repentance is but attrition only, and not contrition, and consequently believes that if he be not absolved really by a true Priest, he cannot possibly escape damnation. Such a man for his comfort, you tell, first (you that will have *mens Salvation depend upon no uncertainties*,) that though he verily believe that his sorrow for sins is a true sorrow, and his purpose of amendment a true purpose; yet he may deceive himself, perhaps it is not, and if it be not, he must be damned. Yet you bid him hope well: But *Spes est rei incertæ nomen.* You tell him secondly, that though the party he confesses to, seem to be a true Priest, yet for ought he knows, or for ought himself knows, by reason of some secret undiscernable invalidity in his Baptism or Ordination, he may be none: and if he be none, he can do nothing. This is a hard saying, but this is not the worst. You tell him thirdly, that he may may be in such a state that he cannot, or if he can, that he will not give the Sacrament with due Intention: and if he does not, all's in vain. Put case a man by these considerations should be cast into some agonies; what advice, what comfort would you give him? Verily I know not what you could say to him, but this; that first for the Qualification required on his part, he might know that he desired to have true sorrow, and that that is sufficient. But then if he should ask you, why he might not know his sorrow to be a true sorrow, as well as his desire to be sorrowful, to be a true desire, I believe you would be put to silence. Then secondly, to quiet his fears, concerning the Priest and his intention you should tell him, by my advice, that Gods goodness (which will not suffer him to damn men for not doing better than their best,) will supply all such defects as to humane endeavours were unavoidable. And therefore though his Priest were indeed no Priest, yet to him: he should be as if he were one: and if he gave Absolution

with-

without Intention, yet in doing so he should hurt himself only and not his penitent. This were some comfort indeed, and this were to settle mens Salvation upon reasonable certain grounds. But this I fear you will never say; for this were to reverse many Doctrines established by your Church, and besides to degrade your Priesthood from a great part of their honour, by lessening the strict necessity of the Laities dependance upon them. For it were to say, that *the Priests Intention is not necessary to the obtaining of absolution*; which is to say, that it is not in the Parsons power to damn whom he will in his Parish, because by this Rule, God should supply the defect which his malice had caused. And besides it were to say, that *Infants dying without Baptism might be saved*, God supplying the want of Baptism which to them is unavoidable. But beyond all this, it were to put into my mouth a full and satisfying answer to your Argument, which I am now returning, so that in answering my objection you should answer your own. For then I should tell you, that it were altogether as abhorrent from the goodness of God, and as repugnant to it, to suffer an ignorant Lay-mans Soul to perish, meerly for being misled by an undiscernable false Translation, which yet was commended to him by the Church, which (being of necessity to credit some in this matter) he had reason to rely upon either above all other, or as much as any other, as it is to damn a penitent sinner for a secret defect in that desired Absolution, which his Gostly Father perhaps was an *Atheist* and could not give him, or was a villain and would not. This answer therefore, which alone would serve to comfort your penitent in his perplexities, and to assure him that he cannot fail of Salvation if he will not, for fear of inconveniencies you must forbear. And seeing you must, I hope you will come down from the Pulpit, and Preach no more against others for *making mens Salvation depend upon fallible and uncertain grounds*, lest by judging others, you make your selves and your own Church inexcusable, who are strongly guilty of this fault, above all the men and Churches of the World: whereof I have already given you two very pregnant demonstrations, drawn from your presumptions tying God and Salvation to your Sacraments; And the efficacy of them to your Priests Qualifications and Intentions.

69. Your making the Salvation of Infants depend on Baptism a Casual thing, and in the power of man to confer, or not confer, would yield me a Third of the same nature. And your suspending the same on the Baptizers intention a Fourth. And lastly your making the Real presence of Christ in the Eucharist depend upon the casualties of the Consecrators true Priesthood and Intention, and yet commanding men to believe it for certain that he is present, and to adore the Sacrament, which according to your Doctrine, for ought they can possibly know, may be nothing else but a piece of Bread, so exposing them to the danger of Idolatry, and consequently of Damnation, doth offer me a Fifth demonstration of the same conclusion, if I thought fit to insist upon them. But I have no mind to draw any more out of this Fountain; neither do I think it Charity to cloy the Reader with uniformity, when the Subject affords variety.

70. Sixthly, therefore I return it thus. The Faith of *Papists* relies alone upon their Churches infallibility. That there is any Church infallible, and that theirs is it, they pretend not to believe, but only upon *prudential motives*. Dependance upon prudential motives they confess to be obnoxious to a possibility of erring. What then remaineth but Truth, Faith, Salvation, and all must in them rely upon a fallible and uncertain ground!

71. Seventhly, The Faith of *Papists* relies upon the Church alone. The Doctrine of the Church is delivered to most of them by their Parish Priest, or Ghostly Father, or at least by a company of Priests, who for the most part sure, are men and not Angels, in whom nothing is more certain than a most certain possibility to Err. What then remaineth but that Truth, Faith, Salvation and all, must in them rely upon a fallible and uncertain ground.

72. Eighthly

72. Eighthly thus. It is apparent and undeniable, that many Thousands there are, who believe your Religion upon no better grounds, than a man may have for the belief almost of any Religion. As some believe it, because their Forefathers did so, and they were good People. Some, because they were Christened, and brought up in it. Some, because it is the Religion of their Country, where all other Religions are persecuted and proscribed. Some, because *Protestants* cannot shew a perpetual succession of Professors of all their Doctrine. Some, because the service of your Church is more stately, and pompous, and magnificent. Some, because they find comfort in it. Some, because your Religion is farther spread, and hath more Professors of it, than the Religion of *Protestants*. Some, because *your* Priests *compass Sea and Land to gain Proselytes to it.* Lastly, an infinite number, by chance, and they know not why, but only because they are sure they are in the right. This which I say is a most certain experimented Truth, and if you will deal ingeniously, you will not deny it. And without question he that builds his Faith upon our *English Translation*, goes upon a more prudent ground than any of these can, with reason, be pretended to be. What then can you alledge but that, with you, rather than with us, Truth and Faith and Salvation and all relies upon fallible and uncertain grounds.

73. Ninthly. Your *Rhemish* and *Doway* Translations are delivered to your Proselytes, (such I mean that are dispenced with for the reading of them,) for the direction of their Faith and Lives. And the same may be said of your Translations of the Bible into other national Languages, in respect of those that are Licensed to read them. This I presume you will confess. And moreover, that these Translations came not by inspiration, but were the productions of humane Industry; and that not Angels, but men were the Authors of them. Men I say, meer men, subject to the same Passions and to the same possibility of erring with our Translators. And then how does it not unavoidably follow, that in them which depend upon these Translations for their direction

rection, Faith, and Truth, and Salvation, and all relies upon fallible and uncertain grounds?

74. Tenthly and lastly (to lay the Axe to the Root of the Tree,) the *Helena* which you so fight for, your vulgar Translation, though some of you believe, or pretend to believe, it to be in every part and particle of it, the pure and uncorrupted Word of God; yet others among you, and those as good and zealous Catholicks as you, are not so confident hereof.

75. First, for all those who have made Translations of the whole Bible or any part of it different many times in sense from the Vulgar, as *Lyranus, Cajetan, Pagnine, Arias, Erasmus, Valla, Steuchus*, and others, it is apparent and even palpable, that they never dreamt of any absolute perfection and authentical Infallibility of the *Vulgar Translation*. For if they had, why did they in many places reject it and differ from it?

76. *Vega* was present at the Council of *Trent*, when that decree was made, which made the *Vulgar Edition* (then not extant any where in the World) *authentical*, and not to be rejected upon any pretence whatsoever. At the forming this decree *Vega* I say was present, understood the mind of the Council, as well as any man, and professes that he was instructed in it by the *President* of it, the *Cardinal S. Cruce*. And yet he hath written that *the Council in this decree, meant to pronounce this Translation free* (not simply from all Error) *but only from such Errors, out of which any opinion pernicious to Faith and Manners might be collected*. This, *Andradius* in his defence of that Council reports of *Vega*, and assents to it himself. *Driedo*, in his *Book of the Translation of Holy Scripture*, hath these Words very pregnant and pertinent to the same purpose; *The See Apostolick, hath approved or accepted* Hieroms *Edition, not as so wholly consonant to the Original, and so entire and pure and restored in all things, that it may not be lawful for any man, either by comparing it with the Fountain to examine it, or in some places to doubt, whether or no* Hierome *did understand the true sense of the Scripture; but only as an Edition to be preferred before all others then extant,*

and

and no where deviating from the Truth in the Rules of Faith and good Life. *Mariana*, even where he is a most earnest Advocate for the Vulgar Edition, yet acknowleges the imperfection of it in these Words, *The faults of the* *Vulgar Edition are not approved by the Decree of the Council of* Trent, *a multitude whereof we did collect from the variety of Copies.* And again, *We maintain that the Hebrew and Greek, were by no means rejected by the* Trent *Fathers: And that the Latin Edition is indeed approved, yet not so, as if they did deny that some places might be Translated more plainly, some more properly; whereof it were easie to produce innumerable examples.* And this he there professes to have learnt of Laines *the then General of the Society:* who was a great part of that Council, present at all the Actions of it, and of very great authority in it. *Pro Edit. vulg. c. 21. p. 99.*

77. To this so great authority he adds a reason of his opinion, which with all indifferent men will be of a far greater authority. *If the Council* (saith he) *had purposed to approve an Edition in all respects, and to make it of equal authority and credit with the Fountains, certainly they ought with exact care first to have corrected the Errors of the Interpreter:* which certainly they did not.

78. Lastly *Bellarmine* himself, though he will not acknowledge any imperfection in the Vulgar Edition, yet he acknowledges that the case may, and does oft-times so fall out, that *it is impossible to discern which is the true reading of the Vulgar Edition, but only by recourse unto the Originals, and dependence upon them.* *Bell. de verbo Dei l. 2. c. 11. p. 120.*

79. From all which it may evidently be collected, that though some of you flatter your selves with a vain imagination of the certain absolute purity and perfection of your Vulgar Edition; yet the matter is not so certain, and so resolved, but that the best Learned men amongst you are often at a stand, and very doubtful sometimes whether your Vulgar Translation be true, and sometimes whether this or that be your Vulgar Translation, and sometimes undoubtedly resolved that your Vulgar Translation is no true Translation, nor consonant to the Original, as it was at first delivered. And what then can be

be alledged, but that out of your own grounds it may be inferred and inforced upon you, that not only in your Lay-men, but your Clergy-men and Scholars, Faith and Truth and Salvation and all depends upon fallible and uncertain grounds? And thus by Ten several retortions of this one Argument, I have endeavoured to shew you, how ill you have complied with your own advice, which was *to take heed of urging Arguments that might be returned upon you.* I should now by a direct answer, shew that it presseth not us at all: but I have in passing done it already, in the end of the second retortion of this Argument, and thither I refer the Reader.

83. Whereas therefore, you exhort them *that will have assurance of true Scriptures, to fly to your Church for it*: I desire to know (if they should follow your advice) how they should be assured that your Church can give them any such assurance; which hath been *confessedly* so negligent, as to suffer many *whole Books of Scripture* to be utterly lost. Again, in those that remain, confessedly so negligent, as to suffer *the Originals of these that remain to be corrupted.* And lastly, so careless of preserving the integrity of the Copies of her Translation, as to suffer *infinite variety of Readings* to come in to them, without keeping *any one perfect Copy,* which might have been as the Standard, and *Polycletus* his Canon to correct the rest by. So that which was the true reading, and which the false, it was utterly undiscernable, but only by comparing them with the Originals, which also she pretends *to be corrupted.*

84. Ad 17. §.] In this Division you charge us *with great uncertainty, concerning the true meaning of Scripture.* Which hath been answered already, by saying, That if you speak of plain places, (and in such all things necessary are contained,) we are sufficiently certain of the meaning of them, neither need they any Interpreter: If of obscure and difficult places, we confess we are uncertain of the sense of many of them. But then we say there is no necessity we should be certain. For if Gods Will had been we should have understood him more certainly, he would have spoken more plainly. And
we

we say besides, that as we are uncertain, so are You too; which he that doubts of, let him read your Commentators upon the Bible, and observe their various and dissonant Interpretations, and he shall in this point need no further satisfaction.

85. *Obj.* But seeing *there are contentions among us, we are taught by nature and Scripture, and experience* (so you tell us out of M. *Hooker*) *to seek for the ending of them, by submitting unto some Judicial sentence, whereunto neither part may refuse to stand.*

Answ. This is very true. Neither should you need to perswade us to seek such a means of ending all our Controversies, if we could tell where to find it. But this we know, that none is fit to pronounce, for all the World, a judicial definitive obliging Sentence in Controversies of Religion, but only such a Man, or such a society of Men, as is authorized thereto by God. And besides we are able to demonstrate, that it hath not been the pleasure of God to give to any Man, or Society of Men any such authority. And therefore though we wish heartily that all Controversies were ended, as we do that all sin were abolisht, yet we have little hope of the one, or the other, till the World be ended. And in the mean while, think it best to content our selves with, and to perswade others unto an *Unity of Charity and mutual Toleration*; seeing God hath authorized no man to force all men to *Unity of Opinion.* Neither do we think it fit to argue thus, To us it seems convenient there should be one Judge of all Controversies for the whole World, therefore God has appointed one: But more modest and more reasonable to collect thus, God hath appointed no such Judge of Controversies, therefore, though it seems to us convenient there should be one, yet it is not so: Or though it were convenient for us to have one, yet it hath pleased God (for Reasons best known to himself) not to allow us this convenience.

87. Ad 18. §.] That the true Interpretation of the Scripture ought to be received from the Church, you need not prove, for it is very easily granted by them, who
profess

profess themselves very ready to receive all Truths, much more the true sense of Scripture, not only from the Church, but from any Society of men, nay from any man whatsoever.

88. That the *Churches Interpretation of Scripture is always true*, that is it which you would have said: and that in some sense may be also admitted. *viz.* If you speak of that Church (which before you speak of in the 14. §.) that is, of the Church of all Ages since the Apostles. Upon the Tradition of which Church, you there told us, *We were to receive the Scripture, and to believe it to be the Word of God.* For there you teach us, that *our Faith of Scripture depends on a Principle which requires no other proof,* And that, *such is Tradition, which from Hand to Hand, and Age to Age bring us up to the Times and Persons of the Apostles and our Saviour himself, cometh to be confirmed by all those Miracles, and other Arguments whereby they convinced their Doctrine to be true.* Wherefore the Ancient Fathers avouch that we must receive the Sacred Scripture upon the Tradition of this Church. The Tradition then of this Church you say must teach us what is Scripture: and we are willing to believe it. And now if you make it good unto us, that the same Tradition down from the Apostles, hath delivered from Age to Age, and from Hand to Hand, any Interpretation of any Scripture, we are ready to embrace that also. But now, if you will argue thus: The Church in one sense, tells us what is Scripture, and we believe, therefore if the Church taken in another sense, tell us, this or that is the meaning of the Scripture, we are to believe that also; this is too transparent Sophistry, to take any but those that are willing to be taken.

89. If there be any Traditive Interpretation of Scripture, produce it, and prove it to be so; and we embrace it. But the Tradition of all Ages is one thing; and the authority of the present Church, much more of the *Roman Church*, which is but a Part, and a corrupted Part of the *Catholick Church*, is another. And therefore though we are ready to receive both Scripture and
the

Scripture the only Rule for Judging Controversies.

the sense of Scripture upon the authority of *Original Tradition,* yet we receive neither the one, nor the other, upon the Authority of your Church.

90. First for the Scripture, how can we receive them upon the Authority of your Church: who hold now those Books to be Canonical, which formerly you rejected from the Canon? I instance, in the *Book of Macchabees,* and the *Epistle to the Hebrews.* The first of these you held not to be Canonical in S. *Gregories* time, or else he was no member of your Church, for it is apparent [a] He held otherwise. The second you rejected from the Canon in S. *Hieroms* time, as it is evident out of [b] many places of his Works.

91. If you say (which is all you can) that *Hierom* spake this of the particular Roman Church, not of the Roman Catholick *Church*; I answer, there was none such in his time, None that was called so. Secondly, what he spake of the *Roman Church,* must be true of all other Churches, if your Doctrine of the necessity of the Conformity of all other Churches to that Church were then Catholick Doctrine. Now then choose whether you will, either that the particular *Roman Church,* was not then believed to be the Mistris of all other Churches (notwithstanding, *Ad hanc Ecclesiam necesse est omnem convenire Ecclesiam, hoc est, omnes qui sunt undique fideles,*; which Card. *Perron,* and his *Translatress* so often translates false:) Or if you say she was, you will run into a greater inconvenience, and be forced to say, that all the Churches of that time, rejected from the Canon the Epistle to the *Hebrews,* together with the *Roman Church.* And consequently that the *Catholick Church* may Err in rejecting from the Canon Scriptures truly Canonical.

[a] See *Greg. Mor. l. 19. c. 13.*
[b] Thus he testifies. *Com. in Esa. c. 6.* in these words. *Unde & Paulus Apost. in Epist. ad Heb. quam Latina consuetudo non recipit:* and again in c. 8. in these, *In Ep. quæ ad Hebræos scribitur, licet eam Latina Consuetudo inter Canonicas Scripturas non recipiat.*) &c.

92. Secondly, How can we receive the Scripture upon the authority of the *Roman Church,* which hath delivered at several times Scriptures in many places, different and repugnant, for Authentical and Canonical? which is most evident out of the place of *Malachy,* which is so quoted for the Sacrifice of the Mass, that either all the Ancient Fathers had false Bibles, or yours is false.

Q   Most

Most evident likewise from the comparing of the story of *Jacob* in *Genesis*, with that which is cited out of it, in the *Epistle to the Hebrews*, according to the vulgar Edition. But above all, to any one, who shall compare the Bibles of *Sixtus* and *Clement*, so evident, that the wit of man cannot disguise it.

93. Thus you see what reason we have to believe your Antecedent, *That your Church it is which must declare, what Books be true Scripture.* Now for the consequence, that certainly is as liable to exception as the Antecedent. For if it were true, that God had promised to assist you, for the delivering of true Scripture, would this oblige him, or would it follow from hence that He had obliged himself, to teach you, not only sufficiently, but *effectually* and *irrisistably* the true sense of Scripture? God is not defective in things necessary: neither will he leave himself without witness, nor the World without means of knowing his will and doing it. And therefore it was necessary that by his Providence he should preserve the Scripture from any undiscernable corruption, in those things which he would have known: otherwise it is apparent, it had not been his will, that these things should be known, the only means of continuing the knowledg of them being perished. But now neither is God lavish in superfluities, and therefore having given us means sufficient for our direction, and power sufficient to make use of these means, he will not constrain or necessitate us to make use of these means. For that were to cross the end of our Creation, which was to be glorified by our free obedience: whereas necessity and freedom cannot stand together. That were to reverse the Law which he hath prescribed to himself in his dealing with men, and that is, *to set Life and Death before him, and to leave him in the hands of his own Counsel.* God gave the Wisemen a Star to lead them to *Christ*, but he did not necessitate them to follow the guidance of this Star: that was left to their liberty. God gave the Children of *Israel a Fire to lead them by Night, and a Pillar of Cloud by Day*, but he constrained no man to follow them: that was left to
their

their liberty. So he gives the Church, the Scripture: which in those things which are to be believed or done, are plain and easie to be followed, like the Wisemens Star. Now that which he desires of us on our part, is the Obedience of Faith, and love of the Truth, and desire to find the true sense of it, and industry in searching it, and humility in following, and Constancy in professing it: all which if he should work in us by an absolute irresistible necessity, he could no more require of us, as our duty, than he can of the Sun to shine, of the Sea to Ebb and Flow, and of all other Creatures to do those things which by meer necessity they must do, and cannot choose. Besides, what an impudence is it to pretend that *your Church is infallibly directed concerning the true meaning of the Scripture*, whereas there are Thousands of places of Scripture, which you do not pretend certainly to understand, and about the Interpretation whereof, your own Doctors differ among themselves? If your Church be infallibly directed concerning the true meaning of Scripture, why do not your Doctors follow her infallible direction? And if they do, how comes such difference among them in their Interpretations?

94. Again, why does your Church thus put her Candle under a Bushel, and keep her Talent of interpreting Scripture infallibly, thus long wrapt up in Napkins? Why sets she not forth Infallible Commentaries or Expositions upon all the Bible? Is it because this would not be profitable for Christians, that Scripture should be Interpreted? Is it blasphemous to say so. The Scripture it self tells us, *All Scripture is profitable.* And the Scripture is not so much the Words as the Sense. And if it be not profitable, why does she imploy particular Doctors to interpret Scriptures fallibly? unless we must think that fallible Interpretations of Scripture are profitable, and infallible Interpretations would not be so?

95. If you say *the Holy Ghost, which assists the Church in interpreting, will move the Church to interpret when he shall think fit, and that the Church will do it when the Holy Ghost shall move her to do it:* I demand whether the Ho-

ly Ghosts moving of the Church to such works as these be resistible by the Church, or irresistible. If resistible, then the Holy Ghost may move, and the Church may not be moved. As certainly the Holy Ghost doth always move to an Action, when he shews us plainly that it would be for the good of men, and Honour of God. As he that hath any sense will acknowledge that an infallible exposition of Scripture could not but be, and there is no conceivable reason, why such a work should be put off a day, but only because you are conscious to your selves, you cannot do it, and therefore make excuses. But if the moving of the Holy Ghost be irresistible, and you are not yet so moved to go about this work; then I confess you are excused. But then I would know, whether those *Popes* which so long deferred the calling of a Council for the Reformation of your Church, at length pretended to be effected by the Council of *Trent*, whether they may excuse themselves, for that they were not moved by the Holy Ghost to do it? I would know likewise, as this motion is irresistible when it comes, so whether it be so simply necessary to the moving of your Church to any such publick Action, that it cannot possibly move without it? That is, whether the *Pope* now could not, if he would, seat himself *in Cathedra*, and fall to writing expositions upon the Bible for the directions of Christians to the true sense of it? If you say he cannot, you will make your self ridiculous. If he can, then I would know, whether he should be infallibly directed in these expositions, or no? If he should, then what need he to stay for irresistible motion? Why does he not go about this noble work presently? If he should not, How shall we know that the calling of the Council of *Trent* was not upon his own voluntary motion, or upon humane importunity and suggestion, and not upon the motion of the Holy Ghost? And consequently how shall we know whether he were assistant to it or no, seeing he assists none but what he himself moves to? And whether he did move the *Pope* to call this Council, is a secret thing, which we cannot possibly know, nor perhaps the *Pope* himself.

96. If

96. If you say, your meaning is only, *That the Church shall be infallibly guarded from giving any false sense of any Scripture, and not infallibly assisted positively to give the true sense of all Scripture:* I put to you your own Question, why should we believe the Holy Ghost will stay there? Or, why may we not as well think he will stay at the first thing, that is, in teaching the Church what Books be true Scripture? For if the Holy Ghosts assistance be promised to all things profitable, then will he be with them infallibly, not only to guard them from all Errors, but to guide them to all profitable truths, such as the true senses of all Scripture would be. Neither could he stay there, but defend them irresistibly from all Vices; Nor there neither, but infuse into them irresistibly all Vertues: for all these things would be much for the benefit of Christians. If you say, he cannot do this without taking away their free-will in living; I say neither can he necessitate men to believe aright, without taking away their free-will in believing and in professing their belief.

97. *Obj.* To the place of S. *Austin,* (*I would not believe the Gospel, unless the Authority of the Church did move me.* Contr. ep. Fund. c. 5.)

Answ. I answer, That not the Authority of the present Church, much less of a Part of it (as the *Roman Church* is) was that which alone moved Saint *Austin* to believe the Gospel, but the perpetual Tradition of the Church of all Ages. Which you your self have taught us to be the *only Principle by which the Scripture is proved, and which it self needs no proof*; and to which you have referred this very saying of S. *Austin,* Ego vero Evangelio non crederem nisi, &c. p. 55. And in the next place which you cite out of his Book *De Util. Cred.* c. 14. he shews, that his *motives to believe, were, Fame, Celebrity, Consent, Antiquity.* And seeing this Tradition, this Consent, this Antiquity did as fully and powerfully move him not to believe *Manichæus,* as to believe the Gospel, (the Christian Tradition being as full against *Manichæus* as it was for the Gospel) therefore he did well to conclude upon these
grounds,

grounds, that he had as much reason to disbelieve *Manichæus*, as to believe the Gospel. Now if you can truly say, that the same Fame, Celebrity, Consent, Antiquity, that the same Universal and Original Tradition, lies against *Luther* and *Calvin*, as did against *Manichæus*, you may do well to apply the Argument against them; otherwise it will be to little purpose to substitute their names instead of *Manichæus*, unless you can shew the things agrees to them as well as him.

98. If you say, that S. *Austin speaks here of the Authority of the Present Church, abstracting from consent with the Ancient*, and therefore you, seeing you have the present Church on your side against *Luther* and *Calvin*, as S. *Austin* against *Manichæus*, may urge the same words against them which S. *Austin* did against him;

99. I answer, First that it is a vain presumption of yours that the *Catholick Church is of your side*. Secondly, that if S. *Austin* speak here of that present Church, which moved him to believe the Gospel, without consideration of the Antiquity of it, and its both Personal and Doctrinal succession from the Apostles; His Argument will be like a *Buskin* that will serve any leg. It will serve to keep an *Arrian*, or a *Grecian* from being a *Roman Catholick*, as well as a Catholick from being an *Arrian*, or a *Grecian*? In as much as the *Arrians* and *Grecians*, did pretend to the Title of Catholicks, and the Church, as much as the *Papists* now do. If then you should have come to an Ancient *Goth* or *Vandal*, whom the *Arrians* converted to Christianity, and should have moved him to your Religion; might he not say the very same words to you as S. *Austin* to the *Manichæans*? *I would not believe the Gospel, unless the Authority of the Church did move me. Them therefore whom I obeyed, saying believe the Gospel, why should I not obey saying to me, do not believe the* Homoousians? *Choose what thou pleasest: If thou shalt say believe the* Arrians, *they warn me not to give any Credit to you. If therefore I believe them, I cannot believe thee. If thou say do not believe the* Arrians, *thou shalt not do well to force me to the Faith of the* Homoousians, *because by the Preaching of the* Arrians

Scripture the only Rule for Judging Controversies.

I believed the Gospel it self. If you say, you did well to believe them, commending the Gospel, but you did not well to believe them discommending the Homoousians: Doest thou think me so very foolish, that without any reason at all, I should believe what thou wilt, and not believe what thou wilt not? It were easie to put these words into the mouth of a *Grecian*, *Abyssine*, *Georgian*, or any other of any Religion. And I pray bethink your selves, what you would say to such a one in such a case, and imagine that we say the very same to you.

101. And whereas you say, S. *Austin* may seem to have spoken Prophetically against Protestants, when he said, *Why should I not most diligently inquire, what Christ commanded, of them before all others, by whose Authority I was moved to believe, that Christ Commanded any good thing?*

Answ. I answer, Until you can shew that *Protestants* believe that Christ commanded any good thing, that is, That they believe the truth of Christian Religion upon the Authority of the Church of *Rome*, this place must be wholly impertinent to your purpose; which is to make *Protestants* believe your Church to be the infallible expounder of Scriptures and judge of Controversies: nay rather is it not directly against your purpose? For why may not a member of the Church of *England*, who received his Baptism, Education and Faith from the Ministry of this Church, say just so to you as S. *Austin* here to the *Manichees*? Why should I not most diligently inquire, what Christ commanded, of them (the Church of *England*) before all others, by whose authority I was moved to believe, that Christ commandded any good thing, Can you, F. or K. or whosoever you are, better declare to me what he said, whom I would not have thought to have been or to be, if the belief thereof had been recommended by you to me? This therefore (that *Christ Jesus* did those miracles, and taught that Doctrine which is contained evidently in the undoubted Books of the *New Testament*) I believed by Fame, strengthened with Celebrity and Consent, (even of those which in other things are at infinite variance one with another,) and lastly by Antiquity (which gives an Universal and a constant attestation to them) But

every

every one may see that you, so few (in comparison of all those upon whose consent we ground our belief of Scripture,) so turbulent, (that you damn all to the Fire, and to Hell, that any way differ from you; that you profess it is lawful for you, to use violence and power whensoever you can have it, for the planting of your own Doctrine, and the extirpation of the contrary;) lastly so new in many of your Doctrines, (as in the lawfulness, and expedience of debarring the Laity the Sacramental Cup; the lawfulness and expedience of your Latine Service, Transubstantiation, Indulgences, Purgatory, the *Popes* infallibility, his Authority over Kings, &c) so new I say, in comparison of the undoubted Books of Scripture, which evidently containeth, or rather is our Religion, and the sole, and adequate object of our Faith: I say every one may see that you, so few, so turbulent, so new, can produce nothing deserving authority (with wise and considerate men) What madness is this? Believe them the consent of Christians which are now, and have been ever since Christ in the World, that we ought to believe Christ; but learn of us what Christ said, which contradict and damn all other parts of Christendom. Why I beseech you? Surely if they were not at all, and could not teach me any thing, I would more easily persuade my self, that I were not to believe in Christ, than that I should learn any thing concerning him, from any other, than them by whom I believed him: at least, than that I should learn what his Religion was from you, who have wronged so exceedingly his Miracles and his Doctrine, by forging so evidently so many false Miracles for the Confirmation of your new Doctrine; which might give us just occasion, had we no other assurance of them but your Authority, to suspect the true ones. Who with forging so many false Stories, and false Authors, have taken a fair way to make the Faith of all Stories questionable; if we had no other ground for our belief of them but your Authority: who have brought in Doctrines plainly and directly contrary to that which you confess to be the Word of Christ, and which, for the most part, make either for the honour

or

or profit of the Teachers of them: which (if there were no difference between the Christian and the *Roman* Church) would be very apt to make suspicious men believe that Christian Religion was a humane invention, taught by some cunning Impostors, only to make themselves rich and powerful; who make a profession of corrupting all sorts of Authors: a ready course to make it justly questionable whether any remain uncorrupted. For if you take this Authority upon you, upon the six Ages last past; how shall we know, that the Church of that time, did not Usurp the same Authority upon the Authors of the six last Ages before them, and so upwards until we come to Christ himself? Whose questioned Doctrines, none of them came from the Fountain of Apostolick Tradition, but have insinuated themselves into the Streams, by little and little, some in one Age, and some in another, some more Anciently, some more lately, and some yet are Embrio's, yet hatching, and in the Shell; as the *Popes* Infallibility, the Blessed Virgins immaculate conception, the *Popes* power over the Temporalities of Kings, the Doctrine of Predetermination, &c. all which yet are, or in time may be imposed upon Christians under the Title of *Original and Apostolick Tradition*; and that with that necessity, that they are told, they were as good believe nothing at all, as not believe these things to have come from the Apostles, which they know to have been brought in but yesterday: which whether it be not a ready and likely way to make men conclude thus with themselves--- I am told, that I were as good believe nothing at all, as believe some points which the Church teaches me, and not others: and some things which she teaches to be Ancient and Certain, I plainly see to be New and False, therefore I will believe nothing at all. Whether I say the foresaid grounds be not a ready and likely way to make men conclude thus, and whether this conclusion be not too often made in *Italy*, and *Spain*, and *France*, and in *England* too, I leave it to the judgment of those that have Wisdom and Experience. Seeing therefore the *Roman Church* is so far from being a sufficient

ent Foundation for our belief in Christ, that it is in sundry regards a dangerous temptation against it; why should I not much rather conclude, Seeing we receive not the knowledg of Christ and Scriptures from the Church of *Rome*, neither from her must we take his Doctrine, or the Interpretation of Scripture?

102. Ad §. 19. In this number, this Argument is contained. *The Judge of Controversies ought to be intelligible to learned and unlearned; The Scripture is not so, and the Church is so; Therefore the Church is the Judge, and not the Scripture.*

103. To this I answer: As to be understandible is a condition requisite to a Judge, so is not that alone sufficient to make a Judge; otherwise you might make your self Judge of Controversies, by arguing; The Scripture is not intelligible by all, but I am, therefore I am Judge of Controversies. If you say your intent was to conclude against the Scripture, and not for the Church: I demand why then, but to delude the simple with Sopistry, did you say in the close of this §. *Such is the Church, and the Scripture is not such?* but that you would leave it to them to infer in the end, (which indeed was more than you undertook in the beginning) *Therefore the Church is Judge and the Scripture not.* I say Secondly; that you still run upon a false supposition: that God hath appointed some Judge of all Controversies that may happen among Christians, about the sense of obscure Texts of Scripture: whereas he has left every one to his liberty herein, in those words of S. *Paul, Quisque abundet in sensu suo,* &c. I say Thirdly. Whereas some *Protestants* make the Scripture Judge of Controversies, that they have the Authority of Fathers to warrant their manner of speaking: as of * *Optatus.*

* *Contra Parmen. l. 5. in Prin.*

104. But speaking truly and properly the Scripture is not a Judge nor cannot be, but only, a *sufficient Rule*, for those to judge by, that believe it to be the word of God (as the Church of *England* and the Church of *Rome* both do,) what they are to believe, and what they are not to believe. I say sufficiently perfect, and sufficiently intelligible in things necessary, to all that have understanding,

whether

whether they be learned or unlearned. And my reason hereof is convincing and demonstrative; because nothing is necessary to be believed, but what is plainly revealed. For to say, that when a place of Scripture, by reason of ambiguous terms, lies indifferent between divers senses, whereof one is true, and the other is false, that God obliges men under pain of damnation, not to mistake through error and humane frailty, is to make God a Tyrant, and to say that he requires us certainly to attain that end, for the attaining whereof we have no certain means; which is to say, that, like *Pharaoh*, he gives no straw, and requires brick; that he reaps where he sows not; that he gathers where he strews not, that he will not be pleased with our utmost endeavors to please him, without full and exact and never failing performance; that his will is we should do what he knows we cannot do; that he will not accept of us according to that which we have, but requireth of us what we have not. Which whether it can consist with his goodness, with his wisdom, and with his word, I leave it to honest men to judge. If I should send a Servant to *Paris*, or *Rome*, or *Jerusalem*, and he using his utmost diligence not to mistake his way, yet notwithstanding, meeting often with such places where the road is divided into several ways, whereof every one is as likely to be true, and as likely to be false as any other, should at length mistake and go out of the way; would not any man say that I were an impotent, foolish and unjust Master, if I should be offended with him for doing so? And shall we not tremble to impute that to God, which we would take in foul scorn, if it were imputed to our selves? Certainly, I for my part fear I should not love God if I should think so strangely of him.

105. Again, When you say, *that unlearned, and ignorant men cannot understand Scripture*, I would desire you to come out of the Clouds, and tell us what you mean: Whether, that they cannot understand all Scripture, or that they cannot understand any Scripture, or that they cannot understand so much as is sufficient for their direction to Heaven. If the first; I believe the Learned are in the

same Case. If the Second; every mans experience will confute you: for who is there that is not capable of a sufficient understanding of the Story, the Precepts, the Promises, and the Threats of the Gospel? If the Third; that they may understand something, but not enough for their Salvations; I ask you, first. Why then doth Saint *Paul* say to *Timothy, The Scriptures are able to make him wise unto Salvation?* Why does Saint *Austin* say, *Ea quæ manifestè posita sunt in sacris Scripturis, omnia continent quæ pertinent ad Fidem Moresque vivendi?* Why does every one of the four *Evangelists* Intitle their Book *The Gospel,* if any necessary and essential part of the Gospel were left out of it? Can we imagine, that either they omitted something necessary, out of ignorance not knowing it to be necessary? Or knowing it to be so, maliciously concealed it? Or out of negligence, did the work they had undertaken by halfes? If none of these things can without Blasphemy be imputed to them, considering they were assisted by the Holy Ghost in this work, then certainly it most evidently follows, that every one of them writ the whole Gospel of Christ; I mean all the essential and necessary parts of it. So that if we had no other Book of Scripture, but one of them alone, we should not want any thing necessary to Salvation. And what one of them has more than another, it is only profitable, and not necessary. Necessary indeed to be believed, because revealed; but not therefore revealed, because necessary to be believed.

106. Neither did they write only for the Learned, but for all men. This being one especial means of the Preaching of the Gospel, which was commanded to be Preached, not only to Learned men but *to all men*. And therefore, unless we will imagine the Holy Ghost and them to have been wilfully wanting to their own desire and purpose, we must conceive, that they intended to speak plain, even to the capacity of the simplest; at least touching all things necessary to be published by them, and believed by us.

107. And

107. And whereas you pretend it *is so easie, and obvious both for the Learned and the ignorant, both to know which is the Church, and what are the Decrees of the Church, and what is the sense of those Decrees*: I say, this is a vain pretence.

108. For First; How shall an unlearned man whom you have supposed now ignorant of Scripture, how shall he know which of all the Societies of Christians is indeed the Church? You will say perhaps, *he must examine them by the notes of the Church, which are perpetual Visibility, Succession, Conformity with the ancient Church*, &c. But how shall he know, first, that these are the notes of the Church, unless by Scripture, which you say he understands not? You may say perhaps, he may be told so. But seeing men may deceive, and be deceived, and their words are no demonstrations, how shall he be assured that what they say is true? So that at the first he meets with an impregnable difficulty, and cannot know the Church but by such notes, which whether they be the notes of the Church he cannot possibly know. But let us suppose this *Isthmus* digged through, and that he is assured these are the notes of the true Church: How can he possibly be a competent Judge, which Society of Christians hath Title to these notes, and which hath not? Seeing this Trial of necessity requires a great sufficiency of knowledge of the monuments of Christian Antiquity, which no unlearned can have, because he that hath it cannot be unlearned. As for example, how shall he possibly be able to know whether the Church of *Rome* hath had a perpetual Succession of Visible Professors, which held always the same Doctrine which they now hold, without holding any thing to the contrary; unless he hath first examined, what was the Doctrine of the Church in the first Age, what in the second, and so forth? And whether this be not a more difficult work, than to stay at the first Age, and to examine the Church by the conformity of her Doctrine, with the Doctrine of the first Age, every man of ordinary understanding may Judge.

Let us imagine him advanced a step farther, and to know which is the Church: how shall he know what that Church hath Decreed, seeing the Church hath not been so careful in keeping of her Decrees, but that many are lost, and many corrupted? Besides, when even the Learned among you are not agreed concerning divers things, whether they be *De Fide* or not; how shall the unlearned do? Then for the sense of the Decrees, how can he be more capable of the understanding of them, then of plain Texts of Scripture, which you will not suffer him to understand? Especially, seeing the Decrees of divers *Popes* and Councils are conceived so obscurely, that the Learned cannot agree about the sense of them. And then they are written all in such Languages which the ignorant understand not, and therefore must of necessity rely herein upon the uncertain and fallible authority of some particular men, who inform them that there is such a Decree. And if the Decrees were Translated into Vulgar Languages, why the Translators should not be as fallible as you say the Translators of Scripture are, who can possibly imagine?

109. Lastly, how shall an unlearned man, or indeed any man, be assured of the certainty of that Decree, the certainty whereof depends upon suppositions which are impossible to be known whether they be true or no? For it is not the Decree of a Council, unless it be confirmed by a true *Pope*. Now the *Pope* cannot be a true *Pope* if he came in by Simony: which whether he did or no, who can answer me? He cannot be a true *Pope* unless he were Baptized, and Baptized he was not, unless the Minister had due Intention. So likewise he cannot be a true *Pope*, unless he were rightly ordained Priest, and that again depends upon the Ordainers secret Intention, and also upon his having the Episcopal Character. All which things, as I have formerly proved, depend upon so many uncertain suppositions, that no humane judgment can possibly be resolved in them. I conclude therefore, that not the learnedst man amongst you all, no not the *Pope* himself, can, according to the grounds you go upon, have any certainty,

certainty, that any Decree of any Council is good and valid, and consequently, not any assurance that it is indeed the Decree of a Council.

110. Ad §. 20.] C. M. *By referring Controversies to Scripture alone, all is finally reduced to the internal private Spirit.*

CHIL. If by a *private Spirit*, you mean, a particular persuasion that a Doctrine is true, which some men pretend, but cannot prove to come from the Spirit of God : I say, to refer Controversies to the Scripture, is not to refer them to this kind of private Spirit. For is there not a manifest difference between saying, *the Spirit of God tells me that this is the meaning of such a Text* (which no man can possibly know to be true, it being a secret thing) and between saying, *these and these Reasons I have to shew, that this or that is true Doctrine, or that this or that is the meaning of such a Scripture?* Reason being a publick and certain thing and exposed to all mens Trial and Examination. But now if by *private Spirit* you understand every Mans particular Reason, then your first and second inconvenience will presently be reduced to one, and shortly to none at all.

111. Ad §. 21.] C. M. *By taking the Office of Judicature from the Church, it is Conferred upon every particular Man.*

CHIL. And does not also giving the Office of Judicature to the Church, come to confer it upon every particular Man? For before any man believes the Church Infallible, must he not have reason to induce him to believe it to be so ? and must he not judge of those reasons, whether they be indeed good and firm, or Captious and Sophistical ? Or would you have all men believe all your Doctrine upon the Churches Infallibility, and the Churches Infallibility they know not why ? .

112. Secondly, supposing they are to be guided by the Church, they must use their own particular reason to find out which is the Church. And to that purpose you your selves give a great many Notes, which you pretend first to be Certain Notes of the Church, and then to be peculiar to your Church, and agreeable to none else;
but

but you do not so much as pretend, that either of those pretences is evident of it self, and therefore you go about to prove them both by reasons; and those reasons I hope every particular man is to judge of, whether they do indeed conclude and convince that which they are alledged for: that is, that these marks are indeed certain Notes of the Church, and then that your Church hath them, and no other.

113. One of these Notes, indeed the only Note of a true and uncorrupted Church, is conformity with Antiquity; I mean the most Ancient Church of all, that is the Primitive and Apostolick. Now how is it possible any man should examine your Church by this Note, but he must by his own particular judgment, find out what was the Doctrine of the Primitive Church, and what is the Doctrine of the present Church, and be able to answer all these Arguments which are brought to prove repugnance between them? otherwise he shall but pretend to make use of this Note for the finding the true Church, but indeed make no use of it, but receive the Church at a venture, as the most of you do; not one in a Hundred being able to give any tolerable reason for it. So that instead of reducing Men to particular reason, you reduce them to none at all, but to chance and passion, and prejudice and such other ways, which if they lead one to the Truth, they lead Hundreds, nay Thousands to Falshood. But it is a pretty thing to consider, how these men can blow Hot and Cold out of the same mouth to serve several purposes. Is there hope of gaining a Proselyte? Then they will tell you, God hath given every every man Reason to follow; and if the Blind lead the Blind, both shall fall into the Ditch. That it is no good reason for a mans Religion, that he was Born and brought up in it: For then a *Turk* should have as much reason to be a *Turk*, as a Christian to be a Christian. That every man hath a judgment of Discretion; which if they will make use of, they shall easily find: that the true Church hath always such and such marks, and that their Church has them, and no other but theirs. But then

then if any of theirs be perſuaded to a ſincere and ſufficient Trial of their Church, even by their own Notes of it, and to try whether they be indeed ſo conformable to Antiquity as they pretend, then their Note is changed: you muſt not uſe your own reaſon nor your judgment, but refer all to the Church, and believe her to be conformable to Antiquity, though they have no reaſon for it, nay though they have evident reaſon to the contrary. For my part I am certain that God hath given us our Reaſon to diſcern between Truth and Falſhood, and he that makes not this uſe of it, but believes things he knows not why, I ſay it is by chance that he believes the Truth, and not by choice: and that I cannot but fear, that God will not accept of this *Sacrifice of Fools*.

114. But you that would not have men follow their Reaſon, what would you have them to follow? their Paſſion? Or pluck out their eyes and go blindfold? *No*, you ſay *you would have them follow Authority*. On Gods name let them; we alſo would have them follow Authority; for it is upon the Authority of Univerſal Tradition, that we would have them believe Scripture. But then as for the Authority which you would have them follow, you will let them ſee reaſon why they ſhould follow it. And is not this to go a little about? to leave reaſon for a ſhort turn, and then to come to it again, and to do that which you condemn in others? It being indeed a plain impoſſibility for any man to ſubmit his reaſon but to reaſon: for he that does it to Authority, muſt of neceſſity think himſelf to have greater reaſon to believe that Authority. Therefore the confeſſion cited by *Brerely*, you need not think to have been extorted from *Luther* and the reſt. It came very freely from them, and what they ſay, you practiſe as much as they.

115. And whereas you ſay that *a Proteſtant admits of Fathers, Councils, Church, as far as they agree with Scripture, which upon the matter is himſelf*: I ſay you admit neither of them, nor the Scripture it ſelf, but only ſo far as it agrees with your Church: and your Church you admit becauſe you think you have reaſon to do ſo:

so that by you as well as by *Protestants* all is finally resolved into your own reason.

116. Nor do *Hereticks* only but *Romish Catholicks* also set up as many Judges, as there are Men and Women in the Christian World. For do not your Men and Women Judge your Religion to be true, before they believe it, as well as the Men and Women of other Religions? Oh but you say, *They receive it not because they think it agreeable to Scripture, but because the Church tells them so.* But then I hope they believe the Church because their own reason tells them they are to do so. So that the difference between a *Papist* and a *Protestant* is this, not that the one judges and the other does not judge, but that the one judges his guide to be infallible, the other his way to be manifest. *This same pernitious Doctrine is taught by* Brentius, Zanchius, Cartwright, *and others*. It is so in very deed: But it is taught also by some others, whom you little think of. It is taught by S. *Paul*, where he says, *Try all things, hold fast that which is good*. It is taught by S. *John*, in these words, *Believe not every Spirit, but try the Spirits whether they be of God or no*. It is taught by S. *Peter*, in these, *Be ye ready to render a reason of the hope that is in you*. Lastly, this very pernitious Doctrine is taught by our *Saviour*, in these words, *If the Blind lead the Blind, both shall fall into the Ditch*. And *why of your selves judge you not what is right?* All which speeches, if they do not advise men to make use of their Reason for the choice of their Religion, I must confess my self to understand nothing. Lastly, not to be infinite, it is taught by M. *Knot* himself, not in one Page only, or Chapter of his *Book*, but all his Book over; the very writing and publishing whereof, supposeth this for certain, that the Readers are to be Judges, whether his Reasons which he brings, be strong and convincing; of which sort we have hitherto met with none: or else captious, or impertinences, as indifferent men shall (as I suppose) have cause to judge them.

117. But you demand, *What good Statesmen would they be, who should ideate, or fancy such a Commonwealth, as these men have*

have framed to themselves a Church? Truly if this be all the fault they have, that they say, *Every man is to use his own judgment in the choice of his Religion, and not to believe this or that sense of Scripture, upon the bare Authority of any Learned man or men, when he conceives he has reasons to the contrary, which are of more weight than their Authority*: I know no reason, but notwithstanding all this, they might be as good Statesmen as any of the Society. But what has this to do with Common-wealths, where men are bound only to external obedience, unto the Laws and Judgments of Courts, but not to an internal approbation of them, no nor to conceal their Judgment of them, if they disapprove them? As if I conceived I had reason to mislike the Law of punishing simple Theft with Death, as Sir *Thomas Moore* did, I might profess lawfully my judgment, and represent my reasons to the King or Common-wealth in a Parliament, as Sir *Thomas Moore* did, without committing any fault, or fearing any punishment.

118. To that place of S. *Austin* you cite (lib. 32. cont. Faust. *You see that you go about to overthrow all Authority of Scripture, and that every mans mind may be to himself a Rule, what he is to allow or disallow in every Scripture:*) I shall need give no other Reply, but only to desire you to speak like an honest man, and to say, whether it be all one for a man, *to allow and disallow in every Scripture what he pleases,* which is, either to dash out of Scripture such Texts or such Chapters, because they cross his opinion? or to say (which is worse,) *Though they be Scripture they are not true?* Whether, I say, for a man thus to allow and disallow in Scripture what he pleases, be all one, and no greater fault, than to allow that sense of Scripture which he conceives to be true and genuine, and deduced out of the words, and to disallow the contrary? for Gods sake, Sir, tell me plainly; In those Texts of Scripture, which you alledge for the infallibility of your Church, do not you allow what sense you think true, and disallow the contrary? And do you not this by the direction of your private reason? If you do, why do you condemn it in others? If you do not, I pray you tell me what direction you follow? or whether you

follow

follow none at all? If none at all, this is like drawing Lots, or throwing the Dice for the choice of a Religion. If any other: I beseech you tell me what it is. Perhaps you will say, *the Churches Authority*; and that will be to dance finely in a round, thus, To believe the Churches Infallible Authority, because the Scriptures avouch it; and to believe that Scriptures say and mean so, because they are so expounded by the Church. Is not this for a Father to beget his Son, and the Son to beget his Father? For a foundation to support the house, and the house to support the foundation? Would not *Campian* have cryed out at it, *Ecce quos gyros, quos Mæandros*? And to what end was this going about, when you might as well at first have concluded the Church infallible because she says so; as thus to put in Scripture for a meer stale, and to say, the Church is infallible because the Scripture says so, and the Scripture means so because the Church says so, which is infallible? Is it not most evident therefore to every intelligent man, that you are enforced of necessity to do that your self, which so Tragically you declaim against in others? The Church, you say, is Infallible; I am very doubtful of it: How shall I know it? The Scripture you say affirms it, as in the 59. of *Esau, My spirit that is in thee, &c.* Well I confess I find there these words: but I am still doubtful, whether they be spoken of the Church of Christ: and if they be, whether they mean as you pretend. You say, the Church says so, which is infallible. Yea but that is the Question, and therefore not to be begged but proved. Neither is it so evident as to need no proof: otherwise why brought you this Text to prove it? Nor is it of such a strange quality, above all other Propositions, as to be able to prove it self. What then remains but that you say, Reasons drawn out of the Circumstances of the Text, will evince that this is the sense of it. Perhaps they will. But Reasons cannot convince me, unless I judge of them by my Reason; and for every man or woman to relie on that, in the choice of their Religion, and in the interpreting of Scripture, you say is a horrible absurdity; and therefore must neither make use of your own in this matter, nor desire me to make use of it.

119. But *Universal Tradition* (you say, and so do I too,) *is of it self credible: and that has in all Ages taught the Churches Infallibility with full consent.* If it have, I am ready to believe it. But that it has I hope you would not have me take upon your word: for that were to build my self upon the Church, and the Church upon You. Let then the Tradition appear; for a secret Tradition is somewhat like a silent Thunder. You will perhaps produce, for the confirmation of it, some sayings of some Fathers, who in every Age taught this Doctrine; (as *Gualterius* in his Chronology undertakes to do, but with so ill success, that I heard an able Man of your Religion profess, that *in the first three Centuries, there was not one Authority pertinent:*) but how will you warrant that none of them teach the contrary? Again, how shall I be assured that the places have indeed this sense in them? Seeing there is not one Father for 500 years after Christ, that does say in plain terms, *The Church of Rome is Infallible.* What, shall we believe your Church that this is their meaning? But this will be again to go into the Circle, which made us giddy before; To prove the Church Infallible because Tradition says so, Tradition to say so, because the Fathers say so, The Fathers to say so, because the Church says so, which is Infallible. Yea, *but reason will shew this to be the meaning of them.* Yes, if we may use our Reason, and rely upon it. Otherwise, as light shews nothing to the Blind, or to him that uses not his eyes; so reason cannot prove any thing to him that either has not, or uses not his reason to judge of them.

120. Thus you have excluded your self from all proof of your Churches Infallibility from Scripture or Tradition. And if you fly lastly to Reason it self for succour, may not it justly say to you, as *Jephte* said to his Brethren, *Ye have cast me out and banished me, and do you now come to me for succour?* But if there be no certainty in Reason, how shall I be assured of the certainty of those which you aledge for this purpose? Either I may judge of them, or not: if not, why do you propose them? If I may, why

do you say I may not, and make it such a monstrous absurdity, That men in the choice of their Religion should make use of their Reason? which yet, without all question, none but unreasonable men can deny, to have been the chiefest end why Reason was given them.

121. Ad §. 22.] An Heretick *he is* (saith D. Potter) *who opposeth any truth, which to be a Divine Revelation, he is convinced in Conscience by any means whatsoever: Be it by a Preacher or Lay-man, be it by reading Scripture, or hearing them read.* And from hence you infer, that he makes all these safe propounders of Faith. A most strange and illogical deduction! For may not a private man by evident reason convince another man, that such or such a Doctrine is Divine Revelation, and yet though he be a true propounder in this point, yet propound another thing falsely, and without proof, and consequently not be a safe propounder in every point? Your Preachers in their Sermons, do they not propose to men Divine Revelations, and do they not sometimes convince men in Conscience, by evident proof from Scripture, that the things they speak are Divine Revelations? And whosoever being thus convinced, should oppose this Divine Revelation, should he not be an *Heretick*, according to your own grounds, for calling Gods own Truth into question? And would you think your self well dealt with, if I should collect from hence, that you make every Preacher a safe, that is, an *infallible* Propounder of Faith? Be the means of Proposal what it will, sufficient or insufficient, worthy of credit, or not worthy, though it were, if it were possible, the barking of a Dog, or the chirping of a Bird, or were it the Discourse of the Devil himself, yet if I be, I will not say convinced, but persuaded, though falsly, that it is a Divine Revelation, and shall deny to believe it, I shall be a formal, though not a material *Heretick*. For he that believes, though falsly any thing to be Divine Revelation, and yet will not believe it to be true, must of necessity believe God to be false, which according to your own Doctrine, is the formality of an *Heretick*.

122. And

Scripture the only Rule for Judging Controversies. 135

122. And how it can be any way advantagious to Civil Government, that men without warrant from God should Usurp a Tyranny over other mens Consciences, and prescribe unto them without reason, and sometimes against reason, what they shall believe, you must shew us plainer if you desire we should believe. For to say, *Verily I do not see but that it must be so*, is no good demonstration. For whereas you say, *that a Man may be a passionate and Seditious Creature,* from whence you would have us infer, that he may make use of his interpretation to satisfie his Passion, and raise Sedition: There were some colour in this consequence, if we (as you do) made private men infallible interpreters for others; for then indeed they might lead Disciples after them, and use them as Instruments for their vile purposes: But when we say they can only interpret for themselves, what harm they can do by their passionate or seditious interpretations, but only endanger both their Temporal and Eternal happiness, I cannot imagine. For though we deny the *Pope* or Church of *Rome* to be an infallible Judge, yet we do not deny, but that there are Judges which may proceed with certainty enough against all Seditious Persons, such as draw men to disobedience either against Church or State, as well as against Rebels, and Traytors, and Thieves, and Murderers.

123. Ad §. 23.] The next § argues thus: *For many Ages there was no Scripture in the World: and for many more, there was none in many places of the World: yet men wanted not then and there some certain direction what to believe: Therefore there was then an Infallible Judge.* Just as if I should say, *York* is not my way from *Oxford* to *London*, therefore *Bristol* is: Or a Dog is not a Horse, therefore he is a Man. As if God had no other ways of revealing himself to men, but only by Scripture and an infallible Church. *S. *Chrysostome* and *Isidorus Pelusiota* conceived he might use other means. And S. *Paul* telleth us that the γνωστὸν τοῦ Θεοῦ *might be known by his Works*; and that *they had the Law written in their Hearts*. Either of these ways might make some faithful men without either necessity of Scripture or Church. 124. But

* See *Chrysost.* Hom. 1. in Mat. *Isidor.* Pelus. l. 3. ep. 106. and also *Basil.* in Ps. 28. and then you shall confess that by other means besides these, God did communicate himself unto men and made them receive and understand his Laws: see also to the same purpose *Heb.* 1. 1.

124. *But D.* Potter *says (you say,) In the Jewish Church there was a living Judge, indowed with an absolute infallible direction in cases of moment: as all points belonging to Divine Faith are.* And where was that infallible direction in the Jewish Church when they should have received Christ for their *Messias*, and refused him? Or perhaps this was not a case of moment. D. *Potter* indeed might say very well, not that the high Priest was infallible, (for certainly he was not) but that his determination was to be of necessity obeyed, though for the justice of it there was no necessity that it should be believed. Besides, it is one thing to say, that the living judge in the Jewish Church, had an infallible direction: another, that he was necessitated to follow this direction. This is the priviledge which you challenge. But it is that, not this, which the Doctor attributes to the *Jews*. As a man may truly say, the Wise men had an infallible direction to Christ, without saying or thinking that they were constrained to follow it, and could not do otherwise.

125. *But either the Church retains still her infallibility, or it was devested of it upon the receiving of Holy Scripture; which is absurd.* An Argument methinks like this, Either you have Horns or you have lost them: but you never lost them, therefore you have them still. If you say you never had Horns; so say I, for ought appears by your reasons, the Church never had infallibility.

126. *But some Scriptures were received in some places and not in others: therefore if Scriptures were the Judge of Controversies, some Churches had one Judge and some another.* And what great inconvenience is there in that, that one part of *England* should have one Judge, and another another? especially seeing the Books of Scripture which were received by those that received fewest, had as much of the Doctrine of Christianity in them, as they all had which were received by any; all the necessary parts of the Gospel being contained in every one of the four Gospels, as I have proved: So that they which had all the Books of the *New Testament* had nothing superfluous: For it was not superfluous but profitable, that the

same

same thing should be said divers times, and be testified by divers witnesses: And they that had but one of the four Gospels wanted nothing necessary: and therefore it is vainly inferred by you, that *with Months and Years, as new Canonical Scriptures grew to be published, the Church altered her rule of Faith and judge of Controversies.*

127. *Heresies*, you say, *would arise after the Apostles time and after the writing of Scriptures: These cannot be discovered, condemned and avoided, unless the Church be Infallible; Therefore there must be a Church infallible.* But I pray tell me, Why cannot *Heresies* be sufficiently discovered, condemned, & avoided, by them which believe Scripture to be the rule of Faith? If Scripture be sufficient to inform us what is the Faith, it must of necessity be also sufficient to teach us what is *Heresie*: seeing *Heresie* is nothing but a manifest deviation from, and an opposition to the Faith. That which is straight will plainly teach us what is crooked; and one contrary cannot but manifest the other. If any one should deny, that there is a God: That this God is omnipotent, omniscient, good, just, true, merciful, a rewarder of them that seek him, a punisher of them that obstinately offend him; that Jesus Christ is the Son of God, and the Saviour of the World: that it is he by obedience to whom men must look to be saved: If any man should deny either his Birth, or Passion, or Resurrection, or Ascension, or sitting at the right Hand of God: his having all Power given him in Heaven and Earth: That it is he whom God hath appointed to be Judge of the Quick and the Dead: that all men shall Rise again at the last Day: That they which believe and repent shall be saved: That they which do not believe or repent shall be damned: If a man should hold, that either the keeping of the *Mosaical* Law is necessary to Salvation: or that good works are not necessary to Salvation: In a word, if any man should obstinatly contradict the truth of any thing plainly delivered in Scripture, who does not see, that every one which believes the Scripture, hath a sufficient means to discover, and condemn, and avoid that *Heresie*, without

any need of an infallible guide? If you say, that *the obscure places of Scripture contain matters of Faith*: I answer, that it is a matter of Faith to believe that the sense of them, whatsoever it is, which was intended by God is true; for he that does not do so calls Gods Truth into question. But to believe this or that to be the true sense of them, or, to believe the true sense of them, and to avoid the false, is not necessary either to Faith or Salvation. For if God would have had his meaning in these places certainly known, how could it stand with his wisdom, to be so wanting to his own will and end, as to speak obscurely? or how can it consist with his Justice, to require of men to know certainly the meaning of those words, which he himself hath not revealed? Suppose there were an absolute Monarch, that in his own absense from one of his Kingdoms, had written Laws for the Government of it, some very plainly, and some very ambiguously, and obscurely, and his Subjects should keep those that were plainly written with all exactness, and for those that were obscure, use their best diligence to find his meaning in them, and obey them according to the sense of them which they conceived? should this King either with justice or wisdom be offended with these Subjects, if by reason of the obscurity of them, they mistook the sense of them, and fail of performance, by reason of their Error?

128. But, *It is more useful & fit*, you say, *for the deciding of Controversies, to have besides an infallible Rule to go by, a living infallible Judge to determine them: & from hence you conclude, that certainly there is such a Judge*. But why then may not another say, that it is yet more useful for many excellent purposes, that all the Patriarchs should be infallible, than that the *Pope* only should? Another, that it would be yet more useful, that all the Archbishops of every Province should be so, than that the Patriarchs only should be so. Another, that it would be yet more useful, if all the Bishops of every Diocess were so. Another, that it would be yet more available, that all the Parsons of every Parish should be so. Another,

ther, that it would be yet more excellent, if all the Fathers of Families were so. And lastly, another, that it were much more to be desired that every Man and every Woman were so: just as much as the prevention of Controversies, is better than the decision of them, and the prevention of Heresies better than the condemnation of them; and upon this ground conclude, by your own very consequence, That not only a general Council, nor only the Pope, but all the Patriarchs, Archbishops, Bishops, Pastors, Fathers, nay all the men in the World are infallible. If you say now, as I am sure you will, that this conclusion is most gross, and absurd against sense and experience, then must also the ground be false, from which it evidently and undeniably follows, *viz.* that, That course of dealing with men seems always more fit to Divine Providence, which seems most fit to humane reason.

129. And so likewise, That there should men succeed the Apostles, which could shew themselves to be their successors, by doing of Miracles, by speaking all kind of Languages, by delivering men to Satan, as S. *Paul* did *Hymenæus*, and the incestuous *Corinthian*, it is manifest in human reason it were incomparably more fit and useful for the decision of Controversies, than that the successour of the Apostles should have none of these gifts, and for want of the signs of Apostleship, be justly questionable whether he be his successor or no: and will you now conclude, That the Popes have the gift of doing Miracles, as well as the Apostles had?

130. It were in all reason very useful and requisite, that the Pope should, by the assistance of Gods Spirit, be freed from the vices and passions of men, lest otherwise, the Authority given him for the good of the Church, he might imploy (as divers Popes you well know have done) to the disturbance, and oppression and mischief of it. And will you conclude from hence, That Popes are not subject to the sins and passions of other men? That there never have been ambitious, covetous, lustful, tyrannous Popes.

131. Who sees not that for mens direction it were much more beneficial for the Church, that Infallibility should

be setled in the Popes Person, than in a general Council: That so the means of deciding Controversies might be speedy, easie and perpetual, whereas that of general Councils is not so. And will you hence infer, that not the Church Representative, but the Pope is indeed the infallible Judge of Controversies? certainly if you should, the *Sorbon* Doctors would not think this a good conclusion.

132. It had been very commodious (one would think) that, seeing either Gods pleasure was the Scripture should be translated, or else in his Providence he knew it would be so, that he had appointed some men for this business, and by his Spirit assisted them in it, that so we might have Translations as Authentical as the Original: yet you see God did not think fit to do so.

133. It had been very commodious (one would think) that the Scripture should have been, at least for all things necessary, a Rule, plain and perfect: And yet you say, it is both imperfect and obscure, even in things necessary.

134. It had been most requisite (one would think) that the Copies of the Bibles, should have been preserved free from variety of Readings, which makes men very uncertain in many places, which is the Word of God, and which is the error or presumption of man: and yet we see God hath not thought fit so to provide for us.

135. Who can conceive, but that an Apostolick Interpretation of all the difficult places of Scripture, would have been strangely beneficial to the Church, especially there being such danger in mistaking the sense of them, as is by you pretended, and God in his providence foreseeing that the greatest part of Christians, would not accept of the Pope for the Judge of Controversies? And yet we see God hath not so ordered the matter.

136. Who doth not see, that supposing the Bishop of *Rome*, had been appointed Head of the Church, and Judge of Controversies, that it would have been infinitely beneficial to the Church, perhaps as much as all the rest of the Bible, that in some Book of Scripture which was to be undoubtedly received, this one Proposition had been set down in Terms, *The Bishops of* Rome *shall be always Monarchs*

narchs of the Church, and they either alone, or with their adherents, the Guides of Faith, and the Judges of Controversies that shall arise amongst Christians? This, if you will deal ingenuously, you cannot but acknowledge; for then all true Christians would have submitted to him, as willingly as to Christ himself, neither needed you and your fellows, have troubled your self to invent so many Sophisms for the proof of it. There would have been no more doubt of it among Christians, than there is of the Nativity, Passion, Resurrection or Ascension of Christ. You were best now rub your forehead hard, and conclude upon us, that because this would have been so useful to have been done, therefore it is done. Or if you be (as I know you are) too ingenuous to say so, then must you acknowledge, that the ground of your Argument, which is the very ground of all these absurdities, is most absurd; and that it is our duty to be humbly thankful for those sufficient, nay abundant means of Salvation, which God hath of his own goodness granted us: and not conclude, he hath done that which he hath not done, because forsooth, in our vain judgments it seems convenient he should have done so.

137. But you demand *what repugnance there is betwixt infallibility in the Church, and existence of Scripture, that the production of the one must be the destruction of the other?* Out of which words I can frame no other argument for you than this. *There is no Repugnance between the Scriptures existence, and the Churches infallibility, therefore the Church is infallible.* Which consequence will then be good, when you can shew, that nothing can be untrue, but that only which is impossible; that whatsoever may be done, that also is done. Which, if it were true, would conclude both you and me to be infallible, as well as either your Church, or Pope: in as much as there is no more repugnance between the Scriptures existence and our infallibility, than there is between theirs.

138. Obj. *But if Protestants will have the Scripture alone for their Judge, let them first produce some Scripture, affirming, that by the entrance thereof, infallibility went out of the Church.* Ans.

Anſ. This Argument put in form runs thus. No Scripture affirms that by the entring thereof, infallibility went out of the Church: Therefore there is an infallible Church, and therefore the Scripture alone is not Judge, that is, the Rule to judge by. But as no Scripture affirms that by the entring of it, Infallibility went out of the Church, ſo neither do we, neither have we any need to do ſo. But we ſay, that it continued in the Church even together with the Scriptures, ſo long as Chriſt and his Apoſtles were living, and then departed: God in his providence having provided a plain and infallible Rule, to ſupply the defect of living and infallible Guides.

141. *But the Jewiſh Church retained Infallibility in her ſelf; and therefore it is unjuſt to deprive the Church of Chriſt of it.*

Anſ. That the Jews had ſometimes an infallible miraculous direction from God, in ſome caſes of moment, he doth affirm and had good warrant: but that the Synagogue was abſolutely Infallible, he no where affirms, and therefore it is unjuſtly and unworthily done of you to obtrude it upon him. And indeed how can the Infallibility of the Synagogue be conceived, but only by ſetling it in the High Prieſt, and the company adhering and ſubordinate unto him? And whether the High Prieſt was Infallible, when he believed not Chriſt to be the *Meſſias*, but condemned and excommunicated them that ſo profeſſed, and cauſed him to be crucified for ſaying ſo, I leave it to Chriſtians to judge. But then ſuppoſe God had been ſo pleaſed to do as he did not, to appoint the Synagouge an infallible guide: Could you by your rules of Logick conſtrain him, to appoint ſuch a one to Chriſtians alſo, or ſay unto him, that, in wiſdom he could not do otherwiſe? Vain man that will be thus always tying God to your imaginations! It is well for us that he leaves us not without directions to him, but if he will do this ſometime by living Guides, ſometime by written Rules, what is that to you? may not he do what he will with his own?

144. *Ad* §. 24 Neither is this Diſcourſe (if you mean your Concluſion, that *Your Church is the infallible Judge*

in Controversies) confirmed by *Irenæus* at all (*Iren.* l.3.c. 3.) For neither has *Irenæus* one syllable to this purpose, neither can it be deduced out of what he says, with any colour of consequence. For first in saying, *What if the Apostles had not left Scripture, ought we not to have followed the Order of Tradition?* And in saying, *That to this Order many Nations yield assent, who believe in Christ, having Salvation written in their hearts, by the Spirit of God, without Letters or Ink, and diligently keeping ancient Tradition*: Doth he not plainly shew, that the Tradition he speaks of, is nothing else, but the very same that is written: nothing but to believe in Christ? To which, whether Scripture alone to them that believe it, be not a sufficient guide, I leave it to you to judge. And are not his words just as if a man should say, If God had not given us the light of the Sun, we must have made use of Candles and Torches: If we had had no Eyes, we must have felt out our way: If we had no Leggs, we must have used Crutches. And doth not this in effect import, that while we have the Sun, we need no Candles? While we have our Eyes, we need not feel out our way? While we enjoy our Leggs, we need not Crutches? And by like reason, *Irenæus* in saying, *If we had no Scripture, we must have followed Tradition, and they that have none, do well to do so*, doth he not plainly import, that to them that have Scripture, and believe it, Tradition is unnecessary? which could not be, if the Scripture did not contain evidently the whole tradition. Which whether *Irenæus* believed or no, these words of his may inform you, *Non enim per alios* &c. *we have received the disposition of our Salvation from no others, but from them, by whom the Gospel came unto us. Which Gospel truly, the Apostles first preached, and afterwards by the will of God, delivered in writing to us, to be the Pillar and Foundation of our Faith.* Upon which place *Bellarmine*'s two observations, and his acknowledgment ensuing upon them, are very considerable, and as I conceive, as home to my purpose as I would wish them. His first *Notandum* is, *That in the Christian Doctrin, some things are simply necessary for the Salvation of all men; as the knowledge of the Articles of the Apostles*

Bellarm. de verbo Dei L. 4. c. 11.

Apostles Creed; and *besides the knowledge, of the ten Commandments, and some of the Sacraments.* Other things not so *necessary, but that a man may be saved, without the explicit knowledge and belief, and profession of them.* His Second Note is, *That those things which were simply necessary, the Apostles were wont to preach to all men; But of other things not all to all, but something to all, to wit, those things which were profitable for all, other things only to Prelats and Priests.* These things premised, he acknowledgeth, *That all those things were written by the Apostles, which are necessary for all, and which they were wont openly to preach to all; But that other things were not all written: And therefore, when* Irenæus *says that the Apostles wrote what they Preach in the World, it is true,* saith he, *and not against Traditions, because they preached not to the People all things, but only those things, which were necessary or profitable for them.*

145. So that at the most, you can infer from hence, but only a suppositive necessity of having an infallible Guide, and that grounded upon a false supposition, In case we had no Scripture, but an absolute necessity hereof, and to them who have and believe the Scripture, which is your assumption, cannot with any colour from hence be concluded, but rather the contrary.

146. Neither because (as he says) it was *then easie to receive the Truth from Gods Church, then,* in the Age next after the Apostles, Then, when all the ancient and Apostolick Churches were at an agreement about the Fundamentals of Faith: Will it therefore follow that now, 1600 years after, when the ancient Churches are divided almost into as many Religions as they are Churches, every one being the Church to it self, and heretical to all other, that it is as easie, but extremely difficult or rather impossible, to find the Church first independently of the true Doctrin, and then to find the truth by the Church.

148. Neither will the *Apostles depositing with the Church, all things belonging to truth,* be any proof that the Church shall certainly keep this *depositum,* entire, and sincere, without adding to it, or taking from it; for this whole *depositum* was committed to every particular Church, nay, to every

every particular Man, which the Apostles converted. And yet no man, I think, will say, that there was any certainty, that it should be kept whole and inviolate by every man, and every Church. It is apparent out of Scripture, it was committed to *Timothy*, and by him consigned to other faithful men: and yet S. *Paul* thought it not superfluous, earnestly to exhort him to the careful keeping of it: which exhortation you must grant had been vain and superfluous, if the not keeping of it had been impossible. And therefore though *Irenæus* says, *The Apostles fully deposited in the Church all truth*, yet he says not, neither can we infer from what he says, that the Church should always infallibly keep this *depositum*, entire without the loss of any truth, and sincere without the mixture of any falshood.

149. Ad §. 25.] *C. M.* proceeds and tells us, *That beside all this, the Doctrine of* Protestants *is destructive of it self. For either they have certain and infallible means not to Err in interpreting; or not. If not, Scripture to them cannot be a sufficient ground for infallible Faith: If they have, and so cannot Err in interpreting Scripture, then they are able with infallibility to hear and determine all Controversies of Faith; and so they may be, and are Judges of Controversies, although they use the Scripture as a Rule. And thus against their own Doctrine, they constitute another Judge of Controversies besides Scripture alone.*

C. H. And may not we with as much reason substitute Church and *Papists*, instead of Scripture and *Protestants*, and say unto you, Besides all this, the Doctrine of *Papists* is destructive of it self. For either they have certain and infallible means not to Err, in the choice of the Church, and interpreting her decrees, or they have not: If not, then the Church to them cannot be a sufficient (but meerly a phantastical) ground for infallible Faith, nor a meet Judge of Controversies: (For unless I be infallibly sure that the Church is infallible, how can I be upon her Authority infallibly sure, that any thing she says is infallible?) If they have certain infallible means, and so cannot Err in the choice of their Church, and in interpreting her decrees, then they are able with Infallibility to hear, examine, and determine all Controversies of Faith, although they pretend to make the Church their Guide, And thus against their own Doctrine, they constitute another Judge of Controversies, besides the Church alone. Nay every one makes himself a chooser of his own Religion, and of his own sense of the Churches decrees, which very thing in *Protestants* they so highly condemn: and so in judging others, condemn themselves.

150. Neither in saying thus have I only cried quittance with you: but that you may see how much you are in my debt, I will shew unto you, that for your Sophism against our way, I have given you a Demonstration against yours. First, I say, your Argument against us, is a transparent fallacy. The first part of it lies thus: *Protestants* have no means to interpret, without Error, obscure and ambiguous places of Scripture; therefore plain places of Scripture cannot be to them a sufficient ground of Faith. But though we pretend not to certain means of not Erring, in interpreting all Scripture, particularly such places as are obscure and ambiguous, yet this methinks should be no impediment but that we may have certain means of not Erring in and about the sense of those places, which are so plain and clear that they need no Interpreters; and in such we say our Faith is contained. If you ask me how I can be sure that I know the true meaning of these places? I ask you again, can you be sure that you understand what I, or any man else says? They that heard our Saviour and the Apostles Preach, could they have sufficient assurance, that they understood at any time, what they would have them do? if not, to what end did they hear them? If they could, why may we not be as well assured, that we understand sufficiently, what we conceive plain in their writings?

151. Again I pray tell us, whether you do certainly know the sense of these Scriptures, with which you pretend you are led to the knowledg of your Church? If you do not, how know you that there is any Church Infallible, and that these are the Notes of it, and that,

this

Scripture the only Rule for Judging Controversies.

this is the Church that hath these Notes? If you do, then give us leave to have the same means, and the same abilities to know other plain places, which you have to know these. For if all Scripture be obscure, how come you to know the sense of these places? If some places of it be plain, why should we stay here?

152. And now, to come to the other part of your dilemma; in saying, *If they have certain means, and so cannot Err,* methinks you forget your self very much, and seem to make no difference, between, having certain means to do a thing, and the actual doing of it. As if you should conclude, because all men have certain means of Salvation, therefore all men certainly must be saved, and cannot do otherwise; as if whosoever had a Horse must presently get up and Ride; Whosoever had means to find out a way, could not neglect those means and so mistake it, God be thanked, that we have sufficient means to be certain enough of the truth of our Faith. But the Priviledge of not being in possibility of Erring, that we challenge not, because we have as little reason as you to do so: and you have none at all. If you ask, seeing we may possibly Err, how can we be assured we do not? I ask you again, seeing your Eye-sight may deceive you, how can you be sure you see the Sun, when you do see it? Perhaps you may be in a dream, and perhaps you, and all the men in the World have been so, when they thought they were awake, and then only awake, when they thought they Dreamt. But this I am sure of, as sure as that God is good, that he will require no impossibilities of us: not an Infallible, nor a certainly-unerring belief, unless he hath given us certain means to avoid Error; and if we use those which we have, will never require of us, that we use that which we have not.

153. Now from this mistaken ground, that it is all one to have means of avoiding Error, and to be in no danger nor possibility of Error; You infer upon us as an absurd conclusion, *That we make our selves able to determine Controversies of Faith with Infallibility, and Judges of Controversies.* For the latter part of this inference, we ac-

knowledge and embrace it. We do make our selves Judges of Controversies: that is, we do make use of our own understanding in the choice of our Religion. But this, if it be a crime, is common to us with you, (as I have proved above) and the difference is, not that we are choosers, and you not choosers, but that we, as we conceive, choose wisely, but you being wilfully blind choose to follow those that are so too; not remembering what our Saviour hath told you, *when the Blind lead the Blind, both shall fall into the Ditch*. But then again I must tell you, you have done ill to confound together, Judges, and infallible Judges; unless you will say, either that we have no Judges in our Courts of Civil judicature, or that they are all Infallible.

154. Thus have we cast off your dilemma, and broken both the Horns of it. But now my retortion lies heavy upon you, and will not be turned off. For first you content not your selves with a moral certainty of the things you believe, nor with such a degree of assurance of them, as is sufficient to produce obedience to the condition of the new Covenant, which is all that we require. Gods Spirit, if he please, may Work more, and certainty of adherence beyond a certainty of evidence. But neither God doth, nor man may require of us, as our Duty, to give a greater assent to the conclusion than the premises deserve; to build an infallible Faith upon Motives that are only highly credible, and not infallible, as it were a great and heavy building upon a Foundation that hath not strength proportionable. But though God require not of us such unreasonable things, You do, and tell men they cannot be saved, unless they believe your Proposals with an infallible Faith. To which end they must believe also your Propounder, your Church, to be simply Infallible. Now how is it possible for them to give a rational assent to the Churches infallibility, unless they have some infallible means to know that she is infallible? Neither can they infallibly know the infallibility of this means, but by some other, and so on for ever: unless they can dig so deep as to come at length to the Rock, that is, *to settle all upon something evident of it self*, which

is

is not so much as pretended. But the last resolution of all is into Motives, which indeed upon examination will scarce appear probable, but are not so much as avouched to be any more than very credible. For example, if I ask you why you do believe Transubstantiation? What can you answer, but because it is a Revelation of the prime Verity. I demand again, how can you assure your self or me of that, being ready to embrace it if it may appear to be so? And what can you say, but that you know it to be so, because the Church says so, which is Infallible. If I ask, what mean You by your Church? You can tell me nothing, but the Company of Christians which adhere to the *Pope*. I demand then lastly: Why should I believe this Company to be the Infallible Propounder of Divine Revelation? And then you tell me, that there are many Motives to induce a Man to this belief. But are these Motives lastly infallible? No say you, but very credible. Well, let them pass for such, because now we have not leisure to examine them. Yet methinks seeing the Motives to believe the Churches infallibility, are only very credible, it should also be but as credible that your Church is Infallible, and as credible, and no more, perhaps somewhat less, that her Proposals, particularly Transubstantiation, are Divine Revelations. And methinks You should require only a Moral, and Modest assent to them, and not a Divine as you call it, and Infallible Faith. But then of these Motives to the Churches Infallibility, I hope you will give us leave to consider, and judge whether they be indeed Motives, and sufficient; or whether they be not Motives at all, or not sufficient; or whether these Motives or Inducements to your Church be not impeached, and opposed with Compulsives, and enforcements, from it; or lastly, whether these Motives which You use, be not indeed only Motives to Christianity, and not to *Popery*: give me leave for distinction sake to call your Religion so. If we may not judge of these things, how can my judgment be moved with that which comes not within its cognizance? If I may, then at least I am to be a Judge of all these

Con-

Controversies. 1. Whether every one of these Motives be indeed a Motive to any Church? 2. If to some, whether to Yours? 3. If to Yours, whether sufficient, or insufficient? 4. Whether other Societies have not as many, and as great Motives to draw me to them? 5. Whether I have not greater reason to believe you do Err, than that you cannot? And now Sir I pray let me trouble You with a few more Questions. Am I a sufficient Judge of these Controversies, or no? If of these, why shall I stay here, why not of others? Why not of all? Nay doth not the true examining of these few, contain and lay upon me the examination of all? What other Motives to your Church have you, but your Notes of it? *Bellarmine* gives some 14. or 15. And one of these fifteen contains in it the examination of all Controversies, and not only so, but of all uncontroverted Doctrines. For how shall I, or can I know the Church of *Romes* conformity with the Ancient Church, unless I know first what the Ancient Church did hold, and then what the Church of *Rome* doth hold; and lastly, whether they be conformable, or if in my judgment they seem not conformable, I am then to think the Church of *Rome* not to be the Church, for want of the Note which she pretends is proper, and perpetual to it. So that for ought I can see, Judges we are and must be of all sides, every one for himself, and God for us all.

155. §. 26.] C. M. *I ask, whether this Assertion (Scripture alone is Judge of all Controversies in Faith) be a Fundamental point of Faith or no?*

CHIL. I answer; This assertion, that *Scripture alone is Judge of all Controversies in Faith*, if it be taken properly, is neither a Fundamental nor Unfundamental point of Faith, nor no point of Faith at all, but a plain falshood. It is not *a Judge of Controversies but a Rule to Judge them by*; and that not an absolutely perfect Rule, but as perfect as a written Rule can be; which must always need something else, which is either evidently true, or evidently credible to give attestation to it, and that in this case is Universal Tradition. So that Universal Tradition

dition is the Rule to judge all Controversies by. But then because nothing besides Scripture, comes to us with as full a stream of Tradition as Scripture, Scripture alone, and no unwritten Doctrine, nor no Infallibility of any Church, having attestation from Tradition truly Universal; for this reason we conceive, as the Apostles persons while they were living were the only Judges of Controversies, so their Writings, now they are dead, are the only Rule for us to judge them by: There being nothing unwritten, which can go in upon half so fair Cards, for the Title of Apostolick Tradition, as these things which by the confession of both Sides are not so: I mean *the Doctrine of the Millinaries, and of the necessity of the Eucharist for Infants.*

156. Yet when we say, the Scripture is the only Rule to Judge all Controversies by, methinks you should easily conceive, that we would be understood of all those that are possible to be Judged by Scripture, and of those that arise among such as believe the Scripture. For if I had a Controversie with an *Atheist* whether there were a God or no, I would not say, that the Scripture were a Rule to judge this by: seeing that doubting whether there be a God or no, he must needs doubt whether the Scripture be the Word of God: or if he does not, he grants the Question, and is not the man we speak of. So likewise, if I had a Controversie about the Truth of Christ with a *Jew*, it would be vainly done of me, should I press him with the Authority of the *New Testament* which he believes not, until out of some Principles common to us both, I had perswaded him that it is the Word of God. The *New Testament* therefore while he remains a *Jew* would not be a fit Rule to decide this Controversie; In as much as that which is doubted of it self, is not fit to determine other doubts. So likewise if there were any that believed Christian Religion, and yet believed not the Bible to be the Word of God, though they believed the matter of it to be true, (which is no impossible supposition, for I may believe a Book of S. *Austines*, to contain nothing but the Truth of God, and yet not to have
been

been inspired by God himself,) against such men therefore there were no disputing out of the Bible; because nothing in question can be a proof to it self. When therefore we say the Scripture is a sufficient means to determine all Controversies, we say not this, either to *Atheists, Jews, Turks,* or such Christians (if there be any such) as believe not Scripture to be the Word of God. But among such men only, as are already agreed upon this, That the Scripture is the Word of God, we say all Controversies that arise about Faith, are either not at all decidable and consequently not necessary to be believed one way or other, or they may be determined by Scripture. In a Word, That all things necessary to be believed are evidently contained in Scripture, and what is not there evidently contained, cannot be necessary to be believed. And our reason hereof is convincing; because nothing can Challenge our belief, but what hath descended to us from Christ by Original and Universal Tradition: Now nothing but Scripture hath thus descended to us, Therefore nothing but Scripture can Challenge our belief. Now then to come up closer to you, and to answer to your Question, not as you put it, but as you should have put it: I say, That this position, *Scripture alone is the Rule whereby they which believe it to be Gods Word are to judge all Controversies in Faith,* is no fundamental point. Though not for your Reasons: For your first and strongest reason you see is plainly voided and cut off by my stating of the Question as I have done, and supposing in it that the parties at variance are agreed about this, That the Scripture is the Word of God; and consequently that this is none of their Controversies. To your second, That *Controversies cannot be ended without some living Authority,* We have said already, that necessary Controversies may be and are decided. And if they be not ended, this is not through defect of the Rule, but through the default of Men. And for these that cannot thus be ended, it is not necessary they should be ended. For if God did require the ending of them, he would have provided some certain means for the ending of them. And to your Third, I say, that

your

your pretence of using these means is but hypocritical: for you use them with prejudice, and with a setled resolution not to believe any thing which these means happily may suggest into you, if it any way cross your pre-conceived perswasion of your Churches infallibility. You give not your selves liberty of judgment in the use of them, nor suffer your selves to be led by them to the Truth, to which they would lead you, would you but be as willing to believe this consequence, Our Church doth oppose Scripture, therefore it doth err, therefore it is not Infallible, as you are resolute to believe this, The Church is Infallible, therefore it doth not err, and therefore it doth not oppose Scripture, though it seem to do so never so plainly.

157. You pray, but it is not that God would bring you to the true Religion, but that he would confirm you in your own. You confer places, but it is that you may confirm, or colour over with plausible disguises your erroneous doctrine, not that you may judge of them and forsake them if there be reason for it. You consult the Originals, but you regard them not when they make against your Doctrin or Translation.

159. Notwithstanding, though not for these reasons, yet for others, I conceive this Doctrin not Fundamental: Because if a man should believe Christian Religion wholly, and entirely, and live according to it, such a man, though he should not know or not believe the Scripture to be a Rule of Faith, no nor to be the Word of God, my opinion is he may be saved; and my reason is, because he performs the entire condition of the new Covenant, which is, that we believe the matter of the Gospel, and not that it is contained in these or these Books. So that the Books of Scripture are not so much the objects of our Faith, as the instruments of conveying it to our understanding; and not so much of the being of the Christian Doctrin, as requisite to the well-being of it. *Iræneus* tells us (as M. K. acknowledgeth) of some barbarous Nations, that *believed the Doctrin of Christ, and yet believed not the Scripture to be the Word of God, for they never heard of it, and Faith comes by hearing*: But these barbarous people might be saved:

therefore men might be saved without believing the Scripture to be the Word of God; much more without believing it to be a Rule, and a perfect Rule of Faith. Neither doubt I, but if the Books of Scripture had been proposed to them by the other parts of the Church, where they had been before received, and had been doubted of, or even rejected by those barbarous Nations, but still by the bare belief and practice of Christianity, they might be saved: God requiring of us under pain of damnation, only to believe the verities therein contained, and not the divine Authority of the Books wherein they are contained. Not but that it were now very strange and unreasonable, if a man should believe the matter of these Books, and not the Authority of the Books: and therefore if a man should profess the not believing of these, I should have reason to fear he did not believe that. But there is not always an equal necessity for the belief of those things, for the belief whereof there is an equal reason. We have I believe as great reason to believe there was such a man as *Henry the VIII. King of England*, as that *Jesus Christ* suffered under *Pontius Pilate:* yet this is necessary to be believed, and that is not so. So that if any man should doubt of or disbelieve that, it were most unreasonably done of him, yet it were no mortal sin, nor no sin at all: God having no where commanded men under pain of damnation to believe all which reason induceth them to believe. Therefore as an Executor, that should perform the whole Will of the dead, should fully satisfie the Law, though he did not believe that Parchment to be his written Will, which indeed is so: So I believe, that he who believes all the particular doctrines which integrate Christianity, and lives according to them, should be saved, though he neither believed nor knew that the Gospels were written by the Evangelists, or the Epistles by the Apostles.

160. This discourse whether it be rational and concluding or no, I submit to better judgment; But sure I am, that the corollary which you draw from this position, *that this point is not Fundamental*, is very inconsequent; that is, *that we are uncertain of the truth of it*, because we say the whole

whole Church, much more particular Churches and private men may err in points not Fundamental. A pretty Sophism, depending upon this Principle, that whosoever possibly may err, he cannot be certain that he doth not err. And upon this ground, what shall hinder me from concluding, that seeing you also hold, that neither particular Churches, nor private men are Infallible even in Fundamentals, that even the Fundamentals of Christianity, remain to you uncertain? A Judge may possibly err in judgment, can he therefore never have assurance that he hath judged right? A Traveller may possibly mistake his way, must I therefore be doubtful whether I am in the right way from my Hall to my Chamber? Or can our *London* Carrier have no certainty, in the middle of the day, when he is sober and in his wits, that he is in the way to *London*? These you see are right worthy consequences, and yet they are as like your own, as an Egg to an Egg, or Milk to Milk.

163. Ad §. 27.] C. M. *S.* Austin *plainly affirms that to oppose the Churches definitions is to resist God himself (speaking of the Controversie of Rebaptization* de Unit. Eccl. cap. 22.) where he saith *that Christ bears witness to his Church, and whosoever refuseth to follow the practice of the Church, doth resist our Saviour himself, who by his testimony recommends the Church, &c.*

CHIL. I Answer, First that in many things you will not be tried by S. *Augustines* judgment, nor submit to his authority; not concerning Appeals to *Rome*, not concerning Transubstantiation, not touching the use and worshiping of Images, not concerning the State of Saints souls before the day of judgment, not touching the Virgin *Maries* freedom from actual and original sin, not touching the necessity of the Eucharist for Infants, not touching the damning Infants to Hell that die without Baptism, not touching the knowledge of Saints departed, not touching Purgatory, not touching the fallibility of Councils, even general Councils, not touching perfection and perspicuity of Scripture in matters necessary to Salvation, not touching Auricular Confession, not touching the half Communion, not touching Prayers in an unknown tongue; In these things, I say, you will not stand to S. *Austines* judgment, and therefore can with no reason or equity require us to do so in this matter. 2. To S. *Augustine* in heat of disputation against the *Donatists*, and ransacking all places for arguments against them, we oppose S. *Austine* out of this heat, delivering the doctrine of Christianity calmly, and moderately; where he says, *In iis quæ apertè posita sunt in sacris Scripturis, omnia ea reperiuntur quæ continent fidem, moresque vivendi.* 3. We say, he speaks not of the *Roman* but the *Catholick Church*, of far greater extent, and therefore of far greater credit and authority than the *Roman* Church. 4. He speaks of a point not expressed, but yet not contradicted by Scripture; whereas the errors we charge you with, are contradicted by Scripture. 5. He says not that Christ has recommended the Church to us for *an Infallible definer of all emergent controversies*, but for a *credible witneß of Ancient Tradition*. Whosoever therefore refuseth to follow the practice of the Church (understand *of all places and ages*) though he be thought to resist our Saviour, what is that to us, who cast off no practices of the Church, but such as are evidently post-nate to the time of the Apostles, and plainly contrary to the practice of former and purer times. Lastly it is evident, and even to impudence it self undeniable, that upon this ground, of believing all things taught by the present Church as taught by Christ, Error was held, for example, the necessity of the Eucharist for Infants, and that in S. *Austines* time, and that by S. *Austine* himself: and therefore without controversie this is no certain ground for truth, which may support falshood as well as truth.

164. To the Argument wherewith you conclude, I Answer, That though the visible Church shall always without fail propose so much of Gods revelation, as is sufficient to bring men to Heaven, for otherwise it will not be the visible Church, yet it may sometimes add to this revelation things superfluous, nay hurtful, nay in themselves damnable, though not unpardonable; and sometimes take from it things very expedient and profitable, and therefore

it is possible, without sin, to resist in some things the Visible Church of Christ. But you press us farther, and demand, *what Visible Church was extant, when* Luther *began, whether it were the* Roman *or* Protestant *Church?* As if it must of necessity either be *Protestant* or *Roman*, or *Roman* of necessity, if it were not *Protestant!* yet this is the most usual fallacy of all your disputers, by some specious Arguments to perswade weak men that the Church of *Protestants* cannot be the true Church; and thence to infer, that without doubt it must be the *Roman.* But why may not the *Roman* be content to be a part of it, and the *Grecian* another? And if one must be the whole, why not the *Greek* Church, as well as the *Roman?* there being not one Note of your Church which agrees not to her as well as to your own; unless it be, that she is poor, and oppressed by the *Turk,* and you are in glory and splendor.

CHAP. III.

The ANSWER to the Third CHAPTER.

Wherein it is maintained, That the distinction of points Fundamental *and not* Fundamental, *is in this present Controversie good and pertinent: And that the Catholick Church may err in the latter kind of the said points.*

1. THis distinction is imployed by *Protestants* to many purposes, and therefore if it be pertinent and good, (as they understand and apply it) the whole Edifice built thereon, must be either firm and stable, or if it be not, it cannot be for any default in this distinction.

2. *If you object to them discords in matter of faith without any means of agreement,* They will answer you, that they want not good and solid means of agreement in matters necessary to salvation, *viz.* Their belief of all those things which are plainly and undoubtedly delivered in Scripture; which who so believes, must of necessity believe all things necessary to salvation: and their mutual suffering one another,

another, *to abound in their several sense*, in matters not plainly and undoubtedly there delivered. And for their agreement in all Controversies of Religion, either they have means to agree about them, or not: If you say they have, why did you before deny it? If they have not means, why do you find fault with them, for not agreeing?

3. You will say, that their fault is, that by *remaining* Protestants *they exclude themselves from the means of agreement, which you have*, and which by submission to your Church they might have also. But if you have means of agreement, the more shame for you that you still disagree. For who, I pray, is more inexcusably guilty, for the omission of any duty; they that either have no means to do it, or else know of none they have, which puts them in the same case as if they had none: or they which profess to have an easie and expedite means to do it, and yet still leave it undone? *If you had been blind* (saith our *Saviour* to the *Pharisees*) *you had had no sin, but now you say you see, therefore your sin remaineth.*

4. If you say, you *do agree in matters of Faith*, I say this is ridiculous: for you define matters of Faith to be those wherein you agree. So that to say, you agree in *matters of Faith*, is to say, you agree in those things wherein you do agree. And do not *Protestants* do so likewise? Do not they agree in those things, wherein they do agree?

5. But *you are all agreed that only those things wherein you do agree are matters of Faith*. And *Protestants* if they were wise, would do so too. Sure I am they have reason enough to do so: seeing all of them agree with explicite Faith in all those things, which are plainly and undoubtedly delivered in Scripture, that is, in all which God hath plainly revealed: and with an implicite Faith, in that sense of the whole Scripture which God intended whatsoever it was. Secondly, That which you pretend is false; for else, why do some of you hold it against Faith, to take or allow the *Oath of Allegiance*, others as learned and honest as they, that it is against Faith and unlawful to refuse it and allow the refusing of it? Why do some of you hold, that it is *de Fide*, that the Pope is Head of the Church by divine Law,

Scripture the only Rule for Judging Controversies.

Law, others the contrary? Some hold it *de Fide*, that the Blessed Virgin was free from Actual sin, others that it is not so. Some, that the *Popes* indirect power over Princes in temporalties is *de Fide*, Others the contrary. Some, that it is Universal Tradition, and consequently *de Fide*, that the *Virgin Mary* was conceived in original sin, others the contrary.

6. But what shall we say now, if you be not agreed touching your pretended means of agreement, how then can you pretend to Unity either Actual or Potential more than *Protestants* may ? Some of you say, the *Pope* alone without a Council may determine all Controversies : But others deny it. Some, that a General Council without a *Pope* may do so : Others deny this. Some, Both in conjunction are infallible determiners : Others again deny this. Lastly, some among you, hold the Acceptation of the decrees of Councils by the Universal Church to be the only way to decide Controversies : which others deny, by denying the Church to be Infallible. And indeed what way of ending Cotroversies can this be, when either part may pretend, that they are part of the Church, and they receive not the decree, therefore the whole Church hath not received it ?

7. Again, Means of agreeing differences are either Rational and well grounded and of Gods appointment, or voluntary and taken up at the pleasure of men. Means of the former nature, we say, you have as little as we. For where hath God appointed, that the *Pope*, or a Council, or a Council confirmed by the *Pope*, or that Society of Christians which adhere to him, shall be the *Infallible Judge of Controversies.* I desire you to shew any one of these Assertions plainly set down in Scripture, (as in all Reason a thing of this nature should be) or at least delivered with a full consent of Fathers, or at least taught in plain terms by any one Father for four Hundred years after *Christ*. And if you cannot do this (as I am sure you cannot) and yet will still be obtruding your selves upon us for our Judges, who will not cry out, ---*perisse frontem de rebus*? that you have lost all modesty ?

8. But

8. But then for means of the other kind, such as yours are, we have great abundance of them. For besides all the ways which you have devised, which we may make use of when we please, we have a great many more, which you yet have never thought of, for which we have as good colour out of Scripture as you have for yours. For first, we could if we would, try it by Lots, whose Doctrine is true, and whose false. And you know it is written, ᵃ *The Lot is cast into the Lap, but the whole disposition of it is from the Lord.* 2. We could refer them to the King, and you know it is written: ᵇ *A Divine sentence is in the Lips of the King, his mouth transgresseth not in judgment.* ᶜ *The Heart of the King is in the hand of the Lord.* We could refer the matter to any assembly of Christians assembled in the name of Christ, seeing it is written, ᵈ *where two or three are gathered together in my name, there am I in the midst of them.* We may refer it to any Priest, because it is written, ᵉ *The Priests Lips shall preserve knowledge.* ᶠ *The Scribes and Pharisees sit in* Moses *Chair,* &c. To any Preacher of the Gospel, to any Pastor, or Doctor, for to every one of them Christ hath promised ᵍ *he will be with them alwaies even to the end of the World*: and of every one of them it is said, ʰ *He that heareth you heareth me,* &c. To any Bishop or Prelate, for it is written, ⁱ *Obey your Prelates,* and again ᵏ *he hath given Pastors and Doctors,* &c. *lest we should be carried about with every wind of Doctrine.* To any particular Church of Christians, seeing it is a particular Church which is called ˡ *The House of God, a Pillar and ground of Truth*: and seeing of any particular Church it is written ᵐ *He that heareth not the Church let him be unto thee as a Heathen or a Publican.* We might refer it to any man that prays for Gods Spirit, for it is written, ⁿ *Every one that asketh receiveth*: and again, ᵒ *If any man want Wisdom let him ask of God, who giveth to all men liberally, and upbraideth not.* Lastly, we might refer it to the *Jews,* for without all doubt of them it is written, ᵖ *my Spirit that is in thee,* &c. All these means of agreement, whereof not any one but hath as much probability from Scripture,

ᵃ Prov. 16. 33.
ᵇ Prov. 16. 10.
ᶜ Prov. 21. 1.
ᵈ Mat. 18. 20.
ᵉ Mat. 2. 7.
ᶠ Mat. 25. 2.
ᵍ Mat. 28. 20.
ʰ Luk. 10. 16.
ⁱ Heb. 13. 17.
ᵏ Eph. 4. 11.
ˡ 1 Tim. 3. 15.
ᵐ Mat. 18. 17.
ⁿ Mat. 7. 8.
ᵒ Jam. 1. 5.
ᵖ Isai. 59. 21.

into Fundamental and not Fundamental.

pture, as that which you obtrude upon us, offer themselves upon a sudden to me: happily many more might be thought on, if we had time, but these are enough to shew, that would we make use of voluntary and devised means to determine differences, we had them in great abundance. And if you say these would fail us, and contradict themselves; so, as we pretend, have yours. There have been *Popes* against *Popes*: Councils against Councils: Councils confirmed by *Popes*, against Councils confirmed by *Popes*: Lastly, the Church of some Ages against the Church of other Ages.

9. Lastly, whereas you find fault, *That* Protestants *upbraided with their discords, answer that they differ only in points not Fundamental,* I desire you tell me whether they do so, or do not so; If they do so, I hope you will not find fault with the Answer: If you say they do not so, but in points Fundamental also; then they are not members of the same Church one with another, no more than with you: And therefore why should you object to any of them, their differences from each other, any more than to your selves, their more and greater differences from you?

10. But *they are convinced sometime even by their own confessions, that the Ancient Fathers taught divers points of Popery: and then they reply, those Fathers may nevertheless be saved, because those Errors were not Fundamental.* And may not you also be convinced by the confessions of your own men, that the Fathers taught divers points held by *Protestants* against the Church of *Rome*, and divers against *Protestants* and the Church of *Rome*? Do not your Purging *Indexes*, clip the Tongues, and seal up the Lips of a great many for such confessions? And is not the above cited confession of your *Doway* Divines, plain and full to the same purpose? And do not you also, as freely as we, charge the Fathers with Errors, and yet say they were saved? Now what else do we understand by an *unfundamental* Error, but such a one with which a man may possibly be saved? So that still you proceed in condemning others for your own faults, and urging argu-

Y ments

ments against us, which return more strongly upon your selves.

11. But your will is, *we should remember that Christ must alwaies have a visible Church.* Answ. Your pleasure shall be obeyed, on condition you will not forget, that there is a difference between perpetual Visibility, and perpetual Purity. As for the answer, which you make for us, true it is, we believe the *Catholick Church cannot perish,* yet that she may, and did Err in points not Fundamental; and that *Protestants* were obliged to forsake these Errors of the Church, as they did, though not the Churh for her Errors, for that they did not, but continued still members of the Church. For it is not all one (though you perpetually confound them) *to forsake the Errors of the Church,* and to *forsake the Church* : or to *forsake the Church in her Errors,* and *simply to forsake the Church* : No more than it is for me to renounce my Brothers or my Friends Vices or Errors, and to renounce my Brother or my Friend. The former then was done by *Protestants,* the latter was not done. Nay not only not from the *Catholick,* but not so much as from the *Roman,* did they separate *per omnia,* but only in those practices which they conceived superstitious or impious. If you would at this time propose a form of Liturgy, which both Sides hold lawful, and then they would not joyn with you in this Liturgy, you might have some colour then to say, they renounce your communion absolutely. But as things are now ordered, they cannot joyn with you in prayers, but they must partake with you in unlawful practices, and for this reason, they *(not absolutely, but thus far)* separate from your communion. And this, I say, they were obliged to do under pain of damnation. *Not as if it were damnable to hold an Error not damnable,* but because it is damnable outwardly to profess and maintain it, and to joyn with others in the practice of it, when inwardly they did not hold it. Now had they continued in your communion, that they must have done, *viz.* have professed to believe and externally practised your Errors, whereof they were

were convinced that they were Errors: which though the matters of the Errors had been not necessary, but only profitable, whether it had not been damnable dissimulation and Hypocrisie, I leave it to you to Judge. You your self tell us within two pages after this, *that you are obliged never to speak any one least lie against your knowledge*, §, 2. now what is this but to live in a perpetual lie?

12. As for that which in the next place you seem so to wonder at, That *both* Catholicks *and* Protestants, *according to the opinion of* Protestants, *may be saved in their several professions, because forsooth, we both agree in all Fundamental points*: I Answer, this proposition so crudely set down, as you have here set it down, I know no *Protestant* will justifie. For you seem to make them teach, that it is an indifferent thing, for the attainment of Salvation, whether a man believe the Truth or the Falshood; and that they care not in whether of these Religions a man live or die, so he die in either of them: whereas all that they say is this, That those amongst you which want means to find the Truth and so die in Error, or use the best means they can with industry, and without partiality to find the Truth, and yet die in Error, these men, thus qualified, notwithstanding these Errors may be saved. Secondly, for those that have means to find the Truth, and will not use them, they conceive, though their case be dangerous, yet if they die with a general repentance for all their sins, known and unknown, their Salvation is not desperate. The Truths which they hold, of Faith in Christ, and Repentance, being as it were an Antidote against their Errors, and their negligence in seeking the Truth. Especially seeing by confession of both sides we agree in much more than is simply, and indispensably necessary to salvation.

13. *Obj. But seeing we make such various use of this distinction, is it not prodigiously strange that we will never be induced to give in a particular Catalogue what points be Fundamental?*

Answ.

Answ. And why I pray is it so *prodigiously strange* that we give no answer to an unreasonable demand? God himself hath told us, ^a *That where much is given, much shall be required; where little is given, little shall be required.* To Infants, Deaf-men, Mad-men, nothing for ought we know, is given, and if it be so, of them *nothing* shall be required. Others perhaps may have means only given them to believe, ^b *That God is, and that he is a rewarder of them that seek him*; and to whom thus much only is given, to them it shall not be damnable, that they believe but only thus much. Which methinks is very manifest from the Apostle, in the *Epist. to the Heb.* where having first said, *that without Faith it is impossible to please God*, he subjoyns as his reason, *for whosoever cometh unto God, must believe that God is, and that he is a rewarder of them that seek him.* Where in my opinion, this is plainly intimated, that this is the *minimum quòd sic*, the lowest degree of Faith, wherewith, in men capable of Faith, God will be pleased: and that with this lowest degree he will be pleased, where means of rising higher are deficient. Besides, if without this belief, *that God is, and that he is a rewarder of them that seek him*, God will not be pleased, then his will is that we should believe it. Now his will it cannot be, that we should believe a falshood: It must be therefore true, that he is a rewarder of them that seek him. Now it is possible that they which never heard of Christ, may seek God, therefore it is true that even they shall please him, and be rewarded by him; I say rewarded, not with bringing them immediately to Salvation without Christ, but with bringing them according to his good pleasure, first, to Faith in Christ, and so to Salvation. To which belief the story of *Cornelius* in the 10. *chap. of the Acts* of the Apostles, and S. *Peters* Words to him, are to me a great inducement. For first it is evident he believed not in Christ, but was a meer Gentile, and one that knew not but men might be worshiped, and yet we are assured *that his Prayers and Alms* (even while he was in that state) *came up for a memorial before God; That his Prayer was heard, and his Alms had in remembrance in the sight of God.* v. 4. that upon this, *Then fearing God*

<small>a Luk. 12. 48.</small>

<small>b Heb. 6. 11.</small>

into Fundamental and not Fundamental.

God and working righteousness, (such as it was) *he was accepted with God.* But how accepted? Not to be brought immediately to Salvation, but to be promoted to a higher degree of the knowledge of Gods will: For so it is in the 4.& 5. v. *Call for Simon whose sirname is* Peter, *he shall tell thee what thou oughtest to do,* and at the 33. verf. *We are all here present before God, to hear all things that are commanded thee of God.* So that though even in his Gentilism, he was accepted in his present state, yet if he had continued in it, and refused to believe in Christ after the sufficient Revelation of the Gospel to him, and Gods will to have him believe it, he that was accepted before, would not have continued accepted still; for then that condemnation had come upon him, *than light was come unto him, and he loved Darkness more that Light.* So that (to proceed a step farther) to whom Faith in Christ is sufficiently propounded, as necessary to Salvation, to them it is simply necessary and Fundamental to believe in Christ, that is, to expect remission of sins, and Salvation from him, upon the performance of the conditions he requires; among which conditions one is, that we believe what he has revealed, when it is suficiently declared, to have been revealed by him: For by doing so, *we set to our Seal, that God is true, and that Christ was sent by him.* Now that may be sufficiently declared to one (all things considered,) which, (all things considered) to another is not sufficiently declared: and consequently that may be Fundamental and necessary to one, which to another is not so. Which Variety of circumstances, makes it impossible to set down an exact Catalogue of Fundamentals, and proves your request as reasonable, as if you should desire us (according to the Fable) to make a Coat to fit the Moon in all her changes; or to give you a Garment that will fit all statures; Or to make you a Dyal to serve all Meridians; or to design particularly, what Provision will serve an Army for a Year: whereas there may be an Army of Ten Thousand, there may be of 100000. And therefore without seting down a Catalogue of Fundamentals in particular (because none that can be given, can Universally

serve

serve for all men, God requiring more of them to whom he gives more, and less of them to whom he gives less) we must content our selves by a general description to tell you what is Fundamental. And to warrant us in doing so, we have your own example, §. 19. where being engaged to give us a Catalogue of Fundamentals, instead thereof you tell us only in general, *that all is Fundamental, and not to be disbelieved under pain of damnation, which the Church hath defined.* As you therefore think it enough to say in general, *that all is Fundamental which the Church has defined,* without setting down in particular a compleat Catalogue of all things, which in any Age the Church has defined (which I believe you will not undertake to do, and if you do, it will be contradicted by your Fellows:) So in reason you might think it enough for us also to say in general, *that it is sufficient for any mans Salvation, to believe that the Scripture is true, and contains all things necessary for Salvation; and to do his best endeavour to find and believe the true sense of it:* without delivering any particular Catalogue of the Fundamentals of Faith.

14. Neither *doth the want of such a Catalogue* leave us in such a *perplexed uncertainty* as you pretend. For though perhaps we cannot exactly distinguish in the Scripture, what *is revealed because it is necessary,* from what is *necessary consequently and accidentally, meerly because it is revealed:* yet we are sure enough, that all that is necessary any way is there, and therefore in believing all that is there, we are sure to believe all that is necessary. And if we Err from the true and intended sense of some, nay of many obscure or ambiguous Texts of Scripture, yet we may be sure enough, that we Err not damnably: because, if we do indeed desire and endeavour to find the Truth, we may be sure we do so, and as sure that it cannot consist with the revealed goodness of God, to damn him for Error, that desires and indeavours to find the Truth.

15. Ad §. 2.] The effect of this Paragraph (for as much as concerns us) is this, *that for any man to deny belief*

to any one thing be it great or small known by him, to be revealed by Almighty God for a truth, is in effect to charge God with falshood: for it is to say that God affirms that to be Truth, which he either knows to be not a Truth, or which he doth not know to be a Truth: and therefore without all Controversie this is a damnable sin. To this I subscribe with Hand and Heart: adding withal, that not only he which knows, but he which believes (nay though it be erroneously) any thing to be revealed by God, and yet will not believe it, nor assent unto it, is in the same case, and commits the same sin of derogation from Gods most perfect and pure Veracity.

16. Ad §. 3.] I said purposely (*known by himself, and believes himself*) For as, without any disparagement of a mans Honesty, I may believe something to be false, which he affirms, of his certain knowledge to be true, provided I neither know nor believe that he has so affirmed: So without any the least dishonour to Gods Eternal never failing Veracity, I may doubt of, or deny some truth revealed by him, if I neither know nor believe it to be revealed by him.

19. But *ignorance of what we are expresly bound to know, is it self a fault, and therefore cannot be an excuse*: and therefore if you could shew the *Protestants* differ in those points, the truth whereof (which can be but one) they were bound expresly to know, I should easily yield that one side must of necessity be in a mortal Crime. But for want of proof of this, you content your self only to say it; and therefore I also might be contented only to deny it, yet I will not, but give a reason for my denial. And my reason is, because our obligation expresly to know any Divine Truth, must arise from Gods manifest revealing of it, and his revealing unto us that he has revealed it, and that his will is, we should believe it: Now in the points controverted among *Protestants*, he hath not so dealt with us, therefore he hath not laid any such obligation upon us. The major of this Syllogism is evident, and therefore I will not stand to prove it. The minor also will be evident to him that

con-

considers, that in all the Controversies of *Protestants*, there is a seeming conflict of Scripture with Scripture, Reason with Reason, Authority with Authority: which how it can consist with the manifest revealing of the truth of either Side, I cannot well understand. Besides, though we grant that Scripture, Reason and Authority, were all on one side, and the apparences of the other side all answerable: yet if we consider the strange power that education and prejudices instilled by it, have over even excellent understandings, we may well imagine, that many truths which in themselves are revealed plainly enough, are yet to such or such a man, prepossest with contrary opinions, not revealed plainly. Neither doubt I but God, who knows whereof we are made, and what passions we are subject unto, will compassionate such infirmities, and not enter into judgment with us for those things, which, all things considered, were unavoidable.

20. *Obj. But till Fundamentals* (say you) *be sufficiently proposed* (*as revealed by God*) *it is not against Faith to reject them*; *or rather it is not possible prudently to believe them: And points unfundamental being thus sufficiently proposed as divine Truths, may not be denied*; *Therefore you conclude there is no difference between them:* *Answ*. A Circumstantial point, may by accident become Fundamental, because it may be so proposed that the denial of it, will draw after it the denial of this Fundamental truth, *that all which God says is true*. Notwithstanding in themselves there is a main difference between them: *Points Fundamental being those only which are revealed by God, and commanded to be Preach'd to all, and believed by all. Points circumstantial being such, as though God hath revealed them, yet the Pastors of the Church are not bound under pain of Damnation particularly to teach them unto all men every where, and the People may be securely ignorant of them.*

21. *Obj*. You say, *Not Erring in points Fundamental, is not sufficient for the preservation of the Church; because any Error maintained by it against Gods Revelation is destructive*. I answer. If you mean against Gods Revelation known by

into Fundamental and not Fundamental.

by the Church to be so, it is true; but impossible that the Church should do so, for *ipso Facto* in doing it, it were a Church no longer. But if you mean against some Revelation, which the Church by error thinks to be no Revelation, it is false. The Church may ignorantly disbelieve such a Revelation, and yet continue a Church; which thus I prove. That the Gospel was to be preached to all Nations, was a Truth revealed before our Saviours Ascension, in these words, *Go and teach all Nations. Mat.* 29. 19. Yet through prejudice or inadvertence, or some other cause, the Church disbelieved it, as it is apparent out of the 11. and 12. Chap. of the *Acts*, until the conversion of *Cornelius*, and yet was still a Church. Therefore to disbelieve some divine Revelation, not knowing it to be so, is not destructive of salvation, or of the being of the Church. Again, It is a plain Revelation of God, that ª the Sacrament of the Eucharist *should be administred in both kinds:* and ᵇ that the publick Hymns and *Prayers of the Church should be in such a language as is most for edification*; yet these Revelations the Church of *Rome* not seeing, by reason of the veil before their eyes, their Churches supposed infallibility, I hope the denial of them shall not be laid to their charge, no otherwise than as *building hay and stubble on the Foundations, not overthrowing the Foundation it self.*

ª 1 Cor. 11. 2.

ᵇ 1 Cor. 14, 15, 16. 26.

24. Ad §. 5. This Paragraph, if it be brought out of the Clouds, will I believe have in it these Propositions. 1. *Things are distinguished by their different natures.* 2. *The Nature of Faith is taken, not from the matter believed, for then they that believed different matters should have different Faiths, but from the Motive to it.* 3. *This Motive is Gods Revelation.* 4. *This Revelation is alike for all objects.* 5. *Protestants disagree in things equally revealed by God: Therefore they forsake the formal motive of Faith: and therefore have no faith nor unity therein.* Which is truly a very proper and convenient argument to close up a weak discourse, wherein both the Propositions are false for matter, confused and disordered for the form, and the conclusion utterly inconsequent. First for the second Proposition, who knows not that the Essence of all Habits (and therefore of Faith

among the rest) is taken from their Act, and their Object? If the Habit be general, from the Act and Object in general, if the Habit be special, from the Act and Object in special. Then for the motive to a thing, that it cannot be of the Essence of the thing to which it moves, who can doubt, that knows that a motive is an efficient cause: and that the efficient is always extrinsecal to the effect? For the fourth, that *Gods Revelation is alike for all Objects,* It is ambiguous: and if the sense of it be, that his Revelation is an equal Motive to induce us to believe all objects revealed by him, it is true, but impertinent: If the sense of it be, that all objects revealed by God are alike (that is, alike plainly and undoubtedly) revealed by him, it is pertinent, but most untrue. Witness the great diversity of Texts of Scripture, whereof some are so plain and evident, that no man of ordinary sense can mistake the sense of them. Some are so obscure and ambiguous, that to say this or this is the certain sense of them, were high presumption. For the 5. *Protestants disagree in things equally revealed by God!* In themselves perhaps, but not equally to them: whose understandings by reason of their different Educations are fashioned, and shaped for the entertainment of various Opinions, and consequently some of them, more inclined to believe such a sense of Scripture, others to believe another; which to say that God will not take into his consideration in judging mens Opinions, is to disparage his goodness. But to what purpose is it, that these things are equally revealed to both, (as the light is equally revealed to all blind men,) if they be not fully revealed to either? The sense of this Scripture, *Why are they then baptized for the dead?* and this, *He shall be saved, yet so as by fire,* and a thousand others, is equally revealed to you and to another interpreter, that is certainly to neither. He now conceives one sense of them, and you another; and would it not be an excellent inference, if I should conclude now as you do; That you forsake the formal motive of Faith, which is Gods Revelation, and consequently lose all faith and unity therein? So likewise the *Jesuits* and *Dominicans,* the *Franciscans* and *Dominicans* disagree about things
equally

equally revealed by Almighty God: and seeing they do so, I beseech you let me understand, why this reason will not exclude them as well as Protestants *from all faith and unity therein?* Thus you have failed of your undertaking in your first part of your Title, and that is a very ill *omen*, especially in points of so streight mutual dependance, that we shall have but slender performance in your second assumpt. Which is, *That the Church is Infallible in all her Definitions, whether concerning points Fundamental, or not Fundamental.*

26. Ad §. 9. 10, 11. I grant that the Church *cannot without damnable sin, either deny any thing to be true, which she knows to be Gods truth:* or propose *any thing as his truth, which she knows not to be so.* But that she may not do this by ignorance or mistake, and so without damnable sin, that you should have proved, but have not. But, say you *this excuse cannot serve: for if the Church be assisted only for points fundamental, she cannot but know that she may err in points not fundamental.* Ans. It does not follow, unless you suppose, that the Church knows that she is assisted no farther. But if, being assisted only so far, she yet did conceive by error her assistance absolute and unlimited, or if knowing her assistance restrained to fundamentals, she yet conceived by error, that she should be guarded, from proposing any thing but what was fundamental, then the consequence is apparently false. *But at least she cannot be certain that she cannot err, and therefore cannot be excused from headlong and pernicious temerity in proposing points not fundamental, to be believed by Christians as matters of Faith.* Ans. Neither is this destruction worth any thing; unless it be understood of such fundamental points, as she is not warranted to propose by evident Text of Scripture. Indeed if she propose such, as *matters of Faith certainly true,* she may well be questioned, *Quo Warranto?* She builds without a foundation, and *says thus saith the Lord, when the Lord doth not say so:* which cannot be excused from rashness and high presumption; such a presumption, as an Embassador should commit, who should say in his Masters name that for which he hath no commission. Of the same nature,

nature, I say, but of a higher strain: as much as the King of Heaven, is greater than any earthly King. But though she may err in some points not fundamental, yet may she have certainty enough in proposing others; as for example, these, *That Abraham begat Isaac*, that *S. Paul had a Cloak*, that *Timothy was sick*; because these, though not fundamental, *i. e.* no essential parts of Christianity, yet are evidently, and undeniably set down in Scripture, and consequently, may be without all rashness proposed by the Church as certain divine Revelations. Neither is your Argument concluding when you say, *If in such things she may be deceived, she must be always uncertain of all such things.* For my sense may sometimes possibly deceive me, yet I am certain enough that I see what I see, and feel what I feel. Our Judges are not infallible in their judgments, yet are they certain enough, that they judge aright, and that they proceed according to the evidence that is given, when they condemn a Thief, or a Murderer to the Gallows. A Traveller is not always certain of his way, but often mistaken; and does it therefore follow that he can have no assurance that *Charing-Cross* is his right way from the *Temple* to *White-Hall* ? The ground of your error here, is your not distinguishing, between actual certainty and absolute infallibility. Geometricians are not infallible in their own Science: yet they are very certain of those things, which they see demonstrated. And Carpenters are not infallible, yet certain of the straightness of those things which agree with their Rule and Square. So though the Church be not infallibly certain, that in all her definitions, whereof some are about disputable and ambiguous matters, she shall proceed according to her Rule, yet being certain of the infallibility of her Rule, and that in this or that thing she doth manifestly proceed according to it, she may be certain of the Truth of some particular Decrees, and yet not certain that she shall never decree but what is true.

27. Ad §. 12. Obj. *But if the Church may err in points not fundamental, she may err in proposing Scripture, and so we cannot be assured whether she have not been deceived already.*

Ans.

Anf. The Church may err in her propofition or cuftody of the Canon of Scripture, if you underftand by the Church, any prefent Church of one denomination, for example, the *Roman*, the *Greek*, or fo. Yet have we fufficient certainty of Scripture, not from the bare teftimony of any prefent Church, but from Univerfal Tradition, of which the teftimony of any prefent Church is but a little part. So that here you fall into the Fallacy, *à dicto fecundum quid ad dictum fimpliciter.* For in effect this is the fenfe of your Argument: Unlefs the Church be infallible, we can have no certainty of Scripture from the authority of the Church: Therefore unlefs the Church be infallible, we can have no certainty hereof at all. As if a man fhould fay; If the Vintage of *France* mifcarry, we can have no Wine from *France*: Therefore if that Vintage mifcarry we can have no Wine at all. And for the incorruption of Scripture, I know no other rational affurance we can have of it, than fuch as we have of the incorruption of other ancient Books, that is, the confent of ancient Copies: fuch I mean *for the kind,* though it be far *greater for the degree of it.* And if the Spirit of God give any man any other affurance hereof, this is not rational and difcurfive, but fupernatural and infufed. An affurance it may be to himfelf, but no argument to another. As for the Infallibility of the Church, it is fo far from being a proof of the Scriptures incorruption, that no proof can be pretended for it, but incorrupted places of Scripture: which yet are as fubject to corruption as any other, and more likely to have been corrupted (if it had been poffible) than any other, and made to fpeak as they do, for the advantage of thofe men, whofe ambition it hath been a long time, to bring all under their authority. Now then, if any man fhould prove the Scriptures uncorrupted, becaufe the Church fays fo which is infallible: I would demand again touching this very thing, that there is an infallible Church, feeing it is not of it felf evident, how fhall I be affured of it? And what can he anfwer, but that the Scripture fays fo in thefe and thefe places? Hereupon I would ask him, how fhall I be affured, that the Scriptures are

are incorrupted in those places? seeing it is possible, and not altogether improbable, that these men, which desire to be thought infallible, when they had the government of all things in their own hands, may have altered them for their purpose. If to this he answer again, that the Church is infallible, and therefore cannot do so. I hope it would be apparent, that he runs round in a circle, and proves the Scriptures incorruption, by the Churches infallibility, and the Churches infallibility by the Scriptures incorruption, and that is in effect the Churches infallibility, by the Churches infallibility, and the Scriptures incorruption by the Scriptures incorruption.

28. Now for your observation, that *some Books, which were not always known to be Canonical, have been afterwards received for such. But never any book or syllable defined for Canonical, was afterwards questioned or rejected for Apocryphal:* I demand, touching the first sort, whether they were commended to the Church by the Apostles as Canonical or not? If not, seeing the whole Faith was preached by the Apostles to the Church, and seeing after the Apostles, the Church pretends to no new Revelations, how can it be an Article of Faith to believe them Canonical? And how can you pretend, that your Church which makes this an Article of Faith, is so assisted as not to propose any thing as a divine Truth which is not revealed by God? If they were, how then is the Church an infallible keeper of the Canon of Scripture, which hath suffered some Books of Canonical Scripture, to be lost? and others to lose for a long time their being Canonical, at least, the necessity of being so esteemed, and afterwards, as it were by the law of *Postliminium* hath restored their Authority and Canonicalness unto them? If this was delivered by the Apostles to the Church, the point was sufficiently discussed, and therefore your Churches omission to teach it for some ages, as an article of faith, nay degrading it from the number of articles of faith, and putting it among disputable problems, was surely not very laudable. If it were not revealed by God to the Apostles, and by the Apostles to the Church, then can it be no Revelation, and therefore

fore her presumption in propoſing it as ſuch, is inexcuſable.

29. And then for the other part of it, *that never any book or syllable defined for Canonical, was afterwards queſtioned or rejected for Apocryphal:* Certainly it is a bold alleveration, but extreamly falſe. For I demand; The Book of *Eccleſiaſticus* and *Wiſdom*, the *Epiſtle of S. James*, and *to the Hebrews*, were they by the Apoſtles approved for Canonical, or no? If not, with what face dare you approve them, and yet pretend that all your doctrin is Apoſtolical? Eſpecially ſeeing it is evident that this point is not deducible by rational diſcourſe from any other defined by them. If they were approved by them, this I hope was a ſufficient definition: and therefore you were beſt rub your forehead hard, and ſay, that theſe Books were never queſtioned. But if you do ſo, then I ſhall be bold to ask you, what Books you meant in ſaying before, *Some Books which were not always known to be Canonical, have been afterwards received?* Then for the Book of *Macchabees*, I hope you will ſay, it was defined for Canonical before S. *Gregories* time: and yet he, lib. 19. Moral. c. 13. citing a teſtimony out of it, prefaceth to it after this matter, *Concerning which matter we do not amiſs if we produce a teſtimony out of Books although not Canonical, yet ſet forth, for the edification of the Church. For Eleazar in the Book of Machabees,* &c. Which if it be not to reject it from being Canonical, is without queſtion, at leaſt to queſtion it. Moreover, becauſe you are ſo punctual, as to talk of words and ſyllables, I would know whether before *Sixtus Quintus* his time, your Church had a defined Canon of Scripture, or not? If not, then was your Church ſurely a moſt vigilant keeper of Scripture, that for 1500. years had not defined what was Scripture, and what was not. If it had, then I demand, was it *that*, ſet forth by *Sixtus*, or *that*, ſet forth by *Clement*, or a *third* different from both? If it were that ſet forth by *Sixtus*, then is it now condemned by *Clement*: if that of *Clement*, it was condemned I ſay, but ſure you will ſay contradicted and queſtioned by *Sixtus*; If different from both, then was it queſtioned and condemned

by

by both, and still lies under the condemnation. But then lastly, suppose it had been true, *That both some Book not known to be Canonical had been received,* and that *never any after receiving had been questioned:* How had this been a sign that the Church is infallibly assisted by the Holy Ghost? In what mood or figure, would this conclusion follow out of these Premises? Certainly your flying to such poor signs, as these are, is to me a great sign, that you labour with penury of better arguments: and that, thus to catch at shadows and bulrushes, is a shrewd sign of a sinking cause.

30. Ad §. 13. We are told here, *That the general promises of Infallibility to the Church, must not be restrained only to points fundamental: Because then the Apostles words and writings may also be so restrained.*

Ans. This also may be done, but if it be done, may easily be confuted. It is done to our hand in this very Paragraph, by five words taken out of Scripture, *All Scripture is divinely inspired.* Shew but as much for the Church: Shew where it is written, *That all the decrees of the Church are divinely inspired*; and the Controversie will be at an end. Besides, there is not the same reason for the Churches absolute Infallibility, as for the Apostles and Scriptures. For if the Church fall into error, it may be reformed by comparing it with the rule of the Apostles doctrine and Scripture. But if the Apostles have erred in delivering the doctrine of Christianity, to whom shall we have recourse, for the discovering and correcting their error? Again, there is not so much strength required in the Edifice as in the Foundation: and if but wise men have the ordering of the building, they will make it much a surer thing, that the foundation shall not fail the building, than that the building shall not fall from the foundation. And though the building be to be of Brick or Stone, and perhaps of Wood, yet if it may be possibly, they will have a Rock for their foundation, whose stability is a much more indubitable thing, than the adherence of the structure to it. Now the Apostles and Prophets, and Canonical Writers, are the foundation of the Church, according to that of S. *Paul,*

built

built upon the foundation of Apostles and Prophets; therefore their stability, in reason ought to be greater than the Churches, which is built upon them. Again, a dependent Infallibility (especially if the dependence be voluntary) cannot be so certain, as that on which it depends: But the Infallibility of the Church, depends upon the Infallibility of the Apostles, and the streightness of the thing regulated, upon the streightness of the Rule: and besides this dependence is voluntary, for it is in the power of the Church to deviate from this Rule; being nothing else but an aggregation of men, of which every one has free will, and is subject to passions and error: Therefore the Churches infallibility, is not so certain as that of the Apostles.

31. Lastly, *Quid verba audiam, cum facta videam?* If you be so infallible as the Apostles were, shew it as the Apostles did; *They went forth* (saith S. *Mark*) *and Preached every where, the Lord working with them, and confirming their words with Signs following.* It is impossible that God should lie, and that the eternal Truth should set his hand and seal to the confirmation of a falshood, or of such Doctrin as is partly true and partly false. The Apostles Doctrin was thus confirmed, therefore it was intirely true, and in no part either false or uncertain. I say in no part of that which they delivered constantly, as a certain divine Truth, and which had the Attestation of Divine Miracles. For that the Apostles themselves, even after the sending of the Holy Ghost, were, and through inadvertence or prejudice, continued for a time in an error, repugnant to a revealed Truth, it is as I have already noted unanswerably evident, from the *story of the Acts of the Apostles*. For notwithstanding our Saviours express warrant and injunction, *to go and preach to all Nations*, yet until S. *Peter* was better informed by a vision from Heaven, and by the conversion of *Cornelius*, both he and the rest of the Church, held it unlawful for them, to go or preach the Gospel to any but the Jews.

32. And for those things which they profess to deliver as the dictates of human reason and prudence, and not as divine Revelations, why we should take them to be divine

A a   revelations,

revelations, I see no reason; nor how we can do so, and not contradict the Apostles, and God himself. Therefore when S. *Paul* says, in the first Epistle to the *Corinth.* 7. 12. *To the rest speak I, not the Lord*; And again, *concerning Virgins I have no commandment of the Lord, but I deliver my Judgment:* If we will pretend, that the Lord did certainly speak, what S. *Paul* spake, and that his judgment was Gods commandment, shall we not plainly contradict S. *Paul,* and that spirit by which he wrote? which moved him to Write, as in other places divine Revelations, which he certainly knew to be such, so in this place, his own judgment, touching some things which God had not particularly revealed unto him.

34. Obj. *But if the Apostles were Infallible, in all things proposed by them as divine Truths, the like must be affirmed of the Church, because* Protestants *teach the promise (of leading into all Truth) to be verified in the Church.*

Ans. It's true that to the Apostles the promise was made, and to them only, yet the words are true also of the Church. But they agree to the Apostles *in a higher,* to the Church *in a lower* sense: to the Apostles *in more absolute,* to the Church in *a more limited* sense. To the Apostles *absolutely,* for the *Churches direction:* to the Church *Conditionally by adherence to that direction, and so far as she doth adhere to it.* In a word, the Apostles were led into all Truths by the Spirit, *efficaciter:* The Church is led also into all Truth by the Apostles *writings, sufficienter.* So that the Apostles and the Church, may be fitly compared to the Star and the Wisemen. The Star was directed by the finger of God, and could not but go right to the place where Christ was: But the Wisemen were led by the Star to Christ; led by it, I say, not *efficaciter,* or *irresistibiliter,* but *sufficienter,* so that if they would they might follow it, if they would not, they might choose. So was it between the Apostles writing Scriptures, and the Church. They in their writing were infallibly assisted to propose nothing as a divine Truth, but what was so. The Church is also led into all Truth, but it is by the intervening of the Apostles writings: But it is, as the Wisemen were led by the

Star,

Star, or as a Traveller is directed by a Mercurial Statue, or as a Pilot by his Card and Compass: led sufficiently, but not irresistibly: led so that she may follow, not so that she must. For seeing the Church is a society of men, whereof every one (according to the Doctrine of the *Romish* Church) hath free-will in believing, it follows, that the whole aggregate has free-will in believing. And if any man say that at least *it is morally impossible, that of so many whereof all may believe aright, not any should do so*: I answer, It is true, if they did all give themselves any liberty of judgment. But if all (as the case is here) captivate their understandings to one of them, all are as likely to err as that one. And he more likely to err than any other, because he may err and thinks he cannot, and because he conceives the Spirit absolutely promised to the succession of Bishops, of which many have been notoriously and confessedly wicked men, *Men of the World:* whereas this Spirit is the *Spirit of Truth, whom the world cannot receive, because he seeth him not, neither knoweth him.*

38. Ad §. 16. To this Paragraph, which pretends to shew, *that if the Catholick Church be fallible in some points, it follows, that no true Protestant can with assurance believe the Universal Church in any one point of Doctrin.*

I *Answer.* Though the Church being not Infallible, I cannot believe her in every thing she says, yet I can and must believe her in every thing she proves, either by Scripture, Reason, or Universal Tradition, be it Fundamental, or be it not Fundamental. This you say, we *cannot, in points not Fundamental, because in such we believe she may err.* But this I know, we can: because though she may err in some things, yet she does not err in what she proves, though it be not Fundamental. Again you say, *we cannot do it in Fundamentals, because we must know what points be Fundamental, before we go to learn of her.* Not so, but I must learn of the Church, or of some part of the Church, or I cannot know any thing Fundamental or not Fundamental. For how can I come to know, that there was such a Man as Christ, that he taught such

Doctrin, that he and his Apostles did such miracles in confirmation of it, that the Scripture is Gods Word, unless I be taught it. So then the Church is, though *not a certain Foundation and proof of my Faith, yet a necessary introduction to it*.

39. But the *Churches infallible direction, extending only to Fundamentals, unless I know them before I go to learn of her, I may be rather deluded than instructed by her.* The reason and connexion of this consequence, I fear neither I nor you do well understand. And besides I must tell you, you are too bold in taking that which no man grants you, *that the Church is an infallible directer in Fundamentals*. For if she were so, then must we not only learn Fundamentals of her, but also *learn of her what is fundamental, and take all for fundamental which she delivers to be such*. In the performance whereof, if I knew any one Church to be infallible, I would quickly be of that Church. But good Sir, you must needs do us this favor, to be so acute, as to distinguish between, being *infallible in fundamentals*, and being an *infallible guide in fundamentals*. That there shall be always *a Church infallible in fundamentals*, we easily grant; for it comes to no more but this, *that there shall be always a Church*. But that there shall be always such a Church, which is an infallible Guide in fundamentals, this we deny. For this cannot be without setling a known infallibility in some one known society of Christians, (as the *Greek* or the *Roman*, or some other Church) by adhering to which Guide, men might be guided to believe aright in all Fundamentals. A man that were destitute of all means of communicating his thoughts to others, might yet in himself, and to himself be infallible, but he could not be a Guide to others. A man or a Church that were invisible, so that none could know how to repair to it for direction, could not be an infallible guide, and yet he might be in himself infallible. You see then there is a wide difference between these two, and therefore I must beseech you not to confound them, nor to take the one for the other.

40. But they that *know what points are Fundamental, otherwise than by the Churches authority, learn not of the Church*

Yes,

into Fundamental and not Fundamental.

Yes, they may learn of the Church, that the Scripture is the word of God, and from the Scripture, that such points are fundamental, others are not so; and consequently learn, even of the Church, even of your Church, that all is not fundamental, nay all is not true, which the Church teacheth to be so. Neither do I see what hinders, but a man may learn of a Church, how to confute the Errors of that Church which taught him: as well as of my Master in Physick, or the Mathematicks, I may learn those rules and principles, by which I may confute my Masters erroneous conclusions.

41. But you ask, *If the Church be not an infallible teacher, why are we commanded to hear, to seek, to obey the Church?* I Answer. For commands *to seek the Church,* I have not yet met with any, and I believe you, if you were to shew them, would be your self to seek. But yet if you could produce some such, we might seek the Church to many good purposes, without supposing her *a Guide infallible*. And then for *hearing and obeying the Church,* I would fain know, whether none may be heard and obeyed, but those that are infallible? Whether particular Churches, Governors, Pastors, Parents, be not to be heard and obeyed? Or whether all these be Infallible? I wonder you will thrust upon us so often, these worn-out Objections, without taking notice of their Answers.

42. Your Argument from S. *Austine*'s first place, is a fallacy, *A dicto secundum quid ad dictum simpliciter*. If the *whole Church practise any of these things (matters of order and decency,* for such only there he speaks of,*) to dispute whether that ought to be done, is insolent madness.* And from hence you infer, *If the whole Church practise any thing, to dispute whether it ought to be done, is insolent madness.* As if there were no difference between *any thing,* and *any of these things?* Or as if I might not esteem it pride and folly, to contradict and disturb the Church for matter of order, pertaining to the time and place, and other circumstances of Gods worship; and yet account it neither pride nor folly, to go about to reform some errors, which the Church hath suffered to come in, and to vitiate the very

substance

substance of Gods worship. It was a practice of the whole Church in Saint *Austines* time, and esteemed an Apostolick Tradition, even by Saint *Austine* himself, *That the Eucharist should be administred to Infants*: Tell me Sir, I beseech you; Had it been insolent madness to dispute against this practice, or had it not? If it had, how insolent and mad are you, that have not only disputed against it, but utterly abolished it? If it had not, then as I say, you must understand Saint *Austines* words, not simply of all things, but (as indeed he himself restrained them) *of these things, of matter of Order, Decency, and Uniformity.*

44. Obj. But the Doctrines, that *Infants are to be baptized, and those that are baptized by Hereticks, are not to be rebaptized, are neither of them to be proved by Scripture: And yet according to S. Austine they are true Doctrins, and we may be certain of them upon the Authority of the Church, which we could not be, unless the Church were Infallible; therefore the Church is Infallible.* I answer, that there is no repugnance but we may be certain enough, of the Universal Traditions of the ancient Church, such as in S. *Austin's* account, these were which here are spoken of, and yet not be certain enough, of the definitions of the present Church. Unless you can shew (which I am sure you can never do) that the Infallibility of the present Church, was always a Tradition of the ancient Church. Now your main business is to prove the present Church Infallible, not so much in consigning ancient Traditions, as in defining emergent controversies. Again, it follows not, because the Churches Authority, is warrant enough for us to believe some Doctrin, touching which the Scripture is silent, therefore it is Warrant enough to believe these, to which the Scripture seems repugnant. Now the Doctrins which S. *Austin* received upon the Churches Authority, were of the first sort; the Doctrins for which we deny your Churches Infallibility are of the second. And therefore though the Churches Authority, might be strong enough, to bear the weight which S. *Austin* laid upon it, yet happily it may not be strong enough, to bear that which

which you lay upon it. Though it may support some Doctrines without Scripture, yet surely not against it. And last of all, to deal ingeniously with you and the world, I am not such an Idolater of S. *Austin*, as to think a thing proved sufficiently because he says it, nor that all his sentences are Oracles; and particularly in this thing, that whatsoever was practised or held by the Universal Church of his time, must needs have come from the Apostles. Though considering the nearness of his time to the Apostles, I think it a good probable way, and therefore am apt enough to follow it, when I see no reason to the contrary. Yet I profess I must have better satisfaction, before I can induce my self to hold it certain and infallible. And this, not because *Popery* would come in at this door, as some have vainly feared, but because by the Church Universal of some time, and the Church Universal of other times, I see plain contradictions held and practised. Both which could not come from the Apostles, for then the Apostles had been teachers of falsehood. And therefore the belief or practice of the present Universal Church, can be no infallible proof, that the Doctrin so believed, or the custom so practised came from the Apostles. I instance in the Doctrine of the *Millenaries*, and the *Eucharists necessity for Infants*: both which Doctrines have been taught by the consent of the eminent Fathers of some ages, without any opposition from any of their Contemporaries: and were delivered by them, not as Doctors, but as Witnesses, not as their own Opinions, but as Apostolick Traditions. And therefore measuring the Doctrin of the Church by all the Rules which Cardinal *Perron* gives us for that purpose, both these Doctrines must be acknowledged to have been the Doctrines of the Ancient Church of some age, or ages; And that the contrary Doctrines were Catholick at some other time, I believe you will not think it needful for me to prove. So that either I must say, the Apostles were fountains of contradictious Doctrines, or that being the Universal Doctrine of the present Church, is no sufficient proof that it came originally from the Apostles. Besides,

sides, who can warrant us, that the Universal Traditions of the Church were all Apostolical? seeing in that famous place for Traditions, in *Tertullian*, [a] *Quicunque traditor*, any Author whatsoever is founder good enough for them. And who can secure us, that Humane inventions, and such as came *à quocunque Traditore*, might not in a short time, gain the reputation of Apostolick? Seeing the direction then was, [b] *Precepta majorum Apostolicas Traditiones quisque existimat.*

[a] *De Corona Militis*, c 3. & 4. Where having recounted sundry unwritten Traditions then observed by Christians, many whereof, by the way, (notwithstanding the Council of Trents profession, *to receive them and the written Word with the like affection of Piety*) are now rejected and neglected by the Church of *Rome*: For example *Immersion in Baptism*; *Tasting a mixture of Milk and Honey presently after*; *Abstaining from Bathes for a week after*; *Accounting it an impiety to pray kneeling on the Lords day, or between Easter and Pentecost*: I say, having reckoned up these and other Traditions in the 3. *chap.* He adds another in the fourth, of *the Veiling of Women*; And then adds, *Since I find no law for this, it follows that Tradition must have given this observation to custom, which shall gain in time, Apostolick authority by the interpretation of the reason of it. By these examples therefore it is declared, that the observing of unwritten Tradition, being confirmed by custom, may be defended. The perseverance of the observation being a good testimony of the goodness of the Tradition. Now custom even in civil affairs where a law is wanting, passes for a law. Neither is it material whether it be grounded on Scripture, or reason; seeing reason is commendation enough for a law. Moreover if law be grounded on reason, all that must be law, which is so grounded.* —— A quocunque productum —— *Whosoever is the producer of it. Do ye think it is not lawful*, Omni fideli, *for every faithful man to conceive and constitute? Provided he constitute only what is not repugnant to Gods will, what is conducible for discipline and available to salvation? seeing the Lord says, why even of our selves, judge ye not what is right? And a little after, This reason now demand, saving the respect of the Tradition,* —— A quocunque Traditore censetur, nec auctorem respiciens sed Auctoritatem; *From whatsoever Traditor it comes; neither regard the Author but the Authority.* [b] Hier.

46. But let us see what S. *Chrysostom* says, *They (the Apostles) delivered not all things in writing* (who denies it?) *but many things also without writing,* (who doubts of it?) *and these also are worthy of belief.* Yes, if we knew what they were. But many things are worthy of belief, which are not necessary to be believed: As that *Julius Cæsar* was Emperor of *Rome* is a thing worthy of belief, being so well testified as it is, but yet it is not necessary to be believed; a man may be saved without it. Those many works which *our Saviour did* (which S. John *supposes, would not have*

have been contained in a World of Books) if they had been written, or if God by some other means had preserved the knowledge of them, had been as worthy to be believed, and as necessary as those that are written. But to shew you how much a more faithful keeper Records are than report, those few that were written are preserved and believed, those infinity more that were not written, are all lost and vanished out of the memory of men. And seeing God in his providence, hath not thought fit to preserve the memory of them, he hath freed us from the obligation of believing them: for every obligation ceases, when it becomes impossible. Who can doubt but the Primitive Christians, to whom the Epistles of the Apostles were written, either of themselves understood, or were instructed by the Apostles, touching the sense of the obscure places of them? These Traditive interpretations, had they been written and dispersed, as the Scriptures were, had without question been preserved, as the Scriptures are. But to shew how excellent a Keeper of the Tradition, the Church of *Rome* hath been, or even the Catholick Church, for want of writing they are all lost, nay were all lost, within a few Ages after Christ. So that if we consult the Ancient Interpreters, we shall hardly find any two of them agree about the sense of any one of them. *Cardinal Perron,* in his discourse of Traditions, having alledged this place for them, *Hold the Traditions,* &c. tell us we *must not answer, that S. Paul speaks here, only of such Traditions, which (though not in this Epist. to the* Thessalonians) *yet were afterwards written, and in other Books of Scripture: because it is upon occasion of Tradition* (touching the *cause* of the *hinderance of the coming of* Antichrist,) *which was never written, that he lays this injunction upon them, to hold the Traditions.* Well, let us grant this Argument good, and concluding; and that the Church of the *Thessalonians,* or the Catholick Church (for what S. *Paul* writ to one Church he writ to all,) were to hold some unwritten Traditions, and among the rest, what was the cause of the hinderance of the coming of *Antichrist.* But what if they did not perform their

their duty in this point, but suffered this Tradition to be lost out of the memory of the Church? Shall we not conclude, that seeing God would not suffer any thing necessary to Salvation to be lost, and he has suffered this Tradition to be lost, therefore the knowledge or belief of it, though it were a profitable thing, yet it was not necessary? I hope you will not challenge such authority over us, as to oblige us to impossibilities, to do that which you cannot do your selves. It is therefore requisite that you make this command possible to be obeyed, before you require obedience unto it. Are you able then to instruct us so well, as to be fit to say unto us, *Now ye know what withholdeth*? Or do you your selves know that ye may instruct us? Can ye, or dare you say, this or this was this hindrance which S. *Paul* here meant, and all men under pain of damnation are to believe it? Or if you cannot, (as I am certain you cannot) go then, and Vaunt your Church, for the only Watchful, Faithful, Infallible Keeper of the Apostles Traditions; when here this very Tradition, which here in particular was deposited with the *Thessalonians* and the Premitive Church, you have utterly lost it, so that there is no Footstep or print of it remaining, which with Divine Faith we may rely upon. Blessed therefore be the goodness of God, who seeing that what was not written, was in such danger to be lost, took order, that what was necessary should be written! S. *Chrysostoms* counsel therefore, of *accounting the Churches Traditions worthy of belief*, we are willing to obey: And if you can of any thing make it appear, that *it is Tradition*, we will seek no farther. But this we say withal, that we are persuaded we cannot make this appear in any thing, but *only the Canon of Scripture*, and that there is nothing now extant, and to be known by us, which can put in so good Plea, to be the unwritten Word of God, as the unquestioned Books of Canonical Scripture, to be the written Word of God.

47. You conclude this Paragraph with a sentence of S. *Austin*'s who says, *The Church doth not approve, nor dissemble, nor do these things which are against Faith*
or

or good Life: and from hence you conclude, *that it never hath done so, nor never can do so.* But though the argument hold in Logick *à non posse, ad non esse*, yet I never heard, that it would hold back again, *à non esse, ad non posse.* The Church cannot do this, therefore it does it not, follows with good consequence: but the Church does not this, therefore it shall never do it, nor can never do it, this I believe will hardly follow. In the Epistle next before to the same *Januarius*, writing of the same matter, he hath these words, *It remains that the thing you inquire of, must be of that third kind of things, which are different in divers places. Let every one therefore do, that which he finds done in the Church to which he comes, for none of them is against Faith or good manners.* And why do you not infer from hence, that *no particular Church can bring up any Custom that is against Faith or good manners?* Certainly this consequence has as good reason for it as the former. If a man say of the Church of *England*, (what S. *Austin* of the Church) that she neither approves, nor dissembles, nor does any thing against Faith or good manners, would you collect presently, that this man did either make or think the Church of *England* infallible? Furthermore, it is observable out of this, and the former Epistle, that this Church *which did not* (as S. *Austin* according to you, thought) *approve or dissemble, or do any thing against Faith or good Life*, did yet tolerate and dissemble vain superstitions, and humane presumptions, and suffer all places to be full of them, and to be exacted, as, nay more severely than the commandments of God himself. This S. *Austin* himself professeth in this very Epistle. *This* (saith he) *I do infinitely grieve at, that many most wholesom precepts of the Divine Scripture, are little regarded; and in the mean time, all is so full of so many presumptions, that he is more grievously found fault with, who during his octaves, toucheth the Earth with his naked Foot, than he that shall bury his Soul in Drunkenness.* Of these he says, *that they were neither contained in Scripture, decreed by Councils, nor corroborated by the Custom of the Universal Church.* And *though not against Faith, yet unprofitable burdens of Christian Liberty, which*

Bb 2 *made*

made the condition of the Jews more tolerable than that of Christians. And therefore he professes of them, *Approbare non possum*, *I cannot approve them*. And *ubi facultas tribuitur, resecanda existimo*, I think they are to be cut off, wheresoever we have power. Yet so deeply were they rooted, and spread so far, through the indiscreet devotion of the People, always more prone to superstion than true Piety, and through the connivence of the Governors, who should have strangled them at their Birth, that himself, though he grieved at them, and could not allow them, yet for fear of offence he durst not speak against them, *multa hujusmodi propter nonnullarum vel sanctarum vel turbulentarum personarum scandala devitanda liberius improbare non audeo*. Many of these things for fear of scandalizing many holy persons, or provoking those that are turbulent, I dare not freely disallow. Nay, the Catholick Church it self, did see and dissemble, and tolerate them; for these are the things of which he presently says after, *the Church of God* (and you will have him speak of the true Catholick Church) *placed between Chaffe and Tares, tolerates many things*. Which was directly against the command of the Holy Spirit, given the Church by S. *Paul*; *To stand fast in that liberty wherewith Christ hath made her free, and not to suffer her self to be brought in bondage to these servile burdens*. Our Saviour tells the Scribes and Pharisees, that in vain they *Worshiped God, teaching for Doctrines mens Commandments: For that laying aside the Commandments of God, they held the Traditions of men, as the washing of Pots, and Cups, and many other such like things*. Certainly that which S. *Austin* complains of, as the general fault of Christians of his time, was parallel to this: *Multa* (saith he) *quæ in divinis libris saluberrima præcepta sunt, minus curantur*; This I suppose I may very well render in our Saviours Words, *The commandments of God are laid aside*; and then; *tam multis presumptionibus sic plena sunt omnia*, all things, or all places, are so full of so many presumptions, and those exacted with such severity, nay with Tyranny, that he was more severely censured, who in the time of his Octaves touched the Earth with his naked Feet, than he which drown-

ed

into Fundamental and not Fundamental.

ed *and buried his Soul in Drink.* Certainly, if this be not to teach for *Doctrines mens Commandments,* I know not what is. And therefore these superstitious Christians might be said, *to Worship God in vain,* as well as Scribes and Pharisees. And yet great variety of superstitions of this kind, were then already spread over the Church, being different in divers place. This is plain from these Words of S. *Austin* of them, *diversorum locorum diversis moribus innumerabiliter variantur*; and apparent, because the stream of them was grown so violent, that he durst not oppose it, *liberius improbare non audeo, I dare not freely speak against them.* So that to say, the Catholick Church tolerated all this, and for fear of offence, durst not abrogate or condemn it, is to say (if we Judge rightly of it) that the Church with silence and connivence generally tolerated Christians to *worship God in vain.* Now how this tolerating of Universal superstition in the Church, can consist with the assistance and direction of Gods omnipotent spirit to guard it from superstition, and with the accomplishment of that pretended Prophesie of the Church, *I have set Watchmen upon thy Walls,* O Jerusalem, *which shall never hold their peace Day nor Night*; besides how these superstitions being thus nourished, cherished, and strengthned by the practice of the most, and urged with great violence upon others as the commandments of God, and but fearfully opposed or contradicted by any, might in time take such deep Root, and spread their Branches so far, as to pass for Universal Customs of the Church, he that does not see, sees nothing. Especially, considering the catching and contagious nature of this sin, and how fast ill Weeds spread, and how true and experimented that rule is of the Historian, *Exempla non consistunt ubi incipiunt, sed quamlibet in tenuem recepta tramitem latissimè evagandi sibi faciunt potestatem.* Examples do not stay where they begin, but tho at first pent up in a narrow Tract, they make themselves room for extravagant wandrings. Nay that some such superstition had not already even in S. *Austins* time, prevailed so far, as to be *Consuetudine universæ Ecclesiæ roboratum,* confirmed by the Custom

Custom of the Universal Church, who can doubt that considers, that the practice of *Communicating Infants*, had even then got the credit, and authority, not only of an Universal Custom, but also of an Apostolick Tradition.

49. But now after all this ado, what if S. *Austin* says not this which is pretended of the Church, *viz. That she neither approves, nor dissembles, nor practises any thing against Faith or good Life,* but only of good men in the Church? Certainly, though some Copies read as you would have it, yet you should not have dissembled, that others read the place otherwise, *vix. Ecclesia multa tolerat, & tamen, quæ sunt contra Fidem & bonam vitam, nec bonus approbat,* &c. *The Church tolerates many things; and yet what is against Faith or good Life, a good man will neither approve, nor dissemble, nor practise.*

50. Ad §. 17. *That* Abraham *begat Isaace*, is a point very far from being Fundamental; and yet I hope you will grant, that *Protestants* believing Scripture to be the Word of God, may be certain enough of the truth and certainty of it. For what if they say *that the Catholick Church, and much more themselves may possibly Err in some unfundamental points*, it is therefore consequent, they can be certain of none such? What if a wiser man than I may mistake the sense of some obscure place of *Aristotle*, may I no: therefore without any arrogance or inconsequence, conceive my self certain that I understand him in some plain places, which carry their sense before them? And then for points Fundamental, to what purpose do you say, *That we must first know what they be, before we can be assured that we cannot Err in understanding the Scripture*; when we pretend not at all to any assurance that we cannot Err, but only to a sufficient certainty, that we do not Err, but rightly understand those things that are plain, whether Fundamental or not Fundamental? That *God is, and is a rewarder of them that seek him:* That *there is no Salvation but by Faith in Christ*: That *by repentance and Faith in Christ Remission of sins may be obtained:* That *there shall be a Resurrection of the Body:* These we conceive both

true,

true, because the Scripture says so, and Truths Fundamental, because they are necessary parts of the Gospel, whereof our Saviour saies, *Qui non crediderit, damnabitur.* All which we either learn from Scripture immediately, or learn of those that learn it of Scripture, so that neither Learned nor Unlearned pretend to know these things independently of Scripture. And therefore in imputing this to us, you cannot excuse your self from having done us a palpable injury.

52. Ad §. 19.] To that which is here urged of the differences amongst *Protestants* concerning many points: I answer, that those differences between *Protestants* concerning Errors damnable and not damnable, Truths Fundamental and not Fundamental, may be easily reconciled. For either the Error they speak of *may be purely and simply involuntary*, or it may be in respect of the *cause of it voluntary*. If the cause of it be some voluntary and avoidable fault, the Error is it self sinful, and consequently in its own nature damnable; As if by negligence in seeking the Truth, by unwillingness to find it, by Pride, by obstinacy, by desiring that Religion should be true which sutes best with my ends, by fear of mens ill opinion, or any other worldly fear, or any other worldly hope, I betray my self to any Error contrary to any Divine revealed Truth, that Error may be justly stiled a sin, and consequently of it self to such a one damnable. But if I be guilty of none of these faults, but be desirous to know the Truth, and diligent in seeking it, and advise not at all with Flesh and Blood about the choice of my opinions, but only with God, and that Reason that he hath given me, if I be thus qualified, and yet through human infirmity fall into Error, that Error cannot be damnable. Again, the party erring may be conceived either to die with contrition for all his sins known and unknown, or without it; If he die without it, this Error in it self damnable, will be likewise so unto him: If he die with contrition (as his Error can be no impediment but he may) his Error though in it self damnable, to him according to your Doctrine, will not prove so. And therefore some

of

of those Authors whom you quote, speaking of Errors whereunto men were betrayed, or wherein they were kept by their Fault, or Vice, or Passion (as for the most part men are:) Others speaking of them, as Errors simply and purely involuntary, and the effects of human infirmity; some as they were *retracted by Contrition* (to use your own phrase) others, as they were not; no marvel though they have past upon them, some a heavier, and some a milder, some an absolving, and some a condemning sentence. The least of all these Errors, which here you mention, having malice enough too frequently mixed with it, to sink a man deep enough into Hell: and the greatest of them all, being according to your Principles, either no fault at all, or very Venial, where there is no malice of the will conjoyned with it. And if it be, yet as the most malignant poyson, will not poyson him that receives with it a more powerful Antidote: so I am confident your own Doctrine will force you to confess, that whosoever dies with Faith in Christ, and Contrition for all sins known and unknown (in which heap all his sinful Errors must be comprized,) can no more be hurt by any the most malignant and pestilent Error, than S. *Paul* by the Viper which he shook off into the fire. Now touching the *necessity of Repentance from Dead works, and Faith in Christ Jesus the Son of God, and Saviour of the World*, they all agree; and therefore you cannot deny, but they agree about all that is simply necessary. Moreover, though, if they should go about to choose out of Scripture all these Propositions and Doctrines which integrate and make up the Body of Christian Religion, peradventure there would not be so exact agreement amongst them, as some say there was between the 70. Interpreters, in Translating the *Old Testament*; yet thus far without Controversie they do all agree, that in the Bible all these things are contained, and therefore, that whosoever does truly and sincerely believe the Scripture, must of necessity either in *Hypothesi*, or at least *in thesi*, either *formally*, or at least *virtually*, either *explicitely*, or at least *implicitely*, either in *Act* or at least in *preparation of mind*, believe
all

all things Fundamental: It being not Fundamental, nor required of Almighty God, to believe the true sense of Scripture in all places, but only that we should endeavour to do so, and be prepared in mind to do so, whensoever it shall be sufficiently propounded to us. Suppose a man in some disease were prescribed a Medicine consisting of twenty ingredients, and he advising with Physitians, should find them differing in Opinion about it, some of them telling him, that all the ingredients were absolutely necessary; some, that only some of them were necessary, the rest only profitable, and requisite *ad melius esse*, lastly some, that some only were necessary, some profitable, and the rest superfluous, yet not hurtful; Yet all with one accord agreeing in this, That the *whole receipt had in it all things necessary* for the recovery of his health, and that if he made use of it, he should infallibly find it successful: what wise man would not think they agreed sufficiently for his direction to the recovery of his health? Just so, these *Protestant* Doctors, with whose discords you make such Tragedies, agreeing in *Thesi* thus far, that the *Scripture evidently contains all things necessary to Salvation*, both for matter of Faith and of practice, and that whosoever believes it, and endeavours to find the true sense of it, and to conform his Life unto it, shall certainly perform all things necessary to Salvation, and undoubtedly be saved; agreeing I say thus far, what matters it for the direction of men to Salvation, though they differ in opinion, touching what points are absolutely necessary, and what not? What Errors absolutely repugnant to Salvation, and what not? Especially considering that although they differ about the Question of the necessity of these Truths, yet for the most part they agree in this that Truths they are, and profitable at least, though not simply necessary. And though they differ in the Question, whether the contrary Errors be destructive of Salvation, or no, yet in this they consent, that Errors they are, and hurtful to Religion, though not destructive of Salvation. Now that which God requires of us is this; That we should believe the Doctrines of the Gospel to be Truths, not all, necessary Truths, for all are not so, and consequently, the repugnant Errors to be falshoods; yet not all such falshoods, as unavoidably draw with them damnation upon all that hold them, for all do not so.

53. Yea but *you say, it is very requisite we should agree upon a particular Catalogue of Fundamental points, for without such a Catalogue, no man can be assured whether or no, he hath Faith sufficient to Salvation.* This I utterly deny as a thing evidently false, and I wonder you should content your self magisterially to say so, without offering any proof of it. I might much more justly, think it enough barely to deny it, without refutation, but I will not. Thus therefore I argue against it. Without being able to make a Catalogue of Fundamentals, I may be assured of the Truth of this Assertion, if it be true, That *the Scripture contains all necessary points of Faith,* and know that I believe explicitely all that is exprest in Scripture, and implicitely all that is contained in them: Now he that believes all this, must of necessity believe all things necessary; Therefore without being able to make a Catalogue of Fundamentals, I may be assured that I believe all things necessary, and consequently that my Faith is sufficient. I said, of the truth of this Assertion, *if it be true*: Because I will not here enter into the Question of the truth of it, it being sufficient for my present purpose, that it may be true, and may be believed without any dependence upon a Catalogue of Fundamentals. And therefore if this be all your reason, to demand a particular Catalogue of Fundamentals, we cannot but think your demand unreasonable. Especially having your self expressed the cause of the difficulty of it, and that is, *Because Scripture doth deliver Divine Truths, but seldom qualifies them, or declares whether they be or be not absolutely necessary to Salvation.* Yet not so seldom, but that out of it I could give you an abstract of the Essential parts of Christianity, if it were necessary, but I have shewed it not so, by confuting your reason, pretended for the necessity of it, and at this time I have no leisure to do you courtesies that are so troublesom to my self. Yet thus much I will promise, that
when

into Fundamental and not Fundamental.

when you deliver *a particular Catalogue of your Church Propofals* with one hand, you shall receive a particular Catalogue of what I conceive Fundamental, with the other. For as yet, I see no such fair proceeding as you talk of, nor any performance on your own part of that which so clamorously you require on ours. For as for the Catalogue which here you have given us, in saying. *You are obliged under pain of damnation to believe whatsoever the Catholick visible Church of Chrift propofeth as revealed by Almighty God,* it is like a covey of one *Patridg*, or a flock of one sheep, or a Fleet composed of one Ship, or an Army of one man. The Author of *Charity Miftaken,* demands a particular Cataloge of Fundamental points ; And *We* (say you *)* *again and again demand such a Catalogue.* And surely, if this one Propofition, which here you think to stop our mouths with, be a Catalogue, yet at least such a Catalogue it is not, and therefore as yet you have not performed what you require. For if to set down such a Propofition, wherein are comprized all points taught by us to be necessary to Salvation, will serve you instead of a Catalogue, you shall have Catalogues enough. As, we are obliged to believe all under pain of damnation which God commands us to believe. There's one Catalogue. We are obliged under pain of damnation , to believe all, whereof we may be sufficiently assured, that Christ taught it his Apoftles, his Apoftles the Church. There's another. We are obliged under pain of damnation to believe Gods Word, and all contained in it to be true. There's a third. If these generalities will not satisfie you, but you will be importuning us to tell you in particular, what they are which Christ taught his Apoftles, and his Apoftles the Church, what points are contained in Gods Word; Then I beseech you do us reason, and give us a particular and *exact Inventory of all your Church Propofals, without leaving out, or adding any,* such a one which all the Doctors of your Church will subscribe to, and if you receive not then a Catalogue of Fundamentals, I for my part will give you leave to proclaim us Banckrupts.

Cc 2   54. Besides

54. Besides this deceitful generality of your Catalogue (as you call it,) another main fault we find with it, that it is extreamly ambiguous; and therefore to draw you out of the Clouds, give me leave to propose some Questions to you concerning it. I would know therefore, whether by believing, you mean explicitely or implicitely? If you mean implicitely, I would know whether your Churches infallibility be under pain of damnation to be believed explicitely, or no? Whether any one point or points besides this, be under the same penalty, to be believed explicitely, or no? And if any, what they be? I would know what you esteem the Proposals of the Catholick Visible Church? In particular, whether the Decree of a *Pope ex Cathedra*, that is, with an intent to oblige all Christians by it, be a sufficient and an obliging proposal? Whether men without danger of damnation may examine such a Decree, and if they think they have just cause, refuse to obey it? Whether the Decree of a Council, without the *Popes* confirmation, be such an obliging Proposal, or no? Whether it be so in case there be no *Pope*, or in case it be doubtful who is *Pope*? Whether the Decree of a general Council confirmed by the *Pope*, be such a Proposal, and whether he be an *Heretick* that thinks otherwise? Whether the Decree of a particular Council confirmed by the *Pope*, be such a Proposal? Whether the General uncondemned practice of the Church for some Ages be such a sufficient Proposition? Whether the consent of the most eminent Fathers of any Age, agreeing in the affirmation of any Doctrine, not contradicted by any of their Contemporaries, be a sufficient Proposition? Whether the Fathers testifying such or such a Doctrine or Practice to be Tradition, or to be the Doctrine or Practice of the Church, be a sufficient assurance that it is so? Whether we be bound under pain of damnation, to believe every Text of the Vulgar Bible, now Authorized by the *Roman Church*, to be the true Translation of the Originals of the Prophets, and Evangelists, and Apostles, without any the least alteration? Whether they that lived when the Bible

Bible of *Sixtus* was set forth, were bound under pain of damnation to believe the same of that? And if not of that, of what Bible they were bound to believe it? Whether the Catholick Visible Church be alwaies that Society of Christians which adheres to the Bishop of *Rome*? Whether every Christian, that hath ability and opportunity, be not bound to endeavour to know Explicitely the Proposals of the Church? Whether Implicite Faith in the Churches Veracity, will not save him that Actually and Explicitely disbelieves some Doctrine of the Church, not knowing it to be so; and Actually believes some damnable *Heresie*, as that God has the shape of a man? Whether an ignorant man be bound to believe any point to be decreed by the Church, when his Priest or Ghostly Father assures him it is so? Whether his Ghostly Father may not Err in telling him so, and whether any man can be obliged under pain of damnation, to believe an Error? Whether he be bound to believe such a thing defined, when a number of Priests, perhaps Ten or Twenty tell him it is so? And what assurance he can have, that they neither Err, nor deceive him in this matter? Why Implicite Faith in Christ, or the Scriptures should not suffice for a mans Salvation, as well as implicite Faith in the Church? Whether when you say, *Whatsoever the Church proposeth*, you mean all that ever she proposed, or that only which she now proposeth; and whether she now proposeth all that ever she did propose? Whether all the Books of Canonical Scripture were sufficiently declared to the Church to be so, and proposed as such by the Apostles? And if not, from whom the Church had this declaration afterwards? If so, whether all men ever since the Apostles time, were bound under pain of damnation to believe the Epistle of S. *James*, and the Epistle to the *Hebrews* to be Canonical; at least, not to disbelieve it, and believe the contrary? Lastly, why it is not sufficient for any mans Salvation to use the best means he can to inform his Conscience, and to follow the direction of it? To all these demands when you have given fair and ingenious answers, you shall hear further from me.

§ 5. Ad

55. Ad §. 20.] At the first entrance into this Parag. from our own Doctrine, *That the Church cannot Err in Points necessary, it is concluded if we are wise, we must forsake it in nothing, least we should forsake it in something necessary.* To which I answer, First, that the supposition as you understand it, is falsly imposed upon us, and as we understand it will do you no service. For when we say, that there shall be *a Church alwaies*, somewhere or other, *unerring in Fundamentals*, our meaning is but this, that *there shall be alwaies a Church*, to the very being whereof it is repugnant that it should Err in Fundamentals; for if it should do so, it would want the very essence of a Church, and therefore cease to be a Church. But we never annexed this priviledg *to any one Church of any one Denomination*, as the *Greek* or the *Roman* Church: which if we had done, and set up some setled certain Society of Christians, distinguishable from all others by adhering to such a Bishop for our Guide in Fundamentals, then indeed, and then only might you with some colour, though with no certainty, have concluded that we could not in Wisdom, *forsake this Church in any point, for fear of forsaking it in a necessary point.* But now that we say not this of any one determinate Church, which alone can perform the Office of Guide or Director, but indefinitely of the Church, meaning no more but this, *That there shall be alwaies in some place or other, some Church that Errs not in Fundamentals*; will you conclude from hence, that we cannot in Wisdom forsake this or that, the *Roman* or the *Greek* Church, for fear of Erring in Fundamentals?

56. Yea, but you may say (for I will make the best I can of all your Arguments,) *That this Church thus unerring in Fundamentals, when* Luther *arose, was by our confession the* Roman; *and therefore we ought not in Wisdom to have departed from it in any thing.* I answer: First, that we confess no such thing, that the Church of *Rome* was then this Church, but only a Part of it, and that the most corrupted and most incorrigible. Secondly, that if by adhering to the Church, we could have been thus far secured, this Argument had some shew of reason. But seeing

seeing we are not warranted thus much by any priviledg of that Church, that she cannot Err Fundamentally, but only from Scripture, which assures us that she doth Err very heinously, collect our hope, that the Truths she retains and the practice of them, may prove an Antidote to her, against the Errors which she maintains in such Persons, as in simplicity of Heart follow this *Absalom*; we should then do against the light of our Conscience, and so sin damnably if we should not abandon the profession of her Errors though not Fundamental. Neither can we thus conclude, we may safely hold with the Church of *Rome* in all her points, for she cannot Err damnably; For this is false, she may, though perhaps she does not: But rather thus, These points of Christianity, which have in them the nature of Antidotes against the Poyson of all Sins and Errors, the Church of *Rome*, though otherwise much corrupted, still retains; therefore we hope she Errs not Fundamentally, but still remains a Part of the Church. But this can be no warrant to us to think with her in all things: seeing the very same Scripture, which puts us in hope she Errs not Fundamentally, assures us that in many things, and those of great moment she Errs very grieviously. And these Errors though to them that believe them, we hope they will not be pernitious, yet the professing of them against Conscience, could not but bring us to certain damnation. *As for the fear of departing from some Fundamental Truths withal, while we depart from her Errors,* Happily it might work upon us, if adhering to her might secure us from it, and if nothing else could: But both these are false. For first, adhering to her in all things cannot secure us from erring in Fundamentals: Because though *de facto* we hope she does not Err, yet we know no priviledges she has, but she may Err in them her self: and therefore we had need have better security hereof than her bare Authority. Then secondly, without dependence on her at all, we may be secured that we do not Err Fundamentally; I mean by believing all those things plainly set down in Scripture, wherein all things necessary, and
most

most things profitable are plainly delivered. Suppose I were Travelling to *London*, and knew two ways thither, the one very safe and convenient, the other very inconvenient, and dangerous, but yet a way to *London*: and that I overtook a Passenger on the way, who himself believed, and would fain perswade me, there was no other way but the worse, and would perswade me to accompany him in it, because I confessed his way, though very inconvenient, yet a way; so that going that way we could not fail of our Journies end, by the consent of both Parties: but he believed, my way to be none at all; and therefore I might justly fear, lest out of a desire of leaving the worst way, I left the true, and the only way: If now I should not be more secure upon my own knowledge, than frighted by this fallacity, would you not beg me for a Fool? Just so might you think of us, if we would be frighted out of our own knowledge by this bugbear. For the only and the main reason why we believe you not to Err in Fundamentals, is your holding the *Doctrines of Faith in Christ and Repentance:* which knowing we hold as well as you, notwithstanding our departure from you, we must needs know that we not Err in Fundamentals, as well as we know that you do not Err in some Fundamentals, and therefore cannot possibly fear the contrary. Yet let us be more liberal to you, and grant that which can never be proved, that God had said in plain terms, *The Church of* Rome *shall never destroy the Foundation*, but withal had said, *that it might and would lay much Hay and Stubble upon it*; That you should never hold any Error destructive of Salvation, but yet many that were prejudicial to Edification: I demand, might we have dispensed with our selves in the believing and professing these Errors in regard of the smalness of them? Or had it not been a damnable sin to do so, though the Errors in themselves were not damnable? Had we not had as plain Direction to depart from you in some things profitable, as to adhere to you in things necessary? In the beginning of your Book, when it was for your purpose to have it so, the greatness or smalness of

the

into Fundamental and not Fundamental.

the matter was not confiderable, the Evidence of the Revelation was all in all. But here we muft err with you in fmall things, for fear of loofing your direction in greater: and for fear of departing too far from you, not go from you at all, even where we fee plainly that you have departed from the Truth.

57. Beyond all this, I fay, that this which you fay *in wifdom we are to do*, is not only unlawful, but, if we will proceed according to reafon, impoffible. I mean to adhere to you in all things, having no other ground for it, but becaufe you are (as we will now fuppofe) Infallible in fome things, that is, in Fundamentals. For, whether by skill in Architecture a large ftructure may be fupported by a narrow foundation, I know not; but fure I am, in reafon, no conclufion can be larger than the Principles on which it is founded. And therefore if I confider what I do, and be perfwaded, that your infallibility, is but limited, and particular, and partial, my adherence upon this ground, cannot poffibly be Abfolute and Univerfal and Total. I am confident, that fhould I meet with fuch a man amongft you (as I am well affur'd there be many) that would grant your Church Infallible only in Fundamentals, which what they are he knows not, and therefore upon this only reafon adheres to you in all things: I fay that I am confident, that it may be demonftrated, that fuch a man adheres to you, with a fiducial and certain affent in nothing. To make this clear (becaufe at the firft hearing it may feem ftrange) give me leave, good Sir, to fuppofe you the man, and to propofe to you a few queftions, and to give for you fuch anfwers to them, as upon this ground you muft of neceffity give, were you prefent with me. Firft, fuppofing you hold your Church Infallible in Fundamentals, obnoxious to Error in other things, and that you know not what points are Fundamental, I demand, C. Why do you believe the Doctrin of Tranfubftantiation? K. becaufe the Church hath taught it, which is Infallible. C. What? Infallible in all things, or only in Fundamentals? K. in Fundamentals only. C. Then in other points fhe may err? K. fhe may. C. and do you know

D d   what

what Points are Fundamental, what not? *K.* No, and therefore I believe her in all things, least I should disbelieve her in fundamentals. *C.* How know you then, whether this be a fundamental point or no? *K.* I know not. *C.* It may be then (for ought you know) an unfundamental point? *K.* yes, it may be so. *C.* And in these you said the Church may err? *K.* yes I did so. *C.* Then possibly it may err in this? *K.* It may do so. *C.* Then what certainty have you, that it does not err in it? *K.* None at all, but upon this supposition, that this is a Fundamental. *C.* And this supposition you are uncertain of? *K.* Yes, I told you so before. *C.* And therefore, you can have no certainty of that, which depends upon this uncertainty, saving only a suppositive certainty, if it be a Fundamental truth, which is in plain English to say, you are certain it is true, if it be both true and necessary. Verily Sir, if you have no better Faith than this, you are no Catholick. *K.* good words I pray! I am so, and God willing will be so. *C.* You mean, in outward profession and practice, but in belief you are not, no more than a *Protestant* is a *Catholick*. For every *Protestant* yields such a kind of assent to all the proposals of the Church, for surely they believe them true, if they be Fundamental Truths. And therefore you must either believe the Church Infallible in all her proposals, be they foundations, or be they superstructions, or else you must believe all Fundamental which she proposes, or else you are no *Catholick*. *K.* But I have been taught, that *seeing I believed the Church Infallible in points necessary, in wisdom I was to believe her in every thing.* *C.* That was a pretty plausible inducement, to bring you hither, but now you are here, you must go farther, and believe her Infallible in all things, or else you were as good go back again, which will be a great disparagement to you, and draw upon you both the bitter and implacable hatred of our part, and even with your own, the imputation of rashness and levity. You see, I hope, by this time, that though a man did believe your Church Infallible in Fundamentals; yet he has no reason to do you the courtesie, of believing all her proposals; nay if he be ignorant what
these

thefe Fundamentals are, he has no certain ground to believe her, upon her Authority in any thing. And whereas you fay, it can be no imprudence to err with the Church; I fay, it may be very great imprudence, if the queftion be, Whether we fhould err with the prefent Church, or hold true with God Almighty.

60. Whereas you add, That *that vifible Church which cannot err in Fundamental, propounds all her definitions without diftinction to be believed under* Anathema's: *Anf.* Again you beg the queftion, fuppofing untruly, that there is, any *that Vifible Church*, I mean any Vifible Church of one Denomination, which cannot err in points Fundamental. Secondly, propofing definitions to be believed under Anathema's, is no good argument, that the Propounders conceive themfelves infallible; but only, that they conceive the Doctrine they condemn is evidently damnable. A plain proof hereof is this, that particular Councils, nay particular men, have been very liberal of their Anathema's, which yet were never conceived infallible, either by others or themfelves. If any man fhould now deny Chrift to be the Saviour of the world, or deny the Refurrection, I fhould make no great fcruple of Anathematizing his Doctrine, and yet am very far from dreaming of Infallibility.

62. The effect of the next Argument is this, *I cannot without grievous fin difobey the Church, unlefs I know fhe commands thofe things which are not in her power to command: and how far this power extends, none can better inform me than the Church. Therefore I am to obey, fo far as the Church requires my obedience.* I Anfwer, Firft, That neither hath the *Catholick Church*, but only a corrupt part of it declared her felf, nor required our obedience, in the points contefted among us. This therefore is falfely, and vainly fuppofed here by you, being one of the greateft queftions amongft us. Then Secondly, That God can better inform us, what are the limits of the Churches power, than the Church her felf, that is, than the *Roman* Clergy, who being men fubject to the fame paffions with other men, why they fhould be thought the beft Judges in their own caufe,

cause, I do not well understand! But yet we oppose against them, no human decisive Judges, nor any Sect or Person, but only God and his Word. And therefore it is in vain to say, That *in following her, you shall be sooner excused, than in following any Sect or Man applying Scriptures against her Doctrine:* In as much as we never went about to arrogate to our selves that Infallibility or absolute Authority, which we take away from you. But if you would have spoken to the purpose, you should have said, that in following her you should sooner have been excused, than in cleaving to the Scripture, and to God himself.

63. Whereas you say, *The fearful examples of innumerable persons, who forsaking the Church, upon pretence of her errors, have failed even in fundamental points, ought to deter all Christians from opposing her in any one doctrine or practice;* This is, just as if you should say, divers men have fallen into *Scylla*, with going too far from *Charybdis*, be sure therefore ye keep close to *Charybdis:* divers leaving prodigality, have fallen into covetousness, therefore be you constant to prodigality; many have fallen from worshipping God perversely and foolishly, not to worship him at all, from worshipping many Gods, to worship none; this therefore ought to deter men, from leaving Superstition or Idolatry, for fear of falling into Atheism and Impiety. This is your counsel and Sophistry: but God says clean contrary; *Take heed you swerve not, either to the right hand or to the left: you must not do evil that good may come thereon;* therefore neither that you may avoid a greater evil, you must not be obstinate in a certain error, for fear of an uncertain. What if some, forsaking the Church of *Rome*, have forsaken Fundamental Truths? Was this because they forsook the Church of *Rome*? No sure, this is *non causa pro causa:* for else all that have forsaken that Church should have done so, which we say they have not. But because they went too far from her, the golden mean, the narrow way is hard to be found, and hard to be kept; hard, but not impossible: hard, but yet you must not please your self out of it, though you err on the right hand, though you offend on the milder part, for this is

the

the only way that leads to life, and few there be that find it. It is true, if we said, there were no danger in being of the *Roman* Church, and there were danger in leaving it, it were madness to perswade any man to leave it. But we protest and proclaim the contrary, and that we have very little hope of their Salvation, who either out of negligence in seeking the truth, or unwillingness to find it, live and die in the errors and impieties of that Church: and therefore cannot but conceive those fears to be most foolish and ridiculous, which perswade men to be constant in one way to hell, lest happily if they leave it, they should fall into another.

64. Obj. *Some Protestants, pretending to reform the Church, are come to affirm that she perished for many Ages, which others cannot deny to be a Fundamental Error against the Article of the Creed, I believe the Catholick Church, and affirm the* Donatists *erred Fundamentally in confining it to* Africa.

To this I Answer, First, that the error of the *Donatists* was not, that they held it possible that some, or many, or most parts of *Christendom*, might fall away from Christianity, and that the Church may loose much of her amplitude, and be contracted to a narrow compass in comparison of her former extent; which is proved not only possible but certain, by irrefragable experience. For who knows not, that *Gentilism*, and *Mahumetism*, mans wickedness deserving it, and Gods providence permitting it, have prevailed to the utter extirpation of Christianity, upon far the greater part of the world? And S. *Austin* when he was out of the heat of Disputation, confesses the Militant Church to be *like the Moon*, sometimes increasing, and sometimes decreasing. This therefore was no error in the *Donatists*, that they held it possible, that the Church, from a larger extent, might be contradicted to a lesser: or that they held it possible to be reduced to *Africa*; (For why not to *Africk* then, as well as within these few ages, you pretend it was to *Europe?*) But their error was, that they held *de facto*, this was done when they had no just ground or reason to do so; and so upon a vain pretence which they could not justify, separated themselves from the communion of all

all other parts of the Church: and that they required it as a necessary condition to make a man a member of the Church, that he should be of their Communion, and divide himself from all other Communions from which they were divided: which was a condition both unnecessary and unlawful to be required, and therefore the exacting of it was directly opposite to the Churches Catholicism; in the very same nature with their Errors who required Circumcision, and the keeping of the Law of *Moses* as necessary to salvation. For whosoever requires harder or heavier conditions of men, than God requires of them, he it is that is properly an Enemy of the Churches Universality, by hindring either Men or Countries from adjoyning themselves to it; which, were it not for these unnecessary and therefore unlawful conditions, in probability would have made them members of it. And seeing the present Church of *Rome* perswades men they were as good (for any hope of Salvation they have) not to be Christians as not to be *Roman* Catholicks, believe nothing at all, as not to believe all which they impose upon them: Be absolutely out of the Churches Communion, as be out of their Communion, or be in any other, whether they be not guilty of the same crime, with the *Donatists* and those Zelots of the Mosaical Law, I leave it to the judgment of those that understand reason! This is sufficient to shew the vanity of this Argument. But I add moreover, that you neither have named those *Protestants* who held the Church to have perished for many ages; who perhaps held not the destruction but the corruption of the Church; not that the true Church, but that the pure Church perished: or rather that the Church perished not from its life and existence, but from its purity and integrity, or perhaps from its splendor and visibility. Neither have you proved by any one reason, but only affirmed it, to be a fundamental Error, to hold that the Church Militant may possibly be driven out of the world, and abolished for a time from the face of the earth.

69. Ad §. 23. In all these Texts of Scripture, which are here alledged in this last Section of this Chapter, or in any one of them, or in any other, doth God say clearly and plainly,

plainly, *The Bishop of* Rome *and that Society of Christians which adheres to him shall be ever the infallible guide of Faith?* You will confess, I presume, he doth not, and will pretend, it was not necessary. Yet if the King should tell us the Lord-Keeper should judge such and such causes, but should either not tell us at all, or tell us but doubtfully who should be Lord-Keeper, should we be any thing the nearer for him to an end of contentions? Nay rather would not the dissentions about the Person who it is, increase contentions, rather than end them? Just so it would have been, if God had appointed a Church to be Judge of Controversies, and had not told us which was that Church. Seeing therefore God does nothing in vain, and seeing it had been in vain, to appoint a Judge of Controversies, and not to tell us plainly who it is, and seeing lastly, he hath not told us plainly, no not at all who it is, is it not evident he hath appointed none? *Obj.* But (you will say perhaps) *if it be granted once, that some Church of one denomination, is the Infallible guide of Faith, it will be no difficult thing to prove, that yours is the Church, seeing no other Church pretends to be so.* Ans. Yes, the Primitive and the Apostolick Church pretends to be so. That assures us, that the *spirit was promised, and given to them, to lead them into all saving truth,* that they might lead others. Obj. *But that Church is not now in the world, and how then can it pretend to be the guide of Faith?* Ans. It is now in the world sufficiently, to be our guide: not by the persons of those men that were members of it, but by their Writings which do plainly teach us, what truth they were led into, and so lead us into the same truth. Obj. *But these Writings, were the Writings of some particular men, and not of the Church of those times: how then doth that Church guide us by these Writings? Now these places shew that a Church is to be our guide, therefore they cannot be so avoided.* Ans. If you regard the conception and production of these Writings, they were the Writings of particular men: But if you regard the reception, and approbation of them, they may be well called the Writings of the Church, as having the attestation of the Church, to have been written by those that were inspired, and
directed

directed by God. As a Statute, though penned by some one man, yet being ratified by the Parliament, is called the Act, not of that man, but of the Parliament. *Obj.* But the *words seem clearly enough to prove, that the Church, the present Church of every Age, is Universally infallible.* *Ans.* For my part, I know I am as willing and desirous, that the Bishop or Church of *Rome* should be Infallible, (provided I might know it) as they are to be so esteemed. But he that would not be deceived must take heed, that he take not his desire that a thing should be so, for a reason that it is so. For if you look upon Scripture, through such Spectacles as these, they will appear to you, of what colour pleases your fancies best: and will seem to say, not what they do say, but what you would have them. As some say the *Manna*, wherewith the *Israelites* were fed in the Wilderness, had in every mans mouth, that very taste which was most agreeable to his palate. For my part I profess, I have considered them a thousand times, and have looked upon them (as they say,) on both sides, and yet to me they seem to say no such matter.

70. Not the First, *Mat.* 16:18.) For the *Church may err, and yet the gates of Hell not prevail against her.* It may err, and yet continue still a true Church, and bring forth Children unto God, and send Souls to Heaven. And therefore this can do you no service, without the plain begging of the point in Question. *Viz.* That every Error is one of the gates of Hell. Which we absolutely deny, and therefore, you are not to suppose, but to prove it. Neither is our denial without reason. For seeing you do, and must grant, that a particular Church may hold some error, and yet be still a true member of the Church: why may not the Universal Church, hold the same error, and yet remain the true Universal?

71. Not the Second or Third. (*John* 14. 16, 17. *John* 16. 13.) For *the spirit of Truth, may be with a Man, or a Church for ever, and teach him all Truth:* And yet he may fall into some error, if this, *all*, be not *simply all*, but all of some kind.

Secondly,

Secondly, he may fall into some Error, even contrary to the truth which is taught him, if it be taught him *only sufficiently, and not irresistibly,* so that he may learn it if he will, not so that he must and shall, whether he will or no. Now who can assertain me, that the Spirits teaching is not of this nature? Or how can you possibly reconcile it, with your Doctrine of free-will in believing, if it be not of this nature? Besides, the word in the Original is ὁδηγήσει, which signifies, to be a guide and director only, not to compel or necessitate. Who knows not, that a guide may set you in the right way, and you may either negligently mistake, or willingly leave it? And to what purpose doth God conplain so often, and so earnestly of some, that *had eyes to see and would not see, that stopped their Ears, and closed their Eyes, lest they should hear and see?* Of others *that would not understand, lest they should do good: that the Light shined, and the Darkness comprehended it not:* That *he came unto his own, and his own received him not: That light came into the World, and Men loved Darkness more than Light:* To what purpose should he wonder, so few believed his report, and that to so few his Arm was revealed: And that when he comes, he should find no Faith upon Earth; If his outward teaching were not of this nature, that it might be followed, and might be resisted? And if it be, then God may teach, and the Church not learn: God may lead, and the Church be refractory and not follow. And indeed, who can doubt, that hath not his Eyes vailed with prejudice, that God hath taught the Church of *Rome* plain enough in the Epistle to the *Corinthians,* that *all things in the Church are to be done for edification,* and that, in any publick Prayers, or Thanks-givings, or Hymns, or Lessons of instruction, to *use a Language,* which the assistants *generally understand not,* is not for edification? Though the Church of *Rome* will not learn this, for fear of confessing an Error, and so overthrowing her Authority; yet the time will come, when it shall appear, that not only by scripture, they were taught this sufficiently, and commanded to believe, but by reason and common sense. And so for the Communion, in both kinds, who can deny but they are taught it by our Saviour *John* 6. in these Words, according to most of your own expositions, *Unless you Eat the Flesh of the Son of Man, and Drink his Blood, you have no Life in you.* (If our Saviour speak there of the Sacrament, as to them he does, because they conceive he does so.) Though they may pretend, that receiving in one kind, they receive the Blood together with the Body, yet they can with no Face pretend that they drink it: And so obey not our Saviours injunction according to the letter, which yet they *profess is literally, always to be obeyed, unless some impiety, or some absurdity force us to the contrary*: and they are not yet arrived to that impudence to pretend, that either there is impiety or absurdity in receiving the Communion in both kinds. This therefore they if not others, are plainly taught by our Saviour in this place. But by S. *Paul* all without exception, when he says, *Let a man examine himself, and so let him Eat of this Bread and Drink of this Chalice.* This (*a Man*) that is to examine himself, is *every man*, that can do it: as is confessed on all hands. And therefore it is all one, as if he had said, *let every man examine himself, and so let him Eat of this Bread, and Drink of this Cup.* They which acknowledg Saint *Pauls* Epistes, and Saint *Johns* Gospel to be the Word of God, one would think should not deny, but that they are taught these two Doctrines plain enough. Yet we see they neither do, nor will learn them. I conclude therefore, that the Spirit may very well teach the Church, and yet the Church fall into and continue in Error, by not regarding what she is taught by the Spirit.

72. But all this I have spoken upon a supposition only, and shewed unto you, that though these promises, had been made unto the present Church of every Age (I might have said though they had been to the Church of *Rome* by name,) yet no certainty of her Universal Infallibility could be built upon them. But the plain truth is, that these Promises are vainly arrogated by you, and were never made to you, but to the Apostles

ſtles only. I pray deal ingenuouſly and tell me, who were they of whom our Saviour ſays, *Theſe things have I ſpoken unto you, being preſent with you.* c. 14. 25. *But the comforter, ſhall teach you all things, and bring all things to your remembrance, whatſoever I have told you* v. 26? Who are they to whom he ſays, *I go away and come again unto you ; and I have told you before it come to paſs :* v. 28. 29. *You have been with me from the beginning :* c. 15. v. 27? And again, *theſe things I have told you, that when the time ſhall come, you may remember that I told you of them : and theſe things I ſaid not to you at the beginning, becauſe I was with you,* c. 16. 4. *And becauſe I ſaid theſe things unto you, ſorrow hath filled your Hearts,* v. 6 ? Laſtly, who are they of whom he ſaith, v. 12. *I have yet many things to ſay unto you, but ye cannot bear them now* ? Do not all theſe circumſtances appropriate this whole diſcourſe of our Saviour to his Diſciples, that were then with him, and conſequently, reſtrain the Promiſes of the Spirit of truth, which was *to lead them into all truth,* to their Perſons only? And ſeeing it is ſo, is it not an impertinent arrogance and preſumption, for you to lay claim unto them, in the behalf of your Church ? Had Chriſt been preſent with your Church ? Did the Comforter bring theſe things to the Remembrance of your Church, which Chriſt had before taught and ſhe had forgotten ? Was Chriſt then departing from your Church ? And did he tell of his departure before it came to paſs ? Was your Church with him from the beginning ? Was your Church filled with ſorrow, upon the mentioning of Chriſts departure ? Or laſtly, did he, or could he have ſaid to your Church, which then was not extant, *I have yet many things to ſay unto you, but ye cannot bear them now* ? as he ſpeaks in the 13. *verſ.* immediately before the words by you quoted. And then goes on, *Howbeit when the Spirit of truth is come, he will guide you into all Truth.* Is it not the ſame *You* he ſpeaks to, in the 13. *verſ.* and that he ſpeaks to in the 14 ? And is it not apparent to any one that has but half an Eye, that in the 13. he ſpeaks only to them that then were with him ? Beſides in the very Text by you alledged, there are things promised, which your Church cannot with any modesty pretend to. For there it is said, *the Spirit of Truth*, not only *will guide you into all Truth*, but also *will shew you things to come.* Now your Church (for ought I could ever understand) does not so much as pretend to the Spirit of Prophesie, and knowledge of future events: And therefore hath as little cause to pretend to the former promise, of being *led by the Spirit into all truth.* And this is the Reason, why both You in this place, and generally, your writers of Controversies, when they entreat of this Argument, cite this Text perpetually by halfs, there being in the latter part of it, a clear, and convincing Demonstration, that you have nothing to do with the former. Unless you will say, which which is most ridiculous, that when our Saviour said, *He will teach you*, &c. and *he will shew you*, &c. He meant one *You* in the former clause, and another *You* in the latter.

73. *Obj.* But this *is to confine Gods Spirit to the Apostles only, or to the Disciples, that then were present with him: which is directly contrary to many places of Scripture.* Ans. I confess, that to confine the Spirit of God to those that were then present with Christ is against Scripture. But I hope it is easie to conceive a difference, between confining the *Spirit of God* to them: and confining *the Promises made in this place* to them. God may do many things which he does not Promise at all: much more, which he does not promise in such or such a place.

74. *Obj.* But *it is promised in the* 14. *Chap. that this Spirit shall abide with them for ever: Now they in their persons were not to abide for ever; and therefore the Spirit could not abide with them, in their Persons for ever, seeing the coexistence of two things, supposes of necessity, the existence of either. Therefore the promise was not made to them only in their Persons, but by them to the Church, which was to abide for ever.* Ans. Your Conclusion is, *not to them only*, but your Reason concludes, either nothing at all, or that this Promise of abiding with them for ever, was not made to their Persons at all; or if it were, that it was not performed. Or if you will not say (as I hope you will not) that it was

not

not performed, nor that it was not made to their Perfons at all; then muft you grant, that the Word *for ever*, is here ufed in a fenfe reftrained, and accommodated to the fubject here entreated of; and that it fignifies, *not Eternally*, without end of time, *but perpetually* without interruption, for the time of their lives. So that the force, and fenfe of the Words is, that they fhould never want the Spirits affiftance, in the performance of their function: And that the Spirit would not (as Chirft was to do,) ftay with them for a time, and afterwards leave them, but would abide with them, if they kept their ftation, unto the very end of their lives, which is mans *for ever*. Neither is this ufe of the word, *for ever*, any thing ftrange, either in our ordinary fpeech, wherein we ufe to fay, this is mine for ever, this fhall be yours for ever, without ever dreaming of the Eternity, either of the thing or Perfons. And then in Scripture, it not only will bear, but requires this fenfe very frequently, as *Exod.* 21. 6. *Deut.* 15. 17. *his Mafter fhall bore his Ear through with an Awl, and he fhall ferve him for ever.* Pfal. 52. 9. *I will praife thee for ever.* Pfal. 61. 4. *I will abide in thy Tabernacle for ever.* Pfal. 119. 111. *Thy Teftimonies have I taken as mine Heritage for ever*: and laftly in the Epiftle to *Philemon*, He therefore departed from thee for a time, that thou fhouldeft receive him for ever.

75. And thus, I prefume, I have fhewed fufficiently, that this *for ever*, hinders not, but that the promife may be appropriated to the Apoftles, as by many other circumftances I have evinced it muft be. But what now, if the place produced by you, as a main pillar of your Churches Infallibility, prove upon Tryal, an Engine to batter and overthrow it, at leaft, (which is all one to my purpofe) to take away all poffibility of our affurance of it? This will feem ftrange news to you at firft hearing, and not far from a prodigy. And I confefs, as you here in this place, and generally all your Writers of Controverfie, by whom this Text is urged, order the matter, it is very much difabled, to do any fervice againft you in this queftion. For with a bold facriledg, and horrible impiety,

piety, somewhat like *Procrustes* his cruelty, you perpetually cut off the Head and Foot, the beginning and end of it; and presenting to your confidents, who usually read no more of the Bible, than is alledged by you, only these words, *I will ask my Father, and he shall give you another Paraclete, that he may abide with you for ever, even the Spirit of Truth*, conceal in the mean time, the words before, and the words after; that so, the promise of Gods Spirit, may seem to be absolute, whereas it is indeed most clearly and expresly conditional: being both in the words before, restrained to those only, that *love God and keep his commandments*: and in the words after, flatly denied to all, whom the Scriptures stile by the name of *the World*, that is, as the very *Antithesis* give us plainly to understand, *to all wicked and worldly men*. Behold the place entire, as it is set down in your own Bible. *If ye love me keep my Commandments, and I will ask my Father, and he shall give you another Paraclete, that he may abide with you for ever, even the spirit of the Truth, whom the World cannot receive.* Now from the place there restored and vindicated from your mutilation, thus I argue against your pretence. We can have no certainty of the Infallibility of your Church, but upon this supposition, that your *Popes* are infallible in confirming the Decrees of General Councils: we can have no certainty hereof, but upon this supposition, that the Spirit of truth is promised to him, for his direction in this work. And of this again we can have no certainty, but upon supposal, that he performs the condition, whereunto the promise of the Spirit of truth is expresly limited, *viz. That he love God and keep his Commandments*; and of this finally, not knowing the *Popes* Heart, we can have no certainty at all; therefore from the first to the last, we can have no certainty at all of your Churches Infallibility. This is my first Argument: From this place another follows, which will charge you as home as the former. If many of the *Roman* See, were such men as could not receive the Spirit of Truth, even men of the World, that is Worldly, Wicked, Carnal, Diabolical men, then

the

into Fundamental and not Fundamental. 215

the Spirit of Truth, is not here promised, but flatly denied them: and consequently we can have no certainty, neither of the Decrees of Councils, which these *Popes* confirm, nor of the Churches Infallibility, which is guided by these Decrees: But many of the *Roman* See, even by the confession of the most zealous Defenders of it, were such men: therefore the Spirit of truth is not here promised but denyed them, and consequently we can have no certainty, neither of the Decrees which they confirm, nor of the Churches Infallibility, which guides her self by these Decrees.

76. You may take as much time as you think fit, to answer these Arguments. In the mean while I proceed to the consideration of the next Text alledged for this purpose by you: out of S. *Paul* 1. Epistle to *Timothy*: cap. 3. 15. where he saith, as you say *the Church is the Pillar and ground of truth*, But the truth is you are somewhat too bold with S. *Paul*. For he says not in formal terms, what you make him say, *the Church is the Pillar and Ground of Truth*, neither is it certain that he means so: for it is neither impossible nor improbable, that the words *the Pillar and Ground of truth*, may have reference not to the Church, but to *Timothy*, the sense of the place *that thou maiest know how to behave thy self, as a Pillar and ground of truth, in the Church of God, which is the house of the living God*, which exposition offers no violence at all to the words, but only supposes an Ellipsis of the Particle ὡς, in the Greek very ordinary. Neither wants it some likelihood, that S. *Paul* comparing the Church to a House, should here exhort *Timothy*, to carry himself, as a Pillar in that House should do, according as he had given other Principal men in the Church, the name of Pillars; rather than, having called the Church a *House*, to call it presently a *Pillar*; which may seem somewhat heterogeneous. Yet if you will needs have S. *Paul* refer this not to *Timothy* but the Church, I will not contend about it any farther, than to say, possibly it may be otherwise. But then secondly, I am to put you in mind, that the Church which S. *Paul* here speaks of, was that in which *Timothy* conversed

versed, and that was a Particular Church, and not the *Roman*; and such you will not have to be Universally Infallible.

77. Thirdly, if we grant you out of Courtesie (for nothing can enforce us to it) that he both speaks of the Universal Church, and says this of it, then I am to remember you, that many Attributes in Scripture are not Notes of Performance but of Duty, and teach us not what the thing or Person is of necessity, but what it should be. *Ye are the Salt of the Earth,* said our Saviour to his Disciples: not that this quality was inseparable from their Persons, but because it was their Office to be so. For if they must have been so of necessity, and could not have been otherwise, in vain had he put them in fear of that which follows, *If the Salt hath lost his savour, wherewith shall it be Salted? it is thenceforth good for nothing, but to be cast forth, and to be trodden under Foot.* So the Church may be by Duty, the Pillar and Ground, that is, the Teacher of Truth, of all truth, not only necessary but profitable to Salvation; and yet she may neglect and violate this Duty, and be in fact, the teacher of some Error.

78. Fourthly and lastly, if we deal most liberally with you, and grant that the Apostle here speaks of the Catholick Church, calls it the *Pillar and ground of Truth*, and that not only because it should, but because it always shall and will be so, yet after all this, you have done nothing; your Bridge is too short, to bring you to the Bank where you would be, unless you can shew that by truth here, is certainly meant, not only *all necessary* to Salvation, but all that is profitable, absolutely and *simply All*. For that the true Church alwaies shall be the maintainer and teacher of all necessary truth, you know we grant and must grant, for it is of the essence of the Church to be so, and any company of Men were no more a Church without it, than any thing can be a Man, and not be reasonable. But as a Man may be still a Man, though he want a Hand or an Eye, which yet are profitable parts, so the Church may be still a
Church

Church, though it be defective in some profitable truth. And as a Man may be a Man, that has some Boyls and Botches on his Body, so the Church may be the Church, though it have many corruptions both in Doctrine and practice.

79. And thus you see we are at liberty from the former places; having shewed that the sense of them, either must or may be such as will do your Cause no service. But the last you suppose, will be a *Gordian* knot, and ties us fast enough: The words are, *Eph.* 4. 11, 12, 13. *He gave some Apostles, and some Prophets,* &c. *to the consummation of Saints, to the work of the Ministry,* &c. *Until we all meet into the Unity of Faith,* &c. *That we be not hereafter Children, wavering and carried up and down with every wind of Doctrine.* Out of which words, this is the only argument which you collect, or I can collect for you. There is no means to conserve unity of Faith, against every wind of Doctrine, unless it be a Church universally Infallible. But it is impious to say there is no means to conserve unity of Faith against every wind of Doctrine: Therefore there must be a Church universally Infallible. Whereunto I answer, that your major is so far from being confirmed, that it is plainly confuted, by the place alledged. For that tells us of another means for this purpose, to wit, the *Apostles, and Prophets, and Evangelists, and Pastors, and Doctors,* which Christ gave upon his Ascension, and that their *consummating the Saints, doing the work of the Ministry,* and *Edifying the body of Christ,* was the means to bring those (which are there spoken of, be they who they will,) to *the unity of Faith, and to perfection in Christ,* that they might not be *wavering, and carried about, with every wind of false Doctrine.* Now the Apostles, and Prophets, and Evangelists, and Pastors, and Doctors, are not the present Church; therefore the Church is not the only means for this end, nor that which is here spoken of.

80. Peradventure by, *he gave,* you conceive, is to be understood, *he promised that he would give unto the worlds end.* But what reason have you for this conceit? Can you shew that the word, ἔδωκε, hath this signification in other places,

places, and that it muſt have it in this place? Or will not this interpretation drive you preſently to this blaſphemous abſurdity, that God hath not performed his promiſe? Unleſs you will ſay, which for ſhame I think you will not, that you have now, and in all Ages ſince Chriſt have had Apoſtles, and Prophets, and Evangeliſts: for as for Paſtors, and Doctors alone, they will not ſerve the turn. For if God promiſed to give all theſe, then you muſt ſay he hath given all, or elſe that he hath broke his promiſe. Neither may you pretend, that the *Paſtors and Doctors were the ſame with the Apoſtles, and Prophets, and Evangeliſts, and therefore having Paſtors and Doctors, you have all.* For it is apparent, that by theſe names, are denoted ſeveral Orders of men, clearly diſtinguiſhed and diverſified by the Original Text; but much more plainly by your own Tranſlations, for ſo you read it, *ſome Apoſtles, and ſome Prophets, and other ſome Evangeliſts, and other ſome Paſtors and Doctors*: and yet more plainly in the parallel place, 1 *Cor.* 12. to which we are referred by your Vulgar Tranſlation, *God hath ſet ſome in the Church, firſt Apoſtles, ſecondarily Prophets, thirdly Teachers*, therefore this ſubterfuge is ſtopped againſt you. Obj. But *how can they, which died in the firſt Age, keep us in Unity, and guard us from Error, that live now, perhaps in the laſt? This ſeems to be all one, as if a Man ſhould ſay, that* Alexander, *or* Julius Cæſar *ſhould quiet a mutiny in the King of* Spains *Army.* Anſ. I hope you will grant, that *Hippocrates,* and *Galen,* and *Euclid,* and *Ariſtotle,* and *Saluſt,* and Cæſar, and *Livie,* were dead many Ages ſince; and yet that we are now preſerved from Error by them, in a great part of Phyſick, of Geometry, of Logick, of the *Roman* ſtory. But what if theſe men had writ by divine Inſpiration, and writ compleat bodies of the Sciences they profeſſed, and writ them plainly and perſpicuouſly? You would then have granted, I believe, that their works had been ſufficient to keep us from error, and from diſſention in theſe matters. And why then ſhould it be incongruous to ſay, that the Apoſtles, and Prophets, and Evangeliſts, and Paſtors, and Doctors, which Chriſt gave upon his Aſcenſion, by their writings, which

which some of them writ but all approved, are even now sufficient means, to conserve us in Unity of Faith, and guard us from Error? Especially seeing these writings are, by the confession of all parts, true and divine, and as we pretend and are ready to prove, contain a plain and perfect Rule of Faith; and as the *Chiefest of you acknowledge, *contain immediatly, all the Principal and Fundamental points of Christianity,* referring us to the Church and Tradition only for some minute particularities. But tell me I pray, the Bishops that composed the Decrees of the Council of *Trent,* and the Pope that confirmed them, are they means to conserve you in Unity, and keep you from Error, or are they not? Peradventure you will say, *their Decrees are, but not their Persons:* but you will not deny I hope, that you owe your unity, and freedom from Error, to the Persons that made these Decrees: neither will you deny, that the writings which they have left behind them, are sufficient for this purpose. And why may not then the Apostles writings be as fit for such a purpose, as the Decrees of your Doctors? Surely their intent in writing was to conserve us in unity of Faith, and to keep us from Error, and we are sure God spake in them; but your Doctors from whence they are, we are not so certain. Was the Holy Ghost then unwilling, or unable to direct them so, that their writings should be fit and sufficient to attain that end they aimed at in writing? For if he were both able and willing to do so, then certainly he did do so. And then their writings may be very sufficient means, if we would use them as we should do, to preserve us in unity, in all necessary points of Faith, and to guard us from all pernitious Error.

* *Perron.*

81. If yet you be not satisfied, but will still pretend that, *all these words by you cited, seem clearly enough to prove, that the Church is Universally infallible, without which Unity of Faith could not be conserved against every wind of Doctrin:* I *Ans.* That to you, which will not understand, that there can be any means to conserve the unity of Faith, but only that which conserves your authority over the Faithful, it is no marvel that these words seem to prove, that the

Church, nay that your Church is universally Infallible. But we that have no such end, no such desires, but are willing to leave all men to their liberty, provided they will not improve it to a Tyranny over others, we find it no difficulty to discern between *dedit* and *promisit*, *he gave at his Ascension*, and *he promised to the Worlds end*. Besides, though you whom it concerns, may happily flatter your selves, that you have not only Pastors, and Doctors, but Prophets, and Apostles, and Evangelists, and those distinct from the former still in your Church; yet we that are disinteressed persons, cannot but smile at these strange imaginations. Lastly, though you are apt to think your selves such necessary instruments for all good purposes, and that nothing can be well done unless you do it; that no unity or constancy in Religion can be maintained, but inevitably Christendom must fall to ruin, and confusion, unless you support it: yet we that are indifferent and impartial, and well content, that God should give us his own favours, by means of his own appointment, not of our choosing, can easily collect out of these very words, that not the Infallibility of your, or of any Church, but the *Apostles, and Prophets, and Evangelists, &c. which Christ gave upon his Ascension*, were designed by him, for the compassing all these excellent purposes, by their preaching while they lived, and by their writings for ever. And if they fail hereof, the Reason is not any insufficiency or invalidity in the means, but the voluntary perversness of the Subjects they have to deal with: who, if they would be themselves, and be content that others should be, in the choice of their Religion the servants of God and not of men; if they would allow, that the way to Heaven is no narrower now, than Christ left it, his yoak no heavier than he made it; that the belief of no more difficulties, is required now to Salvation, than was in the Primitive Church; that no Error is in it self destructive, and exclusive from Salvation now, which was not then; if instead of being zealous *Papists*, earnest *Calvinists*, rigid *Lutherans*, they would become themselves, and be content that others should be plain and honest Christians;

if

into Fundamental and not Fundamental.

if all men would believe the Scripture, and freeing themselves from prejudice and paſſion, would ſincerely endeavour to find the true ſenſe of it, and live according to it, and require no more of others, but to do ſo; nor denying their Communion to any that do ſo; would ſo order their publick ſervice of God, that all which do ſo may without ſcruple, or hypocriſie, or proteſtation againſt any part of it, joyn with them in it: who does not ſee that (ſeeing as we ſuppoſe here, and ſhall prove hereafter,) all neceſſary Truths, are plainly and evidently ſet down in Scripture, there would of neceſſity be among all men, in all things neceſſary, unity of Opinion? And notwithſtanding any other differences that are or could be, unity of Communion and Charity and mutual Toleration? By which means, all Schiſm and Hereſie, would be baniſhed the World, and thoſe wretched contentions which now rend and tear in pieces, not the Coat, but the Members and Bowels of Chriſt, which mutual pride and Tyranny, and curſing, and killing, and damning, would fain make immortal, ſhould ſpeedily receive a moſt bleſſed Cataſtrophe. But of this hereafter, when we ſhall come to the queſtion of Schiſm, wherein I perſwade my ſelf, that I ſhall plainly ſhew, that the moſt vehement accuſers, are the greateſt offenders, and that they are indeed at this time, the greateſt Schiſmaticks, who make the way to Heaven narrower, the yoak of Chriſt heavier, the differences of Faith greater, the conditions of Eccleſiaſtical Communion harder, and ſtricter, than they were made at the beginning by Chriſt and his Apoſtles: they who talk of Unity, but aim at Tyranny, and will have peace with none, but with Slaves and Vaſſals. In the mean while, though I have ſhewed how Unity of Faith, and Unity of Charity too, may be preſerved without your Churches Infallibility, yet ſeeing you modeſtly conclude from hence, not that your Church is, but only *ſeems to be* univerſally Infallible, meaning to your ſelf, of which you are a better judge than I: Therefore I willingly grant your concluſion, and proceed.

86. As

86. As for your pretence, That *to find the meaning of those places, you confer divers Texts, you consult Originals, you examin Translations, and use all the means by Protestants appointed,* I have told you before, that all this is vain and hypocritical, if (as your manner and your doctrin is) you give not your self liberty of judgment in the use of these means; if you make not your selves Judges of, but only Advocates for the doctrin of your Church, refusing to see what these means shew you, if it any way make against the doctrin of your Church, though it be as clear as the light at noon. Remove prejudice, even the ballance, and hold it even, make it indifferent to you which way you go to heaven, so you go the true, which Religion be true so you be of it, then use the means and pray for Gods assistance, and as sure as God is true, you shall be lead into all necessary Truth.

88. Whereas you say, that *it were great impiety to imagin that God, the lover of Souls, hath left no certain infallible means to decide both this and all other differences arising about the interpretation of Scripture, or upon any other occasion:* I desire you to take heed, you commit not an impiety in making more impieties than Gods Commandments make. Certainly God is no way obliged either by his promise or his love to give us all things, that we may imagine would be convenient for us, as formerly I have proved at large. It is sufficient that he denies us nothing necessary to Salvation. *Deus non deficit in necessariis, nec redundat in superfluis:* So D. *Stapleton.* But that the ending of all Controversies, or having a certain means of ending them, is necessary to Salvation, that you have often said and supposed, but never proved, though it be the main pillar of your whole discourse. So little care you take how slight your foundations are, so your building make a fair show. And as little care, how you commit those faults your self, which you condem in others. For you here charge them with great impiety, who imagine that *God the lover of Souls hath left no infallible means to determine all differences arising about the interpretation of Scripture, or upon any other occasion:* And yet afterwards being demanded by D. *Potter*, why the Questions

into Fundamental and not Fundamental.

stions between the Jesuits and Dominicans remain undetermined? You return him this cross interrogatory, *Who hath assured you that the point wherein these learned men differ, is a revealed Truth, or capable of definition, or is not rather by plain Scripture indeterminable, or by any Rule of Faith?* So then when you say, *it were great impiety to imagine that God hath not left infallible means to decide all differences;* I may answer, It seems you do not believe your self. For in this controversie, which is of as high consequence as any can be, you seem to be doubtful whether there be any means to determin it. On the other side, when you ask D. *Potter, who assured him that there is any means to determine this Controversie?* I answer for him, that you have, in calling *it a great impiety to imagine that there is not some infallible means to decide this and all other differences arising about the Interpretation of Scripture, or upon any other occasion.* For what trick you can devise to shew that this difference, between the *Dominicans* and *Jesuits*, which includes a difference about the sense of many Texts of Scripture, and many other matters of moment, was not included under *this and all other differences*, I cannot imagine. Yet if you can find out any, thus much at least we shall gain by it, *that general speeches are not always to be understood generally, but sometimes with exceptions and limitations.*

89. But if there be any infallible means to decide all differences, I beseech you name them. *You say it is to consult and hear Gods Visible Church with submissive acknowledgment of her Infallibility.* But suppose the difference be (as here it is) *whether your Church be Infallible*, what shall decide that? If you would say (as you should do) Scripture and Reason, then you foresee that you should be forced to grant that these are fit means to decide this Controversie, and therefore may be as fit to decide others. Therefore to avoid this, you run into a most ridiculous absurdity, and tell us that this difference also, whether the Church be Infallible, as well as others, must be agreed by *a submissive acknowledgment of the Churches Infallibility.* As if you should have said, My Brethren, I perceive this is a great contention amongst you, whether the *Roman* Church

be

be Infallible? If you will follow my advice, I will shew you a ready means to end it; you must first agree that the *Roman* Church is Infallible, and then your contention whether the *Roman* Church be Infallible, will quickly be at an end. Verily a most excellent advice, and most compendious way of ending all Controversies, even without troubling the Church to determine them! For why may not you say in all other differences, as you have done in this? Agree that the *Pope* is supream head of the Church: That the substance of Bread and Wine in the Sacrament is turned into the body, and blood of Christ: That the Communion is to be given to Lay-men but in one kind: That Pictures may be worshipped: That Saints are to be invocated; and so in the rest, and then your differences about the Popes Supremacy, Transubstantiation, and all the rest will speedily be ended. If you say, the advice is good in this, but not in other cases, I must request you not to expect always, to be believed upon your word, but to shew us some reason, why any one thing, namely the Churches Infallibility, is fit to prove it self; and any other thing, by name the Popes Supremacy, or Transubstantiation is not as fit? Or if for shame you will at length confess, that the Churches Infallibility is not fit to decide this difference, whether the Church be infallible, then you must confess it is not fit to decide all: Unless you will say, it may be fit to decide all, and yet not fit to decide this, or pretend that this is not comprehended under all. Besides if you grant that your Churches infallibility cannot possibly be well grounded upon, or decided by it self, then having professed before, that *there is no possible means besides this, for us to agree hereupon*, I hope you will give me leave to conclude, that it is impossible upon good ground for us to agree that the *Roman* Church is Infallible. For certainly light it self, is not more clear than the evidence of this syllogism: If there be no other means to make men agree upon your Churches Infallibility, but only this, and this be no means, then it is simply impossible for men upon good grounds to agree that your Church is Infallible: But there is (as you have granted) no other possible

sible means to make men agree hereupon, but only a submissive acknowledgment of her Infallibility, And this is apparently no means; Therefore it is simply impossible for men upon good grounds to agree that your Church is Infallible.

90. Lastly to the place of S. *Austin, wherein we are advised to follow the way of Catholick Discipline, which from Christ himself by the Apostles hath come down even to us, and from us shall descend to all posterity*: I answer, That the way which S. *Austin* speaks of, and the way which you commend, being divers ways, and in many things clean contrary, we cannot possibly follow them both; and therefore for you to apply the same words to them is a vain equivocation. Shew us any way, and do not say, but prove it *to have come from Christ and his Apostles down to us*; and we are ready to follow it. Neither do we expect demonstration hereof, but such reasons as may make this more probable than the contrary. But if you bring in things into your now Catholick Discipline, which Christians in S. *Austins* time held abominable, (as the Picturing of God,) and which you must confess to have come into the Church Seven Hundred Years after Christ: if you will bring in things, as you have done the half Communion, with a *non obstante, notwithstanding Christ Institution, and the practice of the Primitive Church were to the contrary*: If you will do such things as these, and yet would have us believe, that your whole Religion came from Christ and his Apostles, this we conceive a request too unreasonable for modest men to make, or for wise Men to grant.

Gg   CHAP.

CHAP. IV.

The ANSWER to the Fourth CHAPTER.

Wherein is shewed, that the Creed contains all necessary points of meer Belief.

AD §. 1, 2, 3, 4, 5, 6.] Concerning the Creeds containing the Fundamentals of Christiany, this is D. *Potters* assertion, delivered in the 207. p. of his Book. *The Creed of the Apostles (as it is explained in the latter Creeds of the Catholick Church) is esteemed a sufficient summary or Catalogue of Fundamentals, by the best learned Romanists and by Antiquity.*

2. By *Fundamentals* he understands *not the Fundamental rules of good Life and Action,* (though every one of these is to be believed to come from God, and therefore virtually includes an Article of Faith;) but the Fundamental *Doctrines of Faith*; such, as though they have influence upon our lives, as every essential Doctrine of Christianinity hath, yet we are commanded to believe them, and not to do them. The assent of our understandings is required to them, but no obedience from our wills.

3. But these speculative Doctrines again he distinguishes out of *Aquinas, Occham,* and *Canus* and others, into two kinds: of the fitst are those which are the *Objects of Faith, in, and for themselves,* which by their own nature and Gods prime intention, are essential parts of that Gospel: such as the Teachers in the Church, cannot without Mortal sin omit to teach the Learners: such as are intrinsecal to the Covenant between God and Man; and not only plainly revealed by God, and so *certain* truths, but also commanded to be preacht to all men, and to be believed distinctly by all, and so *necessary truths.* Of the second sort are *Accidental, Circumstantial, Occasional* objects of Faith; Millions whereof there are in Holy Scripture; such as are to be believed, not for themselves,

but

but becaufe they are joyned with others, that are neceffary to be believed, and delivered by the fame Authority which delivered thefe. Such as we are not bound to know to be Divine Revelations, (for without any fault we may be Ignorant hereof, nay believe the contrary;) fuch as we are not bound to examine, whether or no they be Divine Revelations: fuch as Paftors are not bound to teach their Flock, nor their Flock bound to know and remember: no nor the Paftors themfelves to know them, or believe them, or not to disbelieve them abfolutely and always; but then only when they do fee, and know them to be delivered in Scripture, as Divine Revelations.

4. I fay when they do fo, and not only when they may do. For to lay an obligation upon us of believing, or not disbelieving any Verity, fufficient Revelation on Gods part, is not fufficient: For then feeing all the exprefs Verities of Scripture are either to all men, or at leaft to all learned men fufficiently revealed by God, it fhould be a damnable fin, in any learned men actually to disbelieve any one particular Hiftorical verity contained in Scripture, or to believe the contradiction of it, though he knew it not to be there contained. For though he did not, yet he might have known it; it being plainly revealed by God, and this revelation being extant in fuch a Book, wherein he might have found it recorded, if with dilligence he had perufed it. To make therefore any points neceffary to be believed, it is requifite, that either we actually know them to be Divine Revelations: and thefe though they be not Articles of Faith, nor neceffary to be believed, in and for themfelves, yet indirectly, and by accident, and by confequence, they are fo: The neceffity of believing them, being inforced upon us, by a neceffity of believing this Effential, and Fundamental Article of Faith, *That all Divine Revelations are true*, which to disbelieve, or not to believe, is for any Chriftian not only impious, but impoffible. Or elfe it is requifite that they be, Firft actually revealed by God. Secondly, commanded under pain of damnation, to be particularly

The Creed contains all necessary points of meer Belief.

particularly known (I mean known to be Divine Revelations,) and distinctly to be believed. And of this latter sort of speculative Divine Verities, *D. Potter* affirmed, *that the Apostles Creed was a sufficient summary*: yet he affirmed it, not as his own opinion, but as the Doctrine of the *Ancient Fathers, and your own Doctors.* And besides, he affirmed it not as absolutely certain, but very probable.

5. In brief, all that he says is this: It is *very probable, that according to the judgment of the* Roman *Doctors, and the Ancient Fathers, the Apostles Creed is to be esteemed a sufficient summary of all those Doctrines which being meerly* Credenda, *and not* Agenda, *all men are ordinarily, under pain of Damnation, bound particularly to believe.*

6. Now *this assertion* (you say) *is neither pertinent to the question in hand, nor in it self true.* Your Reasons to prove it impertinent, put into form and divested of impertinencies are these. 1. *Because the question was not, what points were necessary to be explicitly believed, but what points were necessary not to be disbelieeved after sufficient proposal. And therefore to give a Catalogue of points, necessary to be explicitly believed is impertinent.*

7. *Secondly, because Errors may be damnable, though the contrary truths be not of themselves Fundamental; as that* Pontius Pilate *was our Saviours Judge, is not in it self a Fundamental truth, yet to believe the contrary were a damnable Error. And therefore to give a Catalogue of Truths in themselves Fundamental, is no pertinent satisfaction to this demand, what Errors are damnable?*

8. *Thirdly, because if the Church be not Universally infallible, we cannot ground any certainty upon the Creed, which we must receive upon the Credit of the Church: and if the Church be Universally Infallible, it is damnable to oppose her declaration in any thing, though not contained in the Creed.*

9. *Fourthly, Because not to believe the Articles of the Creed in the true sense is damnable, therefore it is frivolous to say the Creed contains all Fundamentals, without specifying in what sense the Articles of it are Fundamental.*

10. *Fifthly, because the Apostles Creed (as* D.Potter *himself confesses) was not a sufficient Catalogue, till it was explained*

by

The Creed contains all necessary points of meer Belief.

by the first Council; nor then until it was declared in the second, &c. by occasion of emergent Heresies: Therefore now also as new Heresies may arise, it will need particular explanation, and so is not yet, nor ever will be a compleat Catalogue of Fundamentals.

11. Now to the first of these objections I say: First, that your distinction between points necessary to be believed, and necessary not to be disbelieved, is more subtil than sound, a distinction without a difference: There being no point necessary to be believed, which is not necessary not to be disbelieved: Nor no point to any man, at any time, in any circumstances necessary not to be disbelieved, but it is to the same man, at the same time, in the same circumstances, necessary to be believed. Yet that which (I believe) you would have said, I acknowledge true, that many points which are not necessary to be believed absolutely, are yet necessary to be believed upon a supposition, that they are known to be revealed by God: that is, become then necessary to be believed, when they are known to be Divine Revelations. But then I must needs say, you do very strangly, in saying, that *the question was, what points might lawfully be disbelieved, after sufficient Proposition that they are Divine Revelations.* You affirm, that none may, and so does D. Potter, and with him all Protestants, and all Christians. And how then is this the question? Who ever said or thought, that of Divine Revelations, known to be so, some might safely and lawfully be rejected, and disbelieved, under pretence that they are not Fundamental? which of us ever taught, that it was not damnable, either to deny, or so much as doubt of the Truth of any thing, whereof we either know, or believe that God hath revealed it? What Protestant ever taught that it was not damnable, either to give God the lie, or to call his Veracity into question? Yet you say, *The demand of Charity mistaken was, and it was most reasonable, that a list of Fundamentals, should be given, the denial whereof destroys Salvation, whereas the denial of other points may stand with Salvation, although both kinds be equally proposed, as revealed by God.*

12. Let

12. Let the reader peruse *Charity Mistaken*, and he shall find that this qualification, *although both kinds of points be equally proposed as revealed by God*, is your addition, and no part of the demand. And if it had, it had been most unreasonable, seeing he and you know well enough, that (though we do not presently without examination, fall down and worship all your Churches proposals, as Divine Revelations) yet, we make no such distinction of known Divine Revelations, as if some only of them were necessary to be believed, and the rest might safely be rejected. So that to demand a particular minute Catalogue of all points that may not be disbelieved after sufficient Proposition, is indeed to demand a Catalogue of all points that are or may be, in as much as none may be disbelieved, after sufficient Proposition, that it is a Divine Revelation. At least it is to desire us, First, to Transcribe into this Catalogue, every Text of the whole Bible. Secondly, to set down distinctly, those innumerous Millions of negative and positive consequences, which may be evidently deduced from it: For these we say, God hath revealed. And indeed you are not ashamed in plain terms to require this of us. For having first told us, *that the demand was, what points were necessary not to be disbelieved, after sufficient proposition that they are Divine Truths*: you come to say, *Certainly the Creed contains not all these*. And this you prove by asking, *how many Truths are there in Holy Scripture, not contained in the Creed, which we are not bound to know and believe, but are bound under pain of damnation not to reject, as soon as we come to know that they are found in Holy Scripture?* So that in requiring a particular Catalogue of all points, not to be disbelieved, after sufficient Proposal, you require us to set you down all points contained in Scripture, or evidently deducible from it. And yet this you are pleased to call a *reasonable*, nay, *a most reasonable Demand*: whereas having ingaged your self to give a Catalogue of your Fundamentals, you conceive your engagement very well satisfied by saying, *all is Fundamental which the Church proposes*, without going about, to give us

an

The Creed contains all necessary points of meer Belief.

an endless Inventory of her Proposals. And therefore from us, instead of a perfect particular of Divine Revelations of all sorts, (of which with a less hyperbole than S. *John* useth, we might say, *If they were to be written, the World would not hold the Books that must be written*;) methinks you should accept of this general, All Divine Revelations are true, and to be believed.

13. The very truth is, the main Question in this business is not, *what Divine Revelations are necessary to be believed, or not rejected when they are sufficiently proposed*: for all without exception, all without question are so; But *what Revelations are simply and absolutely necessary to be proposed to the belief of Christians, so that that Society, which does propose, and indeed believe them, hath for matter of Faith, the essence of a true Church; that which does not, has not*. Now to this question, though not to yours, D. Potter's assertion (if it be true) is apparently very pertinent. And though not a full and total satisfaction to it, yet very effectual, and of great moment towards it. For the main question being, what points are necessary to Salvation: and points necessary to Salvation, being of two sorts, some of *simple belief*, some of *Practice and Obedience*, he that gives you a sufficient summary, of the first sort of necessary points, hath brought you half way towards your Journies end. And therefore that which he does, is no more to be slighted, as vain and impertinent, than an Architects work is to be thought impertinent towards the making of a House, because he does it not all himself. Sure I am, if his assertion be true, as I believe it is, a Corollary may presently be deduced from it, which if it were imbraced, cannot in all reason, but do infinite service, both to the truth of Christ, and the peace of Christendom. For seeing falshood and Error could not long stand against the power of truth, were they not supported by Tyranny and worldly advantages, he that could assert Christians to that liberty which Christ and his Apostles left them, must need do Truth a most Heroical service. And seeing the overvaluing of the differences among Christians, is one of the greatest maintainers of the

Schism

Schism of Christendom, he that could demonstrate that only these points of Belief, are simply necessary to Salvation, wherein Christians generally agree, should he not lay a very fair and firm Foundation of the peace of Christendom? Now the Corollary which I conceive would produce these good effects, and which flowes naturally from D. *Potters* Assertion, is this, *That what Man or Church soever believes the Creed, and all the evident consequences of it sincerely and heartily, cannot possibly (if also he believe the Scripture) be in any Error of simple belief which is offensive to God; nor therefore deserve for any such Error to be deprived of his Life, or to be cut off from the Churches Communion, and the hope of Salvation.* And the production of this again would be this (which highly concerns the Church of *Rome* to think of,) *That whatsoever Man or Church does for any Error of simple belief, deprive any man so quallified as above, either of his temporal life, or livelyhood or liberty, or of the Churches Communion, and hope of Salvation, is for the first unjust, cruel, and Tyrannous: Schismatical, presumptuous, and uncharitable for the second.*

14. Neither yet is this (as you pretend) to take away the necessity of believing those Verities of Scripture, which are not contained in the Creed, when once we come to know that they are written in Scripture, but rather to lay a necessity upon men of believing all things written in Scripture, when once they know them to be there written. For he that believes not all known Divine Revelations to be true, how does he believe in God? Unless you will say, that the same man, at the same time may not believe God, and yet believe in him. The greater difficulty is, how it will not take away the necessity of believing Scripture to be the Word of God? But that it will not neither. For though the Creed be granted a sufficient summary of *Articles of meer Faith*, yet no man pretends that it contains the *Rules of Obedience*, but for them, all men are referred to Scripture. Besides, he that pretends to believe in God, obligeth himself to believe it necessary to obey that which reason assures him to be the Will of God. Now reason will assure him

The Creed contains all necessary points of meer belief.

him that believes the Creed, that it is the Will of God he should believe the Scripture: even the very same Reason which moves him to believe the Creed: Universal, and never failing Tradition, having given this Testimony both to Creed and Scripture, that they both by the works of God were sealed, and testified to be the words of God. And thus much be spoken in Answer to your first Argument; the length whereof will be the more excusable, If I oblige my self to say but little to the rest.

15. I come then *to your second*. And in Answer to it, deny flatly, as a thing destructive of it self, that any Error can be damnable, unless it be repugnant immediatly or mediatly, directly or indirectly, of it self or by accident, to some Truth for the matter of it fundamental. And to your example of *Pontius Pilat's being Judge of Christ*, I say the denial of it in him that knows it to be revealed by God, is manifestly destructive of this Fundamental truth, that *all Divine Revelations are true*. Neither will you find any Error so much as by accident damnable, but the rejecting of it will be necessarily laid upon us, by a real belief of all Fundamentals, and simply necessary Truths. And I desire you would reconcile with this, that which you have said §.15. *Every Fundamental Error must have a contrary Fundamental Truth, because of two Contradictory propositions in the same degree, the one is false, the other must be true*, &c.

16. *To the Third* I Answer; That the certainty I have of the Creed, That it was from the Apostles, and contains the principles of Faith, I ground it not upon Scripture, and yet not upon the Infallibility of any present, much less of your Church, but upon the Authority of the Ancient Church, and written Tradition, which (as D. *Potter* hath proved) gave this constant Testimony unto it. Besides I tell you, it is guilty of the same fault which D. *Potter*'s Assertion is here accused of: having perhaps some colour toward the proving it false, but none at all to shew it impertinent.

17. *To the Fourth*, I Answer plainly thus, That you find fault with D. *Potter* for his Vertues: you are offended with him for not usurping the Authority which he hath not; in

H h   a word

a word for not playing the *Pope*. Certainly if *Protestants* be faulty in this matter, it is for doing it too much, and not too little. This presumptuous imposing of the senses of men upon the words of God, the special senses of men upon the general words of God, and laying them upon mens consciences together, under the equal penalty of death, and damnation; this vain conceit that we can speak of the things of God, better than in the word of God: This Deifying our own Interpretations, and Tyrannous inforcing them upon others; This restraining of the word of God from that latitude and generality, and the understandings of men from that liberty, wherein Christ and the Apostles left them, * is, and hath been the only fountain of all the Schisms of the Church, and that which makes them immortal: the common incendiary of Christendom, and that which (as I said before) tears into pieces, not the coat, but the bowels, and members of Christ: *Ridente Turcâ nec dolente Judæo.* Take away these Walls of separation, and all will quickly be one. Take away this *Persecuting, Burning, Cursing, Damning* of men for not subscribing to the *words of Men,* as the words of God; Require of Christians only to believe Christ, and to call no man master but him only: Let those leave claiming Infallibility that have no title to it, and let them that in their words disclaim it, disclaim it likewise in their actions; In a word, take away Tyranny, which is the Devils instrument to support errors, and superstitions, and impieties, in the several parts of the World, which could not otherwise long withstand the power of Truth, I say take away Tyranny, and restore Christians to their just and full liberty of captivating their understanding to Scripture only, and as Rivers when they have a free passage, run all to the Ocean, so it may well be hoped by Gods blessing, that Universal Liberty thus moderated, may quickly reduce Christendom to Truth and Unity. These thoughts of peace (I am perswaded) may come from the God of peace, and to his blessing I commend them, and proceed.

* This perswasion is no singularity of mine but the Doctrin which I have learnt from Divines of great learning and judgment. Let the Reader be pleased to peruse the seaventh book of *Acontius de Stratag. Satanæ.* And *Zanchius* his last *Oration* delivered by him after the composing of the discord between him and *Amerbachius,* and he shall confess as much.

18. Your *fifth and last objection* stands upon a false and dangerous supposition: That *new Heresies may arise.* For

an Heresie being in it self nothing else but a Doctrine Repugnant to some Article of the Christian Faith, to say that new Heresies may arise, is to say, that new Articles of Faith may arise: and so some great ones among you stick not to profess in plain terms, who yet at the same time are not ashamed to pretend that your whole Doctrin is Catholick and Apostolick. So *Salmeron*: *Non omnibus omnia dedit Deus, ut quælibet ætas suis gaudeat veritatibus, quas prior ætas ignoravit.* God hath not given all things to All: So that every age hath its proper Verities, which the former age was ignorant of: *Disp.* 57. *In Ep. ad Rom.* And again in the Margent: *Habet Unumquodq; sæculum peculiares Revelationes Divinas*, Every age hath its peculiar Divine Revelations. Where that he speaks of such Revelations as are, or may by the Church be made matters of Faith, no man can doubt that reads him; an example whereof, he gives us a little before in these words. *Unius Augustini doctrina Assumptionis B. Deiparæ cultum in Ecclesiam introduxit.* The Doctrin of *Augustin* only, hath brought in to the Church the Worship of the Assumption of the Mother of God, *&c.* Others again mince and palliate the matter with this pretence, that your Church undertakes not to coyn new Articles of Faith, but only to declare those that want sufficient declaration. But if sufficient declaration be necessary to make any Doctrin an Article of Faith, then this Doctrin which before wanted it, was not before an Article of Faith; and your Church by giving it the Essential form, and last complement of an Article of Faith, makes it, though not a Truth, yet certainly an Article of Faith. But I would fain know, whether Christ and his Apostles knew this Doctrin, which you pretend hath the matter, but wants the form of an Article of Faith, that is, *sufficient declaration,* whether they knew it to be a necessary Article of the Faith, or no! If they knew it not to be so: then either they taught what they knew not, which were very strange; or else they taught it not: and if not, I would gladly be informed, seeing you pretend to no new Revelations from whom you learnt it? If they knew it, then either they concealed or declared it. To say they concealed any necessary part of the Gospel, is to charge them with far greater Sacriledg, than what was punished in *Ananias* and *Saphira.* It is to charge these glorious Stewards, and dispensers of the Mysteries of Christ, with want of the great vertue requisite in a Steward, which is *Fidelity.* It is to charge them with presumption for denouncing Anathema's, even to Angels, in case they should teach any other doctrin, than what they had received from them, which sure could not merit an Anathema, if they left any necessary part of the Gospel untaught. It is in a word, in plain terms to give them the lie, seeing they profess plainly and frequently, that they taught Christians *the whole Doctrin of Christ.* If they did know and declare it, then was it a full and formal Article of Faith; and the contrary a full and formal Heresie, without any need of further declaration: and then their Successors either continued the declaration of it, or discontinued: If they did the latter, how are they such faithful depositaries of Apostolick Doctrin as you pretend? Or what assurance can you give us, that they might not bring in new and false Articles, as well as suffer the old and true ones to be lost? If they did continue the declaration of it, and deliver it to their Successors, and they to theirs, and so on perpetually, then continued it still a full and formal Article of faith, and the repugnant doctrin a full and formal Heresie, without and before the definition or declaration of a Council. So that Councils, as they cannot make that a truth or falshood, which before was not so: so neither can they make or declare that to be an Article of Faith, or an Heresie, which before was not so. The supposition therefore on which this argument stands, being false and ruinous, whatsoever is built upon it, must together with it fall to the ground. This explication therefore, and restriction of this doctrin, (whereof you make your advantage) was to my understanding unnecessary. The Fathers of the Church in after times might have just cause to declare their judgment, touching the sense of some general Articles of the Creed: but to oblige others to receive their declarations under pain of damnation, what warrant they had I

know

The Creed contains all necessary points of meer belief. 237

know not. He that can shew, either that the Church of all Ages was to have this Authority; or that it continued in the Church for some Ages, and then expired: He that can shew either of these things let him: for my part I cannot. Yet I willingly confess the judgment of a Council, though not infallible, is yet so far directive and obliging that without apparent reason to the contrary, it may be sin to reject it, at least not to afford it an outward submission for publick peace sake.

20. Ad §. 7. 8, 9. I come now to shew that you also have requited D. *Potter* with a mutual courteous acknowledgment of his assertion, That the Creed is a sufficient summary of all the necessary Articles of Faith, which are meerly *Credenda*.

21. First then, §. 8. You have these words, *That it cannot be denied that the Creed is most full and compleat to that purpose, for which the holy Apostles, inspired by God, meant that it should serve, and in that manner as they did intend it, which was, not to comprehend all particular points of Faith, but such general heads as were most befitting and requisite for preaching the Faith of Christ, to Jews and Gentiles, and might be briefly, and compendiously set down, and easily learnt and remembred.* These words I say, being fairly examined, without putting them on the rack, will amount, to a full acknowledgment of D. *Potters* Assertion. But before I put them to the question, I must crave thus much right of you, to grant me this most reasonable postulate, that the doctrin of *repentance from dead works*, which S. *Paul* saith, was one of the two only things which he preacht, and the doctrin *of Charity, without which* (the same S. *Paul* assures us that) *the knowledge of all mysteries, and all faith is nothing*, were doctrins more necessary and requisite, and therefore more fit to be preacht to *Jews* and *Gentiles*, than these, *under what judge our Saviour suffered, that he was buried*, and *what time he rose again*: which you have taught us cap. 3. §. 2. *for their matter and nature in themselves not to be Fundamental.*

22. And upon this grant, I will ask no leave to conclude, that, whereas you say, *the Apostles Creed was intended for a comprehension, of such heads of faith, as were most befitting*

and

and requisite, for preaching the faith of Christ, &c. You are now, for fear of too much debasing those high doctrines as Repentance and Charity, to restrain your assertion, as D. *Potter* does his, (and though you speak indefinitely) to say you meant it, only of those heads of faith, which are *meerly Credenda.* And then the meaning of it, (if it have any,) must be this, That the Creed is full for the Apostles intent, which was to comprehend all such general heads of faith, which being points of *simple belief,* were most fit and requisite, to be preached to Jews and Gentiles, and might be briefly and compendiously set down, and easily learned and remembred. Neither I nor you, I believe, can make any other sence of your words than this. And upon this ground thus I subsume. But all the points of belief, which were necessary, under pain of damnation, for the Apostles to preach, and for those to whom the Gospel was preached, particularly to know and believe, were most fit and requisite, nay more than so, necessary to be preached to all both Jews and Gentiles, and might be briefly and compendiously set down, and easie learn'd and remembred: therefore the Apostles intent by your confession, was in this Creed, to comprehend all such points. And you say, *the Creed is most full and complete, for the purpose which they intended.* The Major of this Syllogism is your own. The Minor I should think needs no proof, yet because all men may not be of my mind, I will prove it by its parts; and the first part thus, There is the same necessity, for the doing of these things, which are commanded to be done, by the same Authority, under the same penalty: But the same Authority, *viz.* Divine, under the same penalty, to wit, of damnation, commanded the Apostles, to preach all these Doctrines which we speak of, and those to whom they were preached, particularly to know and believe them: For we speak of those only, which were so commanded, to be preached and believed: Therefore all these points were alike necessary to be preached to all both Jews and Gentiles. Now that all these doctrines we speak of, may be briefly and compendiously set down, and easily learned and remembred, he that remembers, that we spake

only

only of such Doctrines as are necessary to be taught and learned, will require hereof no farther demonstration. For, (not to put you in mind of what the Poet says, *Non sunt longa quibus nihil est quod demere possis,*) who sees not, that seeing the greatest part of men are of very mean capacities, that it is necessary that that may be learnt easily, which is to be learn'd of all? What then can hinder me from concluding thus, all the Articles of simple belief, which are fit and requisite to be preached, and may easily be remembred, are by your confession comprized in the Creed: but all the necessary Articles of Faith are requisite to be preached, and easie to be remembred; therefore they are all comprized in the Creed? Secondly, from grounds granted by you, I argue thus, Points of belief in themselves fundamental, are more requisite to be preached than those which are not so: (this is evident.) But the Apostles have put into their Creed some points that are not in themselves fundamental: (so you confess, *ubi supra.*) Therefore if they have put in all, most requisite to be preached, they have put in all, that in themselves are fundamental. Thirdly and lastly, from your own words Sect. 26. thus I conclude my purpose, *The Apostles intention was, particularly to deliver in the Creed such Articles as were fittest for those times, concerning the Deity, Trinity, and Messias*; (thus you, now I subsume,) but all points simply necessary, by vertue of Gods command, to be preached and believed in particular, were as fit for those times as these here mentioned; therefore their intention was, to deliver in it particularly all the necessary points of belief.

23. And certainly he that considers the matter advisedly, either must say that the Apostles were not the Authors of it, or that this was their design in composing it, or that they had none at all. For whereas you say, *their intent was, to comprehend in it such general heads as were most besitting and requisite for preaching the faith*; and elsewhere, *Particularly to deliver such Articles as were fittest for those times*; Every wise man may easily see that your desire here was, to escape away in a cloud of indefinite terms. For otherwise, instead of such general heads, and such Articles,

why did not you say plainly, all such, or some such? This had been plain dealing, but I fear, cross to your design: which yet you have failed of. For that which you have spoken (though you are loath to speak out,) either signifies nothing at all; or that which I and D. *Potter* affirm: *viz.* That the Apostles Creed contains all those points of belief, which were by Gods command, of necessity to be preached to all, and believed by all. Neither when I say so, would I be so mistaken, as if I said, that all points in the Creed are thus necessary: For Punies in Logick, know that universal affirmatives, are not simply converted. And therefore it may be true, that all such necessary points, are in the Creed; though it be not true, that all points in the Creed are thus necessary: which I willingly grant, of the points by you mentioned. But this rather confirms, than any way invalidates my assertion. For how could it stand with the Apostles wisdom, to put in any points circumstantial and not necessary, and at the same time, to leave out any that were essential and necessary for that end, which you say they proposed to themselves, in making the Creed, that is, *The preaching of the Faith, to Jews and Gentiles?*

31. Ad §.11.12,13,14,15. Obj. *Summaries and Abstracts are not intended to specifie all the particulars of the science or subject to which they belong.*

Ans. Yes if they be intended for perfect Summaries, they must not omit any necessary doctrin of that Science whereof they are Summaries; though the Illustration and Reasons of it they may omit. If this were not so, a man might set down forty or fifty of the Principal definitions and divisions, and rules of Logick, and call it a Summary or Abstract of Logick. But sure, this were no more a Summary, than that were the picture of a man in little, that wanted any of the parts of a man; or that a total sum wherein all the particulars were not cast up. Now the Apostles Creed you here intimate that it was intended for a Summary: otherwise why talk you here of Summaries, and tell us that they need not contain all the particulars of their Science? And of what I pray may it be a
Sum-

The Creed contains all necessary points of meer Belief.

Summary, but of the Fundamentals of Christian Faith? Now you have already told us, *That it is most full and compleat to that purpose for which it was intended.* Lay all this together, and I believe the product will be; That the Apostles Creed is a perfect Summary of the Fundamentals of the Christian Faith: and what the duty of a perfect Summary is, I have already told you.

32. Whereas therefore to disprove this Assertion, in divers particles of this Chapter, but especially the Fourteenth, you muster up whole Armies of Doctrines, which you pretend are necessary, and not contained in the Creed; I answer very briefly thus: That the Doctrines you mention, are either concerning matters of practice, and not simple belief; or else they are such Doctrines wherein God has not so plainly revealed himself, but that honest and good men, true Lovers of God and of Truth, those that desire above all things to know his will and do it, may Err, and yet commit no sin at all, or only a sin of infirmity, and not destructive of Salvation; or lastly, they are such Doctrines which God hath plainly revealed, and so are necessary to be believed when they are known to be Divine, but not necessary to be known and believed, not necessary to be known for Divine, that they may be believed. Now all these sorts of Doctrines are impertinent to the present Question.

33. First, the Questions touching the Conditions to be performed by us to obtain remission of sins; the Sacraments; the Commandments, and the possibility of keeping them, the necessity of imploring the Assistance of Gods Grace and Spirit for the keeping of them: how far obedience is due to the Church: Prayer for the Dead: The cessation of the Old Law: are all about *Agenda*, and so cut off upon the first consideration.

34. Secondly, the Question touching Fundamentals, is profitable but not Fundamental. He that believes all Fundamentals, cannot be damned for any Error in Faith, though he believe more or less to be Fundamental than is so. That also of the procession of the Holy Ghost from the Father and the Son: of Purgatory; of the Churches

I i   Visibility:

Visibility: of the Books of the *New Testament* which were doubted of by a considerable part of the Primitive Church: (until I see better reason for the contrary than the bare authority of men,) I shall esteem of the same condition.

35. Thirdly, These Doctrines that *Adam* and the Angels sinned: that there are Angels good and bad: that those Books of Scripture which were never doubted of by any considerable part of the Church, are the word of God: that S. *Peter* had no such primacy as you pretend: that the Scripture is a perfect rule of Faith, and consequently that no necessary Doctrine is unwritten: that there is no one Society or succession of Christians absolutely Infallible: These to my understanding are truths plainly revealed by God, and necessary to be believed by them who know they are so. But not so necessary, that every Man and Woman is bound under pain of damnation particularly to know them to be Divine Revelations, and explicitely to believe them. And for this reason, these with innumerable other points, are to be referred to the third sort of Doctrines above mentioned, which were never pretended to have place in the Creed. There remains one only point of all that Army you Mustred together, reducible to none of these Heads, and that is, that God is, and is a Remunerator, which you say is questioned by the denial of merit. But if there were such a necessary indissoluble coherence between this point and the Doctrine of merit, methinks with as much reason, and more charity you might conclude, That we hold merit, because we hold this point; Then that we deny this point, because we deny merit. Beside, when *Protestants* deny the Doctrine of Merits, you know right well, for so they have declared themselves a thousand times, that they mean nothing else, but with *David*, that *their well doing extendeth not, is not truly beneficial to God*: with our Saviour, *when they have done all which they are commanded, they have done their duty only*, and no courtesie: And lastly, with S. *Paul*, that *all which they can suffer for God* (and yet suffering is more than doing) *is not worthy to be compared*

The Creed contains all necessary points of meer Belief.

pared to the glory that shall be revealed. So that you must either misunderstand their meaning in denying Merit, or you must discharge their Doctrine of this odious consequence, or you must charge it upon *David* and *Paul* and *Christ* himself. Nay you must either grant their denial of true Merit just and reasonable, or you must say, that our good actions are really profitable to God: that they are not debts already due to him, but voluntary and undeserved Favours: and that they are equal unto and well worthy of Eternal Glory which is prepared for them. As for the inconvenience which you so much fear, That the denial of Merit makes God a giver only, and not a rewarder; I tell you, good Sir, you fear where no fear is, and that it is both most true on the one side, that you in holding good Works meritorious of Eternal Glory make God a rewarder only and not a giver, contrary to plain Scripture, affirming that *The gift of God is Eternal Life*; And that it is most false on the other side, that the Doctrine of *Protestants* makes God a giver only and not a rewarder: In as much as their Doctrine is, That God gives not Heaven but to those which do something for it, and so his gift is also a Reward; but withal that whatsoever they do is due unto God beforehand, and worth nothing to God, and worth nothing in respect of Heaven, and so Mans work is no Merit, and Gods reward is still a Gift.

36. Put the case the *Pope*, for a reward of your Service done him in writing this Book, had given you the Honour and means of a Cardinal, would you not, not only in humility but in sincerity have professed, that you had not merited such a reward? And yet the *Pope* is neither your Creator nor Redeemer, nor Preserver, nor perhaps your very great Benefactor, sure I am, not so great as God Almighty, and therefore hath no such right and title to your Service as God hath in respect of precedent obligations. Besides, the work you have done him hath been really advantagious to him: and lastly, not altogether unproportionable to the forementioned reward. And therefore if by the same work you will pretend that either you have or hope to have deserved immortal

Happiness, I beseech you consider well whether this be not to set a higher value upon a Cardinals Cap, than a Crown of immortal Glory, and with that Cardinal to prefer a part in *Paris* before a part in *Paradise*.

37. As for your distinction, between Heresies that have been, and Heresies that are, and Heresies that may be, I have already proved it vain; and that whatsoever may be an Heresie, that is so; and whatsoever is so, that always hath been so, ever since the publication of the Gospel of Christ. The Doctrine of your Church may like a Snow-ball increase with rouling, and again if you please melt away and decrease: But as *Christ Jesus*, so his Gospel, *is yesterday and to day, and the same for ever.*

38. Our Saviour sending his Apostles to preach, gave them no other Commission than this: *Go teach all Nations, Baptizing them in the Name of the Father, the Son, and the Holy Ghost, teaching them to observe all things, whatsoever I have commanded you.* These were the bounds of their Commission. If your Church have any larger, or if she have a Commission at large, to teach what she pleases, and call it the Gospel of Christ, let her produce her Letters patents, from Heaven for it. But if this be all you have, then must you give me leave to esteem it both great sacriledg in you to forbid any thing, be it never so small or ceremonious, which Christ hath commanded: as the receiving of the Communion in both kinds: and as high a degree of presumption, to enjoyn men to believe, that there are or can be any other Fundamental Articles of the Gospel of Christ, than what Christ himself commanded his Apostles to teach all men; or any damnable Heresies, but such as are plainly repugnant to these prime Verities.

39. Ad §. 16, 17.] The saying of the most Learned *Prelate* and excellent man the *Arch-Bishop* of *Armach* (which shall be set down at the end of *N*. 43.) is as great and as good a Truth, and as necessary for these miserable times as can possibly be uttered: For this is most certain, and I believe you will easily grant it, that to reduce Christians to Unity of Communion, there are but two ways

The Creed contains all necessary points of meer Belief.

that may be conceived probable: The one, by taking away diversity of opinions touching matters of Religion: The other by shewing that the diversity of Opinions, which is among the several Sects of Christians, ought to be no hindrance to their Unity in Communion.

40. Now the former of these is not to be hoped for without a miracle, unless that could be done, which is impossible to be performed, though it be often pretended; that is, unless it could be made evident to all men, that God hath appointed some visible Judge of Controversies, to whose judgment all men are to submit themselves. What then remains, but that the other way must be taken, and Christians must be taught to set a higher value upon these high points of Faith and obedience wherein they agree, than upon those matters of less moment wherein they differ, and understand that agreement in those, ought to be more effectual to joyn them in one Communion, than their difference in other things of less moment to divide them? When I say, *in one Communion*, I mean, in a common Profession of those articles of Faith, wherein all consent: A joynt worship of God, after such a way as all esteem lawful; and a mutual performance of all those works of Charity, which Christians owe one to another. And to such a Communion what better inducement could be thought of, than to demonstrate that what was Universally believed of all Christians, if it were joyned with a love of truth, and with holy obedience, was sufficient to bring men to Heaven? For why should men be more rigid than God? Why should any Error exclude any man from the Churches Communion, which will not deprive him of Eternal Salvation? Now that Christians do generally agree in all those points of Doctrine, which are necessary to Salvation, it is apparent, because they agree with one accord, in believing all those Books of the *Old* and *New Testament*, which in the Church were never doubted of to be the undoubted Word of God. And it is so certain that in all these Books, all necessary Doctrines are evidently contained, that of all the four Evangelists this is ve-

ry.

ry probable, but of S. *Luke* most apparent, that in every one of their Books they have comprehended the whole substance of the Gospel of Christ. For what reason can be imagined, that any of them should leave out any thing which he knew to be necessary, and yet (as apparently all of them have done) put in many things which they knew to be only profitable and not necessary? What wise and honest man that were now to write the Gospel of Christ, would do so great a work of God after such a negligent fashion? Suppose *Xaverius* had been to write the Gospel of Christ for the *Indians*, think you he would have left out any Fundamental Doctrine of it? If not, I must beseech you to conceive as well of S. *Matthew*, and S. *Mark*, and S. *Luke*, and S. *John*, as you do of *Xaverius*. Besides, if every one of them have not in them all necessary Doctrines, how have they complied with their own design, which was, as the Titles of their Books shew, to write *the Gospel of Christ*, and not a part of it? Or how have they not deceived us, in giving them such Titles? By the whole Gospel of Christ, I understand not the whole History of Christ, but all that makes up the Covenant between God and Man. Now if this be wholly contained in the Gospel of Saint *Mark* and Saint *John*, I believe every considering man will be inclinable to believe that then without doubt, it is contained, with the advantage of many other very profitable things, in the larger Gospels of Saint *Matthew*, and Saint *Luke*. And that Saint *Marks* Gospel wants no necessary Article of this Covenant, I presume you will not deny, if you believe *Irenæus* when he says, *Matthew to the* Hebrews *in their Tongue published the Scripture of the Gospel: When* Peter *and* Paul *did Preach the Gospel, and found the Church or a Church at* Rome, *or of* Rome, *and after their departure* Mark *the Scholar of* Peter, *delivered to us in writing those things which had been Preached by* Peter; *and* Luke, *the follower of* Paul, *compiled in a Book the Gospel which was Preached by him: And afterwards* John, *residing in* Asia, *in the City of* Ephesus, *did himself also set forth a Gospel.*

41. In

The Creed contains all necessary points of meer Belief.

41. In which words of *Irenæus*, it is remarkable that they are spoken by him against some Hereticks, that pretended (as you know who do now adaies) that *some necessary Doctrines of the Gospel were unwritten*, and that *out of the Scriptures, truth* (he must mean sufficient truth,) *cannot be found by those which know not Tradition.* Against whom to say, that part of the Gospel which was Preached by S *Peter* was written by S *Mark*, and so other necessary parts of it omitted, had been to speak impertinently, and rather to confirm than confute their Error. It is plain therefore, that he must mean, as I pretend, that all the necessary Doctrine of the Gospel, which was Preached by Saint *Peter*, was written by Saint *Mark*. Now you will not deny, I presume, that Saint *Peter*, Preached all, therefore you must not deny that S. *Mark* wrote all.

Lib. 3. c. 2.

42. Our next inquiry let it be touching S. *Johns* intent in writing his Gospel, whether it were to deliver so much truth, as being believed and obeyed would certainly bring men to Eternal Life, or only part of it, and to leave part unwritten? A great man there is, but much less than the Apostle, who saith, that *writing last, he purposed to supply the defects of the other Evangelists, that had wrote before him*: which (if it were true) would sufficiently justifie what I have undertaken, that at least all the four Evangelists have in them, all the necessary parts of the Gospel of Christ. Neither will I deny, but S. *Johns* secondary intent might be to supply the defects of the former three Gospels, in some things very profitable. But he that pretends, that any necessary Doctrine is in S. *John* which is in none of the other Evangelists, hath not so well considered them as he should do, before he pronounce sentence of so weighty a matter. And for his prime intent in writing his Gospel, what that was, certainly no Father in the World understood it better than himself. Therefore let us hear him speak: *Many other signs* (saith he) *also did Jesus in the sight of his Disciples, which are not written in this Book: But these are written, that you may believe that Jesus is Christ the Son of God, and that believing you may have Life in his name.*

By

By *(these are written)* may be understood, either *these things* are written, or *these signs* are written. Take it which way you will, this conclusion will certainly follow, That either all that which S. *John* wrote in his Gospel, or less than all, and therefore all much more was sufficient to make them believe that which being believed with lively Faith, would certainly bring them to Eternal Life.

43. This which hath been spoken (I hope) is enough to justifie my undertaking to the full, that it is very probable that every one of the four Evangelists has in his Book the whole substance, all the necessary parts of the Gospel of Christ. But for Saint *Luke*, that he hath written such a perfect Gospel, in my judgment it ought to be with them that believe him, no manner of question. Consider first the introduction to his Gospel, where he declares what he intends to write, in these Words, *For as much as many have taken in hand to set forth in order a Declaration of those things, which are most surely believed amongst us, even as they delivered unto us, which from the beginning were Eye-witnesses, and Ministers of the Word, it seemed good to me also, having had perfect understanding of things from the first, to write to thee in order, most excellent* Theophilus, *that thou mightest know the certainty, of those things wherein thou hast been instructed.* Add to this place, the entrance to his *History of the Acts of the Apostles: The former Treatise have I made,* O Theophilus, *of all that Jesus began both to do and teach, until the day in which he was taken up.* Weigh well these two places, and then answer me freely and ingenuously to these demands. 1. Whether S. *Luke* does not undertake the very same thing which he says, *many had taken in hand?* 2. Whether this were not *to set forth in order, a Declaration of those things which are most surely believed amongst Christians?* 3. Whether the whole Gospel of Christ, and every necessary Doctrine of it, were not surely believed among Christians? 4. Whether they which were *Eye-witnesses and Ministers of the Word from the beginning, delivered not the whole Gospel of Christ?* 5. Whether he does not undertake to write in order these
things

The Creed contains all necessary points of meer belief.

things whereof he had perfect understanding from the first? 6. Whether he had not perfect understanding of the whole Gospel of Christ? 7. Whether he doth not undertake to write to *Theophilus* of all those things wherein he had been instructed? 8. And whether he had not been instructed in all the necessary parts of the Gospel of Christ? 9. Whether in the other Text, *All things which Jesus began to do and teach,* must not at least imply, all the principal and necessary things? 10. Whether this be not the very interpretation of your *Rhemish* Doctors, in their Annotation upon this place? 11. Whether all these Articles of the Christian Faith, without the belief whereof, no man can be saved, be not the principal and most necessary things which *Jesus* taught? 12. And lastly, whether many things which S. *Luke* has wrote in his Gospel, be not less principal, and less necessary than all and every one of these? When you have well considered these proposals, I believe you will be very apt to think (if S. *Luke* be of credit with you) That all things necessary to salvation, are certainly contained in his writings alone. And from hence you will not choose but conclude, that seeing all the Christians in the world, agree in the belief of what S. *Luke* hath written, and not only so, but in all other Books of Canonical Scripture, which were never doubted of in and by the Church, the Learned Arch-Bishop had very just, and certain ground to say, *That in these Propositions, which without Controversie are universally received in the whole Christian world, so much truth is contained, as being joyned with holy obedience, may be sufficient to bring a man to everlasting Salvation; and that we have no cause to doubt, but that as many as walk according to this rule, neither overthrowing that which they have builded, by superinducing any damnable Heresie thereupon, nor otherwise vitiating their holy faith, with a lewd and wicked conversation, peace shall be upon them, and upon the Israel of God.*

44. Against this, you object two things. The one, that by this Rule, *seeing the Doctrin of the Trinity is not received universally among Christians, the denial of it shall not exclude Salvation.* The other, that the *Bishop contradicts himself,*

self, in supposing a man may believe all necessary Truths, and yet superinduce some damnable Heresies.

45. To the first I answer, what I conceive he would, whose words I here justify, that he hath declared plainly in this very place, that he meant, not an absolute, but a limited Universality, and speaks not of propositions universally believed by all Professions of Christianity that are, but only, by all those several Professions of Christianity, that have any large spread in *any part of the world*. By which words he excludes from the universality here spoken of, the denyers of the Doctrin of the Trinity, as being but a handful of men, in respect of all, nay in respect of any of these professions which maintain it. And therefore it was a great fault in you, either willingly to conceal these words, which evacuate your objection, or else negligently to oversee them.

46. Now for the foul Contradiction, wherein I pray does it lie? *In supposing* (say you) *a man may believe all Truths necessary to salvation, and yet superinduce a damnable Heresie.* I answer, It is not certain that his words do suppose this: neither if they do, does he contradict himself. I say it is not certain that his words import any such matter. For ordinarily men use to speak and write so as here he does, when they intend not to limit or restrain, but only to repeat and press and illustrate what they have said before.

S. *Athanasius* in his Creed tells us, *The Catholick Faith is this, that we worship one God in Trinity, and Trinity in Unity, neither confounding the Persons nor dividing the Substance*; and why now do you not tell him that he contradicts himself, and supposes that we may worship a Trinity of Persons, and one God in substance, and yet confound the Persons, or divide the Substance; which yet is impossible, because Three remaining Three, cannot be confounded, and One remaining One cannot be divided? If a man should say unto you, he that keeps all the Commandments of God, committing no sin either against the love of God, or the love of his neighbour, is a perfect man: Or thus, he that will live in constant health had need be exact in his diet, neither eating too much, nor too little: Or thus, he
that

The Creed contains all necessary points of meer belief.

that will come to *London* must go on straight forward in such a way, and neither turn to the right hand or to the left; I verily believe you would not find any contradiction in his words, but confess them as coherent and consonant as any in your Book. And certainly if you would look upon this saying of the Bishop with any indifference, you would easily perceive it to be of the very same kind, and capable of the very same construction. And therefore one of the grounds of your accusation is uncertain; Neither can you assure us, that the Bishop supposes any such matter as you pretend. Neither if he did suppose this (as perhaps he did) were this to contradict himself. For though there can be no damnable Heresie, unless it contradict some necessary Truth, yet there is no contradiction but the same man may at once believe this Heresie and this Truth; because there is no contradiction that the same man, at the same time, should believe contradictions. For, first, whatsoever a man believes true, that he may and must believe; but there have been some who have believed and taught that contradictions might be true, against whom *Aristotle* disputes in the third of his *Metaphysicks*; Therefore it is not impossible that a man may believe contradictions. Secondly, they which believe there is no certainty in Reason, must believe that contradictions may be true: For otherwise there will be certainty in this Reason; This contradicts Truth, therefore it is false. But there be now divers in the world who believe there is no certainty in reason, (and whether you be of their mind or no, I desire to be informed;) Therefore there be divers in the world who believe contradictions may be true. Thirdly, They which do captivate their understandings to the belief of those things which to their understanding seem irreconcileable contradictions, may as well believe real contradictions: (For the difficulty of believing arises not from their being repugnant, but from their seeming to be so:) But you do captivate your understandings to the belief of those things which seem to your understandings irreconcileable contradictions; therefore it is as possible and easie for you to believe those that indeed

K k 2   are

are so. Fourthly, some men may be confuted in their Errors, and perswaded out of them; but no mans Error can be confuted, who together with his Error doth not believe and grant some true principle that contradicts his Error: for nothing can be proved to him who grants nothing, neither can there be (as all men know) any rational discourse but out of grounds agreed upon by both parts. Therefore it is not impossible but absolutely certain, that the same man at the same time may believe contradictions. Fifthly, It is evident, neither can you without extream madness and uncharitableness, deny, that we believe the Bible, those Books I mean which we believe Canonical: Otherwise why dispute you with us out of them, as out of a common Principle? Either therefore you must retract your opinion, and acknowledge that the same man at the same time may believe contradictions, or else you will run into a greater inconvenience, and be forced to confess, that no part of our Doctrin contradicts the Bible. Sixthly, I desire you to vindicate from contradiction these following Assertions: That there should be Length, and nothing long: Breadth, and nothing broad: Thickness, and nothing thick: Whiteness, and nothing white: Roundness, and nothing round: Weight, and nothing heavy: Sweetness, and nothing sweet: Moisture, and nothing moist: Fluidness, and nothing flowing: many Actions, and no Agent: many Passions, and no Patient: That is, that there should be a long, broad, thick, white, round, heavy, sweet, moist, flowing, active, passive, nothing! That Bread should be turned into the substance of Christ, and yet not any thing of the Bread become any thing of Christ; neither the matter, nor the form, nor the Accidents of Bread, be made either the matter or the Form, or the Accidents of Christ. That Bread should be turned into nothing, and at the same time with the same action turned into Christ, and yet Christ should not be nothing. That the same thing at the same time should have its just dimensions, and just distance of its parts, one from another, and at the same time not have it, but all its parts together in one and the self same point. That the body of

Christ,

The Creed contains all necessary points of meer belief.

Christ, which is much greater, should be contained wholly and in its full dimensions without any alteration, in that which is lesser, and that not once only, but as many times over as there are several points in the bread and wine. That the same thing at the same time should be **wholly above it self**, and wholly below it self, within it self, and without it self, on the right hand, and on the left hand, and round about it self. That the same thing at the same time should move to and from it self, and lie still: Or that it should be carried from one place to another through the middle space, and yet not move. That it should be brought from Heaven to Earth, and yet not come out of Heaven, nor be at all in any of the middle space between Heaven and Earth. That to be one, should be to be undivided from it self, and yet that one and the same thing should be divided from it self. That a thing may be, and yet be no where. That a Finite thing may be in all places at once. That a Body may be in a place, and have there its dimensions, and colour, and all other qualities, and yet that it is not in the power of God to make it visible, and tangible there, nor capable of doing or suffering any thing. That there should be no certainty in our senses, and yet that we should know something certainly, and yet know nothing but by our senses. That that which is, and was long ago, should now begin to be. That that is now to be made of nothing, which is not nothing but something. That the same thing should be before and after it self. That it should be truly and really in a place, and yet without Locality. Nay, that He which is Omnipotent should not be able to give it Locality in this place, where it is, as some of you hold: or if he can, as others say he can, that it should be possible, that the same man, for example You or I, may at the same time, be awake at *London*, & not awake but asleep at *Rome*: There run or walk, here not run or walk, but stand still, sit, or lie along: There study or write, here do neither, but dine or sup: There speak, here be silent. That he may in one place freez for cold, in another burn with heat. That he may be drunk in one place, and sober in another; Valiant in one place, and a Coward in another:

A

A thief in one place, honest in another. That he may be a *Papist* and go to *Mass* in *Rome*; A *Protestant* and go to Church in *England*. That he may die in *Rome*, and live in *England*: or dying in both places may go to Hell from *Rome*, and to Heaven from *England*. That the Body and Soul of Christ should cease to be where it was, and yet not go to another place, nor be destroyed. All these, and many other of the like nature are the unavoidable, and most of them the acknowledged consequences of your doctrin of Transubstantiation, as is explained one where or other by your School-men. Now I beseech you, Sir, to try your skill, and if you can compose their repugnance, and make peace between them; Certainly, none but you shall be *Catholick Moderator*. But if you cannot do it, and that after an intelligible manner, then you must give me leave to believe, that either you do not believe Transubstantiation, or else that it is no contradiction, that men should subjugate their understandings to the belief of contradictions.

48. Ad §. 18. This Paragraph consists of two immodest untruths, obtruded upon us without shew, or shadow of reason: and an evident sophism grounded upon an affected mistake of the sense of the word *Fundamental*.

49. The first untruth is, that *some Protestants make a Church, of men scarcely agreeing in one point of faith; of men concurring in some one or few Articles of belief, and in the rest holding conceits plainly contradictory: agreeing only in this one Article, that Christ is our Saviour*; &c.

Ans. This is a shameless Calumny; because even these men to the constituting of the very essence of a Church, in the lowest degree, require not only *Faith in Jesus Christ the Son of God and Saviour of the World*, but also *submission to his Doctrin in mind and will*. Now I beseech you Sir, tell me ingenuously, whether the Doctrin of Christ may be called without blasphemy, *scarcely one point of Faith?* Or whether it consists only, *of some one or few Articles of belief?* Or whether there be nothing in it, but only this Article, *That Christ is our Saviour?* Is it not manifest to all the world, that Christians of all Professions do agree with one consent, in the belief of all those Books of Scripture,

which

which were not doubted of in the ancient Church, without danger of damnation? Nay is it not apparent, that no man at this time, can without hypocrisie, pretend to believe in Christ, but of necessity he must do so? Seeing he can have no reason to believe in Christ, but he must have the same to believe the Scripture. I pray then read over the Scripture once more, or if that be too much labour, the New Testament only: and then say whether there be nothing there, but *scarcely one point of Faith?* But *some one or two Articles of belief? Nothing but this Article only, that Christ is our Saviour?* Say whether there be not there an infinite number of Divine Verities, Divine precepts, Divine promises, and those so plainly and undoubtedly delivered, that if any sees them not, it cannot be because he cannot, but because he will not! So plainly, that whosoever submits sincerely to the Doctrin of Christ, in mind and will, cannot possibly but submit to these in act and performance. And in the rest, which it hath pleased God, for reasons best known to himself, to deliver obscurely or ambiguously, yet thus far at least they agree, that the sense of them intended by God, is certainly true, and that they are without passion or prejudice to endeavor to find it out: The difference only is, which is that true sense which God intended. Neither would this long continue, if the walls of separation, whereby the Divel hopes to make their Divisions eternal, were pulled down; and Error were not supported against Truth, by human advantages. But for the present, God forbid the matter should be so ill as you make it! For whereas you looking upon their points of difference and agreement, through I know not what strange glasses, have made the first innumerable, and the other scarce a number: the Truth is clean contrary; that those divine Verities, Speculative and Practical, wherein they universally agree (which you will have to be but a few, or but one, or scarcely one) amount to *many millions*, (if an exact account were taken of them:) And on the other side, the Points in variance, are in comparison but few, and those not of such a quality, but the Error in them may well consist with the belief

and

and obedience of the entire Covenant, ratified by Chrift between God and man. Yet I would not be fo miftaken, as if I thought the Errors even of fome *Proteftants* unconfiderable things, and matters of no moment. For the truth is, I am very fearful, that fome of their opinions, either as they are, or as they are apt to be miftaken, (though not of themfelves fo damnable, but that good and holy men may be faved with them, yet) are too frequent occafions of our remifsnefs, and flacknefs, in running the race of Chriftian Perfection, of our deferring Repentance, and converfion to God, of our frequent relapfes into fin, and not feldom of fecurity in finning; and confequently, though not certain caufes, yet too frequent occafions of many mens damnation: and fuch I conceive all thefe Doctrines which either directly or obliquely, put men in hope of Eternal happinefs, by any other means faving only the narrow way *of fincere and Univerfal obedience*, grounded upon a true and lively Faith. Thefe Errors therefore, I do not elevate or extenuate: and on condition the ruptures made by them might be compofed, do heartily wifh, that the cement were made of my deareft Blood, and only not to be an *Anathema* from Chrift! Only this I fay, that neither are their points of agreement fo few, nor their differences fo many, as you make them, nor fo great as to exclude the oppofite Parties from being members of one Church Militant, and Joynt Heirs of the Glory of the Church Triumphant.

50. Your other palpable untruth is, that *Proteftants are far more bold to difagree even in matters of Faith, than Catholick Divines* (you mean your own,] *in Queftions meerly Philofophical, or not determined by the Church.* For neither do they differ at all, in *matters of Faith*, if you take the word in the higheft fenfe, and mean by matters of Faith, fuch Doctrines as are *abfolutely neceffary* to Salvation, to be believed or not to be disbelieved. And then in thofe wherein they do differ, with what colour or fhadow of Argument, can you make good, that *they are more bold to difagree, than you are in Queftions meerly Philofophical, or not determined by the Church?* For is there not as great re-

pug-

pugnancy between your aſſent and diſſent, your affirmation and negation, your *Eſt Eſt, Non Non*, as there is between theirs? You follow your Reaſon, in thoſe things which are not determined by your Church; and they theirs, in things not plainly determined in Scripture. And wherein then conſiſts their greater, *their far greater boldneſs?* And what if they in their contradictory opinnions, pretend both to rely upon the truth of God, doth this make their contradictions ever a whit the more repugnant? I had always thought, that all contradictions had been equally contradictions, and equally repugnant; becauſe the leaſt of them are as far aſunder, as *Eſt* and *Non Eſt* can make them, and the greateſt are no farther. But then you in your differences, (by name, about Predetermination, the Immaculate Conception, the *Popes* Infallibility,) upon what other motive do you rely? Do not you cite Scripture, or Tradition, or both, on both ſides? And do you not pretend, that both theſe are the infallible Truths of Almighty God?

51. You cloſe up this Section with a fallacy, proving forſooth, that *we deſtroy, by our confeſſion, the Church which is the Houſe of God, becauſe we ſtand only upon Fundamental Articles, which cannot make up the whole Fabrick of the Faith, no more than the Foundation of a Houſe alone can be a Houſe.*

52. But I hope, Sir, you will not be difficult in granting, that that is a Houſe which hath all the neceſſary parts belonging to a Houſe: now by Fundamental Articles, we mean all thoſe which are neceſſary; and then I hope you will grant that we may ſafely expect Salvation in a Church, which hath all things Fundamental to Salvation; Unleſs you will ſay, that more is neceſſary, than that which is neceſſary.

53. Ad §. 19.] This long diſcourſe is to ſhew that *Proteſtants give unavoidable occaſion of deſperation to poor Souls,* and brings in a Man deſirous to ſave his Soul, asking Queſtions of *D. P.* and makes anſwers for him. As firſt, if he required, *whoſe directions he might rely upon?* He ſays, the Doctor's Anſwer would be, *upon the truly Catholick Church.*

The Creed contains all necessary points of meer Belief.

But I suppose upon better reason, because I know his mind, that he would advise him to *call no man Master upon Earth*, but according to Chrifts command, to rely upon the *direction of God himself.* If he ask, where he should find this direction? he would anfwer him, *In his Word contained in Scripture.* If he should inquire what affurance he might have that the *Scripture is the Word of God?* He would anfwer him, that the Doctrine it felf is very fit and worthy to be thought to come from God, (*nec vox hominem sonat*) and that they which wrote and delivered it, confirmed it to be the Word of God, by doing such works as could not be done, but by Power from God himself. For affurance of the Truth hereof, he would advife him to rely upon that which all Wife Men, in all matters of belief rely upon; and that is, the confent of Ancient records, and Univerfal Tradition. No Wife Man doubts but there was fuch a man as *Julius Cæfar*, or *Cicero*, that there are fuch Cities as *Rome* or *Conftantinople*, though he have no other affurance for the one or the other, but only the *fpeech* of People. This Tradition therefore he would counfel him to rely upon, and to believe that the Book which we call Scripture, was confirmed abundantly by the Works of God, to be the Word of God. Believing it the Word of God, he muft of neceffity believe it true: and if he believe it true, he muft believe it contains all neceffary directions unto Eternal Happinefs, becaufe it affirms it felf to do fo. Nay he might tell him, that fo far is the whole Book, from wanting any neceffary direction to his Eternal Salvation, that one only Author, that hath writ but two little Books of it, Saint *Luke* by name in the beginning of his *Gofpel*, and in the beginning of his *Story*, fhews plainly that he alone hath written at leaft fo much as is neceffary. And what they wrote, they wrote by Gods direction, for the direction of the World, not only for the Learned, but for all that would do their true endeavour to know the will of God, and to do it; therefore you cannot but conceive, that writing to all and for all, they wrote fo as that in things neceffary they might be underftood by all. Befides that,

here

here he should find, that God himself has engaged himself by promise, that if he would love him, and keep his Commandments, and pray earnestly for his Spirit, and be willing to be directed by it, he should undoubtedly receive it, even the *Spirit of Truth which shall lead him into all Truth*; that is certainly, into all necessary Truths, and suffer him to fall into no pernitious Error. The sum of his whole direction to him briefly would be this, Believe the Scripture to be the Word of God, use your true endeavour to find the true sense of it, and to live according to it, and then you may rest securely that you are in the true way to Eternal Happiness. This is the substance of that Answer which the Doctor would make to any man in this case; and this is a way so plain, that Fools, unless they will, cannot Err from it. Because not knowing absolutely all truth, nay not all profitable truth, and not being free from Error; but endeavouring to know the truth and obey it, and endeavouring to be free from Error, is by this way made the only condition of Salvation.

56. Neither is this to drive any man to desparation; unless it be such a one as hath such a strong affection to this word, *Church*, that he will not go to Heaven, *unless he hath a Church to lead him thither*. For what though a Council may Err, and the whole Church cannot be consulted with, yet this is not to send you on the Fools *Pilgrimage for Faith*, and bid you go and *confer with every Christian Soul, Man and Woman, by Sea and by Land, close Prisoner, or at Liberty*, as you dilate the matter: But to tell you very briefly, that Universal Tradition directs you to the Word of God, and the Word of God directs you to Heaven.

57. To the next demand, *How shall I know whether he hold all Fundamental points or no?* When *Protestants* answer, *If he truly believe the undoubted Books of Canonical Scripture, he cannot but believe all Fundamentals*, and that it is *very probable* that the *Creed contains all the Fundamentals of simple belief:* The Jesuite takes no notice of the former, but takes occasion from the latter to ask. *Shall I hazard my Soul*

on Probabilities, or even Wagers? As if whatfoever is but probable, though in the higheft degree of Probability, were as likely to be falfe as true! or becaufe it is but *Morally*, not Mathematically certain, that there was fuch a Woman as *Q. Elizabeth,* fuch a man as *Hen.* the 8*th.* that is in the higheft degree probable, therefore it were an even Wager there were none fuch! By this Reafon feeing the truth of your whole Religion depends finally upon *Prudential motives,* which you do but pretend to be very credible, it will be *an even Wager that your Religion is falfe.* And by the fame Reafon, or rather infinitely greater, feeing it is impoffible for any man (according to the grounds of your Religion) to know himfelf, much lefs another to be a true *Pope,* or a true Prieft; nay to have a Moral certainty of it, becaufe thefe things are obnoxious to innumerable fecret and undifcernable nullities, it will be an even Wager, nay (if we proportion things indifferently, a hundred to one, that every Confecration and Abfolution of yours is void, and that whenfoever you adore the Hoft, you and your Affiftants commit Idolatry: That there is a nullity in any decree that a *Pope* fhall make, or any Decree of a Council which he fhall confirm: Particularly it will be at leaft an even Wager, that all the decrees of the Council of *Trent* are void, becaufe it is at moft but very probable that the *Pope* which confirmed them was true *Pope.*

62. *Obj.* But *unlefs this Queftion be anfwered,* (what points of the Creed are, and what are not Fundamentals?) *the* Proteftant *Doctrine ferves only either to make men defpare, or elfe to have recourfe to thofe called* Papifts.

Anfw. It feems a little thing will make you defpair, if you be fo fullen as to do fo, becaufe men will not trouble themfelves to fatisfie your curious queftions. And I pray be not offended with me for fo efteeming it, becaufe as before I told you, if you will believe all the points of the Creed, you cannot choofe but believe all the points of it that are Fundamental, though you be ignorant which are fo, and which are not fo. Now I believe your defire to know which are Fundamentals, proceeds

only

only from a defire to be affured that you do believe them; which feeing you may be affured of, without knowing which they be, what can it be but curiofity to defire to know it? Neither may you think to mend your felf herein one whit by having recourfe to them whom we call *Papifts*; for they are as far to feek as we in this point, which of the Articles of the Creed are, for their nature and matter, Fundamental, and which are not. Particularly, you will fcarce meet with any amongft their Doctors, fo adventurous, as to tell you for a certain, whether or no the conception of Chrift by the Holy Ghoft, his being born of a Virgin, his Burial, his defcent into Hell, and the Communion of Saints, be points of their own nature and matter Fundamental. Such I mean, as without the diftinct and explicite knowledge of them no man can be faved.

63. *Obj.* We give this certain Rule, *that all points defined by Chrifts Vifible Church, belong to the Foundation of Faith, in this fenfe, that to deny any fuch, cannot ftand with Salvation.*

Anfw. So alfo Proteftants give you this more certain rule, That whofoever believes heartily thofe Books of Scripture, which all the Chriftian Churches in the World acknowledge to be Canonical, and fubmits himfelf indeed to this, as to the rule of his belief, muft of neceffity believe all things Fundamental, and if he live according to his Faith, cannot fail of Salvation. But befides, what certainty have you, that that rule of *Papifts* is fo certain? By the vifible Church it is plain, they mean only their own: and why their own only fhould be the Vifible Church, I do not underftand: and as little, why all points defined by this Church fhould belong to the Foundation of Faith. Thefe things you had need fee well and fubftantially proved, before you rely upon them, otherwife you expofe your felf to danger of imbracing damnable Errors inftead of Fundamental Truths.

67. Ad §. 23, 24, 25.] *D. P.* demands, *How it can be neceffary for any Chriftian, to have more in his Creed than the Apoftles had.* And this he enforces with many Arguments

ments, thus. *May the Church of after Ages make the narrow way to heaven, narrower than our Saviour left it? Shall it be a fault to straiten and encumber the Kings high way with publick nuisances; and is it lawful by adding new Articles to the Faith, to retrench any thing from the Latitude of the King of Heavens high way to Eternal happiness? The Yoak of Christ, which he said was easie, may it be justly made heavier by the Governors of the Church in after Ages? The Apostles profess they revealed to the Church the whole Counsel of God, keeping back nothing needful for our Salvation. What Tyranny then to impose any new unnecessary matters on the Faith of Christians, especially (as the late* Popes *have done) under the high commanding form,* Qui non crediderit, damnabitur? *He that believeth not, shall be damned. If this may be done, why then did our Saviour reprehend the Pharisees so sharply, for binding heavy burdens, and laying them on mens shoulders? And why did he teach them, that in vain they worshiped God, teaching for Doctrines mens Traditions? And why did the Apostles call it tempting of God, to lay those things upon the Necks of Christians, that were not necessary?*

68. All which interrogations seem to me to contain so many plain and convincing Arguments of the premised Assertion; and if you can devise no fair and satisfying answer to them, then be so ingenuous as to grant the Conclusion, *That no more can be necessary for Christians to believe now, than was in the Apostles time.* A conclusion of great importance, for the deciding of many Controversies, and the disburdening of the Faith of Christ from many incumbrances.

70. The Doctor to make good this conclusion argues further thus, S. *Paul* declared to the *Ephesians* the whole Counsel of God touching their Salvation. Therefore that which S. *Paul* did not declare, can be no part of the Counsel of God, and therefore not necessary. And again; S. *Paul* kept back nothing from the *Ephesians* that was profitable; Therefore he taught them all things necessary to Salvation.

71. Neither is it material, that these words were particularly directed by S. *Paul*, to the Pastours of the Church:

For

The Creed contains all necessary points of meer Belief.

For (to say nothing that the point here issuable, is not, Whom he taught, whether Priests or *Laymen*? But how much he taught, and whether all things necessary?) it appears plainly out of the Text, and I wonder you should read it so negligently as not to observe it, that though he speaks now to the Pastors, yet he speaks of what he taught not only them, but also the Laity as well as them. *I have kept back nothing* (says S. *Paul*) *that was profitable, but have shewed, and have taught you publickly, and from House to House*; *Testifying* (I pray observe) *both to the* Jews, *and also to the* Greeks *Repentance towards God, and Faith towards our Lord Jesus Christ.* And a little after, *I know that ye all, among whom I have gone Preaching the Kingdom of God, shall see my Face no more: Wherefore I take you to record this day, that I am Innocent from the Blood of all men; for I have kept nothing back, but have shewed you all the Counsel of God.* And again, *Remember that by the space of three Years I ceased not to warn every one Night and Day with Tears.* Certainly though he did all these things to the Pastors among the rest, nay above the rest, yet without Controversie, they whom he taught publickly, and from House to House: The *Jews* and *Greeks* to whom he *Testified* (i. e.) *Preached* Faith and Repentance: Those all, amongst whom he went preaching the Kingdom of God: Those, Every one, whom for three Years together he warned, were not Bishops and Pastors only.

72. Neither is this to say, that the Apostles taught Christians nothing but their Creed, nothing of the Sacraments, Commandments, &c. for that is not here the point to be proved: but only, that they taught them all things necessary, so that nothing can be necessary which they did not teach them. But how much of this they put into their Creed, whether *all the necessary points of simple belief*, as we pretend, or only as you say, *I know not what*, is another Question now to be examined.

73. We urge against you, *That if all necessary points of simple belief be not comprized in the Creed, it can no way deserve the name of the Apostles Creed, as not being their Creed in any sense, but only a part of it.* To

To this you say, *That the Faith of the Apostles is of larger extent, than their Creed.* Answer, It is very true that their whole Faith was of a larger extent, but that was not the Question; but whether all points of simple belief which they taught as necessary to be explicitely believed, be not contained in it? And if thus much at least of Christian Religion be not comprized in it, I again desire you to inform me how it could be called the Apostles Creed?

74. To other Reasons grounded upon the practice of the Ancient Church; appointing her Infants to be instructed (for matters of simple belief,) only in the Creed: From her admitting Catechumens unto Baptism: and of Strangers unto her Communion, upon their only profession of the Creed, you have not, that I perceive, thought fit to make any kind of answer.

75. Ad §. 26.] In this Section you practise that trick of a Caviller, which is to answer Objections by other Objections; an excellent way to make Controversies endless! D. *Potter* desires to be resolved, *Why amongst many things of equal necessity to be believed, the Apostles should distinctly set down some in the Creed, and be altogether silent of others?* Instead of resolving him in this difficulty, you put another to him, and that is, *Why are some points not Fundamental expressed in it, rather than others of the same quality?* Which demand is so far from satisfying the former doubt, that it makes it more intricate. For upon this ground it may be demanded, How was it possible that the Apostles should leave out any Articles simply necessary, and put in others not necessary, especially if their intention were (as you say it was) to deliver in it such Articles as were fittest for those times? Unless (which were wondrous strange) unnecessary Articles were fitter for those times, than necessary. But now to your Question, the Answer is obvious: These unnecessary things might be put in, because they were circumstances of the necessary, *Pontius Pilate* of Christs passion, The third day of the Resurrection; neither doth the adding of them make the Creed ever a whit the less probable, the less fit

to

to be understood, and remembered. And for the contrary reasons, other unnecessary things might be left out. Besides, who sees not that the addition of some unnecessary circumstances is a thing that can hardly be avoided without affectation! And therefore not so great a fault, nor deserving such a censure, as the omission of any thing essential to the work undertaken, and necessary to the end proposed in it.

76. You demand again (as it is no hard matter to multiply demands,) *why our Saviours descent into Hell, and Burial was expressed, and not his circumcision, his manifestation to the three Kings, and working of Miracles?* I answer: His Resurrection, Ascension, and sitting at the right hand of God, are very great Miracles, and they are expressed. Besides, S. *John* assures us, *That the Miracles which Christ did, were done and written not for themselves that they might be believed,* but for a further end, that *we might believe that Jesus was the Christ, and believing have eternal life.* He therefore that believes this may be saved, though he have no explicite and distinct Faith of any Miracle that our Saviour did. His Circumcision and Manifestation to the Wise men (for I know not upon what grounds you call them *Kings*) are neither things simply necessary to be known, nor have any near relation to those that are so. As for his Descent into Hell, it may (for ought you know) be put in as a thing necessary of it self to be known. If you ask why more than his Circumcision, I refer you to the Apostles for an answer, who put that in, and left this out of their Creed: and yet sure, were not so *forgetful after the receiving of the Holy Ghost, as to leave out any prime and principal foundation of the faith,* which are the very words of your own *Gordonius Huntlæus, Cont.* 2. *c.* 10. *num.* 10. Likewise his Burial was put in perhaps as necessary of it self to be known. But though it were not, yet hath it manifestly so neer relation to these that are necessary, (his Passion and Resurrection, being the Consequent of the one, and the Antecedent of the other,) that it is no marvel if for their sakes it was put in. For though I verily believe that there is no necessary point of this nature, but

what

what is in the Creed, yet I do not affirm, becaufe I cannot prove it, that there is nothing in the Creed but what is neceffary. You demand thirdly, *Why did they not expreſs Scriptures, Sacraments, and all Fundamental points of faith tending to practice, as well as thofe which reft in Belief?* I anfwer; Becaufe their purpofe was to comprize in it only thofe neceffary points which reft in belief: which appears, becaufe of practical points there is not in it fo much as one.

77. We affirm, That if your Doctrin were true, this fhort Creed, *viz. I believe the Roman Church to be Infallible*, would have been better, that is, more effectual to keep the believers of it from Herefie, and in the true Faith, than this Creed which now we have. A propofition fo evident, that I cannot fee how either you, or any of your Religion, or indeed any fenfible man can from his heart deny it. Yet becaufe you make a fhew of doing fo, or elfe, which I rather hope, do not rightly apprehend the force of the Reafon, I will endeavour briefly to add fome light and ftrength to it, by comparing the effects of thefe feveral fuppofed Creeds.

78. The former Creed therefore would certainly produce thefe effects in the believers of it: An impoffibility of being in any formal Herefie: A neceffity of being prepared in mind to come out of all Error in Faith, or material Herefie; which certainly you will not deny, or if you do, you pull down the only pillar of your Church and Religion, and deny that which is in effect the only thing you labour to prove through your whole Book.

79. The latter Creed which now we have, is fo uneffectual for thefe good purpofes, that you your felf tell us of innumerable, grofs, damnable Herefies, that have been, are, and may be, whofe contrary Truths are neither explicitly, nor by confequence comprehended in this Creed: So that no man by the belief of this Creed without the former, can be poffibly guarded from falling into them, and continuing obftinate in them. Nay, fo far is this Creed from guarding them from thefe mifchiefs, that it is more likely to enfnare them into them, by feeming and

yet

The Creed containſ all neceſſary points of meer belief.

yet not being a full comprehenſion of all neceſſary points of Faith: which is apt (as experience ſhews,) to miſguide men into this pernitious error, That believing the Creed, they believe all neceſſary points of faith, whereas indeed they do not ſo. Now upon theſe grounds I thus conclude: That Creed which hath great commodities and no danger, would certainly be better then that which hath great danger, and wants many of theſe great commodities; But the former ſhort Creed propoſed by me, *I believe the Roman Church to be Infallible,* (if your doctrin be true,) is of the former condition, and the latter, that is, the Apoſtles Creed, is of the latter, Therefore the former (if your doctrin be true) would without controverſie be better than the latter.

83. Whereas you ſay, *If the Apoſtles had expreſt no Article but that of the Catholick Church, ſhe muſt have taught us the other Articles in particular by Creeds, or other means:* This is very true, but no way repugnant to the truth of this which follows, that the Apoſtles (if your doctrin be true) had done better ſervice to the Church, though they had never made this Creed of theirs which now we have, if inſtead thereof, they had commanded in plain terms that for mens perpetual direction in the faith, this ſhort Creed ſhould be taught all men, *I believe the Roman Church ſhall be for ever Infallible.* Yet you muſt not ſo miſtake me, as if I meant, that they had done better not to have taught the Church the ſubſtance of Chriſtian Religion; for then the Church not having learnt it of them, could not have taught it us. This therefore I do not ſay: but ſuppoſing they had written theſe Scriptures as they have written, wherein all the Articles of their Creed are plainly delivered, and preached that Doctrin which they did preach, and done all other things as they have done, beſides the compoſing their Symbol: I ſay, if your doctrin were true, they had done a work infinitely more beneficial to the Church of Chriſt, if they had never compoſed their Symbol, which is but an imperfect comprehenſion of the neceſſary points of ſimple belief, and no diſtinctive mark (as a Symbole ſhould be) between thoſe that are good Chriſtians, and thoſe that are not ſo; but

instead thereof, had delivered this one Proposition, which would have been certainly effectual for all the aforesaid good intents and purposes, *The Roman Church shall be forever Infallible in all things, which she proposes as matters of Faith.*

84. Whereas you say, *If we will believe we have all in the Creed, when we have not all, it is not the Apostles fault but our own:* I tell you plainly, if it be a fault, I know not whose it should be but theirs. For sure it can be no fault in me to follow such Guides whether soever they lead me: Now I say, they have led me into this perswasion, because they have given me great reason to believe it, and none to the contrary. The reason they have given me to believe it, is, because it is apparent and confest, they did propose to themselves in composing it, some good end or ends: As *that Christians might have a form, by which* (for matter of Faith) *they might profess themselves Catholicks,* So Putean out of Thomas Aquinas: *That the faithful might know, what the Christian people is to believe explicitly,* So Vincent Filiucius: *That being separated into divers parts of the world, they might preach the same thing*: *And that that might serve as a mark to distinguish true Christians from Infidels,* So Cardinal Richlieu. Now for all these and for any other good intent, I say, it will be plainly uneffectual, unless it contain at least all points of simple belief, which are in ordinary course, necessary to be explicitly known by all men. So that if it be a fault in me to believe this, it must be my fault to believe the Apostles, wise and good men: which I cannot do if I believe not this. And therefore what *Richardus de sancto Victore* says of God himself, I make no scruple at all to apply to the Apostles, and to say, *Si error est quod credo, à vobis deceptus sum:* If it be an Error which I believe, it is you, and my reverend esteem of you and your actions that hath led me into it. For as for your suspicion, *That we are led into this perswasion, out of a hope that we may the better maintain by it some opinions of our own,* It is plainly uncharitable. I know no opinion I have, which I would not as willingly forsake as keep, if I could see sufficient reason to induce me to believe, that it is the will of God I should

should forsake it. Neither do I know any opinion I hold against the Church of *Rome*, but I have more evident grounds than this whereupon to build it. For let but these Truths be granted: That the authority of the Scripture is independent on your Church, and dependent only in respect of us upon universal Tradition; That Scripture is the only Rule of Faith: That all things necessary to salvation are plainly delivered in Scripture: Let I say these most certain and divine Truths be laid for foundations, and let our superstructions be consequent and coherent to them; and I am confident Peace would be restored, and Truth maintained against you, though the Apostles Creed were not in the world.

CHAP. V.

The ANSWER to the Fifth CHAPTER.

Shewing that the separation of Protestants from the Roman Church, being upon just and necessary causes, is not any way guilty of Schism.

1. AD §. 1.2,3,4,5,6,7. In the seven first Sections of this Chapter, there be many things said and many things supposed by you which are untrue, and deserve a censure. As

2. First, *That Schism could not be a Division from the Church, or that a Division from the Church could not happen, unless there always had been and should be a visible Church.* Which Assertion is a manifest falsehood: For although there never had been any Church Visible or Invisible before this age, nor should be ever after, yet this could not hinder, but that a Schism might now be, and be a Division from the present Visible Church. As though in *France* there never had been until now a lawful Monarch, nor after him ever should be, yet this hinders not, but that now there might be a Rebellion, and that Rebellion might be an Insurrection against Sovereign Authority.

3. *That*

3. *That it is a point to be granted by all Christians, that in all ages there hath been a visible Congregation of faithful people.* Which Proposition howsoever you understand it, is not absolutely certain. But if you mean by *Faithful*, (as it is plain you do) *free from all error in faith*, then you know all Protestants with one consent affirm it to be false; and therefore without proof to take it for granted is to beg the Question.

4. *That supposing Luther and they which did first separate from the Roman Church were guilty of Schism, it is certainly consequent, that all who persist in this division must be so likewise.* Which is not so certain as you pretend. For they which alter without necessary cause the present government of any state Civil or Ecclesiastical, do commit a great fault; whereof notwithstanding they may be innocent who continue this alteration, and to the utmost of their power oppose a change though to the former state, when continuance of time hath once setled the present. Thus have I known some of your own Church condemn the Low-country-men who first revolted from the King of *Spain*, of the sin of Rebellion, yet absolve them from it who now being of your Religion there, are yet faithful maintainers of the common liberty against the pretences of the King of *Spain*.

5. *That all those which a Christian is to esteem neighbors do concur to make one company, which is the Church.* Which is false: for a Christian is to esteem those his neighbors, who are not members of the true Church.

6. *That all the members of the Visible Church, are by charity united into one Mystical body.* Which is manifestly untrue; for many of them have no Charity.

7. *That the Catholick Church, signifies one company of faithful people,* which is repugnant to your own grounds. For you require not true faith, but only the Profession of it, to make men members of the Visible Church.

8. *That every Heretick is a Schismatick.* Which you must acknowledge false in those, who though they deny, or doubt of some point professed by your Church, and so are Hereticks: yet continue still in the Communion of the Church.

9. *That*

9. *That all the members of the Catholick Church, must of necessity be united in external Communion.* Which though it were much to be desired it were so, yet certainly cannot be perpetually true. For a man unjustly excommunicated, is not in the Churches Communion, yet he is still a member of the Church: and divers times it hath happened, as in the case of *Chrisostom* and *Epiphanius*, that particular men, and particular Churches, have upon an overvalued difference, either renounced Communion mutually, or one of them separated from the other, and yet both have continued members of the Catholick Church. These things are in those *seven Sections*, either said or supposed by you untruly, without all shew, or pretence of proof. The rest is an impertinent common place, wherein Protestants and the cause in hand, are absolutely unconcerned. And therefore I pass to the *eighth Section*.

10. Ad §. 8.] Here you obtrude upon us, a double fallacy; One, in supposing and taking for granted, that whatsoever is affirmed by *three Fathers*, must be true; whereas your selves make no scruple of condemning many things of falsehood, which yet are maintained, by more than thrice three Fathers. Another, in pretending their words to be spoken absolutely, which by them are limited and restrained to some particular cases. Thus the words of S. *Austin* (cap. 11. lib. 2. *cont. Parm.*) *That there is no necessity to divide Unity;* are not spoken absolutely, that there never is, nor can be any necessity to divide Unity (which only were for your purpose) but only in such a special case as he there sets down: That is, *When good men tolerate bad men, which can do them no spiritual hurt, to the intent they may not be separated from those, who are spiritually good: Then* (saith he) *there is no necessity to divide Unity.* Which very words do clearly give us to understand, that it may fall out (as it doth in our case) that we cannot keep Unity with bad men, without spiritual hurt, *i. e.* without partaking with them in their impieties, and that then there is a necessity to divide Unity from them: I mean, to break off conjunction with them in their impieties. Which that it was S. *Austins* mind, it is most evident out of the 21. c. of

the

the same book: where to *Parmenian* demanding, *how can a man remain pure, being joyned with those that are corrupted?* He answers, *Very true, this is not possible, if he be joyned with them, that is, if he commit any evil with them, or favour them which do commit it. But if he do neither of these, he is not joyned with them.* And presently after, *these two things retained, will keep such men pure and uncorrupted; that is, neither doing ill, nor approving it.* And therefore seeing you impose upon all men of your Communion, a necessity of *doing* or at least *approving* many things unlawful, certainly there lies upon us an unavoidable necessity of dividing Unity, either with you, or with God; and whether of these is rather to be done, be ye judges.

11. *Irænæus* also says not simply (which only would do you service, (there cannot possibly be any so important Reformation, as to justifie a Separation from them who will not reform: But only, *they cannot make any corruption so great, as is the pernitiousness of a Schism*: Now, *They*, here is a relative, and hath an antecedent expressed in *Irænæus*, which if you had been pleased to take notice of, you would easily have seen, that what *Irenæus* says, falls heavy upon the Church of *Rome*, but toucheth Protestants nothing at all. For the men he speaks of, are such as *Propter modicas & quaslibet causas, for trifling or small causes, divide the body of Christ; such as speak of peace and make war; such as strain at Gnats, and swallow Camels. And these* saith he, *can make no reformation of any such importance, as to countervail the danger of a division.* Now seeing the causes of our separation from the Church of *Rome*, are (as we pretend, and are ready to justify,) because we will not be partakers with her in Superstition, Idolatry, Impiety, and most cruel Tyranny, both upon the bodies and souls of men. Who can say, that the causes of our separation, may be justly esteemed *Modicæ & quælibet causæ?* On the other side, seeing the Bishop of *Rome*, who was contemporary to *Irenæus*, did as much (as in him lay) cut off from the Churches unity, many great Churches, for not conforming to him in an indifferent matter, upon a difference, *Non de Catholico dogmate, sed de Ritu, vel Ritus potiùs tempore, not about any Catholick Doctrin,*

but

but only a *Ceremony*, *or rather about the time of observing it*; so *Petavius* values it: which was just all one, as if the Church of *France* should excommunicate those of their own Religion in *England*, for not keeping *Christmas* upon the same day with them: And seeing he was reprehended sharply and bitterly for it, by most of the Bishops of the World, as * *Eusebius* testifies, and (as Cardinal *Perron* though mincing the matter, yet confesseth) by this very *Irenæus* himself in particular admonished, that for so small a cause (*propter tam modicam causam,*) he should not have cut off so many Provinces from the Body of the Church: and lastly, seeing the Ecclesiastical story of those times, mentions no other notable example of any such Schismatical presumption, but this of *Victor*: certainly we have great inducement to imagin, that *Irenæus* in this place by you quoted, had a special aim at the Bishop and Church of *Rome*. Once, this I am sure of, that the place fits him, and many of his successors, as well as if it had been made purposely for them. And this also, that he which finds fault with them *who separate upon small causes*, implies clearly, that he conceived, their might be such causes as were great and sufficient: And that then a Reformation was to be made, notwithstanding any danger of division that might insue upon it.

* *Euseb. hist. l. 5 c. 24. Perron. Replic. l. 3. c. 2.*

12. Lastly, S. *Denis* of *Alexandria*, says indeed and very well, *that all things should be rather indured, than we should consent to the division of the Church*: I would add, Rather than consent to the continuation of the division, if it might be remedied. But then, I am to tell you, that he says not All things should rather *be done*, but only, All things should rather *be indured or suffered*: wherein he speaks not of the evil of Sin, but of Pain and Misery: Not of tolerating either Error or Sin in others (though that may be lawful,) much less of joyning with others for quietness sake, (which only were to your purpose) in the profession of Error and practice of sin: but of suffering any affliction, nay even Martyrdom in our own persons, rather than consent to the division of the Church. *Omnia incommoda*, so your own *Christophorson*, enforced by

the circumstances of the place, translates *Dionysius* his words, All *miseries should rather be endured, then we should consent to the Churches division.*

13. Ad §. 9.] In this Paragraph you tell us first, *that the Doctrine of the total deficiency of the visible Church, maintained by many chief* Protestants *implies in it vast absurdity, or rather sacrilegious Blasphemy.*

Answ. But neither do the *Protestants* alledged by you, maintain the deficiency of the Visible Church, but only of the Churches Visibility, or of the Church as it is visible; neither do they hold that the Visible Church hath failed totally from its essence, but only from its purity; and that it fell into many corruptions, but yet not to nothing. You say secondly, *that the Reason which cast them upon this wicked Doctrine, was a desperate voluntary necessity, because they were resolved not to acknowledge the* Roman *to be the true Church, and were convinced by all manner of evidence, that for diverse Ages before* Luther *there was no other.* But this is not to dispute but to Divine, and take upon you the property of God which is to know the Hearts of Men. For why I pray, might not the Reason hereof rather be, because they were convinced by all manner of evidence, as Scripture, Reason, Antiquity, that all the Visible Churches in the World, but above all the *Roman*, had degenerated from the purity of the Gospel of Christ, and thereupon did conclude there was no Visible Church, meaning by *no Church, none free from corruption*, and conformable in all things to the Doctrine of Christ.

14. Ad §. 10. Neither is there any repugnance (but in words only) between these (as you are pleased to stile them) *exterminating Spirits*, and those other, whom out of courtesie you intitle, in your 10. §. *more moderate Protestants*. For these affirming the Perpetual Visibility of the Church, yet neither deny, nor doubt of her being subject to manifold and grievous corruptions, and those of such a nature, as were they not mitigated by invincible, or at least a very probable ignorance, none subject to them could be saved. And they on the other side, denying the Churches Visibility

Visibility, yet plainly affirm, that they conceive very good hope of the Salvation of many, of their ignorant and honest Fore-fathers. Thus declaring plainly, though in words they denied the Visibility of the true Church, yet their meaning was not to deny the perpetuity, but the perpetual purity and incorruption of the Visible Church.

17. Ad §. 11.] You ask, *To what Congregation shall a man have recourse for the affairs of his Soul; if upon Earth there be no visible Church of Christ?*

Answ. If some one Christian lived alone among *Pagans* in some Country, remote from Christendom, shall we conceive it impossible for this man to be saved, because he cannot have recourse to any Congregation for the affairs of his Soul? Will it not be sufficient, for such a ones Salvation, to know the Doctrine of Christ, and live according to it?

18. *Obj. To imagine a company of Men believing one thing in their Heart, and with their Mouth professing the contrary (as they must be supposed to do, for if they had professed what they believed, they would have become visible) is to dream of a damned crew of dissembling Sycophants, but not to conceive aright of the Church of Christ.* Answ. What is this to the Visibility of the Church? May not the Church be Invisible, and yet these that are of it profess their Faith? No, say you: Their profession will make them visible. Very true, visible in the places where, and in the times when they live, and to those persons, unto whom they have necessary occasion, to make their profession: But not visible to all, or any great, or considerable part of the World while they live, much less conspicuous to all Ages after them. Now it is a Church thus illustriously and conspicuously visible that you require: by whose splendour, all men may be directed and drawn to repair to her, for the affairs of their Souls: Neither is it the Visibility of the Church absolutely, but this degree of it, which the most rigid Protestants deny: which is plain enough out of the places of *Napper,* cited by you in your 9. Part. of this chapt. Where his words are, *God hath withdrawn his visible Church from open Assemblies, to the Hearts of par-*

ticular godly men. And this Church which had not open Assemblies, he calls *The latent and Invisible Church.* Now I hope *Papists* in *England* will be very apt to grant, men may be so far Latent and Invisible, as not to profess their Faith in open Assemblies, nor to proclaim it to all the World, and yet not deny, nor dissemble it; nor deserve to be esteemed a *damned crew of dissembling Sycophants.*

Obj. *But Preaching of the Word, and administration of the Sacraments, cannot but make a Church Visible: and these are inseparable Notes of the Church.* I answer, they are so far inseparable, that wheresoever they are, there a Church is: But not so, but that in some cases there may be a Church, where these Notes are not. Again, these Notes will make the Church visible: But to whom? certainly not to all men, nor to most men: But to them only to whom the Word is Preached, and the Sacraments are administred. They make the Church Visible to whom themselves are visible, but not to others. As where your Sacraments are administred, and your Doctrine Preached, it is visible, that there is a Popish Church. But this may perhaps be visible to them only, who are present at these performances, and to others, as secret, as if they had never been performed.

20. Obj. *But S.* Austin *saith, it is an impudent, abominable, detestible speech,* &c. *to say the Church hath Perished.* Answ. 1. All that S. *Austin* says is not true. 2. Though this were true, it were nothing to your purpose, unless you will conceive it all one not to be, and not to be conspicuously visible. 3. This very speech that the Church Perished, might be false and impudent in the *Donatists,* and yet not so in the Protestants. For there is no incongruity, that what hath lived 500. Years, may perish in 1600.

21. Obj. *While Protestants deny the perpetuity of a visible Church, they destroy their own present Church.* Answ. I do not see, how the Truth of any present Church depends upon the perpetual Visibility, nay nor upon the perpetuity of that which is past or future. For what sense is there, that it should not be in the power of God Almighty, to restore to a flourishing Estate, a Church which oppres-

sion hath made Invisible? to repair that which is ruined; to reform that which was corrupted, or to revive that which was dead? Nay what reason is there, but that by ordinary means this may be done, so long as the Scriptures by Divine Providence are preserved in their integrity and Authority? As a Common-wealth though never so far collapsed and overrun with disorders, is yet in possibility of being reduced unto its Original State, so long as the Ancient Laws, and Fundamental Constitutions are extant, and remain inviolate, from whence men may be directed how to make such a Reformation. *But S. Austin urges this very Argument against the* Donatists, *and therefore it is good.* I answer, that I doubt much of the Consequence, and my Reason is, because you your selves acknowledge, that even general Councils (and therefore much more particular Doctors) though Infallible in their determinations, are yet in their Reasons and Arguments, whereupon they ground them, subject to like Passions and Errors with other men.

22. *Obj.* Lastly whereas you say, *That all Divines define Schism a Division from the true Church,* and from thence collect, That *there must be a known Church from which it is possible for men to depart.* Answer, I might very justly question your Antecedent, and desire you to consider, whether Schism be not rather, or at least be not as well a division of the Church, as from it? A separation not of a part from the whole, but of some parts from the other. And if you liked not this definition, I might desire you to inform me in those many Schisms, which have happened in the Church of *Rome,* which of the parts was the Church, and which was divided from it. But to let this pass, certainly your consequence is most unreasonable. For though whensoever there is a Schism, it must necessarily suppose a Church existent there, yet sure we may define a Schism, that is, declare what the word signifies (for Defining is no more) though at this present there were neither Schism nor Church in the World. Unless you will say, that we cannot tell wat a Rose is, or what the word Rose signifies, but only in the Summer when we have Roses: or

that

that in the World to come, when men shall not Marry, it is impossible to know, what it is to Marry: or that the Plague is not a Disease, but only when some Body is infected: or that Adultery is not a sin, unless there be Adulterers: or that before *Adam* had a Child, he knew not, and God could not have told him, what it was to be a Father. Certainly Sir, you have forgot your Metaphysicks, which you so much glory in, if you know not, that the connexions of essentiall predicates with their subjects, are Eternal, and depend not at all upon the actual existence in the thing defined. This Definition therefore of Schism, concludes not the existence of a Church, even when it is defined: much less the perpetual continuance of it, and least of all the continuance of it in perpetual visibility and purity, which is the only thing that we deny, and you are to prove.

23. Ad §. 12. 47, 48, 49, 50, 51, 52, 53, 54, 55. The remainder of this Chapter, offers Arguments to convince *Luther* and all that follow him to be Schismaticks.

24. First then to prove us Schismaticks, you urge from the nature of Schism thus.

Whosoever leave the external Communion of the visible Church, are Schismaticks: But Luther *and his followers left the external Communion of the visible Church of Christ: Therefore they are Schismaticks.*

The Minor or second Proposition of this Argument, you prove by two other. The first is this.

They which forsook the external Communion of all Visible Churches, must needs forsake the external Communion of the true visible Church of Christ. But Luther *and his followers forsook the external Communion of all Visible Churches: Therefore they forsook the external Communion of the true visible Church.*

The Second Argument stands thus.

The Roman *Church, when the separation was made by* Luther, *&c. was the true Visible Church of Christ.*

But Luther, *&c. forsook the external Communion of the* Roman *Church. Therefore they forsook the external Communion of the true Visible Church of Christ.*

The

of Rome, *not guilty of Schism.*

The Propofition you confirm by thefe Reafons.

1. The Roman *Church had the Notes of the Church affign-ed by* Proteftants, *viz. The true Preaching of the Word, and due adminiftration of Sacraments: Therefore fhe was the true Church.*

2. *Either the* Roman *Church was the true vifible Church, or* Proteftants *can name and prove fome other difagreeing from the* Roman, *and agreeing with* Proteftants, *in their particular Doctrine: or elfe they muft fay there was no vifible Church: But they will not fay, there was no Church: They cannot name and prove any other difagreeing from the* Roman, *and agreeing with the* Proteftants *in their particular Doctrines; becaufe this cannot be the* Greek *Church, nor that of the* Waldenfes, Wickliffites, Huffites, *nor that of the* Mufcovites, Armenians, Georgians, Æthiopians, (*which you confirm by feveral Arguments:) Therefore they muft grant, that the* Roman *Church was the true Vifible Church.*

25. Now to all this I briefly anfwer thus: That you have played the unwife builder, and erected a ftately ftructure upon a falfe Foundation. For whereas you take for granted as an undoubted Truth, *That whofoever leave the external Communion of the vifible Church, are Schifmatical,* I tell you Sir, you prefume too much upon us, and would have us grant, that which is the main point in Queftion. For either you fuppofe the external Communion of the Church corrupted, and that there was a neceffity for them, that would Communicate with this Church, to Communicate in her corruptions: Or you fuppofe her Communion uncorrupted. If the former, and yet will take for granted, that all are Schifmaticks, that leave her Communion though it be corrupted, you beg the Queftion in your propofition. If the latter, you beg the Queftion in your fuppofition, for *Proteftants,* you know, are Peremptory and Unanimous in the Denial of both thefe things: Both that the Communion of the Vifible Church, was then uncorrupted; And that they are truly Schifmaticks, who leave the Commumion of the Vifible Church, if corrupted; efpecially, if the cafe be fo (and *Luthers* was fo) that they muft either leave her Communion

or

or of necessity Communicate with her in her corruptions.

26. Besides although it were granted Schism, to leave the external Communion of the Visible Church in what state or case so ever it be, and that *Luther* and his followers were Schismaticks, for leaving the external Communion of all Visible Churches: yet you fail exceedingly of clearing the other necessary point undertaken by you, *That the Roman Church was then the Visible Church*. For neither do *Protestants* (as you mistake) *make the true preaching of the Word, and due administration of the Sacraments, the notes of the Visible Church*, but only of a Visible Church: now these you know are very different things, the former signifying *the Church Catholick*, or the whole Church: the latter a *Particular Church*, or a part of the Catholick. And therefore suppose out of courtesie, we should grant, what by argument you can never evince, that your Church had these notes, yet would it by no means follow, that your Church were *the Visible Church*, but only *a Visible Church*: not the whole Catholick, but only a part of it.

27. Lastly, whereas *you say, that* Protestants *must either grant that your Church then was the Visible Church, or name some other, disagreeing from yours and agreeing with* Protestants *in their particular doctrin, or acknowledge there was no Visible Church*. It is all one as if (to use S. *Pauls* similitude) the head should say to the foot, either you must grant that I am the whole body, or name some other member that is so, or confess that there is no body. To which the foot might answer; I acknowledge there is a body: and yet, that no member beside you is this body: nor yet that you are it, but only a part of it. And in like manner say we. We acknowledge a Church there was, corrupted indeed universally, but yet such a one as we hope by Gods gracious acceptance, was still a Church. We pretend not to name any one Society that was this Church, and yet we see no reason, that can enforce us to confess that yours was the Church but only a part of it, and that one of the worst then extant in the World. In vain therefore have you troubled your self in proving, that we *cannot pretend, that either the Greeks, Waldenses, Wickliffites, Hussites, Muscovites, Armenians, Georgians,*

Georgians, Abyssines, were then the Visible Church. For all this discourse proceeds from a false & vain supposition, and begs another point in Question between us, which is, that *some Church of one denomination and one Communion* (as the Roman, the Greek, &c.) *must be always*, exclusively to all other Communions, *the whole Visible Church.* And though perhaps some weak *Protestant* having this false principle setled in him, that there was to be always some Visible Church of one denomination, pure from all error in doctrin, might be wrought upon, and prevailed with by it, to forsake the Church of *Protestants*: yet why it should induce him to go to yours, rather than the *Greek* Church, or any other, which pretends to perpetual succession as well as yours, that I do not understand; unless it be for the reason which *Æneas Sylvius* gave, why more held the Pope above a Council, than a Council above the Pope: which was because *Popes did give Bishopricks, and Archbishopricks, but Councils gave none,* and therefore suing in *Forma Pauperis,* were not like to have their cause very well maintained. For put the case, I should grant of meer favour, that there must be always some Church of one Denomination and Communion, free from all errors in doctrin, and that Protestants had not always such a Church: it would follow indeed from thence, that I must not be a Protestant: But that I must be a Papist, certainly it would follow by no better consequence than this; if you will leave *England,* you must of necessity go to *Rome.* And yet with this wretched fallacy, have I been sometimes abused my self, and known many other poor souls seduced, not only from their own Church and Religion, but unto yours. I beseech God to open the eyes of all that love the truth, that they may not always be held captive, under such miserable delusions.

28. Let us come now to the Arguments which you build upon D. *Potters* own words, out of which you promise unanswerable reasons to convince Protestants of Schism.

29. But these reasons will easily be answered, if the Reader will take along with him these three short Memorandums.

30. First,

30. First, That not every separation, but only a causeless separation from the external Communion of any Church, is the Sin of Schism.

31. Secondly, That imposing upon men under pain of Excommunication a necessity of professing known errors, and practising known corruptions, is a sufficient and necessary cause of separation, and that this is the cause the Protestants alledge to justifie their separation from which Church of *Rome.*

32. Thirdly, That to leave the Church, and to leave the external Communion of a Church, is not the same thing: That being done by ceasing to be a member of it, by ceasing to have those requisites which constitute a man a member of it, as faith and obedience: This by refusing to communicate with any Church in her Liturgies and publick worship of God. This Armour if it be rightly placed, will repel all those Batteries which you threaten us withall.

33. Ad §. 13. 14, 15.] The first is a sentence of S. *Austin* against *Donatus,* applied to *Luther* thus. *If the Church perished, what Church brought forth* Donatus, *(you say* Luther*?) If she could not perish, what madness moved the sect of* Donatus *to separate, upon pretence to avoid the Communion of bad men?* Whereunto, one fair answer (to let pass many others) is obvious out of the second observation: That this sentence though it were Gospel, as it is not, is impertinently applied to *Luther* and *Lutherans.* Whose pretence of separation (be it true or be it false, was not (as that of the *Donatists,*) only to avoid the Communion of bad men: but to free themselves from a necessity (which but by separating was unavoidable,) of joyning with bad men in their impieties.

34. Ad §. 16. Your second onset drives only at those *Protestants, who hold the true Church was invisible for many ages.* Which Doctrin (if by the *true Church* be understood, the *pure Church,* as you do understand it) is a certain truth, & it is easier for you to declaim (as you do) than to dispute against it. But *these men you say must be Hereticks because they separated from the Communion of the Visible Church: and*
there-

therefore also from the Communion of that which they say was invisible: In as much as the invisible Church communicated with the visible.

35. *Ans.* I might very justly desire some proof of that which so confidently you take for granted: That, there were no persecuted and oppressed maintainers of the Truth in the days of our Fore-fathers, but only such as dissembled their opinions, and lived in your Communion. And truly if I should say there were many of this condition, I suppose I could make my Affirmative much more probable, than you can make your Negative. We read in Scripture, that *Elias* conceived *there was none left besides himself in the whole Kingdom of Israel,* who had not revolted from God: and yet God himself assures us that he was deceived. And if such a man, a Prophet, and one of the greatest, erred in his judgment touching his own time, and his own Country, why may not you, who are certainly but a man, and subject to the same passions as *Elias* was, mistake in thinking, that in former ages, in some Countrey or other, there were not always some good Christians, which did not so much as externally bow their knees to your *Baal*? But this answer I am content you shall take no notice of, and think it sufficient to tell you, that if it be true, that this supposed invisible Church did hypocritically communicate with the visible Church, in her corruptions, then *Protestants* had cause, nay necessity, to forsake their Communion also, for otherwise they must have joyned with them in the practice of impieties: and seeing they had such cause to separate, they presume their separation cannot be Schismatical.

36. Yes, you reply, *to forsake the external Communion of them with whom they agree in faith, is the most formal and proper sin of Schism.* *Answ.* Very true, but I would fain know *wherein.* I would gladly be informed, whether I be bound for fear of Schism, to communicate with those that believe as I do, only in lawful things, or absolutely in every thing; whether I am to joyn with them in Superstition and Idolatry, and not only in a common profession of the Faith wherein we agree, but in a common dissimula-

tion or abjuration of it. This is that which you would have them do, or elſe, forſooth, they muſt be Schiſmaticks. But hereafter I pray remember, that there is no neceſſity of communicating even with true Believers in wicked actions. Nay that there is a neceſſity herein to ſeparate from them. And then I dare ſay, even you being their judge, the reaſonableneſs of their cauſe to ſeparate ſhall, according to my firſt obſervation, juſtifie their ſeparation from being Schiſmatical.

37. Arg. *But the property of Schiſm according to D. Potter is to cut off from the hope of ſalvation, the Church from which it ſeparates: And theſe Proteſtants have this property, therefore they are Schiſmaticks.*

38. *Anſ.* I deny the Syllogiſm, it is no better than this: One Simptom of the Plague is a Feaver, but ſuch a man hath a Feaver, therefore he hath the Plague. The true concluſion which iſſues out of theſe Premiſſes, ſhould be this. Therefore he hath one Symptom of the plague. And ſo likewiſe in the former, therefore they have one property or one quality of Schiſmaticks. And as in the former inſtance, The man that hath one ſign of the plague, may by reaſon of the abſence of other requiſites, not have the plague: So theſe Proteſtants may have ſomething of Schiſmaticks, and yet not be Schiſmaticks. A Tyrant ſentencing a man to death for his pleaſure, and a juſt judge that condemns a malefactor, do both ſentence a man to death, and ſo for the matter do both the ſame thing: yet the one does wickedly, the other juſtly. What's the reaſon? becauſe the one hath cauſe, the other hath not. In like manner Schiſmaticks, either always or generally denounce damnation to them from whom they ſeparate. The ſame do theſe Proteſtants, & yet are not Schiſmaticks. The Reaſon: becauſe Schiſmaticks do it, and do it without cauſe, and Proteſtants have cauſe for what they do. The impieties of your Church, being, generally ſpeaking, damnable, unleſs where they are excuſed by ignorance, and expiated at leaſt by a general repentance. In fine, though perhaps it may be true, that all Schiſmaticks do ſo: yet univerſal affirmatives are not converted, and therefore it
follows

follows not by any good Logick, that all that do so, when there is just cause for it, must be Schismaticks. The cause in this matter of separation is all in all, and that for ought I see, you never think of. But *if these rigid Protestants have just cause to cut off your Church from the hope of salvation: How can the milder sort allow hope of salvation to the Members of this Church?* Ans. Distinguish the quality of the Persons censured, and this seeming repugnance of their censures will vanish into nothing. For your Church may be considered either in regard of those, in whom, either negligence, or pride, or worldly fear, or hopes, or some other voluntary sin, is the cause of their ignorance, which I fear is the case of the generality of men amongst you: or in regard of those who owe their Errors from Truth, to want of capacity, or default of instruction; either in respect of those that might know the truth and will not, or of those who would know the truth but (all things considered) cannot: In respect of those that have eyes to see, and will not see, or those that would gladly see, but want eyes, or light. Consider the former sort of men, (which your more rigid censures seem especially to reflect upon,) and the heaviest sentence will not be too heavy. Consider the latter, and the mildest will not be too mild. So that here is no difference but in words only, neither are you flattered by the one, nor uncharitably censured by the other.

39. Your next blow is directed against the milder sort of Protestants, *who you say involve themselves in the sin of Schism by communicating with those (as you call them) exterminating Spirits, whom you conceive your self to have proved Schismaticks:* And now load them further with the crime of Heresie. For, say you, *if you held your selves obliged under pain of damnation, to forsake the Communion of the* Roman *Church by reason of her Errors, which yet you confess were not fundamental: shall it not be much more damnable, to live in confraternity with these, who defend an Error of the failing of the Church, which in the* Donatists *you confess to have been properly Heretical?*

40. Ans. You mistake in thinking that Protestants hold themselves obliged not to communicate with you, only or

principally by reason of your Errors and Corruption. For the true reason according to my third observation, is not so much because you *maintain* Errors and Corruptions, as because you *impose* them: and will allow your Communion to none but to those that will hold them with you; and have so ordered your Communion, that either we must communicate with you in these things, or nothing. And for this very reason, though it were granted, that these Protestants held this Doctrin which you impute to them; And though this Error were as damnable and as much against the Creed as you pretend: Yet after all this, this disparity between you and them, might make it more lawful for us to communicate with them than you: because what they hold, they hold to themselves, and refuse not (as you do) to communicate with them that hold the contrary.

41. Thus we may answer your Argument, though both your former Suppositions were granted, But then for a second answer, I am to tell you that there is no necessity of granting either of them. For neither do these Protestants hold the failing of the Church from its being, but only from its visibility: which if you conceive all one, then must you conceive that the Stars fail every day, and the Sun every night. Neither is it certain that the Doctrin of the Churches failing is repugnant to the Creed. For as the truth of the Article of the Remission of sins, depends not upon the actual remission of any mans sins, but upon Gods readiness and resolution to forgive the sins of all that believe and repent; so that, although unbelief or impenitence should be universal, and *the Faithful should absolutely fail from the children of men*, and *the son of man should find no faith on the earth*, yet should the Article still continue true, that God would forgive the sins of all that repent: In like manner, it is not certain that the truth of the Article of the Catholick Church depends upon the actual existence of a Catholick Church, but rather upon the right, that the Church of Christ, or rather (to speak properly) the Gospel of Christ hath to be universally believed. And therefore the Article may be true, though there

there were no Church in the world. In regard, this notwithstanding, it remains still true that there ought to be a Church, and this Church ought to be Catholick. For as, of these two Propositions, There is a Church in *America,* and, There should be a Church in *America,* The truth of the latter depends not upon the truth of the former, so neither does it in these two: There is a Church diffused all the world over, and, There should be a Church diffused all the world over.

44. Ad §. 17. The next Section in three long leaves delivers us this short sense. *That those Protestants which say they have not left the Churches external Communion, but only her corruptions pretend to do that which is impossible. Because these corruptions were inherent in the Churches external Communion: and therefore he that forsakes them cannot but forsake this.*

45. *Ans.* But who are they that pretend, they forsook the Churches corruptions, and not her external communion? Some there be that say, they have not left the Church, that is, not ceased to be members of the Church, but only left her corruptions: some, that they have not left the communion, but the corruptions of it; meaning the internal communion of it, and conjunction with it by faith and obedience: which disagree from the former only in the manner of speaking: for he that is in the Church, is in this kind of communion with it: and he that is not in this internal communion, is not in the Church. Some perhaps, that they left not your external communion in all things; meaning, that they left it not voluntarily being not *fugitivi* but *fugati,* as being willing to joyn with you in any act of piety; but were by you necessitated & constrained to do so, because you would not suffer them to do well with you, unless they would do ill with you. Now to do ill that you may do well, is against the will of God, which to every good man is a high degree of necessity. But for such Protestants, as pretend that *de facto, they forsook your corruptions only and not your external communion,* that is, such as pretend to communicate with you in your Confessions and Liturgies, and participation of Sacraments, I cannot but

Casaubon in Ep. ad Card. Perron.

but doubt very much, that neither you nor I have ever met with any of this condition. And if perhaps you were led into error, by thinking that to leave the Church, and to leave the external communion of it, was all one in sense and signification, I hope by this time you are disabused, and begin to understand, that as a man may leave any fashion or custom of a Colledge, and yet remain still a member of the Colledge; so a man may possibly leave some opinion or practice of a Church formerly common to himself and others, and continue still a member of that Church: Provided that what he forsakes be not one of those things wherein the essence of the Church consists. Whereas peradventure this practice may be so involved with the external communion of this Church, that it may be simply impossible, for him to leave this practice, and not to leave the Churches external communion.

46. You will reply perhaps, *That the difficulty lies as well against those who pretend to forsake the Churches corruptions and not the Church: as against those who say, they forsook the Churches corruptions, and not her external communion. And that the reason is still the same: because these supposed corruptions, were inherent in the whole Church, and therefore by like reason with the former, could not be forsaken, but if the whole Church were forsaken.*

47. *Ans.* A pretty Sophism, and very fit to perswade men that it is impossible for them, to forsake any Error they hold, or any Vice they are subject to, either peculiar to themselves, or in common with others: Because forsooth, they cannot forsake themselves, and Vices and Errors are things inherent in themselves. The deceit lies, in not distinguishing between a Local and a Moral forsaking of any thing. For as it were an absurdity, fit for the maintainers of Transubstantiation to defend, that a man may locally and properly depart from the accidents of a subject, and not from the subject it self: So is it also against reason to deny, that a man may (by an usual phrase of speech) forsake any custom, or quality, good or bad, either proper to himself, or common to himself with any company, and yet never truly or properly forsake either his company or himself.

himself. Thus if all the Jesuites in the Society, were given to write Sophistically, yet you might leave this ill custome, and yet not leave your Society. If all the Citizens of a City, were addicted to any vanity, they might either, all, or some of them forsake it, and yet not forsake the City. If all the parts of a mans Body were dirty or filthy, nothing hinders but that all or some of them might cleanse themselves, and yet continue parts of the Body. And what reason then in the World is there, if the whole visible Church were overcome with Tares and Weeds of superstitions; and corruptions, but that some members of it might reform themselves, and yet continue still true members of the Body of the Church, and not be made no members, but the better by their Reformation?

50. We acknowledge, that we cannot (as matters now stand) *Separate from your corruptions, but we must depart from your External Communion.* For you have so ordered things, that whosoever will Communicate with you at all, must Communicate with you, in your corruptions. But it is you that will not perceive the difference, between, being a part of the Church, and being in external Communion with all the other parts of it: taking for granted, that which is certainly false, that no two men or Churches, divided in external Communion, can be both true parts of the Catholick Church.

51. We are not *to learn the difference between* Schism *and* Heresie, for *Heresie* we conceive, an obstinate defence of any Error, against any necessary Article of the Christian Faith: And *Schism*, a causless separation of one part of the Church from another. But this we say, That if we convince you of Errors and corruptions, professed and practised in your Communion, then we cannot be Schismaticks, for refusing to joyn with you in the profession of these Errors, and the practice of these corruptions. And therefore you must free your selves from Error, or us from *Schism*.

52. Lastly, whereas you say, *That you have demonstrated against us, that* Protestants *divided themselves from the*
external

external Communion of the Visible Church, add, *which external communion was corrupted*, and we shall confess the accusation, and glory in it. But this is not that *Quod erat demonstrandum*, but that we divided our selves from the Church, that is, made our selves Out-laws from it, and no members of it. And moreover, in the Reason of your separation from the external Communion of your Church you are mistaken: for it was not so much because she, your Church, as because your Churches external Communion was corrupted, and needed Reformation.

53. *That a pretence of Reformation will acquit no man from Schism,* we grant very willingly, and therefore say, that it concerns every man who separates from any Churches Communion, even as much as his Salvation is worth, to look most carefully to it, that the cause of his separation be just and necessary: For unless it be necessary, it can very hardly be sufficient. But whether a true Reformation of our selves from Errors, superstitions and impieties, will not justifie our separation in these things; our separation, I say, from them who will not reform themselves, and as much as in them lies, hinder others from doing so: This is the point you should have spoken to, but have not. As for the sentences of the Fathers to which you refer us, for the determination of this Question, I suppose by what I have said above, the Reader understands, by alledging them you have gained little credit to your cause or person. And that, if they were competent Judges of this Controversie, their sentence is against you much rather than for you.

56. But your Argument you conceive, will be more convincing, *if we consider that when* Luther *appeared, there were not two distinct Visible true Churches, one Pure, the other Corrupted, but one Church only.* *Ans.* The ground of this is no way certain, nor here sufficiently proved. For, whereas you say, Histories are silent of any such matter: I answer, there is no necessity, that you or I should have read all Histories, that may be extant of this matter; nor that all should be extant that were written, much less extant uncorrupted: especially considering your Church, which had

had lately all power in her hands, hath been so pernitiously industrious, in corrupting the monuments of Antiquity that made against her; nor that all Records should remain which were written; nor that all should be recorded which was done.

Lastly, whereas you say, that supposing a visible pure Church, *Luther* must be a Schismatick, who separated from all visible Churches: I tell you, if you will suppose a Visible Church extant before and when *Luther* arose, conformable to him in all points of Doctrine, necessary and profitable, then *Luther* separated not from this Church, but adjoyned himself to it: Not indeed in place, which was not necessary, not in external Communion which was impossible, but by the Union of Faith and Charity. Upon these grounds I say, that the ground of this Argument is no way made certain, yet because it is not manifestly false, I am content to let it pass. And for ought I see, it is very safe for me to do so: for you build nothing upon it, which I may not fairly grant. For what do you conclude from hence, but that seeing there was no Visible Church but corrupted, *Luther* forsaking the external Communion of the corrupted Church, could not but forsake the external Communion of the Catholick Church? Well, let this also be granted, what will come of it? What, that *Luther* must be a Schismatick? By no means: For not every separation, but only a causeless separation from the Communion of the Church we maintain to be Schismatical. Hereunto may be added, that though the whole Church were corrupted, yet properly speaking, it is not true, that *Luther* and his Followers forsook the whole corrupted Church, or the external Communion of it: But only that he forsook that Part of it which was corrupted, and still would be so, and forsook not, but only reformed another Part, which Part they themselves were, and I suppose you will not go about to persuade us, that they forsook themselves or their own Communion. And if you urge that they joyned themselves to no other part, therefore they separated from the whole: I say it follows not, in as much as themselves were a part of it, and still continued so : and therefore could no more separate from the whole than from themselves. Thus though there were no part of the People of *Rome*, to whom the *Plebeians* joyned themselves, when they made their Secession into the *Aventine Hill*, yet they divided themselves from the *Patricians* only, and not from the whole People, because themselves were a part of this People, and they divided not from themselves.

57. Ad §. 18.] Here you prove that which no man denies, that *corruption in manners yields no sufficient cause to leave the Church*: yet sure it yields sufficient cause to cast them out of the Church, that are after the Churches publick admonition obstinate in notorious impieties. Neither doth the cutting off such men from the Church, lay any necessity upon us, either to go out of the World, or out of the Church, but rather puts these men out of the Church into the World, where we may converse with them freely, without scandal to the Church, *Our Blessed Saviour foretold,* you say, *that there should be in the Church Tares with choice Corn.* Look again I pray, and you shall see, that the field he speaks of, is not the Church, but *the World* : and therefore neither doe You obey our Saviours command, *Let both grow up till the Harvest,* who teach it to be lawful to root these Tears (such are *Hereticks*) out of the World : neither do *Protestants* disobey it; if they eject manifest Heresies and notorious sinners out of the Church.

58. Ad §. 19.] In the 19. you are so courteous as to suppose *corruptions in your Doctrine,* and yet undertake to prove that, *neither could they afford us any sufficient cause, or colourable necessity to depart from them.* Your reason is, *because damnable Errors there were none in your Church, by D. Potters confession, neither can it be damnable in respect of Error, to remain in any Churches Communion, whose Errors are not damnable. For if the Error be not damnable, the belief thereof cannot.* Answ. *D. Potter* confesseth no such matter : but only that *he hopes that your Errors, though in themselves sufficiently damnable, yet by accident did not damn all that held them*: such he means and says, as were excusably ignorant

norant of Truth, and amongst the number of their unknown sins, repented daily of their unknown Errors. The truth is, he thinks as ill of your Errors and their desert, as you do of ours: only he is not so peremptory and presumptuous in judging your persons, as you are in judging ours, but leaves them to stand or fall to their own Master, who is infinitely merciful, and therefore will not damn them for meer Errors, who desire to find the truth and cannot: and withal infinitely just, and therefore (is it to be feared) will not pardon them, who might easily have come to the knowledge of the truth, and either through Pride, or obstinacy, or neligence would not.

59. To your minor also, I answer almost in your own Words, §. 42. of this Chap. I thank you for your courteous supposal, that your Church may Err, and in recompence thereof, will do you a Charity, by putting you in mind, into what *Labyrinths* you cast your self, by supposing that the Church may Err in some of her Proposals, and yet denying it lawful for any man though he know this, which you suppose, to oppose her judgment, or leave her communion. Will you have such a man dissemble against his Conscience, or externally deny that which he knows true? No, that you will not, for them that do so, you your self have pronounced *A damned Crew of dissembling Sycophants*. Or would you have him continue in your Communion, and yet profess your Church to Err? This you your selves have made to him impossible. Or would you have him believe those things true, which together with him you have supposed to be Errors? This in such a one, as is assured or perswaded of that, which you here suppose, that your Church doth Err, (and such only we say, are obliged to forsake your Communion,) is, as Schoolmen speak, *Implicatio in terminis*, a contradiction so plain, that one word destroyeth another; as if one should say, a living dead man. For it is to require that they which believe some part of your Doctrine false, should withal believe it all true. Seeing therefore, for any man to believe your Church in Error, and profess the contrary, is damnable Hypocrisie; to believe

lieve it and not believe it, a manifest repugnancy; and thirdly, to profess it and to continue in your Communion (as matters now stand) a plain impossibility; what remains, but that whosoever is supposed to have just reason to disbelieve any Doctrine of your Church, must of necessity forsake her Communion? Unless you would remit so far from your present rigour, as to allow them your Churches Communion, who publickly profess that they do not believe every Article of her established Doctrine. Indeed, if you would do so, you might with some coherence suppose your Church in Error, and yet find fault with men for abandoning her Communion, because they might continue in it, and suppose her in Error. But to suppose your Church in Error, and to excommunicate all those that believe your own supposition, and then to complain that they continue not in your Communion, is the most ridiculous incongruity that can be imagined. And therefore though your corruptions in Doctrine, in themselves (which yet is false) did not, yet your obliging us, to profess your Doctrine uncorrupted against knowledge and Conscience, may induce an obligation to depart from your Communion. As if there were any Society of Christians, that held there were no Antipodes; notwithstanding this Error I might communicate with them. But if I could not do so, without professing my self of their belief in this matter, then I suppose I should be excused from Schism, if I should forsake their Communion, rather than profess my self to believe that which I do not believe. Neither is there any contradiction, or shadow of contradiction, that it may be necessary for my Salvation, to depart from this Churches Communion: And that this Church (though Erring in this matter) wants nothing necessary to Salvation.

60. *That there might be necessary cause to depart from the Church of* Rome *in some Doctrine and practices, though she wanted nothing necessary to Salvation as Dr.* Potter *holds, and you call a contradiction*, will appear by setting down his Words, which are these; *To forsake the Errors of that Church, and not to joyn with her in those practices which we*
account

account erroneous, we are enforced by necessity. For though in the issue they are not damnable to them which believe as they profess, yet for us to profess and avow by Oath (as the Church of Rome enjoyns) what we believe not, were without question damnable. And they with their Errors, by the grace of God might go to Heaven, when we for our Hypocrisie and dissimulation (he might have added, and Perjury) *stould certainly be condemned to Hell.*

61. Ad §. 20.] *Obj.* But *a Church not Erring in Fundamentals, though Erring in other matters, doth what our Saviour exacts at her hands, doth as much as lies in her power to do: Therefore the Communion of such a Church is not upon pretence of Error to be forsaken.* The consequence is manifest. The Antecedent is proved, because *God, by D. Potters confession, hath promised his assistance no further, nor is it in her power to do more than God doth assist her to do.* Pag. 151. 153.

Answ. The promise of Divine Assistance is twofold: Absolute, or Conditional. That there shall be by Divine providence preserved in the World to the Worlds end, such a company of Christians, who hold all things precisely and indispensably necessary to Salvation, and nothing inevitably destructive of it: This and no more the Doctor affirms that God hath promised absolutely. Yet he neither doubts nor denys, but that a farther assistance is conditionally promised us, even such an assistance as shall lead us, if we be not wanting to it and our selves, into all not only necessary, but very profitable truth, and guard us from all not only destructive, but also hurtful Errors. This, I say, he neither denies nor questions. And should he have done so, he might have been confuted by evident and express Texts of Scripture. When therefore you say, That *a Church not Erring in Fundamentals, doth as much as by Gods assistance lies in her power to do*; This is manifestly untrue. For Gods assistance is alwaies ready to promote her farther. It is ready, I say, but on condition the Church does implore it: on condition, that when it is offerred in the Divine directions of Scripture and reason, the Church be not negligent to follow it. If therefore there be any Church, which retaining the foundation,

builds

builds *Hay and Stubble* upon it: which believing what is precisely necessary, Errors shamefully and dangerously in other things very profitable: This by no means argues defect of Divine assistance in God, but neglect of this assistance in the Church. Neither is there any reason, why such a Church should please her self too much, for retaining Fundamental truths, while she remains so regardless of others. For though the simple defect of some truths profitable only and not simply necessary, may consist with Salvation; Yet who is there that can give her sufficient assurance, that the neglect of such truths is not damnable? Besides, who is there that can put her in sufficient caution, that these Errors about profitable matters may not according to the usual fecundity of Error, bring forth others of a higher quality, such as are pernitious and pestilent, and undermine by secret consequences the very foundations of Religion and Piety? Lastly, who can say that she hath sufficiently discharged her duty to God and man by avoiding only Fundamental Heresies, if in the mean time she be negligent of others, which though they do not plainly destroy Salvation, yet obscure and hinder, and only not block up the way to it? Which though of themselves and immediately they damn no man, yet are causes and occasions that many men run the race of Christian Piety more remisly than they should, many defer their repentance, many go on securely in their sins, and so at length are damned by means and occasion of these Errors, though not for them. Such Errors as these (though those of the *Roman Church* be much worse, even *in themselves damnable, and by accident only pardonable*) yet I say such Errors as these, if any Church should tolerate, dissemble and suffer them to reign, and neglect to reform them, and not permit them to be freely, yet peaceably, opposed and impugned; will any wise man say, that she hath sufficiently discharged her duty to God and man? That she hath with due fidelity dispensed the Gospel of Christ? That she hath done what she could, and what she ought? What shall we say then, if these Errors be taught by her, and commanded to be taught? What if she thunder

der out her curses against those that will not believe them? What if she rave and rage against them, and persecute them with Fire and Sword, and all kinds of most exquisite torments? Truly I do much fear, that from such a Church (though it hold no Error absolutely unconsistent with Salvation,) the Candlestick of God, either is already removed, or will be very shortly, and because she is negligent of profitable truths, that she will lose those that are Necessary, and because she will not be led into all truths, that in short time she shall be led into none. And although this should not happen, yet what mortal man can secure us, that not only a probable unaffected ignorance, nor only a meer neglect of profitable truths, but also a wretchless supine negligence, manifest contempt, Dissimulation, Opposition, Oppression of them, may consist with Salvation? I truly for my part, though I hope very well of all such as seeking all truth, find that which is necessary; who endeavouring to free themselves from all Errors, any way contrary to the purity of Christianity, yet fail of performance and remain in some: yet if I did not find in my self a love and desire of all profitable truth; If I did not put away idleness, and prejudice, and worldly affections, and so examine to the bottom all my opinions of Divine matters, being prepared in mind to follow God, and God only which way soever he shall lead me; If I did not hope, that I either do, or endeavour to do these things, certainly I should have little hope of obtaining Salvation.

62. *Obj. But to oblige any man under pain of damnation to forsake a Church by reason of such Errors, against which Christ thought it superfluous to promise his assistance, and for which he neither denies his grace here, nor his glory hereafter, what is it but to make the narrow way to Heaven, narrower than Christ left it?* *Answ.* It is not: for Christ himself hath obliged us hereunto: He hath forbidden us under pain of damnation to profess what we believe not, and consequently under the same penalty, to leave that Communion, in which we cannot remain without this hypocritical profession of those things, which we are convinced to be

erroneous. But then besides, it is here falsely supposed, (as hath been shewed already) that Christ hath not promised assistance to those that seek it, but only in matters simply necessary. Neither is there any reason, why any Church, even in this World, should despair of Victory over all Errors pernitious or noxious; provided she humbly and earnestly implore Divine assistance, depend wholly upon it, and be not wanting to it. Though a *Triumph over all sin and Error*, that is, security that she neither doth nor can Err, be rather to be desired than hoped for on Earth, being a felicity reserved for Heaven.

63. Ad §. 21.] Obj. *But at least the* Roman *Church is as infallible as* Protestants, *and* Protestants *as fallible as the* Roman *Church: therefore to forsake the* Roman *Church for Errors, what is it but to flit from one Erring Society to another?* Ans. The inconsequence of this Argument is too apparent: *Protestants* may Err as well as the Church of *Rome*, therefore they did so! Boys in the Schools know, that *à Posse ad Esse*, the Argument follows not. He is equally fallible that believes twice two to be four, as he that believes them to be twenty: yet in this, he is not equally deceived, and he may be certain that he is not so. One Architect is no more infallible than another, and yet he is more secure that his work is right and streight who hath made it by the level, than he which hath made it by guess and by chance. So he that forsakes the Errors of the Church of *Rome*, and therefore renounceth her Communion, that he may renounce the profession of her Errors, though he knows himself fallible, as well as those whom he hath forsaken, yet he may be certain (as certain as the nature of the thing will bear) that he is not herein deceived: because he may see the Doctrine forsaken by him repugnant to Scripture, and the Doctrine embraced by him consonant to it. At least, this he may know, that the Doctrine which he hath chosen to him seems true, and the contrary which he hath forsaken, seems false: And therefore without remorse of Conscience, he may profess that, but this he cannot.

46. Obj.

64. *Obj.* But *we are to remember, that according to Doctor* Potter *the Visible Church hath a blessing not to Err in Fundamentals, in which any private Reformer may fail, therefore there was no necessity of forsaking the Church, out of whose Communion they were exposed to danger of falling into many more, and even into damnable Errors.* *Answ.* The Visible Church is free indeed from all Errors absolutely destructive and unpardonable, but not from all Error which in it self is damnable: not from all which will actually bring damnation upon them, that keep themselves in them, by their own voluntary and avoidable fault.

Besides, any private man who truly believes the Scripture, and seriously endeavours to know the will of God, and to do it, is as secure as the Visible Church, more secure than your Church from the danger of Erring in Fundamentals: for it is impossible, that any man so quallified should fall into any Error which to him will prove damnable. For God requires no more of any man to his Salvation, but his true endeavour to be saved. Lastly, abiding in your Churches Communion is so far from securing me or any man from damnable Error, that if I should abide in it, I am certain I could not be saved. For abide in it I cannot, without professing to believe your entire Doctrine true: profess this I cannot, but I must lie perpetually, and exulcerate my Conscience. And though your Errors were not in themselves damnable, yet to resist the known Truth, and to continue in the profession of known Errors and falshoods, is certainly a capital sin, and of great affinity with the sin which shall never be forgiven.

65. *Obj. But neither is the* Protestant *Church free from corruptions and Errors: And what man of Judgment will be a* Protestant, *since that Church is confessedly a corrupted one?*

Answ. And yet you your self make large discourses in this very Chapter, to persuade *Protestants* to continue in the Church of *Rome*, though supposed to have some corruptions. And why I pray, may not a man of judgment continue in the Communion of a Church confessedly corrupted, as well as in a Church supposed to be corrupted? Especially when this Church supposed to be corrupted, requires the belief and profession of her supposed corruptions, as the condition of her Communion: which this Church confessedly corrupted, doth not. What man of judgment will think it any disparagement, to his judgment, to prefer the better, though not simply the best, before that which is stark naught? To prefer indifferrent good health, before a diseased and corrupted state of Body? To prefer a field not perfectly weeded, before a field that is quite over-run with Weeds and Thorns? and therefore though *Protestants* have some Errors, yet seeing they are neither so great as yours, nor imposed with such Tyranny, nor maintained with such obstinacy; he that conceives it any disparagement to his judgment, to change your Communion for theirs, though confessed to have some corruptions, it may well be presumed that he hath but little judgment.

66. Ad §. 22.] Obj. *But* Protestants *say, it is comfort enough for the Church to be secured from all capital dangers (which can only arise from Error in Fundamental points) and not hope to Triumph over all sin and Error, till she be in Heaven; why therefore were not the first Reformers content with enough, but would dismember the Church, out of greediness of more than enough?*

Answ. I have already shewed sufficiently, how capital danger may arise from Errors, though not Fundamental. I add now, that what may be enough for men in ignorance, may be to knowing men not enough: according to that of the Gospel, *to whom much is given, of him much shall be required:* That the same Error may be not capital to those who want means of finding the truth, and capital to others who have means, and neglect to use them: That to continue in the profession of Error discovered to be so, may be damnable, though the Error be not so. These I presume are reasons enough, and enough why the first Reformers might think, and justly, that not enough for themselves, which yet to some of their Predecessors they hope might be enough. This very Argument was objected to [a] S. *Cyprian* upon another occasion,

[a] S. *Cyprian: Ep.*63. In these words. *Siquis de antecessoribus nostris, vel ignoranter vel simpliciter non observavit, & tenuit quod res Dominus facere exemplo & Magisterio suo docuit, potest simplicitati ejus de indulgentia Domini, venia conceda: nobis verò non potest ignosci, qui nunc à Domino admoniti & instructi sumus.*

sion, and also by the [b] Brittish *Quartodecimans*, to the maintainers of the Doctrine of your Church ; and [c] by both this very answer was returned; and therefore I cannot but hope that for their sakes you will approve it.

[b] *Wilfridus*, to *Abbat Colman* alledging that he followed the example of his predecessors famous for Holiness, and famous for Miracles, in these Words, *De Patre Vestro Columba & sequacibus ejus, quorum sanctitatem vos imitari & regulam ac præcepta cœlestibus signis confirmata sequi perhibetis, possum respondere ; Quia multis in judicio dicentibus Domino Quòd in nomine ejus prophetaverint & dæmonia ejecerint, & virtutes multas fecerint, responsurus sit Dominus, quia nunquam eos noverit. Sed absit ut de patribus vestris hoc dicam, quia justius multo est de incognitis bonum credere quam malum. Unde & illos Dei famulos & Deo dilectos esse non nego, qui simplicitate rustica, sed intentione pia Deum dilexerunt : Neque illis multum obesse Paschæ talem reor observantiam, quandiu nullus advenerat qui eis instituti perfectioris decreta quæ sequerentur, ostenderet. Quos utique credo, si qui tunc ad eos Catholicus calculator adveniret, sic ejus monita fuisse secu turos, quomodo ea quæ noverant ac didicerunt Dei mandata, probantur fuisse secuti. Tu autem & socii tui si audita decreta sedis Apostolicæ, imo universalis Ecclesiæ & hæc literis sacris confirmata contemnitis, absque ulla dubietate peccatis.* [c] Beda : *lib.* 3. *Eccl. Hist. c.* 25.

67. *Obj. But if no Church may hope to Triumph over Error, till she be in Heaven, then we must either grant, that Errors not Fundamental cannot yield sufficient cause to forsake the Church, or affirm that all communities may and ought to be forsaken.*

Answ. We do not say, that no Church may hope to be free from all Error, either pernitious or any way noxious : But that *no Church may hope to be secure from all Error simply,* for this were indeed truly to triumph over all. But then we say not, that the Communion of any Church is to be forsaken for Errors unfundamental, unless it exact with all either a dissimulation of them being noxious ; or a Profession of them against the dictate of Conscience, if they be meer Errors. This if the Church does (as certainly yours doth,) then her Communion is to be forsaken, rather than the sin of Hypocrisie to be committed. Whereas to forsake the Churches of *Protestants* for such Errors, there is no necessity, because they Err to themselves, and do not under pain of Excommunication exact the profession of their Errors.

68. *Obj. But the Church may not be left by reason of sin, therefore neither by reason of Errors not Fundamental : in as much*

much as both sin and Error are impossible to be avoided till she be in Heaven. Answ. The reason of the consequence does not appear to me: But I answer to the Antecedent: Neither for sin or Errors, ought a Church to be forsaken, if she does not impose and joyn them: but if she do, (as the *Roman* does,) then we must forsake men rather than God; leave the Churches Communion rather than commit sin, or profess known Errors, to be Divine truths. For the Prophet *Ezekiel* hath assured us, that to say, *the Lord hath said so, when the Lord hath not said so,* is a great sin and a high presumption, be the matter never so small.

69. Ad §. 23.] Obj. *But neither the Quality nor the number of your Churches Errors, could warrant our forsaking of it. Not the Quality, because we suppose them not Fundamental. Not the number because the Foundation is strong enough to support them. Answ.* Here again you vainly suppose, that we conceive your Errors in themselves not damnable: Though we hope they are not absolutely unpardonable: but to say they are pardonable, is indeed to suppose them damnable. Secondly, though the Errors of your Church did not warrant our departure, yet your Tyrannous imposition of them, would be our sufficient justification. For this lays necessity on us, either to forsake your company, or to profess what we know to be false.

70. Obj. *Our Blessed Saviour hath declared his Will, that we forgive a private offender Seventy Seven times, that is, without limitation of quantity of time, or quality of Trespasses; and then how dare we alledge his command, that we must not pardon his Church for Errors acknowledged to be not Fundamental? Answ.* He that commands us to pardon our Brother sinning against us so often, will not allow us for his sake to sin with him, so much as once. He will have us do any thing but sin, rather than offend any man. But his will is also, that we offend all the World, rather than sin in the least matter. And therefore though his will were, and it were in our power (which yet is false) to pardon the Errors of an Erring Church; yet certainly it is not his will, that we should Err with the Church, or if we do

not,

not, that we should against Conscience profess the Errors of it.

71. Ad §. 24.] Obj. *But Schismaticks from the Church of England or any other Church, with this very Answer, that they forsake not the Church but the Errors of it, may cast off from themselves the imputation of Schism.* Answ. True, they may make the same Answer, and the same defence as we do, as a Murtherer can cry not guilty, as well as an Innocent person, but not so truly nor so justly. The question is, not what may be pretended, but what can be proved by Schismaticks. They may object Errors to other Churches, as well as we do to yours, but that they prove their accusation so strongly as we can, that appears not. To the Priests and Elders of the *Jews*, imposing that sacred silence mentioned in the *Acts* of the Apostles, S. *Peter* and S. *John* answered *they must obey God rather than men.* The three Children to the King of *Babylon*, gave in effect the same answer. Give me now any factious Hypocrite, who makes Religion the pretence and Cloke of his Rebellion, and who sees not that such a one may answer for himself, in those very formal words, which the Holy Apostles and Martyrs made use of. And yet I presume no Christian will deny, but this answer was good, in the mouth of the Apostles and Martyrs, though it were obnoxious to be used, by Traitors and Rebels. Certainly therefore, it is no good consequence to say, Schismaticks may make use of this Answer, therefore all that do make use of it are Schismaticks. But moreover, it is to be observed, that the cheif part of our defence, that you deny your Communion to all that deny or doubt of any part of your Doctrine, cannot with any colour be imployed against *Protestants*: who grant their Communion to all who hold with them, not all things, but things necessary, that is, such as are in Scripture plainly delivered.

72. Obj. *But the forsaking the* Roman *Church opens a way to innumerable Sects and Schisms, and therefore it must not be forsaken.* Answ. We must not do evil to avoid evil: neither are all courses presently lawful, by which inconveniencies may be avoided. If all men would submit them-

themselves to the chief Mufty of the *Turks*, it is apparent, there would be no divisions; yet Unity is not to be purchased at so dear a rate. It were a thing much to be desired, that there were no divisions: yet difference of opinions touching points controverted, is rather to be chosen, than unanimous concord in damned Errors: As it is better for men to go to Heaven by diverse ways, or rather by divers Paths of the same way, than in the same path to go on peaceably to Hell. *Amica Pax, magis amica Veritas*! Peace is dear to me, but Truth is dearer.

74. Ad §. 26. 27.] Here you make D. *Potter* to say, *that Protestants did well to forsake the Church of* Rome, *because they judged she retained all means necessary to Salvation. Answ.* Who was ever so stupid as to give this ridiculous reason? D. *Potter* Vindicates *Protestants* for Schism two ways: The one is, because they had just and great and necessary cause to separate, which Schismaticks never have; because they that have it are no Schismaticks: For Schism is always a causeless separation. The other is, because they did not joyn with their separation, an uncharitable damning of all those from whom they did divide themselves, as the manner of Schismaticks is. Now that which he intends for a circumstance of our separation, you make him make the cause of it, and the motive to it. And whereas he says, *though we separate from you in some things, yet we acknowledge your Church a member of the Body of Christ, and therefore are not Schismaticks:* You make him say most absurdly, *we did well to forsake you, because we judged you a member of the Body of Christ.* Just as if a Brother should leave his Brothers company in some ill courses, and should say to him, Herein I forsake you, yet I leave you not absolutely, for I acknowledge you still to be my Brother, and shall use you as a Brother: And you perverting his speech, should pretend that he had said, I leave your company in these ill courses, and I do well to do so, because you are my Brother: so making that the cause of his leaving him, which indeed is the cause that he left him no farther.

75. Obj. But you say, *The very reason for which he acquitteth himself for Schism, is because he holds that the Church*

Church which they forsook, is not cut off from the Body of Christ?

Ans. This is true: But can you not perceive a difference between justifying his separation from Schism by this reason, and making this the reason of his separation? If a man denying obedience in some unlawful matter to his lawful Sovereign, should say to him, herein I disobey you, but yet I am no Rebel, because I acknowledge you my Sovereign Lord, and am ready to obey you in all things lawful, should not he be an egregious Sycophant, that should accuse him as if he had said, I do well to disobey you, because I acknowledge you my lawful Soveraign? Certainly he that joyns this acknowledgment with his necessitated disobedience, does well; but he that makes this consideration the reason of his disobedience, doth ill.

76. Obj. *It is an unspeakable comfort to Catholicks* (you say) *that we cannot clear our selves from Schism otherwise, than by acknowledging that* we do *not, nor cannot cut off your Church from the hope of salvation.*

Ans. I beseech you to take care that this false comfort cost you not too dear. For why this good opinion of God Almighty, that he will not damn men for error, who were without their own fault ignorant of the truth, should be any consolation to them, who having the key of knowledge, will neither use it themselves, nor permit others to use it; who have eyes to see and will not see, who have ears to hear and will not hear! this I assure you passeth my capacity to apprehend. Neither *is this to make our salvation depend on yours,* but only ours and yours not desperatly inconsistent. Nor to say we *must be damned unleß you may be saved*; but that we assure our selves, if our lives be answerable, we shall be saved by our knowledge. And that we hope (and I tell you again *Spes est rei incertæ nomen,*) that some of you may possibly be the rather saved by occasion of their unaffected Ignorance.

80. Ad §. 28. 29. Whereas D. *Potter says, There is a great difference between a Schism from them, and a Reformation of our selves: this* you say *is a quaint subtilty by which all Schism and sin may be as well excused.*

Ans.

Anf. It seems then in your judgment, that Thieves and Adulterers, and Murtherers, and Traytors may say with as much probability as Protestants, that they did no hurt to others, but only reform themselves. But then methinks it is very strange, that all Protestants should agree with one consent in this defence of themselves from the imputation of Schism: and that to this day, never any Thief or Murtherer should have been heard of to make use of this Apology! And then for Schismaticks I would know, whether *Victor* Bishop of *Rome*, who excommunicated the Churches of *Asia* for not conforming to his Church in keeping *Easter*; whether *Novatian* that divided from *Cornelius*, upon pretence that himself was elected Bishop of *Rome*, when indeed he was not; whether *Felicissimus* and his Crew, that went out of the Church of *Carthage*, and set up altar against altar, because having fallen in persecution, they might not be restored to the peace of the Church presently, upon the intercession of the Confessors; whether the *Donatists*, who divided from, and damned all the world, because all the world would not excommunicate them who were accused only and not convicted to have been Traditors of the sacred Books; whether they which for the slips and infirmity of others, which they might and ought to tolerate, or upon some difference in matters of Order and Ceremony, or for some error in Doctrin, neither pernitious nor hurtful to faith or piety, separate themselves from others, or others from themselves; or lastly, whether they that put themselves out of the Churches unity and obedience, because their opinions are not approved there, but reprehended and confuted, or because being of impious conversation, they are impatient of their Churches censure: I would know I say, whether all, or any of these, may with any face or without extream impudency, put in this plea of Protestants, and pretend with as much likelihood as they, that they did not separate from others, but only reform themselves? But suppose they were so impudent as to say so in their own defence falsely, doth it follow by any good Logick, that therefore this Apology is not to be imployed by Protestants, who may say

so

of Rome, *not guilty of Schism.*

so truly? *We make* (say they) *no Schism from you, but only a reformation of our selves:* This, you reply, *is no good justification, because it may be pretended by any Schismatick.* Very true, any Schismatick that can speak may say the same words, (as any Rebel that makes conscience the cloak of his impious disobedience, may say with S. *Peter* and S. *John, we must obey God rather than men;*) But then the question is, whether any Schismatick may say so truly? And to this question you say just nothing: but conclude, because this defence may be abused by some, it must be used by none. As if you should have said, S. *Peter* and S. *John* did ill to make such an answer as they made, because impious Hypocrites might make use of the same to palliate their disobedience and rebellion against the lawful commands of lawful Authority.

81. Obj. *But seeing their pretended Reformation consisted in forsaking the Churches corruptions, their Reformation of themselves, and their division from you, falls out to be one and the same thing.*

Ans. Just as if two men having been a long while companions in drunkenness, one of them should turn sober; this Reformation of himself, and desertion of his companion, in this ill custom, would be one and the same thing, and yet there is no necessity that he should leave his love to him at all, or his society in other things. So Protestants forsaking their own former corruptions, which were common to them with you, could not choose but withal forsake you in the practice of these corruptions: yet this they might, and would have done without breach of Charity towards you; and without a renunciation of your company in any act of piety and devotion, confessedly lawful. And therefore though both these were by accident joyned together, yet this hinders not but that the end they aimed at, was not a separation from you, but a reformation of themselves.

82. Neither *doth their disagreement in the particulars of the Reformation,* (which yet when you measure it without partiality, you'll find to be far short of infinite) *nor their symbolizing in the general of forsaking your corruptions,* prove

R r 2 any

any thing to the contrary, or any way advantage your design or make for your purpose. For it is not any sign at all, much less an evident sign, that they had no setled design, but only to forsake the Church of *Rome:* for nothing but malice can deny, that their intent at least was, to reduce Religion to that original purity from which it was fallen. The declination from which, some conceiving to have begun (though secretly) in the Apostles times, *(the mystery of iniquity being then in work;)* and after their departure to have shewed it self more openly: others again believing, that the Church continued pure for some Ages after the Apostles, and then declined: And consequently some aiming at an exact conformity with the Apostolick times: Others thinking they should do God and men good service, could they reduce the Church to the condition of the fourth and fifth ages: Some taking their direction in this work of Reformation, only from Scripture; others from the Writings of Fathers, and the Decrees of Councils of the first five Ages: certainly it is no great marvel, that there was, as you say, disagreement between them, in the particulars of their Reformation; nay morally speaking, it was impossible it should be otherwise. Yet let me tell you, the difference between them (especially in comparison of your Church and Religion,) is not the difference between good and bad, but between good and better: And they did best that followed Scripture, interpreted by Catholick written Tradition: which rule the Reformers of the Church of *England,* proposed to themselves to follow.

83. Ad 30. 31, 32.] D. *Potter,* p. 81. 82. of his Book, speak thus. *If a Monastery should reform it self, and should reduce into practice ancient good discipline, when others would not: In this case could it be charged with Schism from others, or with Apostacy from its rule and order? So in a society of men universally infected with some disease, they that should free themselves from it, could they be therefore said to separate from the society?* He presumes they could not, and from hence concludes, *That neither can the Reformed Churches be truly accused for making a Schism,* (that is separating
from

from the Church, and making themselves no members of it) if all they did was (as indeed it was) to reform themselves.

84. Now instead of these two instances, which plainly shewed it possible in other societies, and consequently in that of the Church, to leave the faults of a Society, and not leave being of it, you disingenuously foist in two other instances, clean cross to the Doctors purpose, of men under colour of faults, abandoning the Society wherein they lived.

85. But that no suspicion of tergiversation may be fastned upon me, I am content to deal with you a little, at your own weapons. Put the case then, though not just as you would have it, yet with as much favour to you, as in reason you can expect, That a Monastery did observe her substantial vows, and all principal statutes, but yet did generally practise, and also enjoyn the violation of some lesser, yet obliging observances, and had done so time out of mind. And that some inferiour Monks more conscientious than the rest, discovering this abuse, should first with all earnestness sollicite their Superiors for a general and orderly reformation of these, though small and venial corruptions, yet corruptions: But finding they hoped and laboured in vain to effect this, should reform these faults in themselves, and refuse to joyn in the practice of them, with the rest of their Confraternity, and persisting resolutely in such a refusal, should by their Superiors be cast out of their Monastery, and being not to be re-admitted without a promise of remitting from their stiffness in these things, and of condescending to others in the practice of their small faults, should choose rather to continue exiles, than to re-enter upon such conditions: I would know whether you would condemn such men of Apostacy from the Order? Without doubt if you should, you would find the stream of your Casuists against you, and besides, involve S. *Paul* in the same condemnation, who plainly tells, that *we may not do the least evil, that we may do the greatest good.* Put case again, you should be part of a Society universally infected with some disease, and discovering

vering a certain remedy for this disease, should perswade the whole company to make use of it, but find the greatest part of them so far in love with their disease, that they were resolved to keep it; and besides, should make a decree, that whosoever would leave it, should leave their company. Suppose now that your self and some few others, should notwithstanding their injunction to the contrary, free your selves from this disease, and thereupon they should absolutely forsake and reject you: I would know in this case who deserves to be condemned, whether you of uncharitable desertion of your company, or they of a tyrannical peevishness? And if in these cases you will (as I verily believe you will,) acquit the inferiors and condemn the superiors, absolve the minor part and condemn the major, then can you with no reason condemn Protestants, for choosing rather to be ejected from the communion of the *Roman* Church, than with her to persist (as of necessity they were to do, if they would continue in her Communion) in the profession of Errors, though not destructive of salvation, yet hindering edification, and in the practice, or at least approbation of many, (suppose not mortal) but venial corruptions.

86. Besides, you censure too partially the corrupt estate of your *Church in comparing it to a Monastery, which did confessedly observe their substantial Vows, and all principal Statutes of their order; and moreover was secured by an infallible assistance, for the avoiding of all substantial corruptions*: for of your Church we confess no such matter, but say plainly, That she not only might fall into substantial corruptions, but did so; that she did not only generally violate, but of all the members of her Communion, either in act or approbation, require and exact the violation of many substantial Laws of Christ, both Ceremonial and Moral, which though we hope it was pardonable in them, who had not means to know their error, yet of its own nature, and to them who did or might have known their error, was certainly damnable. And that it was not the *Tything of Mint and Annise, and Cummin*, the neglect whereof

we

we impute unto you, but *the neglect of judgment, justice, and the weightier matters of the Law.*

87. Again, you compare Proteſtants to *ſuch a Company as acknowledge that themſelves, as ſoon as they were gone out of the Monaſtery that deferred to reform, muſt not hope to be free from thoſe or the like Errors and Corruptions for which they left their Brethren.* Which is very ſtrange, ſeeing this very hope and nothing elſe, moved them to leave your Communion: and this ſpeech of yours, ſo far as it concerns the ſame Errors, plainly deſtroys it ſelf. For how can they poſſibly fall into the ſame Errors by forſaking your Communion, which that they may forſake they do forſake your Communion? And then for other errors of the like nature and quality, or more enormous than yours, though they deny it not poſſible, but by their negligence and wickedneſs they may fall into them, yet they are ſo far from acknowledging that they have no hope to avoid this miſchief, that they proclaim to all the world, that it is moſt prone and eaſie to do ſo, to all thoſe that fear God and love the truth; and hardly poſſible for them to do otherwiſe, without ſupine negligence and extream impiety.

89. Obj. *But when* Luther *began, he being but one, oppoſed himſelf to all, as well Subjects as Superiors.*

Anſ. If he did ſo in the cauſe of God, it was heroically done of him. This had been without hyperbolizing, *Mundus contra Athanaſium,* and *Athanaſius contra Mundum;* the *world againſt* Athanaſius, *and* Athanaſius *againſt the world:* neither is it impoſſible, that *the whole world ſhould ſo far lie in wickedneſs* (as S. *John* ſpeaks) that it may be lawful and noble for one man to oppoſe the world. But yet were we put to our Oaths, we ſhould ſurely not teſtifie any ſuch thing for you; for how can we ſay properly and without ſtreining, that *he oppoſed himſelf to All,* unleſs we could ſay alſo, that All oppoſed themſelves to him? And how can we ſay ſo, ſeeing the world can witneſs, that ſo many thouſands, nay millions followed his ſtandard as ſoon as it was advanced.

90. But

90. *But none that lived immediatly before him thought or spake as he did.* This first is nothing to the purpose. The Church was then corrupted, and sure it was no dishonour to him to begin the Reformation. In the Christian warfare, every man ought to strive to be foremost. Secondly, it is more than you can justifie. For though no man before him lifted up his voice like a Trumpet, as *Luther* did, yet who can assure us, but that many before him, both thought and spake in lower voice of Petitions and Remonstrances, in many points, as he did?

91. Obj. *Many chief learned Protestants, are forced to confess the Antiquity of your Doctrin and practice.*

Ans. Of many Doctrins and practices of yours this is not true; for I pray inform me, what confessions of Protestants have you, for the Antiquity of the Doctrin of the Communion in one kind: the lawfulness and expedience of the *Latin Service*: For the present use of Indulgences: For the Popes power in Temporalties over Princes: For the picturing of the Trinity: For the lawfulness of the worship of Pictures: For your Beads and Rosary, and Ladies Psalter; and in a word, for your whole worship of the Blessed Virgin: For your oblations by way of consumption, and therefore in the quality of Sacrifices to the Virgin *Mary* and other Saints: For your saying of *Pater nosters*, and Creeds to the honour of Saints, and of *Ave-Maries* to the honour of other Saints besides the Blessed Virgin: For infallibility of the Bishop or Church of *Rome*: For your prohibiting the Scripture to be read publickly in the Church, in such Languages as all may understand: For your Doctrin of the Blessed Virgins immunity from actual sin; and for your doctrin and worship of her Imaculate conception: For the necessity of Auricular Confession: For the necessity of the Priests intention to obtain benefit by any of your Sacraments: And lastly (not to trouble my self with finding out more) for this very doctrin of Licentiousness, That though a man live and die without the practice of Christian vertues, and with the habits of many damnable sins unmortified, yet if he in the last moment of life, have any sorrow for his sins, and joyn con-

confession with it, certainly he shall be saved? Besides, though some *Protestants* confess some of your Doctrine to be Ancient, yet this is nothing, so long as it is evident, even by the confession of all sides, that many Errors, I instance in that of the *Millenaries*, and the Communicating of Infants, were more Ancient. Not any antiquity thereof, unless it be absolute and primitive, is a certain sign of true Doctrine. For if the Church were obnoxious to corruption (as we pretend it was,) who can possible warrant us that part of this corruption, might not get in and prevail in the 5. or 4. or 3. or 2. Age? Especially seeing the Apostles assure us that the *mystery of iniquity was working*, though more secretly even in their times. If any man ask how could it become Universal in so short a time? Let him tell me how the Error of the *Millenaries*, and the Communicating of Infants, became so soon Universal, and then he shall acknowledge, what was done in some, was possible in others. Lastly, to cry quittance with you: As there are *Protestants* who confess the Antiquity, but always post-nate to Apostolick, of some points of your Doctrine: so there want not *Papists* who acknowledge as freely, the novelty of many of them, and the Antiquity of ours. A collection of whose Testimony, we have (without thanks to you) in your *Indices expurgatorii*. The Divine Providence, blessedly abusing for the readier manifestation of the Truth this Engine intended by you for the subversion and suppression of it. Here is no place to stand upon particulars: only one general ingenuous confession of that great *Erasmus*, may not be passed over in silence. *Non desunt magni Theologi, qui non verentur affirmare, nihil esse in* Luthero, *quin per probatos authores defendi possit.* There want not great Divines, which stick not to affirm, that there is nothing in Luther, which may not be defended by good and allowed authors.

Erasm. Ep. lib. 15. Ep. ad Godeschalcum. Ros.

92. After this you compose a heap of vain suppositions, pretended to be grounded on our confessions. As first, that your *Defeases* which we forsook, neither were nor could be mortal: whereas we assure our selves, and are ready to justifie, that they are and were mortal in themselves,

and would have been so to us, if when light came to us we had loved Darkness more than Light. Secondly, *that we had no hope to avoid other Diseases like those for which we forsook your company, nor to be secure out of it from damnable Errors:* whereas, in truth, the hope hereof was the only motive of our departure; and we assure our selves that the means to be secured from damnable Error, is not to be secure as you are, but carefully to use those means of avoiding it, to which God hath promised, and will never fail to give a blessing. Thirdly, that *those innumerable mischiefs which followed upon the departure of* Protestants, *were caused by it as by a proper cause*: whereas their Doctrine was no otherwise the occasion of them, than the Gospel of Christ was of the division of the World. The only Fountain of all these mischiefs, being indeed no other than your pouring out a Flood of persecutions against *Protestants*, only because they would not sin & be damned with you for company. Unless we may add the impatience of some *Protestants*, who not enduring to be Torn in peeces like Sheep by a company of Wolves without resistance, chose rather to die like Soldiers than Martyrs.

96. Obj. *But they endeavoured to force the Society whereof they were parts to be healed and reformed as they were; and if it refused, they did, when they had power drive them away, even their superiours both Spiritual and Temporal as is notorious.* The proofs hereof are wanting and therefore I might defer my answer until they were produced; yet take this beforehand: If they did so, then herein, in my opinion, they did amiss; for I have learnt from the Ancient Fathers of the Church, that *nothing is more against Religion than to force Religion*, and of S. Paul, *the Weapons of the Christian Warfare are not carnal.* And great reason: For humane violence may make men counterfeit, but cannot make them believe, and is therefore fit for nothing but to breed form without, and *Atheism* within. Besides, if this means of bringing men to embrace any Religion were generally used (as if it may be justly used in any place by those that have power, and think they have truth, certainly they cannot with reason deny but that it may be used in every place,

place, by those that have power as well as they, and think they have truth as well as they,) what could follow but the maintainance perhaps of truth, but perhaps only of the profession of it in one place, and the oppression of it in a hundred? What will follow from it but the preservation peradventure of Unity, but peradventure only of uniformity in particular States and Churches; but the immortallizing the greater and more lamentable divisions of Christendom and the World? And therefore what can follow from it, but perhaps in the judgment of carnal policy, the temporal benefit and tranquillity of temporal States and kingdoms, but the infinit prejudice, if not the desolation of the kingdom of Christ? And therefore it well becomes them who have their portions in this life, who serve no higher State than that of *England*, or *Spain*, or *France*, nor this neither any further than they may serve themselves by it; who think of no other happiness but the preservation of their own fortunes and tranquillity in this World; who think of no other means to preserve States, but humane power and Machiavillian policy; and believe no other Creed but this, *Regi aut Civitati imperium habenti nihil injustum, quod utile*! that to a King or City that has Ruling Power, nothing that is profitable is unjust. Such men as these it may become to maintain by worldly power and violence their State-instrument, Religion. For if all be vain and false, (as in their judgment it is) the present whatsoever, is better than any, because it is already setled: and alteration of it may draw with it change of States, and the change of State the subversion of their fortune. But they that are indeed Servants and lovers of Christ, of Truth, of the Church, and of Man-kind, ought with all courage to oppose themselves against it, as a common Enemy of all these. They that know there is a King of Kings, and Lord of Lords, by whose will and pleasure Kings and Kingdoms stand and fall, they know, that to no King or State any thing can be profitable which is unjust; and that nothing can be more evidently unjust, than to force weak men by the profession of a Religion which they believe not, to lose their own Eternal Happiness, out of a vain and needless fear, lest they may possibly disturb their temporal quietness. There is no danger to any state from any mans opinion; unless it be such an opinion by which disobedience to authority, or impiety is taught or licenced, which sort, I confess may justly be punished as well as other faults; or unless this sanguinary Doctrine be joyned with it, that it is lawful for him by humane violence to enforce others to it. Therefore if *Protestants* did offer violence to other Mens Consciences and compel them to embrace their Reformation, I excuse them not: much less if they did so to the sacred Persons of Kings, and those that were in authority over them, who ought to be so secured from violence, that even their unjust and Tyrannous violence, though it may be avoided (according to that of our Saviour, *When they persecute you in one Citty fly into another,*) yet may it not be resisted by opposing violence against it. *Protestants* therefore that were guilty of this crime, are not to be excused, and blessed had they been, had they chosen rather to be Martyrs than Murtherers, and to die for their Religion rather than to fight for it. But of all the men in the World you are the most unfit to accuse them hereof, against whom the Souls of Martyrs from under the Altar cry much louder than against all their other Persecutors together: Who for these many Ages together have daily sacrificed *Hecatombs* of Innocent Christians, under the name of Hereticks, to your blind zeal and furious superstition. Who teach plainly, that you may propagate your Religion whensoever you have power by deposing of Kings and Invasion of Kingdoms, and think when you kill the Adversaries of it, you do God good service. But for their departing corporally from them, whom mentally they had forsaken: For their forsaking the external Communion and company of that part of the unreformed part of the Church, in their superstitions and impieties: thus much of your accusation we embrace and glory in it; And say though some Protestants might offend in the manner or the degree of their separation, yet certainly their separation it self was not Schismatical, but Innocent, and not only so, but just and necessary.

99. Ad

of Rome, *not guilty of Schism.*

99. Ad §. 36.] What you cite out of *Optatus* (*l.* 2. *cont. Parm. Thou canst not deny but that thou knowest, that in the City of* Rome *there was first an Episcopal Chair placed for* Peter, *wherein* Peter *the head of the Apostles sate, whereof also he was called* Cephas; *in which one Chair Unity was to be kept by all, lest the other Apostles might attribute to themselves each one his particular Chair; and that he should be a Schismatick and sinner, who against that one single Chair should erect another.* All this is impertinent, if it be well lookt into. The truth is the *Donatists* had set up at *Rome* a Bishop of their faction: not with intent to make him Bishop of the whole Church but of that Church in particular. Now *Optatus* going upon S. *Cyprians* ground *of one Bishop in one Church*, proves them Schismatick for so doing, by this Argument: S. *Peter* was first Bishop of *Rome*, neither did the Apostles attribute to themselves each one his particular Chair, (viz. *in that City*, for in other places others I hope had Chairs besides S. *Peter*) and therefore he is a Schismatick, who against that one single Chair erects another (viz. *in that place*) making another Bishop of that Diocess besides him who was lawfully elected to it.

100. *Obj.* But *he stiles S.* Peter *Head of the Apostles, and says that from thence he was called* Cephas.

Answ. Perhaps he was abused into this opinion, by thinking *Cephas* derived from the Greek word Κεφαλὴ a head: whereas it is a *Syriack* word and signifies a Stone. Besides S. *Peter* might be head of the Apostles, that is first in order and honour among them, and not have supream Authority over them. And indeed that S. *Peter* should have authority over all the Apostles, and yet exercise no one Act of Authority over any one of them, and that they should shew to him no sign of subjection, methinks is as strange, as that a King of *England* for twenty five years should do no Act of Regality, nor receive any one acknowledgment of it. As strange methinks it is, that you so many Ages after, should know this so certainly, as you pretend to do. and that the Apostles (after that those words were spoken in their hearing, by vertue whereof S. *Peter* is pretended to

have

have been made their Head,) should still be so ignorant of it, as to question *which of them should be the greatest?* yet more strange, that our Saviour should not bring them out of their Error, by telling them S. *Peter* was the man, but rather confirm it by saying, *the Kings of the Gentiles exercise authority over them, but it should not be so among them.* No less a wonder was it that S. *Paul* should so far forget S. *Peter* and himself, as that first mentioning him often, he should do it without any Title of Honour. Secondly, speaking of the several degrees of men in the Church, he should not give S. *Peter* the highest, but place him in equipage with the rest of the Apostles, and say, *God hath appointed* (not *first* Peter, *then the rest* of the Apostles, but) *first Apostles, secondly Prophets.* Certainly if the Apostles were *all first*, to me it is very probable, that no one of them was before the rest. For by *First*, all men understand either that which is before all, or that before which is nothing. Now in the former sense, the Apostles could not be all first, for then every one of them must have been before every one of the rest. And therefore they must be *First* in the other sense. And therefore, No man, and therefore not S. *Peter*, must be before any of them. Thirdly and Lastly, that speaking of himself in particular, and perhaps comparing himself with S. *Peter* in particular, rather than any other, he should say in plain terms, *I am in nothing inferior to the very Chiefest Apostles.* But besides all this, though we should grant against all these probabilities and many more, that *Optatus* meant that S. *Peter* was head of the Apostles, not in our but in your sense, and that S. *Peter* indeed was so; yet still you are very far from shewing, that in the judgment of *Optatus*, the Bishop of *Rome*, was to be at all, much less by Divine right, successor to S. *Peter* in this his Headship and Authority. For what incongruity is there, if we say, that he might succeed S. *Peter* in that part of his care, the Government of that particular Church, (as sure he did even while S. *Peter* was living,) and yet that neither he nor any man was to succeed him in his Apostleship, nor in his Government

of

of the Church Univerfal? Efpecially feeing S. *Peter* and the reft of the Apoftles, by laying the Foundations of the Church, were to be the *Foundations of it,* and accordingly are fo called in Scripture. And therefore as in a building it is incongruous that Foundations fhould fucceed Foundations: So it may be in the Church, that any other Apoftle fhould fucceed the firft.

101. Ad §. 37.] *Obj.* What you here cite out of S. *Auft.n*; if it be applied to *Luther*'s Separation, is impertinent. For it is one thing to feparate from the Communion of the whole World, another to feparate from all the Communions in the World: One thing to divide from them who are United among themfelves, another to divide from them who are divided among themfelves. Now the *Donatifts* feparated from the whole World of Chriftians, United in one Communion, profeffing the fame Faith, ferving God after the fame manner, which was a very great Argument, that they could not have juft caufe to leave them: according to that of *Tertullian, Variaſſe debuerat error Eccleſiarum, quod autem apud multos unum eſt, non eſt Erratum ſed Traditum.* But *Luther* and his followers did not fo. The World, I mean of Chriftians and Catholicks, was divided and fubdivided long before he divided from it; and by their divifions had much weakened their own Authority, and taken away from you this Plea of S. *Auſtin,* which ftands upon no other Foundation, but the Unity of the whole Worlds Communion.

102. Ad §. 38.] *Obj. If Luther were in the right, moſt certain thoſe* Proteſtants *that differed from him were in the wrong.*

Anſw. But that either he or they were Schifmaticks, it follows not. Or if it does, then either the Jefuits are Schifmaticks from the *Dominicans,* or they from the Jefuites; The *Canoniſts* from the Jefuits, or the Jefuits from the *Canoniſts*: The *Scotiſts* from the *Thomiſts,* or they from the *Scotiſts*: The *Franciſcans* from the *Dominicans,* or the *Dominicans* from the *Franciſcans.* For between all thefe the World knows, that in point of Doctrine, there is plain and irreconcileable contradiction, and therefore one Part muſt be in Error, at leaſt not Fundamental. Thus your Argument

gument returns upon your self, and if it be good, proves the *Roman* Church in a manner to be made up of Schismaticks. But the answer to it is, that it begs this very false and vain supposition; That whosoever Errs in any point of Doctrine is a Schismatick.

103. Ad §. 39.] In the next place you number up your Victories, and tell us, *that out of these premises, this conclusion follows, That* Luther *and his followers were Schismaticks from the Visible Church, the* Pope, *the Diocess wherein they were baptized, from the Bishop under whom they lived, from the Country to which they belonged, from their Religious order, wherein they were professed, from one another, and lastly, from a mans self: Because the self same* Protestant *is convicted to day, that his yesterdays opinion was an Error.* To which I answer, that *Luther* and his followers separated from many of these, in some opinions and practices: But that they did it without cause, which only can make them Schismaticks, that was the only thing you should have proved, and to that you have not urged one reason of any moment. All of them for weight and strength, were cousin-germans to this pretty device, wherewith you will prove them Schismaticks from themselves, *because the self same* Protestant *to day is convicted in Conscience, that his yesterdays opinion was an Error.* It seems then that they that hold Errors, must hold them fast, and take especial care of being convicted in Conscience, that they are in Error, for fear of being Schismaticks! *Protestants* must continue *Protestants*, and *Puritans* Puritans, and *Papists* Papists, nay *Jews*, and *Turks*, and *Pagans*, must remain *Jews*, and *Turks*, and *Pagans*, and go on constantly to the Devil, or else forsooth they must be *Schismaticks*, and that *from themselves*. And this perhaps is the cause that makes *Papists* so obstinate, not only in their common superstition, but also in adhering to the proper fancies of their several Sects, so that it is a miracle to hear of any Jesuit, that hath forsaken the opinion of the Jesuits: or any *Dominican* that hath changed his or the Jesuits.

But sure the forsaking of error cannot be a sin, unless to be in error be a vertue. And therefore, to do as you do, do, to damn men for false opinions, and to call them Schismaticks for leaving them; to make pertinacy in error, that is, an unwillingness to be convicted, or a resolution not to be convicted, the form of Heresies, and to find fault with men, for being convicted in conscience that they are in error, is the most incoherent and contradictious injustice that ever was heard of. But Sir, if this be a strange matter to you, that which I shall tell you will be much stranger. I know a man that of a moderate Protestant turned a Papist, and the day that he did so, (as all things that are done are perfected some day or other,) was convicted in conscience, that his yesterdays opinion was an error, and yet thinks he was no Schismatick for doing so, and desires to be informed by you, whether or no he was mistaken? The same man afterwards upon better consideration, became a doubting Papist, and of a doubting Papist, a confirmed Protestant. And yet this man thinks himself no more to blame for all these changes, than a Traveller, who using all diligence to find the right way to some remote City, where he never had been, (as the party I speak of had never been in Heaven,) did yet mistake it, and after find his error, and amend it. Nay he stands upon his justification so far, as to maintain that his alterations, not only to you, but also from you by Gods mercy, were the most satisfactory actions to himself, that ever he did, and the greatest victories that ever he obtained over himself, and his affections to those things which in this world are most precious; as wherein for Gods sake and (as he was verily perswaded,) out of love to the Truth, he went upon a certain expectation of those inconveniences, which to ingenuous natures are of all most terrible. So that though there were much weakness in some of these alterations, yet certainly there was no wickedness. Neither does he yield his weakness altogether without apology, seeing his deductions were rational, and out of Principles commonly received by Protestants as well as Papists, and which by his education had got possession of his understanding.

107. Ad §. 41.] Obj. *Though the first Reformers had conceived their own opinions to be true, yet they might and ought to have doubted, whether they were certain; since they affirm, that Infallibility was not promised to particular persons or Churches.*

Ans. This is to say, that they ought to have doubted of the certainty of Scripture, which in formal and express terms, contains many of these opinions. And your reason is vain; for *though they had not an absolute infallibility promised unto them,* yet may they be of some things infallibly certain. As *Euclide* sure was not infallible, yet he was certain enough, that *twice two were four,* and *that every whole was greater than a part of that whole.* And so though *Calvin* and *Melancton* were not infallible in all things, yet they might and did know well enough, that your *Latin-Service* was condemned by S. *Paul,* and that the Communion in both kinds was taught by our Saviour.

Obj. But *your Church was in peaceable possession* (you must mean of her Doctrin and the Professors of it) *and enjoyed prescription for many Ages.*

Ans. The possession which the Governors of your Church held for some ages, of the party governed, was not peaceable, but got by fraud and held by violence.

108. Obj. You say that *a pretence of Conscience will not serve to justifie separation from being Schismatical.*

Ans. This is very true but little to the purpose, seeing it is not an erroneous perswasion, much less an hypocritical pretence, but a true and well grounded conviction of Conscience, which we alledge to justifie Protestants from being Schismatical. And therefore though Seditious men in Church and State, may pretend conscience for a cloak of their rebellion: yet this I hope hinders not, but that an honest man ought to obey his rightly informed conscience, rather than the unjust commands of his Tyrannous Superiors. Otherwise with what colour can you defend either your own refusing the Oaths of Allegiance and Supremacy? Or the ancient Martyrs, and Apostles, and Prophets, who oftentimes disobeyed the commands of men in authority, and for their disobedience

made

made no other but this Apology, *We must obey God rather than men?* It is therefore most apparent that this answer must be meerly impertinent: seeing it will serve against the Martyrs and Apostles and Prophets, and even against your selves, as well as against Protestants. To as little purpose is your rule out of *Lyrinensis* against them that followed *Luther*, seeing they pretend and are ready to justifie, that they forsook not, with the Doctors, the faith, but only the corruption of the Church. As vain altogether is that which follows: That *in cases of uncertainty we are not to leave our Superior, or cast off his obedience, nor publickly oppose his decrees.* From whence it will follow very evidently, that seeing it is not a matter of faith, but a disputed question among you, whether the Oath of Allegiance be lawful: that either you acknowledge not the King your Superior, or do against conscience, in opposing his and the kingdoms decree, requiring the taking of this Oath. This good use, I say, may very fairly be made of it, and is by men of your own Religion.

109 Ad §. 42.] Obj. *It is not fit,* you say, *for any private man to oppose his judgment to the publick.*

Ans. Not his own judgment and bare authority; but occasions may happen, wherein it may be very warrantable, to oppose his reason or the authority of Scripture against it: and is not then to be esteemed to oppose his own judgment to the publick, but the judgment of God to the judgment of men.

Neither will Mr. *Hookers* words you cite do you any service. For though he says (*Pref.* to *Eccles. polit.* sec 6. *pag.* 28.) that *men are bound to do whatsoever the sentence of judicial and final decision shall determine;* as it is plain men are bound to yield such an obedience to all Courts of civil judicature: yet he says not, they *are bound to think* that determination lawful and that sentence just. Nay it is plain he says, that *they must do according to the Judges sentence, though in their private opinion it seem unjust.* As if I be wrongfully cast in a suit at Law, and sentenced to pay an hundred pound, I am bound to pay the money, yet I know no Law of God or man, that binds me in conscience to acquit the Judge of error in his sentence. Neither is there any *necessity*, as you say, *that he must either acknowledge the Universal Infallibility of the Church, or drive men into dissembling against their Conscience*; seeing nothing hinders, but I may obey the sentence of a Judge, paying the mony he awards me to pay, or forgoing the house or land which he hath judged from me, and yet withal plainly profess, that in my Conscience I conceive his Judgment erroneous. To which purpose they have a saying in *France*, that *whosoever is cast in any cause, hath liberty for ten days after, to rail at his Judges*.

110. But observe, I pray, that Mr. *Hooker* says not absolutely and in all their causes; but onely *in litigious causes, of the quality of those whereof he* there treats; In such matters as have plain Scripture or reason neither for them nor against them, and wherein men are perswaded this or that way, *upon their own only probable collection*; in such cases, *This perswasion* (saith he) *ought to be fully setled in mens hearts, that the will of God is, that they should not disobey the certain commands of their lawful Superiors, upon uncertain grounds: But do that which the sentence of judicial and final decision shall determin.* For the purpose, a Question there is, whether a Surplice may be worn in Divine Service: The authority of Superiors injoyns this Ceremony, and neither Scripture nor reason plainly forbids it. *Sempronius* notwithstanding, is by some inducements, which he confesses to be onely probable, lead to this perswasion that the thing is unlawful. The *quære* is, whether he ought for matter of practice follow the injunction of authority, or his own private and only probable perswasion? M. *Hooker* resolves for the former, upon this ground, that *the certain commands of the Church we live in, are to be obeyed in all things, not certainly unlawful*.

As for requiring a blind and an unlimited obedience, to Ecclesiastical decisions universally and in all cases, even when plain Text or reason seems to controul them, M. *Hooker* is as far from making such an Idol of Ecclesiastical Authority, as the Puritans whom he writes against. *I grant* (saith he,) *that proof derived from the authority of*

mans

mans judgment, is not able to work that assurance which doth grow by a stronger proof. *And therefore although ten thousand General Councils would set down one and the same definitive sentence, concerning any point of Religion whatsoever, yet one demonstrative reason alledged, or one manifest testimony cited from the word of God himself, to the contrary, could not choose but over-weigh them all: in as much as for them to be deceived it is not impossible, it is that Demonstrative Reason, or Divine Testimony should deceive.* And again, *Whereas it is thought, that especially with the Church, and those that are called, mans authority ought not to prevail: It must and doth prevail even with them, yea with them especially, as far as equity requireth, and farther we maintain it not. For men to be tied and led by authority, as it were with a kind of captivity of judgment, and though there be reason to the contrary, not to listen to it, but to follow like beasts, the first in the Herd, this were brutish. Again, that authority of men should prevail with men either against or above reason, is no part of our belief. Companies of learned men, be they never so great and reverend, are to yield unto reason, the weight whereof, is no whit prejudiced by the simplicity of his person which doth alledge it, but being found to be sound and good, the bare opinion of men to the contrary, must of necessity stoop and give place.* Thus M. *Hooker* in his Seventh Section of his Second Book.

112. Ad §. 43.] The next Section hath in it some objections against *Luthers* person, but none against his cause, which alone I have undertaken to justifie, and therefore I pass it over. Yet this I promise, that when you, or any of your side, shall publish a good defence, of all that your Popes have said and done, especially of them whom *Bellarmine* believes, in such a long train *to have gone to the Devil:* then you shall receive an ample Apology for all the actions and words of *Luther.* In the mean time, I hope all reasonable and equitable Judges, will esteem it not unpardonable in the great and Heroical spirit of *Luther*, if being oposed, and perpetually baited with a world of Furies, he were transported sometimes, and made somewhat furious. As for you, I desire you to be quiet, and to demand no more, whether God be wont to send such Furies

ries to preach the Gospel? Unless you desire to hear of your killing of Kings: Massacring of Peoples; Blowing up of Parliaments: and have a mind to be ask't, whether it be probable, that that should be Gods cause, which needs to be maintained by such Devilish means?

CHAP. VI.

The ANSWER to the Sixth CHAPTER.

Shewing that Protestants are not Hereticks.

Ad §. 1. HE that will accuse any one man, much more any great multitude of men of any great and horrible crime, should in all reason and justice take care that the greatness of his evidence do equal, if not exceed the quality of the crime. And such an accusation you would here make shew of, by pretending, first, *to lay such grounds of it, as are either already proved, or else yielded on all sides:* and after to raise a firm and stable structure of convincing arguments upon them. But both these I find to be meer and vain pretences, and having considered this Chapter also without prejudice or passion, as I did the former, I am enforced by the light of Truth, to pronounce your whole discourse, a painted and ruinous Building upon a weak and sandy foundation.

2. Ad §. 2, 3. First for your grounds, a great part of them, is falsely said to be either proved or granted. It is true indeed that *Man by his natural wit and industry could never have attained to the knowledge of Gods will to give him a supernatural and eternal happiness,* nor of the means by which his pleasure was to bestow this happiness upon him. And therefore your first ground is good, *That it was requisite his understanding should be enabled to apprehend that end and means by a knowledge supernatural.* I say this is good, if you mean by *knowledge,* an apprehension or belief.

3. But

The nature of Faith. 327

3. But then whereas you add, *that if a such a knowledge were no more than probable, it could not be able sufficiently to overbear our will, and encounter with human probabilities, being backed with the strength of flesh and blood, and therefore conclude, that it was farther necessary, that this supernatural knowledge should be most certain and infallible:* To this I answer, that I do heartily acknowledge and believe the Articles of our Faith be in themselves Truths, as certain and infallible as the very common Principles of Geometry and Metaphysicks. But that there is required of us a knowledge of them, and an adherence to them, as certain as that of sense or science, that such a certainty is required of us under pain of damnation, so that no man can hope to be in the state of salvation, but he that finds in himself such a degree of faith, such a strength of adherence: This I have already demonstrated to be a great error, and of dangerous and pernitious consequence. And because I am more and more confirmed in my perswasion that the Truth which I there delivered, is of great and singular use, I will here confirm it with more reasons. And to satisfie you that this is no singularity of my own my Margent presents you with a ᵃ Protestant Divine of great authority, and no way singular in his opinions, who hath long since preached and justified the same doctrin.

ᵃ M. *Hooker* in his answer to *Travers* his supplication.—

I have taught that the assurance of things which we believe by the word, is not so certain as of that we perceive by sence. And is it as certain? Yea I taught, that the things which God doth promise in his word are surer unto us than any thing we touch, handle or see. But are we so sure and certain of them? If we be, why doth God so often prove his promises unto us, as he doth by arguments taken from our sensible experience? We must be surer of the proof than the thing proved, otherwise it is no proof. How is it that if ten men do all look upon the Moon, every one of them knows it as certainly to be the Moon as another: but many believing one and the same promises all have not one and the same fulnes of perswasion? How falleth it out that men being assured of any thing by sence, can be no surer of it than they are? whereas the strongest in faith that liveth upon the earth, had always need to labour, and strive, and pray, that his assurance concerning heavenly and spiritual things may grow, increase, and be augmented.

4. I say that every Text of Scripture which makes mention of any that were *weak*, or of any that were *strong in faith*: of any that were *of little*, or any that were *of great faith*:

of

of any that *abounded*, or any that were *rich* in faith: of *encreasing, growing, rooting, grounding, establishing, confirming in faith:* Every such Text, is a demonstrative refutation of this vain fancy: proving that faith, even true and saving faith, is not a thing consisting in such an indivisible point of perfection as you make it, but capable of augmentation and diminution. Every Prayer you make to God to encrease your faith (or if you conceive such a prayer derogatory from the perfection of your faith, (*The Apostles praying to Christ to encrease their Faith,* is a convincing argument of the same conclusion. Moreover if this doctrin of yours were true, then seeing not any the least doubting can consist with a most infallible certainty, it will follow that every least doubting in any matter of faith, though resisted and involuntary, is a damnable sin, absolutely destructive, so long as it lasts, of all true and saving faith: which you are so far from granting, that you make it no sin at all, but only an occasion of merit: and if you should esteem it a sin, then must you acknowledge, contrary to your own Principles, that there are Actual sins meerly involuntary. The same is furthermore invincibly confirmed by every deliberate sin that any Christian commits; by any progress in Charity that he makes. For seeing, as S. *John* assures us, *our faith is the victory which overcomes the world,* certainly if the faith of all true Believers were perfect, (and if true faith be capable of no imperfection, if all faith be a knowledge most certain and infallible, all faith must be perfect, for the most imperfect that is, according to your doctrin, if it be true, must be *most certain,* and sure the most perfect that is, cannot be more than most certain,) then certainly their victory over the World, and therefore over the flesh, and therefore over sin, must of necessity be perfect, and so it should be impossible for any true believer to commit any deliberate sin, and therefore he that commits any sin, must not think himself a true believer. Besides seeing Faith worketh by Charity, and Charity is the effect of Faith: certainly if the cause were perfect, the effect would be perfect, and consequently as you make no degrees in Faith, so there would be none in Charity, and so no

man

man could possibly make any progress in it, but all true believers should be equally in Charity, as in Faith you make them equal: and from thence it would follow unavoidably, that whosoever finds in himself any true Faith, must presently persuade himself that he is perfect in Charity: and whosoever on the other side, discovers in his Charity any imperfection, must not believe that he hath any true Faith. These you see are strange and portentous consequences, and yet the deduction of them from your Doctrine is clear and apparent; which shews this Doctrine of yours, which you would fain have true, that there might be some necessity of your Churches Infallibility, to be indeed plainly repugnant not only to Truth but even to all Religion and Piety, and fit for nothing but to make men negligent of making any Progress in Faith or Charity.

5. As for that one single reason which you produce to confirm it, it will appear upon examination to be resolved finally into a groundless Assertion of your own, contrary to all Truth and experience, and that is, *That no degree of Faith, less than a most certain and infallible knowledge, can be able sufficiently to overbear our will and encounter with humane probabilities, being backt with the strength of Flesh and Blood.* For who sees not that many Millions in the World forgoe many times their present ease and pleasure, undergo great and toilsom labours, encounter great difficulties, adventure upon great dangers, and all this not upon any certain expectation, but upon a probable hope of some future gain and commodity, and that not infinite and Eternal, but finite and temporal? Who sees not that many men abstain from many things they exceedingly desire, not upon any certain assurance, but a probable fear of danger that may come after? What man ever was there so madly in love with a present penny, but that he would willingly spend it upon any little hope, that by doing so he might gain an hundred thousand pound? And I would fain know *what gay probabilities* you could devise to dissuade him from this Resolution. And if you can devise none, what reason then, or sense is there, but that

The nature of Faith.

a probable hope of infinite and Eternal Happiness, provided for all those that obey *Chrift Jefus*, and much more a firm Faith, though not so certain, in some sort, as sense or science, may be able to sway our will to obedience, and encounter with all those temptations which Flesh and Blood can suggest to avert us from it? Men may therefore talk their pleasure of an absolute and most infallible certainty, but can they generally believe that obedience to Chrift were the only way to present and eternal felicity, but as firmly and undoubtedly as that there is such a City as *Conftantinople*, nay but as much as *Cæsars* Commentaries, or the History of *Salust*, I believe the lives of most men, both *Papifts* and *Proteftants* would be better than they are. Thus therefore out of your own Words I argue againft you: He that requires to true Faith, an absolute and infallible certainty, for this only Reason, *becaufe any lefs degree could not be able to overbear our will*, &c. imports, that if a less degree of Faith were able to do this, then a less degree of Faith may be true and Divine and saving Faith: But experience shews, and reason confirms, that a firm Faith, though not so certain as sense or science, may be able to encounter and overcome our will and affections: And therefore it follows from your own reason, that Faith which is not a most certain and infallible knowledge may be true and Divine and saving Faith.

6. All these Reasons I have imployed to shew that such a most certain and infallible Faith as here you talk of, is not so necessary, but that without such a high degree of it, it is possible to please God. And therefore the Doctrines delivered by you S. 25. are most presumptuous and uncharitable: *viz. That fuch a moft certain and infallible Faith is* ———*to Salvation, nec non Fide, & Moribus*, so necessary, that *after a man is come to the ufe of reafon, no man ever was or can be faved without it*. Wherein you boldly intrude into the judgment seat of God, and damn men for breaking Laws, not of Gods, but your own making. But withal, you clearly contradict your self, not only where you affirm, *That your Faith depends finally upon the Tradition of age to Age, & Father to Son*, which cannot be a fit ground,

but

but only for a Moral Assurance; nor only, where you pretend, that *not alone Hearing and Seeing,* but also *Histories, Letters, Relations of many* (which certainly are things not certain and infallible,) *are yet Foundations good enough to support your Faith*; Which Doctrine, if it were good and allowable, *Protestants* might then hope that their Histories and Letters and Relations might also pass for means sufficient of a sufficient Certainty, and that they should not be excluded from Salvation for want of such a Certainty. But indeed the pressure of the present difficulty compelled you to speak here, what I believe you will not justifie, and with a pretty tergiversation to shew D. *Potter* your means of moral certainty; whereas the Objection was that you had no means or possibility of infallible certainty, for which you are plainly at as great a loss and as far to seek as any of your Adversaries. And therefore it concerns you highly not to damn others for want of it, lest you involve your selves in the same condemnation; according to those terrible Words of S. *Paul, Inexcusabilis es,* &c. In this therefore you plainly contradict your self. And lastly most plainly, in saying as you do here, you contradict and retract your pretence of Charity to *Protestants* in the beginning of your Book: For there you make profession, that *you have no assurance but that* Protestants *dying* Protestants, *may possibly die with contrition, and be saved:* And here you are very Peremptory, that *they cannot but want a means absolutely necessary to Salvation, and wanting that cannot but be damned.*

7. The third Condition you require to Faith, is, that our assent to Divine Truths should *not only be unknown and unevident by any humane discourse,* but that *absolutely also it should be obscure in it self, and ordinarily speaking, be void even of supernatural evidence.* Which words must have a very favourable construction, or else they will not be sense. For who can make any thing of these words taken properly, that *Faith must be an unknown unevident assent, or an assent absolutely obscure?* I had always thought that known and unknown, obscure and evident had been affections, not of our Assent, but the Object of it, not of

our belief, but the thing believed. For well may we aſſent to a thing unknown, obſcure, or unevident; but that our aſſent it ſelf ſhould be called therefore unknown or obſcure, ſeems to me as great an impropriety, as if I ſhould ſay, your ſight were green or blew, becauſe you ſee ſomething that is ſo. In other places therefore I anſwer your words, but here I muſt anſwer your meaning: which I conceive to be, That it is neceſſary to Faith that the Objects of it, the points which we believe ſhould not be ſo evidently certain, as to neceſſitate our underſtandings to an Aſſent, that ſo their might be ſome merit in Faith, as you love to ſpeak (who will not receive no not from God himſelf, but a penny-worth for a penny,) but as we, ſome obedience in it, which can hardly have place where there is no poſſibility of diſobedience, as there is not where the underſtanding does all, and the will nothing. Now ſeeing the Religion of *Proteſtants*, though it be much more credible than yours, yet is not pretended to have the abſolute evidence of ſenſe or demonſtration; therefore I might let this Doctrine paſs without exception, for any prejudice that can redound to us by it. But yet I muſt not forbear to tell you, that your diſcourſe proves indeed this condition requiſite to the merit, but yet not to the eſſence of Faith: without it Faith were not an act of obedience, but yet Faith may be Faith without it; and this you muſt confeſs, unleſs you will ſay either the Apoſtles believed not the whole Goſpel which they preached, or that they were not eye-witneſſes of a great part of it: unleſs you will queſtion S. *John* for ſaying *that which we have ſeen with our Eyes, and which our hands have handled,* &c. *declare we unto you:* nay our Saviour himſelf for ſaying, Thomas *becauſe thou ſeeſt thou believeſt, Bleſſed are they which have not ſeen and yet have believed.* Yet if you will ſay that in reſpect of the things which they ſaw, the Apoſtles aſſent was not pure and proper and meer Faith, but ſomewhat more; an aſſent containing Faith but ſuperadding to it, I will not contend with you, for it will be a contention about words. But then again I muſt crave leave to tell you,

that

that the requiring this condition, is in my judgment a plain revocation of the former. For had you made the matter of Faith either naturally or supernaturally evident, it might have been a fitly attempered and duly proportioned object for an absolute certainty natural or supernatural: But requiring as you do, *that Faith should be an absolute knowledge of a thing not absolutely known, an infallible certainty of a thing which though it is in it self, yet is it not made appear to us to be infallibly certain,* to my understanding you speak impossibilities. And truly for one of your Religion to do so, is but a good *Decorum*. For the matter and object of your Faith being so full of contradictions, a contradictious Faith may very well become a contradictious Religion. Your Faith therefore, if you please to have it so, let it be a free, necessitated, certain, uncertain, evident, obscure, prudent and foolish, natural and supernatural unnatural assent. But they which are unwilling to believe nonsense themselves, or to persuade others to do so, it is but reason they should make the Faith wherewith they believe, an intelligible, compossible, consistent thing, and not define it by repugnances. Now nothing is more repugnant, than that a man should be required to give most certain credit unto that which cannot be made apppear most certainly credible : and if it appear to him to be so, then is it not obscure that it is so. For if you speak of an acquired, rational, discursive Faith, certainly these Reasons which make the object seem credible, must be the cause of it, and consequently the strength and firmity of my assent must rise and fall together with the apparent credibility of the object. If you speak of a supernatural infused Faith, then you either suppose it infused by the former means, and then that which was said before must be said again : for whatsoever effect is wrought meerly by means, must bear proportion to, and cannot exceed the vertue of the means, by which it is wrought : As nothing by water can be made more cold than water, nor by fire more hot than fire, nor by honey more sweet than honey, nor by gall more bitter than gall: Or if you will suppose it infused with-

out

out means, then that power which infuseth into the understanding assent which bears Analogy to sight in the eye, must also infuse evidence, that is, Visibility into the Object: and look what degree of assent is infused into the understanding, at least the same degree of evidence must be infused into the Object. And for you to require a strength of credit beyond the appearance of the Objects credibility, is all one as if you should require me to go Ten Miles an hour upon a Horse that will go but five: to discern a man certainly through a mist or cloud that makes him not certainly discernable; To hear a sound more clearly than it is audible; to understand a thing more fully than it is intelligible: and he that doth so, I may well expect that his next injunction will be, that I must see something that is invisible, hear something inaudible, understand something that is wholly unintelligible. For he that demands ten of me, knowing I have but five, does in effect, as if he demanded five, knowing that I have none: and by like reason, you requiring that I should see things farther than they are visible, require I should see something invisible, and in requiring that I believe something more firmly than it is made to me evidently credible, you require in effect that I believe something which appears to me incredible, and while it does so. I deny not but that I am bound to believe the truth of many Texts of Scripture the sense whereof is to me obscure and the Truth of many Articles of Faith the manner whereof is obscure, and to humane understandings incomprehensible; But then it is to be observed, that not the sense of such Texts, not the manner of these things is that which I am bound to believe, but the truth of them. But that I should believe the Truth of any thing, the truth whereof cannot be made evident with an evidence proportionable to the degree of Faith required of me, this I say for any man to be bound to, is unjust and unreasonable, because to do it is impossible.

8. Ad §. 4, 5, 6, 7, 8, 9, 10, 11, 12.] Yet though I deny that it is required of us to be certain in the highest degree;
infallibly

infallibly certain of the truth of the things which we believe, for this were to know and not believe, neither is it possible unless our evidence of it, be it natural or supernatural, were of the highest degree; yet I deny not but that we are to believe the Religion of Christ, we are and may be infallibly certain. For first, this is most certain, that we are in all things to do according to wisdom and reason rather than against it. Secondly, this is as certain, That wisdom and reason require that we should believe these things which are by many degrees more credible and probable than the contrary. Thirdly, this is as certain, that to every man who considers impartially what great things may be said for the truth of Christianity, and what poor things they are which may be said against it, either for any other Religion or for none at all, it cannot but appear by many degrees more credible, that Christian Religion, is true than the contrary. And from all these premises, this conclusion evidently follows, that it is infallibly certain, that we are firmly to believe the truth of Christian Religion.

9. Your discourse therefore touching the fourth requisite to Faith which is Prudence, I admit so far as to grant. 1. That if we were required to believe with certainty (I mean a Moral certainty,) things no way represented as infallible and certain, (I mean Morally,) an unreasonable obedience were required of us. And so likewise were it, were we required to believe as absolutely certain, that which is no way represented to us as absolutely certain. 2. That whom God obligeth to believe any thing, he will not fail to furnish their understandings with such inducements, as are sufficient (if they be not negligent or perverse) to persuade them to believe. 3. That there is an abundance of Arguments exceedingly credible, inducing men to believe the Truth of Christianity: I say so credibile, that though they cannot make us evidently see what we believe, yet they evidently convince that in true Wisdom and Prudence, the Articles of it deserve credit, and ought to be accepted as things revealed by God. 4. That without such reasons and inducements, our choice even of the true Faith, is not to be commended

mended as prudent, but to be condemned of rashness and levity.

10. But then for your making Prudence, not only a commendation of a believer, and a justification of his Faith, but also essential to it, and part of the definition of it, in that, questionless you were mistaken, and have done as if being to say what a man is, you should define him, A Reasonable creature that hath skill in Astronomy. For as all Astronomers are men, but all men are not Astronomers, and therefore Astronomy ought not to be put into the definition of men, where nothing should have place, but what agrees to all men: So though all that are truly wise (that is, wise for Eternity,) will believe aright, yet many may believe aright which are not wise. I could wish with all my Heart as *Moses* did, *that all the Lords People could Prophesie*: That all that believe the true Religion *were able* (according to S. *Peters* injunction) *to give a reason of the hope that is in them*, a reason why they hope for Eternal Happiness by this way rather than any other! neither do I think it any great difficulty that men of ordinary capacities, if they would give their mind to it, might quickly be enabled to do so. But should I affirm that all true believers can do so, I suppose it would be as much against experience and modesty, as it is against Truth and Charity, to say as you do, that *they which cannot do so, either are not at all, or to no purpose true believers.* And thus we see that the foundations you build upon, are ruinous and deceitful, and so unfit to support your Fabrick that they destroy one another. I come now to shew that your Arguments to prove *Protestants Hereticks* are all of the same quality with your former grounds: which I will do by opposing clear and satisfying Answers in order to them.

11. Ad §. 13.) To the first then, delivered by you §. 13. *That* Protestants *must be* Hereticks, *because they opposed divers Truths propounded for Divine by the Visible Church*: I Answer, It is not *Heresie* to oppose any Truth propounded by the Church, but only such a Truth as is an essential part of the Gospel of Christ. 2. The Doctrines which *Protestants* opposed, were not Truths, but
plain

plain and impious falshoods: Neither thirdly, were they propounded as Truths by the Visible Church, but only by a Part of it, and that a corrupted Part.

12. Ad §. 14. The next *Argument, in the next Particle tells us,* That *every error against any doctrin revealed by God is damnable Heresie: Now either Protestants or the* Roman *Church must err against the word of God: But the* Roman *Church we grant (perforce) doth not err damnably, neither can she, because she is the Catholick Church, which we (you say) confess cannot err damnably: Therefore Protestants must err against Gods word, and consequently are guilty of formal Heresie.* Whereunto I answer plainly, that there be in this argument almost as many falshoods as assertions. For neither is every error against any Doctrin revealed by God a damnable Heresie, unless it be revealed publickly, and plainly with a command that all should believe it. 2. D. *Potter* no where grants, that the Errors of the *Roman* Church are *not in themselves damnable*, though he hopes by accident they may not actually damn some men amongst you: and this you your self confess in divers places of your book, where you tell us, that he *allows no hope of Salvation to those amongst you, whom ignorance cannot excuse.* 3. You beg the Question twice in taking for granted, First that *the* Roman *Church is the truly Catholick Church*; which without much favour can hardly pass for a part of it: And again, that the *Catholick Church cannot fall into any error of it self damnable:* for it may do so, and still be the Catholick Church, if it retain those Truths which may be an antidote against the malignity of this error, to those that held it out of a simple un-affected ignorance. Lastly, though the thing be true, yet I might well require some proof of it from you, that either *Protestants* or the *Roman* Church must err against Gods word. For if their contradiction be your only reason, then also you or the *Dominicans* must be *Hereticks,* because you contradict one another as much as *Protestants* and *Papists.*

13. Ad §. 15. The third Argument pretends that *you have shewed already, that the Visible Church is Judge of Controversies, and therefore Infallible*; *from whence you suppose that*

it follows, that to oppose her, is to oppose God. To which I answer, that you have said onely, and not shewed that *the Visible Church is Judge of Controversies.* And indeed how can she be judge of them if she cannot decide them? And how can she decide them, if it be a question whether she be judge of them? That which is questioned it self, cannot with any sense be pretended to be fit to decide other questions; and much less this question, whether it have Authority to judge and decide all questions? 2. If she were judge, it would not follow that she were infallible, for we have many Judges in our Courts of Judicature, yet none infallible. Nay you cannot with any modesty deny, that every man in the world ought to judge for himself, what Religion is truest, and yet you will not say that every man is infallible. 3. If the Church were supposed Infallible, yet it would not follow at all, much less manifestly, that to oppose her declaration is to oppose God: unless you suppose also that as she is infallible, so by her opposers, she is known or believed to be so. Lastly, If all this were true (as it is all most false) yet were it to little purpose, seeing you have omitted to prove that the Visible Church is the *Roman*.

14. Ad §. 16. Instead of a fourth Argument this is presented to us, *That if Luther were an Heretick, then they that agreed with him must be so.* And that *Luther* was a formal Heretick, you endeavor to prove by this most formal Syllogism; *To say the Visible Church is not Universal, is properly an Heresie: but* Luthers *Reformation was not Universal, Therefore it cannot be excused from formal Heresie.* Whereunto I Answer, first to the first part, that it is no way impossible that *Luther*, had he been the inventer and first broacher of a false Doctrin, (as he was not) might have been a formal Heretick, and yet that those who follow him may be only so materially and improperly, and indeed no Hereticks. Your own men out of S. *Augustin* distinguish between *Hæretici* & *Hæreticorum sequaces*: And you your self though you pronounce *the leaders among the* Arrians *formal Hereticks*, yet confess that *Salvian* was at least doubtful whether these *Arrians*, who in simplicity followed

ed their Teachers, might not be excused by ignorance. And about this suspension of his you also seem suspended, for you neither approve nor condemn it. Secondly, to the second part I say, that had you not presumed upon our ignorance in Logick as well as Metaphysicks and School Divinity, you would never have obtruded upon us this rope of sand for a formal Syllogism. It is even Cousin-German to this, To deny the Resurrection is properly an Heresie, But *Luthers* Reformation was not Universal, Therefore it cannot be excused from formal Heresie! Or to this, To say the Visible Church is not Universal is properly an Heresie: But the preaching of the Gospel at the beginning was not Universal; therefore it cannot be excused from formal Heresie. For as he whose Reformation is but particular, may yet not deny the Resurrection, so may he also not deny the Churches Universality. And as the Apostles who preached the Gospel in the beginning, did believe the Church Universal, though their preaching at the beginning was not so: So *Luther* also might and did believe the Church Universal, though his Reformation were but particular. I say he did believe it Universal, even in your own sense, that is, Universal *de jure*, though not *de facto*. And as for universality in fact, he believed the Church much more Universal than his Reformation: For he did conceive (as appears by your own Allegations out of him) that only the Part reformed was the true Church, but also that they were Part of it who needed reformation. Neither did he ever pretend to make a new Church but to reform the old one. Thirdly and lastly, to the first proposition of this unsyllogistical syllogism, I answer, That to say the true Church is not always *de facto* universal, is so far from being an Heresie, that it is a certain Truth known to all those that know the world, and what Religions possess far the greater part of it. *Donatus* therefore was not to blame, for saying, that the Church might possibly be confined to *Africk*; but for saying without ground, that then it was so. And S. *Austin*, as he was in the right, in thinking that the Church was then extended farther than *Africk*; so was he in the wrong if he thought that of neceffity it always muft be fo; but moft palpably miftaken in conceiving that it was then fpread over the whole earth, and known to all nations, which if paffion did not trouble you, and make you forget how lately almoft half the world was difcovered, and in what eftate it was then found, you would very eafily fee and confefs.

16. *The* Donatifts *might do ill in calling the Chair of* Rome *the Chair of Peftilence, and the* Roman *Church an Harlot,* and yet the ftate of the Church being altered, *Proteftants* might do well to do fo, and therefore though, S. Auftin *might perhaps have reafon to perfecute the* Donatifts *for detracting from the Church,* and calling her Harlot, when fhe was not fo; yet you may have none to threaten D. *Potter* that you would perfecute him (as the Application of this place intimates you would,) if it were in your power: plainly fhewing that you are a curft Cow though your horns be fhort, feeing the *Roman* Church is not now what it was in S. *Auftins* time. And hereof the conclufion of your own book affords us a very pregnant teftimony: where you tell us out of Saint *Auftin,* that one grand impediment, which among many kept the feduced followers of the faction of *Donatus* from the Churches Communion, was a vifible calumny raifed againft the Catholicks, that *they did fet fome ftrange thing upon their Altar. To how many* (faith Saint *Auftin*) *did the reports of ill Tongues fhut up the way to enter, who faid, that we put, I know not what upon the Altar?* Out of deteftation of the calumny, and juft indignation againft it, he would not fo much as name the impiety wherewith they were charged, and therefore by a Rhetorical figure calls it, *I know not what.* But compare with him *Optatus,* writing of the fame matter, and you fhall plainly perceive that this *(I know not what)* pretended to be fet upon the Altar, was indeed a picture, which the *Donatifts* (knowing how deteftable a thing it was to all Chriftians at that time, to fet up any pictures in a Church to worfhip them, as your new fafhion is) bruited abroad to be done in the Churches of the Catholick Church. But what anfwer do S. *Auftin* and *Optatus* make

make to this accusation? Do they confess and maintain it? Do they say, as you would now, It is true we do set Pictures upon our Altar, and that not only for ornament or memory, but for worship also; but we do well to do so, and this ought not to trouble you, or affright you from our Communion? What other answer your Church could now make to such an objection, is very hard to imagine: And therefore were your Doctrin the same with the Doctrin of the Fathers in this point, they must have answered so likewise. But they to the contrary not only deny the crime, but abhor and detest it. To little purpose therefore do you hunt after these poor shadows of resemblances between us and the *Donatists*: unless you could shew an exact resemblance between the present Church of *Rome* and the Ancient: which seeing by this, and many other particulars it is demonstrated to be impossible; that Church which was then a Virgin may be now a Harlot, and that which was detraction in the *Donatists*, may be in *Protestants* a just accusation.

18. But the main point you say is, that *since Luthers Reformed Church was not in being for divers Centuries before Luther, and yet was in the Apostles time, they must of necessity affirm heretically with the* Donatists, *that the true unspotted Church of Christ perished, and that she which remained on earth, was (O Blasphemy!) an Harlot.* By which words it seems you are resolute perpetually to confound *True* and *Unspotted*; and to put no difference between a corrupted Church and none at all. But what is this, but to make no difference between a diseased and a dead man? Nay what is it but to contradict your selves, who cannot deny but that sins are as great stains and spots and deformities in the sight of God, as errors; and confess your Church to be a Congregation of men, whereof every particular, not one excepted, (and consequently the generality which is nothing but a collection of them) is polluted and defiled with sin?

19. You ask, How *can the Church more truly be said to perish, than when she is permitted to maintain a damnable Heresie?* I Answer, she may be more truly said to perish, when she

she is not only permitted to do so, but *de facto* doth maintain a damnable Heresie. Again, she may be more truly said to perish, when she falls into an Heresie, which is not only damnable in it self, and *ex natura rei*, as you speak, but such an Heresie, the belief of whose contrary Truth is necessary, not only *necessitate præcepti* but *medii*, and therefore the Heresie so absolutely and indispensably destructive of salvation, that no ignorance can excuse it, nor any general repentance, without a dereliction of it, can beg a pardon for it. Such an heresie if the Church should fall into, it might be more truly said to perish, than if it fell only into some heresie of its own nature damnable. For in that state all the members of it, without exception, all without mercy must needs perish for ever: In this, although those that might see the truth and would not, cannot upon any good ground hope for salvation, yet without question, it might send many souls to heaven, who would gladly have embraced the Truth, but that they wanted means to discover it. Thirdly and lastly, she may yet more truly be said to perish when she Apostates from Christ absolutely, or rejects even those Truths out of which her Heresies may be reformed; as if she should directly deny *Jesus to be the Christ*, or the Scripture to be the Word of God. Towards which state of Perdition it may well be feared that the Church of *Rome* doth somewhat incline, by her superinducing upon the rest of her Errors the Doctrin of her own Infallibility, whereby her errors are made incurable; and by her pretending that the Scripture is to be interpreted according to her doctrin, and not her doctrin to be judged of by Scripture, whereby she makes the Scripture uneffectuall for her Reformation.

20. Ad §. 18. I was very glad when I heard you say *The Holy Scripture and ancient Fathers do assign Separation from the Visible Church as a mark of Heresie*: for I was in good hope, that no Christian would so belie the Scripture, as to say so of it, unless he could have produced some one Text at least, wherein this was plainly affirmed, or from whence it might be undoubtedly and undeniably collected. For assure your self, good Sir, it is a very heinous crime

to say, *thus saith the Lord, when the Lord doth not say so.* I expected therefore some Scripture should have been alledged, wherein it should have been said, *whosoever separates from the* Roman *Church is an Heretick:* or *the* Roman *Church is infallible,* or *the guide of Faith:* or at least, *There shall be always some Visible Church infallible in matters of Faith.* Some such direction as this I hoped for: And I pray consider whether I had not reason! The Evangelists and Apostles who wrote the New Testament, we all suppose were good men, and very desirous to direct us the surest and plainest way to Heaven; we suppose them likewise very sufficiently instructed by the Spirit of God in all the necessary points of the Christian Faith, and therefore certainly not ignorant of this *Unum Necessarium,* this most necessary point of all others, without which as you pretend and teach, all faith is no Faith, that is, that *the Church of* Rome *was designed by God the guide of Faith.* We suppose them lastly wise men, especially being assisted by the spirit of wisdom, and such as knew that a doubtful and questionable guide was for mens direction as good as none at all. And after all these suppositions, which I presume no good Christian will call into question, is it possible that any Christian heart can believe, that not one amongst them all should *ad rei memoriam* write this necessary doctrin plainly so much as once? Certainly in all reason they had provided much better for the good of Christians if they had wrote this, though they had writ nothing else. Methinks the Evangelists undertaking to write the Gospel of Christ, could not possibly have omitted, any one of them, this most necessary point of faith, had they known it necessary, (S. *Luke* especially, who plainly professeth that *his intent was to write all things necessary.*) Methinks S. *Paul* writing to the *Romans* could not but have congratulated this their Priviledge to them! Methinks instead of saying, *Your Faith is spoken of all the world over* (which you have no reason to be very proud of, for he says the very same thing to the *Thessalonians,*) he could not have failed to have told them once at least in plain terms, that *their Faith was the Rule for all the World for ever.* But then sure he would have forborn to put them

in

in fear of an impossibility, as he doth in his eleventh Chap. that they also, nay the whole Church of the *Gentiles if they did not look to their standing, might fall away to infidelity* as the *Jews* had done. Methinks in all his other Epistles, at least in some, at least in one of them, he could not have failed to have given the world this direction, had he known it to be a true one, that *all men were to be guided by the Church of* Rome, *and none to separate from it under pain of damnation.* Methinks writing so often of Hereticks and Antichrist, he should have given the world this (as you pretend) only sure preservative from them. How was it possible that S. *Peter* writing two Catholick Epistles, mentioning his own departure, writing to preserve Christians in the Faith, should in neither of them commend them to the guidance of his pretended Successors, the Bishops of *Rome?* How was it possible that S. *James,* and S. *Jude* in their Catholick Epistles should not give this Catholick direction? Methinks S. *John* instead of saying, *he that believeth that Jesus is the Christ, is born of God,* (The force of which direction, your glosses do quite enervate, and make unavailable to discern who are the sons of God,) should have said, *He that adheres to the doctrin of the* Roman *Church, and lives according to it, he is a good Christian, and by this Mark ye shall know him!* What man not quite out of his wits, if he consider as he should, the pretended necessity of this doctrin, that without the belief hereof no man ordinarily can be saved, can possibly force himself to conceive that all these good and holy men, so desirous of mens salvation, and so well assured of it (as it is pretended,) should be so deeply and affectedly silent in it, and not one say it plainly so much as once, but leave it to be collected from uncertain principles, by many more uncertain consequences? Certainly he that can judge so uncharitably of them, it is no marvel if he censure other inferior servants of Christ as Atheists, and Hypocrites, and what he pleases. Plain places therefore I did and had reason to look for, when I heard you say, *the holy Scripture assigns Separation from the visible Church as a mark of Heresie.* But instead hereof what have

have you brought us, but meer impertinences? S. *John* saith of some who pretended to be Christians and were not so, and therefore when it was for their advantage forsook their Profession, *They went out from us, but they were not of us; for if they had been of us, they would no doubt have continued with us.* Of some, who before the decree of the Council to the contrary, were perswaded and accordingly taught, that the convert Gentiles were to keep the Law of *Moses*, it is said in the *Acts, Some who went out from us.* And again S. *Paul* in the same Book forewarns the *Ephesians* that *out of them should arise men speaking perverse things.* And from these places which it seems are the plainest you have, you collect *that separation from the Visible Church is assigned by Scripture as a Mark of* Heresie. Which is certainly a strange and unheard of strain of Logick. Unless you will say that every Text wherein it is said, that some Body goes out from some Body, affords an Argument for this purpose! For the first place there is no certainty that it speaks of *Hereticks*, but, *no Christians*, of *Antichrists, of such as denied Jesus to be the Christ*: See the place and you shall confess as much. The second place, it is certain, you must not say it speaks of *Hereticks*, for it speaks only of some who believed and taught an Error, while it was yet a question and not evident, and therefore according to your Doctrine, no formal *Heresie*. The third says indeed, that of the Professors of Christianity, some shall arise that shall teach *Heresie*: But not one of them all that says or intimates, that whosoever separates from the Visible Church, in what state soever, is certainly an *Heretick. Hereticks* I confess do always do so; But they that do so are not always *Hereticks,* for perhaps the State of the Church may make it necessary for them to do so; as Rebels always disobey the command of their King, yet they which disobey a Kings Command (which perhaps may be unjust) are not presently Rebels.

22. In the 19. §. We have the Authority of eight Fathers urged to prove *that the separation from the Church of Rome as it is the Sea of S.* Peter (I conceive you mean as it is the Particular Church) *is the mark of* Heresie. Which kind of Argument I might well refuse to answer,

Y y unless

unless you would first promise me, that whensoever I should produce as plain sentences, of as great a number of Fathers, as Ancient, for any Doctrine whatsoever, that you will subscribe to it, though it fall out to be contrary to the Doctrine of the *Roman* Church. For I conceive nothing in the World more unequal or unreasonable, than that you should press us with such Authorities as these, and think your selves at liberty from them; and that you should account them Fathers when they are for you, and Children when they are against you. Yet I would not you should interpret this as if I had not great assurance, that it is not possible for you ever to gain this cause at the Tribunal of the Fathers, nay not of the Fathers whose sentences are here alledged. Let us consider them in order, and I doubt not to make it appear that far the greater part of them, nay all of them that are any way considerable fall short of your purpose.

23. Obj. S. *Hierome* (you say Ep. 57. ad *Damasum*) professes, *I am in the Communion of the Chair of* Peter, *&c.* But then I pray consider he saith it to *Pope Damasus*: and this will much weaken the Authority, with them who know how great over-truths men usually write to one another in letters. Consider again, that he says only, that *he was then in Communion with the Chair of* Peter, Not that he always would, or of necessity must be so: for his resolution to the contrary is too evident out of that which he saith elswhere which shall be produced hereafter. He says that the *Church at that present was built upon that Rock*; but not that only, Nor that alwaies. Nay his judgment as shall appear is express to the contrary. And so likewise the rest of his expressions (if we mean to reconcile *Hierome* with *Hierome*) must be conceived as intended by him, of that Bishop and Sea of *Rome*, at that present time, and in the present State, and in respect of that Doctrine which he there intreats of. For otherwise had he conceived it necessary for him and all men to conform their judgments in matters of Faith, to the judgment of the Bishop and Church of *Rome*, how came it to pass that he chose rather to believe the Epistle to the

Hebrews

Hebrews Canonical, upon the Authority of the Eastern Church, than to reject it from the Canon upon the Authority of the *Roman*? How comes it to pass that he dissented from the Authority of that Church, touching the Canon of the *Old Testament*? For if you say, that the Church, then consented with S. *Hierome*, I fear you will lose your Fort by maintaining your ¦Out-works, and by avoiding this, run into a greater danger of being forced to confess the present *Roman* Church opposite herein to the Ancient. How was it possible, that he should ever believe that *Liberius* Bishop of *Rome* either was or could have been wrought over by *the follicitation of Fortunatianus Bishop of Aquileia, and brought after two Years Banishment to subscribe* Heresie? Which Act of *Liberius* though some fondly question, being so vain as to expect we should rather believe them that lived but yesterday, thirteen hundred Years almost after the thing is said to be done, and speaking for themselves in their own Cause, rather than the dis-interessed time-fellows or immediate Successors of *Liberius* himself: yet I hope they will not proceed to such a degree of immodesty, as once to question whether S. *Hierome* thought so. And if this cannot be denied, I demand then if he had lived in *Liberius* his time, could he or would he have written so to *Liberius* as he does to *Damasus*? would he have said to him, *I am in the Communion of the Chair of* Peter, *I know that the Church is built upon this Rock, Whosoever gathereth not with thee scattereth.* Would he then have said, the *Roman* Faith and the *Catholick* were the same: or, that the *Roman* Faith received no delusions, no not from an Angel? I suppose he could not have said so with any coherence to his own belief; and therefore conceive it undeniable that what he said then to *Damasus*, he said it (though perhaps he strained too high) only of *Damasus*, and never conceived that his words would have been extended to all his Predecessors and all his Successors.

Hierom. de scrip. Eccle. Fortunatianus.

24. Obj. S. *Ambrose* (de obitu Satyri fratris) *saith* of his Brother *Satyrus*, that *inquiring for a Church wherein to give thanks for his delivery from Shipwreck, he called to him the*

Bishop,

Bishop, and he asked him whether he agreed with the *Catholick Bishops,* that is, *with the* Roman *Church? And when he understood that he was a Schismatick,* that is, *Separated from the* Roman *Church, he abstained from Communicating with him.*

Answ. No more can be certainly concluded from it, but that the *Catholick* Bishops and the *Roman* Church were then at Unity; so that whosoever agreed with the latter could not then but agree with the former. But that this Rule was perpetual, and that no man could ever agree with the *Catholick* Bishops, but he must agree with the *Roman* Church, this he says not, nor gives you any ground to conclude from him. *Athanasius* when he was excommunicated by *Liberius,* agreed very ill with the *Roman* Church, and yet you will not gainsay, but he agreed well enough with the *Catholick* Bishops.

24. Obj. S. *Cyprian saith* (*Epist.* 55. *ad Cornel.*) They are bold to Sail to the *Chair of S.* Peter, *and to the principal Church, from whence Priestly Unity hath sprung. Neither do they consider that they are* Romans, *whose Faith was commended by the Preaching of the Apostle, to whom falshood cannot have access.*

Answ. For S. *Cyprian* all the World knows that he [b] resolutely opposed a Decree of the *Roman* Bishop, and all that adhered to him in the point of Re-baptizing, which that Church at that time delivered as a necessary tradition. So necessary, that by the Bishop of *Rome Firmilianus* and other Bishops of *Cappadocia, Cilicia* and *Galatia,* and generally all who persisted in the contrary opinion, [c] were therefore deprived of the Churches Communion, (which excommunication could not but involve S. *Cyprian,* who defended the same opinion as resolutely as *Firmilianus,* though Cardinal *Perren* magisterially and without all colour of proof affirm the contrary,) and *Cyprian* in particular so far cast off, as for it to be pronounced by *Stephen a false Christ.* Again so necessary that the Bishops which were sent by *Cyprian* from *Africk* to *Rome,* were not admitted to the Communion of ordinary conference: But all men who were subject to the Bishop of *Romes* Authority, were commanded by him not only to deny them the

[b] It is confessed by *Baronius Anno.* 238. N. 41. By *Bellarm. l.* 4. *de R. Pont. c.*7. §. *Tertia ratio.*

[c] Confessed by *Baronius An,* 258. N. 14. & 15. By *Card. Perron. Repl. l.* 1. *c.* 25. *Ibid.*

the Churches peace and Communion, but even lodging and entertainment: manifestly declaring, that they reckoned them among those whom S. *John* forbids *to receive to house, or to say God speed to them.* All these terrors notwithstanding S. *Cyprian* holds still his former opinion, and though out of respect to the Churches peace ᵈ *he judged no man, nor cut off any man from the right of Communion, for thinking otherwise than he held,* yet he conceived *Stephen* and his adherents, ᵉ to hold a pernitious Error. And S. *Austin*, (though disputing with the *Donatists* he useth some Tergiversation in the point,) yet confesseth elsewhere, that *it is not found that* Cyprian *did ever change his opinion.* And so far was he from conceiving any necessity of doing so, in submitting to the judgment of the Bishop and Church of *Rome*, that he plainly professeth that no other Bishop, but our *Lord Jesus only, had power to Judge* (with Authority) *of his Judgment,* and as plainly intimates that *Stephen,* for usurping such a power, and making himself *a Judge over Bishops, was little better than a Tyrant:* and as heavily almost he censures him, and peremptorily opposes him as obstinate in Error, in that very place where he delivers that famous saying, *How can he have God for his Father, who hath not the Church for his Mother?* little doubting it seems but a man might have the Church for his Mother, who stood in opposition to the Church of *Rome*, and far from thinking what you fondly obtrude upon him, that to be United to the *Roman* Church, and to the Church was all one, and that separation from S. *Peters* Chair was a mark, I mean a certain mark, either of Schism or *Heresie.*

ᵈ *Vide Con. Carth. apud Sur. To.* 1:

ᵉ *Bell. l.* 2. *de Conc. c.* 5.

Aug. ep. 48. *& lib.* 1. *de Bapt. c.* 18.

26. But you have given a false or at least a strained Translation of S. *Cyprians* forecited Words; for *Cyprian* faith not *to whom falshood cannot have access,* as if he had exempted the *Roman* Church from a possibility of Error, but to whom *perfidiousness cannot have access,* meaning those perfidious Schismaticks, whom he there complains of; and of these by a Rhetorical insinuation, he says that *with such good Christians as the* Romans *were, it was not possible they should find favourable entertainment.* As for his joyning the *Principal Church* and the *Chair of* Peter, how that will
serve

serve to prove separation from the *Roman* Church to be a mark of *Heresie*, it is hard to understand. Though we do not altogether deny, but that the Church of *Rome* might be called the *Chair of S.* Peter, in regard he is said to have Preached the Gospel there; and the *principal Church*, because the City was the principal and imperial City, which prerogative of the City, if we believe the Fathers of the Council of *Chalcedon*, was the ground and occasion, why the Fathers of former times (I pray observe) conferred upon this Church this prerogative above other Churches.

27. Obj. *But in another place* (Epist. 52.) S. Cyprian *makes Communicating with* Cornelius *(the Bishop of Rome) and with the* Catholick *Church to be the same.*

Answ. This does not prove that to Communicate with the Church and *Pope* of *Rome*, and to Communicate with the *Catholick* Church, is *always* (for that you assume) one and the same thing. S. *Cyprian* speaks not of the Church of *Rome* at all, but of the Bishop only, who when he doth Communicate with the *Catholick* Church, as *Cornelius* at that time did, then whosoever Communicates with him, cannot but Communicate with the *Catholick* Church: and then by accident one may truely say, such a one Communicates with you, that is, with the *Catholick* Church, and that to Communicate with him is to Communicate with the *Catholick* Church. As if *Titius* and *Sempronius* be together, he that is in company with *Titius*, cannot but be at that time in company with *Sempronius*. As if a General be marching to some place with an Army, he that then is with the General must at that time be with the Army: And a man may say without absurdity, such a time I was with the General, that is, with the Army, and that to be with the General is to be with the Army. Or as if a mans hand be joyned to his Body, the finger which is joyned to the hand is joyned to the Body, and a man may say truly of it, this finger is joyned to the hand, that is, to the Body, and to be joyned to the hand is to be joyned to the Body; because all these things are by accident true. And yet I hope you would not deny,

but

The nature of Faith. 351

but the finger might poſſibly be joyned to the hand, and yet not to the Body, the hand being cut off from the Body; and a man might another time, be with his General and not with his Army, he being abſent from the Army. And therefore by like Reaſon your collection is Sophiſtical, being in effect but this, to communicate with ſuch a Biſhop of *Rome,* who did Communicate with the *Catholick* Church, was to Communicate with the *Catholick* Church, therefore abſolutely and always it muſt be true, that to Communicate with him, is by conſequent to Communicate with the *Catholick* Church, and to be divided from the Communion, is to be an *Heretick.*

28. Obj. S. Irenæus *faith,* (lib. 3. cont. hær : c. 3.) *Becauſe it were long to number the ſucceſſions of all Churches, we declaring the Tradition of the moſt great moſt Ancient and known Church, founded by the two glorious Apoſtles* Peter *and* Paul, *which Tradition it hath from the Apoſtles, coming to us by ſucceſſion of Biſhops, we confound all thoſe who any way either by vain Glory, Blindneſs, or ill Opinion do gather otherwiſe than they ought. For to this Church for a more powerful Principality, it is neceſſary that all Churches reſort, that is, all faithful People* (undique) *of what place ſoever : In which* (Roman Church) *the Tradition from the Apoſtles hath always been conſerved from thoſe who are* (undique) *every where.*

Anſw. Though at the firſt, hearing the Glorious Attributes here given (and that juſtly) to the Church of *Rome, the confounding* Hereticks *with her Tradition, and ſaying it is neceſſary for all Churches to reſort to her,* may ſound like Arguments for you : yet he that is attentive I hope will eaſily diſcover, that it might be good and rational in *Irenæus* having to do with Hereticks, who, ſomewhat like thoſe who would be the only *Catholicks,* declining a tryal by Scripture as not containing the Truth of Chriſt perfectly, and not fit to decide Controverſies without recourſe to Tradition: I ſay he will eaſily perceive that it might be rational in *Irenæus* to urge them with any Tradition of more credit than their own, eſpecially a Tradition conſonant to Scripture, and even contained in it ; and yet that it may be irrational in you to urge us, who do not decline Scripture but appeal to it as a perfect rule of Faith, with a Tradition which we pretend is many ways repugnant to Scripture, and repugnant to a Tradition far more general than it self, which gives testimony to Scripture, and lastly repugnant to it self as giving attestation both to Scripture and to Doctrines plainly contrary to Scripture. Secondly, that the Authority of the *Roman* Church was then a far greater Argument of the Truth of her Tradition when it was United with all other Apostolick Churches, than now when it is divided from them, according to that of *Tertullian*, *Had the Churches Erred they would have varied, but that which is the same in all, cannot be Error but Tradition*; and therefore though *Irenæus* his Argument may be very probable, yet yours may be worth nothing. Thirdly, that fourteen hundred years may have made a great deal of alteration in the *Roman* Church: as Rivers, though near the Fountain they may retain their native and unmixt sincerity, yet in long Progress cannot but take in much mixture that came not from the Fountain. And therefore the *Roman* Tradition though then pure, may now be corrupt and impure: and so this Argument (being one of those things which are the worse for wearing) might in *Irenæus* his time be strong and vigorous, and after declining and decaying may long since have fallen to nothing. Especially considering that *Irenæus* plays the Historian only and not the Prophet, and says only, that the *Apostolick Tradition had been always there as in other Apostolick Churches conserved or observed*, choose you whether, but that *it should be always so* he says not, neither had he any warrant. He knew well enough that there was foretold a *great falling away of* the Churches of Christ to Antichrist: that the *Roman* Church in particular was forewarned that she also, *nay the whole Church of the Gentiles, might fall if they look not to their standing*: and therefore to secure her that she should stand for ever, he had no reason, nor Authority. Fourthly, that it appears manifestly out of this Book of *Irenæus* quoted by you, that the Doctrine of the *Chiliasts* was in his Judgment Apostolick Tradition, as also

it

it was esteemed (for ought appears to the contrary) by all the Doctors, and Saints, and Martyrs of or about his time, for all that speak of it, or whose judgments in the point are any way recorded, are for it: and *Justin Martyr* professeth that *all good and Orthodox Christians of his time believed it*, and those that did not, he reckons amongst Hereticks. Now I demand, was this Tradition one of those that was conserved, and observed in the Church of *Rome*, or was it not? If not, had *Irænens* known so much, he must have retracted this commendation of that Church. If it was, then the Tradition of the present Church of *Rome* contradicts the Ancient, and accounts it Heretical, and then sure it can be no certain note of Heresie to depart from them, who have departed from themselves, and prove themselves subject unto error by holding contradictions. Fifthly and lastly, that out of the Story of the Church it is as manifest as the light at noon, that though *Irænens* did esteem the *Roman* Tradition, a great Argument of the Doctrin which he there delivers and defends against the Hereticks of his time, viz. *that there was one God*, yet he was very far from thinking that Church was, and ever should be a safe keeper, and an infallible witness of Tradition in general: Inasmuch as in his own life, his action proclaimed the contrary. For when *Victor* Bishop of *Rome* obtruded the *Roman* Tradition touching the time of *Easter* upon the *Asian* Bishops under the pain of Excommunication, *and damnation, Irænens*, and all the other Western Bishops, though agreeing with him in his observation yet sharply reprehended him for Excommunicating the *Asian* Bishops for their disagreeing, plainly shewing, that they esteemed that not a necessary doctrin and a sufficient ground of excommunication, which the Bishop of *Rome* and his adherents did so account of: For otherwise how could they have reprehended him for excommunicating them, had they conceived the cause of his excommunication just and sufficient? And besides evidently declaring that they esteemed not separation from the *Roman* Church a certain mark of Heresie, seeing they esteemed not them Hereticks though separated and cut off from the *Roman* Church.

31. Obj. S. *Austin* saith (in Psalm *cont. partem Donati*) *It grieves us to see you so to lie cut off. Number the Priests even from the Sea of* Peter; *and consider in that order of Fathers who succeeded; to whom she is the Rock which the proud gates of Hell do not overcome*: Where he seems to say, that the Succession in the Sea of *Peter*, was the Rock which our Saviour means when he said, *upon this Rock will I build my Church*.

Ans. I answer, First, We have no reason to be confident of the truth hereof, because S. *Austin* himself was not, but retracts it as uncertain, and *leaves to the Reader whether he will think that, or another more probable.* Retr. *l.* 1. *c.* 26. Secondly, what he says of the Succession in the *Roman* Church in this place, he says it elsewhere, of all the Successions in all other Apostolick Churches. Thirdly, that as in this place he urgeth the *Donatists* with separation from the *Roman* Church, as an argument of their Error: So elsewhere he presseth them with their Separation from other Apostolick Churches, nay more from these than from that, because in *Rome* the *Donatists* had a Bishop, though not a perpetual Succession of them, but in other Apostolick Churches they wanted both. *These scattered men* (saith he of the *Donatists* Epist. 165.) *read in the holy Books the Churches to which the Apostles wrote, and have no Bishop in them: But what is more perverse and mad, than to the Lectors reading these Epistles to say, Peace with you, and to separate from the peace of these Churches, to which these Epistles were written?* So *Optatus* having done you (as it might seem) great service, in upbraiding the *Donatists* as Schismaticks, because they had not Communion with the Church of *Rome*, overthrows and undoes it all again, and as it were with a spunge wipes out all that he had said for you, by adding after, that they were Schismaticks, because *they had not the fellowship of Communion with the seven Churches of* Asia, *to which S.* John *writes*: whereof he pronounces confidently, (though I know not upon what ground) *Extra septem Ecclesias quicquid foris est, alienum est*. Now I pray tell me, do you esteem the Authority of these Fathers a sufficient assurance, that separation from these other

A-

Apostolick Churches, was a certain mark of Heresie, or not? If so, then your Church hath been for many Ages heretical. If not, how is their authority, a greater argument for the *Roman*, than for the other Churches? If you say, they conceived separation from these Churches a note of Schism, only when they were united to the *Roman*: so also they might conceive of the *Roman*, only when it was united to them. If you say, they urged this only as a probable, and not as a certain Argument, so also they might do that. In a word, whatsoever answer you can devise to shew, that these Fathers made not separation from these other Churches a mark of Heresie, apply that to your own Argument, and it will be satisfied.

33. You see S. *Austins* words make very little, or indeed nothing for you. But now his Action, (which according to Cardinal *Perrons* rule, is much more to be regarded than his words, as not being so obnoxious to misinterpretation) [a] I mean his famous opposition of three Bishops of *Rome* in Succession, touching the great question of Appeals, wherein he and the rest of the *African* Bishops proceeded so far in the first or second *Milevitan* Council, as to [b] decree any African *Excommunicate, that should appeal to any man out of* Africk, and therein continued resolute unto death: I say this famous Action of his, makes clearly and evidently and infinitely against you. For had *Boniface*, and the rest of the *African* Bishops, a great part whereof were Saints and Martyrs, believed as an Article of Faith, that Union and Conformity with the Doctrin of the *Roman* Church, in all things which she held necessary, was a certain note of a good Catholick, and by Gods command necessary to Salvation, how was it possible they should have opposed it in this? Unless you will say they

[a] You do ill to translate it, *the Principality of the Sea Apostolick*, as if there were but one: whereas S. *Austin* presently after speaks of Apostolical Churches, in the plural number, and makes the Bishops of them, joynt Commissioners for the judging of Ecclesiastical causes. [b] The words of the Decree (which also *Bellarmine* l.1.de *Matrim.*c. 17. assures us to have been formed by S. *Austin*) are these. *Si qui (Africani,) ab Episcopis provocandum putaverint, non nisi ad Africana provocent Concilia, vel ad Primates provinciarum suarum. Ad transmarina antem, qui putaverit appellandum, à nullo intra Africam in Communionem suscipiatur.* This Decree is by *Gratian* most impudently corrupted. For whereas the Fathers of that Council intended it particularly against the *Church of Rome*, he tells us they forbad Appeals to all, *excepting only the Church of Rome*.

were all so foolish as to believe at once direct contradictions, *viz.* that conformity to the *Roman* Church was necessary in all points, and not necessary in this: or else so horribly impious, as believing this doctrin of the *Roman* Church true, and h● power to receive Appeals derived from divine Authority, notwithstanding to oppose and condemn it, and to Anathematize all those *Africans*, of what condition soever, that should appeal unto it. I say *of what condition soever*: For it is evident, that they concluded in their determination, Bishops as well as the inferior Clergy and Laity: And Cardinal *Perrons* pretence of the contrary, is a shameless falshood, repugnant to the plain * words of the Remonstrance of the *African* Bishops to *Celestine* Bishop of *Rome*.

* The words are these, *Præfato debito salutationis officio, impendio deprecamur; ut deinceps ad aures vestras hinc venientes, non facilius admittatis; nec à nobis excommunicatos u'tra in Communionem velitis recipere, quia hoc etiam Niceno Concilio definitum facile advertet venerabilitas tua. Nam si de inferioribus Clericis vel Laicis videtur id præcaveri, quanto magis hoc de Episcopis voluit observari.*

34. Obj. *Tertullian* saith (Præscrip. cap. 36.) *If thou be near* Italy, *thou hast* Rome, *whose Authority is near at hand to us: a happy Church, into which the Apostles have poured all Doctrin, together with their blood.*

Ans. Your allegation of *Tertullian* is a manifest conviction of your want of sincerity: For you produce with great ostentation what he says of the Church of *Rome*, but you and your fellows always conceal and dissemble, that immediately before these words he attributes as much for point of direction to any other Apostolick Church, and that as he sends them to *Rome* who lived near *Italy*, so those near *Achaia* he sends to *Corinth*, those about *Macedonia* to *Philippi*, and *Thessalonica*, those of *Asia* to *Ephesus*. His words are, *Go to now thou that wilt better imploy thy curiosity in the business of thy salvation, run over the Apostolical Churches, wherein the Chairs of the Apostles are yet sate upon in their places, wherein their Authentick Epistles are recited, sounding out the voyce, and representing the face of every one! Is Achaia near thee? there thou hast* Corinth*: If thou art not far from* Macedonia, *thou hast* Philippi, *thou*

thou haft Theſſalonica: *If thou canſt go into* Aſia, *there thou haft* Epheſus: *If thou be adjacent to* Italy, *thou haft* Rome, *whoſe Authority is near at hand to us* (in *Africk*;) *A happy Church, into which the Apoſtles poured forth all their Doctrine together with their Blood,* &c. Now I pray Sirtell me, if you can for bluſhing, why this place might not have been urged by a *Corinthian,* or *Philippian,* or *Theſſalonian,* or an *Epheſian,* to ſhew that in the Judgment of *Tertullian,* ſeparation from any of their Churches is a certain mark of Hereſie, as juſtly and rationally as you alledge it to vindicate this priviledge to the *Roman* Church only? Certainly if you will ſtand to *Tertullians* judgment, you muſt either grant the authority of the *Roman* Church (though at that time a good Topical Argument, and perhaps a better than any the Hereticks had, eſpecially in conjunction with other Apoſtolick Churches:) yet, I ſay you muſt grant it perforce but a Fallible Guide as well as that of *Epheſus,* and *Theſſalonica,* and *Philippi,* and *Corinth:* or you muſt maintain the authority of every one of theſe infallible, as well as the *Roman.* For though he make a *Panegyrick* of the *Roman* Church in particular, and of the reſt only in general, yet as I have ſaid, for point of direction he makes them all equal; and therefore makes them (chooſe you whether) either all fallible, or all infallible: Now you will and muſt acknowledge that he never intended to attribute infallibility to the Churches of *Epheſus,* or *Corinth,* or if he did, that (as experience ſhews) he Erred in doing ſo; and what can hinder, but then we may ſay alſo that he never intended to attribute infallibility to the *Roman* Church, or if he did that he Erred in doing ſo?

38. Ad §. 20, 21, 22, 23.] The ſum of your diſcourſe in theſe Sections, if it be pertinent to the Queſtion, muſt be this. *Want of Succeſſion of Biſhops and Paſtors holding always the ſame Doctrine, and of the forms of ordaining Biſhops and Prieſts which are in uſe in the* Roman *Church, is a certain mark of Hereſie: But* Proteſtants *want all theſe things: Therefore they are Hereticks.* To which I anſwer, That nothing but want of truth and holding Error, can make or prove

any

any man or Church Heretical. For if he be a true *Aristotelian*, or *Platonist*, or *Pyrrhonian*, or *Epicurean*, who holds the Doctrine of *Aristotle*, or *Plato*, or *Pirrho*, or *Epicurus*, although he cannot assign any that held it before him for many Ages together, why should I not be made a true and Orthodox Christian, by believing all the Doctrine of Christ, though I cannot derive my descent from a perpetual Succession that believed it before me? By this reason you should say as well, that no man can be a good Bishop or Pastor, or King or Magistrate, or Father that succeeds a bad one. For if I may conform my will and actions to the Commandments of God, why may I not embrace his Doctrine with my understanding, although my predecessor do not so? You have above in this Chapter defined *Faith a free Infallible, obscure, supernatural assent to Divine Truths, because they are revealed by God and sufficiently propounded:* This definition is very phantastical; but for the present I will let it pass, and desire you to give me some piece of shadow or reason, why I may not do all this without a perpetual Succession of Bishops and Pastors that have done so before me? You may judge as uncharitably, and speak as maliciously of me, as your blind zeal to your Superstition shall direct you, but certainly I know, (and with all your Sophistry you cannot make me doubt of what I know,) that I do believe the Gospel of Christ (as it is delivered in the undoubted Books of Canonical Scripture, as verily as that it is now day, that I see the light, that I am now writing: and I believe it upon this Motive, because I conceive it sufficiently, abundantly, superabundantly proved to be Divine Revelation: And yet in this, I do not depend upon any Succession of men that have always believed it without any mixture of Error; nay I am fully persuaded, there hath been no such Succession, and yet do not find my self any way weakned in my Faith by the want of it; but so fully assured of the truth of it, that not only, though your Devils at *Lowden* do tricks against it, but though an Angel from Heaven should gainsay it or any part of it, I persuade my self that I should not be moved. This I say, and this I am sure is true: and if you will be so Hypersceptical

sceptical as to perſuade me, that I am not ſure that I believe all this, I deſire you to tell me, how are you ſure that you believe the Church of *Rome*? For if a man may perſuade himſelf he doth believe what he doth not believe, then may you think you believe the Church of *Rome*, and yet not believe it. But if no man can Err concerning what he believes, then you muſt give me leave to aſſure my ſelf that I do believe, and conſequently that any man may believe the aforeſaid truths upon the aforeſaid motives, without any dependence upon any Succeſſion that hath believed it always. And as from your definition of Faith, ſo from your definition of Hereſie, this fancy may be refuted. For queſtionleſs no man can be an Heretick but he that holds an Hereſie, and an Hereſie you ſay *is a Voluntary Error*; therefore no man can be neceſſitated to be an Heretick whether he will or no, by want of ſuch a thing that is not in his power to have: But that there ſhould have been a perpetual Succeſſion of Believers in all points Orthodox, is not a thing which is in your power, therefore our being or not being Hereticks depends not on it. Beſides, what is more certain, than that he may make a ſtreight line, who hath a Rule to make it by, though never man in the World had made any before: and why then may not he that believes the Scripture to be the Word of God, and the Rule of Faith, regulate his Faith by it, and conſequently believe aright without much regarding what other men either will do or have done? It is true indeed there is a neceſſity that if God will have his Words believed, he by his Providence muſt take order, that either by Succeſſion of men, or by ſome other means natural or ſupernatural, it be preſerved and delivered, and ſufficiently notified to be his Word; but that this ſhould be done by a Succeſſion of men that holds no Error againſt it, certainly there is no more neceſſity, than that it ſhould be done by a Succeſſion of men that commit no ſin againſt it. For if men may preſerve the Records of a Law, and yet tranſgreſs it, certainly they may alſo preſerve directions for their Faith, and yet not follow them. I doubt not but Lawyers at the Barr do find by frequent experience, that

that many men preserve and produce evidences, which being examined oftimes make against themselves. This they do ignorantly, it being in their power to suppress, or perhaps to alter them. And why then should any man conceive it strange, that an erroneous and corrupted Church should preserve and deliver the Scriptures uncorrupted, when indeed for many reasons which I have formally alleged, it was impossible for them to corrupt them? Seeing therefore this is all the necessity that is pretended of a perpetual Succession of men Orthodox in all points, certainly there is no necessity at all of any such, neither can the want of it prove any man or any Church Heretical.

39. When therefore you have produced some proof of this, (which was your Major in your former Syllogism,) That want of Succession is a certain mark of Heresie, you shall then receive a full answer to your Minor. We shall then consider whether your indelible Character be any reality, or whether it be a Creature of your own making, a fancy of your own imagination? And if it be a thing, and not only a Word, whether our Bishops and Priests have it not as well as yours; and whether some mens persuasion that there is no such thing, can hinder them from having it, or prove that they have it not if there be any such thing? (Any more than a mans persuasion that he has not taken Physick or Poyson, will make him not to have taken it if he has, or hinder the operation of it?) And whether *Tertullian* in the place quoted by you, speak of a Priest made a Lay-man, by a just deposition or degradation, and not by a voluntary desertion of his Order? And whether in the same place he set not some mark upon Hereticks that will agree to your Church? Whether all the Authority of our Bishops in *England* before the Reformation, was conferred on them by the *Pope*? And if it were, whether it were the *Popes* right, or an Usurpation? If it were his right, whether by Divine Law or Ecclesiastical? And if by Ecclesiastical only, whether he might possibly so abuse his power, as to deserve to lose it? Whether *de facto* he had done so? Whether supposing he had deserved to lose it, those that deprived him of it had power to take it from him?

him? Or if not, whether they had power to suspend him from the use of it, until good caution were put in, and good assurance given, that if he had it again, he would not abuse it as he had formerly done? Whether in case they had done unlawfully that took his power from him, it may not (things being now setled, and the present Government established) be as unlawful to go about to restore it? whether it be not a Fallacy to conclude, because we believe the *Pope* hath no power in *England*, now when the King and State and Church hath deprived him upon just grounds of it, therefore we cannot believe that he had any before his deprivation? Whether without Schism, a man may not withdraw obedience from an Usurped Authority commanding unlawful things? Whether the *Roman* Church might not give Authority to Bishops and Priests to oppose her Errors, as well as a King gives Authority to a Judge to judge against him, if his cause be bad; as well as *Trajan* gave his Sword to his Prefect, with this commission, that *if he Governed well, he should use it for him, if ill against.* Whether the *Roman* Church gave not Authority to her Bishops and Priests to Preach against her corruptions in manners? And if so, why not against her Errors in Doctrine, if she had any? Whether she gave them not Authority to Preach the whole Gospel of Christ, and consequently against her Doctrine, if it should contradict any part of the Gospel of Christ? Whether it be not acknowledged lawful in the Church of *Rome*, for any Lay-man or Woman that has ability to perswade others by Word or by Writing from Error, and unto truth? And why this Liberty may not be practised against their Religion, if it be false, as well as for it if it be true? Whether any man need any other Commission or Vocation than that of a Christian, to do a work of Charity? And whether it be not one of the greatest works of Charity (if it be done after a peaceable manner, and without any unnecessary disturbance of order,) to perswade men out of a false, unto a true way of Eternal happiness? Especially the Apostle having assured us, that he, (whosoever he is) *who converteth a sinner from the Error of his way, shall save a Soul from*

A a a *Death,*

Death, and shall hide a multitude of Sins? Whether the first Reformed Bishops died all at once, so that there were not enough to ordain others in the places that were vacant? Whether the Bishops of *England* may not Consecrate a Metropolitan of *England*, as well as the Cardinals do the *Pope?* whether the King or Queen of *England*, or they that have the Government in their Hands, in the minority of the Prince, may not lawfully commend one to them to be consecrated, against whom there is no Canonical exception? Whether the Doctrine, that the King is supream head of the Church of *England*, (as the Kings of *Judah*, and the first Christian Emperors were of the Jewish and Christian Church,) be any new found Doctrine? Whether it be not true, that Bishops being made Bishops, have their Authority immediately from Christ, though this or that man be not made Bishop without the Kings Authority; as well as you say, the *Pope* being *Pope*, has Authority immediately from Christ, and yet this or that man cannot be made *Pope* without the Authority of the Cardinals? Whether you do well to suppose, that Christian Kings have no more Authority in ordering the affairs of the Church, than the great *Turk*, or the *Pagan* Emperors? Whether the King may not give Authority to a Bishop to exercise his function in some part of his Kingdom, and yet not be capable of doing it himself: as well as a Bishop may give Authority to a Physician, to practice Physick in his Diocess, which the Bishop cannot do himself? Whether if *Nero* the Emperor would have commanded S. *Peter* or S. *Paul* to Preach the Gospel of Christ, and to exercise the office of a Bishop of *Rome*, whether they would have questioned his Authority to do so? Whether there were any Law of God or man, that prohibited K. JAMES to give Commission to Bishops, nay to lay his injunction upon them, to do any thing that is lawful? Whether a casual irregularity may not be lawfully dispenced with? Whether the *Popes* irregularities if he should chance to incur any, be indispensable? And if not, who is he, or who are they, whom the *Pope* is so subject unto, that they may dispense with him? Whether that

that be certain which you take for granted; *That your Ordination imprints a Character and ours doth not?* Whether the power of Consecrating and Ordaining by imposition of hands, may not reside in the Bishops, and be derived unto them, not from the King but God; and yet the King have Authority to command them to apply this power to such a fit person, whom he shall commend unto them: As well as if some Architects only had the faculty of *Architecture*, and had it immediately by infusion from God himself, yet, if they were the Kings Subjects, he wants not authority to command them to build him a Palace for his use, or a fortress for his service: Or as the King of *France* pretends not to have power to make Priests himself, yet I hope, you will not deny him power to command any of his Subjects that has this power, to ordain any fit person Priest, whom he shall desire to be ordained? Whether it do not follow, that whensoever the King commands an House to be Built, a Message to be delivered, or a Murtherer to be Executed, that all these things are presently done without intervention of the Architect, Messenger, or Executioner: As well as, that they are *ipso facto* Ordained and Consecrated, who by the Kings Authority are commended to the Bishops to be Ordained and Consecrated: Especially seeing the King will not deny, but that these Bishops may refuse to do what he requires to be done, lawfully if the person be unworthy, if worthy, unlawfully indeed, but yet *de facto* they may refuse: and in case they should do so, whether justly or unjustly; neither the King himself, nor any Body else, would esteem the person Bishop upon the Kings designation? Whether many *Popes*, though they were not Consecrated Bishops by any temporal Prince, yet might not, or did not receive authority from the Emperor to exercise their Episcopal function in this or that place? And whether the Emperors had not authority, upon their desert, to deprive them of their jurisdiction, by imprisonment or banishment? Whether Protestants do indeed pretend that their Reformation is Universal? Whether in saying, the *Donatists Sect was confined to* Africa, you do not forget your self, and contradict

tradict what you said above, in §. 17. of this Chapter, where you tell us, *they had some of their Sect residing in* Rome? Whether it be certain, that none can admit of Bishops willingly, but those that hold them of Divine institution? Whether they may not be willing to have them, conceiving that way of Government the best, though not absolutely necessary? Whether all those *Protestants* that conceive the distinction between Priests and Bishops, not to be of Divine institution, be Schismatical and Heretical for thinking so? Whether your form of ordaining Bishops and Priests, be essential to the constitution of a true Church? Whether the forms of the Church of *England* differ essentially from your forms? Whether in saying, that *the true Church cannot subsist without undoubted true Bishops and Priests*, you have not overthrown the truth of your own Church: wherein I have proved it plainly impossible, that any man should be so much as morally certain, either of his own Priesthood or any other mans? Lastly, whether any one kind of these external Forms and Orders, and Government be so necessary to the being of a Church, but that they may not be diverse in diverse places, and that a good and peaceable Christian may and ought to submit himself to the Government of the place where he lives whatsoever it be? All these Questions will be necessary to be discussed for the clearing of the truth of the *Minor* proposition of your former Syllogism, and your proofs of it: and I will promise to debate them fairly with you, if first you will bring some better proof of the *Major*, *That want of Succession is a certain note of Heresie*, which for the present remains both unproved and unprobable.

40. *Obj.* You say, *The Fathers assign Succession as one mark of the true Church.*

Answ. I confess they did urge Tradition as an Argument of the Truth of their Doctrine and of the falshood of the contrary; and thus far they agree with you. But now see the difference: They urged it not against all Hereticks that ever should be, but against them who rejected a great part of the Scripture, for no other reason but *because it was repugnant to their Doctrine, and corrupted other parts with*

with their additions and detractions, and perverted the remainder with divers absurd interpretations: So *Tertullian* not a leaf before the words by you cited. Nay they urged it against them who *when they were confuted out of Scripture, fell to accuse the Scriptures themselves as if they were not right, and came not from good authority, as if they were various one from another, and as if truth could not be found out of them, by those who know not Tradition, for that it was not delivered in writing,* (they did mean wholly,) *but by word of mouth: And that thereupon* Paul *also said, we speak wisdom amongst the perfect.* So *Irenæus* in the very next Chapter before that which you alledge. Against these men being thus necessitated to do so, they did urge Tradition, but what or whose Tradition was it? Certainly no other but the joynt Tradition of all the Apostolick Churches, with one Mouth and one Voice teaching the same Doctrine. Or if for brevity sake they produce the Tradition of any one Church, yet is it apparent, that that one was then in conjunction with all the rest; *Irenæus, Tertullian, Origen,* testifie as much in the words cited, and S. *Austin,* in the place before alledged by me. This Tradition they did urge against these men, and in a time, in comparison of ours, almost contiguous to the Apostles: So near, that one them, *Irenæus,* was Scholar to one who was Scholar to S. *John* the Apostle. *Tertullian* and *Origen* were not an Age removed from him: and the last of them all, little more than an Age from them. Yet after all this they urged it not as a demonstration, but only as a very probable argument, far greater than any their Adversaries could oppose against it. So *Tertullian* in the place above quoted, §. 5. *How is it likely that so many and so great Churches should Err in one Faith?* (it should be, should have Erred into one Faith.) And this was the condition of this Argument as the Fathers urged it. Now if you having to deal with us, who question no Book of Scripture, which was not Anciently questioned by some whom you your selves esteem good Catholicks; nay who refuse not to be tried by your own Canons, your own Translations, who in interpreting Scriptures are content to allow of all those rules which you propose, only

except

except that we will not allow you to be our Judges; if you will come fifteen hundred years after the Apostles, a fair time for the purest Church to gather much drofs and corruptions, and for the *mystery of iniquity* to bring its work to some perfection, which *in the Apostles time began to work*, If (I say) you will come thus long after and urge us with the single Tradition of one of these Churches, being now Catholick to it self alone, and Heretical to all the rest: nay not only with her Ancient Original Traditions, but also with her post-nate and introduced Definitions, and these as we pretend, repugnant to Scripture, and Ancient Tradition, and all this to decline an indifferent Trial by Scripture, under pretence (wherein also you agree with the calumny of the Old Hereticks) that *all necessary truth cannot be found in them without recourse to Tradition:* If, I say, notwithstanding all these differences, you will still be urging us with this argument, as the very same and of the same force with that wherewith the fore-mentioned Fathers urged the Old Hereticks, certainly this must needs proceed from a confidence you have, not only that we have no School-Divinity, nor Metaphysicks, but no Logick or common sense, that we are but Pictures of men, and have the definition of rational creatures given us in vain.

41. But now suppose I should be liberal to you, and grant what you cannot prove, that the Fathers make Succession a certain and perpetual mark of the true Church; I beseech you what will come of it? What, that want of Succession is a certain sign of an Heretical company? Truly if you say so, either you want Logick, which is a certain sign of an ill disputer; or are not pleased to use it, which is a worse. For speech is a certain sign of a living man, yet want of speech is no sure argument that he is dead, for he may be dumb and yet living still, and we may have other evident tokens that he is so, as Eating, Drinking, Breathing, Moving: So, though the constant and Universal delivery of any Doctrine by the Apostolick Churches ever since the Apostles, be a very great argument of the truth of it, yet there is no certainty, but that

that truth, even Divine truth, may through mens wickedneſs, be contracted from its univerſality, and interrupted in its perpetuity, and ſo loſe this argument, and yet not want others to juſtifie and ſupport it ſelf. For it may be one of thoſe principles which God hath written in all mens Hearts, or a concluſion evidently ariſing from them: It may be either contained in Scripture in expreſs terms, or deducible from it by apparent conſequence. If therefore you intend to prove want of a perpetual Succeſſion of Profeſſors a certain note of Hereſie, you muſt not content your ſelf to ſhew, that having it is one ſign of truth; but you muſt ſhew it to be the only ſign of it and inſeparable from it. But this, if you be well adviſed, you will never undertake. Firſt becauſe it is an impoſſible attempt: and then becauſe if you do it you will marr all: for by proving this an inſeparable ſign of Catholick Doctrine, you will prove your own, which apparently wants it in many points, not to be Catholick. For whereas you ſay *this Succeſſion requires two things, agreement with the Apoſtles Doctrine, and an uninterrupted conveyance of it down to them that challenge it:* It will be proved againſt you that you fail in both points; and that ſome things wherein you agree with the Apoſtles have not been held alwaies, as your condemning the Doctrine of the *Chiliaſts*, and holding the Euchariſt not neceſſary for Infants; and that in many other things you agree not with them nor with the Church for many Ages after. For example; In mutilation of the Communion, in having your Service in ſuch a Language as the Aſſiſtants generally underſtand not, your offering to Saints, your Picturing of God, your worſhiping of Pictures.

42. Ad §. 24.] Obj. *The true Church muſt have Univerſality of place which* Proteſtants *wanting cannot avoid the juſt note of Hereſie.*

Anſw. You have not ſet down clearly and univocally what you mean by it, whether Univerſality of fact or of right: and if of fact, whether abſolute or comparative: and if comparative, whether of the Church in compariſon of any other Religion, or only of Heretical Chriſtians: or if in compariſon of theſe, whether in compariſon

of

of all other Sects conjoyned, or in comparison only of any one of them. Nor have you proved it by any good argument in any sense to be a certain mark of Heresie: For those places of S. *Austin* do not deserve the name. And truly in my judgment you have done advisedly in proving it no better. For as for Universality of right, or a right to Universality, all Religions claim it, but only the true has it, and which has it cannot be determined, unless it first be determined which is the true. An absolute Universality, and diffusion through all the World if you should pretend to, all the World would laugh at you. If you should contend for latitude with any one Religion, *Mahumetism* would carry the Victory from you. If you should oppose your selves against all other Christians besides you, it is certain you would be cast in this suit also. If lastly, being hard driven you should please your selves with being more than any one Sect of Christians, it would presently be replied, that it is uncertain whether now you are so, but most certain that the time has been when you have not been so. Then when the

^a *Hierom. Cont. Luciferianos.*

^a *whole World wondered that it was become Arrian*: then when *Athanasius opposed the World, and the World Athanasius*: then

^b *In Theodoret. Hist. 16. c. l. 2.*

when ^b *your Liberius* having the contemptible paucity of his adherents objected to him as a note of Error, answered for himself, *There was a time when there were but three opposed the decree of the King, and yet those three were in the right, and the rest in the wrong*: then when the *Professors of Error surpassed the number of the Professors of truth in proportion, as the sands of the Sea do the Stars of the Heaven.* (As

^c *In ep. 48. ad Vincentium.*
^d *Commenitorii. lib. 1. c. 4.*
^e *In vita Nazianz.*

^c S. *Austin* acknowledgeth:) then when ^d *Vincentius* confesseth, that *the Poyson of the Arrians had contaminated, not now some certain portion, but almost the whole World*: then when the Author of *Nazianzens* Life testifies, *That* ^e *the Heresie of Arrius, had possessed in a manner the whole extent of the World*; and when *Nazianzen* found cause to cry out,

^f *In Orat. Arian. & pro se ipso.*

^f *Where are they who reproach us with our poverty, who define the Church by the multitude, and despise the little flock? They have the People, but we the Faith.* And lastly when *Athanasius* was so overborn with Sholes and Floods of

Arrians,

Arrians, that he was enforced to write a Treatise on purpose ᵍ against those, *who judge of the truth only by plurality of adherents*. So that if you had proved want of Univerſality even thus reſtrained, to be an infallible note of Hereſie, there would have been no remedy but you muſt have confeſſed, that the time was when you were Hereticks. And beſides, I ſee not how you would have avoided this great inconvenience, of laying grounds and ſtoring up arguments for Antichriſt, againſt he comes, by which he may prove his Company the true Church. For it is evident out of Scripture, and confeſſed by you, that though his time be not long, his dominion ſhall be very large; and that the true Church ſhall be then, the *woman driven into the wilderneſſ*.

ᵍ Tom. 2.

45. *Ad §. 25. 26*] You endeavor to prove that the Faith of Proteſtants is no Faith, being deſtitute of its due qualifications.

Obj. *Firſt*, you ſay, *their belief wanteth certainty, becauſe they denying the Univerſal Infallibility of the Church, can have no certain ground to know what Objects are revealed or teſtified by God.*

Anſ. But if there be no other ground of certainty but your Churches infallibility, upon what certain ground do you know that your Church is infallible? Upon what certain ground do you know all thoſe things which muſt be known before you can know that your Church is infallible? As that there is a God: that God hath promiſed his aſſiſtance to your Church in all her Decrees: that the Scripture wherein this promiſe is extant is the word of God: that thoſe Texts of Scripture which you alledge for your infallibility are incorrupted: that that which you pretend is the true ſenſe of them? When you have produced certain grounds for all theſe things, I doubt not but it will appear, that we alſo may have grounds certain enough to believe our whole Religion, which is nothing elſe but the Bible, without dependence on the Churches infallibility. Suppoſe you ſhould meet with a man that for the preſent, believes neither Church, nor Scripture, nor God, but is ready and willing to believe them all, if you can

Bbb   ſhew

shew some sufficient grounds to build his faith upon; will you tell such a man there are no certain grounds, by which he may be converted; or there are? If you say the first, you make all Religion an uncertain thing: If the second, then either you must ridiculously perswade, that your Church is infallible, because it is infallible, or else that there are other certain grounds besides your Churches infallibility.

46. Obj. *The Holy Scripture is in it self most true and infallible, but without the direction and declaration of the Church, we can neither have certain means to know what Scripture is Canonical, nor what Translations be faithful, nor what is the true meaning of Scripture.*

Ans. But all these things must be known, before we can know the direction of your Church to be infallible, for no other proof of it can be pretended, but only some Texts of Canonical Scripture, truly interpreted: Therefore either you are mistaken, in thinking there is no other means to know these things, but your Churches infallible direction, or we are excluded from all means of knowing her direction to be infallible.

47. Obj. *But Protestants, though they are perswaded their own opinions are true, and that they have used such means as are wont to be prescribed for understanding the Scripture, as Prayer, conferring of Texts, &c. Yet by their disagreement shew, that some of them are deceived. Now they hold all the Articles of their faith, upon this only ground of Scripture, interpreted by these rules, and therefore it is clear, that the ground of their faith is infallible in no point at all.*

Ans. The first of these suppositions must needs be true, but the second is apparently false: I mean, that every Protestant is perswaded that he hath used those means which are prescribed for understanding of Scripture. But that which you collect from these suppositions is clearly inconsequent: and by as good Logick you might conclude, that Logick and Geometry stand upon no certain grounds, that the rules of the one, and the principles of the other do sometimes fail, because the disagreement of Logicians and Geometricians shew, that some of them are deceived.

ceived. Might not a Jew conclude as well against all Christians, that they have no certain ground whereon to relie in their understanding of Scripture; because their disagreements shew that some are deceived; because some deduce from it the infallibility of a Church, and others no such matter? So likewise a Turk might use the same argument against both Jews and Christians, and an Atheist against all Religions, and a Sceptick against all reason. Might not the one say, Mens disagreement in Religion, shews that there is no certainty in any; and the other, that experience of their contradictions teacheth, that the rules of reason do sometimes fail? Do not you see and feel how void of reason and how full of impiety your sophistry is? And how transported with zeal against Protestants, you urge arguments against them, which if they could not be answered, would overthrow not only your own, but all Religion? But God be thanked, the answer is easie and obvious! For let men but remember not to impute the faults of men but only to men, and then it will easily appear, that there may be sufficient certainty in reason, in Religion, in the rules of interpreting Scripture, though men through their faults, take not care to make use of them, and so run into divers errors and dissentions.

48. *Obj.* But *Protestants cannot determine what points be fundamental, and therefore must remain uncertain, whether or no they be not in some fundamental error.*

Ans. By like reason since you acknowledge, that every error in points defined and declared by your Church destroys the substance of Faith, and yet cannot determine what points be defined, it followeth that you must remain uncertain, whether or no you be not in some fundamental error, and so want the substance of Faith, without which there can be no hope of Salvation.

But though we cannot perhaps say in particular, thus much, and no more is fundamental, yet believing all the Bible, we are certain enough that we believe all that is fundamental. As he that in a receipt, takes twenty ingredients whereof ten only are necessary, though he know not which those ten are, yet taking the whole twenty he is sure enough that he has taken all that are necessary.

49. Ad §. 29. Obj. *It is generally delivered by Catholick Divines that he who erreth against any one revealed truth, loseth all Divine Faith. Now certainly some Protestants must do so, because they hold contradictions, which cannot all be true. Therefore some of them at least, have no divine faith.*

Ans. I pass by your weakness in urging Protestants with the authority of your Divines. Yet if the Authority of your Divines were even Canonical, certainly nothing could be concluded from it in this matter, there being not one of them, who delivers for true doctrin this position of yours, thus nakedly set down, *That any error against any one revealed truth destroys all divine faith.* For they all require (not your self excepted) that this truth must not only be revealed, but revealed publickly, and (all things considered) sufficiently propounded to the erring party, to be one of those, which God under pain of damnation commands all men to believe.

But if the Reader will be at the pains he may see this vain fancy confuted, out of one of the most rational and profound Doctors of your own Church, I mean *Estius*, upon the third Book of the Sententes, the 23. Distinct. and the 13. Section, beginning thus. *It is disputed whether in him who believes some of the Articles of our Faith, and disbelieves others, or perhaps some one, there be faith properly so called in respect of that which he does believe?*

50. *But if Protestants have certainty, they want obscurity, and so have not that faith, which as the Apostle saith is of things not appearing.* This argument you prosecute in the next Paragraph; but I can find nothing in it, to convince or perswade me that Protestants cannot have as much certainty as is required to faith, of an object not so evident as to beget science. If obscurity will not consist with certainty in the highest degree, then you are to blame for requiring to faith contradicting conditions. If certainty and obscurity will stand together, what reason can be imagined that a Protestant may not entertain them both as well as a Papist? Your bodies and souls, your understandings and
wills

wills are, I think, of the same condition with ours: And why then may not we be certain of an obscure thing as well as you?

51. But then besides, I am to tell you, that you are here, every where, extreamly, if not affectedly mistaken in the Doctrin of Protestants; who though they acknowledge, that the things which they believe are in themselves as certain as any demonstrable or sensible verities, yet pretend not that their certainty of adherence is most perfect and absolute, but such as may be perfected and increased as long as they *walk by faith and not by sight*. And consonant hereunto is their doctrin touching the evidence of the objects whereunto they adhere. For you abuse the world and them, if you pretend that they hold the first of your two principles, That these particular Books are the word of God, (for so I think you mean) either to be in it self evidently certain, or of it self and being devested of the motives of credibility, evidently credible: For they are not so fond as to be ignorant, nor so vain as to pretend, that all men do assent to it, which they would if it were evidently certain, nor so ridiculous as to imagine, that if an *Indian* that never heard of Christ or Scripture, should by chance find a Bible in his own Language, and were able to read it, that upon the reading it he would certainly without a miracle believe it to be the word of God: which he could not chuse if it were evidently credible. What then do they affirm of it? Certainly no more than this, that whatsoever man that is not of a perverse mind, shall weigh with serious and mature deliberation, those great moments of reason which may incline him to believe the Divine authority of Scripture, and compare them with the light objections that in prudence can be made against it, he shall not chuse but find sufficient nay abundant inducements to yield unto it firm faith and sincere obedience. Let that learned man *Hugo Grotius* speak for all the rest, in his Book *of the Truth of Christian Religion*; which Book whosoever attentively peruses shall find that a man may have great reason to be a Christian without dependence upon your Church for any part of it: and that your Religion

ligion is no foundation of, but rather a scandal and an objection against Christianity. He then in the last Chapter of his second Book hath these excellent words, 'If 'any be not satisfied with these arguments abovesaid, but 'desires more forcible reasons for confirmation of the ex- 'cellency of Christian Religion, let such know that as 'there are variety of things which be true, so are there di- 'vers ways of proving or manifesting the truth. Thus is 'there one way in Mathematicks, another in Physicks, a 'third in Ethicks, and lastly another kind when a matter 'of fact is in question: wherein verily we must rest con- 'tent with such Testimonies as are free from all suspicion 'of untruth; otherwise down goes all the frame and use 'of History, and a great part of the art of Physick, toge- 'ther with all dutifulness that ought to be between parents 'and children: for matters of practice can no way else be 'known but by such Testimonies. Now it is the pleasure 'of Almighty God that those things which he would have 'us to believe (so that the very belief thereof may be im- 'puted to us for obedience) should not so evidently ap- 'pear, as those things which are apprehended by sense 'and plain demonstration, but only be so far forth reveal- 'ed as may beget faith, and a perswasion thereof, in the 'hearts and minds of such as are not obstinate: That so 'the Gospel may be as a touchstone for tryal of mens 'judgments, whether they be sound or unsound. For see- 'ing these arguments, whereof we have spoken, have in- 'duced so many honest, godly, and wise men to approve 'of this Religion, it is thereby plain enough that the fault 'of other mens infidelity is not for want of sufficient testi- 'mony, but because they would not have that to be had 'and embraced for truth which is contrary to their wilful 'desires; it being a hard matter for them to relinquish 'their honours, and set at naught other commodities; 'which thing they know they ought to do, if they admit of 'Christs Doctrin and obey what he hath commanded. 'And this is the rather to be noted of them, for that ma- 'ny other historical narrations are approved by them to be 'true, which notwithstanding are only manifest by autho-
'rity,

'rity, and not by any such strong proofs, and perswasi-
'ons, or tokens, as do declare the history of Christ to be
'true; which are evident, partly by the confession of
'those Jews that are yet alive; and partly in those compa-
'nies and congregations of Christians which are any where
'to be found; whereof doubtless there was some cause.
'Lastly, seeing the long duration or continuance of Chri-
'stian Religion, and the large extent thereof can be ascri-
'bed to no human power, therefore the same must be at-
'tributed to miracles: or if any deny that it came to pass
'through a miraculous manner; this very getting so great
'strength and power without a miracle, may be thought to
'surpass any miracle.

52. And now you see I hope that Protestants neither do nor need to pretend to any such evidence in the doctrin they believe, as cannot well consist both with the essence and the obedience of faith. Let us come now to the last nullity which you impute to the faith of Protestants, and that it is *want of prudence*. Touching which point, as I have already demonstrated, that wisdom is not essential to faith, but that a man may truly believe truth, though upon insufficient motives; So I doubt not but I shall make good, that if prudence were necessary to faith, we have better title to it than you; and that if a wiser than *Solomon* were here, he should have better reason to believe the Religion of Protestants than Papists, the Bible rather than the Council of *Trent*. But let us hear what you can say!

53. Ad §. 31. You demand then first of all, *What wisdom was it to forsake a Church confessedly very ancient, and besides which there could be demonstrated no other Visible Church of Christ upon earth?* I answer: Against God and truth there lies no prescription, and therefore certainly it might be great wisdom to forsake ancient Errors for more ancient Truths. One God is rather to be followed than innumerable worlds of men: And therefore it might be great wisdom either for the whole Visible Church, nay for all the men in the world, having wandred from the way of Truth, to return unto it; or for a part of it, nay for one man to do so, although all the world besides were madly

resolute

resolute to do the contrary. It might be great wisdom to forsake the Errors though of the only Visible Church, much more the *Roman*, which in conceiving her self the whole Visible Church, does somewhat like the Frog in the Fable, which thought the Ditch he lived in to be all the World.

54. You demand again, *What wisdom was it to forsake a Church acknowledged to want nothing necessary to Salvation, indued with Succession of Bishops*, &c. usq, ad *Election or Choice?* I answer: Yet might it be great wisdom to forsake a Church not acknowledged to want nothing necessary to Salvation, but accused and convicted of many damnable errors: certainly damnable to them who were convicted of them, had they still persisted in them after their conviction; though perhaps pardonable (which is all that is acknowledged) to such as ignorantly continued in them. A Church vainly arrogating without possibility of proof a perpetual Succession of Bishops, holding always the same doctrine; and with a ridiculous impudence pretending perpetual possession of all the world: whereas the world knows, that a little before *Luthers* arising, your Church was confined to a part of a part of it. Lastly a Church vainly glorying in the dependence of other Churches upon her, which yet she supports no more than those crouching Anticks which seem in great buildings to labour under the weight they bear, do indeed support the Fabrick. For a corrupted and false Church may give authority to preach the Truth, and consequently against her own falshoods and corruptions. Besides, a false Church may preserve the Scripture true, (as now the Old Testament is preserved by the Jews,) either not being arrived to that height of impiety as to attempt the corruption of it, or not able to effect it, or not perceiving, or not regarding the opposition of it to her corruptions. And so we might receive from you lawful Ordination and true Scriptures, though you were a false Church; and receiving the Scriptures from you (though not from you alone, I hope you cannot hinder us, neither need we ask your leave to believe and obey them. And this, though you be a false
Church,

Church; and receiving the Scriptures from you (though not from you alone,) I hope you cannot hinder us, neither need we ask your leave, to believe and obey them. And this, though you be a false Church, is enough to make us a true one. As for a *Succession of men that held with us in all points of Doctrine*, it is a thing we need not, and you have as little as we. So that if we acknowledge that your Church before *Luther* was a true Church, it is not for any ends, for any dependence that we have upon you; but becaufe we conceive that in a charitable conftruction, you may pafs for a true Church. Such a Church (and no better) as you do fometimes acknowledge *Proteftants* to be, that is, a Company of men, wherein fome ignorant Souls may be faved. So that in this ballancing of Religion againft Religion, and Church againft Church, it feems you have nothing of weight and moment to put into your Scale; nothing but Smoak and Wind, vain fhadows and phantaftical pretences. Yet if *Proteftants* on the other fide, had nothing to put in their Seal but thofe negative commendations which you are pleafed to afford them; nothing but, no Unity, nor means to procure it; no farther extent when *Luther* arofe than *Luthers* Body; no Univerfality of time or place; no vifibility or being, except only in your Church; no Succeffion of Perfons or Doctrine; no leader but *Luther*, in a quarrel begun upon no ground but paffion; no Church, no Ordination, no Scriptures but fuch as they received from you; if all this were true, and this were all that could be pleaded for Proteftants, poffibly with an allowance of three grains of partiality your Scale might feem to turn. But then if it may appear that part of thefe objections are falfly made againft them, the reft vainly; that whatfoever of truth is in thefe imputations, is impertinent to this Tryal, and whatfoever is pertinent is untrue; and befides, that plenty of good matter may be alledged for Proteftants which is here diffembled: then I hope, our Caufe may be good notwithftanding thefe pretences.

55. I fay then, that want of Univerfality of time and place, The invifibility or not exiftence of the profeffors of

Protestant Doctrine before *Luther*, *Luthers* being alone when he first opposed your Church, Our having our Church, Ordinations, Scriptures, personal and yet not Doctrinal Succession from you, are vain and impertinent allegations, against the truth of our Doctrine and Church. That the entire truth of Christ without any mixture of Error should be professed or believed in all places at any time, or in any place at all times, is not a thing evident in reason, neither have we any Revelation for it. And therefore in relying so confidently on it, you build your House upon the Sand. And what obligation we had either to be so peevish, as to take nothing of yours, or so foolish as to take all, I do not understand. For whereas you say that *this is to be choosers and therefore Hereticks*, I tell you that though all Hereticks are choosers, yet all choosers are not Hereticks, otherwise they also, which choose your Religion must be Hereticks. As for *our wanting Unity and Means of proving it*, Luthers *opposing your Church upon meer passion, our following private men rather than the Catholick Church*; the first and last are meer untruths, for we want not Unity, nor means to procure it in things necessary. Plain places of Scripture, and such as need no interpreter are our means to obtain it. Neither do we follow any private men, but only the Scripture, the Word of God as our rule, and reason, which is also the gift of God given to direct us in all our actions, in the use of this rule. And then for *Luthers opposing your Church upon meer passion*, it is a thing I will not deny because I know not his Heart, and for the same reason you should not have affirmed it. Sure I am, whether he opposed your Church upon reason or no, he had reason enough to oppose it. And therefore if he did it upon passion, we will follow him only in his action and not in his passion, in his opposition, not in the manner of it; and then I presume you will have no reason to condemn us, unless you will say that a good action cannot be done with reason, because some Body before us hath done it upon passion. You see then how imprudent you have been in the choice of your arguments,

to

to prove *Protestants* unwise in the choice of their Religion.

56. It remains now, that I should shew that many reasons of moment may be alledged for the justification of *Protestants*, which are dissembled by you, and not put into the Balance. Know then, Sir, that when I say, the Religion of *Protestants*, is in prudence to be preferred before yours: as on the one side I do not understand by your Religion, the Doctrine of *Bellarmine* or *Baronius*, or any other private man amongst you, nor the Doctrine of the *Sorbon*, or of the *Jesuits*, or of the *Dominicans*, or of any other particular Company among you, but that wherein you all agree, or profess to agree, *the Doctrine of the Council of Trent*: so accordingly on the other side, by the *Religion of Protestants*, I do not understand the Doctrine of *Luther* or *Calvin*, or *Melancthon*; nor the Confession of *Augusta*, or *Geneva*, nor the Catechism of *Heidelburg*, nor the Articles of the Church of *England*, no nor the *Harmony* of *Protestant* Confessions; but that wherein they all agree, and which they all subscribe with a greater *Harmony*, as a perfect rule of their Faith and Actions, that is, The *Bible*. The *Bible*, I say, The *Bible* only is the Religion of *Protestants*! Whatsoever else they believe besides it, and the plain, irrefragable, indubitable consequences of it, well may they hold it as a matter of Opinion; but as matter of Faith and Religion, neither can they with coherence to their own grounds believe it themselves, nor require the belief of it of others, without most high and most Schismatical presumption. I for my part after a long (and as I verily believe and hope,) impartial search of *the true way to Eternal Happiness*, do profess plainly that I cannot find any rest for the sole of my Foot, but upon this Rock only. I see plainly and with mine own eyes, that there are *Popes* against *Popes*, Councils against Councils, some Fathers against others, the same Fathers against themselves, a Consent of Fathers of one Age against a Consent of Fathers of another Age, the Church of one Age against the Church of another Age. Traditive interpretations of Scripture are pretended, but there are few or none to be found: No Tradition but only of

Scripture, can derive it self from the Fountain, but may be plainly proved, either to have been brought in, in such an Age after Christ; or that in such an Age it was not in. In a word, there is no sufficient certainty but of Scripture only, for any considering man to build upon. This therefore, and this only I have reason to believe: This I will profess, according to this I will live, and for this, if there be occasion, I will not only willingly, but even gladly lose my life, though I should be sorry that Christians should take it from me. Propose me any thing out of this Book, and require whether I believe it or no, and seem it never so incomprehensible to humane reason, I will subscribe it with Hand and Heart, as knowing no demonstration can be stronger than this, God hath said so therefore it is true. In other things I will take no mans liberty of judgment from him; neither shall any man take mine from me. I will think no man the worse man, nor the worse Christian: I will love no man the less, for differing in opinion from me. And what measure I mete to others I expect from them again. I am fully assured that God does not, and therefore that men ought not to require any more of any man, than this, To believe the Scripture to be Gods word, to endeavour to find the true sense of it, and to live according to it.

57. This is the Religion which I have chosen after a long deliberation, and I am verily perswaded that I have chosen wisely, much more wisely than if I had guided my self according to your Churches authority. For the Scripture being all true, I am secured by believing nothing else, that I shall believe no falshood as matter of Faith. And if I mistake the sense of Scripture, and so fall into Error, yet am I secure from any danger thereby, if but your grounds be true: because endeavouring to find the true sense of Scripture, I cannot but hold my Error without pertinacy, and be ready to forsake it when a more true and a more probable sense shall appear unto me. And then all necessary truth being as I have proved, plainly set down in Scripture, I am certain by believing Scripture, to believe

all

all necessary Truth: And he that does so, if his life be answerable to his Faith, how is it possible he should fail of Salvation?

58. Besides, whatsoever may be pretended to gain to your Church the credit of a Guide, all that and much more may be said for the Scripture. Hath your Church been Ancient? The Scripture is more Ancient. Is your Church a means to keep men at Unity? So is the Scripture to keep those that believe it and will obey it, in Unity of belief, in matters necessary or very profitable, and in Unity of Charity in points unnecessary. Is your Church Universal for time or place? Certainly the Scripture is more Universal. For all the Christians in the World (those I mean that in truth deserve this name,) do now, and always have believed the Scripture to be the Word of God: whereas only you say that you only are the Church of God, and all Christians besides you deny it.

59. Thirdly, following the Scripture, I follow that whereby you prove your Churches infallibility, (whereof were it not for Scripture what pretence could you have, or what notion could we have?) and by so doing tacitely confess, that your selves are surer of the Truth of the Scripture than of your Churches authority. For we must be surer of the proof than of the thing proved, otherwise it is no proof.

60. Fourthly, following the Scripture, I follow that which must be true if your Church be true: for your Church gives attestation to it. Whereas if I follow your Church, I must follow that which, though Scripture be true, may be false; nay which if Scripture be true must be false, because the Scripture testifies against it.

61. Fifthly, to follow the Scripture I have Gods express warrant and command, and no colour of any prohibition: But to believe your Church infallible, I have no command at all, much less an express command. Nay I have reason to fear that I am prohibited to do so in these Words: *call no man Master on Earth: They fell by infidelity, Thou standest by Faith, Be not high minded but fear: The Spirit of truth The World cannot receive.*

62. Following

62. Following your Church I must hold many things not only above reason but against it, if any thing be against it: whereas following the Scripture I shall believe many mysteries but no impossibilities; many things above reason, but nothing against it; many things which had they not been revealed, reason could never have discovered, but nothing which by true reason may be confuted: many things which reason cannot comprehend how they can be, but nothing which reason can comprehend that it cannot be. Nay I shall believe nothing which reason will not convince that I ought to believe it: For reason will convince any man, unless he be of a perverse mind, that the Scripture is the Word of God: And then no reason can be greater than this, God says so, therefore it is true.

63. Following your Church I must hold many things which to any mans judgment that will give himself the liberty of judgment, will seem much more plainly contradicted by Scripture, than the infallibility of your Church appears to be confirmed by it; and consequently must be so foolish as to believe your Church exempted from Error upon less evidence, rather than subject to the common condition of mankind upon greater evidence. Now if I take the Scripture only for my Guide, I shall not need to do any thing so unreasonable.

64. If I will follow your Church I must believe impossibilities, and that with an absolute certainty, upon motives which are confessed to be but only *Prudential* and probable: That is, with a weak Foundation I must firmly support a heavy, a monstrous heavy building: Now following the Scripture I shall have no necessity to undergo any such difficulties.

65. Following your Church I must be servant of Christ and a Subject of the King, but only *Ad placitum Papæ*. I must be prepared in mind to renounce my allegiance to the King, when the *Pope* shall declare him an Heretick and command me not to obey him: And I must be prepared in mind *to esteem Vertue Vice, and Vice Vertue, if the* Pope *shall so determine*. Indeed you say it is impossible he should do the latter; but that you know is a great question, neither is it fit my obedience to God and the King should depend upon

upon a questionable Foundation. And howsoever, you must grant that if by an impossible supposition the *Popes* commands should be contrary to the law of Christ, that they of your Religion must resolve to obey rather the commands of the *Pope* than the law of Christ. Whereas if I follow the Scripture, I may, nay I must obey my Sovereign in lawful things, though an Heretick, though a Tyrant, and though, I do not say the *Pope*, but the Apostles themselves, nay *an Angel from Heaven should teach any thing against the Gospel of Christ*, I may, nay I must denounce Anathema to him.

66. Following the Scripture I shall believe a Religion, which being contrary to Flesh and Blood, without any assistance from worldly power, wit or policy; nay against all the power and policy of the World prevailed and enlarged it self in a very short time all the World over. Whereas it is too too apparent, that your Church hath got and still maintains her authority over mens Consciences, by counterfeiting false miracles, forging false stories, by obtruding on the World suppositious writings, by corrupting the monuments of former times, and defacing out of them all which any way makes against you, by Wars, by persecutions, by Massacres, by Treasons, by Rebellions; in short, by all manner of Carnal means whether violent or fraudulent.

67. Following the Scripture I shall believe a Religion, the first Preachers of Professors whereof, it is most certain they could have no worldly ends upon the World, that they could not project to themselves by it any of the profits or honours or pleasures of this World, but rather were to expect the contrary, even all the miseries which the World could lay upon them. On the other side, the Head of your Church, the pretended Successor of the Apostles, and Guide of Faith, it is even palpable, that he makes your Religion the instrument of his ambition, and by it seeks to entitle himself *directly or indirectly to the Monarchy of the World*. And besides, it is evident to any man that has but half an eye, that most of those Doctrines which you add to the Scripture do make one way or other, for the honour or temporal profit of the Teachers of them.

68. Fol-

68. Following the Scripture only, I shall embrace a Religion of admirable simplicity, consisting in a manner wholly in the worship of God in Spirit and Truth. Whereas your Church and Doctrine is even loaded with an infinity of weak, childish, ridiculous, unsavoury superstitions and ceremonies, and full of that *righteousness* for which *Christ shall Judge the World.*

69. Following the Scripture, I shall believe that which Universal, never-failing Tradition assures me, that it was by the admirable supernatural Work of God confirmed to be the Word of God: whereas never any miracle was wrought, never so much as a lame Horse cured in confirmation of your Churches authority and infallibility. And if any strange things have been done, which may seem to give attestation to some parts of your Doctrine, yet this proves nothing but the truth of the Scripture, which foretold that (Gods providence permitting it, and the wickedness of the World deserving it) *strange signs and wonders should be wrought to confirm false Doctrine, that they which love not the Truth, may be given over to strange delusions.* Neither does it seem to me any strange thing, that God should permit some true wonders to be done to delude them who have forged so many to deceive the World.

70. If I follow the Scripture, I must not promise my self Salvation without effectual dereliction and mortification of all Vices, and the effectual Practice of all Christian Vertues: But your Church opens an easier and a broader way to Heaven, and though I continue all my life long in a course of sin, and without the Practice of any Vertue, yet gives me assurance that I may be let into Heaven, at a Postern-gate, even by any Act of Attrition at the hour of Death, if it be joyned with confession, or by an Act of Contrition without confession.

71. Admirable are the Precepts of piety and humility, of innocence and patience, of liberality, frugality, temperance, sobriety, justice, meekness, fortitude, constancy and gravity, contempt of the World, love of God and the love of mankind; In a Word, of all Vertues, and

against

against all vice, which the Scriptures impose upon us, to be obeyed under pain of damnation: The sum whereof is in manner comprised in our *Saviours Sermon upon the Mount,* recorded in the 5, 6, and 7. of S. *Matthew,* which if they were generally obeyed, could not but make the world generally happy, and the goodness of them alone were sufficient to make any wise and good man believe that this Religion rather than any other, came from God the fountain of all goodness. And that they may be generally obeyed, our Saviour hath ratified them all in the close of his Sermon, with these universal Sanctions, *Not every one that saith Lord Lord, shall enter into the Kingdom, but he that doth the will of my Father which is in Heaven:* and again, *whosoever heareth these sayings of mine and doth them not, shall be likned unto a foolish man which built his house upon the sand, and the rain descended, and the flood came, and the winds blew, and it fell, and great was the fall thereof.* Now your Church, notwithstanding all this, enervates and in a manner dissolves and abrogates many of these precepts, teaching men that they are not Laws for all Christians, but Counsels of perfection and matters of Supererrogation: that a man shall do well if he do observe them, but he shall not sin if he observe them not; that they are for them who aim at high places in heaven, who aspire with the two sons of *Zebede,* to the right hand or to the left hand of Christ: But if a man will be content barely to go to heaven, and to be a doorkeeper in the house of God, especially if he will be content to taste of Purgatory in the way, he may obtain it at any easier purchase. Therefore the Religion of your Church is not so holy nor so good as the doctrin of Christ delivered in Scripture, and therefore not so likely to come from the Fountain of holiness and goodness.

72. Lastly, if I follow your Church for my Guide, I shall do all one, as if I should follow a Company of blind men in a judgment of colours, or in the choice of a way. For every unconsidering man is blind in that which he does not consider. Now what is your Church but a Company of unconsidering men, who comfort themselves be-

cause they are a great company together, but all of them, either out of idleness refuse the trouble of a severe tryal of their Religion, (as if heaven were not worth it,) or out of superstition fear the event of such a tryal, that they may be scrupled and staggered and disquieted by it; and therefore, for the most part do it not all. Or if they do it, they do it negligently and hypocritically, and perfunctorily, rather for the satisfaction of others than themselves: but certainly without indifference, without liberty of judgment, without a resolution to doubt of it, if upon examination the grounds of it prove uncertain, or to leave it, if they prove apparently false. My own experience assures me, that in this imputation I do you no injury: but it is very apparent to all men from your ranking, *doubting of any part of your Doctrin,* among mortal sins. For from hence it follows, that seeing every man must resolve that he will never commit mortal sin, that he must never examine the grounds of it at all, for fear he should be moved to doubt: or if he do, he must resolve that no motives, be they never so strong shall move him to doubt, but that with his will and resolution he will uphold himself in a firm belief of your Religion, though his reason and his understanding fail him. And seeing this is the condition of all those whom you esteem good Catholicks, who can deny, but you are a Company of men unwilling and afraid to understand, lest you should do good! That have eyes to see and will not see, that have *not the love of truth* (which is only to be known by an indifferent tryal,) and therefore deserve *to be given over to strong delusions*; men that love darkness more than light: in a word, that you are *the blind leading the blind,* and what prudence there can be, in following such Guides, our Saviour hath taught us in saying, *If the blind lead the blind, both shall fall into the ditch.*

74. Ad §. 32. Your next and last argument against the faith of Protestants is, because *wanting certainty and prudence, it must also want the fourth condition, Supernaturality. For that being a humane perswasion, it is not in the essence of it Supernatural: and being imprudent and rash, it cannot proceed from*

from Divine motion, and so is not supernatural in respect of the cause from which it proceedeth.

Ans. This little discourse stands wholly upon what went before, and therefore must fall together with it. I have proved the Faith of Protestants as certain, and as prudent as the faith of Papists; and therefore if these be certain grounds of supernaturality, our faith may have it as well as yours. I would here furthermore be informed how you can assure us that your faith is not your perswasion or opinion (for you make them all one,) that your Churches doctrine is true? Or if you grant it your perswasion, why is it not the perswasion of men, and in respect of the subject of it, an humane perswasion? I desire also to know, what sense there is in pretending that your perswasion is, not in regard of the object only and cause of it, but in nature or essence of it supernatural? Lastly, whereas you say, that *being imprudent it cannot come from divine motion:* certainly by this reason all they that believe your own Religion, and cannot give a wise and sufficient reason for it, (as millions amongst you cannot) must be condemned to have no supernatural faith: or if not, then without question nothing can hinder, but that the imprudent faith of Protestants may proceed from divine motion, as well as the imprudent faith of Papists.

75. And thus having weighed your whole discourse, and found it altogether lighter than vanity, why should I not invert your conclusion, and say, Seeing you have not proved that whosoever errs against any one point of Faith loseth all divine Faith: nor that any error whatsoever concerning that which by the Parties litigant may be esteemed a matter of faith is a grievous sin, it follows not at all, that when two men hold different doctrines concerning Religion, that but one can be saved? Not that I deny, but that the sentence of S. *Chrysost.* with which you conclude this Chapter may in a good sense be true: for oftimes by *the faith* is meant only that Doctrin which is *necessary to salvation,* and to say that salvation may be had without any the least thing which is necessary to salvation, implies a repugnance and destroys it self. Besides, not to

believe all necessary points, and to believe none at all, is for the purpose of salvation all one; and therefore he that does so, may justly be said to destroy the Gospel of Christ, seeing he makes it uneffectual to the end for which it was intended, the Salvation of mens souls. But why you should conceive that all differences about Religion are concerning matters of faith, in this high notion of the word, for that I conceive no reason.

CHAP. VII.

The ANSWER to the Seventh CHAPTER.

Shewing that Protestants are not bound by the Charity which they owe to themselves, to reunite themselves to the Roman *Church.*

6. Ad §. 2.] Whereas you say, *it is directly against Charity to our selves, to adventure the omitting of any means necessary to salvation,* this is true: But so is this also, that it is directly against the same Charity, to adventure the omitting any thing, that may any way help or conduce to my salvation, that may make the way to it more secure or less dangerous. And therefore if the errors of the *Roman* Church do but hinder me in this way, or any way endanger it, I am in Charity to my self bound to forsake them, though they be not destructive of it. Again, whereas you conclude, *That if by living out of the* Roman *Church we put our selves in hazard to want something necessary to Salvation, we commit a grievous sin against the vertue of Charity as it respects our selves:* This consequence may be good in those which are thus perswaded of the *Roman* Church, and yet live out of it. But the supposition is certainly false. We may live and die out of the *Roman* Church, without putting our selves in any such hazard: Nay to live and die in it is as dangerous as to shoot a gulf, which though some good ignorant souls may do

and

and escape, yet it may well be feared that not one in a hundred but miscarries.

7. *Ad* §. 5.] In this Section I observe, first, this acknowledgment of yours, *That in things necessary only because commanded, a probable ignorance of the commandment excuses the party from all fault, and doth not exclude Salvation.* From which Doctrin it seems to me to follow, that seeing obedience to the *Roman* Church cannot be pretended to be necessary, but only because it is commanded, therefore not only an invincible, but even a probable ignorance of this pretended command, must excuse us from all faulty breach of it, and cannot exclude Salvation. Now seeing this command is not pretended to be expresly delivered, but only to be deduced from the word of God, and that not by the most clear and evident consequences that may be; and seeing an infinity of great objections lies against it, which seem strongly to prove that there is no such command; with what Charity can you suppose that our ignorance of this comand, is not at the least probable, if not all things consider'd, plainly invincible? Sure I am, for my part, that I have done my true endeavour to find it true, and am still willing to do so; but the more I seek, the farther I am from finding, and therefore if it be true, certainly my not finding it is very excusable, and you have reason to be very charitable in your censures of me. 2. Whereas you say, That *besides these things necessary because commanded, there are other things, which are commanded because necessary: of which number you make Divine infallible faith, Baptism in Act for Children, and in desire for those who are come to the use of Reason, and the Sacrament of Confession, for those who have committed mortal sin*: In these words you seem to me to deliver a strange Paradox, *viz.* That Faith, and Baptism, and Confession are not therefore necessary for us, because God appointed them, but are therefore appointed by God because they were necessary for us, antecedently to his appointment; which if it were true, I wonder what it was beside God that made them necessary, and made it necessary for God to command them! Besides, in making faith one of these necessary means, you seem to exclude Infants from

from Salvation: For *Faith comes by hearing*, and they have not heard. In requiring that this Faith should be *divine and infallible*, you cast your *Credentes* into infinite perplexity, who cannot possibly by any sure mark discern whether their Faith be Divine or human, or if you have any certain sign, whereby they may discern, whether they believe your Churches infallibility with Divine or only with humane faith, I pray produce it, for perhaps it may serve us to shew, that our Faith is Divine as well as yours. Moreover in affirming that *Baptism in act is necessary for Infants, and for men only in desire*, You seem to me in the latter to destroy the foundation of the former. For if a desire of Baptism will serve men in stead of Baptism, then those words of our Saviour, *Unless a man be born again of water*, &c. are not to be understood literally and rigidly of external Baptism; for a desire of Baptism is not Baptism, and so your foundation of the absolute necessity of Baptism is destroyed. And if you may gloss the Text so far, as that men may be saved by the desire, without Baptism it self, because they cannot have it, why should you not gloss it a little farther, that there may be some hope of the salvation of unbaptized infants: to whom it was more impossible to have a desire of Baptism, than for the former to have the thing it self? Lastly, for your *Sacrament of Confession*, we know none such, nor any such absolute necessity of it. They that confess their sins and forsake them shall find mercy, though they confess them to God only and not to men. They that confess them both to God and men, if they do not effectually and in time forsake them, shall not find mercy. 3. Whereas you say, that *supposing these means once appointed as absolutely necessary to salvation, there cannot but arise an obligation of procuring to have them*, you must suppose I hope, that we know them to be so appointed, and that it is in our power to procure them: otherwise though it may be our ill fortune to fail of the end, for want of the means, certainly we cannot be obliged to procure them. For the rule of the law is also the dictate of common reason and equity, That *no man can be obliged to what is impossible*. We can be obliged to nothing but
by

by vertue of some command: now it is impossible that God should command in earnest any thing which he knows to be impossible. For to command in earnest, is to command with an intent to be obeyed; which is not possible he should do, when he knows the thing commanded to be impossible. Lastly, whosoever is obliged to do any thing, and does it not, commits a fault; but Infants commit no fault in not procuring to have Baptism, therefore no obligation lies upon them to procure it. 4. Whereas you say, that *if Protestants dissent from you in the point of the necessity of Baptism for Infants, it cannot be denied but that our disagreement is in a point fundamental*; If you mean a point esteemed so by you, this indeed cannot be denied: But if you mean a point that indeed is fundamental, this may certainly be denied, for I deny it, and say, that it doth not appear to me any way necessary to Salvation to hold the truth, or not to hold an error, touching the condition of these Infants. This is certain, and we must believe that God will not deal unjustly with them, but how in particular he will deal with them concerns not us, and therefore we need not much regard it. 5. Whereas you say the like of your *Sacrament of Pennance*, you only say so, but your proofs are wanting. Lastly, whereas you say, *This rigour ought not to seem strange or unjust in God, but that we are rather to bless him for ordaining us to Salvation by any means:* I answer, that it is true, we are not to question the known will of God of injustice; yet whether that which you pretend to be Gods will, be so indeed, or only your presumption, this I hope may be questioned lawfully and without presumption; and if we have occasion we may safely put you in mind of *Ezekiel's* commination, against all those who say, *thus saith the Lord*, when they have no certain warrant or authority from him to do so.

8. *Ad* §. 4. In the fourth Paragraph you deliver this false and wicked Doctrin, *that for the procuring our own salvation we are always bound under pain of mortal sin, to take the safest way, but for avoiding sin we are not bound to do so, but may follow the opinion of any probable Doctors,* though the contrary may be certainly free from sin, and theirs be
doubt-

doubtful. Which doctrin in the former part of it is apparently false: For though wisdom and Charity to our selves would perswade us always to do so, yet many times, that way which to our selves and our salvation is more full of hazard, is notwithstanding not only lawful, but more Charitable and more noble. For example, to flie from a persecution and so to avoid the temptation of it, may be the safer way for a mans own salvation; yet I presume no man ought to condemn him of impiety, who should resolve not to use his liberty in this matter; but for Gods greater glory, the greater honour of truth, and the greater confirmation of his brethren in the faith, choose to stand out the storm and endure the fiery tryal, rather than avoid it; rather to put his own soul to the hazard of a temptation, in hope of Gods assistance to go through with it, than to baulk the opportunity of doing God and his brethren so great a service. This part therefore of this Doctrin is manifestly untrue. The other not only false but impious; for therein you plainly give us to understand, that in your judgment, a resolution to avoid sin, to the uttermost of our power, is no necessary means of Salvation, nay that a man may resolve not to do so, without any danger of damnation. Therein you teach us, that we are to do more for the love of our selves, and our own happiness than for the love of God; and in so doing contradict our Saviour, who expresly commands us, *to love the Lord our God with all our heart, with all our soul, and with all our strength*; and hath taught us *that the love of God consists in avoiding sin and keeping his commandments.* Therein you directly cross S. *Pauls* Doctrin, who though he were a very probable Doctor, and had delivered his judgment for the *lawfulneß of eating meats offered to Idols*; yet he assures us that he which should make scruple of doing so, and forbear upon his scruple, should not sin, but only be *a weak brother*; whereas he, who should do it with a doubtful conscience, (though the action were by S. *Paul* warranted lawful, yet) *should sin and be condemned for so doing.* You pretend indeed to be rigid defenders and stout champions for the necessity of

good

good works; but the truth is, *you speak lies in Hypocrisie*, and when the matter is well examined, will appear to make your selves and your own functions necessary, but obedience to God unnecessary: Which will appear to any man who considers what strict necessity the Scripture imposes upon all men, of effectual mortification of the habits of all Vices, and effectual Conversion to newness of Life, and Universal obedience, and withal remembers that an act of Attrition, which you say with Priestly absolution is sufficient to Salvation, is not mortification, which being a work of difficulty and time, cannot be performed in an instant. But for the present, it appears sufficiently out of this impious assertion, which makes it absolutely necessary for men, either in Act if it be possible, or if not, in Desire, to be Baptized and Absolved by you, and that with Intention: and in the mean time warrants them that for avoiding of sin, they may safely follow the uncertain guidance of a vain man, who you cannot deny may either be deceived himself, or out of malice deceive them, and neglect the certain direction of God himself, and their own Consciences. What wicked use is made of this Doctrine, your own long experience can better inform you, than it is possible for me to do: yet my own little conversation with you affords me one memorable example to this purpose. For upon this ground I knew a young Scholar in *Doway*, licensed by a great Casuist to swear a thing as upon his certain knowledge, whereof he had yet no knowledge but only a great presumption, because (forsooth) *it was the opinion of one Doctor that he might do so*. And upon the same ground, whensoever you shall come to have a prevailing party in this Kingdom, and power sufficient to restore your Religion, you may do it by deposing or killing the King, by blowing up of Parliaments, and by rooting out all others of a different Faith from you. Nay this you may do, though in your own opinion it be unlawful, because ª *Bellarmine*, a

[a] *Bellar. Cont. Barcl. c. 7. In 7. c. refutare conatur Barcl. verba illa Romuli. Veteres illos Imperatores Constantinum Valentem & Cæteros non ideo toleravit Ecclesia quod legitime successissent, sed quod illos sine populi detrimento coercere non poterat. Et miratur hoc idem scripsisse Bellarminum. l. 5. de Pontif. c. 7. Sed ut magis miretur, sciat hoc idem sensisse S. Thomam. 2. 2. q. 12. art. 2. ad 1. Ubi dicit Ecclesiam tolerasse ut fideles obedirent Juliano Apostatæ, quia in sui novitate non-*
dum habebant vires compescendi Principes terrenos. Et postea, Sanctus Gregorius dicit, nullum adversus Juliani persecutionem fuisse remedium præter lacrymas, quoniam non habebat Ecclesia vires quibus illus tyrannidi resistere posset.

man with you of approved Vertue, Learning and Judgment, hath declared his opinion for the lawfulness of it, in saying, that *want of power to maintain a Rebellion, was the only reason that the Primitive Christians did not Rebel against the persecuting Emperors.* By the same rule, seeing the Priests and Scribes and Pharisees, men of greatest repute among the *Jews* for Vertue, Learning and Wisdom, held it a lawful and a pious work to persecute Christ and his Apostles, it was lawful for the People to follow their Leaders: for herein, according to your Doctrine, they proceeded prudently, and according to the conduct of opinion, maturely weighed and approved by men as it seemed to them of Vertue, Learning and Wisdom; nay by such as sate in *Moses* Chair, and of whom it was said, *whatsoever they bid you observe, that observe and do:* which Universal you pretend is to be understood Universally, and without any restriction or limitation. And as lawful was it for the *Pagans* to persecute the Primitive Christians, because *Trajan* and *Pliny*, men of great Vertue and Wisdom were of this opinion. Lastly, that most impious and detestable Doctrine, (which by a foul calumny you impute to me, who abhor and detest it,) that *men may be saved in any Religion*, follows from this ground unavoidably. For certainly Religion is one of those things which is necessary only because it is commanded: for if none were commanded under pain of damnation, how could it be damnable to be of any? Neither can it be damnable to be of a false Religion, unless it be a sin to be so. For neither are men saved by good luck, but only by obedience; neither are they damned for their ill Fortune but for sin and disobedience. Death is the wages of nothing but sin: and S. *James* sure intended to deliver the adequate cause of sin and Death in those words, *Lust when it hath conceived bringeth forth sin, and sin when it is finished bringeth forth Death.* Seeing therefore in such things, according to your Doctrine, it is sufficient for avoiding of sin, that we proceed prudently, and by the conduct of some probable opinion, maturely weighed and approved by men of

Learning,

Learning, Vertue and Wisdom: and seeing neither *Jews* want their *Gamaliels*, nor *Pagans* their *Antoninus*'s nor any Sect of Christians such professors and maintainers of their several Sects, as are esteemed by the People, which know no better (and that very reasonably) men of Vertue, Learning, and Wisdom, it follows evidently that the embracing their Religion proceeds upon such reason as may warrant their action to be prudent, and this is sufficient for avoiding of sin, and therefore certainly for avoiding damnation, for that in humane affairs, & discourse, evidence and certainty cannot be always expected. I have stood the longer upon the refutation of this Doctrine, not only because it is impious, and because bad use is made of it, and worse may be, but only because the contrary position, *That men are bound for avoiding sin always to take the safest way*, is a fair and sure Foundation, for a clear confutation of the main conclusion, which in this Chapter you labour in vain to prove, and a certain proof that in regard of the precept of Charity towards ones self, and of obedience to God, *Papists* (unless ignorance excuse them) are in state of sin as long as they remain in subjection to the *Roman* Church.

9. for if the safer way for avoiding sin, be also the safer way for avoiding damnation, then certainly the way of *Protestants* must be more secure, and the *Roman* way more dangerous; take but into your consideration these ensuing Controversies: Whether it be lawful to worship Pictures? to Picture the Trinity? to invocate Saints and Angels? to deny Lay-men the Cup in the Sacrament? to adore the Sacraments? to prohibit certain Orders of Men and Women to Marry? to Celebrate the publick service of God in a language which the assistants generally understand not? and you will not choose but confess that in all these you are on the more dangerous side for the committing of sin, and we on that which is more secure. For in all these things, if we say true, you do that which is impious: on the other side if you were in the right, yet we might be secure enough, for we should only not do something which you confess not necessary to be done.

We pretend, and are ready to juſtifie out of principles agreed upon between us, that in all theſe things, you violate the manifeſt commandments of God; and alledge ſuch Texts of Scripture againſt you, as, if you would weigh them with any indifference, would put the matter out of queſtion, but certainly you cannot with any modeſty deny, but that at leaſt they make it queſtionable. On the other ſide, you cannot with any face pretend, and if you ſhould, know not how to go about to prove, that there is any neceſſity of doing any of theſe things; that it is unlawful not to worſhip Pictures, not to Picture the Trinity, not to invocate Saints and Angels, not to give all men the entire Sacrament, not to adore the Eucharist, not to prohibit Marriage, not to Celebrate Divine Service in an unknown Tongue : I ſay you neither do nor can pretend that there is any law of God which enjoyns us, no nor ſo much as an Evangelical Council that adviſes us to do any of theſe things. Now *where no law is there can be no ſin, for ſin is the tranſgreſſion of the Law*; It remains therefore that our forbearing to do theſe things, muſt be free from all danger and ſuſpicion of ſin; whereas your acting of them, muſt be, if not certainly impious, without all contradiction queſtionable and dangerous. I conclude therefore that which was to be concluded, that if the ſafer way for avoiding ſin, be alſo (as moſt certainly it is,) the ſafer way for avoiding damnation, then certainly the way of *Proteſtants* muſt be more ſafe, and the *Roman* way more dangerous.

12. Ad §. 5.] Here you begin to make ſome ſhew of arguing; and the firſt Argument put into form ſtands thus, *Every leaſt Error in Faith deſtroys the nature of Faith; It is certain that ſome* Proteſtants *do Err, and therefore they want the ſubſtance of Faith.* The Major of which Syllogiſm I have formerly confuted by unanſwerable Arguments out of one of your own beſt Authors, who ſhews plainly that he hath amongſt you, as ſtrange as you make it, many other Abettors. Beſides, if it were true, it would conclude that either you or the *Dominicans* have no Faith, in as much as you oppoſe one another as much as *Arminians* and *Calviniſts*.

13. The

13. The Second Argument stands thus, *Since all* Protestants *pretend the like certainty, it is clear that none of them have any certainty at all* : Which Argument if it were good, then what can hinder but this must also be so, Since *Protestants* and *Papists* pretend the like certainty ; it is clear that none of them have any certainty at all ! And this too : Since all Christians pretend the like certainty, it is clear that none of them have any certainty at all ! And thirdly this : Since men of all Religions pretend a like certainty, it is clear that none of them have any at all ! And lastly this : Since oft-times they which are abused with a specious Paralogism, pretend the like certainty with them which demonstrate, it is clear that none of them have any certainty at all ! Certainly Sir, Zeal and the Devil did strangely blind you, if you did not see that these horrid impieties were the immediate consequences of your positions, if you did see it, and yet would set them down, you deserve worse censure. Yet such as these, are all the Arguments wherewith you conceive your self to have proved undoubtedly, that *Protestants have reason at least to doubt in what case they stand.*

14. Your third and fourth Argument may be thus put into one ; *Protestants cannot tell what points in particular be Fundamental; therefore they cannot tell whether they or their Brethren do not Err Fundamentally, and whether their difference be not Fundamental.* Both which deductions I have formerly shewed to be most inconsequent ; for knowing the Scripture to contain all Fundamentals, (though many more points besides, which makes it difficult to say precisely what is Fundamental and what not,) knowing this I say and believing it, what can hinder but that I may be well assured, that I believe all Fundamentals, and that all who believe the Scripture sincerely as well as I, do not differ from me in any thing Fundamental ?

15. In the close of this Section, you say, *that you omit to add that we want the Sacrament of Repentance instituted for the remission of sins, or at least we must confess that we hold it not necessary: and yet our own Brethren the Century writers acknowledge that in the times of* Cyprian

and

and Tertullian, *private Confession even of thoughts was used, and that it was then commanded and thought necessary; and then our Ordination*, you say, *is very doubtful and all that depends upon it.* Answer, I also omit to answer, 1. That your Brother *Rhenanus*, acknowledges the contrary, and assures us that the Confession then required and in use, was publick, and before the Church, and that your auricular Confession was not then in the World; for which his Mouth is stopped by your *Index Expurgatorius*. 2. That your Brother *Arcudius* acknowledges, that the Eucharist was in *Cyprians* time given to Infants, and esteemed necessary, or at least profitable for them, and the giving it shews no less; and now I would know whether you will acknowledg your Church bound to give it, and to esteem so of it? 3. That it might be then commanded, and being commanded be thought necessary, and yet be but a Church Constitution. Neither will I deny, if the present Church could, and would so order it, that the abuses of it might be prevented, and conceiving it profitable, should enjoyn the use of it, but that being commanded it would be necessary. 4. Concerning our Ordinations, besides that I have proved it impossible that they should be so doubtful as yours, according to your own principles; I answer, that experience shews them certainly sufficient to bring men to Faith and Repentance, and consequently to Salvation; and that if there were any secret defect of any thing necessary, which we cannot help, God will certainly supply it.

19. It is remarkable against what you say, §. 7. *That any small Error in Faith destroys all Faith*, that S. *Austin*, whose authority is here stood upon, thought otherwise: He conceived the *Donatists* to hold some Error in Faith and yet not to have no Faith. His words of them to this purpose are most pregnant and evident, *you are with us* (saith he to the *Donatist*. Ep. 48.) *in Baptism, in the Creed, in the other Sacraments*: And again. *Super gestis cum emerit: Thou hast proved to me that thou hast Faith; prove to me likewise that thou hast Charity.* Parallel to which words are these of *Optatus*, *Amongst us and you is one Ecclesiastical conversation*,

Lib. 5. prope initium.

versation, common lessons, the same Faith, the same Sacraments. Where by the way we may observe, that in the judgments of these Fathers, even the *Donatists*, though Hereticks and Schismaticks, gave true Ordination, the true Sacrament of Matrimony, true Sacramental Absolution, Confirmation, the true Sacrament of the Eucharist, true extream Unction; or else (choose you whether) some of these were not then esteemed Sacraments. But for Ordination, whether he held it a Sacrament or no, certainly he held that it remained with them entire: for so he says in express terms, in his Book against *Parmenianus* his Epistle. Which Doctrine if you can reconcile with the present Doctrine of the *Roman* Church, *Eris mihi magnus Apollo.*

20. Ad §. 8.] *Obj.* You say there is *an inevitable necessity for us, either to grant Salvation to your Church, or to entail certain damnation upon our own, because ours can have no being till* Luther, *unless yours be supposed to have been the true Church.* I answer, this cause is no cause: For first, as *Luther* had no being before *Luther,* and yet he was when he was, though he was not before; so there is no repugnance in the terms, but that there might be a true Church after *Luther,* though there were none for some Ages before; as since *Columbus* his time, there have been Christians in *America,* though before there were none for many Ages. For neither do you shew, neither does it appear, that the generation of Churches is Univocal, that nothing but a Church can possibly beget a Church: nor that the present being of a true Church, depends necessarily upon the perpetuity of a Church in all Ages; any more than the present being of Peripateticks or Stoicks depends upon a perpetual pedigree of them. For though I at no hand deny the Churches perpetuity, yet I see nothing in your Book to make me understand, that the truth of the present depends upon it, nor any thing that can hinder, but that a false Church, (Gods providence overwatching and over-ruling it,) may preserve the means of confuting their own Heresies, and reducing men to truth, and so raising a true Church, I mean the integrity

and

The Religion of Protestants a safer way

and the Authority of the word of God with men. Thus the *Jews* preserve means to make men Christians, and *Papists* preserve means to make men *Protestants*, and *Protestants* (which you say are a false Church) do, as you pretend, preserve means to make men *Papists*; that is, their own Bibles, out of which you pretend to be able to prove that they are to be *Papists*. Secondly, you shew not, nor does it appear that the perpetuity of *the Church* depends on the truth of *yours*. For though you talk vainly, as if you were the only men in the World before *Luther*, yet the World knows that this is but talk, and that there were other Christians besides you, which might have perpetuated the Church though you had not been. Lastly, you shew not, neither doth it appear, that your being acknowledged in some sense a true Church, doth necessarily import, that we must grant Salvation to it, unless by it you understand the ignorant members of it, which is a very unusual *Synechdoche*.

21. Whereas you say, *that Catholicks never granted that the* Donatists *had a true Church or might be saved.* I answ. S. *Austin* himself granted that those among them, who sought the Truth, being *ready when they found it to correct their Error were not Hereticks, and therefore notwithstanding their Error might be saved.* And this is all the Charity that *Protestants* allow to *Papists*.

Therefore the Argument of the *Donatists*, is as good as that of the *Papists* against *Protestants*. For the *Donatists* argued thus, speaking to the *Catholicks*, *Your selves confess our Baptism, Sacraments and Faith good and available. We deny yours to be so, and say there is no Church, no Salvation amongst you; Therefore it is safest for all to joyn with us.*

22. S. *Austins* words are (cont. lit. petil. l. 2. c. 108.) *Petilianus dixit, venite ad Ecclesiam populi & aufugite Traditores, si perire non vultis*: Petilian *saith, come to the Church ye People, and fly from the Traditours, if ye will not be damned; for that ye may know that they being guilty, esteem well of our Faith, behold I Baptize these whom they have infected, but they receive those whom we have Baptized.* Where

Cont. lit. Petil. l. 2. c. 108.

it

it is plain, that *Petilian* by his words makes the *Donatists* the Church, and excludes the *Catholicks* from salvation absolutely. And whereas you say, *the* Catholicks *never yielded that among the* Donatists *there was a true Church and hope of Salvation,* I say it appears by what I have alledged out of S. *Austin,* that they yielded both these were among the *Donatists,* as much as we yield them to be among the *Papists.* As for D. *Potters* acknowledgment, *that they maintained an error in the matter and nature of it Heretical:* This proves them but material Hereticks, whom you do not exclude from possibility of Salvation. So that all things considered, this argument must be much more forcible from the *Donatists* against the *Catholicks,* than from *Papists* against *Protestants,* in regard *Protestants* grant *Papists* no more hope of salvation than *Papists* grant *Protestants*: whereas the *Donatists* excluded absolutely all but their own part from hope of Salvation, so far as to account them no Christians that were not of it: the Catholicks mean while accounting them Brethren, and freeing those among them, from the imputation of Heresie, who being in error *quærebant cautâ sollicitudine veritatem corrigi parati cùm invenerint*; *sought for truth carefully, being ready when they found it to correct their errors.*

23. Whereas you say, *That the Argument for the certainty of their Baptism (because it was confessed good by Catholicks, whereas the Baptism of Catholicks was not confessed by them to be good,) is not so good as yours, touching the certainty of your Salvation grounded on the confession of Protestants, because we confess there is no damnable error in the doctrin or practice of the* Roman *Church:* I Answer, no: we confess no such matter, and though you say so a hundred times, no repetition will make it true. We profess plainly, that many damnable errors plainly repugnant to the precepts of Christ both Ceremonial and Moral, more plainly than this of Rebaptization, and therefore more damnable, are believed and professed by you. And therefore seeing this is the only disparity you can devise, and this is vanished, it remains that as good an answer as the Catholicks made touching the certainty of their Baptism, as good may we make,

make, and with much more evidence of Reason, touching the security and certainty of our Salvation.

24. By the way I desire to be informed, seeing you affirm that *Rebaptizing those whom Hereticks had baptized was a sacriledge, and a profession of a damnable Heresie,* when it began to be so? If from the beginning it were so, then was *Cyprian* a sacrilegious professor of a damnable heresie, and yet a Saint and a Martyr. If it were not so, then did your Church excommunicate *Firmilian* and others, and separate from them without sufficient ground of Excommunication or Separation, which is Schismatical. You see what difficulties you run into on both sides; choose whether you will, but certainly both can hardly be avoided.

27. What S. *Austin* answers to the *Donatists* argument, fits us in answer to yours, as if it had been made for it; for as S. *Austin* says, *that Catholicks approve the Doctrin of* Donatists, *but abhor their Heresie of Re-baptization:* So we say, that we approve those fundamental and simple necessary Truths which you retain, by which some good souls among you may be saved, but abhor your many Superstitions and Heresies. And as he says, that as gold is good, yet ought not to be sought for among a company of thieves, and Baptism good but not to be sought for in the Conventicles of *Donatists*: so say we, that the Truths you retain are good, and as we hope sufficient to bring good ignorant souls among you to salvation, yet are not to be sought for in the Conventicle of *Papists*, who hold with them a mixture of many vanities, and many impieties.

30. Obj. *But* Protestants *do either exclude Hope by Despair, with the Doctrin that our Saviour died not for all, and that such want grace sufficient to salvation; or else by vain* presumption *grounded upon a fantastical perswasion that they are predestinate, which Faith must exclude all fear and trembling;* and you add, *though some* Protestants *may relent from the rigour of the aforesaid doctrin, yet none of them can have true hope while they hope to be saved in the Communion of those, who defend such Doctrins.*

Ans.

Anf. * All this may be as forcibly returned upon Papists, as it is urged against Protestants; in as much as all Papists either hold the Doctrine of Predetermination and absolute Election, or Communicate with those that do hold it. Now from this Doctrin what is more prone and obvious, than for every natural man (without Gods especial preventing grace) to make this practical collection; either I am elected, or not elected; if I be, no impiety possible can ever damn me: If not, no possible industry can ever save me? Now whether this disjunctive perswasion be not as likely (as any doctrin of Protestants) to extinguish Christian Hope and filial fear, and to lead some men to despair, others to presumption, all to a wretchless and impious life, I desire you ingenuously to inform me; and if you deny it, assure your self, you shall be contradicted and confuted, by men of your own Religion and your own society; and taught at length this charitable doctrin, that though mens opinions may be charged with the absurd consequences which naturally flow from them, yet the men themselves are not; I mean, if they perceive not the consequence of these absurdities, nor do not own and acknowledge, but disclaim and detest them.

* *See numb.* 4. *in the* fol. edit.

I add 1. That there is no *Calvinist* that will deny the truth of this proposition, *Christ died for all,* nor to subscribe to that sense of it, which your Dominicans put upon it; neither can you with coherence to the received Doctrine of your own Society, deny that they as well as the *Calvinists,* take away the distinction of sufficient and effectual grace, and indeed hold none to be sufficient, but only that which is effectual. 2. Whereas you say, *They cannot make their calling certain by good works, who do certainly believe that before any good works they are justified, and justified by faith alone, and by that faith whereby they certainly believe they are justified:* I answer, There is no *Protestant* but believes that Faith, Repentance, and universal Obedience, are necessary to the obtaining of Gods favour and eternal happiness. This being granted, the rest is but a speculative Controversie, a Question about words which would quickly vanish, but that men affect not to understand

stand one another. As if a company of Physicians were in consultation, and should all agree, that three Medicins and no more were necessary for the recovery of the Patients health, this were sufficient for his direction towards the recovery of his health; though concerning the proper and specifical effects of these three Medicins, there should be amongst them as many differences as men: So likewise being generally at accord that these three things, Faith, Hope, and Charity, are necessary to salvation, so that whosoever wants any of them cannot obtain it, and he which hath them all cannot fail of it, is it not very evident that they are sufficiently agreed for mens directions to eternal Salvation? And seeing Charity is a full comprehension of all good works, they requiring Charity as a necessary qualification in him that will be saved, what sense is there in saying, *they cannot make their calling certain by good works?* They know what salvation is as well as you, and you have as much reason to desire it: They believe it as heartily as you, that there is no good work but shall have its proper reward, and that there is no possibility of obtaining the eternal reward without good works: and why then may not this Doctrin be a sufficient incitement and provocation unto good works?

31. You say, that *they certainly believe that before any good works they are justified:* But this is a calumny. There is no Protestant but requires to Justification, Remission of sins, and to Remission of sins they all require Repentance, and Repentance I presume may not be denied the name of a good work, being indeed, if it be rightly understood, and according to the sense of the word in Scripture, an effectual conversion from all sin to all holiness. But though it be taken for meer sorrow for sins past, and a bare purpose of amendment, yet even this is a good work, and therefore Protestants requiring this to Remission of sins, and Remission of sins to justification, cannot with candor be pretended to believe, that they are justified before any good work.

32. Obj. You say, *They believe themselves justified by faith alone, and that by that faith whereby they believe themselves justified:* Ans.

Answ. Some peradventure do so, but withal they believe that that faith which is alone, and unaccompanied with *sincere* and universal obedience, is to be esteemed not faith but presumption, and is at no hand sufficient to justification: that though Charity be not imputed unto justification, yet it is required as a necessary disposition in the person to be justified, and that though in regard of the imperfection of it, no man can be justified by it, yet that on the other side, no man can be justified without it. So that upon the whole matter, a man may truly and safely say, that the Doctrin of these Protestants taken altogether, is not a Doctrin of Liberty, nor a Doctrin that turns hope into presumption, and carnal security, though it may justly be feared, that many licentious persons, taking it by halves, have made this wicked use of it. For my part, I do heartily wish, that by publick Authority it were so ordered, that no man should ever Preach or Print this Doctrin that Faith alone justifies, unless he joyns this together with it, that universal obedience is necessary to salvation. And besides that those Chapters of S. *Paul* which intreat of justification by faith, without the works of the Law, were never read in the Church, but when the thirteenth Chapter of the first Epistle to the *Corinthians* concerning the absolute necessity of Charity should be, to prevent misprision, read together with them.

33. Obj. Whereas you say, that *some Protestants do expresly affirm the former point to be the soul of the Church*, &c. *and that therefore they must want the Theological vertue of Hope, and that none can have true hope, while they hope to be saved in their Communion.*

I *Answer*, They have great reason to believe the Doctrin of Justification by faith only, a point of great weight and importance, if it be rightly understood: that is, they have reason to esteem it a principal and necessary duty of a Christian, to place his hope of justification and salvation, not in the perfection of his own righteousness (which if it be imperfect will not justifie,) but only in the mercies of God through Christs satisfaction: and yet notwithstanding this, nay the rather for this, may preserve themselves

selves in the right temper of good Christians, which is a happy mixture and sweet composition of confidence and fear. If this Doctrin be otherwise expounded than I have here expounded, I will not undertake the justification of it, only I will say (that which I may do truly) that I never knew any Protestant such a soli-fidian, but that he did believe these divine Truths; *That he must make his calling certain by good works: That he must work out his salvation with fear and trembling, and that while he does not so, he can have no well-grounded hope of Salvation*: I say I never met with any who did not believe these divine Truths, and that with a more firm, and a more unshaken assent, than he does that himself is predestinate, and that he is justified by believing himself justified. I never met with any such, who if he saw there were a necessity to do either, would not rather forgo his belief of these Doctrins than the former: these which he sees disputed and contradicted and opposed with a great multitude of very potent Arguments; then those, which being the express words of Scripture, whosoever should call into question, could not with any modesty pretend to the title of Christian. And therefore there is no reason but we may believe, that their full assurance of the former Doctrins doth very well qualifie their perswasion of the latter, and that the former (as also the lives of many of them do sufficiently testifie) are more effectual to temper their hope, and to keep it at a stay of a filial and modest assurance of Gods favor, built upon the conscience of his love and fear, than the latter can be to swell and puff them up into vain confidence and ungrounded presumption. This reason, joyned with our experience of the honest and religious conversation of many men of this opinion, is a sufficient ground for Charity, to hope well of their hope: and to assure our selves that it cannot be offensive, but rather most acceptable to God, if notwithstanding this diversity of opinion, we embrace each ether with the strict embraces of love and Communion. To you and your Church we leave it, to separate Christians from the Church, and to prescribe them from heaven upon trivial and trifling causes: As for

our

our selves, we conceive a charitable judgment of our Brethren and their errors, though untrue, much more pleasing to God than a true judgment, if it be uncharitable; and therefore shall always chuse (if we do err) to err on the milder and more merciful part, and rather to retain those in our Communion which deserve to be ejected, than eject those that deserve to be retained.

34. Lastly, whereas you say, that *seeing Protestants differ about the point of Justification, you must needs infer that they want unity in faith, and consequently all faith, and then that they cannot agree what points are fundamental*: I Answer, to the first of these inferences, that as well might you infer it upon *Victor* Bishop of *Rome* and *Policrates*; upon *Stephen* Bishop of *Rome* and S. *Cyprian*: inasmuch as it is undeniably evident, that what one of those esteemed necessary to salvation the other esteemed not so. But points of Doctrin (as all other things) are as they are, and not as they are esteemed: neither can a necessary point be made unnecessary by being so accounted, nor an unnecessary point be made necessary by being overvalued. But as the ancient Philosophers, (whose different opinions about the soul of man you may read in *Aristotle de Anima*, and *Cicero's Tusculan Questions,*) notwithstanding their divers opinions touching the nature of the soul, yet all of them had souls, and souls of the same nature: Or as those Physicians who dispute whether the brain or heart be the principal part of a man, yet all of them have brains and have hearts, and herein agree sufficiently: So likewise, though some Protestants esteem that Doctrin the soul of the Church, which others do not so highly value, yet this hinders not but that which is indeed the soul of the Church may be in both sorts of them; and though one account that a necessary truth which others account neither necessary nor perhaps true, yet this notwithstanding, in those Truths which are truly and really necessary they may all agree. For no Argument can be more sophistical than this: They differ in some points which they esteem necessary; Therefore they differ in some that indeed and in truth are so.

35. Now

35. Now as concerning the other inference, *That they cannot agree what points are fundamental:* I have said and proved formerly that there is no such necessity as you imagin or pretend, that men should certainly know what is, and what is not fundamental. They that believe all things plainly delivered in Scripture, believe all things fundamental, and are at sufficient Unity in matters of Faith, though they cannot precisely and exactly distinguish between what is fundamental and what is profitable: nay though by error they mistake some vain, or perhaps hurtful opinions for necessary and fundamental Truths. Besides, I have shewed above, that as Protestants do not agree (for you over-reach in saying they cannot) touching what points are fundamental; so neither do you agree what points are defined and so to be accounted, and what are not: nay, nor concerning the subject in which God hath placed this pretended Authority of defining: some of you setling it in the Pope himself, though alone without a Council: Others in a Council, though divided from the Pope: Others only in the conjunction of Council and Pope: Others not in this neither, but in the acceptation of the present Church Universal: Lastly, others not attributing it to this neither, but only to the perpetual Succession of the Church of all Ages: of which divided Company it is very evident and undeniable, that every former may be and are obliged to hold many things defined and therefore necessary, which the latter, according to their own grounds, have no obligation to do, nay cannot do so upon any firm and sure and infallible foundation.

Cap. 3. §. 53. & alibi.

FINIS.

OUT OF
Mr. *Chillingworth's* Manuscript.

A LETTER TO
Mr. LEWGAR,
CONCERNING THE
𝕮𝖍𝖚𝖗𝖈𝖍 𝖔𝖋 𝕽𝖔𝖒𝖊𝖘
Being the Guide of Faith and Judge of Controversies.

Good Mr. LEWGAR,

Though I am resolved not to be much afflicted for the loss of that which is not in my power to keep, yet I cannot deny, but the loss of a friend goes very near unto my heart: and by this name of a friend, I did presume till of late, that I might have called you, because, though perhaps for want of power and opportunity, I have done you no good office, yet I have been always willing and ready to do you the best service I could: and therefore I cannot but admire at that affected strangeness which, in your last Letter to me, you seem to take upon you, renouncing in a manner all relation to me, and tacitly excommunicating me from all interest in you: the *Superscription* of your Letter

Letter is to Mr. *William Chillingworth*, and your *Subscription John Lewgar*, as if you either disdained or made a conscience of stiling me your friend, or your self mine. If this proceed from passion and weakness, I pray mend it; if from reason I pray shew it: If you think me one of those to whom Saint *John* forbids you to say *God save you*, then you are to think and prove me one of those Deceivers which deny Christ Jesus to be *come in the flesh*. If you think me an Heretick and therefore to be avoided, you must prove me αὐτοκατάκριτον, condemned by my own judgment; which I know I cannot, and therefore I think you cannot: If you say I *do not hear the Church*, and therefore am to be esteemed an *Heathen* or *Publican*; you are to prove that by the Church there is meant the Church of *Rome*: and yet when you have done so, I hope Christians are not forbidden to shew humanity and civility, even to *Pagans*: for Gods sake, Mr. *Lewgar*, free your self from this blind zeal, at least for a little space; and consider with reason and moderation what strange crime you can charge me with, that should deserve this strange usage, especially from you: Is it a crime to endeavour with all my understanding to find your Religion true, and to make my self a believer of it, and not be able to do so? Is it a crime to imploy all my reason upon the justification of the Infallibility of the *Roman* Church, and to find it impossible to be justified? I will call God to witness, who knows my heart better than you do, that I have evened the scale of my judgment as much as possibly I could, and have not willingly allowed any one grain of worldly motives on either side; but have weighed the Reasons for your Religion and against with such indifference, as if there were nothing in the world but God and my self; and is it my fault, that that scale goes down which hath the most weight in it? that that building falls, which has a false foundation? have you such power over your understanding, that you can believe what you please, though you see no reason, or that you can suspend your belief when you do see reason? If you have, I pray for our old friend-

friendships sake teach me that trick; but until I have learnt it, I pray blame me not for going the ordinary way; I mean for believing or not believing as I see reason: If you can convince me of wilful opposition against the known truth, of negligence in seeking it, of unwillingness to find it, of preferring temporal respects before it, or of any other fault, which is in my power to amend, that is indeed a fault, if I amend it not, be as angry with me as you please. But to impute to me involuntary errors; or that I do not see that which I would see, but cannot; or that I will not profess that which I do not believe; certainly this is far more unreasonable error, than any which you can justly charge me with; for let me tell you, the imputing *Socinianism* to me, whosoever was the author of it, was a wicked and groundless slander.

Perhaps you will say, for this is the usual song on that side, that pride is a voluntary fault, and with this I am justly chargeable for forsaking that guide which God has appointed me to follow: But what if I forsook it, because I thought I had reason to fear, it was one of those blind guides which whosoever blindly follows, is threatned by our Saviour that both he and his guide shall fall into the Ditch; then I hope you will grant it was not pride, but Conscience that moved me to do so; for as it is wise humility to obey those whom God hath set over me, so it is sinful credulity to follow every man or every Church, that without warrant will take upon them to guide me: shew me then some good and evident title which the Church of *Rome* has to this office, produce but one reason for it which upon trial will not finally be resolved and vanish into uncertainties; and if I yield not unto it, say if you please I am as proud as Lucifer: in the mean time give me leave to think it strange and not far from a Prodigee, that this Doctrin of the *Roman* Churches being the guide of faith, if it be true doctrin, should either not be known to the four Evangelists, or if it were known to them, that being wise and good men, they should either
be

be so envious of the Churches happiness; or so forgetful of the work they took in hand, which was to write the Gospel of Christ, as that not so much as one of them should mention so much as once, this so necessary part of the Gospel, without the belief whereof there is no salvation, and with the belief whereof, unless men be snatcht away by sudden death, there is hardly any damnation. It is evident they do all of them, with one consent, speak very plainly of many things of no importance in comparison hereof: and is it credible or indeed possible that with one consent or rather conspiracy, they should be so deeply silent concerning this *unum necessarium*? You may believe it if you can, for my part I cannot, unless I see demonstration for it: for if you say they send us to the Church, and consequently to the Church of *Rome*: this is to suppose that which can never be proved, that the Church of *Rome* is the only Church; and without this supposal, upon Division of the Church, I am as far to seek for a guide of my Faith as ever. As for example,

In that great division of the Church when the whole world wondred, saith Saint *Hierom*, that it was become *Arrian*: when *Liberius* Bishop of *Rome* (as S. *Athanasius*, and S. *Hilary* testifie) subscribed their Heresie, and joyned in Communion with them: Or in the division between the *Greek* and the *Roman* Church, about the procession of the Holy Ghost, when either side was the Church to it self, and each part Heretical and Schismatical to the other; what direction could I then an ignorant man have found from that Text of Scripture, *Unless he hear the Church, let him be to thee as a Heathen or a Publican*: or *Upon this Rock will I build my Church and the Gates of Hell shall not prevail against it*.

Again, give me leave to wonder, that neither S. *Paul* writing to the *Romans* should so much as intimate this their priviledge of Infallibility, but rather on the contrary put them in fear in the eleventh Chapter, that they as well as the Jews were in danger of falling away.

That

That Saint *Peter*, the pretended Bishop of *Rome*, writing two Catholick Epistles, mentioning his departure, should not once acquaint the Christians whom he writes to, what guide they were to follow, after he was taken from them.

That the writers of the New Testament, should so frequently forewarn men of Hereticks, false Chrifts, false prophets, and not once arm them against them, with letting them know this onely sure means of avoiding their danger.

That so great a part of the New Testament should be imployed about Antichrist, and so little or indeed none at all, about the Vicar of Christ, and the guide of the faithful.

That our Saviour should leave this onely means for the ending of Controversies, and yet speak so obscurely and ambiguously of it, that now our Judge is the greatest Controversie, and the greatest hinderance of ending them.

That there should be better evidence in the Scripture to intitle the *King* to this Office who disclaims it, than the *Pope* who pretends it.

That S. *Peter* should not ever exercise over the Apostles, any one act of Jurisdiction, nor they ever give him any one Title of Authority over them.

That if the Apostles did know S. *Peter* was made head over them, when our Saviour said, *Thou art Peter,* &c. they should still contend who should be the first; and that our Saviour should never tell them S. *Peter* was the man.

That S. *Paul* should say, he was in nothing inferiour to the very chief Apostles.

That the Catechumenists in the primitive Church should never be taught this foundation of their Faith, that the Church of *Rome* was Guide of their Faith.

That the Fathers, *Tertullian*, S. *Hierom* and *Optatus*, when they flew highest in commendation of the *Roman* Church, should attribute no more to her than to all other Apostolical Churches.

That

That in the Controverfie about *Easter*, the Bifhops and Churches of *Afia*, fhould be fo ill Catechifed as not to know this Principle of Chriftian Religion——The neceffity of Conformity in Doctrin with the Church of *Rome*. That they fhould never be preffed with any fuch neceffity of conformity in all things, but onely with the Tradition of the Weftern Churches in that point.

That *Irenæus* and many other Bifhops (notwithftanding *ad hanc Ecclefiam neceffe eft omnem convenire Ecclefiam*) fhould not yet think that a neceffary Doctrin, nor a fufficient ground of Excommunication, which the Church of *Rome* thought to be fo.

That S. *Cyprian* and the Bifhops of *Africk*, fhould be fo ill inftructed in their Faith, as not to know this foundation of it. That they likewife were never urged with any fuch neceffity of Conformity with the Church of *Rome*, nor ever charged with herefie or error for denying it.

That when *Liberius* joyned in Communion with the *Arrians* and fubfcribed their herefie, the *Arrians* then fhould not be the Church, and the Guide of Faith.

That never any Hereticks for three Ages after Chrift, were preffed with this Argument of the Infallibility of the prefent Church of *Rome*, or charged with denyal of it, as a diftinct Herefie; fo that *Æneas Sylvius* fhould have caufe to fay, *Ante tempora Concilii Niceni, quifq; fibi vivebat, & parvus refpectus habebatur ad Ecclefiam Romanam*. That the Ecclefiaftical Story of thofe times mentions no Acts of Authority of the Church of *Rome* over other Churches; as if there fhould be a Monarchy, and the Kings for fome Ages together fhould exercife no act of Jurifdiction in it.

That to fupply this defect, the Decretal Epiftles fhould be fo impudently forged, which in a manner fpeak nothing elfe but *Reges & Monarchas*; I mean, the Popes making Laws for exercifing authority over all other Churches.

That the *African* Churches in S. *Auftins* time fhould be ignorant that the Pope was Head of the Church and Judge of Appeals *jure divino*; and that there was a neceffity cessity of Conformity with the Church, in this and all other points of Doctrin.

Nay that the *Popes* themselves should be so ignorant of the true ground of this their Authority, as to pretend to it, not upon Scripture or universal Tradition, but upon an imaginary pretended none-such Canon of the Council of *Nice*.

That *Vincentius Lirinensis* seeking for a guide of his Faith and a preservative from Heresie, should be ignorant of this so ready one, The Infallibility of the Church of *Rome*.

All these things and many more are very strange to me, if the Infallibility of the *Roman* Church be indeed and were always by Christians acknowledged the foundation of our Faith: And therefore I beseech you pardon me, if I choose to build mine, upon one that is much firmer and safer, and lies open to none of these objections, which is Scripture and universal Tradition; and if one that is of this Faith may have leave to do so; I will subscribe with hand and heart,

Your very loving and true Friend

W. C.

A TABLE

A TABLE OF Contents.

Note that the first Figure refers to the Chapter, the other to the divisions of each Chapter.

A.

Protestants *agree* in more things than they differ in, by believing the Scripture. *chap.* 4. *div.* 49. 50.

We have as many rational means of *Agreement* as the Papists. *c.* 3. 7, 8.

Papists pretend to means of *agreement*, and do not agree. *c.* 3. 3,4,5,6.

Not necessary to find a Church *agreeing* with Protestants in all points. Ans. pref. 19. & *c.* 5. 27.

Antiquity vainly pleaded for *Romish* Doctrins and Practices, since many Errors are more ancient than some of their Doctrins. *c.* 5. 91.

The *Apostolick* Church an Infallible Guide to which we may resort, being present to us by her Writings. *c.* 3. 69, 80.

That the Church has power to make new *Articles* of Faith, asserted by the *Romish* Doctors. *c.* 4. 18.

This one *Article*, I *believe the Roman Catholick Church to be Infallible*, if their Doctrin were true, would secure against heresie, more than the whole Creed. *c.* 4. 77, 78, 79, 83.

Christs *assistance* promised to the Church, to lead her into more than necessary truths. *c.* 5. 61, 62.

Atheism and irreligion springs easily from some *Romish* Doctrins and Practices. Pref. 7, 8.

A Table of Contents.

S. *Austins* saying, *Evangelio non crederem*, &c. how to be understood. *c.* 2. 54, 97, 98, 99.

S. *Austins* Testimony against the *Donatists*, not cogent against *Protestants*. *c.* 2. 163.

S. *Austins* words, *No necessity to divide unity*, explained. *c.* 5. 10.

The *Authors* vindication from suspition of Heresie, *Pref.* 28.

The *Authors* motives to turn a Papist, with answers to them. *Pref.* 42. 43.

B.

The *Bible* which is the Religion of Protestants, to be preferred before the way of *Romish* Religion, shewed at large. *c.* 6. from 56. to 72. Inclusive.

C.

The *Calvinists* rigid Doctrin of Predetermination, unjustly reproached by Papists, who communicate with those that hold the same. *c.* 7. 30.

To give a *Catalogue* of our Fundamentals not necessary nor possible. *Ans. Pref.* 27. & *c.* 3. 13, 53.

Want of such a *Catalogue*, leaves us not uncertain in our Faith. *c.* 3. 14.

Papists as much bound to give a *Catalogue* of the Churches proposals, which are their Fundamentals, and yet do it not. *c.* 3. 53.

Our general *Catalogue* of Fundamentals as good as theirs. *c.* 4. 12. *c.* 7. 35.

Moral *certainty* a sufficient Foundation of Faith. *c.* 2. 154.

A Protestant may have *certainty*, though disagreeing Protestants all pretend to like certainty. *c.* 7. 13.

What *Charity* Papists allow to us Protestants, and we to them. *c.* 1. 1, 3, 4, 5.

A *Charitable* judgment should be made of such as err, but lead good lives. *c.* 7. 33.

Protestant *Charity* to Ignorant Papists; no comfort to them that will not see their errors. *c.* 5. 76.

The *Church* how furnished with means to determin Controversies. *c.* 1. 7, 11.

Commands in Scripture to hear the Church and obey it, suppose it not infallible. *c.* 3. 41.

We may be a *true Church*, though deriving Ordination and receiving Scripture from a false one. *c.* 6. 54.

Common truths believed, may preserve them good that otherwise err. *c.* 7. 33.

Conscience in some cases will justifie separation, though every pretence of it will not. *c.* 5. 108.

Concord in damned errors, worse than disagreement in controverted points *c.* 5. 72.

The *Consequences* of mens Opinions, may be unjustly charged upon them. *c.* 1. 12. *c.* 7. 30.

What *Contradictions* Papists believe, who hold Transubstantiation. *c.* 4. 46.

All

A Table of Contents.

All *Controversies* in Religion not necessary to be determined. *c.* 1.7,156. & *c.* 3.88.

How *Controversies* about Scripture it self are to be decided. *c.* 2. 27.

Controversies not necessary to be decided by a Judicial sentence, without any appeal. *c.* 2. 85.

That the *Creed* contains all necessary points, and how to be understood. *c.* 4. 23, 73, 74.

Not necessary that our *Creed* should be larger than that of the Apostles. *c.* 4. 67, 70, 71, 72.

Whether it be contrary to the *Creed*, to say the Church may fail. *c.* 5. 31.

D.

S *Dennis* of *Alexandria's* saying explained, about not dividing the Church. *c.* 5. 12.

To *deny* a Truth witnessed by God, whether always damnable —— *Ans. Pref.* 9.

The Apostles *depositing* Truth with the Church, no argument that she should always keep it sincere and intire. *c.* 2. 148.

Of *Disagreeing* Protestants, though one side must err, yet both may hope for salvation. *Ans. Pref.* 22. & *c.* 1. 10, 13, 17.

Two may *disagree* in a matter of faith, and yet neither be chargeable with denying a declared Truth of Gods. *Ans. Pref.* 10.

Differences among Protestants vainly objected against them. *c.* 3.2; 3.5. & *c.* 5. 72.

No reason to reproach them for their *differences* about necessary Truths and damnable Errors. *c.* 3. 52.

What is requisite to convince a man that a *Doctrin* comes from God. *Ans. Pref.* 8.

Believing the *Doctrin* of Scripture, a man may be saved, though he did not believe it to be the word of God. *c.* 2. 159.

The *Donatists* error about the Catholick Church, what it was and was not. *c.* 3. 64.

The *Donatists* case and ours not alike. *c.* 5. 103.

The *Roman* Church guilty of the *Donatists* Error, in perswading men as good not to be Christians, as not *Roman* Catholicks. *c.* 3. 64.

Papists liker to the *Donatists* than we, by their uncharitable denying salvation out of their Church. *c.* 7. 21, 22, 27.

E.

English Divines vindicated from inclining to Popery, and for want of skill in School-Divinity. *Pref.* 19.

How *Errors* may be damnable. *Ans. Pref.* 22.

In what case *Errors* damnable, may not damn those that hold them. *c.* 5. 58. & *c.* 6. 14.

In what case *Errors* not damnable, may be damnable to those that hold them. *c.* 5. 66.

A Table of Contents.

No man to be reproached for quitting his *Errors*. *c.* 5. 103.
Though we may pardon the *Roman* Church for her *Errors*, yet we may not sin with it. *c.* 5. 70.
Errors of the *Roman* Church that endanger salvation to be forsaken, though they are not destructive of it. *c.* 7. 6.
Erring persons that lead good lives, should be judged of charitably. *c.* 7. 33.
A man may learn of the Church to confute its *Errors*. *c.* 3. 40.
We did well to forsake the *Roman* Church for her *Errors*, though we afterwards may err out of it. *c.* 5. 63, 64, 65, 67, 87, 92.
We must not adhere to a Church in professing the least *Errors*, lest we should not profess with her necessary Doctrin. *c.* 3. 56.
The *Examples* of those that forsaking Popish Errors, have denied necessary Truths, no Argument against Protestants. *c.* 3. 63.
External Communion of a Church may be left without leaving a Church. *c.* 5. 32, 45, 47.

F.

Whether *Faith* be destroyed, by denying a Truth testified by God. *Ans.* Pref. 25. *c.* 6. 49. *c.* 7. 19.
The Objects of *Faith* of two sorts, essential and occasional. *c.* 4. 3.
Certainty of *Faith* less than the highest degree, may please God and save a man. *c.* 1. 8. & 6. 3, 4, 5.
Faith less than infallibly certain may resist temptations & difficulties. *c.* 6. 5.
There may be *Faith* where the Church and its infallibility begets it not. *c.* 2. 49.
Faith does not go before Scripture, but follows its efficacy. *c.* 2. 48.
Protestants have sufficient means to know the certainty of their *Faith* *c.* 2. 152.
In the *Roman* Church, the last resolution of *Faith* is into Motives of Credibility. *c.* 2. 154.
The *Fathers* declared their Judgment of Articles, but did not require their declarations to be received under Anathema. *c.* 4. 18.
Protestants did not *forsake* the Church, though they forsook its errors. *c.* 3. 11.
Sufficient *Foundation* for faith without infallible certainty. *c.* 6. 6, 45.
What Protestants mean by *Fundamental Doctrins*. *c.* 4. 52.
In what sense the Church of *Rome* errs not *Fundamentally*. *Ans.* Pref. 20.
To be unerring in *Fundamentals*, can be said of no Church of one denomination. *c.* 3. 55.
To say that there shall be always a Church not erring in *Fundamentals*, is to say that there shall be always a Church. *c.* 3. 55.
A Church is not safe, though retaining *Fundamentals*, when it builds hay and stubble on the foundation, and neglects to reform her Errors. *c.* 5. 61.
Ignorance of what points in particular are *fundamental*, does not make it uncertain whether we do not err fundamentally, or differ in fundamentals among our selves. *c.* 7. 14.

A Table of Contents.

G.

The four *Gospels* contain all necessary Doctrins. *c.* 4.40,41,42,43.
An *Infallible Guide* not necessary for avoiding Heresie. *c.* 2. 127.
The Apostolick Church an *Infallible Guide* to which we may resort. *c.* 3.69.
The Church may not be an *Infallible Guide* in fundamentals, though it be infallible in fundamentals. *c.* 3.39.
That the *Roman* Church should be the only *infallible Guide* of Faith, and the Scriptures say nothing concerning it, is incredible. *c.* 6. 20.

H.

The difference betwixt *Heresie* and Schism. *c.* 5. 51.
There are no New *Heresies*, no more than new Articles of Faith. *c.* 4. 18,37,38.
Separation from the Church of *Rome* no mark of *Heresie* by the Fathers, whose Citations are answered. *c.* 6.22,23,24,25,26,27,2 ,30,31,33,34.
No mark of *Heresie* to want succession of Bishops, holding the same Doctrin. *c.* 6.18,41.
We are not *Hereticks* for opposing things propounded by the Church of *Rome* for divine Truth. *c.* 6. 11, 12.
Whether Protestants Schismatically cut off the *Roman* Church from hopes of salvation. *c.* 5. 38.

I.

The *Jewish Church* had no *Infallibility* annexed to it, and if it had, there is no necessity that the Christian Church should have it. *c.* 2. 141.
The *Imposing* a necessity of professing known errors, and practising known corruptions, is a just cause of separating from a Church. *c.* 5. 31,36,40,50,59,60,68,69.
Indifferency to all Religions falsely charged upon Protestants. *Ans. Pref.* 3. & *c.* 3. 12.
The belief of the Churches *Infallibility* makes way for Heresie. *Pref.* 10.
An *Infallible Guide* not needful for avoiding Heresies. *c.* 2. 127.
The Churches *Infallibility* has not the same Evidence, as there is for the Scriptures. *c.* 3. 30, 31.
The Churches *Infallibility* can no way be better assured to us, than the Scriptures incorruption. *c.* 2.25. & *c.* 3. 27.
The Churches *Infallibility* is not proved from the promise that *the Gates of Hell shall not prevail against it.* c. 3. 70.
Nor from the promise of the *Spirits leading into all Truth*, which was made onely to the Apostles. *c.* 3. 71, 72.
The Churches infallibility not proved from *Ephes.*4.11,12,13. *He gave some Apostles* &c. *till we all come in the Unity of the Faith*, &c. *c.*3. 79, 80.
That God has appointed an *Infallible Judge* of Controversies, because such a one is desirable and useful, is a weak conclusion. *c.*2. from 128. to 136. inclusive.
Infallibility in fundamentals, no warrant to adhere to a Church in all that she proposes. *c.* 3. 57.

A Table of Contents.

Infallible interpretations of Scripture vainly boasted of by the *Roman* Church. *c.* 2. 93, 94, 95.

Whether the denial of the Churches *Infallibility* leaves men to their private spirit, reason and discourse, and what is the harm of it. *Pref.* 12. 13. & *c.* 2. 110.

Traditional *Interpretations* of Scripture how ill preserved. *c.* 2. 10.

Interpretations of Scripture which private men make for themselves (not pretending to prescribe their sense to others) though false or seditious, endanger onely themselves. *c.* 2. 122.

Allow the Pope or *Roman* Church to be a decisive *Interpreter* of Christs Laws, and she can evacuate them, and make what Laws she pleases. *Pref.* 10. 11. & *c.* 2. 1.

S. *Irenæus*'s account of Tradition favours not Popery. *c.* 2. 144, 145, 146.

His saying that no Reformation can countervail the danger of a Schism, explained. *c.* 5. 11.

A living *Judge* to end Controversies about the sense of Scripture, not necessary. *c.* 2. 12, 13.

If Christ had intended such a *Judge* in Religion, he would have named him, which he has not done. *c.* 2. 23. *c.* 3. 69. *c.* 6. 20.

Though a living *Judge* be necessary to determin Civil causes, yet not necessary for Religious causes. *c.* 2. from 14. to 22. inclus.

If there be a *Judge* of Controversies, no necessity it should be the *Roman* Church. *c.* 3. 69.

Roman Catholicks set up as many Judges in Religion as Protestants. *c.* 2. 116, 118, 153.

A *Judgment of discretion* must be allowed to every man for himself, about Religion. *c.* 2. 11.

The Protestant Doctrin of *Justification*, taken altogether, not a licentious doctrin. *c.* 7. 30.

When they say they are *justified by faith alone*, yet they make good works necessary to salvation. *c.* 7. 30.

K.

Our obligation to *know* any divine truth, arises from Gods manifest revealing it. *c.* 3. 19.

L.

How we are assured in what *Language* the Scripture is uncorrupted. *c.* 2. 55, 56, 57.

To *leave* a Church, and to leave the external Communion of a Church, is not the same thing. *c.* 5. 32, 45, 47.

Luthers separation not like that of the *Donatists*, and why. *c.* 5. 33. 101.

Luther and his followers did not divide from the whole Church, being a part of it, but onely reformed themselves, forsaking the corrupt part. *c.* 5. 56.

Luthers opposing himself to all in his reformation, no objection against him. *c.* 5. 89, 90.

We are not bound to justifie all that *Luther* said and did, no more than Papists are bound to justifie what several Popes have said and done. *c.* 5. 112.

M.

A Table of Contents.

M.

They may be *members* of the Catholick Church, that are not united in external Communion. *c.* 5. 9.
The Proteſtant Doctrin of *Merit* explained. *c.* 4. 35, 36.
The Authors *Motives* to change his Religions, with Anſwers to them. Pref. 42. 43.
The Faith of Papiſts reſolved at laſt into the *Motives* of Credibility. *c.* 2. 154.
The *Miſchiefs* that followed the Reformation, not imputable to it. *c.* 5. 92.

N.

What make points *neceſſary* to be believed. *c.* 4. 4, 11. No more is *neceſſary* to be believed by us, than by the Apoſtles. *c.* 4. 67, 70, 71, 72.
Papiſts make many things *neceſſary* to ſalvation, which God never made ſo. *c.* 7. 7.
All *neceſſary* points of Faith are contained in the Creed. *c.* 4. 73, 74.
Why ſome points not ſo *neceſſary* were put into the Creed. *c.* 4. 75, 76.
Proteſtants may agree in *neceſſary* points, though they may overvalue ſome things they hold. *c.* 7. 34.
To impoſe a *neceſſity* of profeſſing known errors, and practiſing known corruptions, is a juſt cauſe of ſeparation. *c.* 5. 31, 36, 40, 50, 59, 60, 68, 69.

O.

A blind *obedience* is not due to Eccleſiaſtical deciſions, though our practiſe muſt be determined by the ſentence of ſuperiours in doubtful caſes. *c.* 5. 110.
A probable *opinion* may be followed (according to the *Roman* Doctors) though it be not the ſafeſt way for avoiding ſin. *c.* 7. 8.
Optatus's ſaying impertinently urged againſt Proteſtants. *c.* 5. 99, 100.
Though we receive *Ordination* and Scripture from a falſe Church, yet we may be a true Church. *c.* 6. 54.

P.

Whether *Papiſts* or *Proteſtants* moſt hazard their ſouls on probabilities. *c.* 4. 57.
What we believe concerning the *Perpetuity* of the Viſible Church. Anſ. Pref. 18.
Whether 1 Tim. 3. 15. *The Pillar and ground of Truth*, belong to *Timothy* or to the Church. *c.* 3. 76.
If thoſe words belong to the Church, whether they may not ſignifie her duty, and yet that ſhe may err in neglecting it. *c.* 3. 77.
A *poſſibility* of being deceived, argues not an uncertainty in all we believe. *c.* 3. 26, 50, *c.* 5. 107. *c.* 6. 47.
By joyning in the *Prayers* of the *Roman* Church, we muſt joyn in her unlawful practices. *c.* 3. 11.
Preaching of the Word and adminiſtring the Sacrament, how they are inſeparable notes of the Church, and how they make it viſible. *c.* 5. 19.

A Table of Contents.

Private Spirit, how we are to understand it. *c.* 2. 110.

Private Spirit is not appealed to (*i. e.* to dictates pretending to come from Gods spirit) when Controversies are referred to Scripture. *c.*2.110.

Whether one is left to his *private* spirit, reason and discourse, by denying the Churches infallibility, and the harm of it. *Pref.*12,13. & *c.* 2.110.

A mans *private judgment* may be opposed to the publick, when Reason and Scripture warrant him. *c.* 5. 109.

A *probable opinion*, according to the *Roman* Doctors, may be followed, though it is not the safest way for avoiding sin. *c.* 7. 8.

It's hard for Papists to resolve, what is a *sufficient proposal* of the Church. *c.* 3. 54.

Protestants are on the surer side for avoiding sin, and *Papists* on the more dangerous side to commit sin, shewed in instances. *c.* 7. 9.

R.

Every man by *Reason* must judge both of Scripture and the Church. *c.* 2. 111, 112, 113, 118, 120, 122.

Reason and judgment of discretion, is not to be reproached for the private spirit. *c.* 2. 110.

If men must not follow their *Reason*, what they are to follow. *c.*2.114,115.

Some kind of *Reformation* may be so necessary, as to justifie separation from a corrupt Church, though every pretence of reformation will not. *c.* 5. 53.

Nothing is more against *Religion*, than using violence to introduce it. *c.* 5. 96.

The *Religion* of Protestants (which is the belief of the Bible) a wiser and safer way than that of the *Roman* Church, shewed at large. *c.* 6. from 56. to 72. Inclus.

All Protestants require *Repentance* to remission of sins, and remission of sins to Justification. *c.* 7. 31.

No *Revelations* known to be so, may be rejected as not Fundamental. *c.* 4. 11.

A Divine *revelation* may be ignorantly disbelieved by a Church, and yet it may continue a Church. *c.* 3. 20.

Things equally *revealed*, may not be so to several persons. *c.* 3. 24.

Papists cannot have *Reverence* for the Scripture, whilst they advance so many things contrary to it. *c.* 2. 1.

No argument of their *reverence* to it, that they have preserved it intire. *c.* 2. 2.

The *Roman Church*, when *Luther* separated, was not *the visible Church*, though a *visible* Church, and part of the Catholick. *c.* 5. 26, 27.

The present *Roman Church* has lost all Authority to recommend what we are to believe in Religion. *c.* 2. 101.

The properties of a *perfect Rule*. *c.* 2. 5. 6, 7.

Whether the Popish *Rule* of Fundamentals, or ours is the safest. *c.* 4. 63.

S.

Right administration of *Sacraments* uncertain in the *Roman* Church. *c.* 2. from 63. to 68. inclusive.

A Table of Contents.

In what sense *Salvation* may be had in the *Roman* Church. *Ans.Pref.* 5,7.
Salvation depends upon great uncertainties in the *Roman* Church. *c.* 2. from 63. to 73. inclus.
Schisms whence they chiefly arise, and what continues them. *c.* 4. 17.
Schism may be a Division of the Church, as well as from it. *c.* 5. 22.
He may be no *Schismatick*, that forsakes a Church for Errors not damnable. *Ans. Pref.* 2.
No *Schism* to leave a corrupted Church, when otherwise we must communicate in her corruptions. *c.* 5. 25.
Not every separation from the external Communion of the Church, but a causeless one, is the sin of *Schism*. *c.* 5. 30.
They may not be *Schismaticks* that continue the separation from *Rome*, though *Luther* that began it, had been a *Schismatick*. *c.* 5. 4. & *c.* 6. 14.
The *Scripture* cannot be duly reverenced by Papists. *c.* 2. n. 1.
The *Scripture* how proved to be the word of God. *c.* 4. 53.
The Divine Authority of the *Scripture* may be certain, though it be not self-evidently certain, that it is Gods word. *c.* 6. 51.
Books of *Scripture* now held for Canonical, which the *Roman* Church formerly rejected. *c.* 2. 90, 91.
Whether some Books of *Scripture* defined for Canonical, were not afterward rejected. *c.* 3. 29.
The *Scripture* in things necessary is intelligible to learned and unlearned. *c.* 2. 104, 105, 106.
Some Books of *Scripture* questioned by the Fathers as well as by Protestants. *c.* 2. 34.
The *Scripture* has great Authority from internal Arguments. *c.* 2. 47.
The Truth of *Scripture* inspiration depends not on the authority of the *Roman* Church. Pref. 14. & *c.* 6. 45.
If the *Scriptures* contain all necessary truths, Popery is confuted. *Pref.* 30. to 38. inclusive.
The true meaning of *Scripture* not uncertain in necessary points. *c.* 2. 84.
A determinate sense of obscure places of *Scripture*, is not needful. *c.* 2. 127, 150.
The sense of plain places of Scripture, may be known by the same means, by which the Papists know the sence of those places that prove the Church. *c.* 2. 150, 151.
God may give means to the Church to know the true sense of *Scripture*, yet it is not necessary it should have that sense. *c.* 2. 93.
It is easier to know the *Scripture* and its sense, than for the ignorant in the *Roman* Church which is the Church, and what are her decrees, and the sense of them. *c.* 2. 107, 108, 109.
In what Language the *Scripture* is incorrupted, and the assurance of it. *c.* 2. 55, 56, 57.
The *Scripture* is capable of the properties of a perfect Rule. *c.* 2. 7.
In what sense we say the *Scripture* is a perfect Rule of Faith. *c.* 2. 8.
The *Scripture* not properly a judge of Controversies, but a Rule to judge by. *c.* 2. 11, 104, 155.

A Table of Contents.

The *Scriptures* incorruption more secured by providence, than the *Roman* Churches vigilancy. *c.* 2. 24.

When *Scripture* is made the Rule of Controversies, those that concern it self are to be excepted. *c.* 2. 8, 27, 156.

The *Scripture* contains all necessary material objects of Faith, of which the Scripture it self is none, but the means of conveying them to us. *c.* 2. 32. 159.

The *Scripture* must determine some Controversies, else those about the Church and its Notes are undeterminable. *c.* 2. 3.

The *Scripture* unjustly charged with increasing Controversies and Contentions. *c.* 2. 4.

The *Scripture* is a sufficient means for discovering Heresies. *c.* 2. 127.

When Controversies are referred to Scripture, it is not referring them to the private spirit, understanding it of a perswasion pretending to come from the Spirit of God. *c.* 2. 110.

Protestants that believe *Scripture*, agree in more things than they differ in, and their differences are not material. *c.* 4. 49, 50.

Private men, if they interpret *Scriptures* amiss and to ill purposes, endanger only themselves, when they do not pretend to prescribe to others. *c.* 2. 122.

The Protestants *Security* of the way to happiness. *c.* 2. 53.

Want of Skill in *School-Divinity* foolishly objected against *English* Divines. *Pref.* 19.

The Principles of the Church of *Englands separating* from *Rome*, will not serve to justifie Schismaticks. *c.* 5. 71, 74, 80, 81, 82, 85, 86.

Socinianism and other Heresies countenanced by *Romish* Writers, who have undermined the Doctrin of the Trinity. *Pref.* 17. 18.

The promise of the *Spirits leading into all truth*, proves not Infallibility. *c.* 3. 71.

The promise of the *Spirits abiding with them for ever*, may be personal. *c.* 3. 74.

And it being a conditional promise, cuts off the *Roman* Churches pretence to infallibility. *c.* 3. 75.

Want of *Succession* of Bishops, holding always the same Doctrin, is not a mark of Heresie. *c.* 6. 38, 41.

In what sense *Succession* is by the Fathers made a mark of the true Church. *c.* 6. 40.

Papists cannot prove a perpetual *Succession* of Professors of their Doctrin. *c.* 6. 41.

T.

Tradition proves the Books of Scripture to be Canonical, not the Authority of the present Church. *c.* 2. 25, 53, 90, 91, 92. & *c.* 3. 27.

Traditional Interpretations of Scripture how ill preserved by the *Roman* Church. *c.* 2. 10. & *c.* 3. 46.

No *Traditional Interpretations* of Scripture, though if there were any remaining we are ready to receive them. *c.* 2. 88, 89. & *c.* 3. 46.

The *Traditions* distinct from Scripture which *Irenæus* mentions, do not favour Popery. *c.* 2. 144, 145, 146.

The asserting unwritten *Traditions*, though not inconsistent with the truth of Scripture, yet disparages it as a perfect Rule. *c.* 2. 10.

Though our *Translations* of the Bible are subject to error, yet our salvation is not thereby made uncertain. *c.* 2. 68, 73.

Different *Translations* of Scripture may as well be objected to the Ancient Church, as to Protestants. *c.* 2. 58, 59.

The Vulgar *Translation* is not pure and uncorrupted. *c.* 2. 75, 76, 77, 78, 79, 80.

To believe *Transubstantiation*, how many contradictions one must believe. *c.* 4. 46.

The Doctrin of the Trinity undermined by *Roman* Doctors. Pref. 17, 18.

The Church may *tolerate* many things, which she does not allow. *c.* 3. 47.

Gods *Truth* not questioned by Protestants, though they deny points professed by the Church. *c.* 1. 12.

Protestants question not Gods *Truth*, though denying some truth revealed by him, if they know it not to be so revealed. *c.* 3. 16.

The *Truth* of the present Church, depends not upon the visibility or perpetuity of the Church in all Ages. *c.* 5. 21. & *c.* 7. 20.

The Apostles depositing *Truth* with the Church, is no argument that she should always keep it intire and sincere. *c.* 2. 148.

The promise of being *led into all truth*, agrees not equally to the Apostles and to the Church. *c.* 3. 34.

A *Tryal* of Religion by Scripture, may well be refused by Papists. *c.* 2, 3.

U.

Violence and force to introduce Religion, is against the nature of Religion, and unjustly charged upon Protestants. *c.* 5. 96.

What *Visible Church* was before *Luther*, disagreeing from the *Roman*. Ans. Pref. 19. & *c.* 5. 27.

That there should be always a *visible* unerring Church, of one denomination, is not necessary. *c.* 5. 27.

The *Visible Church* may not cease, though it may cease to be visible. *c.* 5. 13, 14, 41.

The Church may not be *Visible* in the Popish sense, and yet may not dissemble but profess her faith. *c.* 5. 18.

The great *uncertainties* salvation in the *Roman* Church depends on. *c.* 2. 63. to 73. inclusive.

Their *uncertainty* of the right administration of Sacraments. *c.* 2. 63. to 68. inclusive.

The Churches *Unity*, by what means best preserved. *c.* 3. 81. *c.* 4. 13, 17, 40.

Pretence of Infallibility a ridiculous means to *Unity*, when that is the chief question to be determined. *c.* 3. 89.

Unity of Communion how to be obtained. *c.* 4. 39, 40.

A Table of Contents.

Unity of external Communion not necessary to the being a Member of the Catholick Church. *c.* 5. 9.

Universality of a Doctrin, no certain sign that it came from the Apostles. *c.* 3. 44.

Want of *Universality* of place, proves not Protestants to be Hereticks, and may as well be objected against the *Roman* Church. *c.* 6. 42, 55.

We would receive *unwritten Traditions* derived from the Apostles, if we knew what they were. *c.* 3. 46.

The *Vulgar Translation* not pure and incorrupted. *c.* 2. 75, 76, 77, 78, 79, 80.

W.

The *whole Doctrin* of Christ was taught by the Apostles, and an Anathema denounced against any that should bring in new doctrins. *c.* 4. 18.

The *wisdom* of Protestants justified, in forsaking the errors of the *Roman* Church. *c.* 6. 53, 54.

The wisdom of Protestants shewed at large against the Papists, in making the Bible their Religion. *c.* 6. from 56. to 72. inclusive.

F I N I S.

ADDITIONAL DISCOURSES OF Mr. Chillingworth NEVER BEFORE PRINTED.

Imprimatur.

Ex Ædib. Lambeth.
Jun. 14. 1686.

GUIL. NEEDHAM R R.
in Christo P. ac D. D. Wilhelmo
Archiep. Cant. à Sacr. Domesticis.

LONDON,
Printed for *Richard Chiswell* at the *Rose* and *Crown* in S. *Pauls* Church-Yard, 1687.

CONTENTS.

I. *A Conference betwixt Mr. Chillingworth and Mr. Lewgar, whether the Roman Church be the Catholick-Church, and all out of her Communion Hereticks or Schismaticks.* p. 1.

II. *A Discourse against the Infallibility of the Roman Church, with an Answer to all those Texts of Scripture that are alledged to prove it.* p. 26.

III. *A Conference concerning the Infallibility of the Roman Church; proving that the present Church of Rome either errs in her worshiping the Blessed Virgin; or that the Ancient Church did err in condemning the Collyridians as Hereticks.* p. 41.

IV. *An Argument drawn from Communicating of Infants, as without which they could not be saved against the Churches Infallibility.* p. 68.

V. *An Argument against Infallibility, drawn from the Doctrin of the Millenaries.* p. 80.

VI. *A Letter relating to the same subject.* p. 89.

VII.

CONTENTS.

VII. *An Argument against the* **Roman** *Churches Infallibility, taken from the Contradictions in their Doctrin of Transubstantiation.* p. 91.

VIII. *An account of what moved the Author to turn a Papist, with his Confutation of the Arguments that perswaded him thereto.* p. 94.

IX. *A Discourse concerning Tradition.* p. 103.

The Reader is desired to take notice of a great mistake of the Printer and to Correct it, That he has made this the running Title over most of the Additional Pieces, *viz.* *A Conference betwixt* Mr. *Chillingworth* and Mr. *Lewgar*; which should only have been set over the first: there are also some literal mistakes, as pag. 65. ἐνεργεῖν twice for ἐνεργεῖν and such like, not to be imputed to the Author.

A CON-

A CONFERENCE BETWIXT Mr. *CHILLINGWORTH* AND Mr. *LEWGAR.*

Thesis. THE Church of *Rome* (taken diffusively for all Christians communicating with the Bishop of *Rome*) was the Judge of Controversies at that time, when the Church of *England* made an alteration in her Tenents.

Argu. She was the Judge of Controversies at that time, which had an Authority of deciding them. But the Church of *Rome* at that time had the Authority of deciding them. Ergo.

Answ. A limited Authority to decide Controversies according to the Rule of Scripture and Universal Tradition, and to oblige her own Members (so long as she evidently contradicted not that Rule) to obedience I grant she had: but an unlimited, an infallible Authority, or such as could not but proceed according to that Rule, and such as should bind all the Churches in the World to Obedience (as the *Greek* Church) I say she had not.

Quest. When your Church hath decided a Controversie, I desire to know whether any particular Church or person hath Authority to reexamine her decision, whether she hath observed her Rule or no; and free himself from the obedience of it, by his or her particular judgment?

Answ. If you understand by your Church, the Church Catholick, probably I should answer no: but if you understand by your Church, that only which is in Subordination to the See of *Rome*, or if you understand a Council of this Church, I answer, yea.

Arg. That was the Catholick Church, which did abide in the Root of Apostolick Unity: But the Church of *Rome* at that time was the only Church that did abide in the Root of Apostolick Unity. *Ergo.*

Quest. What mean you by Apostolick Unity?

Answ. I mean the Unity of that Fellowship wherein the Apostles Lived and Died.

Quest. Wherein was this Unity?

Answ. Herein it consisted, that they all professed one Faith, obeyed one Supream Tribunal, and communicated together in the same Prayers and Sacraments.

Solut. Then the Church of *Rome* continued not in this Apostolick Unity; for it continued not in the same Faith, wherein the Apostles Lived and Died: for though it retained so much (in my judgment) as was essential to the being of a Church, yet it degenerated from the Church of the Apostles times, in many things which were very profitable; as in Latin Service, and Communion in one kind.

Argu. Some Church did continue in the same Faith wherein the Apostles lived and died: But there was no Church at that time which did continue in the Apostles Faith besides the *Roman* Church. *Ergo.*

Answ. That some Church did continue in the Apostles Faith in all things necessary, I grant it: that any did continue in the Integrity of it, and in a perfect conformity with it in all things expedient and profitable, I deny it.

Quest. Is it not necessary to a Churches continuing in the Apostles Faith, that she continue in a perfect conformity with it in all things expedient and profitable?

Answ. A perfect conformity in all things is necessary to a perfect continuance in the Apostles Faith; but to

an

an imperfect continuance, an imperfect conformity is sufficient; and such I grant the *Roman* Church had.

Quest. Is not a perfect continuance in the Apostles Faith necessary to a Churches continuance in Apostolick Unity?

Asw. It is necessary to a perfect continuance in Apostolick Unity.

Argu. There was some one company of Christians at the time of *Luthers* rising, which was the *Catholick Church*; But there was no other company at that time besides the *Roman*: *Ergo,* the *Roman* at that time was the *Catholick Church.*

Answ. There was no one company of Christians, which in opposition to and Exclusion of all other companies of Christians was the Catholick Church.

Argu. If the *Catholick Church* be some one company of Christians in opposition to and exclusion of all other companies, then if there was some one company, she was one in opposition to and exclusion of all other companies: But the *Catholick Church* is one company of Christians in opposition to and exclusion of, *&c.* *Ergo,* There was then some one company which was the *Catholick Church* in opposition to and exclusion of all other companies.

The *Minor* proved by the Testimonies of the Fathers, both Greek and Latin, testifying that they understood the Church to be *one* in the sense alledged.

1. If this Unity which cannot be separated at all or divided, is also among Hereticks, what contend we farther? Why call we them Hereticks, S. *Cypr. Epist.* 75.

2. But if there be but one Flock, how can he be accounted of the Flock, which is not within the number of it? *Id: Ibid.*

3. When *Parmenian* commends one Church, he condemns all the rest; for besides one, which is the true *Catholick,* other Churches are esteemed to be among Hereticks, but are not. S. *Optat. lib.* 1.

4. The Church therefore is but one, this cannot be among all Hereticks and Schismaticks. *Ibid.*

5. You

5. You say you offer for the Church, which is *one*; this very thing is part of a lie to call it one, which you have divided into two: *Id: Ibid*.

6. The Church is *one*, which cannot be amongst us and amongst you; it remains then, that it be in one only place. *Id: Ibid.*

7. Although there be many Heresies of Christians, and that all would be called *Catholicks*, yet there is always one Church, &c. *S. August. de util. credend. c. 7.*

8. The question between us is, where the Church is, whether with us or with them, for she is but *one. Id : de unitat. c. 2.*

9. The proofs of the *Catholick* prevailed, whereby they evicted the Body of Christ to be with them, and by consequence not to be with the *Donatists*; for it is manifest that she is *one* alone. *Id. Collat. Carthag. lib. 3.*

10. In illud cantic. 6. 7. *There are 60 Queens and 80 Concubines and Damosels without number, but my Dove is one*, &c. He said not, *my* Queens are 60, and *my Concubines*, &c. but he said my Dove is but one; because all the Sects of Philosophers and Heresies of Christians are none of his; his is but one, to wit, the *Catholick* Church, &c. *S. Epiphan. in fine Panar.*

11. A man may not call the Conventicles of Hereticks (I mean *Marcionites, Manichees*, and the rest) Churches; therefore the Tradition appoints you to say, *I believe one Holy Catholick Church*, &c. *S. Cyrill. Catech. 18.*

And these Testimonies I think are sufficient to shew the judgment of the Ancient Church, that this Title of the Church *one*, is directly and properly exclusive to all companies besides one; to wit, that where there are diverse professions of Faith, or diverse Communions, there is but one of these, which can be the *Catholick Church*. Upon this ground I desire some company of Christians to be named, professing a diverse Faith, and holding a diverse Communion from the *Roman*, which was the *Catholick Church* at the time of *Luthers* rising: and if no other in this sense can be named, than was she the *Catholick Church* at that time, and therefore her judgment to be rested in, and

Mr. Chillingworth *and Mr.* Lewgar.

and her Communion to be embraced upon peril of Schism and Heresie.

Mr. *Chillingworths* Answer.

Upon the same ground, if you pleased, you might desire a Protestant to name some Company of Christians, professing a diverse Faith, and holding a diverse Communion from the *Greek* Church, which was the Catholick Church at the time of *Luthers* rising; and seeing he could name no other in this sense, concludes that the *Greek* Church was the Catholick Church at that time. Upon the very same ground you might have concluded for the Church of the *Abyssines,* or *Armenians,* or any other society of Christians extant before *Luthers* time. And seeing this is so, thus I argue against your ground.

1. That ground which concludes indifferently for both parts of a contradiction, must needs be false and deceitful, and conclude for neither part: But this ground concludes indifferently both parts of a contradiction; *viz.* That the *Greek* Church is the Catholick Church, and not the *Roman,* as well as, That the *Roman* is the Catholick Church, and not the *Greek*: Therefore the ground is false and deceitful, seem it never so plausible.

2. I answer Secondly, that you should have taken notice of my Answer, which I then gave you; which was, that your *major,* as you then framed your Argument, but as now, your *minor* is not always true, if by *one* you understand *one* in external Communion; seeing nothing hindred in my Judgment, but that one Church excommunicated by another upon an insufficient cause, might yet remain a true member of the Catholick Church; and that Church, which upon the overvaluing this cause doth excommunicate the other, though in fault, may yet remain a member of the Catholick Church: which is evident from the difference about *Easter-day* between the Church of *Rome* and the Churches of *Asia*; for which vain matter *Victor* Bishop of *Rome* excommunicated the Churches of *Asia*. And yet I believe you will not say, that either the Church excommunicating, or the Church excommunicated, ceased

sed to be a true member of the Church Catholick. The case is the same between the *Greek* and the *Roman* Church; for though the difference between them be greater, yet it is not so great, as to be a sufficient ground of excommunication: and therefore the excommunication was causeless, and consequently *Brutum fulmen*, and not ratified or confirmed by God in Heaven; and therefore the Church of *Greece* at *Luthers* rising might be, and was a true member of the Catholick Church.

As concerning the places of Fathers, which you alledge; I demand, 1. If I can produce you an equal, or greater number of Fathers, or more ancient than these, not contradicted by any that lived with them or before them, for some doctrin condemned by the *Roman* Church, whether you will subscribe it? If not, with what face or conscience can you make use of, and build your whole Faith upon the Authority of Fathers in some things, and reject the same authority in others?

2. Secondly, because you urge S. *Cyprians* Authority, I desire you to tell me, whether this Argument in his time would have concluded a necessity of resting in the Judgement of the *Roman* Church, or no? If not, how should it come to pass, that it should serve now, and not then, fit this time and not that? as if it were like an Almanack, that would not serve for all Meridians? If it would, why was it not urged by others upon S. *Cyprian*, or represented by S. *Cyprian* to himself for his direction, when he differed from the *Roman* Church, and all other that herein conformed unto her, touching the point of Re-baptizing Hereticks; which the *Roman* Church held unlawful and damnable, S. *Cyprian* not only lawful, but necessary; so well did he rest in the Judgment of that Church: *Quid verba audiam, cùm facta videam*, says he in the Comedy? And Cardinal *Perron* tells you in his Epistle to *Casaubon*, that nothing is more unreasonable, than to draw consequences from the words of Fathers, against their lively and actual practice.

The same may be said in refutation of the places out of S. *Austin*; who was so far from concluding, from them or
any

Mr. Chillingworth *and Mr.* Lewgar.

any other, a neceſſity of reſting in the Judgment of the *Roman* Church, that he himſelf, as your Authors teſtifie, lived and died in oppoſition of it; even in that main fundamental point, upon which Mr. *Lewgar* hath built the neceſſity of his departure from the Church of *England*, and embracing the Communion of the *Roman* Church, that is, The Supream Authority of that Church over other Churches, and the power of receiving Appeals from them. Mr. *Lewgar*, I know, cannot be ignorant of theſe things; and therefore I wonder, with what conſcience he can produce their words againſt us, whoſe Actions are for us.

If it be ſaid, that S. *Cyprian* and S. *Auſtin* were Schiſmaticks for doing ſo; it ſeems then Schiſmaticks may not only be members of the Church, againſt Mr. *Lewgars* main concluſion, but Canoniz'd Saints of it; or elſe S. *Auſtin* and S. *Cyprian* ſhould be raſed out of the *Roman* Kalendar.

If it be ſaid, that the point of Re-baptization was not defined in S. *Cyprians* time; I ſay that in the Judgment of the Biſhop and Church of *Rome* and their adherents, it was: For they urged it as an Original and Apoſtolick Tradition, and conſequently at leaſt of as great force as any Church definition. They excommunicated *Firmilianus* and condemned S. *Cyprian*, as a falſe Chriſt, and a falſe Apoſtle, for holding the contrary; and urged him *Tyrannico terrore* to conform his judgment to theirs, as he himſelf clearly intimates.

If it be ſaid, they differed only from the particular Church of *Rome*, and not from the *Roman* Church, taking it for the univerſal ſociety of Chriſtians in Communion with that Church: I Anſwer,

1. They know no ſuch ſenſe of the word, I am ſure never uſed it in any ſuch; which whether it had been poſſible, if the Church of *Rome* had been in their judgment to other Churches in ſpiritual matters, as the City was to other Cities and Countries in temporals, I leave it to indifferent men to judge.

2. Secondly,

2. Secondly, that they differed not only from the particular *Roman* Church, but also from all other Churches, that agreed with it in those doctrins.

3. Thirdly, I desire you would answer me directly, whether the *Roman* Church, taking it for that particular Church, be of necessity to be held Infallible in Faith by every *Roman* Catholick, or not. To this Question I instantly desire a direct answer without tergiversation, that we may at length get out of the cloud, and you may say, *Coram, quem quæritis, adsum.* If you say, they are not bound to believe so; then it is no Article of Faith, nor no certain truth upon which men may safely rest without fluctuation or fear of error: And if so; I demand

1. Why are all your Clergy bound to swear, and consequently your Laity (if they have Communion of Faith with them) by your own grounds, bound to believe, That the *Roman* Church is the Mistris of all other Churches? where it is evident from the relation and opposition of the *Roman* to other Churches, that the *Roman* Church is there taken for that particular Church.

2. Secondly, why then do you so often urge that mistaken saying of *Irænæus*, *Ad hanc Ecclesiam necesse est omnem convenire Ecclesiam?* falsely translating it, as Cardinal *Perron* in *French*, and my *L. F.* in *English*——*All Churches must agree with this Church*; for *convenire ad* signifies not *to agree with*, but *to come unto*; whereas it is evident for the aforesaid reason, that the *Roman* is here taken for that particular Church.

3. Thirdly, if that particular Church be not certainly infallible, but subject to error in points of faith; I would know, if any division of your Church should happen, in which the Church of *Rome* either alone, or with some others should take one way; the Churches of *Spain* and *France*, and many other Churches another, what direction should an ignorant Catholick have then from the pretended Guide of Faith? How shall he know which of these Companies is the Church? seeing all other Churches distinguished from the *Roman* may err, and seeing the *Roman* Church is now supposed subject to error, and consequently

ly not certain to guard those men, or those Churches that adhere unto it from erring.

4. Fourthly, if that particular Church be not infallible in Faith, let us then suppose that *de facto* it does err in faith; shall we not then have an Heretical head upon a Catholick body? A head of the Church, which were no member of the Church? which sure were a very strange and heterogeneous Monster! If to avoid these inconveniences you will say, that *Roman* Catholicks must of necessity hold that particular Church infallible in faith; I suppose it will evidently follow, that S. *Austin* and S. *Cyprian* (notwithstanding those sentences you pretend out of them) were no *Roman* Catholicks; seeing they lived and died in the contrary belief and profession. Let me see these absurdities fairly and clearly avoided, and I will dispute no more, but follow you whithersoever you shall lead me.

3. Thirdly, I answer, that the places alledged are utterly impertinent to the conclusion you should have proved; which was, That it was impossible, that two Societies of Christians divided upon what cause soever in external Communion, may be in truth and in Gods account, both of them parts of the Catholick Church: whereas your testimonies, if we grant them all, say no more but this; That the Societies of Hereticks, which are such as overthrow any doctrin necessary to salvation; and of Schismaticks, which are such as separate from the Churches Communion without any pretence of error in the Church or unlawfulness in the conditions of her Communion; I say, they prove only this, that such Societies as these, are no parts of the Church: which I willingly grant of all such, as are properly and formally Hereticks and Schismaticks; from which number I think (with S. *Austin*) they are to be exempted, *Qui quærunt cautâ sollicitudine veritatem, corrigi parati, cùm invenerint.* Whereas I put the case of such two Societies, which not differing indeed in any thing necessary to salvation, do yet erroneously believe that the errors wherewith they charge one another, are damnable, and so by this opinion of mutual error, are kept on both sides from being Hereticks.

Because I desire to bring you and others to the truth, or to be brought to it by you, I thought good for your direction in your intended Reply, to acquaint you with these things:

1. That I conceive the ———— in your discourse is this. That whensoever any two Societies of Christians differ in external Communion, one of them must be of necessity Heretical or Schismatical. I conceive there is no such necessity; and that the stories of *Victor* and the Bishops of *Asia*, S. *Cyprian* and Pope *Stephen* make it evident; and therefore I desire you to produce some convincing argument to the contrary; and that you may the better do it, I thought good to inform you what I mean by an *Heretick*, and what by a *Schismatick*.

An *Heretick* therefore I conceive him, that holds an Error against Faith with obstinacy. Obstinate I conceive him, who will not change his Opinion, when his reasons for it are so answered, that he cannot reply; and when the reasons against it are so convincing, that he cannot answer them. By the Faith I understand all those Doctrines and no more, which Christ taught his Apostles, and the Apostles the Church; yet I exclude not from this number the certain and evident deductions of them.

A *Schismatick* I account him, (and *Facundus Hermianensis* hath taught me to do so) who, without any supposing of error in the conditions of a Churches Communion, divides himself either from the obedience of that Church to which he owes obedience; or from the Communion of that Church to which he owes Communion.

2. Another thing, which I thought fit to acquaint you with, is this: That you go upon another very false and deceitful supposition; *viz.* that if we will not be *Protestants*, presently we must be *Papists*; if we forsake the Church of *England*, we must go presently to the Church of *Rome*: Whereas if your Arguments did conclude (as they do not) that before *Luthers* time, there was some Church of one Denomination, which was the Catholick Church; I should much rather think it were the Church of *Greece*, than the Church of *Rome*; and I believe others also would think

think so as well as I, but for that reason which one gives, why more men hold the Pope above a Council, than a Council above a Pope, that is, because Councils give no maintenance or preferment, and the Popes do.

 Think not yet, I pray, that I say this, as if I conceived this to be your reason for preferring the *Roman* Church before the *Greek*; (for I protest I do not) but rather, that conceiving verily you were to leave the Church of *England*, to avoid trouble you took the next Boat, and went to the Church of *Rome*, because that bespake you first.

 You impute to me (as I hear) that the way I take is destructive only, and that I build nothing; which first, is not a fault; for Christian Religion is not now to be built; but only I desire to have the rubbish and impertinent Lumber taken off, which you have laid upon it, which hides the glorious simplicity of it from them which otherwise would embrace it. Remember, I pray, *Averroes* his saying; *Quandoquidem Christiani adorant quod comedunt, sit anima mea cum Philosophis*; and consider the swarms of Atheists in *Italy*, and then tell me, whether your unreasonable and contradictious Doctrines, your forged Miracles and counterfeit Legends have not in all probability produced this effect. Secondly, if it be a fault, it is certainly your own; for your discourse intended for the proof of a positive conclusion —— *That we must be Papists* —— proves *in deed and in truth* nothing; but even *in shew and appearance* no more but this Negative, that we must not be Protestants; but what we must be, if we must not be Protestants, God knows; you in this Discourse (I am sure) do not shew it.

 Mr. *Lewgars* Reply.
 §. 1. The minor of Mr. *Chillingworths* Argument against my ground is very weak, being framed upon a false supposition, that a Protestant could name no other Church professing a diverse Faith, &c. from the *Greek* Church, which was the Catholick Church: for if he could not indeed name any other, the title would remain to the *Greek* Church: But he hath the *Roman* to name, and so my ground cannot conclude, either for the *Greek* or *Abyssine* or

any other, besides the *Roman*, but for that it does, except he can name some other.

§. 2. His second answer is weak likewise; for my Minor is always true; at least they thought it to be so, whose Authorities I produce in confirmation of it, as will appear to any one that considers them well; how their force lies in *Thesi*, not in *Hypothesi*; not that the Church was not then divided into more Societies than one, but that she could never be.

§. 3. As for his Instance to the contrary, wherein he believes I will not say the Churches excommunicated by *Victor* ceased to be a true member of the Catholick: If I say so, I say no more than the Ancient Fathers said before me. *Iræneus* when he desired *Victor* μὴ ἀποκόπτειν, not to cut off so many and great Churches; and *Ruffinus, reprehendit eam, quod non benè fecisset abscindere ab unitate corporis*, &c.

§. 4. But howsoever the case of Excommunication may be, the division of external Communion which I intended, and the Fathers spake of in the alledged Authorities, was that which was made by voluntary separation.

§. 5. Whereby the Church (before one Society) is divided into several distinct Societies, both claiming to be the Church; of which Societies so divided, but one can be the Catholick; and this is proved by the Authorities alledged; which Authorities must not be answered by disproving them, as he does (for that is to change his Adversary, and confute the Fathers sayings, instead of mine) but by shewing their true sense or judgment to be otherwise than I alledged it.

§. 6. To his demand upon the places alledged I Answer, that I do not build my whole faith of this conclusion upon the Authority of those Fathers; for I produce them, not for the Authority of the thing, but of the Exposition. The thing it self is an Article of the Creed, *Unam Catholicam*; grounded in express Scripture, *Columba mea unica*: but because there is difference in understanding this Prophesie, I produce these Authorities, to shew the Judgment of the Ancient Church how they understood it; and the proper answer to this is either to shew, that these words were

were not there, or at least, not this meaning; and so to shew their meaning out of other places more pregnant.

§. 7. And I promise, that whensoever an equal consent of Fathers can be shewed for any thing, as I can shew for this, I will believe it as firmly as I do this.

§. 8. But this is not the Answerers part, to propound doubts and difficulties, but to satisfie the proof objected.

§. 9. And if this course be any more taken, I will save my self all farther labour in a business so likely to be endless.

§. 10. His second Answer to the places is wholly impertinent; for therein would he disprove them from watching a necessity of resting in the judgment of the *Roman Church*; whereas I produced them only to shew, that among several Societies of Christians, only *one* can be the *Catholick*; and against this his second Answer saith nothing.

§. 11. In his third Answer he makes some shew of reply to the Authorities themselves; but he commits a double Error: One, that he imposes upon me a wrong conclusion to be proved, as will appear by comparing my conclusion in my Paper, with the conclusion he would appoint me.

§. 12. Another, that he imposes upon the Authorities a wrong Interpretation, no way grounded in the words themselves, nor in the places whence they were taken, nor in any other places of the same Fathers, but meerly forged out of his own Brain. For first, the places do not only say, that the Societies of Hereticks and Schismaticks are no part of the Church; but that the Church cannot be divided into more Societies than *one*; and they account Societies divided, which are either of a diverse Faith or a diverse Communion. Neither do they define *Hereticks* or *Schismaticks* in that manner as he does.

§. 13. For an *Heretick* in their Language is he, that opposes partinaciously the Common Faith of the Church: and a *Schismatick*, he that separates from the *Catholick* Communion; never making any mention at all of the cause.

§. 14. And if his definition of a *Schismatick* may stand, then certainly there was no *Schismatick* ever in the World, nor none are at this day: for none did, none does separate without some pretence of Error, or unlawfulness in the Conditions of the Churches Communion.

§. 15. And so I expect both a fuller and directer answer to my Argument, without excursions, or diversions into any other matter, till the judgment of Antiquity be cleared in this point.

Mr. *Chillingworths* Answer.

Ad §. 1. The *Minor* of my Argument, you say, is very weak, being grounded upon a false Supposition, That a Protestant could name no other Church professing a diverse Faith from the *Greek*, which was the *Catholick* Church: And your reason is, because he might name the *Roman*. But in earnest, Mr. *Lewgar*, do you think that a Protestant remaining a Protestant, can esteem the *Roman* Church to be the Catholick Church? or do you think to put tricks upon us, with taking your proposition one while *in sensu composito*, another while *in sensu diviso*? For if your meaning was, that a Protestant not remaining, but ceasing to be a Protestant, might name the *Roman* for the *Catholick*; so I say also to your discourse, that a Protestant ceasing to be a Protestant, might name a *Greek* to be the *Catholick* Church; and if there were any necessity to find out one Church of one denomination, as the *Greek*, the *Roman*, the Abyssine, which *one* must be the *Catholick*? I see no reason, but he might pitch upon the *Greek* Church, as well as the *Roman*; I am sure your discourse proves nothing to the contrary. In short, thus I say, if a *Grecian* should go about to prove to a Protestant, that his Church is the *Catholick*, by saying (as you do for the *Roman*) some one was so before *Luther*, and you can name no other, therefore ours is so: Whatsoever may be answered to him, may be answered to you. For as you say, a Protestant, ceasing to be a Protestant, may name to him the *Roman*; so I say, a Protestant, ceasing to be a Protestant, may name to you the *Grecian*. If
you

you say, a Proteſtant, remaining a Proteſtant, can name no other but the *Roman*, for the *Catholick*; I may (very ridiculouſly I confeſs, but yet as truly) ſay, he can name no other but the *Grecian*. If you ſay, he cannot name the *Greek Church* neither, remaining a Proteſtant; I ſay likewiſe, neither remaining a Proteſtant, can he name the *Roman* for the *Catholick*. So the Argument is equal in all reſpects on both ſides; and therefore either concludes for both parts (which is impoſſible, for then contradictions ſhould be both true) or elſe (which is certain) it concludes for neither. And therefore I ſay, your ground you build on, That before *Luther* ſome Church of one denomination was the *Catholick* (if it were true, as it is moſt falſe) would not prove your intent. It would deſtroy perhaps our Church, but it would not build yours. It would prove peradventure, that we muſt not be Proteſtants, but it will be far from proving that we muſt be *Papiſts*. For after we have left being Proteſtants (I tell you again that you may not miſtake) there is yet no neceſſity of being *Papiſts*; no more than if I go out of *England*, there is a neceſſity of going to *Rome*. And thus much to ſhew the poorneſs of your ground, if it were true. Now in the ſecond place, I ſay it is falſe, neither have you proved any thing to the contrary.

Ad §. 2. You ſay, the Authorities you have produced, ſhew to any that conſider them well, That the Church could never be divided into more Societies than *one*; and you mean (I hope) *one* in external Communion, or elſe you dally in ambiguities; and then I ſay, I have well conſidered the alledged authorities, and they appear to me to ſay no ſuch thing; but only, that the Societies of Hereticks and Schiſmaticks are no true members of the Church: Whereas I put the caſe of two ſuch Societies, which were divided in external Communion by reaſon of ſome over-valued difference between them, and yet were neither of them Heretical or Schiſmatical. To this I know you could not anſwer, but only by ſaying, That this ſuppoſition was impoſſible; *viz.* That of two Societies divided in external Communion, neither ſhould be Heretical nor Schiſmatical;

Schismatical; and therefore I desired you to prove by one convincing Argument, that this is impossible. This you have not done, nor I believe can do; and therefore all your places fall short of your intended conclusion; and if you would put them into Syllogistical form, you should presently see you conclude from them Sophistically in that fallacy, which is called *A dicto secundum quid, ad dictum Simpliciter.* Thus, — No two divided Societies, whereof one is Heretical or Schismatical, can be both members of the *Catholick Church*: therefore simply no two divided Societies can be so: the Antecedent I grant, which is all that your places say, as you shall see anon; but the consequence is Sophistical, and therefore that I deny: It is no better nor worse than if you should argue thus; No true divided Societies, whereof one is Out-lawed and in Rebellion, are both members of the same Commonwealth; therefore simply no two divided Societies.

But against this you pretend, That the alledged places say not only, that the Societies of Hereticks and Schismaticks are no parts of the Church; but that the Church cannot be divided into more Societies than *one*: And they account Societies divided, which are either of a diverse Faith, or of a diverse Communion: This is that which I would have proved, but as yet I cannot see it done. There be Eleven Quotations in all; seven of them speak expressly and formally of division made by Hereticks and Schismaticks, *viz.* 1. 3, 4. 7. 9, 10, 11. Three other of them, (*viz.* 5, 6. 8.) though they use not the word, yet Mr. *Lewgar* knows they speak of the *Donatists*, which were Schismaticks; and that by the relative particles *you* and *them* are meant the *Donatists*. And lastly, the second, Mr. *Lewgar* knows, says nothing but this, That an Hereticks cannot be accounted of that one Flock, which is the Church.

But to make the most of them that can be: The first saith, the Unity of the Church cannot be separated at all, nor divided. This I grant, but then I say, every difference does not in the sight of God divide this Unity: for then diversity of Opinions should do it; and so the *Jesuits and*

and *Dominicans* should be no longer members of the same Church. Or if every difference will not do it, why must it of necessity be always done by difference in Communion, upon an insufficient ground, yet mistaken for sufficient? (for such only I speak of.) Sure I am, this place says no such matter. The next place saies, the Flock is but one; and all the rest, that the Church is but *one*, and that Hereticks and Schismaticks are not of it; which certainly was not the thing to be proved, but that of this one Flock, of this one Church, two Societies divided without just cause in Communion, might not be true and lively members; both in one Body Mystical in the sight of God, though divided in Unity in the sight of men: It is true indeed, whosoever is shut out from the Church on Earth, is likewise cut off from it before God in Heaven: but you know it must be *Clave non errante*; when the cause of abscission is true and sufficient.

Ad §. 3. If you say so, *you say no more than the Fathers*: but what evasions and tergiversations are these? Why do you put us off with *ifs* and *ands*? I beseech you tell me, or at least him that desires to reap some benefit by our Conference, directly and Categorically, —— Do you say so, or do you say, it is not so? Were the Excommunicated Churches of *Asia* still members of the *Catholick Church* (I mean in Gods account) or were they not? but all damned for that horrible Heresie of celebrating the Feast of *Easter* upon a diverse day from the Western Churches? If you mean honestly and fairly, answer directly to this Question, and then you shall see what will come of it. Assure your self, you have a Wolf by the Ears: If you say they were, you overthrow your own conclusions, and say that Churches divided in Communion may both be members of the *Catholick*. If they were not; then shall we have Saints and Martyrs in Heaven, which were no members of the *Catholick Roman Church*.

As for *Irenæus* his μὴ προσκόπτειν; and *Ruffinus* his —— *Abscindere ab unitate corporis*; they imply no more but this at the most; That *Victor* (*quantum in se fuit*) did cut them off from the *External* Communion of the *Catholick Church*;

supposing, that for their Obstinacy in their Tradition, they had cut themselves off from the *internal* Communion of it: but that this sentence of *Victors* was ratified in Heaven, and that they were indeed cut off from the mystical Body of Christ, so far was *Irenæus* from thinking, that he, and in a manner all the other Bishops, reprehended *Victor* for pronouncing this Sentence on them, upon a cause so insufficient: which how they could say, or possibly think of a Sentence ratified by God in Heaven, and not reprehend God himself, I desire you to inform me: and if they did not intend to reprehend the Sentence of God himself, together with *Victors*, then I believe it will follow unavoidably, that they did not conceive, nor believe *Victors* Sentence to be ratified by God; and consequently did not believe, that these excommunicated Churches were not in Gods account true members of the Body of Christ.

Ad §. 4. And here again, we have another subterfuge, by a Verbal distinction between Excommunication, and voluntary separation: As if the separation, which the Church of *Rome* made in *Victors* time from the *Asian Churches*, were not a voluntary separation; or as if the Churches of *Asia*, did not voluntarily do that which was the cause of their separation; or as if (though they sepated not themselves indeed, conceiving the cause to be insufficient) they did not yet remain voluntarily separated, rather than conform themselves to the Church of *Rome*: Or lastly, as if the *Grecians* of Old, or the Protestants of Late, might not pretend as justly as the *Asian* Churches, that their Separation too was not voluntarily, but of necessity; for that the Church of *Rome* required of them under pain of Excommunication such conditions of her Communion, as were neither necessary nor lawful to be performed.

Ad §. 5. And here again the matter is streightned by another limitation. Both sides (say you) must claim to be the Church: but what then, if one of them only claim (though vainly) to be the Church, and the other content it self with being a part of it? These then it seems
for

(for any thing you have said to the contrary) may be both members of the *Catholick Church*: And certainly this is the case now, between the Church of *England* and the Church of *Rome*: and for ought I know, was between the Church of *Rome* and the Church of *Greece*: For I believe, it will hardly be proved, that the Excommunication between them was mutual; nor that the Church of *Greece* esteems it self the whole Church, and the Church of *Rome* no Church but it self a sound member of the Church, and that a corrupted one.

Again, whereas you say, the Fathers speak of a voluntary separation; certainly they speak of any Separation by Hereticks; and such were (in *Victors* judgment) the Churches of *Asia*, for holding an opinion contrary to the Faith, as he esteemed: Or if he did not, why did he cut them from the Communion of the Church? But the true difference is, The Fathers speak of those, which by your Church are esteemed Hereticks, and are so; whereas the *Asian* Churches were by *Victor* esteemed Hereticks, but were not so.

Ad §. 6. But their Authorities produced shew no more, than what I have shewed; that the Church is but one in exclusion of Hereticks and Schismaticks; and not that two particular Churches divided by mistake upon some overvalued difference, may not be both parts of the *Catholick*.

Ad §. 7. But I desire you to tell me, whether you will do this, if the Doctrines produced and confirmed by such a consent of Fathers, happen to be in the judgment of the Church of *Rome*, either not *Catholick*, or absolutely Heretical. If you will undertake this, you shall hear farther from me: But if, when their places are produced, you will pretend (as some of your side do) that surely they are corrupted, having neither reason nor shew of reason for it; unless this may pass for one (as perhaps it may, where reasons are scarce) that they are against your Doctrine; or if you will say, they are to be interpreted according to the pleasure of your Church, whether their words will bear it or no; then I shall but lose my Labour;

for this is not to try your Church by the Fathers, but the Fathers by your Church.

The Doctrines which I undertake to juſtifie, by a greater conſent of Fathers than here you produce, for inſtance ſhall be theſe.

1. That Gods Election ſuppoſeth preſcience of mans Faith and perſeverance.
2. That God doth not predetermine men to all their Actions.
3. That the *Pope* hath no power in temporalties over Kings either directly or indirectly.
4. That the Biſhop of *Rome* may Err in his publick determinations of matters of Faith.
5. That the B. *Virgin* was guilty of Original ſin.
6. That the B. *Virgin* was guilty of actual ſin.
7. That the Communion was to be adminiſtred to the Laity in both kinds.
8. That the reading of the Scripture was to be denied to no man.
9. That the Opinion of the Millenaries is true.
10. That the Euchariſt is to be adminiſtred to Infants.
11. That the ſubſtance of Bread and Wine remains in the Euchariſt of her Conſecration.
12. That the Souls of the Saints departed enjoy not the Viſion of God before the Laſt day.
13. That at the day of judgment, all the Saints ſhall paſs through a purging fire.

All theſe propoſitions are held by your Church either Heretical, or at leaſt not *Catholical*; and yet in this promiſe of yours you have undertaken to believe them as firmly, as you now do this, That two divided Societies cannot be both members of the *Catholick Church*.

Ad §. 8. Is it not then the Anſwerers part to ſhew, that the proofs pretended are indeed no proofs? and doth not he prove no proofs (at leaſt in your mouth) who undertakes to ſhew, that an equal or greater number of the very ſame witneſſes is rejected by your ſelves in many other things? Either the conſent of the Fathers, in any Age or Ages, is infallible, and then you are to reject

Mr. Chillingworth *and Mr.* Lewgar.

ject it in nothing; or it is not so, and then you are not to urge it in any thing: As if the Fathers Testimonies against us were Swords and Spears, and against you bul-rushes.

Ad §. 9. In effect as if you should say, If you answer not as I please, I will dispute no longer. But you remember the proverb, ⸺ will think of it. ⸺ *Occasionem quærit, qui cupit discedere.*

Ad §. 10. I pray tell me, Is not *Therefore* a note of an Illation, or a conclusion? And is not your last *therefore* this, *Therefore her judgment is to be rested in?* which though it be not your first conclusion, yet yours it is, and you may not declaim it: and it is so near of kin to the former (in your judgment I am sure) that they must stand or fall together: therefore he that speaks pertinently for the disproving of the one, cannot speak impertinently towards the disproving the other: and therefore you cannot so shift it off, but of necessity you must answer the Argument there urged, or confess it ingenuously to be unanswerable.

Or if you will not answer any thing, where the contradiction of your first conclusion is not in terms inferred, then take it thus: If S. *Cyprian* and S. *Austin* did not think it necessary in matters of Faith to rest in the judgment of the *Roman* Church and the adherents of it; Then either they thought not the *Catholick Churches* judgment necessary to be rested on, or they thought not *that* the *Catholick Church.* But the Antecedent is true, and undeniably proved so by their Actions, and the consequence Evident: Therefore the consequent must be true in one or other part: But you will not say the former is true; it remains therefore, the latter must be, and that is ⸺ That S. *Austin* and S. *Cyprian* did not think the Church of *Rome* and the adherents of it to be the Catholick Church.

Ad §. 11. But I tell you now, and have already told you, that in our discourse before Mr. *Skinner* and Dr. *Sheldon* I answered your Major, as then you framed your Argument, as now your Minor thus ⸺ If you understand

by

by *one company* of Christians, *one* in External Communion, I deny your Major. For I say, that two several Societies of Christians, which do not externally communicate together, may be both parts of the same Catholick Church: and what difference there is between this, and the conclusion I told you, you should have proved, I do not well understand.

Ad §. 12. And is it possible you should say so, when every one of the places carry this sense in their forehead, and 7 of the 11 in terms express it ―― That they intended only to exclude Hereticks and Schismaticks from being parts of the Church: For if they did not, against whom did they intend them? *Pagans* lay no claim to the Church, therefore not against them: *Catholicks* they did not intend to exclude: I know not who remains besides, but Hereticks and Schismaticks. Besides the frequent opposition in them between ―― *One Church* on the one side, and Hereticks and Schismaticks; who sees not, that in these places they intended to exclude only these pretenders out of the Churches Unity?

Lastly, whereas you say, that the places say ―― That the Church cannot be divided; and that they account those divided who are of a diverse Faith, or a diverse Communion: I tell you, that I have read them over and over, and unless my Eyes deceive, they say not one word of a *diverse Communion*.

Ad §. 13. Whereas a *Heretick* in your Language, is he that opposeth pertinaciously the common Faith of the Church; ―― In mine ―― He is such a one, as holds an Error against Faith with Obstinacy: Verily a monstrous difference between these definitions. To oppose and hold against (I hope) are all one: *Faith* and the *common Faith of the Church*, sure are not very different: *pertinaciously* and *with Obstinacy*, methinks might pass for Synonimous; and seeing the parts agree so well, methinks the Total should not be at great hostility. And for the definition of a *Schismatick*, if you like not mine (which yet I give you out of a Father) I pray take your own; and then shew me, (if you mean to do any thing) that wheresoever

soever there are two Societies of Christians, differing in external Communion, one of them most be of necessity either Heretical, or Schismatical in your own sense of these words. To the contrary, I have said already, (and say it now again, that you may not forget it) the *Roman* and the *Asian* Churches in *Victors* time, the *Roman* and the *African* in S. *Stephens* time differed in external Communion; and yet neither of them was *Heretical*; For they did not oppose pertinaciously the commonFaith of theChurch: Neither of them was *Schismatical*; for they did not separate (never making mention of the cause at all) but were separated by the *Roman* Church, and that upon some cause, though it were not sufficient.

Ad §. 14. The *Donatist* did so (as *Facundus Hermianensis* testifies:) but you are abused, I believe, with not distinguishing between these two — They did pretend, that the Church required of them some unlawful thing among the conditions of her Communion: and they did pretend, that it was unlawful for them to communicate with the Church. This I confess they did pretend; but it was in regard of some Persons in the Church, with whom they thought it unlawful to communicate: But the former they did not pretend, (I mean while they continued meer Schismaticks,) *viz.* That there was any Error in the Church, or impiety in her publick service of God: And this was my meaning in saying, — A Schismatick is he, which separates from the Church without pretence of Error, or unlawfulness in the conditions of her Communion: Yet if I had left out the term *unlawfulness*, the definition had been better, and not obnoxious to this Cavillation; and so I did in the second Paper which I sent you for your direction; which if you had dealt candidly, you should have taken notice of.

Ad §. 15. I have replied (as I think) fully to every part and particle of your Argument. Neither was the History of S. *Cyprians* and S. *Austins* opposition to the Church of *Rome* an excursion or diversion; but a cleer demonstration of the contradictory of your conclusion: (*viz. That the Roman Church, &c. and therefore her judgment not to be re-*
sted

ted upon) For an answer hereto I shall be very importunate with you; and therefore, if you desire to avoid trouble, I pray come out of my debt as soon as may be.

If it be said, that my Argument is not contradictory to your conclusion; because it shews only, that the *Roman* Church with her adherents was not in S. *Cyprians* or S. *Austins* time the Catholick Church, but was at the time before *Luther*; I say, to conclude the one is to conclude the other. For certainly, if it were then at *Luthers* time so, it was always so; if it was not always, it was not then: for if it be of the essence, or necessary to the Church (as is pretended) to be a Society of Christians joyned in Communion with the Church and Bishop of *Rome*; then did it always agree to the Church; and therefore in S. *Cyprians* and S. *Austins* time, as well as at *Luthers* rising: if it were not always, particularly not in S. *Cyprians* time, of the Essence or necessary to the Church to be so; then it was impossible the Church should acquire this Essence, or this property afterwards, and therefore impossible it should have it at the time of *Luthers* rising. *Necessarium est, quod non aliquando inest, aliquando non inest, alicui inest, alicui non inest; sed quod semper & omni.* Arist. Post. Analyt.

Again, every Sophister knows, that of Particulars nothing can be concluded; and therefore he that will shew, that the Church of *Rome* and the adherents of it was the Catholick Church at *Luthers* rising; He must argue thus:
—— It was always so, therefore then it was so: Now this Antecedent is overthrown by any Instance to the contrary; and so, the first Antecedent being proved false, the first consequent cannot but be false; for what Reason can be imagined, that the Church of *Rome* and the Adherents of it, was not the whole Catholick Church at S. *Cyprians* time, and was at *Luthers* rising? If you grant (as I think you cannot deny) that a Church divided from the Communion of the *Roman*, may be still in truth and in Gods account a part of the Catholick (which is the thing we speak of:) then I hope Mr. *Lewgars* Argument from Unity of Communion is fallen to the ground; and it will be no good Plea to say, Some

Some one Church, not consisting of divers Communions, was the Catholick Church at *Luthers* rising:

No one Church can be named to be the Catholick Church, but the *Roman*:

Therefore the *Roman* Church was the Catholick at *Luthers* rising.

For Mr. *Lewgar* hath not nor cannot prove the Major of this syllogism certainly true; but to the contrary I have proved, that it cannot be certainly true, by shewing divers instances, wherein divers divided Communions have made up the Catholick Church: and therefore not the dividing of the Communions, but the cause and ground of it, is to be regarded, whether it be just and sufficient, or unjust and insufficient.

Neither is the Bishop or Church of *Rome*, with the Adherents of it, an infallible Judge thereof; for it is evident, both he and it have erred herein divers times; which I have evinced already by divers examples, which I will not repeat; but add to them one confessed by Mr. *Lewgar* himself in his discourse upon the Article of the Catholick Church, pag. 84. S. Athanasius *being excommunicated (though by the* [a] *whole Church) yet might remain a member of Christs body, (not visible, for that is impossible,* [b] *that a person cut off from visible Communion, though unjustly, should be a visible member of the Church, but) by invisible Communion, by reason of the invalidity of the sentence; which being unjust, is valid enough to visible excision, but not farther.*

[a] How by the whole Church, when himself was part of it, and communicated still with divers other parts of it?
[b] What not to them who know and believe him to be unjustly Excommunicated?

II. *A Discourse against the Infallibility of the Roman Church, with an Answer to all those Texts of Scripture that are alledged to prove it.*

THE Condition of Communion with the Church of *Rome*, without the performance whereof no man can be received into it, is this, That he believe firmly and without doubting, whatsoever that Church requires him to believe.

It is impossible that any man should certainly believe any thing, unless that thing be either evident of it self (as that twice two are four; that every whole is greater than a part of it self) or unless he have some certain reason (at least some supposed certain reason) and infallible guide for his belief thereof.

The Doctrins which the Church of *Rome* requireth to be believed are not *evident of themselves*; for then every one would grant them at first hearing without any further proof. He therefore that will believe them, must have some certain and infallible ground whereupon to build his belief of them.

There is no other ground for a mans belief of them, especially in many points, but only an assurance of the Infallibility of the Church of *Rome*.

Now this point of that Churches Infallibility, is not evident of it self; for then no man could chuse but in his heart believe it without farther proof. Secondly, it were in vain to bring any proof of it, as vain as to light a Candle to shew men the Sun. Thirdly, it were impossible to bring any proof of it, seeing nothing can be more evident, than that which of it self is evident: and nothing can be brought in proof of any thing which is not more evident than that matter to be proved: But now experience teacheth that millions there are, which have heard talk of the Infallibility of the *Roman* Church, and yet do not believe that the defenders of it do not think it either vain or impossible to go about to prove it; and from hence it follows plainly, that this point is not evident of it self.

Neither

Neither is there any other certain ground for any mans belief of it: or if there be, I desire it may be produced, as who am ready and most willing to submit my judgment to it, fully perswaded that none can be produced, that will endure a severe and impartial examination.

If it be said, The *Roman* Church is to be believed infallible because the Scripture says it is so.

1. I demand how shall I be assured of the Texts that be alledged, that they are indeed Scripture, that is, the Word of God? And the answer to this must be either because the Church tells me so, or some other: if any other be given, then all is not finally resolved into, and built upon that Churches Authority; and this answer then I hope a Protestant may have leave to make use of, when he is put to that perillous Question; *How know you the Scripture to be the Scripture?* If the answer be, because the Church tells me so: my reply is ready; that to believe that Church is infallible, because the Scriptures say so: and that the Scripture is the word of God, because the same Church says so, is nothing else but to believe the Church is infallible, because the Church says so, which is infallible.

2. I could never yet from the beginning of *Genesis*, to the end of the *Apocalypse*, find it written so much as once in express terms, or equivalently, that the Church in subordination to the Sea of *Rome* shall be always infallible.

3. If it be said, that this is drawn from good consequence from Scripture truly interpreted; I demand, what certain ground have I to warrant me, that this consequence is good and this interpretation true: and if answer be made, that reason will tell me so: I reply, 1. That this is to build all upon my own reason and private interpretation. 2. I have great reason to fear, that reason assures no man, that the infallibility of the Church of *Rome* may be deduced from Scripture, by good and firm consequence.

4. If it be said, that a Consent of Fathers do so interpret the Scripture. I answer, 1. That this is most false and cannot without impudence be pretended, as I am ready to justifie to any indifferent Hearer. 2. I demand, who shall be judge whether the Fathers mean as is pretended.

If it be said, reason will tell me so: I say, 1. this is false. 2. This is again to do that which is objected to Protestants for such a horrid crime, that is, to build all finally upon reason.

If it be said, they are so interpreted by the Catholick Church; I demand, whether by the Catholick Church be meant that onely that is in subordination to the Bishop of *Rome*, or any other with that, or besides that. If any other, it is false and impudent to pretend that they so understand the Fathers or Scriptures: If that only, then this is to say, that that Church is infallible, because it may be deduced from Scripture that it is so; and to prove that it may be deduced from Scripture, because the Fathers say so; and to prove the Fathers do say and mean so, because the Church of *Rome* says they do so. And then what a stir and trouble was here to no purpose; why was it not rather said plainly at the beginning; The Church of *Rome* is certainly infallible, because she her self says so; and she must say true because she is infallible: and that is as much to say as unless you grant me the Question, I neither can nor will dispute with you.

If it is said, indeed the Fathers do not draw this doctrin from Scripture, but yet they affirm it with a full consent, as a matter of Tradition. I reply. 1. That this pretence also is false, and that upon tryal it will not appear to have any colour of probability to any who remembers, that it is the present *Roman* Church, and not the Catholick Church whose infallibility is here disputed. 2. I demand, who shall be judge, whether the Fathers do indeed affirm this or no: If reason, then again we are fallen upon that dangerous Rock, that all must be resolved into private reason: If the Church I ask again, what Church is meant? If the Church of the *Grecians* or *Abyssines* or Protestants, or any other but the *Roman*, it is evident they deny it. If the Church of *Rome*, then we are again very near the head of the Circle. For I ask, how shall I be assured this Church will not err and deceive me in interpreting the Fathers; and th Answer must be either none, or this, that the Churcl   infallible.

Obj.

Obj. If it be said, that the Infallibility of the *Roman* Church would yield the Church so many commodities, and that the want of an infallible Church to guide men in the way to Heaven, would bring so many mischiefs upon the world, that it cannot be thought but that God out of his love to men, hath appointed this Church as an infallible guide to all other Churches; seeing it is so necessary there should be some such guide, and so evident there is no other.

Ans. I answer; that this argument would serve the Church of *Greece*, or *England*, or *Geneva*, to prove it self infallible, and the guide of all other Churches, would they but take upon them to be so. For every one might say for it self; It is necessary there should be some Guide; it is evident there is no other; *Ergo* I am appointed by God to be that Guide. The same argument any man might use, to make himself Monarch of any popular State: for first he might represent unto them the commodities of a Monarchy, and the mischiefs of a Democracy: then he might say, That God surely out of his Love to them hath appointed some remedy for their inconveniences: And lastly, that he hath ordained no other to redress them but himself, and then conclude, that he alone must of necessity be the man appointed to rule over them.

I answer Secondly, that here also we must resolve all into Reason and the private Spirit, or that we are still in the Circle. For I demand, how do you know that these pretended commodities are to be compassed, and these pretended mischiefs are to be avoided, only by the Infallibility of the Church of *Rome* or some other Church, and not by any other means which God hath provided. If you say, reason tells you so; I say 1. This is to make reason your last and lowest foundation. 2. I assure you Reason tells me no such matter, and yet I know that I am as willing to hear it as you are. If you say, the Church tells you so, and she is infallible; this, I say, is to prove the Church infallible because she is so.

Thirdly, I demand, How it is possible you should know, that these pretended commodities might not be gained,
and

and these mischiefs which you fear avoided, without any assistance of the Church of *Rome*'s infallibility, if all men in the world did believe the Scripture, and live according to it, and would require no more of others, but to do so? If you say, that notwithstanding this, there would be no unity in Doctrin: I answer 1. It is impossible you should know this; considering that there are many places in Scripture, which do more than problably import, that the want of piety in living, is the cause of want of unity in believing. 2. That there would be unity of Opinion in all things necessary: and that in things not necessary unity of Opinion is not necessary. But lastly, that notwithstanding differences in these things of lesser importance, there might and would be unity of Communion, unity of charity and affection, which is one of the greatest blessings which the world is capable of; absolute unity of opinion being a matter rather to be desired than hoped for.

Obj. Against this it has been objected, that the Scripture cannot be the guide, because many men have used their best endeavors to follow it, and yet have fallen, some into *Arianism*, others into *Pelagianism*, others into other damnable Heresies, and how can I secure any man, but he may do the like?

Ans. To this I answer, by distinguishing the persons which are pretended to have made use of this Guide, and yet to have fallen into Heresie, that they were either such as did love the truth sincerely and above all things, as did seek it diligently and with all their power, to this intent that they might conform their belief and life unto it; such as following S. *Pauls* direction, did first try all things deliberately, and then chose what in their conscience they thought was best: or they were such as for want of the love of the truth, God suffered to fall into strong delusions, to fall to a false Religion, because they brought not forth the fruits of the true; to make shipwreck of their faith, because they had cast away a good conscience; to have their Eyes blinded, and their light taken away, because they made not the right use of it, but were idle and un-

Mr. Chillingworth *and Mr.* Lewgar.

unprofitable, and set their hearts upon vanity, and had only a form of Religion, but denied the effect of it in their lives and conversations; in a word, such as were betrayed to their Error, and kept for ever in it, either by negligence in seeking the Truth, or unwillingness to find it, or by some other voluntary sin: And for these I dare not flatter them with hope of pardon; but let me tell you, it is not the error of the understanding, but the sin of their will that truly and properly damns them: But for the former I am confident, that nothing is more contumelious to the goodness of God, than to think that he will damn any such; for he should damn men that truly love him, and desire to serve him, for doing that which all things considered, was impossible for them not to do.

Obj. If it is said, that pride of their own understanding made them not submit to the Church of *Rome*, and to her guidance, and that for this, being a voluntary sin, they may be justly damned.

Ans. I answer, that whether the Church of *Rome* be the guide of all men is the Question, and therefore not to be begged but proved: that the man we speak of is very willing to follow this Guide, could he find any good ground to believe it is his Guide; and therefore the reason he follows her not, is not pride but ignorance: that as it is humility to obey those whom God hath set over us, so it is credulity to follow every one that will take upon him to lead us: that if the *blind lead the blind*, not only the *leader* but the *follower* shall perish: Lastly, that the present Church of *Rome* pretends very little and indeed nothing of moment, to get the office of being Head and Guide of the Church, which Antichrist when he cometh, may not and will not make use of, for the very same end and purpose; and therefore he had reason, not to be too sudden and precipitate, in committing himself to the conduct of the Pope, for fear of mistaking Antichrist for the Vicar of Christ.

Obj. But in all Commonwealths, it is necessary there should be not only a Law for men to live by, but also a living and speaking Judge to decide their differences arising
about.

about the various Interpretations of the Law, and otherwise Controversies would be endless: therefore if such a judge be so necessary in civil affairs, for the procuring and preserving our temporal peace and happiness; how much more necessary is he, for the deciding of those Controversies, that concern the saving and damning of our souls for ever.

Ans. Hereunto I answer, 1. That if it were as evident and certain that God hath appointed the Pope or Church of *Rome* to be the Guide of Faith, and Judge of Controversies, as that the King hath appointed such a one to be Lord Chief Justice, the having of such a Guide would be very available, for to preserve the Church in Unity, and to conduct mens souls to Heaven: but a Judge that has no better title or evidence to his place, than the Pope has to that which he pretends to, a Judge that is doubtful and justly questionable whether he be the Judge or no, is in all probability likely to produce clean contrary effects, and to be himself one of the Apples of strife, one of the greatest subjects of Controversie, and occasion of dissentions.

And to avoid this great inconvenience, if God had intended the Pope or Church of *Rome* for this great Office, certainly he would have said so very plainly and very frequently; if not frequently, certainly sometimes, once at least he would have said so in express terms: but he does not say so, no not so much as once, nor any thing from whence it may be collected, with any sure or firm consequence: therefore if it be not certain, certainly it is very probable he never meant so.

Again, in Civil Controversies the case can hardly be so put, that there should be any necessity that the same man should be Judge and Party: but in matters of Religion, wherein all have equal interest, every man is a party, and engaged to judge for temporal respects, this way or that way, and therefore not fit to be a Judge. But what then if he which was with so much clamor and so little reason vouched, for the Infallibility of the *Roman* Church, do tell you plainly, there is no living Judge on Earth appointed by God, to decide the Controversies arising amongst
Christians;

Christians; nor no way to determine them but Scripture. His words are express and formal, and need no other commentary but a true interpretation.

Optatus Melevit. *lib.* 5. ad princip.

Vos dicitis, Licet; *nos, non* Licet: *inter Vestrum* Licet, & *nostrum* non Licet, *nutant & remigant animæ populorum. Nemo vobis credat, nemo nobis; omnes contentiosi homines sumus. Quærendi sunt judices: si Christiani, de utrâque parte dari non possunt: de foris quærendus est Judex. Si* Paganus, *non potest nosse Christiana Secreta: Si* Judæus, *inimicus est Christiani Baptismatis. Ergo in terris de hac re nullum poterit reperiri judicium: de cœlo quærendus est Judex. Sed ut quid pulsamus cælum, cum habeamus hic in Evangelio Testamentum? Quia hoc loco rectè possunt terrenæ cœlestibus comparari; tale est, quod quivis hominum habens numerosos filios: His, quamdiu presens est, ipse imperat singulis; non est adhuc necessarium Testamentum. Sic & Christus, quamdiu præsens in terris fuit (quamvis nec modo desit) pro tempore quicquid necessarium erat, Apostolis imperavit. Sed quomodo terrenus pater cùm se in confinio senserit mortis, timens ne post mortem suam ruptâ pace litigent fratres, adhibitis testibus voluntatem suam de pectore morituro transfert in tabulas diù duraturas; & si fuerit inter fratres contentio nata, non itur ad tumulum, sed quæritur Testamentum, & qui in tumulo quiescit, tacitis de tabulis loquitur vivus. Is, cujus est testamentum, in cœlo est: Ergo voluntas ejus velut in Testamento sic in Evangelio inquiratur.*

That is, "You say such a thing is *Lawful*; we say it is
"*Unlawful*: the minds of the People are doubtful and
"wavering between your *lawful* and our *unlawful*. Let
"no man believe either *you* or *us*; we are all contentious
"men. We must seek therefore for Judges between us.
"If Christians are to be our Judges; both sides will not af-
"ford such. We must seek for a Judge abroad. If he be
"a *Pagan*, he cannot know the secrets of Christianity:
"If he be a *Jew*, he is an Enemy to Christian Baptism.
"Therefore there is no judgment of this matter can be
"found on Earth. We must seek for a Judge from Hea-
"ven.

"ven. But to what end do we follicite Heaven, when
"we have here in the Gospel a Will and Testament? And
"becaufe here we may fitly compare Earthly things with
"Heavenly; The cafe is juft as if a man had many Sons:
"while he is prefent with them, he commands every one
"what he will have done; and there is no need as yet of
"making his laft Will. So alfo Chrift, as long as he was
"prefent on Earth (though neither now is he wanting)
"for a time commanded his Apoftles, whatfoever was
"neceffary. But juft as an Earthly Father, when he
"feels his Death approaching, fearing left after his Death
"the Brothers fhould fall out and quarrel, he calls in Wit-
"neffes, and tranflates his Will from his dying Heart into
"Writing-Tables that will continue long after him: Now
"if any controverfie arifes among the Brothers; they do
"not go to his Tomb, but confult his laft Will; and thus
"he whilft he refts in his Grave, does fpeak to them in thofe
"filent Tables as if he were alive. He whofe Tefta-
"ment we have, is in Heaven. Therefore we are to en-
"quire his pleafure in the Gofpel, as in his laft Will and
"Teftament.

It is plain from hence, that he knew not of any living, fpeaking, audible Judge, furnifhed with Authority and infallibility to decide this controverfie: had he known any fuch affifted with the Spirit of God for this purpofe, it had been horrible impiety againft God and the Churches peace, to fay there was none fuch: or the Spirit of God was not able by his affiftance to keep this Judge from being hindred with partiality, from feeing the Truth. Had he thought the Bifhop of *Romes* fpeaking *ex Cathedra* to be this Judge, now had been the time to have faid fo: but he fays directly the contrary, and therefore it is plain, he knew of no fuch Authority he had.

Neither is there the like reafon for a Judge finally and with Authority to determine controverfies in Religion and civil differences: For if the controverfie be about *Mine* and *Thine*, about Land or Money or any other thing, it is impoffible that both I fhould hold the poffeffion of it and my adverfary too: and one of us muft do injury
to

to the other, which is not fit it should be Eternal: But in matters of Doctrine the case is clean contrary; I may hold my opinion and do my Adversary no wrong, and my Adversary may hold his and do me none.

[*Texts of Scripture alledged for Infallibility.*]

The Texts alledged for it by *Cardinal Perren* and Mr. *Stratford*, are partly Prophecies of the *Old Testament*, partly promises of the *New*.

1. Esa. 1. 26. *Thou shalt be called the City of Justice, the faithful City.*
2. Esa. 52. 1. *Through thee shall no more pass any that is uncircumcised, or unclean.*
3. Esa. 59. 21. *As for me, this is my Covenant with them, saith the Lord, my spirit that is upon thee, and my Words which I have put in thy mouth, shall not depart out of thy mouth, nor out of the mouth of thy seed, nor out of the mouth of thy seeds seed, saith the Lord, from henceforth and for ever.*
4. Esa. 62. 6. *Upon thy Walls* Hierusalem *I have appointed Watchmen all the day and all the night for ever, they shall not hold their peace.*
5. Jerem. 31. 33. *This shall be the Covenant which I will make with the House of* Israel, *saith the Lord, I will give my Law in their Bowels, and in their Heart I will write it, and I will be their God, and they shall be my People.*
6. Ezek. 36. 27. *I will put my Spirit within you, and cause you to walk in my Statutes, and ye shall keep my judgments and do them.*
7. Ezek. 37. 26. *I will give my Sanctification in the midst of them for ever.*
8. Ose. 2. 19, 20. *I will dispouse thee to me for ever; and I will dispouse thee to me in Justice and judgment, and in mercy and commiserations; I will Espouse thee to me in Faith, and thou shalt know that I am the Lord.*
9. Cant. 4. 7. *Thou art all fair my Love, and there is no spot in thee.*

Now before we proceed further, let us reflect upon these places, and make the most of them for the behoof of the *Roman* Church; and I believe it will then appear to any one not veil'd with prejudice, that not one of them reaches home to the conclusion intended, which is, That the *Roman* Church is infallible.

The first place perhaps would do something, but that there are Three main exceptions against it. 1. That here is no evidence, not so much as that of probability, that this is here spoken of the Church of *Rome*. 2. That it is certain that it is not spoken of the Church of *Rome*; but of the Nation of the *Jews*, after their conversion, as is apparent from that which follows. *Zion shall be redeemed with judgment, and her converts with righteousness.* 3. That it is no way certain, that whatsoever Society may be called, *the City of righteousness, the faithful City*, must be infallible in all her Doctrine: with a great deal more probability, it might challenge from hence the priviledg of being *Impeccable*; which yet *Roman Catholicks* I believe do not pretend to.

The Second place is liable to the same exceptions; the Church of *Rome* is not spoken of in it: but *Zion* and *Hierusalem*; and it will *serve as well nay* better to prove *Impeccability* than *Infallibility*.

The third place is the *Achilles* for this opinion, wherein every writer Triumphs; but I wonder they should do so; considering the Covenant here spoken of is made, not with the Church of *Rome*, but with *Zion* and them that turn from transgression in *Jacob*, the words are: *And the Redeemer shall come out of* Zion, *and unto them that turn from transgression in* Jacob *saith the Lord. As for me, this is my Covenant with them saith the Lord; My Spirit that is in thee and my Words,* &c. Now if the Church of *Rome* be *Zion* and they that turn from iniquity in *Jacob*, they may have Title to this Covenant; if not they must forbear, and leave it to the *Jews* after their Conversion; to whom it is appropriated by a more Infallible Interpreter than the *Pope*; I mean S. *Paul*, Rom. 11. 26. And it seems the Church of *Rome* also believes as much: for otherwise why does she in the Margent of her Bible, send us to that place of S. *Paul* for an exposition.

Read

Read the 4th place, and you shall find nothing can be made of it but this: that the Watchmen of *Hierusalem* shall never cease importuning God, for the sending of the *Messias*: To this purpose speaks the Prophet in *ver.* 1. For *Zions sake I will not hold my peace, and for Hierusalems sake I well not rest, until the righteousness thereof go forth as brightness*: And the *Gentiles shall see thy righteousness.* But the words following these that are objected, make it most evident, which are, *ye that make mention of the Lord keep not silence, and give him no rest, till he establish and till he make* Hierusalem *a praise in the Earth.*

The 5th place had they set down entirely, for very shame they could not have urged it for the Infallibility of the *Roman* Church. The words are, *Behold the days come, saith the Lord, that I will make a new Covenant with the House of* Israel, *and with the House of* Judah; *not according to the Covenant which I made with their Fathers ——— But this shall be the Covenant that I will make with the House of* Israel ——— *After those days, saith the Lord, I will put my Law in their inward parts and write it in their Hearts, and I will be their God and they shall be my People; and they shall teach no more every man his Neighbour and every man his Brother, saying, know the Lord; for they shall all know me from the least of them to the greatest of them, saith the Lord.* And now I have transcribed the place, I think it superfluous to make any other answer.

The same Answer and no other will I make also to the 6th place. The words are, *Therefore say unto the House of* Israel; *thus saith the Lord God, I do not this for your sakes O House of* Israel, *but for my holy names sake,* ver. 22. *I will take you from among the Heathen, and gather you out of all Countries, and will bring you into your own Land,* v. 24. *Then will I sprinkle clean Water upon you,* ver. 25. *A new heart also will I give you,* ver. 26. *And I will put my Spirit in you and cause you to walk in my Statutes, and ye shall keep my judgments and do them,* ver. 27. *And ye shall dwell in the Land that I gave to your Fathers: I will also save you from all your uncleannesses, and I will call for the Corn and will encrease it, and lay no Famine upon you. And the desolate Land shall be tilled*, ver. 34. *And they shall say, this Land that was desolate, is become like the Garden of* Eden.

The 7th place also carries its answer in its forehead: *Thus saith the Lord God, behold I will take the Children of* Israel *from among the* Heathen *whether they be gone; and I will make them one Nation in the Land upon the mountains of* Israel: *and one King shall be King to them all*, &c. to the end of the Chapter. In all which place, he that can find a Syllable of the Church of *Rome*, he must have better eyes than I have.

The next (8th) place would be very pregnant for the Church of *Rome*, if of courtesie we would grant, that whatsoever is promised to *Israel*, is intended to them. As you may see in the place at large, from *ver.* 17. to the end of the Chapter.

The 9th and last place out of the *Canticles*, had it been urged by a Protestant; it would have been thought a sufficient Answer to have said, That Mystical Texts are not fit to argue upon; but if this will not serve, then we answer. 1. That there is no mention nor intimation of the Church of *Rome*. 2. That it proves either too much or nothing at all: that is, that the *Roman* Church is impeccable, as well as infallible; unless we will say that Errors only are Spots, and impieties are not.

Out of the New Testament *they alledge these Texts.*

Matth. 16. 18. *Upon this Rock I will build my Church, and the Gates of Hell shall not prevail against it.*

But this is said of the Catholick, not of the *Roman* Church: nor can it ever be proved that the Church in Communion with the See of *Rome* is the Catholick Church. Secondly, it says something for the *perpetuity* of the Church, but not for the *Infallibility* of it: unless you will take for granted what can never be proved, That a Church that teaches any Erroneous Doctrine, is a Church no longer; which is all one, as if you should say, a man that has the *Stone*, or *Gout*, or any other Disease, is not a man.

They

They urge, Matth. 28. 19, 20.

And I am with you all days, even unto the consummation of the World.

And here also if we will grant, 1. That by *you*, is meant you and only you of the Church of *Rome*. 2. That our Saviour has here obliged himself to assist, not only *Sufficienter*, but also *irresistibiliter*, not only to preserve in the Church a light of sufficient direction, as he provided a Star for the Wise Men, and a Pillar of Fire and a cloud for the conduct of the *Israelites*; but also compel or at least necessitate them to follow it. 3. That he will be with them, not only to keep them from all damnable and destructive Errors, but absolutely form all erroneous Doctrines: If these things I say were granted, some good might be done. But certainly these are μεγάλα λίαν αἰτήματα, too great favours to be lookt for by strangers: And yet if all this be granted, we should run into this inconvenience on the other side; that if the promise be absolute, not only the whole Church of *Rome*; not only a general Council; not the *Pope* alone; but every Bishop, every Priest, every one who is sent by Christ to Baptize and Preach the Gospel, might claim this assistance by vertue of Christs words, and consequently *Infallibility*.

They urge, Matth. 18. 17.

If he will not hear the Church, let him be to thee as the Heathen *and the* Publican. And here again the Church must be the Church of *Rome*, or we are as far to seek as ever. But what if by it be meant, which is most evident out of the place, every particular Church of Christians, whereunto any one Christian injured by another, may address himself for remedy. Certainly whosoever reads the place without prejudice, I am confident that he shall not deny, but that the sense of the Words is. That if any Christian injure another, and being first admonished of it by him in private; then by him before two or

three

three Witnesses; Lastly, by the Church he lives in; and yet still proceeds on obstinately in doing injury to his Brother, he is to be esteemed as a *Heathen*, or a *Publican*: and then if Infallibility may be concluded, what a multitude of Infallible Churches shall we have?

They urge, Matth. 18. 20.

Where two or three are gathered together in my name, there am I in the midst of them.

But this also either shoots short, or over; either proves nothing, or too much: Either it proves not the Infallibility of the whole Church, or it proves the Infallibility of every part of it: Either not the Infallibility of General Councils, or the infallibility of particular Councils; for there two or three at least are assembled in Christs name. But then besides these two or three for ought I can see or gather from the Text, they may as well be of any other Church as the *Roman*.

They urge, Luke 10. 16.

He that heareth you heareth me, and he that despiseth you despiseth me.

But this will not do you any service, unless of favour we grant, that *you* here, is *you* of the Church of *Rome*; and but very little if that be granted: for then every Bishop, every Priest must be Infallible. For there is not the meanest of the Messengers of Christ, but this may be verified of him, That he that heareth him, heareth Christ, and he that despiseth him, despiseth Christ.

They urge out of John 14. *ver.* 15, 16.

I will ask my Father, and he will give you another Paraclete, that he may abide with you for ever, even the Spirit of Truth.

But here also, what warrant have we, by *you* to understand the Church of *Rome*: whereas he that compares *v*. 26.

with

with this, shall easily perceive, that our Saviour speaks only of the Apostles in their own persons; for there he says going on in the same discourse. *The Holy Ghost whom the Father will send in my name, he shall teach you all things, and bring all things to your remembrance, whatsoever I have said to you:* which cannot agree but to the Apostles themselves in person; and not to their Successors, who had not yet been taught and therefore not forgotten any thing, and therefore could not have them brought to their remembrance. But what if it had been promised to them and their Successors? had they no Successors but them of the *Roman* Church? this indeed is pretended and cried up, but for proofs of it, *desiderantur*.

Again, I would fain know whether there be any certainty, that every Pope is a good Christian, or whether he may not be in the sence of the Scripture, *of the World?* If not, how was it that *Bellarmine* should have cause to think, that such a rank of them went successively to the Devil?

III. *A Conference, concerning the Infallibility of the* Roman *Church:* Proving *that the present Church of* Rome *either errs in her worshipping the Blessed Virgin* Mary, *or that the Ancient Church did err in condemning the* Collyridians *as* Hereticks.

1. *Demand.* WHether the Infallibility of the *Roman* Church, be not the foundation of their Faith which are members of that Church?

Answ. The Infallibility of the Church is (not the foundation but) a part of their Faith who are members of the Church. And the *Roman* Church is held to be the Church, by all those who are members of it.

Reply. That which is the last Reason, why you believe the Scripture to be the written Word of God and unwritten Traditions his unwritten word; and this or that to be the true sense of Scripture, that is to you the foundation of your Faith, and such unto you is the Infallible Authority of the *Roman* Church. Therefore unto you it is not only a part of your faith, but also such a part as is the foundation of all other parts. Therefore you are deceived if you think, there is any more opposition between being a part of the faith and the foundation of other parts of it; than there is between being a part of a house and the foundation of it. But whether you will have it the foundation of your faith, or only a part of it, for the present purpose it is all one.

2. *Demand.* Whether the Infallibility of the *Roman* Church be not absolutely overthrown, by proving the *present Roman* Church is in error, or that the *Ancient* was?

Answ. It is, if the Error be in those things wherein she is affirmed to be infallible; *viz.* in points of Faith.

Reply. And this here spoken of, whether it be lawful to offer Tapers and Incense to the honour of the Blessed Virgin, is I hope a Question concerning a point of Faith.

3. *Demand.* Whether offering a Cake to the Virgin *Mary*, be not as lawful, as to offer Incense and Tapers and divers other oblations to the same Virgin?

Answ. It is as lawful to offer a Cake to her honour as Wax-Tapers, but neither the one, nor the other may be offered to her, or her honour, as the term or object of the Action. For to speak properly, nothing is offered to her or to her honour, but to God in the honour of the Blessed Virgin. For Incense, it is a foul slander that it is offered any way to the Blessed Virgin; for that incensing which is used in the time of Mass, is ever understood by all sorts of people to be directed to God only.

Reply. If any thing be offered to her, she is the Object of that oblation; as if I see water, and through water something else, the water is the object of my sight, though not the last object. If I honour the Kings Deputy, and by him the King, the Deputy is the object of my action, though not the final object: And to say these things may

be

be offered to her, but not as to the object of the action, is to say they may be offered to her, but not to her. For what else is meant by the object of an action, but that thing on which the action is imployed, and to which it is directed?

If you say, that by the object of the action, you mean the final object only wherewith the action is terminated; you should then have spoken more properly and distinctly, and not have denied her simply to be the object of this action, when you mean only she is not such a kind of object: no more than you may deny a man to be a living creature, meaning only that he is not a horse.

Secondly, I say, it is not required of *Roman* Catholicks when they offer Tapers to the Saints, that by an actual intention they direct their action actually to God; but it is held sufficient, that they know and believe that the Saints are in Subordination and near Relation to God, and that they give this honour to the Saints because of this relation: And to God himself rather habitually and interpretative, than actually, expresly and formally. As many men honour the Kings Deputy, without having any present thought of the King, and yet their action may be interpreted an honour to the King, being given to his Deputy, only because he is his Deputy, and for his relation to the King.

Thirdly, I say, there is no reason or ground in the world, for any man to think, that the *Collyridians* did not chuse the Virgin *Mary* for the object of their worship, rather than any other Woman or any other Creature, meerly for her relation to Christ; and by consequence there is no ground to imagine, but that at least habitually and interpretative, they directed their action unto Christ, if not actually and formally. And *Ergo*, if that be a sufficient defence for the Papists, that they make not the Blessed Virgin the final object of their worship, but worship her not for her own sake, but for her relation unto Christ: *Epiphanius* surely did ill to charge the *Collyridians* with Heresie, having nothing to impute to them, but only that he was informed, that they offered a Cake to the honour of the Blessed Virgin, which honour yet they might, and without question did give unto her for her relation unto Christ, and so made her not the last object and term of their worship: and from hence it is evident, that he conceived the very action it self, substantially and intrinsically malitious, *i. e.* he believed it a sin that they offered to her at all: and so by their action put her in the place of God, by giving unto her this worship proper to God; and not that they terminated their action finally in her, or did in very deed think her to be a God, and not a Creature.

But to speak properly, you say, *nothing is offered to her or to her honour, but to God in honour of the Blessed Virgin.*

Belike then if through *Henly* I go from hence to *London*, I may not be said properly to go to *Henly*, but only to *London:* or if through Water I see the Sand, I may not be properly said to see the Water, but only the Sand. Away with such shifting Sophistry; either leave your practice of offering to Saints if it be naught, or colour it not over with such empty distinctions if it be good: Christ saith to his Apostles in regard of their relation to him, *He that heareth you heareth me, and he that despiseth you despiseth me:* and yet who doubts, but they that heard the Apostles did properly hear them, and they that despised them did properly despise them, though their action staid not in them, but reached up to Heaven and to Christ himself. You pray to Saints and Angels, though you do not terminate your prayers in them; and yet I doubt not but your prayers to Saints, may be as properly called prayers, as those you make to God himself. For though these be of a more excellent nature than they, yet do they agree in the general nature, that they are both prayers. As though a Man be a more excellent living creature than a horse, yet he agrees with him in this, that both are living creatures. But if nothing be properly offered to her or to her honor, why do you in your sixth Answer say, you may offer any thing to the Virgin *Mary*, by way of presents and gifts by the doctrin of the *Roman* Church? Certainly he that offers by way of gift or present, offers as properly as he that offers by way of sacrifice; as a horse is as properly a living creature as a Man.

But

But if it were so as you say (which is most false) that you did not properly offer to the Blessed Virgin, but to God in honour of her; yet in my judgment, this would not qualifie or mend the matter but make it worse. For first, who taught you, that in the time of the Gospel (after the accomplishment of the prediction, *sacrifice and offering thou wouldest not but a body hast thou prepared me*: after this Interpretation of it in the Epistle to the *Hebrews*, *He taketh away the first that he may establish the second*) that it is still lawful to offer Tapers or Incense to God. Secondly, in my understanding, to offer to God in honour of the Virgin, is more derogatory from Gods honour, than to offer to her in the honour of God. For this is in my apprehension to subordinate God to her, to make her the terminating and final object of the action; to make God the way and her the end, and by and through God to conveigh the worship unto her.

But *for incense*, you say, *it is a foul slander, that it is offered any way to the Blessed Virgin*.

To this I answer, that your imputing slander to me, is it self a slander: For, In your 5th Answer, you have given a clear intimation that you have never been out of *England*: so that you cannot certainly know, what is the practice of your Church in this point beyond Sea. And he that lives amongst you, and has but half an Eye open and free from prejudice, cannot but see, that the *Roman* Religion is much more exorbitant in the general practice of it, than it is in the Doctrine published in Books of Controversie; where it is delivered with much caution and moderation, nay cunning and dissimulation that it may be the fitter to win and engage Proselytes; who being once ensnared, though they be afterwards startled with strange and unlookt-for practices, yet a hundred to one, but they will rather stifle their Conscience, and dash all scruples against the pretended Rock of their Churches Infallibility, and blindly follow those guides, to whose Conduct they have unadvisedly committed themselves, than come off again with the shame of being reputed weak and inconstant: so terrible an Idol is this vain nothing, *the opinion and censure of foolish men*. But

But to return again to you, I say your ignorance of the practice of the *Roman* Church beyond the Seas, does plainly convince that you have rashly and therefore slanderously charged me with the Crime of slander. As for your reason you add, consider it again, and you will see it is worth nothing. For what if incensing in time of Mass, be understood by all sorts of People to be directed to God alone (which yet you cannot possibly know) yet this I hope hinders not, but that in Processions, you may Incense the Images of the Saints, and consequently (according to your Doctrine) do this Honour to the Saints themselves represented by the Images. I my self (unless I am very much mistaken) was present when this very thing was done to the Picture of Saint *Benet* or Saint *Gregory* in the Cloyster of Saint *Vedastus* in the Monastery in *Doway*.

But indeed what a ridiculous inconsequence is it, to think that Wax Tapers may lawfully be offered to the Saints and incense may not: or if Incense may not, which you seem to disclaim as impious, that Wax Tapers may.

4. *Demand.* Whether the *Collyridians* were not condemned as Hereticks by the Ancient Church. First, for offering a Cake upon a Anniversary Feast to the Blessed Virgin. Secondly for that they did this not being Priests.

Answ. The *Collyridians* were condemned as Hereticks for two things. First, for imploying Women in the place and Office of Priests to offer a Cake (not in the nature of a gift or present,) but in the nature of a [a] Sacrifice, which was never lawful for any but [b] men, and those [c] consecrated.

[a] *Ut in nomen Virginis Collyridem quandam Sacrificarent.* Epiph. hær. 78. *Offerunt panem in nomen* Mariæ, *omnes autem pane participant* — [b] *Deo enim ab æterno nulla tenus mulier Sacrificavit.* Idem hæres. 79. [c] *Diaconissarum ordo est in Ecclesia, sed non ad Sacrificandum, nam neque Diaconis concreditum est, ut aliquod mysterium perficiant.* Id. Ibid.

Secondly, for offering this [a] Sacrifice εἰς ὄνομα in the name of the Blessed Virgin, *i. e.* unto her, her self directly and terminatively, as an act of [b] Divine Worship and ado-

[a] *vid. sup. litera* (a)
[b] *Mortuis cultum divinum*

adoration, due unto her, as unto a Sovereign 'Power and *præstantes*. Id. Deity. Ibid. *And again*: *Revera virgo erat honorata, sed non ad adorationem nobis data, sed ipsa adorans Deum.* And again: *Non ut adoretur Virgo, nec ut Deum hanc efficeret*, &c. *Sit in honore Maria; Pater & Filius & Spiritus S. adoretur, Mariam nemo adoret. Deo debetur hoc mysterium* Id. Ibid. ' *Pro Deo hanc introducere statuerant.* Id. Ibid. *Revera Sanctum erat Mariæ corpus non tamen Deus.* And again. *Mulierem eam appellavit* Joh. 2. *Velut prophetans: & ne aliqui nimium admirati Sanctum, in hanc hæresin dilabantur.* And again. *Non tamen aliter genita est præter hominis naturam, sed sicut omnes ex semine viri & utero Mulieris.* Id. Ibid.

Reply. It seems then these Women might offer this Cake to the honour and name of the Virgin *Mary*, if they had done it as a *Gift* or *Present* and not as a *Sacrifice*. *Epiphanius* then surely was too hasty to condemn them, being informed of nothing, but that they offered a Cake unto her. Methinks before he had put them in his Catalogue, he should have enquired whether they offered this Cake as a *Gift* only, or as a *Sacrifice*. Certainly had the practice of offering to Saints by way of gifts, been the practice of the Church in his time, he would not have been so uncharitable, as to condemn that action as impious and Heretical, which might have received so lawful and pious a construction. But he, good man, it seems could not conceive a difference between a Sacrifice, and the offering a Creature by way of Consumption to the Honour of that to which it is offered. The subtle Wits of our times I hope have found out another definition for it, and I shall understand by you what it is. But if you can find no other, then certainly, though setting up a Picture or hanging up a Leg or Eye or Ear in memory of some miraculous cure, obtained by a Saints intercession, would be a *Gift* or *Present* only; yet offering of Incense, or burning a Taper in the honour of a Saint, daub the matter how you will, will be without Question a *Sacrifice*. If you say, that there may be such an offering and yet no Sacrifice; I would know then, how you would prove that the *Collyridians* offering was indeed a Sacrifice? All that *Epiphanius* says of them is but this —— *Panem proponunt & in Mariæ nomen offerunt.* And though
this

this offering of theirs was indeed a Sacrifice in the notion of the word which I have given it, yet doth he not any where say expresly, *That they did Sacrifice, or offer it as a Sacrifice,* but only and barely that they did *offer it* : not using (as good fortune would have it) any word which doth of necessity and properly signifie *to Sacrifice*: and therefore you are fain to help the Dice, and alter every place for your advantage. *Epiphanius* says not, as you translate him, *ut in nomen Virginis Collyridem quendam Sacrificent*; nor *Sacrificantes offerunt*, as *Petavius*: but ὡς ἐπιτελεῖν, which may as well signifie, to *consecrate* or *offer*, as to *Sacrifice*, if there be any difference between them. So the next place, *offerunt panem in nomen Mariæ, omnes autem pane participant*; proves not I hope offering by way of *Sacrifice*, unless the Consumption of the oblation make it a *Sacrifice*; which if it do, how your Tapers can be kept from being Sacrifices I cannot imagine; unless again perhaps Consumption by way of *Eating* will make it a *Sacrifice,* and by *Burning* will not; which cannot be, because the whole Burnt-offerings were Sacrifices as well as any other.

Your third place is, *Deo autem ab æterno nullatenus mulier Sacrificavit.* But ἱεραδύω signifies not *to Sacrifice,* but only to *perform the Office of a Priest,* and so *Petavius* translates the place. *Nunquam sacerdotio functa est mulier.* And though Sacrificing be *one* perhaps, yet will you not say it is the *only* Office of a Priest: as your next and last place would have declared, had you set it down faithfully; but in that also you juggle again, and force it to speak to your purpose thus. *Diaconissarum ordo est in Ecclesia, sed non ad Sacrificandum*: but *Petavius* hath translated it truly thus: *Quanquam vero Diaconissarum in Ecclesia ordo sit, non tamen ad sacerdotii functionem, aut ullam administrationem institutus est.* And now though by an usual Synechdoche the name of the *Genus* be given to the *Species,* and therefore had a man fairly and candidly translated ἱεραδύω by *Sacrifico,* I should not have much condemned him, yet to do it when the Question is, whether this their offering, confessed to be an offering, were in propriety of speech
a Sa-

a Sacrifice, to do it for Ends, to shift off a convincing argument, to palliate over a foul matter, by putting a verbal difference where there is none indeed, and all that you may, *Imperitos rerum in fraudem illicere*; that is ——— But I forbear you.

But Secondly it is pretended, [*they offered this Sacrifice* εἰς ὄνομα *in the name of the Blessed Virgin: i. e. unto her, her self, directly and terminately as an act of Divine Worship and adoration due unto her, as unto a Sovereign Power and Deity.*] And to colour and countenance this strange gloss, many places are quoted out of *Epiphanius*, which I will examine in order as they lie.

The first place is, *mortuis cultum Divinum præstantes*, where your meaning is, I believe, that *Epiphanius* says the *Collyridians* did so: but the truth is he says only, *mortuos colentes*; as *Petavius* translates it: and therefore here once again you help the Dice; yet if he had said so, why should you rather from *cultum divinum* collect that, that they thought her *God*, than from *mortuis*, that they thought her *Dead*, and therefore certainly not a God? Certainly this can be no warrant to you, that *Epiphanius* charges them with so thinking: For *Protestants* you know impute to *Papists* that they give to Saints *cultum divinum*, and yet they do not impute to them the Heresie of thinking, that the Saints are Sovereign Powers and Deities: But as S. *Paul* accuseth the Gentiles, for that knowing God to be God, *they did not worship him as God*, so on the other side, *Protestants* condemn *Papists*, and *Epiphanius* for ought we can see hitherto, might condemn the *Collyridians*, for that knowing the Blessed Virgin not to be God, they yet worship'd her as God. That is, gave her that worship which is Gods own peculiar, which yet they might do, not because they thought her God, but because this worship, which was indeed proper to God, they might think not proper, but communicable to such Creatures as were high in his favour.

The next place is ——— *Revera virgo erat honorata, sed non ad adorationem nobis data, sed ipsa adorans Deum*, &c.

I answer that the *&c.* perhaps conceals something more pertinent to your purpose, but in the Words set down there appears to me just nothing; for I can frame out of them no other Syllogism but this.

Whatsoever *Epiphanius* in this place says is not to be adored, that the *Collyridians* thought to be God.

But *Epiphan.* here says the Virgin is not to be adored.

Ergo. The *Collyridians* thought her God.

Of this Syllogism I deny the Major proposition, and I believe shall stay as long for a proof of it, as I have done for an answer to some other discourses, which being written in a few days, have waited now with a longing expectation for a promised answer many months. If you say, you would conclude from these Words, that they did adore her and therefore thought her God, I have answered already, that they might do this, not because they thought her God, but because they thought Creatures high in Gods favour capable of adoration.

The next place —— *Non ut adoretur Virgo, nec ut deum hanc efficeret* —— tells us that Christ took Flesh of the Virgin, not that she should be adored, nor to make her God: And this you think imports, that they conceive her God. Yet if I should, condemning your Practice of offering Tapers to her, use the same Words and say, —— *Christ took Flesh of the Virgin, not that she should be adored, or to make her God*: You would not yet conceive that I charged you with the Heresie of believing her God, but only of the impiety of giving to her that worship which was peculiar to God: and why then might not *Epiphanius*, having like occasion, use the same words to the *Collyridians* upon the same, and no other ground.

The next place —— *Mariam nemo adoret, Deo debetur hoc mysterium,* —— is so far from proving your imagination, that it strongly confirms my assertion, that *Epiphanius* did not impute to the *Collyridians* the opinion, *that the Virgin Mary was God*. If I should say to a *Papist*, the Blessed Virgin is not to be worshiped with the worship of *Hyperdaulia*, because such worship is due only to the Mother of God, would they not say I were mad and argued against
my

my self, for that they believed she was the Mother of God. By like reason, if *Epiphanius* knew, that the *Collyridians* believed the Virgin *Mary* to be God, he reasoned as wildly against himself in saying —— *Mariam nemo adoret, Deo debetur hoc mysterium* —— For it is very true (might they have said) this service is due to God alone, but you know our Belief and Profession that she is God, and therefore by your own rule capable of this worship.

The next place is —— *Pro Deo hanc introducere studuerunt*. And may not this be justly said to any man, who to any thing besides God, gives that worship which is proper and peculiar unto God? What if to man that should teach — *The* Pope *had power to dispense with men for the keeping of Gods Laws* —— I should say, *pro Deo Papam introducis*. Must I of necessity mean that that man did verily believe the *Pope* not a man but a Sovereign Power and Deity? S. *Paul* tells us that *Covetousness is Idolatry*; he tells us of some, *whose God is their Belly*; is it therefore consequent, that every covetous man doth indeed believe his *Gold*, and every Glutton his *Belly*, to be indeed a Sovereign Power and Deity? Away with such fopperies. Whosoever loves, or fears, or trusts in any thing more than God, may yet be justly said to make that his God, and whosoever should worship any Creature with that external worship which God has appropriated to himself, might justly be said to bring in that Creature for God. S. *Paul* tells us of some, who *in words professed God, yet factis negabant, in their deeds deny him*: so these on the contrary, may in their words deny this Creature to be God, and in their Hearts not think it so, yet seeing their actions to it are as if it were God, they may be justly charged, that with their deeds they make this Creature God.

Qui fingit Sacros ex auro & marmore vultus,
Non facit ille Deos, qui colit ille facit.

What if upon consideration of the strangely enormous worship which *Papists* give to the Virgin *Mary* (swearing by her name, making Vows unto her, offering Tapers to her Honour, attributing a kind of Communicated omniscience and almost omnipotence to her, as I can easily make good they do, partly out of the Offices of their Church, partly out of private mens Works, but set out with Licence and approbation) what I say, if upon this consideration I should affirm, *pro Deo ipsam introducere conantur*. Would it therefore be consequent, that I must impute this Blasphemy to them, that they believed and taught her to be a Sovereign Power and Deity? I trow not. And therefore *Epiphanius* might say the same of the *Collyridians* considering their *Action*, without any intent of imputing to them any such *opinion*. This *Petavius* sure saw well enough, and therefore (as I shall hereafter demonstrate to the Eye) to countenance his Marginal Annotation, *Quidam Mariam Deum esse crediderunt*, he cunningly abuses and perverts *Epiphanius* his Text with false Translation. —— *Sic pugnat, Sic est metuendus Ulysses*. —— The next place is, *revera sanctum erat* Mariæ *corpus non tamen Deus*. (*The Body of* Mary *was truly holy, but not a God.*) As much to the purpose as — *Tityre tu patulæ* —— for what if *Epiphanius* say, she is not God, and therefore not to be adored, does it therefore follow that the *Collyridians* believed she was a God? He that knows Logick or sense, cannot but know, that he that will confute an Adversaries conclusion, must choose such principles to do it, to which his Adversary consents, and out of that which he grants prove that which he denies; or if his first propositions be not agreed to by his Adversary, he must prove them in the end by such as are agreed to; or else he does nothing. And therefore seeing *Epiphanius* thinks it sufficient for the convincing of the *Collyridians*, of the unlawfulness of the practice, to say, she was not God: it is evident, that so far was he from imputing to them the belief that she was God, that he seems rather to take the contrary for a principle agreed upon between them, which it was sufficient to say and superfluous to prove. This answer I thought good to make, while I conceived that here *Epiphanius* had denied the Person of the Virgin Mary to be God; but after upon better consideration I found that *Petavius* had abused me with adding to *Epi-*

phanius

phanius of his own —— *Illa fuit* —— and that *Epiphanius* says not here, *non tamen Deus* (*she was not God*) of her *Person*, but of her *Body*; and as yet I do not understand that you impute to the *Collyridians* the belief, that her Body was God.

The next place —— *Mulierem eam appellavit*, &c. —— says no more but this; that our Saviour calls the Blessed Virgin *Woman*, that no man might think her any thing more than a Woman, as it were prophetically refuting the Schisms and Heresies which would be in the World : lest some out of excess of admiration of her, might fall into the Dotage of this Heresie. Thus far *Epiphanius*: but then the Question will be, what was this Heresie. You say the belief that she was God. I say, not that she was God, but that they might lawfully offer to her. And as I deny not but it follows, *she is a Woman, therefore not a God*; so I think you will grant it follows as justly, *she is a Woman, therefore not to be adored with offerings*. And therefore seeing the words lie indifferently between us, and are not expresly and especially here applied, for the refutation of that Heresie which you pretend they were guilty of, I see no reason why *Epiphanius* might not as well intend them for that purpose which I conceive, as for that which you conceive.

The last place alledged tells us, *that she was begotten and Born as other Men and Women are*. Which if the *Collyridians* had thought her God, Eternal and absolutely without beginning, should not have been barely said but proved, as being in effect the very point in question; and therefore seeing *Epiphanius* contents himself with saying so without proof, it is evident he never thought they would make difficulty to grant it, and consequently that they did not believe her to be God Eternal.

But then again, if the Rule be good which part of your proofs depend upon, That whatever *Epiphanius* denies in this discourse, that the *Collyridians* held (for upon that ground from —— *Non & Deum hanc efficeret : & non tamen Deus*, you conclude they believed her God) If I say this Rule be good, then you should be constant to it, and now that he says, —— *Non tamen aliter genita est præter hominum naturam*, *(she was not begotten in a different way from other men)* you should infer, that they believed not that she was God, but that she was otherwise Born and Begotten than the ordinary sort of Men. And so whereas he says before —— *Non tamen corpus de cœlo tulit* —— *(her Body was not from Heaven)* you should infer, that they believed her Body came from Heaven. And again from those —— *Sanctum erat Mariæ corpus non tamen Deus* —— you should collect that they thought not only her person, but her Body to be God: or if these be wild and weak deductions, then you must acknowledge that I have done yours some favour in vouchsafing them a particular answer.

5. *Demand*. Whether in the Church of *Roman*, it be not an approved and perpetually practised worship of the Blessed Virgin, that Incense (which was never anciently offered unto any, either by *Jews* or *Gentiles*, but to the true, or to a supposed true God) and Tapers and divers other oblations, should be offered to her honour?

Answ. A practice of the Church of *Rome*, and approved too by those that practise it, belongs not to her, except it be a practice of the Church and approved by her. What her practice is abroad I know not; here at home I see no such practice; nor do I know any approbation of it, in any of her publick declarations: But this I know, that there is nothing in it unlawful or savouring of the *Collyridian Superstition*, to offer Wax, Tapers or any other thing at the Memories of the Blessed Virgin or any other Canonized Saint, either as means to procure their intercession, by these outward Signs of the Honour and Devotion which they bear to them (as of Old we find by S. *Austin* [a] they did use to adorn their Tombs with Flowers) or as monuments of their thankfulness for some benefits received by their Intercession, as *Theodoret* [b] tells

[a] Ad aquas Tibilotanas, Episcopo offerente Projecto, reliquias martyris gloriosissimi Stephani, ad ejus memoriam veniebat magnæ multitudinis concursus & occursus. Ibi cæca mulier, ut ad episcopum portantem pignora Sacra duceretur, oravit: Flores quos ferebat dedit; recepit, oculis admovit, protenus vidit. August. de Civit. Dei. l. 22. c. 8. abscedens aliquid de Altari (S. Stephani) florum quod occurrit, tulit. Idem. Ibid. &c. [b] Theodoretus de curandis affec: Græc. l. 8.

us of Eyes and Ears and Hands, some of Gold and some of Silver (hung up in the Chappels of the Saints) that had been presented as oblations by those that had recovered health in those Members, according to their Vows made to that purpose in time of Sickness.

Reply. I do not deny, but a practice may be *tolerated* in a Church, and not *approved.* As the *Publick Stews* are in *Italy,* and *Usury* in *England* ? But it is one thing to Tolerate with condemnation, another to Tolerate without condemnation, nay with condemnation of those that should oppose or condemn it. And such I doubt not upon examination, you may find is this practice, general in the Church of *Rome,* offering Tapers to the Saints and for their honour. I say, not only to God, at the Memories of the Saints, as you would mince the matter, which yet were a groundless superstition, (God having appointed no such Sacrifice to be offered to him under the Gospel) but to the Saints themselves and to their honour, prove this lawful for either of those purposes you mention, either to procure their intercession or as Monuments of thankfulness for benefits obtained by it, and then you shall do something. Otherwise you will but trifle as now you have done : For instead of telling us what may be done *de jure,* you tell us what of Old has been done *de facto.* As if *ab antiquo,* and a *principio* were all one ; or as if the Church (as we pretend) being subject to corruption, part of this corruption might not possibly have come in S. *Austins* or *Theodorets* time ; yet this I say not, as if I would decline the Tryal of this cause by S. *Austin* or *Theodoret* ; but because I am sure you will not be Tryed by the Fathers, no not the consent of Fathers in all things : and therefore there is no reason nor equity in the World, that you should serve your selves with their Authority in any thing.

But now what is it, which was done in S. *Austins* time, that may justifie the Practice of the *Roman* Church ? was there then any approved offering of Wax, Tapers and Incense, to the Queen of Heaven, or any other Saint ? *nil horum* : you neither do nor can produce any thing out of S. *Austin* to this purpose. But what then is it ? Why forsooth,

forsooth, they were used to adorn their Tombs: *Egregiam verò laudem & spolia ampla*; of Old in S. *Austins* time they were used to adorn their Tombs with Flowers, therefore we may offer Tapers to them. Truly an excellent *Enthymeme*, but I fear the concealed proposition which should make it a *Syllogism*, hides its head for shame and dares not appear: yet we will for once make bold to draw it forth into light, that you may look upon it and tell us how you like it. This therefore it is.

Whose soever Tombs we adorn, to them and to their honour we may offer Wax Tapers.

Consider it I pray you, and if you approve it, then approve also of offering Tapers not only to Canonize Saints, but to all Christians that may have Monuments in Churches. For all their Tombs may be adorned, with more pretious and lasting Ornaments than Flowers; yet if you had proved but this only, that in S. *Austins* time, they adorned the Saints Tombs with Flowers by these outward signs to procure their Intercession; this, though not much to the purpose, had been not absolutely to delude us. But your quoted places prove not so much as this; and yet I believe you quoted the best you could find. Nay they prove not they did adorn their Tombs with Flowers at all, much less that they did it for your pretended purpose; such fools you think to deal with, that will take any thing for any thing. Your first place, I say, proves it not, unless out of meer courtesie we understand by *ferebat, she brought to adorn* S. Stephens *Tomb.*

The Second proves it not, unless we give you leave after *Altari* (without warrant from S. *Austin*) to put in, S. *Stephani,* whereas I am yet to seek for any place in S. *Austin,* where he calls any Altar, the Altar of such or such a Saint, which yet I think they forbore not for the unlawfulness, but for fear of misconstruction.

Then for *Theodoret*, he tells us indeed of Vows made, of monuments of thankfulness dedicated, for benefits obtained by the intercession of the Martyrs. But here also I fear your Conscience tells you, that you abuse us and hide your self in ambiguities. For to whom does *Theodoret* say

say these Vows were made? to whom were these monuments of thankfulness dedicated? What, to the Author? or Procurer of the received favours? To God, or to the Martyrs? If to the Martyrs, that had been something towards, though not home to your purpose: For there is a a wide difference between offering of a Creature by way of Consumption (as was never lawfully done but to God alone, as a profession that he is the Lord of the Creature) and erecting a permanent Monument to a Saints honour; which I doubt not but it may lawfully be done to a living Saint, much more to the memory of a Martyr. But *Theodoret* in the place, hath not so much as this: Nay it is evident that these gifts he speaks of, were both Vowed and payed to God himself. His words are —— *Piè precatos ea consequi*, &c. —— that they which pray piously, obtain the things which they desire, they paying of their Vowed presents in the sign of their recovered health, doth abundantly testifie. For their Lord accepts most gratiously these presents how mean so ever.

6. *Demand.* Whether according to the Doctrine of the *Roman* Church, this may not be done lawfully by Women and Children, and men that are not Priests?

Answ. They may offer any thing by way of *gifts* and *presents*, by the Doctrine of the *Roman* Church; But it is contrary to the *Roman* Doctrine, for any other than Priests, to offer any thing by way of *Sacrifice*, as the *Collyridians* did.

Reply. Aristotle says most truly, that true Definitions (he means I think of the terms of the conclusion to be demonstrated) are the best principles of Science: and therefore want of them, must needs be a cause of Error and confusion in any discourse. Let me therefore here request you to set down what is a *Sacrifice*, and how distinguished from an oblation by way of *gift* or *present*, and you will quickly see, that if the *Collyridians* offering a Cake to the Blessed Virgin were indeed a *Sacrifice*, your offering a Taper to her, must likewise be so. For a *Sacrifice* is nothing else (for ought I know) but the oblation of any Creature by way of *Consumption*, to the honour of that, whatsoever it is, to which it is offered. For if you include in the definition, that this offering must be intended to the highest Lord of all: So is, as you pretend, your offering of Tapers to the Blessed Virgin, intended to God finally, though not immediately. If you say it must be directed immediatly to him; and is, not only *no lawful Sacrifice*, but simply *no Sacrifice* unless it be so: I say you may as well require to the essence of a Sacrifice, that it be offered by a Priest, and from thence conclude, because the *Collyridians* were, you say, no Priests, their offering was no Sacrifice. For the object of the Action is as extrinsecal to the essence of it, as the efficient; And therefore if the defect of a due and legitimate Offerer, cannot hinder but that an offering may be a true Sacrifice, neither will the want of a due and lawful object be any hindrance but still it may be so. Secondly, I say, this is to confound the essence of things with the lawful use of them; in effect as if you should say, that a Knife, if misimployed, were a Knife no longer. Thirdly, it is to make it not unlawful, to offer Incense (which yet you seem somewhat scrupulous of) or Burnt-offerings to the Virgin *Mary*, or the Saints, or even to living Men, provided you know and believe and profess them to be Men and not Gods. For this once supposed, these offerings will be no longer Sacrifices, and to offer to Creatures offerings that are not Sacrifices, you say, by the Doctrine of the *Roman* Church is lawful: It is lastly, to deny (which is most ridiculous) that the *Pagans* did indeed Sacrifice to any of their inferiour Gods.

7. *Demand.* If it be said, that this worship which they give to the Blessed Virgin is not that of *Latria*, but that of *Dulia* or *Hyperdulia*, for that they do not esteem her God: or if it be said, that their worship to her is not finally terminated neither, but given her for her relation to Christ. I demand, whether as it is, in S. *Pauls* judgment, a great crime for him that knows God, not to worship him as God, so it be not as great a crime, for him that knows her not to be God, yet to worship her (as if she were God) with the worship which is proper

and

and hath been alwaies appropriated to God alone, such is the *worship of oblations*?

Answ. The *worship of oblations*, as *worship* is taken largly for *honour*, and *oblations* for a *gift* or *present*, was never appropriate to God alone; take *worship* and *oblations* in any higher sense, and so it is not allowed in the Church of *Rome*.

Reply. The *oblation* of things by way of *Consumption*, is the worship I spoke of; this is a higher matter, than that of *gifts* and *presents*, and this is allowed in the Church of *Rome*, to be imployed on, and directed into, (though not terminated in) the Virgin *Mary* and other Saints.

8. *Demand.* Whether any thing can be said for the justifying the Doctrine and practice of the *Roman* Church in this matter, which might not also have been as justly pretended, for the justification of the *Collyridians* in their opinion and practice; seeing it was never imputed to them, that they accounted the Blessed Virgin God, or that they believed in more Gods than one. And seeing their choosing her out, rather than any other Woman or any other Creature for the object of their Devotion, shews plainly, that they gave it her for her Relation to Christ?

Answ. The *Collyridians* could not say this, as appears by what has been said before: As it is a most shameless slander upon Gods Church, and such as (without repentance) will lie heavy upon his Soul that uttered it, that the *Collyridians* might as justly and truly have said all this for themselves as *Papists* for themselves.

Reply. To this I reply four things. 1. That to my last and most convincing reason, you have answered (as much as you could I believe, but yet you have answered) nothing; and I am well content you should do so; for where nothing is to be had, the King himself must lose his right. 2. That if I had thought or spoke better of the *Collyridians* than they deserved, yet I cannot see how this had been to slander the Church of *Rome*. 3. That I did not positively affirm, that the *Collyridians* might do so, but desired only it might be inquired into and examined,

whether

whether for the reasons alledged they might not do so.

4. And lastly, upon a thorow examination of the matter, I do now affirm, what before I did not, that the *Collyridians* for ought appears to the contrary, might justly and truly have said for the justification of their practice, as much, nay the very same things that the *Papists* do for theirs. For they might have said, we are Christians and believe the Scripture, and believe there is but one God. We offer not to the Blessed Virgin, as believing she is God, but the Mother of God: our worship of her is not absolute but relative, not terminated in her, but given to her for her Sons sake: And if our practice may be allowed, we are content to call our Oblation, not a Sacrifice, but a present: neither is there any reason, why it should be called a Sacrifice, more than the Offering and Burning a Taper to the honour of the same Virgin. All this the *Collyridians* might have said for themselves: and therefore I believe, you will have more cause to repent you for daubing over impiety with untempered Morter, than I shall have for slandering the *Roman* Church with a matter of truth.

9. *Demand.* Whether therefore, one of the two must not of necessity follow: that either the Ancient Church Erred in condemning the Opinion and Practice of the *Collyridians* as Heretical, or else that the Church of *Rome* Errs, in approving the same opinion, and the same practice in effect, which in them was condemned. That is, whether the Church of *Rome* must not be Heretical with the *Collyridians*, or else the *Collyridians* Catholicks with the Church of *Rome*?

Answ. It appears by the former answers, that neither did the Ancient Church Err, in condemning the opinion and practice of the *Collyridians*, as Heretical, nor doth the Church of *Rome* approve the same opinion or the same practice.

Reply. The Substance of the former answers is but this. That the *Papists* offer to the Virgin *Mary* and other Saints Wax Tapers by way of *gift* or *present*, not of Sacrifice; and to her not as to a God, but as the Mother of God:

God: but that the *Collyridians* offered to her by way of Sacrifice, as to a Sovereign Power and Deity. To this I have replied and proved, that it no way appears, that the *Collyridians* did believe the Blessed Virgin to be a Sovereign Power and Deity, or that she was not subordinate to God. Then that their offering might be called a *gift*, as well as the *Papists*, and the *Papists* a *Sacrifice* as well as theirs; both of them being a *Consumption* of a Creature in honour of the Blessed Virgin, and neither of them more than so: and therefore either the *Collyridians* must stand with the Church of *Rome*, or the Church of *Rome* fall with the *Collyridians*. It had been perhaps sufficient for me, thus to have vindicated my Assertion from contrary objections, without taking on my self the burden of proving a Negative: yet to free from all doubt the conformity of the *Roman* Church with the *Collyridians*, in this point, I think it will be necessary to shew, and that by many very probable Arguments, that *Epiphanius* did not impute to them the pretended Heresie of *believing* the Virgin *Mary God*: for then that other Evasion, that their oblation is a Sacrifice and the *Papists* is not, together with this pretence will of it self fall to the ground.

Now an opinion may be imputed to a man two ways: either because he holds and maintains it expresly and formally and in terms: or because it may by a rational deduction be collected from some other opinion which he does hold: In this latter sense I deny not but *Epiphanius* might impute this opinion we speak of to the *Collyridians*, as a consequence upon their practice, which practice they esteemed lawful. But that they held it and owned it formally and in terms, this I say *Epiphanius* does not impute to them, which I think for these seven reasons.

My first Reason is, because he could not justly do so, and therefore without evident proof we may not say he did so: for this were to be uncharitable to him, in making him uncharitable to others. Now I say he could not justly charge them with this opinion, because he was not informed of any such opinion that they held, but only of their

their practice, and this practice was no sufficient proof that they held this opinion. That his information reached no further than their Practice, appears out of his own Words. *I have heard* (saith he. Hæres. 78.) *another thing with great astonishment: that some being madly affected to the Blessed Virgin, endeavour to bring her in in Gods place, being mad and besides themselves: For they report that certain Women in* Arabia *have devised this Vanity, to have meetings, and offer a Cake to the Blessed Virgin:* The same practice he sets down *Hæres.* 79. But that he was informed of any such opinion that they held, he has not a Word or Syllable to any such purpose; and yet if he had been informed of any, here had been the place to set it down: which certainly writing his Book rather of Heretical opinions than practices, he would not have omitted to do; if there had been occasion: his silence therefore is a sufficient Argument, that he was not informed of any such opinion that they held.

Now that their practice was no assurance that they held this opinion, it is manifest; because they might ground it not upon this opinion *that she was God,* but upon another as false, though not altogether so impious, *That the Worship of Oblations was not proper to God alone.* And therefore, though *Epiphanius* might think or fear that possibly they might ground their practice upon that other impious opinion, and therefore out of abundant caution confute that also, as he doth obliquely and in a word, and once only in all his long discourse, by telling them that our Saviour called her *Woman*; yet he had no ground from their practice to assure himself, that certainly they did hold so. Nay Justice and Reason and Charity would, that he should incline himself to believe, that they grounded their practice upon that other opinion, which had less impiety in it, that is, that this worship of Oblations, was not proper to God, but communicable to Creatures high in his favour.

My second is, Because if *Epiphanius* had known, that these *Collyridians* held the Blessed Virgin to be a Supream Power and Deity; this being a far greater matter than

offering

offering a Cake to her, should in all probability rather have given them their denomination: at least when he sets down what their Heresie was, he would have made this part of it, that they did believe so: But to the contrary, in his *Anacæphaleosis*, p. 130. he thus describes them. *They that offer to the name of the Blessed Virgin Cakes, who are called* Collyridians. And again, p. 150. *They that offer to the Blessed Virgin Cakes who are called* Collyridians: So to the 79th. Heresie he gives this Title, *Against the* Collyridians *who offer to* Mary: So *Hæres.* 78, and 79. He sets down what he heard of them; but no where that they held this opinion of her: I conclude therefore, that he never conceived this opinion to be a part of their Heresie, and they were no further chargeable with it, than as a probable consequent upon their practice.

My third is, Because had the *Collyridians* held her God, they would have worshiped her all the year long, and not only once a year at a Solemn time, as *Epiphanius* says they did.

My fourth is, Because if *Epiphanius* had known that they held her God, he would questionless have urged them with those Attributes that are given to God in Scripture, as Eternity, Immortallity, Impossibility, Omnipotence, &c. And shewed them, that if they believed the Scripture, they could not think of her any of those things; if they did not, they had no reason to think of her any thing more than of an ordinary Woman.

My fifth is, because had their opinion been, that the Blessed Virgin was God; a great part of *Epiphanius*'s discourse were plainly ridiculous; both where he says only without proof, she was not a God but a Mortal Creature, which to them that held the contrary should not have been said, but proved: But especially where he speaks to this purpose (as he does very frequently) that the honour of Oblations was not to be given to Angels or Men, much less to Women, but only to God: for what had that been to the *Collyridians*, if they thought her (as is pretended) a Sovereign Power and Deity? to what purpose was it for *Epiphanius* to ask, *Quis prophetam*; *What prophet*

prophet ever permitted, that a Man, much less a Woman should be adored, though he be yet alive. Nor John *nor* Tecla, *nor any other Saint. For neither shall the Old Superstition have dominion over us, that leaving the Living God, we should Adore his Creatures.* To what end I say was all this, if they thought her not a Saint nor Creature, but God himself and the Lord of all? How did this Argument touch them? *Ne Angelos quidem* —— *He suffers not the very Angels to be adored, how much less the Daughter of* Anna? if they thought her not the Daughter of *Anna*, but God Eternal; In vain had it been to say to them — *Not to a Woman, no nor to a Man, but to God alone, is this mistery* (of Oblation) *due.* So that the Angels themselves are not fit Subjects for such an honour. Or again, *Let the Creature be turned to the Creator: Let shame at length compel you to worship God alone:* Or lastly, that so often repeated —— *Let* Mary *be honoured, but the Lord only adored.* For they might have answered all this in a word, saying, All this discourse sits besides the Cushion, and concerns us and our offering nothing at all. For we believe the Blessed Virgin to whom we offer neither Man nor Woman, nor Angel, nor Creature, but a Deity.

A Sixth Reason let it be this, If *Epiphanius* did indeed say of the *Collyridians* as is pretended, That they held the Virgin *Mary* God, and so difference their practice from the *Papists*: Then the Author of this Answer and *Petavius* in his Translation, needed not to have dictated to him what he should say, nor make him say so whether he will or no: But it is evident they do so, as of the Author of this Answer I have already shewn: and for *Petavius* his part, I will so present it to your view, that if you will not shut your Eyes, you shall not choose but see it.

First then, *Hæres.* 78. *propè fin.* he (*Petavius*) sets in his Margent, *quidam Deum Mariam esse, crediderunt*; and to countenance this with a *loquuntur* of his own putting in, makes them *speak* of her like mad Men, *i. e.* they said she was God: whereas in *Epiphanius*'s Greek they say just nothing.

Secondly,

Secondly, To fasten the pretended Opinion on them, he translates κενοφώνημα *Novum dogma:* presuming it seems κενοφώνημα would easily be mistaken for καινοφώνημα, and therefore meanes nothing by it, but a vanity or folly.

Thirdly, He translates τólογε, *Illud*; and so makes it look backward to that pretended *Novum dogma* of the *Collyridians*; whereas it signifies there [And] and looks forward to their practice.

Fourthly, With the help of a *Colon*, he stops the sense at *Commentas fuisse*, whereas in *Epiphanius* there is but a *Comma*, and the sense goes on without suspension.

Fifthly, With an *adeo ut*, he brings in their action, as an effect of their former opinion; whereas *Epiphanius* lays nothing to their charge but their Action only: So that whereas *Epiphanius* his words truly translated run thus: *Another thing I have received with great astonishment, that others being mad concerning the Blessed Virgin, have and do go about to bring her in, in the place of God, being mad, I say, and besides themselves: For they report that certain Women in* Arabia *have brought this vanity of offering a Cake to her name.* Petavius makes them thus —— *Not without admiration we have heard another thing, that some in these things that concern the most holy Virgin have proceeded to that degree of madness, that they would obtrude her upon us for a God, and speak of her as madmen: For they report that certain Women in* Arabia, *have invented that new Opinion: so that to the Virgins name and honour, they offer by way of sacrifice a Cake or wreath of Bread.*

Again in the same *Hæres.* ἱερεργεῖν διὰ γυναικῶν, he translates advantageously——*per mulieres sacrificia facere.* Whereas ἱερεργεῖν is more general than *sacrificia facere*, and signifies *sacris operari*, or *sacros ritus peragere*.

Again, in the same place, whereas *Epiphanius* says simply and absolutely——*Let no man offer to her name*, he makes it, *Let no man offer sacrifice to her name;* as if you might lawfully offer any thing provided you do not call it a sacrifice.

So again *Hæref.*79. besides his putting cunningly—*ipsa fuit*—which before we took notice of; he makes no scruple to put in *Dogma* and *Sacrificium*, wheresoever it may be for his purpose. *Epiphanius* his title to this Heresie is, *Against the* Collyridians *who offer to* Mary—*Petavius* puts in—*Sacrifice.*

Again in the same page, before *D.* he puts in his own *illo dogmate*, and whereas *Epiphanius* says—*in all this*, he makes it, *in all this Opinion.*

Pag. 1061. τὸ θηλυσῆς ὑπογοιᾶς, he translates, *this womanish Opinion*, whereas ὑπόγια though perhaps it may signifie a *thought*, or act of thinking, yet I believe it never signifies an *Opinion* which we hold.

Ibid. at *B.* τοῦτο—this—he renders *this Opinion.*

Pag. 1064. at *C. Nor that we should offer to her name,* simply and absolutely: he makes it,—*Nor that we should offer sacrifice to her name.* So many times is he fain to corrupt, and translate him partially, lest in condemning the *Collyridians*, he might seem to have involved the practice of the *Roman Church* in the same Condemnation.

My Seventh and last Reason is this. Had *Epiphanius* known that the *Collyridians* held the *Virgin Mary* to be a Sovereign power and Deity, then he could not have doubted, whether this their offering was to her or to God for her: whereof yet he seems doubtful and not fully resolved, as his own words intimate, *Hæref.*79. *ad fin. Quam multa* &c. *How many things may be objected against this Heresie? for idle Women either worshipping the Blessed Virgin, offer unto her a Cake, or else they take upon them to offer for her this foresaid ridiculous oblation. Now both are foolish and from the Devil.*

These Arguments I suppose do abundantly demonstrate to any man not viel'd with prejudice, that *Epiphanius* imputed not to the *Collyridians* the Heresie of believing the Virgin *Mary* God: and if they did not think her God, there is then no reason imaginable why their oblation of a *Cake*, should not be thought a *Present*, as well as the

Papists offering a *Taper*, or that the Papists offering a *Taper*, should not be thought a *Sacrifice*, as well as their offering a *Cake*; and seeing this was the difference pretended between them, this being vanished there remains none at all; So that my first Conclusion stands yet firm; that either the Ancient Church erred in condemning the *Collyridians*, or the present errs in approving and practising the same worship.

An Advertisement.

The Reader when he meets with the Phrase *Catholick Doctrin*, in the two following Discourses, must remember, that it does not signifie *Articles of Faith* determined in any General Councils, which might be looked upon as the Faith of the whole Church; but the *Current* and *Common Opinion* of the Age, which obtained in it without any known opposition and contradiction. Neither need this be wondred at, since they are about matters far removed from the Common Faith of Christians, and having no necessary influence upon good life and manners, whatsoever necessity, by mistake of some Scriptures, might be put upon them.

IV. *An*

IV. *An Argument drawn from the admitting Infants to the Eucharist, as without which they could not be saved, against the Churches Infallibility.*

THE Condition without the performance whereof no man can be admitted to the Communion of the Church of *Rome*, is this; that he believe firmly and without doubting, whatsoever the Church requires him to believe: More distinctly and particularly thus:

He must believe all that to be divine Revelation which that Church teaches to be such; as the Doctrin of the Trinity, the Hypostatical union of two natures in the person of Christ. The procession of the Holy Ghost from the Father and the Son: the Doctrin of Transubstantiation, and such like.

Whatsoever that Church teaches to be necessary, he must believe to be necessary. As Baptism for Infants; Faith in Christ, for those that are Capable of Faith; Penance for those that have committed mortal sin after Baptism, &c.

Whatsoever that Church declares expedient and profitable, he must believe to be expedient and profitable: as Monastical Life: Prayer to Saints: Prayer for the Dead: going on Pilgrimages: The use of Pardons: Veneration of holy Images and Reliques: Latin Service where the people understand it not: Communicating the Laity in one kind and such like.

Whatsoever that Church holdeth lawful, he must believe lawful: As to Marry: to make distinction of Meats, as if some were clean and others unclean: to flie in time of Persecution: for them that serve at the Altar, to live by the Altar: to testifie a truth by Oath, when a lawful Magistrate shall require it: to possess Riches, &c.

Now is it impossible that any man should certainly believe any thing; unless either it be evident of it self, or he have some certain reason (at least some supposed certain reason) and infallible ground for his belief. Now the

Doctrins which the Church of *Rome* teacheth, it is evident and undeniable that they are not evident of themselves, neither evidently true nor evidently credible. He therefore that will believe them, must of necessity have some certain and infallible ground whereon to build his belief of them.

There is no other ground for a Mans belief of them, especially in many points, but only an assurance of the Infallibility of the Church of *Rome*. No man can be assured that that Church is infallible and cannot err, whereof he may be assured that she hath erred, unless she had some new promise of divine assistance, which might for the future secure her from danger of erring; but the Church of *Rome* pretends to none such.

Nothing is more certain, than that that Church hath erred, which hath believed and taught irreconcileable Contradictions, one whereof must of necessity be an Error.

That the Receiving the Sacrament of the Eucharist is necessary for Infants, and that the receiving thereof is not necessary for them: That it is the will of God, that the Church should administer the Sacrament to them; and that it is not the will of God that the Church should do so; are manifest and irreconcileable Contradictions: Supposing only, (that which is most evident) that the Eucharist is the same thing, of the same vertue and efficacy now, as it was in the primitive Church: That Infants are the same things they were, have as much need, are capable of as much benefit by the Eucharist, now as then: As subject to irreverent carriages, then as now. And lastly, that the present Church is as much bound to provide for the spiritual good of Infants, as the Ancient Church was: I say these things supposed, the propositions before set down are plain and irreconcileable Contradictions: whereof the present *Roman* Church doth hold the Negative, and the Ancient Church of *Rome* did hold the Affirmative; and therefore it is evident, that either the present Church doth err, in holding something not necessary, which is so; or that the Ancient Church did err, in holding something necessary, which was not so. For

For the Negative Propofition, *viz. That the Eucharift is not neceſſary for Infants*; that it is the Doctrin of the prefent Church of *Rome* it is moſt manifeſt. 1. From the difuſe and abolition and prohibition of the contrary Ancient practice. For if the Church did conceive it neceſſary for them, either ſimply for their ſalvation, or elſe for their increaſe or confirmation in grace, and advancement to a higher degree of glory (unleſs ſhe could ſupply ſome other way their damage in this thing, which evidently ſhe cannot) what an uncharitable ſacriledge is it, to debar and defraud them of the neceſſary means of their ſo great ſpiritual benefit? eſpecially ſeeing the adminiſtration of it might be ſo ordered, that irreverent caſualties might eaſily be prevented: which yet ſhould they fall out againſt the Churches and Paſtors intention, certainly could not offend God, and in reaſon ſhould not offend man. Or if the Church do believe, that upon ſuch a vain fear of irreverence (which we ſee moved not the Ancient Church at all) ſhe may lawfully forbid ſuch a general, perpetual and neceſſary charity, certainly herein ſhe commits a far greater error than the former. Secondly, from the Council of *Trents* Anathema, denounced on all that hold the contrary, in theſe words. *If any man ſay that the receiving of the Eucharift, is neceſſary for little children, before they come to years of diſcretion, let him be Anathema.* Concil. Trid. Seſſ. 21. *de communione parvulorum,* Can. 4.

Now for the Affirmative part of the Contradiction, to make it evident that that was the Doctrin of the Ancient Church; I will prove it, Firſt, from the general practice of the Ancient Church for ſeveral Ages. Secondly, by the direct and formal Teſtimonies of the Fathers of thoſe times. Thirdly, by the confeſſion of the moſt learned Antiquaries of the *Roman* Church. My Firſt Argument I form thus. If to communicate Infants was the general practice of the Ancient Church for many Ages; then certainly the Church then believed, that the Eucharift was neceſſary for them, and very available for their Spiritual benefit: But it is certain, that the Communicating of Infants was the general practice of the Church for many Ages

Ages: Therefore the Church of those times thought it necessary for them. To deny the consequence of the proposition, is to charge the Church with extream folly, wilful superstition, and perpetual profanation of the Blessed Sacrament. As for the Assumption, it is fully confirmed by *Clemens Rom. Constit. Apost.* l. 3. c. 20. *Dionysius Areopagita de Eccles. Hierarch.* cap. ult. S. *Cyprian* and a Council of *African* Bishops with him, *Epist.* 59. *ad Fidum*; and in his Treatise *de Lapsis* p. 137. Edit. *Pamel. Paulinus* Bishop of *Nola* in *Italy*, An. 353. in *Epist.* 12. *ad Senem*; out of *Ordo Romanus*, cited by *Alevinus* S. *Bedes* Scholar and Master to *Charlemain* in his Book *de divinis officiis* cap. *de Sab. Sancto Pasc. Gennadius Massiliensis de Eccles. dogmatibus* c. 52. *Concil. Toletanum* 2. Can. 11. It continued in the Western Church, unto the days of *Lewes* the *Debonair*, witness Cardinal *Perron des passages de S. Austin* p. 100. Some footsteps of it remained there in the time of *Hugo de S. Victore*, as you may see *lib.* 1. *de Sacram. & Cærem.* cap. 20. It was the practice of the Church of the *Armenians* in *Waldensis* his time, as he relates out of *Guido* the *Carmelite*, Tom. 2. de *Sacr.* c. 91. *de erroribus Armenorum.* It is still in force in the Church of the *Abyssines*, witness *Franc. Alvarez. Hist. Æthiop.* c. 22. *& Thomas a Jesu de procuranda salute omnium gentium.* It has cotinued without any interruption in the *Greek* Church, unto this present Age, as may be evidently gathered out of *Lyranus* in c. 6. *John. Arcudius* lib. 1. c. 14. & lib. 3. c. 40. *de concord. Eccles. Orient. & Occident. in Sacram. administratione*; Card. *Perron des passages de S. Austin.* p. 100. where he also assures us of the Primitive Church in general, that she gave Infants the Eucharist as soon as they were baptized: and that the custome of giving this Sacrament to little Infants the Church then observed: and before p. 21. That in those Ages it was always given to Infants together with Baptism. The same is likewise acknowledged by *Contzen* in *John* 6. ver. 54. and by *Thomas a Jesu de proc. salute omnium gentium.* So that this matter of the practice of the Ancient Church is sufficiently cleared. Seeing therefore the Ancient Church did use this Custom, and could have no other ground for it,

but

but their belief that this Sacrament was necessary for Infants, it follows necessarily, that the Church then did believe it necessary.

But deductions, though never so evident, are superfluous and may be set aside, where there is such abundance of direct and formal Authentical Testimonies; whereof some speak in *Thesi*, of the necessity of the Eucharist for all men, others in *Hypothesi*, of the necessity of it for Infants.

My Second Argument, from the Testimonies of the Fathers of those times I form thus. That Doctrin, in the affirmative whereof the most eminent Fathers of the ancient Church agree, and which none of their contemporaries have opposed or condemned, ought to be taken for the Catholick Doctrin of the Church of those times.

But the most eminent Fathers of the Ancient Church agree in the Affirmation of this Doctrin, that the Eucharist is necessary for Infants; and none of their contemporaries have opposed or condemned it. *Ergo*, it ought to be taken for the Catholick Doctrin of the Church of their times. The Major of this Syllogism is delivered and fully proved by *Card. Perron*, in his Letter to *Casaubon* 5. obs. and is indeed so reasonable a postulate, that none but a contentious spirit can reject it.

For confirmation of the Minor, I will alledge, first, their sentences, which in Thesi affirm the Eucharist to be generally necessary for all, and therefore for Infants: and then their Suffrages, who in Hypothesi avouch the necessity of it for Infants.

The most pregnant Testimonies of the first rank are these: Of *Irenæus* lib. 4. *cont. Heres.* c. 34. where he makes our Union to Christ by the Eucharist, the foundation of the hope of our resurrection, in these words. *As the bread of Earth, after the Invocation of God, is now not common bread, but the Eucharist, consisting of two things an earthly and an heavenly: so our bodies receiving the Eucharist, are not now corruptible (for ever) but have hope of resurrection.* The like he hath, *lib.* 5. *c.* 2. And hence in probability it is, that the *Nicene Council* stiled this Sacrament, *Symbolum resurrectionis,*

surrectionis, the pledge of our Resurrection. And *Ignatius* Ep. ad Eph. *Pharmacum Immortalitatis*, the Medicine of Immortality.

Cyril. Alex. lib. 4. in Joan. *They shall never partake, nor so much as tast, the life of holiness and happiness, which receive not the Son in the mystical Benediction.* Cyril. lib. 10. in Joan. c. 13. & lib. 11. c. 27. *This corruptible nature of our body, could not otherwise be brought to life and immortality, unless this body of natural life were conjoyned unto it.* The very same things saith *Gregory Nyssen.* Orat. Catech. c. 37. And that they both speak of our conjunction with Christ by the Eucharist, the Antecedents and Consequents do fully manifest, and it is a thing confessed by learned Catholicks.

Cyprian de cæna Domini, and *Tertullian de resur. carnis*, speak to the same purpose: But I have not their Books by me, and therefore cannot set down their words. S. *Chrysostom*, Hom. 47. in Joh on these words, *nisi manducaveritis*, has many pregnant and plain speeches to our purpose. *As, the words here spoken are very terrible: verily, saith he, if a man eat not my flesh, and drink not my blood, he hath no life in him; for whereas they said before, this could not be done, he shews it not only not impossible, but also very necessary.* And a little after; *he often iterates his speech concerning the holy mysteries, shewing the necessity of the thing, and that by all means it must be done.* And again, *what means that which he says, my flesh is meat indeed, and my blood is drink indeed; either that this is the true meat that saves the soul; or to confirm them in the faith of what he had spoken, that they should not think he spoke Enigmatically, or parabolically, but knew that by all means they must eat his body.*

But most clear and unanswerable is that place *lib.* 3. *de Sacerdotio*, where he saith, *If a man cannot enter into the Kingdom of Heaven unless he be born again of water and the holy spirit; and if he which eats not the flesh of our Lord and drinks not his blood, is cast out of eternal life: And all these things cannot be done by any other, but only by those holy hands, the hands, I say of the Priest, how then without their help can any man, either avoid the fire of hell, or obtain the Crowns laid up for us.*

Theophylact. in 6. Joan. *when therefore we hear, that unleß we eat the fleſh of the Son of man, we cannot have life, we muſt have faith without doubting in the receiving of the divine myſteries, and never inquire how: for the natural man, that is he which followeth humane, that is, natural reaſons, receives not the things which are above nature and ſpiritual; as alſo he underſtands not the ſpiritual meat of the fleſh of our Lord, which they that receive not, ſhall not be partakers of eternal life, as not receiving Jeſus, who is the true life.* S. *Auſtin* de pec. mer. & Remiſſ. c. 24. *Very well do the puny Chriſtians call Baptiſm nothing elſe but ſalvation; and the Sacrament of Chriſts Body nothing elſe but Life; from whence ſhould this be, but as I believe from the Ancient and Apoſtolical Tradition, by which this Doctrin is implanted into the Churches of Chriſt, that but by Baptiſm and the participation of the Lords Table, not any man can attain, neither to the Kingdom of God, nor to ſalvation and eternal life.*

Now we are taught by the learned Cardinal; that when the Fathers ſpeak, not as Doctors, but as witneſſes of the Cuſtoms of the Church of their times; and do not ſay, *I believe this ſhould be ſo holden, or ſo underſtood, or ſo obſerved*, but that the Church from one end of the earth to the other believes it ſo, or obſerves it ſo; then we no longer hold what they ſay, for a thing ſaid by them, but as a thing ſaid by the whole Church; and principally when it is in points, whereof they could not be ignorant, either becauſe of the condition of the things, as in matters of fact; or becauſe of the ſufficiency of the perſons: and in this caſe, we argue no more upon their words probably, as we do when they ſpeak in the quality of particular Doctors, but we argue thereupon demonſtratively.

I ſubſume. But S. *Auſtin* the ſufficienteſt perſon which the Church of his time had, ſpeaking of a point, wherein he could not be ignorant; ſays not that I believe the Euchariſt to be neceſſary to ſalvation; but the Churches of Chriſt believe ſo, and have received this doctrin from Apoſtolical Tradition: Therefore I argue upon his words not probably, but demonſtratively, that this was the Catholick doctrin of the Church of his time. And thus much for

for the *Thesis, That the Eucharist was held generally necessary for all*. Now for the *Hypothesis; That the Eucharist was held necessary for Infants in particular*. Witnesses hereof are S. *Cyprian*, Pope *Innocentius* I. and *Eusebius Emissenus*, with S. *Austin* together with the Author of the Book intituled *Hypognostica*.

Cyprian indeed does not in terms affirm it, but we have a very clear intimation of it in his Epistle to *Fidus*. For whereas he and a Council of Bishops together with him, had ordered, that Infants might be *baptized* and *sacrificed*, that is, *communicated* before the eighth day, though that were the day appointed for Circumcision by the old Law. There he sets down this as the reason of their Decree, *that the mercy and grace of God, was to be denied to no man.*

Pope *Innocent* the first, (in *Ep. ad Epis. Conc. Milev. quæ est inter August.*93.) concludes against the *Pelagians*; that Infants could not attain eternal life without Baptism; because without Baptism they were uncapable of the Eucharist, and without the Eucharist could not have eternal life. His words are, *but that which your Fraternity affirms them to Preach, that Infants without the grace of Baptism may have the rewards of eternal life, is certainly most foolish; for unless they eat the flesh of the Son of man and drink his blood; they shall have no life in them.*

Now that this sense which I have given his words, is indeed the true sense of them, and that his judgment upon the point was as I have said; it is acknowledged by *Maldonate* in *Joan.*6.*v.*54. by *Binius* upon the Councils *Tom.*1.p.624. by *Sanctesius, Repet.*6.c.7. and it is affirmed by S. *Austin* who was his Contemporary, held correspondence by Letters with him, and therefore in all probability could not be ignorant of his meaning. I say he affirms it, as a matter out of Question, Epist. 106. and *Cont. Julian.* lib.1.c.4. where he tells that *Pelagius* in denying this, did dispute *contra sedis Apostolicæ authoritatem*; against the authority of the Sea Apostolick; and after, *but if they yield to the Sea Apostolick, or rather to the Master himself and Lord of the Apostles, who says, that they shall not have life in them, unless they* *eat the flesh of the Son of man and drink his blood, which none may do but those that are baptized; then at length they will confess, that Infants not baptized cannot have life.*

Now I suppose no man will doubt, but the belief of the Apostolick Sea; was then (as S. *Austin* assures us *l.* 1. *cont. Jul. c.* 4.) the belief of the Church of *Rome*, taking it for a particular Church: and then it will presently follow, that either other Churches do not think themselves bound in conformity of belief with the *Roman* Church, notwithstanding *Irenæus* his——*necesse est ad hanc Ecclesiam, omnem convenire Ecclesiam*: or that this was then the Doctrin of the Catholick Church. For *Eusebius Emissenus* I cannot quote any particular proof out of him: but his belief in this point is acknowledged by *Sanctes.* Repet. 6. c. 7. Likewise for S. *Austin*, the same *Sanctesius* and *Binius*, and *Maldonate*, either not mindful or not regardful of the Anathema of the Council of *Trent*, acknowledge (in the places above quoted) that he was also of the same belief: and indeed he professeth it so plainly and so frequently, that he must be a meer stranger to him that knows it not, and very impudent that denies it. *Eucharistiam infantibus putet necessariam Augustinus*, say also the Divines of *Lovaine*, in their *Index* to their Edition of S. *Austin*: and they refer us in their *Index* only to Tom. 2. pag. 185. that is, to the 106. Epist. (the words whereof I have already quoted to shew the meaning of *Innocentius*) and to Tom. 7. pag. 282. that is, lib. 1. *de pec. Mer. & remis.* c. 20. where his words are; *Let then all doubt be taken away: Let us hear our Lord I say, saying not of the Sacrament of Holy Baptism, but of the Sacrament of his Table (to which none may lawfully come, but he which has been baptized) unless you eat the flesh of the Son and drink his blood, you shall have no life in you; what seek we any further? what can be answered hereunto? What, will any man dare to say, that this appertains not to little Children, and that without the participation of his body and blood, they may have Life?* &c. with much more to the same effect. Which places are indeed so plain and pregnant for that purpose, that I believe they thought it needless to add more: otherwise had they pleased they might

might have furnished their Index with many more referrences to this point; as *de Pec. Mer. & Rem.* l. 1. c. 24. where of Baptism and the Eucharist he tells us, that *Salus & vita eterna sine his frustra promittitur parvulis.* The same he has *Cont.* 2. *Epist. Pelag. ad Bonifacium* l. 1. c. 22. which yet by *Gratian de Consec. D.* 3. *c. Nulli.* and by *Tho. Aquinas* p. 3. q. 3. *art.* 9. *ad tertiam* is strangely corrupted and made to say the contrary, and *l.* 4. *c.* 4. the same *Cont. Julian. l.* 1. *c.* 4. and *l.* 3. *c.* 11. & 12. *Cont. Pelag. & Celest.* l. 2. c. 8. *de Prædest. Sanctorum ad Prosp. & Hilar. l.* 1. *cap.* 14. Neither doth he retract or contradict this opinion any where, nor mitigate any one of his sentences touching this matter, in his Book of *Retractations. Sanctesius* indeed tells us, that he seems to have departed from his Opinion, in his works against the *Donatists.* But I would he had shewed some probable reason to make it seem so to others; which seeing he does not, we have reason to take time to believe him. For as touching the place mentioned by *Beda* in 1. *ad Corinth.* 10. as taken out of a Sermon of S. *Austins, ad infantes ad Altare.* Besides that it is very strange S. *Austin* should make a Sermon to Infants; and that there is no such Sermon extant in his works; nor any memory of any such in *Possidius,* S. *Austins* Scholars Catalogue of his works, nor in his Book of *Retractaitons*: setting aside all this, I say First, That it is no way certain that he speaks there of Infants, seeing in propriety of speech (as S. *Austin* himself teacheth us *Ep.* 23;) Infants were not *Fideles,* of whom S. *Austin* in that supposed Sermon speaks. Secondly, Admit he does speak of Infants, where he assures us, that in Baptism every faithful man is made partaker of Christs body and blood, and that he shall not be alienated from the benefit of the Bread and Cup, although he depart this life, before he eat of that Bread and drink of that Cup. All this concludes no more, but that the actual participation of the Eucharist, is not a means simply necessary to attain salvation, so that no impossibility shall excuse the failing of it: Whereas all that I aim at is but this, that in the judgment of the Ancient Church, it was believed necessary, in case of possibility; necessary, not *in actu*, but *in voto Ecclesiæ*: not necessary to salvation simply, but necessary for the increase of grace and glory: And therefore, Lastly, though not necessary by *necessity of means*, for Infants to receive it; yet necessary by *necessity of precepts* for the Church to give it.

The last witness I promised, was the Author of the work against the *Pelagians* called *Hypognostica*, who (*l*. 5. *c*. 5.) ask the *Pelagians, Seeing he himself hath said, unleß you eat the flesh*, &c. *How dare you promise eternal life to little Children, not regenerate of water and the Holy Ghost; not having eaten his flesh, nor drank his blood.* And a little after, *Behold then, he that is not Baptized, and he that is destitute of the Bread and Cup of life, is separated from the Kingdom of Heaven.*

To the same purpose he speaks *l*. 6. *c*. 6. But it is superfluous to recite his words, for either this is enough or nothing.

The third kind of proof, whereby I undertook to shew the belief of the ancient Church in this point, was the *Confession of the learnedest Writers and best verst in the Church of* Rome. Who, what the Council of *Trent* forbids under Anathema, that any man should say of any ancient Father, are not yet afraid, nor make no scruple, to say it in plain terms of the whole Church for many Ages together, *viz.* That she believed the Eucharist necessary for Infants. So doth *Maldonate* in *Joan.* 6. *Mitto Augustini & Innocentii sententiam (quæ etiam viguit in Ecclesiâ per sexcentos annos) Eucharistiam etiam Infantibus necessäriam.* I *say nothing* says he, *of Austins* and *Innocentius his opinion, that the Eucharist was necessary even for Infants, which doctrin flourished in the* Church for 600. years.

The same almost in terms hath *Binius,* in his Notes on the Councils, pag. 624. *Hinc constat Innocentii sententia (quæ sexcentos circiter annos viguit in Ecclesiâ, quam Augustinus sectatus est) Eucharistiam etiam infantibus necessariam fuisse.*

Lastly, That treasury of Antiquity Cardinal *Perron,* though he speaks not so home as the rest do, yet he says enough for my purpose: *des passages de S. August.* c. 10. p. 101.

p. 101. *The Custom of giving the Eucharist to Infants the Church then observed as profitable.* This I say is enough for my purpose. For what more contradictious, than the Eucharist being the same without alteration to Infants being the same without alteration, should then be profitable and now unprofitable: then all things considered expedient to be used, if not necessary, and therefore commanded: And now, though there be no variety in the case, all things considered not necessary, nor expedient, and therefore forbidden.

The Issue of all this Discourse, for ought I can see, must be this: That either both parts of a Contradiction must be true, and consequently nothing can be false, seeing that which contradicteth truth is not so: or else, that the Ancient Church did err in believing something expedient which was not so; (and if so, why may not the present Church err, in thinking *Latin* Service, and Communion in one kind expedient:) or that the present Church doth err, in thinking something not expedient, which is so. And if so, why may she not err, in thinking Communicating the Laity in both kinds, and Service in vulgar Languages, not expedient.

V. *Al.*

V. *An Argument drawn from the Doctrin of the Millenaries, against Infallibility.*

THE Doctrin of the *Millenaries* was, *That before the worlds end, Christ should reign upon earth for a thousand years, and that the Saints should live under him in all holiness and happiness.* That this Doctrin is by the present *Roman* Church held false and Heretical, I think no man will deny.

That the same Doctrin, was by the Church of the next Age after the Apostles held true and Catholick I prove by these two Reasons.

The first Reason, Whatsoever doctrin is believed and taught by the most eminent Fathers of any Age of the Church, and by none of their contemporaries opposed or condemned, that is to be esteemed the Catholick Doctrin of the Church of those times.

But the Doctrin of the *Millenaries* was believed and taught by the eminent Fathers of the Age next after the Apostles, and by none of that Age opposed or condemned.

Therefore it was the Catholick Doctrin of the Church of those times. The Proposition of this Syllogism is Cardinal *Perrons* rule, (in his Epistle to *Casaubon*, 5. observ.) And is indeed one of the main pillars, upon which the great Fabrick of his Answer to King *James* doth stand, and with which it cannot but fall; and therefore I will spend no time in the proof of it.

But the Assumption thus I prove.

That Doctrin which was believed and taught by *Papias* Bishop of *Hierapolis*, the disciple of the Apostles disciples (according to *Eusebius*) who lived in the times of the Apostles, saith he, by *Justin Martyr*, Doctor of the Church and Martyr: by *Melito* Bishop of *Sardis*, who had the gift of Prophesie, witness *Tert.* and whom *Bellarmine* acknowledgeth a Saint. By S. *Irenæus* Bishop of *Lyons* and Martyr; and was not opposed and condemned by any one Doctor

Doctor of the Church of those times: That Doctrine was believed and taught by the most Eminent Fathers of that Age, next to the Apostles, and opposed by none.

But the former part of the Proposition is true. *Ergo*, the Latter is also true.

The Major of this Syllogism and the latter part of the Minor, I suppose will need no proof, with them that consider, that these here mentioned were equal in number to all the other Ecclesiastical Writers of that Age, of whom there is any memory remaining; and in weight and worth infinitely beyond them: they were *Athenagoras, Theophilus Antiochenus, Egesippus* and *Hippolitus*: of whose contradiction to this Doctrine there is not extant, neither in their works, nor in story, any Print or Footstep: which if they or any of them had opposed, it had been impossible, considering the Ecclesiastical Story of their time is Written by the professed Enemies of the Millinaries Doctrine; who could they have found any thing in the monuments of Antiquity to have put in the Ballance against *Justin Martyr* and *Irenæus*, no doubt would not have buried it in silence: which yet they do, neither vouching for their opinion any one of more Antiquity than *Dionysius Alexandrinus*, who lived, saith *Eusebius, nostra ætate*, [in our Age] but certainly in the latter part of the third Century. For *Tatianus* because an Heretick I reckon not in this number. And if any man say that before his fall he wrote many Books; I say, it is true; but withal would have it remembred, that he was *Justin Martyrs* Scholar, and therefore, in all probability of his Masters Faith, rather than against it, all that is extant of him one way or other is but this in S. *Hierome, de Script. Ecclef.* Justini Martyris *sectator fuit*.

Now for the other part of the Minor, that the forementioned Fathers did believe and teach this Doctrine. And first for *Papias* that he taught it, it is confessed by *Eusebius* the Enemy of this Doctrine (*Lib.* 3. *Hist. Ecclef.* c. 33.) in these words,—— *Other things besides the same Author* (Papias) *declares, that they came to him as it were by unwritten Tradition, wherein he affirms that after the Resur-*

rection of all Flesh from the Dead, there shall be a Kingdom of Christ continued and established for a thousand years upon Earth, after a humane and corporeal manner. The same is confessed by S. *Hierome*, another Enemy to this opinion, (*descript. Ecclef. S. 9.*) Papias *the Auditor of* John *Bishop of* Hieropolis *is said to have taught the Judaical Tradition of a thousand years, whom* Irenæus *and* Apollinarius *followed.* And in his preface upon the Commentaries of *Victorinus* upon the *Apocalypse*, thus he writes, — *before him* Papias *Bishop of* Hieropolis *and* Nepos *Bishop in the parts of* Egypt *taught as* Victorinus *does touching the Kingdom of the thousand years.*

The same is testified by *Irenæus* (*lib.* 5. *cont. Her. c.* 33.) where having at large set forth this Doctrine, he confirms it by the Authority of *Papias* in these words. Papias *also the Auditor of* John, *the familiar friend of* Policarpus *an Ancient man, hath testified by writing these things in the fourth of his Books, for he hath writtten five.* And concerning *Papias* thus much.

That *Justin Martyr* was of the same belief, it is confessed by *Sixtus Senensis* (*Biblioth. Stæ. l.* 6. *An.* 347.) by *Feverdentius* in his premonition before the five last Chapters of the 5th. Book of *Irenæus*. By *Pamelius* in *Antidoto ad Tertul. parad. paradox.* 14.

That S. *Melito* Bishop of *Sardis* held the same Doctrine is confessed by *Pamelius* in the same place; and thereupon it is that *Gennadius Massiliensis* in his Book *de Eccles. dogmatibus*, calls the followers of this opinion *Melitani*; as the same *Pamelius* testifies in his Notes upon that fragment of *Tertullian de Spe fidelium.*

Irenæus his Faith in this point is likewise confessed by *Eusebius*, in the place before quoted in these words. *He* (Papias) *was the Author of the like Error to most of the Writers of the Church, who alledged the Antiquity of the Man for a defence of their side, as to* Irenæus *and whosoever else seemed to be of the same opinion with him.*

By S. *Hierome* in the place above cited *de script. Ecclef.* S. 29. Again in *Lib. Ezek.* 11. in these words. *For neither do we expect from Heaven a Golden* Hierusalem (*according to the Jewish tales which they call* Duterossis) *which also* so many of our own have followed: *Especially* Tertullian *in his Book* de spe fidelium; *and* Lactantius *in his seventh Book of Institutions, and the frequent expositions of* Victorinus Pictavionensis: *and of late* Severus *in his Dialogue which he calls* Gallus: *and to name the* Greeks *and to joyn together the first and last*, Irenæus *and* Apollinarius. Where we see he acknowledges *Irenæus* to be of this opinion; but that he was the first that held it, I believe that that is more a Christian untruth than *Irenæus* his opinion a Judaical Fable. For he himself acknowledges in the place above cited, that *Irenæus* followed *Papias*; and it is certain and confessed that *Justin Martyr* believed it long before him: and *Irenæus* himself derives it from ——— *Presbyteri qui* Johannem *discipulum Domini viderunt*; from Priests which saw *John* the Disciple of the Lord. Lastly, by *Pamelius, Sixtus Senensis*, and *Faverdentius* in the places above quoted.

Seeing therefore it is certain, even to the confession of the Adversaries, that *Papias, Justin Martyr, Meleto* and *Irenæus*, the most considerable and eminent men of their Age, did believe and teach this Doctrine; and seeing it has been proved as evidently as a thing of this nature can be, that none of their contemporaries opposed or condemned it; It remains according to Cardinal *Perrons* first rule; that this is to be esteemed the Doctrine of the Church of that Age.

My second Reason I form thus. Whatsoever Doctrine is taught by the Fathers of any Age, not as Doctors but as witnesses of the Tradition of the Church, (that is, not as their own opinion, but as the Doctrine of the Church of their times) that is undoubtedly to be so esteemed; especially if none contradicted them in it. But the Fathers above cited teach this Doctrine, not as their own private opinion, but as the Christian Tradition, and as the Doctrine of the Church, neither did any contradict them in it. *Ergo*, it is undoubtedly to be so esteemed.

The Major of this Syllogism, is Cardinal *Perrons* second Rule and way of finding out the Doctrine of the Ancient Church in any Age: and if it be not a sure Rule, farewel the use of all Antiquity.

And for the *Minor*, there will be little doubt of it, to him that considers, that *Papias* professes himself to have received this Doctrine by unwritten Tradition, though not from the Apostles themselves immediately, yet from their Scholars, as appears by *Eusebius* in the forecited third Book 33. Chapter.

That *Irenæus* grounding it upon evident Scripture, professes that he learnt it, (whether mediately or immediately I cannot tell) from (a) *Presbyteri qui* Johannem *Discipulum Domini viderunt*. Priests or Elders who saw *John* the Lords Disciple, and heard of him what our Lord taught of those times (of the thousand years) and also, as he says after, from *Papias* the Auditor of *John* the Chamber-fellow of *Polycarpus*, an Ancient man who recorded it in writing.

(a) *Faverdentius* his Note upon this place is very Notable. *Hinc apparet* (saith he) from hence it appears that *Irenæus* neither first invented this opinion, nor held it as proper to himself, but got this blot and blemish from certain Fathers. *Papias* I suppose and some other inglorious fellows, the familiar Friends of *Irenæus*, are here intended.

I hope then if the Fathers which lived with the Apostles had their blots and blemishes; it is no such horrid Crime for *Calvin* and the *Century writers* to impute the same to their great Grandchildren. *Ætas parentum pejor avis progeniem fert vitiosiorem*. But yet these inglorious Disciples of the Apostles, though perhaps not so learned as *Faverdentius*, were yet certainly so honest, as not to invent lies and deliver them as Apostolick Tradition; or if they were not, what confidence can we place in any other unwritten Tradition.

Lastly, that *Justin Martyr* grounds it upon plain Prophecies of the *Old Testament*, and express words of the *New*: he professeth, *That he, and all other Christians of a right belief in all things, believe it*; joyns them who believe it not, with them who deny the Resurrection; or else says, that none denied this, but the same who denied the Resurrection; and that indeed they were called Christians, but in deed and Truth were none.

Whoso-

Whosoever, I say, considers these things will easily grant, that they held it not as their own opinion, but as the Doctrine of the Church and the Faith of Christians.

Hereupon I conclude, whatsoever they held, not as their private opinion, but as the Faith of the Church, that was the Faith of the Church of their time: But this Doctrine they held, not as *their* private opinion, but as the Faith of the Church. *Ergo*, it was and is to be esteemed the Faith of the Church.

Trypho. "Do ye confess that before ye expect the "coming of Christ, this place *Hierusalem* shall be again "restored, and that your People shall be congregated, and "rejoyce together with Christ, and the Patriarchs and "the Prophets, *&c.*

Justin Martyr. "I have confessed to you before, that "both I and many others do believe, as you well know, "that this shall be; but that many again, who are (not) "of the pure and holy opinion of Christians, do not "acknowledge this, I have also signified unto you: "For I have declared unto you, that some called Christians, "but being indeed *Atheists* and impious *Hereticks*, do gene-"rally teach blasphemous and Atheistical and foolish things: "but that you might know that I speak not this to you on-"ly, I will make a Book as near as I can of these our dis-"putations, where I will profess in writing that which I "say before you; for I resolve to follow not men, and the "Doctrines of men, but God and the Doctrine of God. "For although you chance to meet with some that are "called Christians, which do not confess this, but dare "to Blaspheme the God of *Abraham*, the God of *Isaac*, and "the God of *Jacob*, which also say there is no Resurrecti-"on of the Dead, but that as soon as they die their Souls "are received into Heaven, do not ye yet think them "Christians: as neither if a man consider rightly will he "account the Sadducees and other Sectaries and Hereticks, "as the *Genistæ* and the *Meristæ* and *Galileans*, and *Pharisees* "and *Hellenians* and *Baptists* and other such to be *Jews*; but "only that they are called *Jews*, and the Children of *Abra-*"*ham*, and such as with their lips confess God (as God "himself

"himself cries out) but have their Hearts far from him.
"But I and all Christians that in all things believe aright,
"both know that there shall be a Resurrection of the
"Flesh, and a thousand years in *Hierusalem* restored and
"adorned and inlarged; according as the Prophets, *Ezekiel*
"and *Esay* and others do testifie: for thus saith *Isaiah* of
"the time of this thousand years. *For there shall be a new*
"*Heaven and a new Earth, and they shall not remember the*
former, &c. And after.——"A certain man amongst us
"whose name was *John*, one of the Twelve Apostles of
"Christ, in that *Revelation* which was exhibited unto him,
"hath foretold— That they which believe our Christ
"shall live in *Hierusalem* a thousand years, and that after,
"the Universal and everlasting Resurrection and Judgment
"shall be.

I have presumed in the beginning of *Justin Martyrs* answer to substitute (not) instead of (also) because I am confident, that either by chance, or the fraud of some ill-willers to the Millinaries opinion; the place has been corrupted, and (*u*) turned into (ϰ) (not) into (also.) For if we retain the usual reading——*But that many who are also of the pure and holy opinion of Christians do not acknowledge this, I have also signified unto you*; then must we conclude, that *Justin Martyr* himself did believe the opinion of them which denied the thousand years, to be the pure and holy opinion of Christians: and if so, why did he not himself believe it? nay how could he but believe it to be true, professing it (as he does if the place be right) to be the pure and holy opinion of Christians: for how a false Doctrine can be the pure and holy opinion of Christians, what Christian can conceive? or if it may be so, how can the contrary avoid the being untrue, unholy and not the opinion of Christians?

Again, if we read the place thus ——*That many who are also of the pure and holy opinion of Christians, do not acknowledge this, I have also signified*: certainly there will be neither sense nor reason, neither coherence nor consequence in the words following——*For I have told you of many called Christians, but being indeed Atheists and He-*
reticks,

reticks, that they altogether teach blasphemous and impious and foolish things: for how is this a confirmation or reason of, or any way pertinent unto what went before? if there he speak of none but such as were, *puræ piæque Chriſtianorum ſententiæ,* of the pure and holy opinion of Chriſtians. And therefore to diſguiſe this inconſequence, the Tranſlator has thought fit to make uſe of a falſe Tranſlation, and inſtead of ── *for I have told you,* to make it, ── *beſides I have told you of many,* &c. Again, if *Juſtin Martyr* had thought this *the pure and holy opinion of Chriſtians,* or them good and holy Chriſtians that held it; why does he rank them with them that denyed the Reſurrection? Why does he ſay afterward ── *Although you chance to meet with ſome that are called Chriſtians which do not confeſs this, do not ye think them Chriſtians.* Laſtly, what ſenſe is there in ſaying as he does ── *I and all Chriſtians that are of a right belief in all things, believe the Doctrine of the thouſand years,* and that the Scriptures both of the *Old* and *New Teſtament* teach it, and yet ſay ── *That many of the pure and holy opinion of Chriſtians do not believe it?* Upon theſe reaſons I ſuppoſe it is evident, that the place has been corrupted, and it is to be corrected according as I have corrected it, by ſubſtituting *ε* in the place of *χϳ* (not) inſtead of (alſo.) Neither need any man think ſtrange that this misfortune of the change of a Syllable ſhould befal this place, who conſiders that in this place *Juſtin Martyr* tells us that he had ſaid the ſame things before, whereas nothing to this purpoſe appears now in him. And that in *Victorinus* comment on the *Revelation,* wherein, (by S. *Hieroms* acknowledgment) this Doctrine was ſtrongly maintained, there now appears nothing at all for it, but rather againſt it. And now from the place thus reſtored, theſe Obſervations offer themſelves unto us.

1. That *Juſtin Martyr* ſpeaks not as a Doctor, but as a witneſs of the Doctrine of the Church of his time. I (ſaith he) and all Chriſtians that are of a right belief in all things hold this: And therefore from hence according to Cardinal *Perrons* Rule, we are to conclude, not probably but demonſtratively, that this was the Doctrine of the Church of that time. 2. That

2. That they held it as a necessary matter, so far as to hold them no Christians that held the Contrary: *though you chance to meet with some called Christians that do not confess this, but dare to Blaspheme the God of* Abraham, Isaac and Jacob, *&c. Yet do not ye think them Christians*: Now if *Bellarmines* Rule be true, that Councils then determine any thing as matters of Faith, when they pronounce them Hereticks that hold the Contrary; then sure *Justin Martyr* held this Doctrine as a matter of Faith, seeing he pronounceth them no Christians, that contradict it.

3. That the Doctrine is grounded upon the Scripture of the *Old* and *New Testament* and the *Revelation* of S. *John*, and that by a Doctor and Martyr, of the Church, and such a one as was converted to Christianity within 30 years after the Death of S. *John*, when in all probability there were many alive, that had heard him expound his own words and teach this Doctrine: and if probabilities will not be admitted, this is certain out of the most authentical records of the Church, that *Papias* the Disciple of the Apostles Disciples taught it the Church, professing that he had received it from them that learned it from the Apostles: and if after all this, the Church of those Times might Err in a Doctrine so clearly derived and authentically delivered, how without extream impudence can any Church in after times, pretend to Infallibility.

The *Millinaries* Doctrine was over-born, by imputing to them that which they held not: by abrogating the Authority of S. *John*'s Revelation, as some did: or by derogating from it, as others; ascribing it not to S. *John* the Apostle, but to some other *John*, they know not who: which —— *Dionysius* the first known adversary of this doctrine and his followers; against the Tradition of *Irenæus, Justin Martyr*, and all the Fathers their Antecessors: by calling it a Judaical opinion and yet allowing it as probable by corrupting the Authors for it, as *Justin, Victorinus, Severus*.

VI. *A Letter relating to the same Subject.*

SIR,

I Pray remember, that if a consent of Fathers either constitute or declare a Truth to be necessary, or shew the opinion of the Church of their Time; then that opinion of the Jesuits, concerning Predestination upon prescience (which had no opposer before S. *Austin*) must be so, and the contrary Heretical of the Dominicans; and the present Church differs from the Ancient, in not esteeming of it as they did.

Secondly, I pray remember, that if the Fathers be infallible, (when they speak as witnesses of Tradition) to shew the opinion of the Church of their Time, then the opinion of the *Chiliasts* (which now is a Heresie in the Church of *Rome*) was once Tradition in the Opinion of the Church.

Thirdly, Since S. *Austin* had an opinion, that of whatsoever no beginning was known, that came from the Apostles, many Fathers might say things to be Tradition upon that ground only; but of this Opinion of the *Chiliasts*, one of the ancientest Fathers *Irenæus* says not onely that it was Tradition, but sets down Christs own words when he taught it, and the pedigree of the opinion from Christ to *John* his Disciple; from him to several Priests (whereof *Papias* was one who put it in writing) and so downwards; which can be shewn from no other Father, for no other opinion, either controverted, or uncontroverted.

Fourthly, That if *Papias* either by his own error, or a desire to deceive, could cozen the Fathers of the purest age in this, why not also in other things? why not in twenty as well as one, why not twenty others as well as he.

Fifthly, That if the Fathers could be cozened, how could general Councils scape? who you say make Tradition one of their Rules, which can only be known from the Fathers?

Sixthly, If they object, how could errors come in, and no beginning of them known? I pray remember to ask them the same Question concerning the *Millenaries*, which lasted uncontradicted, until *Dionysius Alexandrinus* two hundred and fifty years after Christ; and if they tell you that *Papias* was the first beginner, look in *Irenæus*, and he will tell you the contrary. (*Loco citato* l. 5. c. 33.)

Seventhly, Remember, that if I ought not to condemn the Church of *Rome* out of Scripture, because my interpretation may deceive me; then they ought not to build their Infallibility upon it (and less upon her own word) because theirs may deceive them: unless the same thing may be a wall when you lean upon it, and a bulrush when we do.

Eighthly, Remember that they cannot say, they trust not their Interpretation in this, but a consent of Fathers; because the Fathers are not said to be infallible, but as they tell the Opinion of the Church of their time, which is infallible: therefore they must first prove out of Scripture that she is infallible, or else she (who is her self the subject of the Question) cannot be allowed till then to give a verdict for her self.

Ninthly, Remember the *Roman* Church claims no Notes of the Church, but what agree with the *Grecian* too (as Antiquity, Succession, Miracles, &c.) but onely Communion with the Pope and Splendor; both which made for the *Arrians* in *Liberius* his time; and it were a hard Case, that because the *Greeks* are poor upon Earth, they should be shut out of Heaven.

Tenthly, Remember that if we have an Infallible way, we have no use (at least no necessity) of an Infallible Guide; for if we may be saved by following the Scripture as near as we can (though we err) it is as good as any Interpreter to keep unity in charity (which is only needful) though not in opinion: and this cannot be ridiculous, because they say, if any man misinterpret the Council of *Trent*, it shall not damn him; and why (without more ado) may not the same be said of Scripture?

VII. *An*

VII. *An Argument against the Infallibility of the present Church of* Rome, *taken from the Contradictions in your Doctrin of Transubstantiation.*

Chillingworth. THat Church is not infallible, which teacheth Contradictions: But the Church of *Rome* teacheth Contradictions. Therefore the Church of *Rome* is not infallible.

Mr. *Daniel.* I deny the Minor.

Chilling. That Church teacheth Contradictions, which teacheth such a Doctrin as contains Contradictions: But the Church of *Rome* teacheth such a Doctrin: Therefore the Church of *Rome* teacheth Contradictions.

Mr. *Daniel.* I deny the Minor.

Chilling. The Doctrin of Transubstantion contains Contradictions: But the Church of *Rome* teacheth the Doctrin of Transubstantiation: Therefore the Church of *Rome* teacheth such a Doctrin as contains Contradictions.

Mr. *Dan.* I deny the Major.

Chilling. That the same thing at the same time should have the true figure of a mans body, and should not have the true figure of a mans body, is a Contradiction: But in the Doctrin of Transubstantiation it is taught, that the same thing, (*viz.* our Saviour present in the Sacrament) has the true figure of a mans body, and has not the true figure of a mans body at the same time; therefore the Doctrin of Transubstantiation contains Contradictions.

Mr. *Dan.* The Major, though not having all rules required to a contradiction (as boys in Logick know) yet let it pass.

Chilling. Boys in Logick know no more conditions required to a Contradiction, but that the same thing should be affirmed and denied of the same thing at the same time. For my meaning was, that that should not be accounted the same thing, which was considered after divers manners.

Mr. *Dan.*

Mr. Dan. I deny the Minor of your syllogism.

Chilling. I prove it, according to the several parts of it: And first, for the first part. He must have the Figure of a mans body in the Eucharist, who is there without any real alteration or difference from the natural body of a man: But our Saviour, according to the *Romish* Doctrin of Transubstantiation, is in the Sacrament without any real alteration or difference from the natural body of a man: Therefore according to this Doctrin he must there have the figure of a mans body. To the second part, that he must not have the figure of a mans body in the Sacrament, according to this Doctrin, thus I prove it. He must not have the figure of a mans body in the Eucharist, which must not have extension there: But our Saviours body, according to the Doctrin of Transubstantiation, must not have extension there; Therefore, according to this doctrin, he must not have the figure of a mans body there. The Major of this Syllogism I proved, because the figure of a mans body could not be without extension. The Minor I proved thus; That must not have extension in the Eucharist, whose every part is together in one and the same point: But according to this Doctrin, every part of our Saviours body must be here in one and the same point: therefore here it must not have extention.

Mr. Dan. Answered, by distinguishing the Major of the first Syllogism, and said; that he must not have the true figure of a mans body, according to the reason of a figure taken in its essential consideration, which is to have *positionem partium sic & sic extra partes*; but not the accidental consideration, which is in *ordine ad locum*. And this answer he applied for the solution of the Minor, saying thus, Our Saviour is there without any real alteration intrinsecal, but not extrinsecal; for he is not changed in order to himself, but in order to place: Or otherwise, he is not altered in his continual existence, which is only *modus essentiæ* and inseparable even by divine power, though altered *in modo existendi*, which is situation and required to figure taken in order to place.

Chilling.

Mr. Chillingworth *and Mr.* Lewgar.

Chill. Against this it was replied by *Chillingworth*: That the distinction of a mans body as considered in it self, and as considered in reference to place, is vain, and no solution of the Argument: And thus he proved it; If it be impossible, that any thing should have several parts one out of another in order, and reference of each to other, without having these parts in several places; then the distinction is vain: But it is impossible, that any thing should have several parts one out of another, without having these parts in several places; Therefore the distinction is vain.

The Major of this Syllogism he took for granted.

The Minor he proved thus: Whatsoever body is in the proper place of another body, must of necessity be in that very body, by possessing the demensions of it: therefore, whatsoever hath several parts one out of the other, must of necessity have them one out of the place of the other; and consequently in several places.

For illustration of this Argument he said; If my head and belly and thighs and legs be all in the very same place; of necessity my head must be in my belly, and my belly in my thighs, and my thighs in my legs, and all of them in my feet, and my feet in all of them; and therefore if my head be out of my belly, it must be out of the place where my belly is; and if it be not out of the place where my belly is, it is not out of my belly but in it.

Again, to shew that according to the Doctrin of Transubstantiation, our Saviours body in the Eucharist hath not the several parts of it out of one another, he disputed thus: Wheresoever there is a body having several parts one out of the other, there must be some middle parts severing the extreme parts: But here, according to this Doctrin, the extreme parts are not severed, but altogether in the same point; Therefore here our Saviours Body cannot have parts one out of other.

Mr. *Dan.* To all this (for want of a better Answer) gave only this. *Let all Scholars peruse this.* After, upon better consideration, he wrote by the side of the last Syllogism this: *Quoad entitatem verum est, non quoad locum*, that is, according to entity it is true, but not according to place.

place. And to (*Let all Scholars peruse these*) he caused this to be added; *And weigh whether there is any new matter, worth a new Answer.*

Chillingworth Replyed, That to say the extreme parts of a body are severed by the middle parts according to their entity, but not according to place, is ridiculous. His reasons are first, Because severing of things is nothing else, but putting or keeping them in several places, as every silly woman knows; and therefore to say, they are severed but not according to place, is as if you should say, They are heated, but not according to heat; they are cooled, but not according to cold: Indeed is it to say, they are severed, but not severed.

VIII. *An account of what moved the Author to turn a Papist, with his own Confutation of the Arguments that perswaded him thereto.*

I Reconciled my self to the Church of *Rome*, because I thought my self to have sufficient reason to believe, that there was and must be always in the World some Church, that could not err: and consequently seeing all other Churches disclaimed this priviledge of not being subject to error; the Church of *Rome* must be that Church which cannot err.

I was put into doubt of this way which I had chosen, by D. *Stapleton* and others; who limit the Churches freedom from Error to things necessary only, and such as without which the Church can be a Church no longer, but granted it subject to error in things that were not necessary: Hereupon considering that most of the differences between *Protestants* and *Roman* Catholicks; were not touching things necessary, but only profitable or lawful; I concluded, that I had not sufficient ground to believe the *Roman* Church either could not or did not err in any thing, and therefore no ground to be a *Roman* Catholick.

Against

Against this again I was perswaded, that it was not sufficient to believe the Church to be an *infallible believer* of all doctrins necessary; but it must also be granted an *infallible teacher* of what is necessary; that is, that we must believe not only that the Church teacheth all things necessary, but that all is necessary to be believed, which the Church teacheth to be so: in effect, that the Church is our Guide in the way to Heaven.

Now to believe that the Church was an infallible Guide, and to be believed in all things which she requires us to believe, I was induced: First, because there was nothing that could reasonably contest with the Church about this Office, but the Scripture: and that the Scripture was this Guide, I was willing to believe, but that I saw not how it could be made good, without depending upon the Churches authority.

1. That Scripture is the Word of God.
2. That the Scripture is a perfect rule of our duty.
3. That the Scripture is so plain in those things that concern our duty, that whosoever desires and endeavors to find the will of God, there shall either find it, or at least not dangerously mistake it.

Secondly, I was drawn to this belief, because I conceived that it was evident, out of the Epistle to the *Ephesians*, that there must be unto the worlds end a Succession of Pastors, by adhering to whom, men might be kept from wavering in matters of faith, and from being carried up and down with every wind of false doctrin.

That no Succession of Pastors could guard their adherents from danger of error, if themselves were subject unto error, either in teaching that to be necessary which is not so, or denying that to be necessary which is so: and therefore,

That there was and must be some Succession of Pastors, which was an infallible guide in the way to Heaven; and which should not possibly teach any thing to be necessary which was not so; nor any thing not necessary which was so: upon this ground I concluded, that seeing there must be such a Succession of Pastors, as was an infallible guide;
and

and there was no other (but that of the Church of *Rome*) even by the confession of all other Societies of Pastors in the world; that therefore that Succession of Pastors is that infallible Guide of Faith which all men must follow.

Upon these grounds I thought it necessary for my salvation, to believe the *Roman* Church, in all that she thought to be, and proposed as necessary.

Against these Arguments it hath been demonstrated unto me; and First against the first. That the reason why we are to believe the Scripture to be the word of God, neither is nor can be the Authority of the present Church of *Rome*, which cannot make good her Authority any other way, but by pretence of Scripture: and therefore stands not unto Scripture (no not in respect of us) in the relation of a Foundation to a building, but of a building to a Foundation, doth not support Scripture, but is supported by it. But the general consent of Christians of all Nations and Ages, a far greater company than that of the Church of *Rome*, and delivering universally the Scripture for the word of God, is the ordinary external reason why we believe it: whereunto the Testimonies of the Jews, enemies of Christ, add no small moment for the Authority of some part of it.

That whatsoever stood upon the same ground of Universal Tradition with Scripture, might justly challenge belief, as well as Scripture: but that no Doctrin not written in Scripture, could justly pretend to as full Tradition as the Scripture, and therefore we had no reason to believe it with that degree of faith, wherewith we believe the Scripture.

That it is unreasonable to think, that he that reads the Scripture, and uses all means appointed for this purpose, with an earnest desire and with no other end, but to find the will of God and obey it, if he mistake the meaning of some doubtful places, and fall unwillingly into some errors, unto which no vice or passion betrays him, and is willing to hear reason from any man that will undertake to shew him his error: I say, that it is unreasonable to think, that a God of goodness will impute such an error to such a man.

Against

Mr. Chillingworth *and Mr.* Lewgar.

Againſt the ſecond it was demonſtrated unto me, that the place I built on ſo confidently, was no Argument at all for the Infallibility of the Succeſſion of Paſtors in the *Roman* Church, but a very ſtrong Argument againſt it.

Firſt, no Argument for it; becauſe it is not certain, nor can ever be proved, that S. *Paul* ſpeaks there of any ſucceſſion; *Epheſ.* 4. 11, 12, 13. For let that be granted which is deſired, that in the 13. ver. by [*until we all meet*] is meant, until all the Children of God meet in the Unity of Faith; that is, unto the Worlds end: yet it is not ſaid there, *that he gave Apoſtles and Prophets,* &c. *which ſhould continue,* &c. *until we all meet,* by connecting the 13. ver. to the 11. But he gave (then upon his Aſcenſion and miraculouſly endowed) Apoſtles and Prophets, *&c.* for the work of the miniſtry, for the Conſummation of the Saints, for the Edification of the Body of Chriſt, until we all meet, that is, if you will, unto the Worlds end. Neither is there any incongruity, but that the Apoſtles and Prophets, *&c.* which lived then, may in good ſenſe be ſaid, now at this time and ever hereafter to do thoſe things which they are ſaid to do: For who can deny but S. *Paul* the Apoſtle and Doctor of the Gentiles, and S. *John* the Evangeliſt and Prophet, do at this very time (by their writings, though not by their perſons) do the work of the miniſtry, conſummate the Saints, and Edifie the body of Chriſt.

Secondly, it cannot be ſhewn or proved from hence, that there is or was to be any ſuch ſucceſſion: becauſe S. *Paul* here tells us only, that he gave ſuch in the time paſt, not that he promiſed ſuch in the time to come.

Thirdly, it is evident, that God promiſed no ſuch ſucceſſion, becauſe it is not certain that he hath made good any ſuch promiſe; for who is ſo impudent as to pretend, that there are now, and have been in all Ages ſince Chriſt, ſome Apoſtles and ſome Prophets and ſome Evangeliſts and ſome Paſtors and Teachers: eſpecially ſuch as he here ſpeaks of, that is, endowed with ſuch gifts as Chriſt gave upon his Aſcenſion; of which he ſpeaks in the 8 *ver.* ſaying; *He led Captivity Captive, and gave gifts unto men*. And that thofe gifts were —— Men endowed with extraordinary Power and Supernatural gifts —— it is apparent, becaufe thefe Words, *and he gave fome Apoſtles, fome Prophets,* &c. are added by way of explication and illuſtration of that which was faid before —— *and he gave gifts unto Men*: And if any man except hereunto, that though the Apoſtles and Prophets and Evangeliſts were extraordinary and for the Plantation of the Gofpel, yet Paſtors were ordinary and for continuance: I anfwer, it is true, fome Paſtors are ordinary and for continuance, but not fuch as are here fpoken of: not fuch as are endowed with the ſtrange and heavenly gifts, which Chriſt gave not only to the Apoſtles and Prophets and Evangeliſts, but to the inferior Paſtors and Doctors of his Church, at the firſt Plantation of it: And therefore S. *Paul* in the 1ſt. to the *Corinth*. 12. 28. (to which place we are referred by the Margent of the Vulgar Tranſlation, for the explication of this,) places this gift of teaching amongſt, and prefers it before many other miraculous gifts of the Holy Ghoſt: Paſtors there are ſtill in the Church, but not fuch as *Titus* and *Timothy* and *Apollos* and *Barnabas*: not fuch as can juſtly pretend to immediate infpiration and illumination of the Holy Ghoſt: And therefore feeing there neither are nor have been for many Ages in the Church, fuch Apoſtles and Prophets, &c. as here are fpoken of, it is certain he promifed none; or otherwife we muſt blafphemouſly charge him with breach of his promife.

Secondly, I anfwer, that if by *dedit he gave*, be meant *promifit*, he *promifed* for ever; then all were promifed and all ſhould have continued. If by *dedit* be not meant *promifit*, then he promifed none fuch, nor may we expect any fuch by vertue of, or warrant from this Text that is here alledged: And thus much for the firſt Affumpt which was, that the place was no Argument for an infallible fucceffion in the Church of *Rome*.

Now for the fecond, That it is a ſtrong Argument againſt it, thus I make it good.

The Apoſtles and Prophets and Evangeliſts and Paſtors, which our Saviour gave upon his Afcenfion, were given

by

by him that they might Confummate the Saints, do the work of the Miniftry, Edifie the Body of Chrift, until we all come into the Unity of Faith, that we be not like Children wavering and carried up and down with every wind of Doctrine. The Apoftles and Prophets, &c. that then were, do not now in their own perfons and by oral inftruction do the work of the Miniftry, to the intent we may be kept from wavering and being carried up and down with every wind of Doctrine: therefore they do this fome other way: Now there is no other way by which they can do it, but by their writings; and therefore by their writings they do it: therefore by their writings and believing of them we are to be kept from wavering in matters of Faith: therefore the Scriptures of the Apoftles and Prophets and Evangelifts are our Guides. Therefore not the Church of *Rome*.

FINIS.

AN ANSWER

To Some

PASSAGES

IN

Rushworths Dialogues.

BEGINNING

At the Third Dialogue Section 12.
p. 181. Ed. *Paris*, 1654.

ABOUT

TRADITIONS.

LONDON,

Printed for *James Adamson*, at the *Angel* in S. Pauls Church-Yard, 1687.

AN ANSWER

To some passages in

Rushworths Dialogues.

BEGINNING AT
The Third Dialogue, §. 12. *p.* 181. Ed. *Paris,* 1654.

ABOUT

TRADITIONS.

Uncle. DO you think there is such a City as *Rome* or *Constantinople?*
Nephew. That I do, I would I knew what I ask as well.

CHILLINGWORTH.

First I should have answered that in propriety of Speech I could not say that I *knew* it, but that I did as undoubtedly *believe* it, as those things which I did know. For though (as I conceive) we may be properly said to believe that which we know, yet we cannot say truly, that we know that which we only believe upon report and hearsay, be it never so constant, never so general: For seeing the generality of men is made up of particulars, and every particular man may deceive and be deceived, it is not impossible, though exceedingly improbable, that all men should conspire

conspire to do so. Yet I deny not that the popular phrase of Speech will very well bear, that we may say we *know* that which in truth we only *believe*, provided the grounds of our belief be morally certain.

Neither do I take any exception to the Nephews answers, made to his Uncles 2, 3, 4. and 5. Interrogatories. But grant willingly as to the first, that it is not much material whether I remember or not any particular Author of such a general and constant report. Then, that the Testimony of one or two Witnesses, though never so credible, could add nothing to that belief which is already at the height, nay perhaps that my own seeing these Cities would make no accession, add no degree to the strength and firmness of my Faith concerning this matter, only it would change the kind of my assent, and make me *know* that which formerly I did but *believe*.

To the fourth, that seeming Reasons are not much to be regarded against sense or experience and moral Certainties (but withal I should have told my Uncle, that I fear his supposition is hardly possible, and that the nature of the thing will not admit, that there should be any great, nay any probable reasons invented to perswade me that there never was such a City as *London*) and therefore if any man should go about to perswade me that there never was such a City as *London*; That there were no such men as called themselves, or were called by others Protestants, in *England*, in the days of Q. *Elizabeth*, perhaps such a mans Wit might delight me, but his reasons sure would never perswade me.

Hitherto we should have gone hand in hand together, but whereas in the next place he says—*In like manner then you do not doubt, but a Catholick living in a Catholick Country, may undoubtedly know what was the publick Religion of his Country in his Fathers days, and that so assuredly that it were a meer madness for him to doubt thereof.*—I should have craved leave to tell my Uncle that he presumed too far upon his Nephews yielding disposition. For that as it is a far more easie thing to know, and more authentically testified, that there were some men called Protestants

stants by themselves and others, than what opinions these Protestants held, divers men holding divers things, which yet were all called by this name. So is it far more easie for a *Roman Catholick* to know that in his Fathers days there were some men, for their outward Communion with and subordination to the Bishop of *Rome* called *Roman Catholicks*, than to know what was the Religion of those men who went under this name, For they might be as different one from another in their belief, as some Protestants are from others.

As for example, had I lived before the *Lateran* Council which condemned *Berengarius*, possibly I might have known that the belief of the *Real presence* of Christ in the Sacrament was part of the publick Doctrine of my Country: But whether the Real absence of the Bread and Wine after Consecration, and their Transubstantiation into Christs Body, were likewise *Catholick* Doctrine at that time, *that*, I could not have known, seeing that all men were at liberty to hold it was so, or it was not so.

Moreover I should have told my Uncle, that living now, I know it is *Catholick* Doctrine, That the Souls of the Blessed enjoy the Vision of God: But if I had lived in the Reign of *Pope John* the XXII, I should not have known that then it was so, considering that many good Catholicks before that time had believed, and then, even the *Pope* himself did believe the contrary: and he is warranted by *Bellarmine* for doing so, because the Church had not then defined it.

I should have told him further that either Catholicks of the present time do so differ in their belief, that what some hold lawful and pious, others condemn as unlawful and impious: or else that all now consent, and consequently make it *Catholick* Doctrine, That it is not unlawful to make the usual Pictures of the *Trinity*, and to set them in Churches to be adored. But had I lived in S. *Austins* time, I should then have been taught another Lesson: To wit, that this Doctrine and practice was impious, and the contrary Doctrine Catholick.

I should have told him that now I was taught that the Doctrine of Indulgences was an Apostolick Tradition: but had I lived 600 years since, and found that in all antiquity there was no use of them: I should either have thought the Primitive Church no faithful Steward in defrauding mens Souls of this Treasure intended by God to them, and so necessary for them, or rather that the Doctrine of Indulgences now practised in the Church of *Rome* was not then Catholick.

I should have told him that the general practice of *Roman* Catholicks now taught me that it was a pious thing to offer Incense and Tapers to the Saints and to their Pictures: But had I lived in the Primitive Church, I should with the Church have condemned it in the *Collyridians* as Heretical.

I should have represented to him *Erasmus* his complaint against the Protestants, whose departing from the *Roman* Church occasioned the determining, and exacting the belief of many points as necessary, wherein before *Luther* men enjoyed the Liberties of their Judgments and Tongues and Pens. *Antea*, saies he, *licebat varias agitare quæstiones, de potestate Pontificis, de Condonationibus, de restituendo, de Purgatorio: nunc tutum non est hiscere, ne de his quidem, quæ piè verèque dicuntur. Et credere cogimur, quod homo gignit ex se opera meritoria, quod benefactis meretur vitam æternam, etiam de condigno, Quòd B. Virgo potest imperare Filio cum Patre regnanti ut exaudiat hujus aut illius preces, aliaque permulta ad quæ piæ mentes inhorrescunt.* And from hence I should have collected, as I think very probably, that it was not then such a known and certain thing, what was the Catholick Faith in many points which now are determined, but that divers men who held external Communion with that Church which now holds these as matters of Faith, conceived themselves no waies bound to do so, but at liberty to hold as they saw reason.

I should have shewed him by the confession of another Learned Catholick, That through the negligence of the Bishops in former Ages, and the indiscreet Devotion of the People many opinions and practices were brought into the Church, which at first perhaps were but wink'd at, after

after tolerated, then approved, and at length after they had spread themselves into a seeming Generality, confirmed for good and Catholick: and that therefore there was no certainty, that they came from the beginning whose beginning was not known.

I should have remembred him that even by the acknowledgment of the Council of *Trent*, many corruptions and superstitions had by insensible degrees insinuated themselves into the very Mass and Offices of the Church, which they thought fit to cast out: and therefore seeing that some abuses have come in, God knows how, and have been cast out again, who can ascertain me that some Errors have not got in, and while men slept (for it is apparent they did sleep) gathered such strength, gotten such deep root, and so incorporated themselves, like Ivy in a Wall, in the State and polity of the *Roman* Church, that to pull them up had been to pull them down, by rasing the Foundation on which it stands, to wit, the Churches Infallibility? Besides as much water passes under the Mill which the Miller sees not, so who can warrant me that some old corruptions, might not escape from them, and pass for Original and Apostolick Traditions? I say *might not*; though they had been as studious to reduce all to the primitive State, as they were to preserve them in the present State, as diligent to cast out all Postnate and introduct opinions, as they were to persuade men that there were none such, but all as truly Catholick and Apostolick as they were *Roman*.

I should have declared unto him that many things reckoned up in the Roll of Traditions are now grown out of fashion and out of use in the Church of *Rome*: and therefore that either they believed them not, whatever they pretended, or were not so obedient to the Apostles command as they themselves interpret it——*Keep the Traditions which ye have received, whether by word or by our Epistle.*

And seeing there have been so many vicissitudes and changes in the *Roman* Church: Catholick Doctrines growing exolete, and being degraded from their Catholicism, and perhaps deprest into the number of Heresies: Points of Indifference, or at least *Aliens* from the Faith, getting first to be Inmates, after, procuring to be made *Denizons*, and in process of time necessary members of the Body of the Faith: Nay Old Heresies sometimes like old Snakes, casting their Skin and their Poyson together, and becoming wholsom and Catholick Doctrines. I must have desired pardon of my Uncle, if I were not so undoubtedly certain what was and what was not Catholick Doctrine in the days of my Fathers.

Nay perhaps I should have gone further and told him, That I was not fully assured what was the Catholick Doctrine in some points, no not at this present time. For instance, to lay the Axe unto the Root of the Tree: the infallibility of the present Church of *Rome*, in determining controversies of Faith, is esteemed indeed by divers that I have met with, not only an Article of Faith, but a Foundation of all other Articles. But how do I know there are not, nay why should I think there are not in the World divers good Catholicks of the same mind touching this matter, which *Mirandula, Panormitan, Cusanus, Florentinus, Clemangis, Waldensis, Occham,* and divers others were of, who were so far from holding this Doctrine the Foundation of Faith, that they would not allow it any place in the Fabrick.

Now *Bellarmine* has taught us that no Doctrine is Catholick, nor the contrary Heretical, that is denied to be so by some good Catholicks. From hence I collect that in the time of the forenamed Authors, this was not Catholick Doctrine, nor the contrary Heretical; and being then not so, how it could since become so, I cannot well understand: If it be said that it has since been defined by a General Council; I say first, This is false, no Council has been so foolish as to define that a Council is Infallible, for unless it were presumed to be Infallible before, who or what could assure us of the Truth of this definition? Secondly if it were true it were ridiculous: for he that would question the Infallibility of all Councils in all their Decrees, would as well question the Infallibility of this Council in this Decree. This therefore was not, is not,

nor

nor ever can be an Article of Faith, unless God himself would be pleased (which is not very likely) to make some new Revelation of it from Heaven.

The πρῶτον ψεῦδος, the Fountain of the Error in this matter is this: That the whole Religion of the *Roman Church* and every point of it, is conceived or pretended to have issued Originally out of the Fountain of Apostolick Tradition, either in themselves or in the principles from which they are evidently deducible. Whereas it is evident that many of their Doctrines, may be Originally derived from the Decrees of Councils, many from Papal definitions, many from the Authority of some great Man; To which purpose it is very remarkable what *Gregory Nazianzen* says of *Athanasius*. *What pleased him was a law to men, what did not please him was as a thing prohibited by Law; his Decrees were to them like* Moses *his Tables; and he had a greater veneration paid him than seems to be due from men to Saints.*

* Τοῦτο ὡς νόμῳ αὐτοῖς ὃ τι ἐκείνῳ ἐδόκει, καὶ τοῦτο ἀπώμοτον πάλιν, ὃ μὴ ἐδόκει, καὶ πλάκες Μωϋσέως αὐτῆς τὰ ἐκείνε δόγματα, καὶ πλέον τὸ σέβας ἢ περὶ ἀνδράσιν τῆς ἀξίοις ὀφείλεται. Orat XXI. in Laudem Athanasii.

And as memorable that in the late great Controversie about Predetermination and Free-will, disputed before *Pope Clement* VII. by the Jesuits and Dominicans, The *Popes* resolution was, if he had determined the matter, to define for that opinion which was most agreeable, not to Scripture, nor to Apostolick Tradition, nor to a consent of Fathers, but to the Doctrine of S. *Austin*: so that if the *Pope* had made an Article of Faith of this Controversie, it is evident S. *Austin* had been the Rule of it.

Sometimes upon erroneous grounds Customs have been brought in, God knows how, and after have spread themselves through the whole Church. Thus *Gordonius Huntleius* confesses, that because Baptism and the Eucharist had been anciently given both together to men of ripe years, when they were converted to Christianity; Afterwards by Error when Infants were Baptized, they gave the Eucharist also to Infants. This Custom in short time grew Universal, and in S. *Austins* time passed currantly for an Apostolick Tradition, and the Eucharist was thought as necessary for them as Baptism. This Custom the Church of *Rome* hath again cast out, and in so doing profest either

ther her no regard to the traditions of the Apostles, or that this was none of that number. But yet she cannot possibly avoid but that this example is a proof sufficient that many things may get in by Error into the Church, and by degrees obtain the esteem and place of Apostolick Traditions which yet are not so.

The Custom of denying the Laity the Sacramental Cup, and the Doctrine that it is lawful to do so, who can pretend to derive from Apostolick Tradition? Especially when the * Council of Constance the Patron of it, confesses that Christs institution was under both kinds, and that the faithful in the Primitive Church received it in both. —— *Licet Christus*, &c. *Although Christ after his Supper instituted and administred this venerable Sacrament under both kinds.*—— *Although in the Primitive Church this Sacrament were received by the faithful under both kinds.*—— Non obstante, &c.—— *Yet all this notwithstanding this Custom for the avoiding of Scandals* (to which the Primitive Church was as obnoxious as the present is) *was upon just reason brought in, that Laicks should receive only under one kind.*

* Sess. XIII.

Brought in therefore it was, and so is one of those Doctrines which *Lerinensis* calls — *inducta non tradita, inventa non accepta*, &c. therefore all the Doctrine of the Roman Church does not descend from Apostolick Tradition.

But if this Custom came not from the Apostles, from what Original may we think that it descended? Certaintainly from no other than from the belief of the substantial presence of whole Christ under either kind. For this opinion being once setled in the Peoples minds, that they had as much by one kind as by both; both Priest and People quickly began to think it superfluous, to do the same thing twice at the same time; and thereupon, being (as I suppose) the Custom required that the Bread should be received first, having received that, they were contented that the Priest should save the pains, and the Parish the charge of unnecessary reiteration. This is my Conjecture which I submit to better judgments; but whether it be true or false, one thing from hence is certain,

That

That immemorial Customs may by degrees prevail upon the Church, such as have no known beginning nor Author, of which yet this may be evidently known, that their beginning whensoever it was, was many years, nay, many Ages after the Apostles.

* *S. Paul* commands that nothing be done in the Church but for edification. He says, and if that be not enough, he proves in the same place, that it is not for edification that either Publick Prayers, Thanksgiving and Hymns to God, or Doctrine to the People should be in any Language which the Assistants generally understand not; and thereupon forbids any such practice though it were in a Language miraculously infused into the speaker by the Holy Ghost: unless he himself or some other present could and would interpret. He tells us that to do otherwise is to speak into the Air: That it is to play the *Barbarians* to one another: That to such Blessings and Thanksgivings, the ignorant for want of understanding cannot say *Amen.* He clearly intimates that to think otherwise is to be Children in understanding. Lastly, in the end of the Chapter he tells all that were Prophets and Spiritual among the *Corinthians,* That the things written by him are the Commandments of God. Hereupon *Lyranus* upon the place acknowledgeth that in the Primitive Church, Blessings and all other Services were done in the Vulgar Tongue. Cardinal *Cajeton* likewise upon the place tells us that out of this Doctrine of S. *Paul* it is consequent, That it were better for the Edification of the Church, that the publick Prayers which are said in the Peoples hearing, should be delivered in a Language common both to the Clergy and the People. And I am confident that the Learnedst Antiquary in the *Roman* Church cannot, nay that *Baronius* himself, were he alive again, could not produce so much as one example of any one Church, one City, one Parish in all the Christian World, for five hundred years after Christ, where the Sermons to the People were in one Language, and the Service in another. Now it is confest on all hands to be against sense and reason, that Sermons should be made to the People in any

1 *Cor.* 14. 26.

27, 23.

9. 11.

16.
20.

37.

any Language not understood by them, and therefore it follows of necessity, that their Service likewise was in those Tongues which the People of the place understood.

But what talk we of 500. years after Christ? when even the *Lateran* Council held in the year 1215. makes this Decree. *Quoniam in plerisque*—— *Because in many parts within the same City and Diocess, People are mixed of divers Languages, having under one Faith divers rites and fashions, we strictly command that the Bishops of the said Cities or Dioceses provide fit and able men, who according to the diversities of their Rites and Languages may celebrate Divine Services and administer the Sacraments of the Church, instructing them both in word and example.*

Now after all this if any man will still maintain, that the Divine Service in unknown Tongues is a matter of Apostolick Tradition, I must needs think the World is grown very impudent.

There are divers Doctrines in the *Roman* Church which have not yet arrived to the honour to be *Donatæ civitate*, to be received into the number of Articles of Faith; which yet press very hard for it, and through the importunity and multitude of their Attorneys that plead for them, in process of time may very probably be admitted. Of this rank are the Blessed Virgins Immaculate conception, The *Popes* Infallibility in determining Controversies, His superiority to Councils, His indirect Power over Princes in Temporalties, *&c.* Now as these are not yet matters of Faith and Apostolick Traditions, yet in after Ages in the days of our great Grandchildren may very probably become so, so why should we not fear and suspect, that many things now pass currantly as points of Faith which *Ecclesia ab Apostolis, Apostoli à Christo, Christus à Deo recepit*, which perhaps in the days of our great Grandfathers had no such reputation.

Cardinal *Perron* teaches us two Rules whereby to know the Doctrine of the Church in any Age. The first is when the most eminent Fathers of any Age agree in the affirmation of any Doctrine, and none of their Contemporaries oppose or condemn them, that is to be accounted

the

the Doctrine of the Church. The second: when one or more of these Eminent Fathers, speak of any Doctrine not as Doctors but as witnesses, and say, not, *I think so, or hold so*, but, *the Church holds and believes this to be Truth*. This is to be accounted the Doctrine of the Church. Now if neither of these Rules be good and certain, then are we destitute of all means to know what was the publick Doctrine of the Church in the days of our Fathers. But on the other side, if either of them be true, we run into a worse inconvenience; for then surely the Doctrine of the Millinaries must be acknowledged to have been the Doctrine of the Church in the very next Age after the Apostles. For both the most eminent Fathers of that time, and even all whose Monuments are extant, or mention made of them, viz. *Justin Martyr, Irenæus, Tertullian, Melito Sardensis*, agree in the affirmation of this point, and none of their contemporary writers oppose or condemn it: And besides they speak not as Doctors but as Witnesses, not as of their own private opinion, but as Apostolick Tradition and the Doctrine of the Church.

Horantius and out of him *Franciscus a Sancta Clara* teach us that under the Gospel there is no where extant any precept of Invocating Saints, and tell us that the Apostles reason of their giving no such precept was, lest the converted Gentiles might think themselves drawn over from one kind of Idolatry to another. If this reason be good, I hope then the position whereof it is the reason is true, viz. that the Apostles did neither command nor teach, nor advise, nor persuade the converted Gentiles to invocate Saints, for the reason here rendred serves for all alike, and if they did not, and for this reason did not so: how then in Gods name comes Invocation of Saints to be an Apostolick Tradition?

The Doctrines of Purgatory, Indulgences, and Prayer to deliver Souls out of Purgatory are so closely conjoyned, that they must either stand or fall together; at least, the first being the Foundation of the other two, if that be not Apostolick Tradition, the rest cannot be so. And if that be so, what meant the Author of the Book of Wisdom to tell us that (after Death) *the Souls of the righteous are in the hand of God, and there shall no torment touch them.* What means S. *John* to teach us, That they are *Bleſſed which Die in the Lord, for that they reſt from their Labours.* But above all what meant Biſhop *Fiſher* in his Confutation of *Luthers* aſſertion ſo to prevaricate as to me he ſeems to do in the 18th. Art. in ſaying, *multos fortaſſe movet,* &c. *Peradventure many are moved not to place too great Faith in Indulgences, becauſe the uſe of them may ſeem not of long ſtanding in the Church, and a very late invention among Chriſtians.* To whom I anſwer that * *it is not certain by whom they began firſt to be taught.* Yet ſome uſe there was of them, as they ſay very Ancient among the Romans, which we are given to underſtand by the Stations which were ſo frequented in that City. Moreover they ſay Gregory the firſt granted ſome in his time. And after *Cæterum ut dicere cœpimus,* &c. ——— *But as we were ſaying, there are many things of which in the Primitive Church no mention was made, which yet upon doubts ariſing are become perſpicuous through the diligence of after times.* Certainly, (to return to our buſineſs) no Orthodox man now doubts whether there be a Purgatory, of which yet among the Ancients there was made very rare or no mention. Moreover the Greeks to this very day believe not Purgatory. Who ſo will let him read the writings of the Ancient Greeks, and I think he ſhall find no ſpeech of Purgatory, or elſe very rarely. The Latines alſo received not this verity all at once but by little and little. Neither was the Faith whether of Purgatory or Indulgences ſo neceſſary in the Primitive Church as now it is, for then Charity was ſo fervent that every one was moſt ready to Die for Chriſt. Crimes were very rare, and thoſe which were, were puniſhed by the Canons with great ſeverity. But now a great part of the People would rather put off Chriſtianity than ſuffer the rigour of the Canons. That not without the great Wiſdom of the Holy Spirit, it hath come to paſs that after the courſe of ſo many years, the Faith of Purgatory and the uſe of Indulgences hath been by the Orthodox generally received as long as there was no care of Purgatory, no man look'd after Indulgences, for all the Credit of Indulgences depends on that. Take away

* *Therefore it is not true that all the Roman Doctrines were taught by Chriſt and his Apoſtles.*

away *Purgatory and what need is there of Indulgences.* We therefore considering that *Purgatory was a long while unknown. That after, partly upon Revelations partly upon Scripture it was believed by some, and that so at length the Faith of it was most generally received by the Orthodox Church,* shall easily find out some reason *of Indulgences. Seeing therefore it was so late ere Purgatory was known and received by the Universal Church, who now can wonder touching Indulgences, that in the Primitive Church there was no use of them? Indulgences therefore began after men had trembled a while at the Torments of Purgatory. For then it is credible the Holy Fathers began to think more carefully by what means they might provide for their Flocks a remedy against those Torments, for them especially who had not time enough to fulfil the Penance which the* Canons *enjoyned.*

Erasmus tell us of himself, that though he did certainly know and could prove, that *Auricular Confession* such as is in use in the *Roman* Church, were not of Divine institution: yet he would not say so, because he conceived Confession a great restraint from sin, and very profitable for the times he lived in, and therefore thought it expedient, that men should rather by Error hold that necessary and commanded, which was only profitable and advised, than by believing, though truly the non-necessity of it to neglect the use of that, as by experience we see most men do which was so beneficial: If he thought so of Confession, and yet thought it not fit to speak his mind, why might he not think the like of other points, and yet out of discretion and Charity hold his peace? And why might not others of his time do so as well as he: and if so, how shall I be assured that in the Ages before him there were not other men alike minded, who though they knew and saw Errors and Corruptions in the Church, yet conceiving more danger in the remedy, than harm in the disease, were contented *hoc Catone* ── to let things alone as they were, left by attempting to pluck the Ivy out of the Wall, they might pull down the Wall it self, with which the Ivy was so incorporated.

Sir *Edwin Sandys* relates that in his Travels he met with

with divers men, who, though they believed the Pope to be Antichrist, and his Church Antichristian, yet thought themselves not bound to separate from the Communion of it : nay thought themselves bound not to do so : because the True Church was to be the Seat of Antichrist, from the Communion whereof no man might divide himself upon any pretence whatsoever.

And much to this purpose is that which *Charron* tells us in his third *Verité, cap.* 4. *§.* 13. 15. That although all that which the Protestants say falsly of the Church of *Rome*, were true, yet for all this they must not depart from it: and again, Though the Pope were Antichrist, and the Estate of the Church, were such (that is as corrupt both in discipline and Doctrine) as they (Protestants) pretend, yet they must not go out of it. Both these assertions he proves at large in the above-cited Paragraphs, with very many and very plausible reasons : which I believe would prove his intent, had not the corruptions of the *Roman* Church possessed and infected even the publick Service of God among them, in which their Communion was required: and did not the Church of *Rome* require the *Belief* of all her Errors, as the condition of her Communion. But howsoever be his reasons conclusive or not conclusive certainly this was the profest opinion of him, and divers others; as by name *Cassander* and *Baldwin*, who though they thought as ill of the Doctrine of the most prevailing part of the Church of *Rome* ; as Protestants do, yet thought it their duty not to separate from her Communion. And if there were any considerable number of considerable men thus minded (as I know not why any man should think there was not) then it is made not only a most difficult, but even an impossible thing to know what was the *Catholick* Judgment of our Fathers in the points of controversie : seeing they might be joyned in Communion, and yet very far divided in opinion. They might all live in obedience to the Pope, and yet some think him head of the Church by Divine right : others (as a great part of the *French Church* at this day) by Ecclesiastical constitution : others by neither, but
by

by Practice and Usurpation, wherein yet because he had Prescription of many Ages for him he might not justly be disturbed.

All might go to Confession and yet some only think it necessary; others only profitable. All might go to Mass and the other Services of the Church, and some only like and approve the Language of it: others only tolerate it and wish it altered if it might be, without greater inconvenience. All might receive the Sacrament, and yet some believe it to be the Body and Blood of Christ, others only a Sacrament of it. Some that the Mass was a true and proper Sacrifice, others only a Commemorative Sacrifice, or the Commemoration of a Sacrifice. Some that it was lawful for the Clergy to deny the Laicty the Sacramental Cup: others that it was lawful for them to receive in one kind only, seeing they could not in both. Some might adore Christ as present there according to his Humanity, others as present according to his Divine Nature only. Some might pray for the Dead as believing them in Purgatory: others upon no certain ground, but only that they should rather have their Prayers and Charity which wanted them not, than that they which did want them should not have them. Some might pray to Saints upon a belief that they heard their Prayers and knew their Hearts; others might pray to them meaning nothing but to pray by them, that God for their sakes would grant their Prayers: others thirdly, might not pray to them at all, as thinking it unnecessary, others as fearing it unlawful, yet because they were not fully resolved, only forbearing it themselves, and not condemning it in others.

Uncle. I pray you then remember also what it is that Protestants do commonly taunt and check Catholicks with, is it not that they believe Traditions?

It is a meer Calumny that Protestants condemn all kind of Traditions, who subscribe very willingly to that of *Vincentius Lerinensis.* That Christian Religion is ——*res tradita non inventa,* a matter of Tradition not of mans invention, is, what the Church received from the Apostles, (and by consequence what the Apostles delivered to the Church)

Church) and the Apostles from Christ, and Christ from God. *Chemnitius* in his Examen of the Council of *Trent* hath liberally granted seven sorts of Traditions, and Protestants find no fault with him for it. Prove therefore any Tradition to be Apostolick, which is not written. Shew that there is some known Word of God which we are commanded to believe, that is not contained in the Books of the *Old* and *New Testament*, and we shall quickly shew that we believe Gods Word because it is Gods, and not because it is written. If there were any thing not written which had come down to us with as full and Universal a Tradition as the unquestioned Books of Canonical Scripture, That thing should I believe as well as the Scripture: but I have long sought for some such thing, and yet I am to seek: Nay I am confident no one point in Controversie between Papists and Protestants can go in upon half so fair Cards, for to gain the esteem of an Apostolick Tradition, as those things which are now decried on all hands, I mean the opinion of the *Chiliasts*; and *the Communicating Infants*. The latter by the confession of Cardinal *Perron*, *Maldonate*, and *Binius* was the Custom of the Church for 600 years at least: It is expresly and in terms vouched by S. *Austin* for the Doctrine of the Church and an Apostolick Tradition: it was never instituted by General Council, but in the use of the Church, as long before the First general Council as S. *Cyprian* before the Council. There is no known Author of the beginning of it: all which are the Catholick marks of an Apostolick Tradition, and yet this you say is not so, or if it be, why have you abolisht it? The former Lineally derives its pedigree from our Saviour to St. *John*: from S. *John* to *Papias*: from *Papias* to *Justin Martyr*, *Irenæus*, *Melito Sardensis*, *Tertullian* and others of the two first Ages: who as they generally agree in the Affirmation of this Doctrine, and are not contradicted by any of their Predecessors: so some of them at least, speak to the point not as Doctors but Witnesses, and deliver it for the Doctrine of the Church and Apostolick Tradition, and condemn the contrary as Heresie. And therefore if
there

there be any unwritten Traditions, thefe certainly muft be admitted firft: or if thefe which have fo fair pretence to it muft yet be rejected: I hope then we fhall have the like liberty to put back Purgatory, and Indulgences, and Tranfubftantiation, and the Latin Service, and the Communion in one kind, &c. none of which is of Age enough to be Page to either of the forenamed Doctrines, efpecially the opinion of the Millenaries.

Uncle. What think you means this word Tradition? No other thing certainly but that we confute all our Adverfaries by the Teftimony of the former Church; faying unto them, this was the belief of our Fathers; Thus were we taught by them and they by theirs, without ftop or ftay till you come to Chrift.

We confute our Adverfaries by faying thus——Truly a very eafie confutation: But faying and proving are two Mens Offices; and therefore though you be excellent in the former, I fear when it comes to the Tryal, you will be found defective in the Latter.

Uncle. And this no other but the *Roman* Church did or could ever pretend to, which being in truth undeniable, and they cannot choofe but grant the thing; Their laft refuge is to laugh, and fay that both Fathers and Councils did Err becaufe they were men, as if Proteftants themfelves were more. Is it not fo as I tell you?

No indeed, it is not by your leave, good *Uncle.* For firft the *Greek* Church as every body knows, pretends to perpetual fucceffion of Doctrine, and undertakes to derive it from Chrift and his Apoftles, as confidently as we do ours: Neither is there any word in all this difcourfe, but might have been urged as fairly and as probably for the *Greek* Church as for the *Roman*: and therefore feeing your Arguments fight for both alike, they muft either conclude for both, which is a direct impoffibility, for then Contradictions fhould be both true: or elfe which is moft certain they conclude for neither and are not Demonftrations as you pretend, (for never any Demonftration could prove both parts of a Contradiction) but meer Sophifms phisms and Captions, as the progress of our answer shall justifie.

Secondly, It is so far from Protestants to grant the thing you speak of, To wit, that the controverted Doctrines of the *Roman* Church came from Apostolick Tradition, that they verily believe should the Apostles now live again, they would hardly be able to find amongst you the Doctrin which they taught by reason of abundance of trash and rubbish which you have laid upon it.

And lastly, They pretend not that Fathers and Councils may err and they cannot, nor that they were men and themselves are not; but that you do most unjustly and vainly to father your inventions of Yesterday upon the Fathers and Councils.

Nephew. I know that we Catholicks do reverence Traditions as much as Scripture it self: neither do I see why we should be blamed for it; for the words which Christ and his Apostles spake, must needs be as infallible as those which were written.

True. But still the question depends, whether Christ and his Apostles did indeed speak those words which you pretend they did: we say with *Irenæus: Præconiaverunt primum, scripserunt postea.* What they preacht first, that they wrote afterwards: we say with *Tertullian*—(*Ecclesias*) *Apostoli condiderunt, ipsi eis prædicando, tam vivâ quod aiunt voce, quam per Epistolas postea.*—The Apostles founded the Churches by their Preaching to them: first by word of mouth, then after by their writings. If you can prove the contrary do so and we yield: but hitherto you do nothing.

Nephew. And as for the keeping of it, I see the Scripture it self is beholden to Tradition (Gods providence presupposed) for the integrity both of the letter, and the sense. Of the letter it is confest: of the sense manifest. For the sense being a distinct thing from the naked letter, and rather fetcht out by force of consequence, than in express and formal terms contained, (which is most true whether we speak of *Protestant* sense or the *Catholick*) it belongeth rather to Tradition than express Text of Scripture.

That

That which you desire to conclude is, That we must be beholden to Tradition for the sense of Scripture: and your reason to conclude this is, because the sense is fetcht out by force of consequence: This of some places of Scripture is not true, especially those which belong to faith and good manners, which carry their meaning in their foreheads. Of others it is true, but nothing to the purpose in hand, but rather directly against it. For who will not say, If I collect the sense of Scripture by Reason, then I have it not from Authority: that is unless I am mistaken. If I fetch it out by force of Consequence, then I am not beholden to Tradition for it. But the letter of Scripture has been preserved by Tradition, and therefore why should we not receive other things upon Tradition as well as Scripture? I answer. The Jews Tradition preserved the books of the Old Testament, and why then doth our Saviour receive these upon their Tradition, and yet condemn other things which they suggested as matters of Tradition? If you say it was because these Traditions came not from *Moses* as they were pretended; I say also that yours are only pretended and not proved to come from the Apostles. Prove your Tradition of these Additions as well as you prove the Tradition of Scripture, and assure your selves, we then according to the injunction of the Council of *Trent* shall receive both with equal reverence.

Nephew. As it may appear by the sense of these few words. *Hoc est corpus meum,* whether you take the *Protestant* or the *Catholick* sense: For the same Text cannot have two contrary senses of it self, but as they are fetcht out by force of Argument; and therefore what sense hath best Tradition to shew for it self that's the Truth.

This is neither Protestant nor Catholick sense, but if we may speak the truth direct nonsense. For what if the same Text cannot have contrary senses: is there therefore no means but Tradition to determin which is the true sense? What connexion or what relation is there between this Antecedent and this Consequent? certainly they are

meer

Have we not reason enough without advising with Tradition about the matter, to reject the Literal sense and embrace the Spiritual ? S. *Austin* certainly thought we had: For he gives us this direction in his Book *de Doctrinâ Christianâ*; and the first and fittest Text that he could choose to exemplifie his Rule, what think you is it? even the Cousin-German to that which you have made choice of. *Unleß you eat the flesh of the Son of Man, &c.* Here saith he, the Letter seems to command impiety. *Figura est ergo.* Therefore it is a Figure commanding to feed devoutly, upon the Passion of our Lord, and to lay up in our memory that Christ was crucified for us.

Uncle. These particulars peradventure would require a further discussion, and now I will take nothing but what is undeniable. As this is, to wit, That what points are in Controversie betwixt us and Protestants, we believe to have been delivered by Christ and his Apostles to our forefathers, and by them delivered from hand to hand to our Fathers, whom we know to have delivered them for such to us, and to have received and believed them for such themselves.

Certainly though Ink and Paper cannot blush, yet I dare say you were fain to rub your forehead over and over before you committed this to Writing. Say what you list, for my part I am so far from believing you, that I verily believe you do not believe your selves, when you pretend that you believe those points of your Doctrin which are in controversie, to have been delivered to your Forefathers by Christ and his Apostles. Is it possible that any sober man who has read the New Testament, should believe that Christ and his Apostles taught Christians, That it
was

was fit and lawful to deny the Laity the Sacramental Cup: That it was expedient and for the edification of the Church, that the Scripture should be read, and the publick worship of God perpetually celebrated in a language which they understand not, and to which for want of understanding, (unless S. *Paul* deceive us) they cannot say *Amen:* Or is it reasonable you should desire us to believe you, when your own Men, your own Champions, your own Councils confess the contrary?

Does not the Council of *Constance* acknowledg plainly, That the custom which they ratified, was contrary to Chrifts institution, and the custom of the Primitive Church? and how then was it taught by Christ and his Apostles?

Do not *Cajetan* and *Lyranus* confess ingenuously, that it follows evidently from S. *Paul,* that it is more for edification, that the Liturgy of the Church should be in such a Language as the Assistants understand?

The like Confession we have from others concerning Purgatory and Indulgences.

Others acknowledges the Apostles never taught Invocation of Saints.

Rhenanus says as much touching Auricular Confession.

It is evident from *Peter Lombard* that the Doctrin of Transubstantiation was not a point of Faith in his time.

From *Pius Mirandula* that the Infallibility of the Church was no Article, much less a foundation of Faith in his time.

Bellarmine acknowledges that the Saints enjoying the Vision of God before the day of judgment was no Article of Faith in the time of Pope *John* the XXII.

But as the Proverb is, when Thieves fall out, true men recover their goods: so how small and heartless the reverence of the Church of *Rome* is to ancient Tradition, cannot be more plainly discovered, than by the Quarrels which her Champions have amongst themselves, especially about the Immaculate conception of the Blessed Virgin.

The Patrons of the Negative opinion, *Cajetan, Bannes, Bandellus* and *Canus*, alledg for it, First an whole army of Scriptures, Councils and Fathers, agreeing unanimously in this Doctrin, That only Christ was free from sin. Then, an innumerous multitude of Fathers expresly affirming the very point in question, not contradicted by any of their Contemporaries, or Predecessors, or indeed of their Successors for many ages.

All the Holy Fathers agree in this, that the Virgin *Mary* was conceived in Original sin. So * *Bannes.*

Cajetan brings for it fifteen Fathers in his judgment irrefragable, others produce two hundred, *Bandellus* almost three hundred. Thus † *Salmeron.*

That all the Holy Fathers who have fallen upon the mention of this matter, with one mouth affirm, that the Blessed Virgin was conceived in Original sin. So ‖ *Canus.*

And after,——That the contrary Doctrin has neither Scripture nor Tradition for it. For (saith he) no Traditions can be derived unto us but by the Bishops and Holy Fathers, the Successors of the Apostles, and it is certain that those ancient writers received it not from their predecessors.

Now against this stream of ancient Writers, *when the contrary new Doctrin came in, and how it prevailed,* it will be worth the considering.

The First that set it abroach was *Richardus de Sancto Victore,* as his country-man * *Johannes Major* testifies of him. ——*He was expresly the first that held the Virgin Mary free from Original sin,* —— *or he was the first that expresly held so.* So after upon this false ground, which had already taken deep root in the heart of Christians, That it was impossible to give too much honour to her that was the Mother of the Saviour of the World; like an ill weed it grew and spread apace. So that in the Council of † *Basil,* (which *Binius* tells us was reprobated but in part, to wit, in the point of the Authority of Councils, and in the deposition of *Eugenius* the Pope) it was defined and declared, to be Holy Doctrin, and consonant to the worship of the Church,

* In part primum q. 1. Art. 8. Dub. 5.
† Disp. 51. in Ep. ad Rom.
‖ Lib. VII. loc. cap. 1. cap. 3. n. 9.

* *Omnium expresse primus Christiferam virginem originalis noxæ expertem tenuit. —De gestis Scotorum.* III. 12.
† Sess. XXXVI.

Church, to the Catholick Faith, to right Reason and the Holy Scripture, and to be approved, held and embraced by all Catholicks: and that it should be lawful for no man for the time to come to preach or teach the contrary. The custom also of keeping the Feast of her Holy Conception, which before was but particular to the *Roman* and some other Churches, and it seems somewhat neglected, was then renewed and made Universal; and commanded to be celebrated——*sub nomine Conceptionis*——*under the name of the Conception*. *Binius* in a Marginal note tells us indeed, That they celebrate not this Feast in the Church of *Rome*, by virtue of this Renovation, —— *cum esset Conciliabalum*——being this was the act not of a Council, but of a Conventicle, yet he himself in his Index, stiles it the Oecomenical Council of *Basil*, and tells that it was reprobated only in two points, of which this is none. Now whom shall we believe, *Binius* in his Margin, or *Binius* in his Index?

Yet in after-times Pope *Sixtus* IV. and *Pius* V. thought not this Decree so binding, but that they might and did again put life into the condemned opinion, giving liberty by their constitutions to all men to hold and maintain either part, either that the Blessed Virgin was conceived with Original sin or was not. Which Constitution of *Sixtus* IV. The * Council of *Trent* renewed and confirmed. * Sess. V.

But the wheel again turning, and the Negative opinion prevailing, The Affirmative was banisht, first by a Decree of *Paul* V. from all publick Sermons, Lectures, Conclusions, and all publick Acts whatsoever: and since by another Decree of *Gregory* XV. from all private Writings, and private Conferences.

But yet all this contents not the University of *Paris*. They, as *Salmeron* tells us, admit none to the Degree of Doctor of Divinity, unless they have first bound themselves by solemn Oath to maintain the Immaculate conception of the Blessed Virgin.

Now I beseech you Mr. R—— consider your courses with some indifference.

First,

First, You take Authority upon you, against the universal, constant, unopposed Tradition of the Church for many ages: to set up as a rival, a new upstart yesterdays invention: and to give all men liberty to hold which they please. So Pope *Sixtus* IV. The Council of *Trent*, and *Pius* V. that is, you make it lawful to hold the ancient Faith, or not to hold it, nay to hold the contrary. This is high presumption. But you stay not here; For,

Secondly, The ancient Doctrin you cloyster and hook up within the narrow, close and dark rooms of the thoughts and brains of the defenders of it, forbidding them upon pain of damnation so much as to whisper it in their private discourses and writings: and in the mean time the New Doctrin you set at full liberty, and give leave, nay countenance and encouragement to all men to employ their time and wits and tongues and pens, in the maintenance and propagation of it. Thus *Paul* V. and *Gregory* XV. Yet this is not all; For,

Thirdly, You bind men by Oaths to defend the new opinion, and to oppose the ancient. So the University of *Paris*. Yet still you proceed further; For,

Fourthly, By your General Councils confirmed by your Popes, you have declared and defined, that this new invention is agreeable, and consequently that the ancient Doctrin is repugnant to the Catholick Faith, to Reason, to the Holy Scripture. So the Council of *Basil*.

These things I entreat you weigh well in your Consideration, and put not into the Scale above a just allowance, not above three grains of partiality, and then tell me whether you can with reason or with modesty suppose or desire that we should believe, or think that you believe, that all the points of Doctrin which you contest against us, were delivered at first by Christ and his Apostles, and have ever since by the Succession of Bishops and Pastors been preserved inviolate and propagated unto you.

The Patrons I confess of this new Invention set not much by the Decree of the Council of *Basil* for it, but plead very hard for a full and final definition of it from the Sea
Apostolick

Apostolick: and finding the conspiring opposition of the ancient Fathers to be the main impediment of their purpose, it is strange to see how confidently they ride over them.

First, Says * *Salmeron in the place forecited, they press us with multitude of Doctors; of whom we must not say that they err in a matter of such moment.* † Disp 51. in Epist. ad Rom.

We answer, says he, out of † *S.* Austin *and the Doctrin of S.* Thomas: *That the argument drawn from Authority is weak. Then to that multitude of Doctors we oppose another multitude.* ‖ De moribus Ecclesia. lib 1. cap. 2.

Thirdly, We object to the contrary the efficacy of reasons, which are more excellent than any Authority.

Some of them reckon two hundred Fathers, other as Bandellus *almost three hundred,* Cajetan *fifteen, but those as he says irrefragable. But as a wise Shepheard said* ⸺⸺ pauperis est numerare pecus. *Some of those whom they produce are of an exolete Authority, and scarce worthy of memory.*

Lastly, Against this objected multitude we answer with the word of God. * *Thou shalt not follow a multitude to do evil. Neither shalt thou in judgment yield to the sentence of many to depart from the truth. For when the Donatists gloried in the multitude of their Authors, S.* Austin *answered it was a sign of a cause destitute of truth, to rely only upon the Authority of many men which may err.* * Exod. 23. 2.

It falls out sometimes also that from some one Doctor, especially if he be famous, proceeds a multitude of followers of his Opinion, and some, taken with an humble and pious fear, choose rather to follow the Opinion of another against their mind, than to bring out of their own wit any thing new, lest they should so bring any new thing into the Church. Whose humility as it is to be praised, so the confidence of others is not to be condemned, who for the love of truth fear not to bring in better things. Thus S. Hierome *in his Sermon of the Assumption, if it be his, fears to affirm that the Virgin* Mary *is assumed into Heaven, and thinks it rather to be piously desired, than rashly defined. But* * *S.* Austin *more happily dared to affirm it, and settle it with many argument, by which adventure this the Church hath gained,* * In the Margint here he says, *The Doctrin of S.* Austin *alone hath brought into the Church the Worship of the blessed Virgins Assumption.*

gained, that perswaded by his reasons she hath believed it, and celebrates it in her worship.

But they fetch their arguments from the Antiquity of the Doctors, to which always greater honour was given than to Novelties. But I answer, old men are praisers of ancient times, but we affirm, the younger the Doctors are, the more perspicacious. Moreover we say that although they were ancient yet they were men, and themselves held under the darkness of Original sin and might err. But go to, who are these Ancients? are they Apostles? are they Ambrose *or* Hierom, *or* Austin? *but none of them discuss'd this Controversie on purpose.*

Chrysostom *is opposed in his Commentary on* S. Matthew, *where he saith though Christ were not a sinner, yet he has humane Nature from a sinner. Understand (says Salmeron) from her who of her self, and according to the condition of nature was a sinner.* Thomas *says that* Chrysostom *speaks exorbitantly, for he constitutes the* Virgin *under actual sin. Or that the Commentaries which go up and down under his name ane not his. Or that these passages are adjectitious. Or if they be indeed his, with the good leave and favour of so great a man, they are to be rejected. Neither ought any man to marvel that he &* Bernard, *and* Thomas, *and* Bonaventure, *and* Alexander *of* Ales, *and* Albert, *and* Durand, *and* Egidius; *and Lastly, The greater part followed that opinion: both because they were men, and because in progress of time, new mysteries are revealed which before were unknown. —— For as holiness of life purgeth no man from sin, so it frees no man from danger of error. —— Every age finds out some verities proper to it self, which the former ages were ignorant of,* —*and there in the* Margin, *Every age hath its peculiar divine revelations.*

Thus far *Salmeron*, by whom we may see, That *Protestants* are not the only men who say that the Fathers may err: but that *Roman Catholicks* too, can and dare valiantly break through, and tread under their feet (though perhaps with cap in hand, and some shew of reverence) and even ride over whole bands of Fathers when they stand in their way.

Another

Another great *Achilles* for the same opinion is one *Joannes Baptista Poza*, a Jesuite, and Professor of Divinity at *Complutum*: He in his fourth Book of his *Elucidarium Deiparæ*, pleads very earnestly to have it defined, and labours very lustily to remove all exceptions to the contrary, but above all those many ones; —That there is no Tradition for it, That the stream of Ancient Tradition is against, and therefore well and worthily may it be condemned for an Heresie: but to be Canonized among the Articles of Faith, it can with no reason expect.

To the Second exception he brings two answers which *Salmeron* it seems forgot, in the prosecution whereof he hath many excellent passages, which I have thought good to cull out of him to evidence the wonderful reverence, and constant regard of the present Church of *Rome*, to the Tradition of the Ancient.

The first, That it is possible the Writings of the Fathers out of which these Testimonies against the *Immaculate conception* are taken, may be corrupted: But to shew it probable they are so in these places, he speaks not one word of sense, nor so much as any colourable reason, unless this may pass for one (as perhaps it may where reasons are scarce.) No proposition, which contradicts the common judgment of the Fathers can be probable, ; * But it is *de fide* that our opinion is probable, for the Council of *Trent* hath made it so by giving liberty to all to hold it. Therefore without doubt we must hold, that it is not (whatsoever it seems) against the common judgment of the Fathers. This argument saith he doth most illustriously convince the followers of the contrary opinion: that they ought not to dare affirm hereafter, that their opinion flowes from the common judgment and writings of the ancient Doctors.

* I should rather subsume, but this does fo. Therefore not probable.

His second answer is, That whereas *Bandillus* and *Cajetan*, &c. produce general sayings of *Irenæus*, *Origen*, *Athanasius*, *Theophilus Alexandrinus*, *Greg. Nyssen*, *Basil*, *Greg. Naz.* *Cyprian*, *Hierom*, *Fulgentius*, and in a manner of all the ancient Fathers, exempting Christ alone from, and consequently concluding the Virgin *Mary* under Original sin

sin, which Argument must needs conclude if the Virgin *Mary* be not Christ. His answer I say is, These Testimonies have little or no strength: for did they conclude, we must then (let us in Gods name) say that the Virgin *Mary* committed also many venial sins: For the Scriptures, Fathers and Councils set forth in propositions as Universal. That there is no man but Christ who is not often defiled at least with smaller sins, and who may not justly say that Petition of our Lords Prayer, *Dimitte nobis debita nostra*.

An answer I confess as fit as a Napkin to stop the mouths of his domestick adversaries, though no way fit to satisfie their reason. But this man little thought there were *Protestants* in the world as well as *Dominicans*, who will not much be troubled by thieves falling out, to recover more of their goods than they expected, and to see a prevaricating Jesuit, instead of stopping one breach in their ruinous cause, to make two. For whereas this man argues from the destruction of the Consequent to the destruction of the Antecedent thus: If these testimonies were good and concluding, then the Virgin *Mary* should have been guilty not only of Original but also of actual sin, But the Consequent is false and blasphemous: Therefore the Antecedent is not true. They on the others side argue, and sure with much more reason, and much more conformity to the Ancient Tradition: From the Assertion of the Antecedent to the Assertion of the Consequent, thus: If these testimonies be good and concluding, then the Blessed Virgin was guilty both of Original sin and Actual; but the Testimonies are good and concluding; therefore she was guilty even of actual sins, and therefore much more of Original.

His Third Answer is, That their Church hath, or may define many other things against which (if their works be not depraved) there lies a greater consent of Fathers, than against the Immaculate Conception, and therefore why not this?

The Instances he gives are four.
1. That the Blessed Virgin committed no actual sin.

2. That

in Rushworth's *Dialogues.*

2. That the Angels were not created before the visible world.

3. That Angels are Incorporeal.

4. That the Souls of Saints departed are made happy by the Vision of God before the day of Judgment.

Against the first Opinion he alledges direct places out of *Origen*, which he says admit no exposition; though *Pamelius* upon *Tertullian*, and *Sixtus Senensis* labour in vain to put a good sense on them. —— Out of *Euthymias* and *Theophylact*: Out of S. *Chrysostom* divers pregnant testimonies, and S. *Thomas* his confession touching one of them, out of the Author of the Questions of the New and Old Testament in S. *Austin* cap. 75. Out of S. *Hilary* upon *Psa.* 118. which words yet says he *Tolet* has drawn to a good construction: yet so much difficulty still remains in them. —— Out of *Tertullian de carne Christi* cap. 7. which he tells us will not be salved by *Pamelius* his gloss. —— Out of *Athanasius*, out of *Irenæus* III. 18. out of S. *Austin* lib. 2. *de Symbolo ad Catech.* cap. 5. Whose words yet, because they admit, says *Poza*, some exposition, I thought fit to suppress, though some think they are very hard to be avoided. Out of *Greg. Nyss.* —— out of S. *Cyprian* in his Sermon on the Passion: Whose words, says he; though they may by some means be eluded, yet will always be very difficult if we examin the Antecedents and Consequents: out of *Anselm*, *Rich. de S. Victor*, S. *Ambrose*, S. *Andrew* of *Hierusalem*, and S. *Bede* and then tells us there are many other Testimonies much resembling these: and besides many Fathers and Texts of Scripture, which exempt Christ only from actual sin, and lastly, many suspicious sayings against her Immunity in them, who use to say that at the Angels Annunciation she was cleansed and purged and expiated from all faults committed by her freewill, which saith he, though *Canisius* and others explicate in a pious sense, yet at least they shew, that either those alledged against the Imaculate conception are as favourable to be expounded: Or we must say, that a verity may be defined by the See Apostolick against the judgment of some Fathers.

From these things, says he, is drawn an unanswerable reason, That for the defining the purity of the conception, nothing now is wanting. For seeing, notwithstanding more and more convincing testimonies of Fathers who either did, or did seem to ascribe actual sin to the Blessed Virgin; notwithstanding the Universal sayings of Scripture and Councils bringing all, except Christ, under sin: Lastly, notwithstanding the silence of the Scriptures and Councils touching her Immunity from actual sin, seeing notwithstanding all this the Council of *Trent* hath either decreed, or hath confirmed, it being before decreed by the consent of the faithful, that the Blessed Virgin never was guilty of any voluntary, no not the least sin: It follows certainly that the Apostolick See, hath as good nay better ground, to enrol amongst her Articles the Virgins Immaculate conception: The reason is clear, for neither are there so many nor so evident sentences of Fathers which impute any fault or blemish to the Conception of the Mother of God, as there are in appearance to charge her with actual offences. Neither are there fewer Universal propositions in Scripture, by which it may be proved that only Jesus was free from actual sin, and therefore that the Virgin *Mary* fell into it. Neither can there at this time be desired a greater consent of the faithful, nor a more ardent desire than there now is, that this verity should be defined, and that the contrary Opinion should be Anathematized for Erroneous and Heretical. The words of the Council of *Trent* on which this reason is grounded are these.

If any man say, That a man all his life long may avoid all, even venial sins, unless by special priviledge from God, as the Church holds of the Blessed Virgin, let him be Anathema. But if the consent of the Church hath prevailed against more clear Testimonies of ancient Fathers, even for that which is favoured with no express authority of Scriptures or Councils: And if the Council of *Trent* upon this consent of the faithful, hath either defined this Immunity of the Virgin, from all actual sin, or declared it to be defined: Who then can

Sess. VI. c. 23. de Justifical.

can deny but that the Church hath Immediate power to define among the Articles of Faith, the pious Opinion of the Immaculate Conception?

His second Example by which he declares the power of their Church to define Articles againſt a multitude of Fathers (and conſequently not only without but againſt Tradition) is the opinion that Angels were not created before the Corporeal world was created: which ſaith he is, or may be defined, though there were more Teſtimonies of Fathers againſt it, than againſt the Immaculate Conception. So he ſays in the Argument of his Fifth Chapter, and in the end of the ſame Chapter: The Council of *Lateran* hath defined this againſt the expreſs judgment of twenty Fathers, of which *Nazianzen*, *Baſil*, *Chryſoſtome*, *Cyrill*, *Hierom*, *Ambroſe*, and *Hillary* are part.

His third Example to the ſame purpoſe, is the opinion that Angels are Incorporeal: againſt which ſaith he, in the Argument of his ſixth Chapter: there are more Teſtimonies of the Fathers, than againſt the Immaculate Conception, and yet it is, or at leaſt may be defined by the Church, and in the end of the Chapter, I have for this Opinion cited twenty three Fathers, which as moſt men think is now condemned in the * *Lateran* Council, or at leaſt as † *Suarez* proves, is to be rejected as manifeſtly temerarious.

*Firm de ſum mâ Trinitate.
† De Angelis. lib. 6.

His fourth and laſt Example to the ſame purpoſe is, The Opinion that the Souls of Saints departed enjoy the Viſion of God before the Reſurrection. Againſt which he tells us in the firſt place was the Judgment of Pope *John* XXI. though not as a Pope but as a private Doctor. Then he muſters up againſt it a great multitude of *Greek* and *Latin* Fathers, touching which he ſays —— All theſe Teſtimonies when * *Vaſquez* has related, at length he † anſwers that they might be ſo explained as to ſay nothing againſt the true and Catholick Doctrin. Yet if they could not be ſo explained, their Authority ought not to hinder us from embracing that which the Church

* 1. 2. D. 29. cap. 1.
† cap 3.

Church hath defined. The same argument I make (says *Poza*) The Fathers and ancient Doctors which are objected against the pious opinion of the Conception of the Virgin, may be commodiously explicated, or at least so handled that they shall not hurt: Notwithstanding though they cannot be explicated, some of them, that their Testimonies ought not to hinder, but that the Sea Apostolick may define the Blessed Virgins preservation from Original sin. In fine, for the close of this Argument he adds, *Nolo per plura.* ——I will not run through more Examples: These that I have reckoned are sufficient, and admonishes learned men to bring together other like proofs, whereby they may promote the desired Determination.

FINIS.

www.ingramcontent.com/pod-product-compliance
Lightning Source LLC
Chambersburg PA
CBHW031937290426
44108CB00011B/590